The Psychology of Music in Multimedia

"This well-edited, laid out, and contextualized collection of essays provides a much needed resource on a topic whose rigorous examination has, until now, been limited to scholarly articles scattered amongst a variety of academic journals. Its appearance could not be more timely, given the steadily increasing interest in cross modal perception, and, specifically, perception of audio-visual composites, as evidenced in university curricula, relevant interdisciplinary research, and the desire of 'sound for visual media' industries to anchor their practice and its effectiveness on empirical research. The book's contributors and editors represent a 'who's who' in the area and their work provides rigorous substance to the ever-growing realization that the presence of an image changes what we 'hear' and the presence of a sound changes what we 'see.' A must-have resource for experts, students, and practitioners of the topic alike!"

Pantelis Vassilakis,
Associate Professor and Chair,
Audio Arts and Acoustics Department,
Columbia College Chicago, USA

"This cutting-edge collection of essays highlights new perspectives, research, and ideas about how music impacts many different kinds of media—from film to video games to television advertisements. Any serious media scholar will want this volume as part of their library."

James C. Kaufman
Professor of Psychology
University of Connecticut, USA
Founding Editor, Psychology
of Popular Media Culture

The Psychology of Music in Multimedia

Edited by

Siu-Lan Tan
Annabel J. Cohen
Scott D. Lipscomb
and
Roger A. Kendall

OXFORD
UNIVERSITY PRESS

OXFORD
UNIVERSITY PRESS

Great Clarendon Street, Oxford, OX2 6DP,
United Kingdom

Oxford University Press is a department of the University of Oxford.
It furthers the University's objective of excellence in research, scholarship,
and education by publishing worldwide. Oxford is a registered trade mark of
Oxford University Press in the UK and in certain other countries

First Edition published in 2013

Impression: 1

British Library Cataloguing in Publication Data
Data available

ISBN 978–0–19–960815–7

Printed and bound in Great Britain by
CPI Group (UK) Ltd, Croydon, CR0 4YY

Foreword

Nowadays music hardly exists in the sense in which it existed, or was thought to exist, a hundred years ago. At that time music was conceived as something exclusively defined by and contained within the auditory realm. Music might be combined with words or images, as in song or opera, but this was the bringing together of distinct media, each with their own independent existence and their own meaning. By contrast, to think of music as an integral element of multimedia is to think about it quite differently. Seen—as well as heard—this way, music becomes a dimension of a larger, complex experience, and it acquires its meaning from the context of that experience, whether in the concert hall, at home watching television, or playing a video game. This book rethinks music from the perspective of today's multimedia-oriented world, explores its psychological underpinnings, and illustrates a wide range of empirical techniques through which it can be investigated.

This is a book about music today. It is also a book about how music always was, but was not understood to be. The conception of music as an independent, exclusively auditory medium—what Peter Kivy (1990) calls 'music alone'—was most perfectly realized in the hi-fi culture of the post-war years, above all in the image of music heard on headphones in a darkened room. But the aesthetic aspiration preceded its technological realization. From the second half of the 19th century, concert halls were designed to minimize social interaction and de-emphasize the visual, fostering instead a direct and purely auditory communion between musical work and listener. This is the aesthetic and conceptual order that is still expressed in the institutions of today's academia: music, words, and moving images are the business respectively of departments of musicology, literature, and film studies.

Outside academia, however, the world moved on. Film and television became the 20th century's dominant forms of entertainment. In the latter decades of the century, video, MTV, and most decisively the development of digital technology normalized the consumption of music in the form of multimedia: not music *and* words *and* moving images (*and* dance *and* tactile stimulation *and*…), but rather music as one dimension of a holistic experience in which meaning emerges from dynamic interactions between multiple media. Multimedia playback has itself converged with computer, Internet, and telephone technologies, resulting in a proliferation of digitally mediated practices of listening and viewing. All this leads us to think of multimedia as a distinctively contemporary cultural phenomenon, perhaps a dimension of the postmodern experience in the same way that the de-socialized listening of concert hall and headphones were symptomatic of modernism.

But there is a sense in which the world never was quite what aestheticians and academics made it out to be. Even during the half century when audio-only technology dominated—say from the 1920s to the 1970s—music was received alongside such paratexts as program notes and LP sleeve images. Concert audiences heard music, but they saw it too, in the sometimes considered and always significant gestures of stage performance. And it goes further than that. Even heard on headphones, music elicits perceptions of space and motion, embodied experience, and emotional empathy: it invokes multiple sensory modalities and engages listeners as inhabitants of a world that is experienced through sight, sound, smell, taste, and touch. In that sense the idea of music *as* multimedia—the phrase is Zohar Eitan's (Chapter 8, this volume)—is not so much the recognition of a new condition as a new and more realistic recognition of something that has always been the case.

The idea of music as an independent, purely auditory medium was protected by walls, ranging from the physical walls of concerts halls that excluded the sounds and sights of the outside world to the conceptual but no less real walls that divide academic disciplines. Seeking to break down such walls, this book concludes with a call for the formation of multidisciplinary research teams in place of the disciplinary fragmentation bequeathed by the old aesthetic and academic order. Just as multimedia is not music *and* words *and* moving images (*and*…), but rather subsists in the meaningful experience that results from their interaction, so a multidisciplinary approach to multimedia means not psychology *and* musicology *and* communication studies *and* film studies *and* semiotics (*and*…), but rather a dynamic process of interaction between different perspectives and methodologies. The book also breaches the walls that have traditionally separated the aesthetic from the applied: as a dimension of multimedia experience, music emerges from the following chapters as a cultural practice as much at home in advertising, data visualization, and the creation of computer and video games as in the concert hall.

At the same time, the transition from music as medium to music as multimedia gives a new significance to the empirical orientation that lies at the heart of the book, with its focus on the perceptions and experiences of real, situated listener-viewers (it is a real problem that there is no one word in English to designate how we perceive multimedia). Under the old order, music was assumed to be always already meaningful: meaning was deposited into the musical artwork by its composer, to be communicated by the performer and reconstructed by the listener, and the analysis of such meaning was the province of the musicologist. Within that paradigm, the role of empirical investigation was basically limited to testing the extent to which that meaning was or was not in fact communicated. Consequently musicologists saw the work of music psychologists as peripheral to their core business.

But in the multimedia experience, as I said, meaning emerges from dynamic interactions between media: it is produced in the real time of listening-viewing. In this context, empirical investigation engages fully with the production of meaning, contributing to an understanding of what music means as well as the processes through which it comes to mean what it means. And that makes it possible for empirical approaches to enter into dialogue with the equally evidence-based but different approaches of historical musicology and of what is sometimes referred to as speculative theory (perhaps more accurately seen as a blending of introspection and systematic analysis).

It was through that kind of speculative approach that I attempted to extend traditional music-theoretical thinking into the field of multimedia in my book *Analysing*

Musical Multimedia (Cook, 1998), first published 15 years before the present book. My aim was to rescue music from the subordinate position in which it had been placed by writing on film that reflected the practices and biases of the Hollywood system (where the music was added at the last minute to an otherwise completed film); prompted by the then dominant phenomenon of the music video, I wanted to show that words and images could themselves be deployed in musical ways. Another example of a speculative approach, coming from a different perspective and informed by the author's experience as an electroacoustic composer and film-maker, was Michel Chion's (1994) influential book *Audio-Vision*. The chapters that follow show how such established approaches can coexist productively with approaches informed by empirical methods: speculative approaches provide material for empirical investigation, while empirical findings prompt new speculation. This kind of dialogue between approaches traditionally associated with the humanities on the one hand, and with scientific investigation on the other, is full of promise as an instrument of disciplinary renewal.

Nicholas Cook
University of Cambridge, UK

References

Chion, P. (1994). *Audio-vision: Sound on screen* (C. Gorbman, Ed. and Trans.). New York, NY: Columbia University Press. (Originally published 1990.)

Cook, N. (1998). *Analysing musical multimedia*. Oxford: Oxford University Press.

Kivy, P. (1990). *Music alone: Philosophical reflections on the purely musical experience*. Ithaca, NY: Cornell University Press.

Acknowledgements

We would like to thank Martin Baum for his support and interest in this book from the beginning and Charlotte Green for illuminating our path through every step of the journey with her expert guidance. Our thanks to all the other splendid staff at Oxford University Press including Emma Lonie, Papitha Ramesh, Fiona Richardson, Lauren Small, Katie Stileman, Nic Williams, Simon Witter, Ben Tiller, and Geraldine Begley. We are also grateful to Nicolas Wehmeier and Sarah Brett at OUP for designing the companion website with multimedia features to supplement the content of this book. At every stage of this venture, we were thoroughly impressed by the warm supportive style, clear communication, and attention to detail of all OUP staff. We express our appreciation to anonymous reviewers for their expertise and valuable insights that helped strengthen and refine this work. We especially thank all chapter authors for their unflagging dedication and enthusiastic involvement; this book would not have been possible without their diverse and vibrant contributions. Our gratitude is also extended to Nicholas Cook for presenting the Foreword for this book. Finally, the editors express personal thanks to their wonderfully supportive colleagues, friends, and families.

ST, AJC, SDL, RAK

Contents

Companion Website

The companion website to *The Psychology of Music in Multimedia* can be found at www.oup.co.uk/companion/tan. This website features over 60 files—including audiovisual materials, sound files, and animations—primarily representing original laboratory stimuli used in some of the empirical studies described in the book. Though not a comprehensive audiovisual companion to all the chapters, the website provides readers with a rare and unique opportunity to see and hear examples of audiovisual stimuli to which participants were exposed in some studies described in this volume. The site serves as a valuable teaching and learning tool, providing an opportunity for the reader to gain a deeper understanding of empirical investigations of music in multimedia. The materials also serve as a valuable resource for present and future researchers.

Connections to relevant materials are indicated within the text, directing the reader to the companion website. Some specific examples of materials to be found on the companion website include numerous excerpts from original auditory and audiovisual stimuli employed in various research studies conducted by chapter authors and their colleagues, video clips of participants responding to tasks while taking part in research studies, and an animated version of an important model capturing the role of music in multimedia. The contents of this website are subject to change and may be updated or expanded over time.

Contributors

David Bashwiner is Assistant Professor of Music Theory at the University of New Mexico, USA. He holds a doctorate in the History and Theory of Music from the University of Chicago, a master's degree in Music Composition from the University of Illinois, and bachelor's degree in Biopsychology from Cornell University. His dissertation, supported by a Whiting Fellowship, was titled *Musical Emotion: Toward a Biologically Grounded Theory* (2010), and his essay, 'Lifting the Foot: The Neural Underpinnings of the "Pathological" Response to Music,' appears in Barbara Stafford's *A Field Guide to a New Meta-Field: Bridging the Humanities-Neurosciences Divide* (University of Chicago Press, 2011). He has presented research nationally and internationally on music as it relates to emotion, neuroscience, syntax, speech, meaning, and attention. In addition to his scholarly work, Bashwiner composes music for films, including the award-winning feature *Crime Fiction* (2007).

Marilyn G. Boltz is Professor of Psychology at Haverford College, Pennsylvania, USA, and is a past Board Member and Secretary/Treasurer for the Society of Music Perception and Cognition. She has published numerous studies in the fields of temporal behavior, music cognition, and cross-modal perception. In the study of temporal behavior, her work has been influential in not only illuminating those cognitive mechanisms that mediate judgments of duration, tempo, and rhythm, but also how these different temporal dimensions of environmental events influence behaviors such as the perception and memory of music, film, and naturalistic sounds; social impression formation; and the detection of lying. A second line of research has explored ways in which the auditory and visual modalities interact with one another. Much of this work has investigated the role of musical soundtracks in the interpretation and remembering of film information, while other studies have examined the interactive influence of facial and vocal information on the impressions we form of others.

Sandra L. Calvert is Professor of Psychology at Georgetown University, USA and Director of the Children's Digital Media Center, a multisite interdisciplinary research center funded by the National Science Foundation. Her research focuses on the effects of media on very early development, the effects of interactive media and food marketing on children's diets and health, and the role that formal features play in children's learning from media. Calvert has authored numerous journal articles, book chapters, and books, including *Children's Journeys Through the Information Age* (McGraw-Hill, 1999). She co-edited *Children in the Digital Age: Influences of Electronic Media on Development* (Greenwood Publishing Group, 2002) and *The Handbook of Children, Media, and Development* (Wiley-Blackwell Publishing, 2008). She has served on two committees for the National Academies, leading to two committee co-authored books: *Food Marketing to Children and Youth: Threat or Opportunity* (2006) and *Youth, Pornography, and the Internet* (2002). Calvert also serves on numerous advisory boards to improve the quality of children's media.

Annabel J. Cohen is Professor of Psychology at the University of Prince Edward Island in Canada. Her doctorate is from Queen's University, BA from McGill, and associate diploma (ARCT) from the Royal Conservatory of Music, Toronto. She has dedicated her career to the study of music perception and cognition, with extensions to multimedia, publishing on such topics as tonality, music transposition, the acquisition of music grammar, and film music, from a cognitive perspective. She has led multi-institutional research projects focusing on harnessing multimedia for education in the context of culture and cognition. On that foundation, she currently directs a major collaborative research initiative (AIRS or Advancing Interdisciplinary Research in Singing). Cohen is the Editor of *Psychomusicology: Music, Mind, & Brain* and serves on the consulting boards of several journals (e.g., *Music and the Moving Image*, *Musicae Scientiae*, *Music Perception*, *Psychology of Music*, *The Soundtrack*). She is an Adjunct Professor at Dalhousie University, Fellow of the Canadian Psychological Association, and Council Member of the American Psychological Association representing the Division for Psychology of Aesthetics, Creativity and the Arts.

Nicholas Cook (Foreword) is 1684 Professor of Music at the University of Cambridge, UK. Born in Athens, Greece, he has taught in Hong Kong and Sydney as well as various British universities, and directed the AHRC Research Centre for the History and Analysis of Recorded Music from 2004 to 2009. His books include *A Guide to Musical Analysis* (1987); *Music, Imagination, and Culture* (1990); *Beethoven: Symphony No. 9* (1993); *Analysis Through Composition* (1996); and *Music: A Very Short Introduction* (1998), which has appeared in 14 different languages. His most recent book, *The Schenker Project: Culture, Race, and Music Theory in Fin-de-siècle Vienna* (2007), won the Society for Music Theory's Wallace Berry Award, while a book on studying music as performance is in press. His work in multimedia includes a monograph (*Analysing Musical Multimedia*, 1998) and articles on classical music video, video mashup, and the participatory video culture that has grown up around 'Bohemian Rhapsody.' A former editor of *Journal of the Royal Musical Association*, he is a Fellow of the British Academy and of Academia Europaea.

Zohar Eitan is Associate Professor of Music Theory at Tel Aviv University in Israel. He studied music composition and music theory at Tel Aviv University and at the University of Pennsylvania, USA. Much of Eitan's research investigates empirically how listeners associate musical features with aspects of non-auditory experience. Among other topics, he examines how musical parameters such as pitch, loudness and tempo are associated with physical space and motion, and how metaphors for musical pitch are applied and understood across cultural barriers. His other research interests include the perception and cognition of similarity in music, the experience of musical tension, the cognition of large-scale musical form, and the implicit perception of absolute pitch. His recent research was published in *Cognition*, *Music Perception*, *Musicae Scientiae*,

Psychomusicology: Music, Mind and Brain, and *Psychology of Music*. Eitan's book, *Highpoints* (1997), published by the University of Pennsylvania Press, investigates the phenomenon of melodic peaks in 18th- to 20th-century music.

Mark Grimshaw is the Obel Professor of Music at Aalborg University in Denmark, where he is co-chair of the Research Laboratory in Art & Technology. He grew up in The Bahamas, Kenya, and Botswana and qualified with a BMus (Hons) at the University of Natal, South Africa, an MSc in Music Technology from the University of York, UK, and a PhD on the acoustic ecology of the First-Person Shooter at the University of Waikato, New Zealand. After working as a sound engineer in Italy, he moved into academia and now writes extensively on sound in computer games and particularly the use of biofeedback for the real-time synthesis of game sound. He also writes free, open source software for virtual research environments (WIKINDX) and is investigating the uses of sonification to facilitate creativity in the context of such knowledge tools. His last book was an anthology on computer game audio published in 2011 and he is currently editing the *Oxford Handbook of Virtuality* for Oxford University Press.

Berthold Hoeckner is Associate Professor of Music and the Humanities at the University of Chicago, USA. He is a music historian specializing in 19th- and 20th-century music. Research interests include aesthetics, Adorno, music and literature, film music and visual culture, and the psychology of music. Awards and fellowships include the Alfred Einstein Award of the American Musicological Society (1998), a Humboldt Research Fellowship (2001–2002), a Mellon New Directions Fellowship (2006–2007), and a Fellowship at the Franke Institute of the Humanities at the University of Chicago (2012–2013). Hoeckner is also a Lead Researcher for the Chicago Wisdom Project at the University of Chicago (2012–2014). Articles and essays have appeared in *The Journal of the American Musicological Society*, *Music Theory Spectrum*, *Music Theory Online*, *The Musical Quarterly*, *Opera Quarterly*, and *Nineteenth-Century Music*. He is the author of *Programming the Absolute: Nineteenth-Century German Music and the Hermeneutics of the Moment* (Princeton, 2002); and the editor of *Apparitions: New Perspectives on Adorno and Twentieth-Century Music* (Routledge, 2006). He is currently working on a monograph entitled *Film, Music, Memory*.

Kineta Hung is Associate Professor of Communication at the Hong Kong Baptist University in Hong Kong (China), where she is Program Director of the Integrated Communication Management Program. She holds a doctorate in Marketing and an MBA, both from York University, Canada; and a bachelor's degree in Piano Performance from Oberlin College, USA. Her research interests include advertising, online communications, celebrity endorsement, and international marketing. She is regarded as one of Asia's top advertising researchers and her works have been funded by multiple competitive research grants provided by the Research Grants Council (RGC). Hung has published in *Journal of Advertising*, *Journal of Advertising Research*, *Journal of Retailing*, *Journal of International Business Studies*, and *Journal of Marketing*. Her work on music in advertising is highly regarded and has been nominated for an award from the *Journal of Advertising*. She reviews regularly for the *Journal of Advertising* and is on the editorial board of the *International Journal of Advertising*.

Shin-ichiro Iwamiya is a Professor of Acoustics at Kyushu University in Japan. He served as President of the Japanese Society for Music Perception and Cognition from 2004 to 2007, and President of the Kyushu Chapter of the Acoustical Society of Japan. He received the Sato Paper Award of the Acoustical Society of Japan in 1993, the Paper Award of the Institute of Noise Control Engineering/Japan in 2000, and the Paper Award of the Japanese Society for Music Perception and Cognition in 2002. Iwamiya has published papers on perceived pitch and timbre of vibrato tones, tone quality of product sounds, functions of ambient music, functional imagery of audio signals, and features of the Japanese soundscape. He has carried out research into the interactions between auditory and visual processing of visual media productions, the effects of music on visual media productions, the effects of color on the impression of music, and the elements needed to create subjective congruence between moving pictures and sounds. Iwamiya is the author of *Sound Ecology* (2000), *Multimodal Communication by Music and Motion Picture* (2000, 2011), *Sound Design* (2007), *Science of Sound Sign* (2012), *Science of Music* (2009), and *Fundamentals of Modern Acoustics* (2007).

Hermann Kappelhoff is Professor of Film Studies at the Film Department and board member as well as Director at the Cluster of Excellence 'Languages of Emotion' (LoE) at Freie Universität Berlin, Germany. His fields of research include inter alia the auteur cinema of the Weimar Republic and the cinematic melodrama as a paradigm for a theory of artificial emotionality. At the LoE, Kappelhoff is directing research projects regarding the mobilization of emotions in Hollywood war films, multimodal metaphors and expressive movement, as well as the dynamics of affective viewer responses to film. In addition, he is directing a subproject on the politics of aesthetics in Western European cinema within the German Research Fellowship's (DFG) special research field (SFB) 626 on aesthetic experience and the dissolution of artistic limits. His essay 'Embodied meaning construction: Multimodal metaphor and expressive movement in speech, gesture, and in feature film' (with Cornelia Müller) has been published in *Metaphor and the Social World* in 2011.

Roger A. Kendall is a Professor in the Department of Ethnomusicology at the University of California, Los Angeles, USA in the specialization of Systematic Musicology. He co-authored an invited chapter on music perception and cognition for the *Ecological Psychology* volume of the *Handbook on Perception*, as well as a chapter on comparative music psychology for *Psychology of Music* (D. Deutsch, Ed. 2nd ed.). His current research interests include comparative perceptual and acoustical analyses of natural versus synthetic and sampled orchestral timbres and spectra, tuning models and perception of the slendro mode in the Gamelan, expressive music performance modeled in terms of communication theory, and perception of meaning in film music. Kendall co-edited *Perspectives in Systematic Musicology* in *Selected Reports in Ethnomusicology*, Volume 12 and contributed a chapter outlining connections of experimental empirical research in meaning to visual and musical elements. His pioneering course in the Psychology of

Film Music has inspired similar courses. His computer program, the Music Experiment Development System (MEDS), is used internationally.

Mark Kerins is Associate Professor of Film & Media Arts at Southern Methodist University in Dallas, USA, where he teaches film production and post-production. He studies surround sound using an interdisciplinary approach combining quantitative empirical investigations, text-based analyses, practitioner interviews, and theory-based examinations of sound design practices. Kerins has authored a number of journal articles and book chapters, presented his work at numerous conferences, and wrote the award-winning book *Beyond Dolby (Stereo): Cinema in the Digital Sound Age* (Indiana University Press, 2010), which examines the effects of 5.1-channel sound on filmmaking practices and the implications of these changes for film scholarship. Kerins is also an active film-maker whose directing credits include major label music videos (The Verve Pipe's 'Happiness Is'; Rachael Yamagata's 'Would You Please') and short films that have played in domestic and international film festivals. Most recently, he received nominations for Best Director of a Short, Best Producer, and Best Script from the Tenerife International Film Festival for the comedy *How NOT to Quit Your Day Job*. His debut feature film is entitled *All the Wrong Friends* (2013).

Stefan Koelsch is Professor for Biological Psychology and Music Psychology and member of the Cluster of Excellence 'Languages of Emotion' at Freie Universität Berlin, Germany. He holds master's degrees in music, psychology, and sociology, as well as a doctorate in neuroscience. He worked at the Max Planck Institute for Human Cognitive and Brain Science (Leipzig, Germany), Harvard Medical School (Boston, MA, USA), and the University of Sussex (Falmer, UK). Koelsch has an international reputation in the field of the neuroscience of music and has published milestone articles on the neural correlates of music-syntactic and music-semantic processing. His main research areas include music and emotion, music and language, development of music perception in children, auditory working memory, auditory sensory memory, as well as music therapy. He has expert knowledge in functional neuroimaging and electrophysiology, and is involved in several projects investigating emotions elicited by music and visual information. Koelsch is author of the book *Brain and Music* (Wiley, 2012).

Lars Kuchinke is Junior Professor (Assistant Professor) of Experimental Psychology and Methods at the Ruhr-Universität Bochum, Germany, and member of the Cluster of Excellence 'Languages of Emotion' at Freie Universität Berlin. His main research interests cover the field of verbal and non-verbal emotion processing, thereby focusing on neurocognitive research of the neural responses elicited by emotional stimuli. In addition to this primary interest he is currently extending his experimental investigations into the field of aesthetic emotions and empathic responding. Kuchinke is a principal investigator of a research project in empirical media science on the dynamics of affective viewer responses to film. This project deals in particular with how the aesthetic expressive quality of audiovisual pictures relates to the narrativity of cinematic fiction regarding the viewers' emotional response and how neural responses in viewing emotional movie clips are modulated when the viewer integrates different types of affective music.

Scott D. Lipscomb is Associate Professor and Division Head of Music Education and Music Therapy in the School of Music at the University of Minnesota, USA. In addition to his primary research interest in 'sound for multimedia,' he is currently pursuing investigations related to surround sound presentation of cinema and musical sound, the effect of music in video game contexts, impact of visual performance information on listener preference for 'complex' music, integration of music across the K-12 curriculum, and the development of interactive instructional media to enhance the music learning experience. Lipscomb served two 3-year terms as Treasurer for the Society for Music Perception and Cognition, four 2-year terms as President of the Association for Technology in Music Instruction (ATMI), and serves as a member of the Executive Board and as Chair of the Research Committee for Technology Institute for Music Educators (TI:ME). He has presented results of his research at numerous regional, national, and international conferences and his work has been published in numerous peer-reviewed journals and edited volumes.

Howard C. Nusbaum is Professor of Psychology and a member of the Committee on Computational Neuroscience at the University of Chicago in Chicago, USA, where he is also Co-Director of the Center for Cognitive and Social Neuroscience. His research interests span topics in cognitive and social neuroscience including auditory cognition, spoken language use, multimedia perception and understanding, attention, learning, evolution of communication, and sleep consolidation of memory. His work uses a wide range of methods from human behavioral testing, neuroimaging, human electrophysiology, cross-species comparisons, and computational modeling. Recent research has focused on questions of the neural mechanisms of integration of auditory and visual signals in perception and comprehension of speech and movies, how sequences of auditory patterns are understood by humans and songbirds, how meaning emerges from experiences and generalizes to new situations, and the affective and social impact of communicative signals.

Agnieszka Roginska is Assistant Professor and Associate Director of Music Technology at New York University (NYU) in New York, USA. She holds a B.M. in Piano Performance and Computer Applications in Music from McGill University, Canada, an M.M. in Music Technology from NYU, and a Ph.D. in Music Technology from Northwestern University, USA. She was born in Poland, lived in Italy, Canada, and moved to the United States to pursue graduate studies. Roginska conducts extensive research in 3D audio, Head-Related Transfer Functions measurement techniques in non-anechoic environments, simulation of virtual auditory environments, the design and implementation of auditory displays for improved information perception, as well as applications of auditory displays in augmented acoustic sensing. Her work includes entertainment as well as mission-critical applications. Before joining NYU, she was the Audio Research Scientist at AuSIM Inc, where she directed research in audio simulation and spatialization for a number of government agencies (including NASA, US Army, US Navy), research centers, and universities.

Mark Shevy is Associate Professor of Mass Communication and Media Production at Northern Michigan University, USA. His research focuses primarily on the psychological effects of music in media, including the cross-cultural meanings of popular music genres and the influence of music on viewers' evaluation of film characters. In addition, he has researched emotional reactions to news coverage, the cognitive process of attending to television, and models of media effects. His work has been published in *Psychology of Music*, *Psychomusicology: Music, Mind, & Brain*, and the *Journal of Broadcasting & Electronic Media*. He also coauthored (with R. P. Hawkins) an entry on attending to mass media in the *International Encyclopedia of Communication*. He holds a doctorate in Mass Communication from the University of Wisconsin-Madison and a Master of Science in Journalism and Technical Communication from Colorado State University.

Siu-Lan Tan is Associate Professor of Psychology at Kalamazoo College in Michigan, USA. Born in Indonesia and raised in Hong Kong, she holds diplomas from the Associated Board of the Royal Schools of Music (England) and degrees in Music and Piano Pedagogy, and taught music in Hong Kong and California for many years before completing a PhD in Psychology at Georgetown University, USA and a term on scholarship at Oxford University in the United Kingdom. Tan's research on video games and virtual reality games has been published in the *Journal of Applied Developmental Psychology*, *International Journal of Gaming and Computer-Mediated Simulations*, *Interacting with Video* (Praeger 1996), and *Interdisciplinary Advancements in Gaming, Simulations and Virtual Environments* (IGI, 2012). Her research on film music and other topics has appeared in *Music Perception*, *Psychology of Music*, *Psychomusicology: Music, Mind, & Brain*, and *College Music Symposium*. She is first author of the book *Psychology of Music: From Sound to Significance* (with P. Pfordresher and R. Harré) published by Routledge/Psychology Press in 2010.

Chapter 1

Introduction: The psychology of music in multimedia

Annabel J. Cohen, Scott D. Lipscomb, Siu-Lan Tan, and Roger A. Kendall

The term 'multimedia' commonly refers to audiovisual presentations in film, television, video, interactive gaming, computer interfaces, and on the Internet. Such multimedia forms are typically created collaboratively by artists and technicians. Multimedia presentations often have the power to engage audiences thoroughly, be it in a narrative, a game, or an advertisement. These spectator-listeners typically take for granted the role played by music and audio; although, if asked, most would agree that the music and sound contribute to the entertainment value, communication function, aesthetic pleasure, or educational purpose that multimedia can provide. In contrast to audiences, however, some researchers across numerous academic disciplines are directing attention to the role of music and sound in the multimedia experience. The present volume gathers the work of leading scholars from these diverse disciplines to inform our understanding of the role of music in the experiences and functions of multimedia.

The primary focus of this book is on the growing body of empirical research investigating the cognition of musical multimedia. The term *empirical* refers to the process of collecting data from human participants via systematically designed experiments. The results of such empirical research provide a framework for understanding the relationships between music, sound, and image in multimedia contexts. The empirical approach can ultimately facilitate the acquisition of knowledge to support or refute insightful speculation proposed in comprehensive theoretical works (e.g., Chion, 1990/1994; Cook, 1998; Gorbman, 1987). Such information is of particular value due to the increasing impact of multimedia in contemporary global wired society. A major goal of the present volume is to demonstrate many aspects of the empirical approach to the study of music and media and to highlight the promise of the empirical approach as an avenue for future research.

The impetus for this book arose independently among the co-editors Siu-Lan Tan and Annabel Cohen from psychology and Scott Lipscomb and Roger Kendall from music. Cohen, Kendall, and Lipscomb had been empirically exploring the functions of film music since the 1980s. The three met for the first time in 1990 at a small symposium on the psychology of film music organized by William Rosar at the University of Southern California. At the time, Lipscomb was initiating his graduate research under the direction of Kendall. Part of this work appeared in a volume of the journal *Psychomusicology* dedicated to the psychology of film music and edited by Cohen (1994). About a decade later, Kendall co-edited a volume of *Selected Reports in Ethnomusicology* (Kendall & Savage, 2005) that also highlighted research in film music.

Cohen, Kendall, Lipscomb, and a growing number of colleagues in the field continued to organize symposia and present their research on the topic of music and film at meetings of the International Conference on Music Perception and Cognition (ICMPC) held in Bologna, Italy (2006), Sapporo, Japan (2008), and Seattle, Washington (2010) and numerous biennial meetings of the Society for Music Perception and Cognition (SMPC). Siu-Lan Tan had written an important paper on film music, and Cohen introduced her to Lipscomb and Kendall at the SMPC meeting in Montreal, Canada, in 2007. As Tan became increasingly intrigued by the topic of film music and began to explore the role of music in video games, while also completing a co-authored text on music psychology (Tan, Pfordresher, & Harré, 2010), she approached Cohen about the possibility of developing a book about music and multimedia. Cohen remembered past conversations with Kendall about a similar idea and suggested that Kendall and Lipscomb be invited to join the endeavor, establishing this long-term project as an interdisciplinary venture from the outset.

Luckily the foursome were attending the 2008 ICMPC meeting in Sapporo, Japan, and, with Tan at the helm, the feasibility and plans for the book were discussed. The following year, SMPC in Indianapolis, Indiana, provided the opportunity to review the prospectus completed under the leadership of Lipscomb, which culminated in the successful acquisition of a book contract from Oxford University Press, UK. The editors were pleased to meet with Martin Baum, Senior Commissioning Editor for Oxford University Press in the areas of Psychology, Psychiatry, and Neuroscience, at the ICMPC meeting in Seattle, Washington (2010). Tan continued to keep the team on track, including planning for a two-day editors' meeting preceding SMPC in Rochester, New York (2011). The outcome of this series of meetings—and many, many rounds of communication in between—is the volume before you.

Multimedia

Combinations of media are common worldwide and have also been prevalent historically. Dance forms, incorporating temporally organized sound and visuals, are ubiquitous. In fact, music without visuals is mostly an artifact of technology; sound recording effectively removes the multisensory aspects of live concerts. Sometimes the term *multimedia* implies a technological combination of sensory art forms, and, even before the term was coined, combinations of music and visual patterns were explored. Light or color keyboards were combined with compositions since at least the 18th century (Cook, 1998, chapter 1; see also the Center for Visual Music library for extensive historical descriptions, <http://www.centerforvisualmusic.org>). Scriabin's 1910 composition *Prometheus* (op. 60) includes a notated light organ part. Such ideas extend themselves to the present day, with both Windows and Macintosh computers offering 'visualization' modes in their media players, producing algorithmic visual patterns to accompany any music selection being played. Multimedia is not of course limited to sound and visuals. It can be easily argued that a book is in fact a multisensory experience involving text, paper texture, illustrations, and the smell of the book itself. The focus of the present book, however, is on music in multimedia.

The term *multimedia* (possibly first spelled *multi-media*) is attributed to Bobb Golsteinn (who has worked in many facets of the entertainment industry) in his description of the show 'LightWorks at L'Oursin,' which integrated music, lights, and film among other mediums (Albarino, 1966). Definitions of the term *multimedia* are legion. Maras (1996), for example, discusses ten different definitions of the term including *multiple media* and describes mixed media as performance art that includes installations of films, videos, actors, and other elements; this construct he calls a *hybrid definition*. He also discusses *megamedium*, a combination of different media into an integrated, unified, or colonized form. Film theorist Monaco (1999) stated that academicians began using the term 'mediums' as a super-intensive plural.

From the field of educational psychology, Mayer (2009) proposed a three-part taxonomy to define the attributes of multimedia. First, the delivery medium involves two or more devices, such as a computer screen and amplified speakers. Second, the presentation mode combines two or more modes, such as printed text and illustrations or on-screen text and animations. Third, two or more sensory modalities are involved. Clearly there are many overlaps among these categories, since a presentation mode involves multiple delivery media and sensory modalities.

This book focuses on a psychological frame of reference in defining multimedia. A primary focus is on cognitive integration in multisensory contexts, with a particular emphasis on temporally organized *auditory* and *visual* structures. The specific elements and the properties of temporal structure and cognitive integration rely on the operational definitions of the individual authors, and the rules of measurement in each domain, rather than descriptive, dictionary definitions. This forms the basis for the process of empirical investigation which informs the research approach of the authors.

Empirical approach

The authors contributing to the volume align themselves with a variety of disciplines—many identifying with multiple disciplines—including musicology, music technology, education, film studies, communication studies, advertising, and several branches of psychology including developmental, cognitive, educational, physiological, and social. However, as the title of the book suggests, the chapter authors all embrace the principles of psychology and value the conducting of experiments as a means of testing theories and assumptions about how music functions in multimedia contexts. In a general sense, psychology is the science of mental life (Miller, 1962), the scientific study of mind and behavior (Doyle, 2000; Schacter, Gilbert, & Wegner, 2011). Knowledge in psychology has progressed by means of the experimental method. More specifically, in experiments, data from humans or animals are gathered under controlled conditions for the purpose of addressing specific questions. Answers to those questions advance the discipline.

For researchers outside the field of psychology, particularly those who are in the fields of music and film studies, connection with the scientific approach can be a challenge from both conceptual and practical standpoints. A few words, then, may be in order to introduce the concept of 'experiment' and its role in the empirical approach, although for more detailed information, there are many sources that might be consulted (e.g., Elmes, Kantowitz, & Roediger, 2005; Harris 2012; McKnight, McKnight, Sidani, & Figueredo, 2007; Vogt, Gardner, & Haeffele, 2012).

An *experiment* is executed for the purpose of testing a hypothesis, that is, a predicted outcome often of the effect of one *independent variable* on a *dependent variable.*[1] For example, in the field of multimedia psychology, potential hypotheses might include: (1) that the emotional meaning of TV music influences the audience member's plot expectations for that scene, (2) that the tempo of music can influence the sense of immersion in a video game environment, or (3) that music aids memory for visual, dramatic, or spoken facts in multimedia advertising or educational content delivery. In these examples, the behavior of interest—audience plot expectations, sense of immersion, and memory for facts, respectively—comprises the dependent variable, that which is measured in the study. The possible causes of that behavior—the meaning of the music, tempo of the music, or the very presence of music compared with none at all, respectively—are under experimental control and individually referred to as the independent variable.

Experiments require measures of operational variables that represent the question(s) of interest. For example, 'attention' in a multimedia context could be *operationally defined* as self-reports of interest in particular sections of a multimedia presentation. 'Memory' for multimedia events could be operationally defined as the number of discrete concepts accurately recalled after viewing an educational video under a variety of test conditions (e.g., presented with director-intended music, with alternative music selections, or without music). Or 'emotional meaning' in a multimedia context could be operationally defined as the most frequent choice from a closed set of categories (e.g., happy, neutral, sad) to describe the emotion that a particular musical excerpt conveys to individuals in a study. The judged mood of a character could be operationally defined as a word or phrase offered by the participant to describe the character's mood, a choice from any number of mood adjectives offered to the participant, or a judgment on a rating scale or series of rating scales for *happy* (where 1 = not happy… 5 = happy) or *loneliness* (where 1 = not lonely… 5 = lonely), or whatever the experimenter decides.

Based on previous research and sometimes also on introspection, the experimenter generally has some intuition about the outcome of the study that is formally stated as a hypothesis, as previously mentioned. Consider the example of a hypothesis that audiences can systematically judge the 'goodness of fit' between musical soundtracks and video excerpts. To test the hypothesis, participants could be asked to rate the goodness of fit of various combinations of music and video excerpts. Judgments of how well a selection of music fits a scene could be measured by participants on a 10-point scale where 1 represents a *very poor fit* and 10 represents a *perfect fit.* Suppose participant ratings of appropriateness for an audiovisual combination are higher for one pairing with a musical soundtrack than with another. This finding would support the original hypothesis. However, a more detailed hypothesis of cause and effect would be needed to account for the fact that certain combinations of music and video lead to higher ratings of goodness of fit while others lead to lower ratings.

Sometimes, the results of experiments are quite different than expected. Experimenters may initially be dejected and discouraged when an experiment does not result in the predicted outcome. The experimenter may think that the experiment failed to support the hypothesis; that months of time and costs of testing and analysis have all been wasted; or that the underlying ideas or the methods employed were all wrong. In reality, however, every such 'failure' constitutes a step forward in advancing current understanding. If the meaning of a multimedia event does not change under contrasting musical conditions, or if the accuracy of memory is unaffected by the presence of music, the experimenter may realize that film music has an influence only when visual information is ambiguous or that visual memory may override any influence that music might have in certain situations.

Thus, the experimental method entails an iterative process in which controlled conditions are established in order to test the researcher's hypothesis, and responses from human participants are obtained and analyzed. On the basis of the data, conclusions may be drawn regarding the success or failure in supporting the hypothesis. The process often does not end there for the conscientious researcher. If the hypothesis is supported by the study, a useful next step is to repeat the study to make absolutely sure that the same results will be obtained under the original conditions, because the first set of results may have happened by chance (although statistical analysis usually is sufficient to rule out that possibility); a replication of these results will assure that the new finding is a real one.

Clear results that support the hypothesis would normally be disseminated to the research community through journal articles and other types of scholarly publications. If the data show that under one condition the audience behaves in one way as predicted and under another condition the audience behaves in a different way, as predicted, the results are of interest. Alternatively, if results reliably show that in fact the opposite happens and the controlled conditions lead to different effects but not the predicted ones, then again, the result is of interest and would be disseminated. However, if there is no difference in the results arising from the different conditions, the results are generally not publishable, because the null findings cannot be related to the variable that was controlled in the study. A null finding encourages great care in the follow-up study and possible re-evaluation of the original method and rationale for the study.

Publication is one of the key goals of research. A new finding deserves to be made accessible to as large an audience as possible so that others can join in moving the research to the next step. Even if they are not conducting research themselves, readers of publications can gain an enhanced understanding of phenomena of interest.

Scope and organization of the book

Multimedia in its many forms (film, animation, TV, video games, the Internet, etc.) has psychological, sociological, and economic significance to contemporary society. According to the Motion Picture Association of America (2013), for example, global box office sales for 2012 totaled $43.7 billion, constituting a rise of 6 percent from the previous year, representing a continuing rise in economic and sociological relevance. It is important to understand the impact of such multimedia exposure on society. On the surface, the role of music and other aspects of audio may seem like 'frills' that are of little consequence; however, understanding the impact of multimedia cannot be complete without understanding the role of music within that context.

Audiences may encounter music and sound in multimedia contexts in an enormous number of ways. To accommodate this variety of settings and situations, the scope of the present volume is intentionally broad, dealing with multiple forms of multimedia, that is, varying combinations of sound, image, tactile stimulation, and/or other elements. However, as stated in the opening of this first chapter, the primary emphasis is on perceptual and cognitive integration of *sound and image.*

The intended audience for this book are those enrolled in undergraduate and graduate music psychology-related courses in institutions of higher learning, primarily within music and psychology departments, but also in departments of film, fine arts, media, and communications. In addition, we hope that our colleagues and other researchers will find the book to serve as a useful reference. Finally, the book is written so as to be accessible to the informed layperson; technical terms related to psychology, music, and/or multimedia are typically defined upon their first appearance, so that the content should be readily understandable to readers with expertise in any of a variety of scholarly disciplines.

Chapters are written by researchers authoritative in their fields—individuals who are actively engaged in research related to their chapter topic. The international collection of authors represents eight countries, consistent with our global village on the one hand but also providing data on similar issues gathered from persons from different cultures and nations. The body of the text is grounded in empirical work, providing a summary of current knowledge based on this past and ongoing research; each chapter constitutes an organized secondary source providing the most current research findings and specifying how they inform our understanding. Every chapter includes a comprehensive literature review on the focused topic and, where appropriate, identifies exemplary models that can be empirically tested.

The organization of the book proceeds logically with coverage that is deep as well as broad, encompassing both cognitive and emotional processes. It begins with chapters that represent contrasting, empirically based, theoretical approaches from cognitive psychology, philosophy, semiotics, communications, musicology, and neuroscience. The early chapters (Part I) elucidate principles underlying the role of music in multimedia. Part II reviews research on the structural aspects of music and multimedia with less emphasis on semantic meaning, and Part III focuses on research that examines the role of music in determining the meaning and interpretation of media to some extent independent of (or with less emphasis on) the structural aspect. Part IV explores applications of music in media including multimedia for children, video games, advertising, auditory displays of information, and the impact of surround sound, showing how theory and principle intertwine in various examples of multimedia in practice. A final chapter considers the entire volume from the perspective of future directions for the psychology of music in multimedia. Right now, however, a brief précis of each chapter, introduced in the immediately following paragraphs, provides an overview of the content of the book.

Part I

Models and multidisciplinary perspectives

The model described in the opening chapter by Annabel Cohen (Canada) entitled 'Congruence-Association Model of music and multimedia: Origin and evolution' joins associationist and Gestalt theoretical psychological perspectives in the Congruence-Association Model (CAM) to accommodate two aspects of media cognition: the structural aspect (often connected to a Gestalt perspective) and meaning (often associationist in nature). This approach paves the way for later sections of the volume that focus primarily on structural aspects (Part II) or on meaning (Part III). To accommodate the narrative element of multimedia, the notion of a conscious *working narrative* arises from the best match between bottom-up processing of sensory information of the film and top-down contextual information based on past experience represented in long-term memory. The chapter also describes Cohen's transition from the original 1988 dichotomy of music and film to six differentiated categories of sensory surface information in the model, as represented in a recent revision of the CAM: music, visual scenes, text, sound effects, speech, and bodily kinesthetic information.

In the next chapter, 'Experimental semiotics applied to visual, sound, and musical structures,' Roger Kendall (USA) and Scott Lipscomb (USA), influenced by the philosopher Charles Peirce and a semiotic theoretical perspective, take a different approach in thinking of structure/meaning as a continuum, rather than a dichotomy. They provide compelling audiovisual examples that fall at various locations along this proposed continuum of referentiality. It is one thing to demonstrate the feasibility of this scheme but another to provide empirical support for it. This they do by showing how music students are able to systematically categorize music and visual interactions in accordance with this continuum.

Audiences are affected by musical multimedia, but they also affect the development of multimedia. In his chapter entitled 'Integrating media effects research and music psychology,' Mark Shevy (USA) introduces the perspectives of communication theory and media studies, both of which aim to determine the effects of media on audiences and the processes underlying audience demand and preference for certain kinds of media. Music plays an important part in such media, and yet, as Shevy emphasizes, the research in this area typically ignores music as an independent component. Shevy reviews theories of communication, social behavior, and personality that are relevant to all audience reaction to, and demand for, music in multimedia.

Logically, the challenge of discovering the psychological processes underlying the role of music in multimedia should benefit from an understanding of the music itself. The fields of music theory and musicology are best suited to provide this knowledge. What does a researcher need to know about music in general when embarking on a study of music in multimedia, and what should or can be known about the particular musical material of interest in a research study? David Bashwiner (USA) introduces this perspective in his chapter 'Musical analysis for multimedia: A perspective from music theory.' He describes several levels of analysis that can apply to complex scenes from mainstream motion pictures; specifically, he provides concurrent analyses of the textual, musical, and visual aspects of a scene. The usefulness of this multilevel analysis is demonstrated by means of a wonderfully original analysis of the climactic scene from the film *The King's Speech*. In his speech, the king refers to the challenges ahead, and Bashwiner extends that same challenge to those who would explain the role of music in film: they must, he contends, first properly analyze the music.

Finally, attention is directed to the field of neuroscience. Whereas information about brain function at one time relied on autopsy results to determine the location of brain lesions or on rare studies of electrical stimulation of human brain cells exposed for brain surgery, technological advances have provided the opportunity to non-invasively capture images of the activity of the brain during various controlled conditions. Lars Kuchinke (Germany) studies many aspects of emotion, Hermann Kappelhoff (Germany) is a well-known film theorist, and Stefan Koelsch (Germany) is a primary contributor to the understanding of brain imaging and music. Together, in their chapter, 'Emotion and music in narrative films: A neuroscientific perspective,' they review current knowledge about the neural mechanisms for processing visual and auditory/musical information. They set the stage with a review of film-theoretic approaches to the issue of visual-musical integration. Just as an appreciation of music theory is crucial to understanding the psychology of music in multimedia, so is an appreciation of film theory. The chapter thus provides a wealth of reference material from the two quite different sources of film theory and neuroscience.

Part II

Cross-modal relations in multimedia

The next three chapters, comprising Part II, focus primarily on the structural aspects of multimedia, in essence, how sound, images, and other stimuli shape the viewer experience. In his chapter entitled 'Perceived congruence between auditory and visual elements in multimedia,' Shin-Ichiro Iwamiya (Japan) reviews the sizeable body of research with a focus on studies conducted in his country. Here, the interest is on the judged meanings of audiovisual composites that arise as a result of the manner in which the auditory and visual components of empirical stimuli are considered to be congruent (i.e., appropriately matched formally or semantically). Iwamiya then moves on to consider the dynamic relationship between changing patterns in the audio and visual domains as well as the role of cultural differences among participants related to perceived congruence. Of particular importance to Western readers interested in this topic are the clear descriptions of numerous studies published in Japanese.

In the chapter entitled 'How pitch and loudness shape musical space and motion,' Zohar Eitan (Israel) investigates the relationship between basic features of sound—specifically, *musical* sound—and aspects of physical space and motion. Such cross-modal research is crucial to understanding the multimedia context and the human cognitive processes involved in its perception. Eitan begins by presenting a general introduction to cross-domain feature correspondence, and then, based on results of empirical research, delves deeper into specific relationships: pitch height (correlated with spatial height, lateral position in space, distance, speed, and physical size) and loudness (correlated with distance, spatial height, speed, and physical size). He addresses an area that has been largely ignored: how these relationships function when perceiving dynamic (i.e., time-varying) stimuli.

Scott Lipscomb (USA), in his chapter entitled 'Cross-modal alignment of accent structures in multimedia,' addresses the synchronization of important events across the aural and visual sensory modalities. On the basis of past research, he identifies specific determinants of 'accent' (salient moments) within each perceptual domain, presenting a tripartite model of accent structure alignment (Yeston, 1976) as a means of systematizing the study of temporal–structural relationships in multimedia contexts. Very few studies have addressed the issue of cross-modal accent structure alignment; even fewer have focused specifically on the empirical bases for determining our current understanding. Lipscomb uniquely reviews perceptual studies of multimedia stimuli that represent varying levels of complexity, some approaching the complexity level of real-world multimedia experiences.

Part III

Interpretation and meaning

Part III includes two chapters that directly address the meaning of multimedia as interpreted by listener-viewers. Marilyn Boltz (USA) presents a chapter entitled 'Music videos and visual influences on music perception and appreciation: Should you want your MTV?'[2] As evident in a number of the previous chapters, a fair amount of research has addressed the ways in which music may influence the cognitive processing of visual information. Boltz's chapter reverses the question by asking: How might visual information influence our perception and appreciation of musical stimuli? This focus is particularly relevant to the music video context in which music is the driving force with video seemingly—and somewhat unusually—in a supportive role. Based on past research, Boltz addresses a number of relevant contexts: the role of the visual component in music learning and in the evaluation of musical performances, the impact of physical appearance on assessments of musical ability, and interrelationships between physical gestures of performers and perception of the musical performance by the audience. After a brief discussion of issues related to the coordination amongst members of performing ensembles, Boltz proceeds to investigate what we know about the experience of music videos for the purpose of artistic expression. She then reviews theoretical foundations relevant to audiovisual interactions, revealing the influence one modality can have on perception in another and the ability for cross-modal information to 'fill in' missing information in another modality to complete an affective response.

In their chapter entitled 'Music and memory in film and other multimedia: The Casablanca effect,' Berthold Hoeckner (USA) and Howard Nusbaum (USA) consider whether music might be a more effective means of cuing visual recall than visual images are for cuing recall of musical sound. Using *Casablanca* (and Max Steiner's well-known musical score for this classic film) as a point of departure, the authors delve into a discussion of films in which memory plays a significant role within the film narrative itself (e.g., Hitchcock's *Spellbound* and Gondry's *Eternal Sunshine of the Spotless Mind*).

Building on the pioneering work of Hugo Münsterberg (1916/1970), they also describe how evolving cinematic techniques that allow film narratives to move freely across time and space (such as cuts and flashbacks) enable film-makers to represent memory in ways that reflect our experiences. Film depictions of memory processes, in turn, have influenced popular notions of how memory works. Hoeckner and Nusbaum then turn to a discussion of the role of different types of memory in processing sound and image in film and other multimedia, including episodic (and autobiographical) memory, semantic memory, and implicit memory. The chapter concludes by revisiting some of the main questions emerging from the empirical studies reviewed.

Part IV

Applications: Music and sound in multimedia

The final section of the book comprises five chapters that present specific applications of multimedia in a variety of contexts. The chapters address topics related to media for children, video games, advertising, and informational displays and surround-sound. The chapter by Sandra Calvert (USA) entitled 'Children's media: The role of music and audio features,' examines the impact of musical multimedia upon infants, children, and adolescents. Young children rarely gaze at the television for extended periods; they play with toys and look only intermittently at the screen. Sound plays an important role in capturing their attention. Calvert's chapter identifies specific auditory formal features that direct children's attention to the screen at important plot points to support comprehension of the story line. The chapter also explores the functions of music in multimedia for infants, children, and adolescents—including effects of background music, sung versus spoken text, and actively singing lyrics—on attention, comprehension, and memory of information presented. Finally, Calvert discusses the creative opportunities available to these 'digital natives' (Prensky, 2001) via a new generation of multimedia authoring tools.

Mark Grimshaw (Denmark), Siu-Lan Tan (USA), and Scott Lipscomb (USA) address the role of the auditory component in computer and video games in a chapter entitled 'Playing with sound: The role of music and sound effects in gaming.' Atari's *Pong* (Alcorn, 1972) was the first game to feature sound, and it is surprising to see just how far game audio has come. No longer consisting of 'bleeps' and 'blips' and trivial melodies, computer and video game music is now frequently compared to orchestral film scores and sound effects are increasingly elaborate and realistic. After a brief description of evolving technological developments and their direct impact on sound design for computer and video games, the authors explore the variety of roles fulfilled by music and sound effects in interactive games. Grimshaw et al. then provide a thorough review of empirical research related to the sonic component of gaming, including the effects of the presence of sound on player performance, subjective aspects of the gaming experience, and players' physiological responses.

In the chapter entitled 'Music in television advertising and other persuasive media,' Mark Shevy (USA) and Kineta Hung (Hong Kong) review empirical research on the role of music in media with the specific intent to influence behavior. Music is prevalent in advertising, but its effects are not always easy to predict. Some studies show that music can sharpen attention and memory for an advertisement and strengthen its persuasive message. However, music can also interfere with efficient processing of information and even weaken the impact of an advertisement. Many variables may interact with listener-viewers' individual traits to ultimately determine how a person will respond to the music in an advertisement. Shevy and Hung's chapter provides the groundwork to understand the complex and often nuanced effects that music may have in persuasive multimedia contexts (e.g., musical preference and familiarity, how well the music seems to fit the product or service being endorsed, and conscious and unconscious associations one has formed for the music).

Agnieszka Roginska (USA) explores the uses and functions of auditory displays in the chapter entitled 'Auditory icons, earcons, and displays: Information and expression through sound.' She begins by presenting a brief history of these phenomena, extending back to the Ancient Greek era. Roginska then provides a detailed discussion of the various types of auditory display, including earcons, auditory icons, spatial auditory displays, and speech-based auditory displays. The author then turns to the sonification of complex data sets in order to facilitate the discovery of patterns as a result of the identification of auditory signatures, a discussion that is complemented by a following section focused on data mapping. The chapter concludes with a set of specific applications within multimedia contexts, including the use of auditory displays for interaction and feedback, alerting, monitoring, navigation, and the augmentation of reality.

In the final chapter of this section, 'Understanding the impact of surround sound in multimedia,' Mark Kerins (USA) investigates the role of multichannel audio playback when experiencing multimedia. Focusing specifically on motion pictures, because this is the medium in which most relevant technological advances occurred, Kerins provides a brief history of the evolution of sound in multimedia. The author then reviews dozens of empirical studies that have informed us about the effect of auditory presentation mode on audience perceptions of the multimedia experience. The author then dissects the manner in which multichannel sound directly impacts the experience, including factors such as presentation context and content of the various multisensory components comprising multimedia. Bringing the chapter to a close, Kerins proposes the existence of what he calls the 'digital surround style,' in which the content of the auditory track and visual images in isolation becomes subordinate to the audiovisual experience as a whole, in essence, the image–sound interrelationship.

Final remarks

From the time of the early Greek dramas through Wagner's *Gesamtkunstwerke* in the 19th century, music performance was a visual-musical experience. The development of sound recording in the 19th century changed this. Music could be presented independently of other modalities, sharing this privilege previously held by visual images that could stand alone as sole objects of appreciation. Now in the digital age, presentation of visual still and moving images increasingly includes music and audio soundtracks. The growing prevalence of multimedia fully justifies both the burgeoning interest in film-music studies and academic programs focusing on multimedia. These and related activities have been on the increase since the 1990s in line with developments in digital technology, but much of this work has been theoretical or practical in orientation rather than empirical.

The collection of chapters in the present volume is the first to gather in one place the body of empirical research in the field of psychology and across numerous other disciplines that refer in one way or another to the impact of music and audio on the experience of multimedia. Our hope is that this volume will fill a gap for the growing numbers of students, scholars, and artists who are intrigued by this field. One of our aspirations is that the book will provide the foundation for future discoveries, discoveries that will elucidate the role of music and sound in multimedia, increase the effectiveness of the auditory component of multimedia, and contribute to our general understanding of the human mind in perceptual, cognitive, emotional, and narrative processes.

Applying the empirical approach to multimedia, as advocated throughout the book, requires much knowledge: knowledge to create multimedia stimuli having particular features, knowledge to measure and analyze listener-viewer responses, knowledge to develop hypotheses based on various disciplinary theories, and knowledge to interpret data in terms of such theories. Such diverse knowledge is more easily found in a research team than in a single researcher. Each member of such a research team offers different areas of expertise across disciplinary boundaries. For success, however, the team members must share a common language. It is our hope that the present volume may help to establish such common ground so as to advance our understanding of the psychology of music in multimedia.

Notes

1. Hypothesis testing, data collection in controlled experimental designs, statistical analysis, and the belief in objective science reflect a particular approach to research and one that is increasingly contrasted with qualitative research methodology. Qualitative methods are equally valid empirical methods for determining the nature of a situation and of gaining knowledge. Focus groups, semi-structured interviews, analysis of diaries and documents are some examples and these methods could be applied to questions about the role of music in multimedia. This is not to suggest necessarily a clearcut distinction between quantitative and qualitative research.
2. MTV is an acronym for 'music television,' a music channel established in the USA in 1981. In its early years, the channel played music videos almost exclusively, interrupted periodically by brief segments of spoken dialogue by video jockeys (VJs) and commercials.

References

Albarino, R. (1966). Goldstein's LightWorks at Southhampton. *Variety*, *213*(12). Cited in *Multimedia*. Retrieved from <http://en.wikipedia.org/wiki/Multimedia> (accessed October 8, 2012).

Alcorn, A. (1972). *Pong* [Computer game]. United States: Atari. Center for Visual Music. Retrieved from <http://www.centerforvisualmusic.org> (accessed October 14, 2012).

Chion, M. (1994). *Audio-vision: Sound on screen* (C. Gorbman, Trans.). New York, NY: Columbia University Press. (Original work published in French in 1990.)

Cohen, A. J. (Ed.) (1994). Special volume on the psychology of film music. *Psychomusicology*, *13*.

Cook, N. (1998). *Analyzing musical multimedia.* New York, NY: Oxford University Press.

Doyle, C. L. (2000). Psychology: Definition. In A. E. Kazdin (Ed.), *Encyclopedia of psychology* (Vol. 6, pp. 374–376). Washington, DC: American Psychological Association.

Elmes, D. G., Kantowitz, B. H., & Roediger III, H. L. (2005). *Research methods in psychology* (8th ed.). Belmont, CA: Wadsworth.

Gorbman, C. (1987). *Unheard melodies: Narrative film music.* Bloomington, IN: Indiana University Press.

Harris, C. (Ed.). (2012). *APA handbook of research methods in psychology.* Washington, DC: American Psychological Association.

Kendall, R. A., & Savage, R. W. (Eds.). (2005). Selected reports in ethnomusicology. Perspectives in Systematic Musicology, *12.*

Maras, S. (1996). Convergence/divergence: Ten definitions of multimedia. *Metro, 108,* 9–13. Retrieved from <http://members.optusnet.com.au/~maras/divergence.html> (accessed September 9, 2012).

Mayer, R. E. (2009). *Multimedia learning* (2nd ed.). New York, NY: Cambridge University Press.

McKnight, P. E., McKnight, K. M., Sidani, S., & Figueredo, A. J. (2007). *Missing data: A gentle introduction.* New York, NY: Guilford Press.

Miller, G. A. (1962). *Psychology: The science of mental.* Reading, MA: Addison Wesley.

Monaco, J. (1999). *The dictionary of new media: The digital world of video, audio, and print.* New York, NY: Harbor Electronic Publishing. Cited in R. Norquist. (n.d.). *Media, medium, mediums: Commonly confused words.* Retrieved from <http://grammar.about.com/od/alightersideofwriting/a/mediagloss.htm> (accessed September 29, 2012).

Motion Picture Association of America (2013). *Theatrical market statistics 2012.* Retrieved from <http://www.mpaa.org/Resources/3037b7a4-58a2-4109-8012-58fca3abdf1b.pdf>.

Münsterberg, H. (1970). *The photoplay: A psychological study.* New York, NY: Arno. (Original work published 1916.)

Prensky, M. (2001). Digital natives, digital immigrants. *On the Horizon, 9*(5), 1–6. Retrieved from <http://www.marcprensky.com/writing/Prensky%20-%20Digital%20Natives,%20Digital%20Immigrants%20-%20Part1.pdf> (accessed October 14, 2012).

Schacter, D. L., Gilbert, D. T., & Wegner, D. M. (2011). *Psychology* (2nd ed.). New York, NY: Worth.

Tan, S. -L., Pfordresher, P. Q., & Harré, R. (2010). *Psychology of music: From sound to significance.* London, UK: Psychology Press.

Vogt, W. P., Gardner, D. C., & Haeffele, L. M. (2012). *When to use what research design.* New York, NY: Guilford Press.

Yeston, M. (1976). *The stratification of musical rhythm.* New Haven, CT: Yale University Press.

Part I

Models and Multidisciplinary Perspectives

Chapter 2

Congruence-Association Model of music and multimedia: Origin and evolution

Annabel J. Cohen

University of Prince Edward Island, Canada

The present chapter describes a research path in the psychology of music and multimedia with a specific focus on the development of the Congruence-Association Model that originated over 25 years ago. The history conveys not only the research and theoretical outcomes but also, and perhaps even more importantly, an example of the process of discovery in this field. Showing how ideas generate experiments and how predicted and unpredicted results of experiments inspire further studies may encourage others to engage in testing their own theories, ideas, and insights.

Background

The late 19th century witnessed the emergence of both the scientific study of behavior and the invention of the moving image. Psychology and the movies had more than a birthday in common. Each exploited new electronic technologies for controlling the presentation of information to human observers. A catalogue of the equipment of the psychology laboratory of Harvard University in 1893 included a long list of basic resources as well as the stereopticon and zoetrope (Münsterberg, 1893), forerunners of the motion picture projector. While for psychology, the technology enabled measurement of the human responses reflecting how the mind worked, for film, the technology engaged the audience and ultimately helped to achieve commercial viability. The success of the moving-picture industry depended on implicit theories of human perception, motivation, and attitude formation, the very aspects of human experience that psychologists would try to make explicit through experiments measuring human responses.

Music played a role in the development of both psychology and the movies. Early psychologists were interested in how we hear, just as they were interested in how we see and in all other mental phenomena including thinking and aesthetics. That first experimental psychology laboratory at Harvard had many collections of tuning forks, organ pipes, and bells as well as a music keyboard, all for the purpose of understanding auditory and musical phenomena. Many early professors of psychology were well versed in music. Only a small percentage of the population attended university in those days. Those so privileged typically also had the opportunity to receive training in music as part of their earlier education. Regarding developments in film, from the start, film exploited music to mask the sound of the film projector but also to serve other aesthetic functions (Langdale, 2002; Marks, 1997; Münsterberg, 1916/1970). The importance of music to early film led to a small industry. Companies published scores of appropriate music for pianists[1] and other musicians employed in the majority of movie theaters. Some theaters had special theater organs or were fit for small orchestras, offering greater sound variety. The emergence of the talking film in 1927, however, heralded the demise of this film-music industry, but to the surprise of many, a new industry soon emerged to supply the recorded orchestral music integral to contemporary motion pictures.

American behaviorism rose to prominence in the 1920s, and for the next four decades it created a less favorable climate for the study of mental phenomena than the climate of earlier days of psychology. Behaviorism, inspired by Pavlovian classical conditioning in Russia, emphasized the value of scientific objectivity and the importance of measuring observable responses. Behaviorists showed, for example, that the number of times a rat pressed a bar in a Skinner box could help disclose natural laws of human learning. Exploring mental imagery, thought, and creativity, however, did not fit this zeitgeist, and neither then did music. The later part of this period also overlapped with World War II when theorists and experimentalists embraced applied psychology in support of the war effort, be it the development of intelligence and personality tests or the measurement of code effectiveness in the transmission of information between allies. In the 1960s, however, the limitations of the behaviorist approach combined with new ideas arising from information theory gave way to cognitive psychology, with a renewed interest in mental activity. Once again psychology of music could begin to flourish but this time with increasingly proficient technologies and methods (cf. Cohen, 2005a, 2009).

Experiments in music and psychology during the early cognitive period of the 1970s and 1980s typically focused on memory, music structure, and the bridging of music theory and psychology (Krumhansl, 1990). The work revealed that concepts from music theory could provide insights into how the mind dealt with music. My research in music psychology during that time initially focused on musical structure (Cohen, 1975), and how the mind represented the elements of music (Cuddy & Cohen, 1976), or how to generate musical sequences for experiments using new computer technology and digital synthesis (Cohen, Isaacs, Flores, Harrison, & Bradley, 1977). The similarities between musical structure and the structure of moving images were also intriguing, and the role of music in film was a curiosity. An opportunity to explore this arose when in 1983 an undergraduate student, Sandra Marshall, who shared my interest in the topic of music and the moving image, approached me to supervise a research project connecting music and psychology.

Around that time, Thayer and Levenson (1983) had reported that background music altered skin conductance level (a measure of emotional arousal) during a short rather gruesome instructional film about industrial workplace safety. Specifically chosen horror-film music and documentary-music when paired with the film increased or reduced respectively the skin conductance measure as compared to a condition without music. In developmental psychology, Spelke (1979) had reported on infants' attention to film that was temporally congruent with background music. The articles by Thayer and Levenson (1983) and Spelke (1979) provided context for our study and for the Congruence-Association Model developed to explain the data.

Frameworks, models, and theories

Before continuing, it is well to consider the terms 'model,' 'theory,' and 'framework.' Each of these terms highlights relevant dimensions of a problem space in order to address questions within that space. Here the problem space must include the role of music in perception of film, and so within the space we need to identify music, film, and the mind. Each of these concepts, 'music,' 'film,' and 'mind,' needs further division. The initial three-part division itself (into *music*, *film*, and *mind*) may not even be the only or best one. The issue of identifying categories and boundaries is complex. The importance of 'carving nature at its joints' was identified in Plato's Phaedrus (360 BCE/2012),[2] so it has been with us for some time. We can think of the goal of empirical work as determining what are the units from which larger units are formed, and how do these units work together to create the phenomena we are trying to explain, in this case how film music works. How should we conceive of film, music, and the mind to account for the function of music in film?

For the purposes of the present chapter, the term *framework* implies the least assumptions of the three terms and simply means a way of looking at a problem or at a set of data. The term *model* suggests the creation of a tangible representation of a complex process, as in an architectural drawing. The notion is that if you can build something, you understand how it works. Finally, a *theory* may be more abstract and may live in the world of logic and mathematics in order to make precise predictions from initial premises.

The initial proposal of the Congruence-Association ideas began as a framework for understanding the role of music in film, but as the idea was sustained, developed, and took more shape, it seemed appropriate, therefore, to call it a model. It can lead to testable hypotheses, with which data can be considered to be consistent or not. As neuroscience progresses, it may be possible to translate the components of the model into brain mechanisms for which precise predictions about perception, memory, and aesthetic response can be made. Currently, the model allows us to consider how these human responses may arise from the flow of information that it depicts. Its great advantage is in providing the scaffolding for considering many factors that simultaneously interact in the *film–music–mind* context.

Congruence-Association Model—iteration 1 (CAM-1)

Upon deciding to work on the problem of film music, Sandra Marshall and I needed a film for use in our experiment. The challenge of choosing stimulus materials faces anyone who intends to carry out research on music and film or music and multimedia (Cohen, 2005b). It is not a trivial problem. Fortuitously, Sandra's first class in Social

Psychology had included a discussion of stereotyping supported by a simple film animation featuring two triangles and a circle. This was the classic 2-minute film from Heider and Simmel (1944) that had been developed to illustrate how attitudes and stereotypes can arise even when observing moving geometric figures.

Heider and Simmel (1944), in their research on attitudes, had observed that persons who watched the film tended to refer to the big triangle as a bully and the two smaller figures as innocent victims. The finding was remarkable because, after all, these moving geometric figures were nothing more than a few lines, and yet their motion patterns provoked attitudes that were normally associated with complex human interactions. Viewers systematically responded as if the geometric figures had personalities and motives. The stable finding allowed us to ask: Could different background music alter the meaning of or attitudes toward these geometric figures?

In order to determine whether music could change the meaning of the geometric figures, two similar experiments were conducted. The first, which was exploratory, entailed classical music by Tchaikovsky, and the second included two contrasting scores that Sandra composed. In both studies, participants were asked to watch the film in only one of two music conditions or in a condition without music, and then rate the three characters and the film overall on bipolar adjective scales (e.g., heroic–villainous, brave–cowardly). In the second experiment, the adjectives were chosen to represent three dimensions of affective (i.e., emotional/connotative as opposed to denotative/dictionary) meaning: *evaluative* (e.g., good–bad), *potency* (e.g., strong–weak), and *activity* (e.g., fast–slow). These three dimensions had evolved through a long program of research on the *semantic differential* (Osgood, Suci, & Tannenbaum, 1957). The three dimensions were considered as independent aspects of affective meaning, and the bipolar adjective pairs chosen in the study were known to load more heavily on one of the three dimensions. Four heavily-loaded bipolar adjective pairs were chosen for each of the three semantic-differential dimensions. The study thus produced 12 bipolar adjective ratings for each of the three figures, for the music, and for film itself. A mean value was calculated using each of the four adjective pairs intended to represent the three semantic dimensions: evaluative, potency, and activity. These three mean values under different music background conditions became the primary data of interest.

Under the two different music conditions, there were significantly different average ratings on a semantic-differential dimension (e.g., the activity dimension) for the three geometric characters. This is illustrated by the fact that the lines in Figure 2.1 are not parallel. We had expected that one type of music would affect all characters the same way, but this is not what happened, and this result made us stop and think about what was going on. The first thing we did was conduct a short follow-up study to show that this effect of interest was repeatable.

Why weren't all the characters affected equally by the meaning of the music? Why was the impact of the music not consistent across all contexts? If you reflect on these questions and take into account the temporal structure and the meaning of the music and film elements, you might come up with the same suggestion as was proposed in our paper—a two-stage mental process. One process exploited the shared (congruent) temporal structure of the music and film, guiding attention to a particular part of the film. The second process directed the meanings (or associations) of the music to the

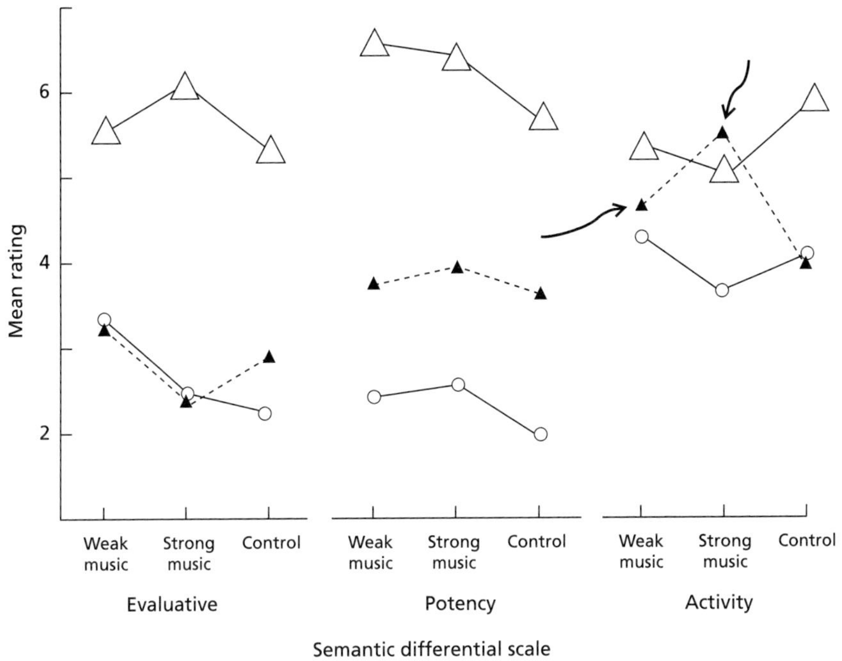

Figure 2.1 Mean rating on the Evaluative, Potency, and Activity dimensions for the three film characters as a function of the Weak, Strong, and Control (no music) soundtrack conditions. The arrows point to the Activity ratings for the small triangle that differ significantly under the two music soundtrack conditions. Data from *Music Perception*, 6(1), Effects of musical soundtracks on attitudes to geometric figures, Marshall, S., & Cohen, A. J., p. 108, figure 7 © 1988, Regents of the University of California.

place on the screen where visual attention had been directed by the first process. The two processes were referred to as Congruence and Association respectively, and led to the Congruence-Association Model—later referred to as CAM for short. Congruence referred to the structural overlap in music and film (see Figure 2.2).[3]

Structure—congruence

Rhythm, beat, and accent pattern are examples of musical structure. There are other kinds of structure as well, for example, harmony and the up and down contour pattern of melody. Perhaps less obvious is this type of structure in the visual domain of film, for example, an accent pattern created by objects moving on the screen, be it human limbs, fluttering leaves, boughs of branches, or, traveling vehicles that create patterns of light and dark that change across time. The brain receives input from these two sensory sources of structure, acoustic and optical. In its attempt to make sense of the world, it is reasonable to assume that the brain would direct more attention to the shared structural (congruent) patterns than to structural patterns that are incongruent.

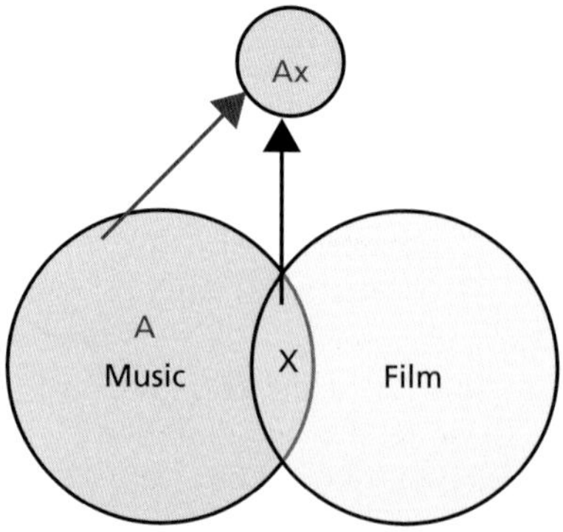

Figure 2.2 Congruence-Association Model—iteration 1 based on figure 8b of Marshall and Cohen (1988, p. 109). The model depicts two channels of information, one for music and one for film represented by respective circles. The overlap in the structure of music and film domains is represented by the overlap in the two circles (at x). Attention is directed to this area of visual overlap, and associations (A) of the music are ascribed to this visual focus of attention. The information flow is in one direction, bottom-up, from sensory coding to interpretation. A second component of the model accounting for how music influences the evaluative meaning judgment of the film is not shown (figure 8a). Adapted from *Music Perception*, 6(1), Effects of musical soundtracks on attitudes to geometric figures, Marshall, S. K., & Cohen, A. J., p. 109, figure 8b © 1988, Regents of the University of California, with permission.

This notion of cross-modal congruence was actually investigated with infants by Spelke (1979) who also showed similar sensitivities in a control group of adults. Spelke's approach was consistent with that of Gibson (1966). Gibson had advanced the notion of perceptual processes constantly in search of regularities in the world, what he termed *affordances* (see also Sirius & Clarke, 1994). The notion of attention directed to shared structure is also consistent with Gestalt principles of good form (Prägnanz), although the Gestalt psychologists typically focused on structure within a single sensory modality. A problem with Gestalt psychological principles is that they are not easily quantified. Garner (1974) directed attention to this problem with the help of simple, clever experiments inspired by his prior applications of the mathematical theory of information to problems of perception and memory (Garner, 1962).

Gestalt principles influenced two major theories of music perception: the Generative Theory of Tonal Music (GTTM) (Lerdahl & Jackendoff, 1983) and the Implication Realization theory (Narmour, 1990). The former focused attention on segmentation of music into meaningful units and phrases, while the latter focused on expectancies while listening to music. Similarly, Bregman's (1990) influential theory of auditory stream segregation owes much to Gestalt principles of grouping. These theories dealt with the acoustic domain, but since the time of the early Gestalt psychologists (e.g., Wertheimer, 1939), Gestalt principles of perceptual organization have been applied to visual stimuli. The study of perceived cross-modal audiovisual correspondence also has a long history. As reviewed by Spence (2011), a relevant question of contemporary neuroscientific interest is that of how the brain knows to combine signals from different sources. Kubovy and Yu (2012) argue in a related context that the 'strongest relation between perceptual organization in vision and perceptual organization in audition is likely to be by way of analogous Gestalt laws' (p. 94). Cross-modal correspondences had also interested a number of composers, for example, Schoenberg and Scriabin, as described by Cook (1998) in his chapter on 'Synesthesia and Similarity.' Part II of the present volume addresses cross-modal correspondence in greater depth through the work of Lipscomb, Iwamiya, and Eitan.

A general cognitive principle is that of limited mental capacity (Cohen, 2005a; Miller, 1956). The mind cannot attend to everything equally. If a choice must be made, it makes sense to direct attention to information that is coordinated between the two modalities. The term *congruence* in the Congruence-Association Model refers to the priority of attention to information that is structurally congruent across two modalities.[3] The focus of attention is an additional aspect. Attention is often directed to vision rather than to audition when both audio and visual stimuli are present (e.g., Colavita, 1974). The phenomenon is referred to as *visual dominance*, although situations can arise in which the auditory sense is primary (cf. Boltz, Chapter 10, this volume; Boltz, Ebendorf, & Field, 2009). Due to the dominance of vision over hearing in many situations, the CAM model[4] initially claimed that structural congruence between the music and the visual structure could control visual attention. Indeed, Spelke (1979) showed such a mechanism in infants and adults.

Many neuroscientists interested in consciousness are also focusing on synchronous activity patterns arising in different parts of the brain (e.g., Edelman & Tononi, 2000). Thus, the notion of congruence across vision and audition is consistent both with evidence of infants' early sensitivities to visual and auditory temporal correspondence and with evidence of remotely located brain rhythms creating a single network of activity. The notion of congruence implies a mechanism for drawing attention to cross-modally correlated information, and it also accommodates the possibility that attention may be directed to that correlated information within a dominant modality. Once attention is directed to a location, there remains the problem of interpreting information at the attended site. So there are three parts to the notion of congruence: (1) a brain response to coordinated information across modalities, (2) assignment of privileged status to this information (it has a higher priority for attention than non-congruent activity), and (3) conscious attention that may be disproportionally directed to the congruent information across modalities. The dominant modality is typically visual, but not necessarily.

Meaning—association

The previous discussion of the role of music has focused on the structure of the music and film. The *meaning* of music is another aspect of music that addresses the problem of interpretation of stimuli to which attention is directed.[5] The music by itself has meaning, where we define meaning here as the associations the music brings to mind. Even during the heyday of behaviorism, research on the meaning of music was conducted. Hevner (1935) showed that listeners agreed on the meaning of the major and minor modes among other features and dimensions of music. Rigg (1937) showed further agreement on the happy/sad meaning of classical works of music as well as more refined judgments (e.g., whether the music reflected death, sorrow, religion, love, activity, or nature). On the basis of intuition and his early findings Rigg said: 'Music enters readily into associative bonds' (p. 223). Later Collier and Hubbard (2001) related specific physical dimensions of pitch height, tempo, and direction to judgments of happiness or sadness (with high pitch, fast tempo, and upward direction being associated with happiness). While it is possible that these meanings may be innate, an experiential account is also available. Here, the human body is regarded as a musical instrument that alters its shape depending on emotion. Happy bodies speak more quickly and at a higher pitch (and possibly with more upward inflections) than sad bodies. Thus, due to this 'body language of emotions which exerts its influence also over the behavior of the voice organs' (Sundberg, 1983, p. 147), the music reflecting these characteristics comes to be associated with a particular feeling of happiness or sadness, and such associations are then learned.

The musicologist Peter Burkholder (2006) has put forward an associationist theory of musical meaning that overlaps with the one espoused here, though it is musicological rather than psychological. Based on experience, some music seems happy, or sad, or fearful, or may remind us of a particular culture, or time of year, or event. The tune 'Auld Lang Syne' reminds Western listeners of New Year's Eve, but in Japan 'Auld Lang Syne' played in a department store signals closing time. Given that music systematically elicits associations, once attention is directed to a particular part of the film, the associations from the music can be ascribed to that focus of attention. That is represented by the Association part of the Congruence-Association Model. Together, congruence and association can explain why an object or action depicted on the cinema screen will be interpreted in one way when accompanied by one music score and in a different way when accompanied by another. Before discussing this model further, it is useful to consider examples of some psychological studies that examined either the congruence or association aspect of film music.

Studies of congruence between music and visual motion patterns

First, let us look at the congruence aspect. As reviewed in this volume, Scott Lipscomb (see also Lipscomb, 1999, 2005, Chapter 9, this volume) created simple auditory and visual motion patterns. For example the auditory pattern consisted of the beginning notes of a scale (*do re mi fa*) repeating over and over again, and the visual pattern consisted of a dot oscillating between two positions. Visual patterning was either synchronous or asynchronous with the auditory patterning. Participants reliably rated the degree of alignment of the patterns, and this degree of alignment correlated highly with the judged 'effectiveness' of the two patterns combined, particularly for simple stimuli.

Iwamiya (2008, see also Chapter 7, this volume) and his students explored congruencies as well, for example, working with auditory patterns that increase and decrease in pitch along with visual patterns that contract or expand in similar ways. Kim and Iwamiya (2008) explored the congruence between auditory patterns and visual transformations of words (called telops) that move about as in television ads. Some of the auditory patterns were correlated in time with the visual transformations and others were not. The authors claimed that the different degrees of auditory-visual structural correlation led to different judgments of the telop patterns.

Hamon-Hall, Cohen, and Klein (in preparation) have been examining perceived boundaries in a Beethoven orchestral excerpt and in the visual pattern of the Heider and Simmel film, used in the Marshall and Cohen (1988) study, in individual auditory and visual modalities, and in combined modalities. The purpose was to determine whether boundaries arising when the modalities are considered separately influence the boundaries perceived when the modalities are combined. Krumhansl and Schenk (1997) carried out a similar study in the realm of dance. They examined the choreography by George Ballantine for a Mozart divertimento. They showed a similarity in judging boundaries (judging section ends) for the visual and music modalities, but also in the bimodal condition, the strength of the boundaries was greater, suggesting additivity across the two modalities. However, as Ballantine believed that dance structure should mirror musical structure, it is difficult to determine from this example whether the boundaries in the music influenced the perceived visual boundaries. This would require examples in which the music and visual boundaries differed in their temporal structures. Vines, Krumhansl, Wanderley, and Levitin (2006) studied the role of music and visual (bodily motion) information in judging the performance by a clarinetist. Participants in the study either heard, saw, or both heard and saw the music and the performer. Of particular interest is that judgments of phrasing were similar for both the visual- and music-only conditions, indicating that bodily motion can reliably represent phrasing or temporal structure found in music. The authors note that 'there is an inherent temporal correspondence between events in a musician's sound and in body movement; some change in body state accompanies every change in sound' (p. 103). They also argued that the ability to perceive the musical phrase structure through visual information shows 'high-level pattern processing in visual perception' (p. 105).

Part of the challenge of studying shared music-visual structure is to create the visual patterns of animations and corresponding musical patterns (unless like Vines et al. (2006), one is filming a performance). Kendall's interest in this problem has recently led to generating fairly complex visual animations that are correlated or are not correlated with the temporal structure of musical patterns (see Kendall, 2005a, 2005b, 2010; Kendall & Lipscomb, Chapter 3, this volume).

Studies of association

Whereas the discussion of the concept of Congruence focused on the separate structure of the musical and visual information, the concept of Association focuses on the semantic aspect, that is, the meaning. As before, it is useful first to determine what each separate modality, visual and musical, means on its own and then to determine what the meaning is when modalities are combined. We then ask: Does the meaning of the combination relate in a systematic way to the meaning of the components? My students and I carried out a series of studies along these lines with a variety of materials ranging from very simple to complex.

The studies have the same basic design. The simplest case consisted of a bouncing ball as the visual material and a simple tone pattern. Both the visual and auditory stimuli varied along two dimensions, tempo and height, in the same way—the ball could bounce at a low, middle, or high height, and it could bounce at a slow, moderate, or fast speed. Similarly, the tone could be low, middle, or high in pitch, or slow, medium, or fast in tempo. Participants were presented with these patterns either alone or in combination, and they were asked to rate either the ball, or the sound, on a numeric scale on the dimension of sadness/happiness. Participants agreed that a high, fast bounce is happy, and a low, slow bounce is sad, while a high, fast pitch is happy, and so on. What we learned was that participants considered the information from the two sources when the ball and sound were combined, so that a low, slow pitch tended to neutralize the happiness of a high, fast bounce.

More recently Jeong et al. (2011) presented happy or sad faces accompanied by happy or sad music and obtained both behavioral measures on a happiness–sadness scale as well as brain images (derived from measurement of blood oxygen level-dependent signal—BOLD). The emotion of the music systematically influenced the ratings of happiness–sadness of the faces consistent with results mentioned earlier, and correlated music-visual meaning led to activity in one area of the brain (superior temporal gyrus), while uncorrelated meaning led to activity in another (the fusiform gyrus).

A similar behavioral study with slightly more realistic stimuli was conducted observing interactions among wolves. Bolivar, Cohen, and Fentress (1994) examined the role of aggressive and friendly music on the judged aggressiveness and friendliness of wolves engaged in social interactions. The music and visual clips selected for the study were independently judged by viewers or listeners and rated on the friendliness–aggressiveness continuum. Based on these average ratings, we chose four music examples regarded as most friendly and four examples regarded as most aggressive, and four most friendly and most aggressive wolf interactions. When the visual and musical information were presented together for aggressiveness–friendliness ratings by another group of participants, meanings from both the music and the video sources influenced the judgments, providing evidence of additivity of the meanings from the two modalities. The visual information contributed more to the judgments than did the music, but both played significant roles.

A final example (cf. Cohen, 1993) in this set of studies made use of two contrasting excerpts from a realistic narrative film. One clip was of an unambiguous fight scene, the other was of an ambiguous interaction between a man and a woman—it was unclear whether they were fighting or engaged in a playful, amorous encounter. Two excerpts of music were chosen, entitled by their composer as 'Say Hello to Love' and 'Conflict.' Listeners judged the titles as highly appropriate for the music. These music stimuli were presented in combination with both the ambiguous and unambiguous scenes. Participants in the study viewed and heard each excerpt in only one combination. Semantic differential judgments (evaluation, potency, activity) and title ratings were obtained for the film and music individually and in combination. It was expected that the presence of both pieces of music would influence the meaning of the visual clips. However, the music influenced only the meaning of the ambiguous interaction but did not influence the meaning of the unambiguous fight scene. In retrospect it was obvious that the meaning of the visual clip of the fight was so clear that no additional background context was likely to change it. This added to the understanding of the conditions in which film music could change meaning.

Other studies have shown the influence of music on film interpretation (e.g., Boltz, 2001; Bullerjahn & Güldenring, 1994; Lipscomb & Kendall, 1994/1996; Shevy, 2007; Thompson, Russo, & Sinclair, 1994). When Eldar, Ganor, Admon, Bleich, and Hendler (2007) presented joyful or fearful music with an emotionally neutral film clip, the type of music influenced behavioral ratings of the meaning of the clip. Brain activity measured by functional magnetic resonance imaging (fMRI) in emotion centers of the brain (amygdala, hippocampus, and lateral prefrontal regions), however, were activated only in the combined condition as compared to either the music or film alone. The emotionality of the music on its own was insufficient to affect a response in the amygdala. It is as if a situation represented by video does not call forth a deep level of emotion without accompanying music that is somehow compelling. See also Baumgartner, Lutz, Schmidt, and Jäncke (2006), and Spreckelmeyer, Kutas, Urbach, Altenmüller, and Münte (2006) for related findings with affective visual still images. Reviews of the neural basis of emotion in music by Koelsch (2010) and of emotion in film music, in particular by Kuchinke, Kappelhoff, and Koelsch (Chapter 6, this volume), suggest that the neuroscientific problem is complex. Consistent with this picture of complexity, Ellis and Simons (2005) showed additivity of music and visual emotional meaning in self-reports of emotion but not in physiological measures of heart rate, electromyography, and skin conductance.

These studies have all examined the influence of music on visual information presented simultaneously. However, music can precede or follow events depicted on the screen. Boltz, Schulkind, and Kantra (1991) showed unique influences of music on meaning and memory of short film scenes depending on whether the music foreshadowed or accompanied the visually depicted event and whether the foreshadowing and accompaniment were consistent or inconsistent with the meaning of the scene. For example, if music foreshadowed a situation that subsequently occurs, the scene was less memorable than a scene which violated the expectation; however, if music accompanied a subsequent scene consistent in meaning, the scene was more memorable than when its meaning was inconsistent with accompanying music. Tan, Spackman, and Bezdek (2007) have shown that music presented either prior to or after a neutral visual event influences the meaning of the image, although the effect is weaker retrospectively. In this case, timing was not critical to the influence of music associations on the interpretation of a film event. By analogy, music here acts like an adverb whose position relative to the verb is somewhat irrelevant, as in the example: Mary *quickly ran* across the street, Mary *ran quickly* across the street or Mary *ran* across the street *quickly*.

All of these experiments provide evidence of the associative influences of music on the interpretation of the moving image, the second of the two processes that explained the original findings of Marshall and Cohen (1988), leading to the first version of the Congruence-Association model (CAM-1). While the focus here has been on the influence of music on the interpretation of visual information, the reverse is also possible, as is demonstrated by Boltz in the present volume (Chapter 10). She reports a series of studies in which visual images influenced the interpretation of music having neutral meaning.

Critique of CAM-1

Looking at CAM-1 (Figure 2.2), we see that congruent structure directs attention to a part of the film (x), and, subsequently associations from the music (A) are ascribed to this focus of attention. The two processes create an interpretation of the film. The model is limited in that it divides the movie into two components: music and everything else filmic. Film is more complex than this. It includes more than two types of components. Specific components of film were categorized by the film theorist Christian Metz (1974; see also 1964, p. 71), as described by New York University film theorist Robert Stam (Stam, Burgoyne, & Flitterman-Lewis, 1992; see also Green, 2010, p. 81) as being of five types: sound effects (referred to as noise), dialogue, visual scenes, and written text, in addition to a fifth, which is music. It is notable that Metz attributed status to music as a separate channel.

Another limitation of the first graphic version of CAM was the unidirectional information flow, from the stimulus to a higher interpretive level. Could it not be that higher-level processes influence perception at the lower level? Aside from innately given perceptual strategies (such as Gestalt principles), humans have only two sources of information available to them: what they receive from the senses, and knowledge derived from experience. The first representation of CAM primarily took into account information received from the senses, although the associative meaning of music would be regarded in part as arising from experience. The role of past experience and long-term memory (LTM) in interpreting the film was ignored in this first representation of the model.

Moreover, the model did not account for audience motivation—what was the audience trying to do when viewing/listening to a film? The audience is not a passive receiver of information but rather an active creator of a story, trying to make sense of the world, or, when situated in a movie theater or home theater, trying to make the most entertaining story out of the information given.

Congruence-Association Model—iteration 2 (CAM-2)

It then seemed prudent to think about the audience member as an active participant in the creation of the film experience, as one might think of an active reader of text. In fact, the approach to text comprehension of cognitive psychologist Walter Kintsch seemed worth considering. Kintsch (1998) argued that text is understood through the reader's integration of two sources of information—the information on the page, and the inferences built up from experience, lodged in LTM, which must be used in order to interpret the text.

Stephen Grossberg (1995, see also 2007) proposed a theory of attention that entailed matching information derived through bottom-up sensory analysis with information derived from higher-order inferential processes. The best match of the inferences to the sensory analysis entered consciousness. In other words what was attended and in short-term memory (STM) was in consciousness. For a discussion of recent approaches to bottom-up top-down inference models (see Clark, in press). This notion of bottom-up and top-down processing seemed applicable to the film situation and to the film-music situation, with viewers analyzing the sensory information and at the same time making inferences about the message it contains. The best match, what makes the most sense, is the narrative, the story that achieves conscious awareness.

This second iteration of the CAM model (CAM-2), as seen in Figure 2.3, added several features. First, the overall structure of the model extends now to top-down processes based on experience and LTM. Bottom-up processes begin at the sensory surfaces for speech, visual images, and music. From here, early pre-processed information that quickly leaks through to higher processes provides sufficient clues for the generation of hypotheses from LTM sent back to match the slower outcomes of bottom-up processes. Following Grossberg (1995), the matching process takes place in STM. The number of channels of information increased from two in CAM-1 to three in CAM-2, including speech in addition to music and film (which is assumed to include the entire visual component of film). The analyses of congruence (formal structure) and association (meaning) that applies to visual scenes and to music applies now also to speech (see adjacent triangle pairs between the two sets of ascending large arrows in Figure 2.3). From a structural standpoint, overlap or congruence in structure between musical and visual features assists in directing visual attention in STM. The same principle of congruence is also assumed to occur between language and film structure; for example, the structural congruence between spoken words and moving facial images associated with speaking would direct attention to a speaker, and the semantic information from the spoken text and from the music could then add narrative context. The congruence principle thus determines in part what information is activated in STM. Because of visual dominance and because the audience is understood as trying to create a narrative out of all the information presented to the senses, the model refers to the *visual narrative*. This is represented in Figure 2.3 in the box designated for visual STM, as the primary outcome of the dynamic matching process arising from the interaction between bottom-up (analysis of sensory information) and top-down (inference) processing. An arrow from Speech STM is directed to the Visual narrative, recognizing the dominance of the visual 'screen' where the narrative takes place. An arrow from the music structure to visual structure identifies the action of the congruence principle and is in one direction due to visual dominance established by the typical narrative film viewing situation The oval represents the part of visual structure that is congruent with the musical structure and that would have priority of transfer to the STM Visual narrative.

A benefit of CAM-2 was its ability to nicely handle the film-music phenomenon of unheard melodies (Gorbman, 1987). Film music is not generally part of the reality of the film story—that is, the world of the film characters (the diegesis). Because there are no top-down expectations of acoustical aspects of music in the scene, the acoustic component of music does not emerge in the narrative. The emotional meaning of music, however, could be matched by expectations and this meaning could then be retained in STM and added to the narrative context. Hence, an arrow from the Music *meaning* analysis is directed to the STM Visual narrative. For simplicity, only a few of the possible interconnections among components are represented by arrows, but the model is viewed as having many connections among components.

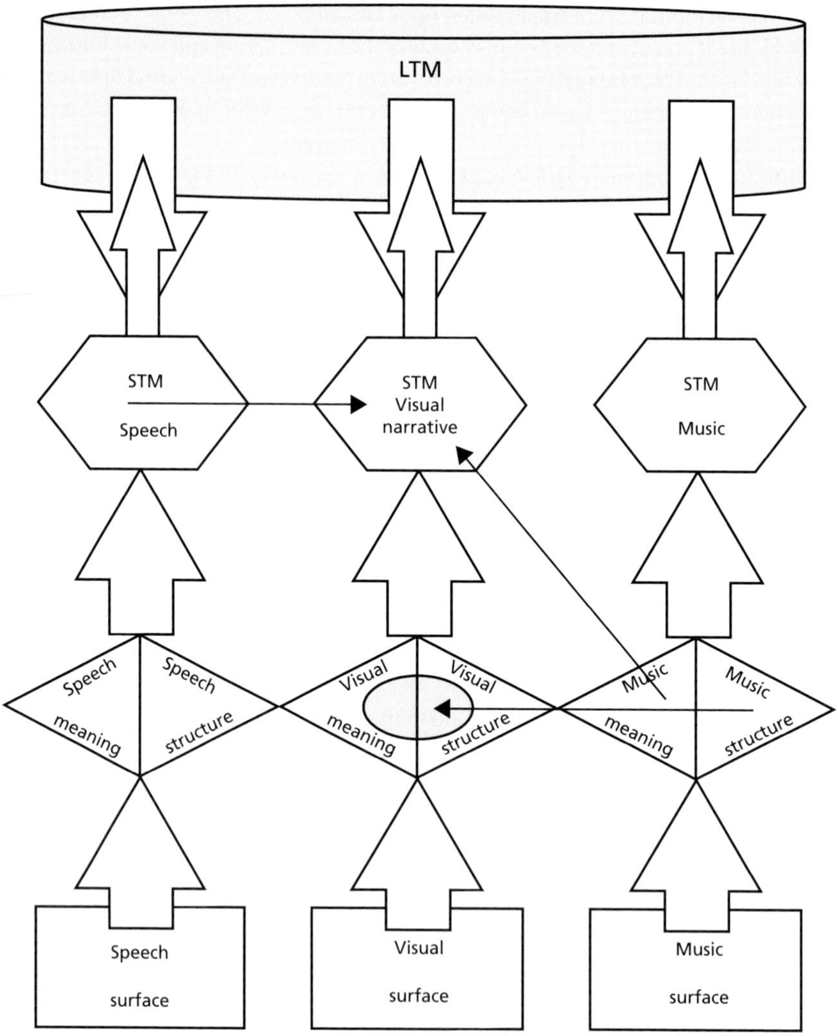

Figure 2.3 Congruence-Association Model—iteration 2. See text for explanation. Reproduced from Cohen, A. J., Music as a source of emotion in film. In Juslin, P. & Sloboda, J., *Handbook of music and emotion: Theory, research, application*, figure 11.3, p. 259 © 2010, Oxford University Press with permission.

Critique of CAM-2

The focus on vision in the narrative captured visual dominance and offered an explanation for the phenomenon of the unheard melody; however, CAM-2 was somewhat vague in regard to how non-visual information of speech and music might enter consciousness as part of the diegesis. The emphasis on visual dominance sparked the inquiry of Marilyn Boltz, who conducted research to determine whether the meaning of a neutral piece of music could be altered through contiguous presentation of meaningful visual material. Boltz, Ebendorf, and Field (2009) discovered that the meaning of neutral music in videos could be altered by the type of visual accompaniment it received (see Boltz, Chapter 10, in this volume). In addition, CAM-2 did not account for sound effects or for text.

Congruence-Association Model—iteration 3 (CAM-3): Five media channels

Iteration 3 incorporated all five of Metz's (1964, 1974) channels, augmenting the previous version now with a channel for sound effects and for text. Adding sound effects to CAM-2's music, film, and speech, seemed straightforward. A text channel also seemed important because reading engages processes quite different from those for scenes and actions (Dehaene, 2009). Initially, that was all that changed and this version was published in a review paper (Cohen, 2005b). However, in that same year, several lines of our research on absorption in film, led to the concept of a single integrated *working narrative* replacing that of *visual narrative* and the other domain specific short-term stores (Cohen, 2006; Cohen, MacMillan, & Drew, 2006).

Because the conscious representation of a film narrative is transient and is always a work in progress, and because of possible connections to Baddeley's (1986) model of working memory, the term *working narrative* was adopted as the conscious experience of the film. I also used the term *working* due to my prior collaboration with Joan E. Foley on the study of wayfinding in large-scale space. Her exposure to Baddeley's ideas during the early 1980s, led to her proposing a notion of the *working map* that an individual mentally generates to guide his or her wayfinding in an environment. Such working maps are continually updated by information received by the senses or by information about large-scale space stored in LTM (e.g., floor plans). Some persons may rely on visual or auditory imagery while others might make use of more abstract constructions based on their individual thinking styles, abilities, and experiences (Foley & Cohen, 1984). The notion of the working narrative captured this dynamic construction of reality, or pseudo-reality, of the film as shown in Figure 2.4 at level C of CAM-3.[6]

The same dual analysis for all modalities

There is one additional feature in CAM-3 to be pointed out. The concepts of congruence and association apply to all the channels of information (level B). Looking first at congruence (here referred to as *structure* at B), all five channels of information have structural characteristics, independent of their specific content. Speech, music, and sound effects, can all have rhythm, but so too can visual motion, as previously described, and text (e.g., letters moving across the screen, or the patterning of font). The sequence of changes in each of the five modalities has specific durational pattern and intensity or accent patterns. Hence, a structural analysis can lead to congruencies across the various channels, as indicated by arrows between modalities at the same level (only one of which is shown, that between music and visual structure). These congruencies can contribute to the direction of attention. This is a parsimonious system, because the same process is carried out on all domains of information. In other words, the model assumes a structural analysis independent of that of meaning.

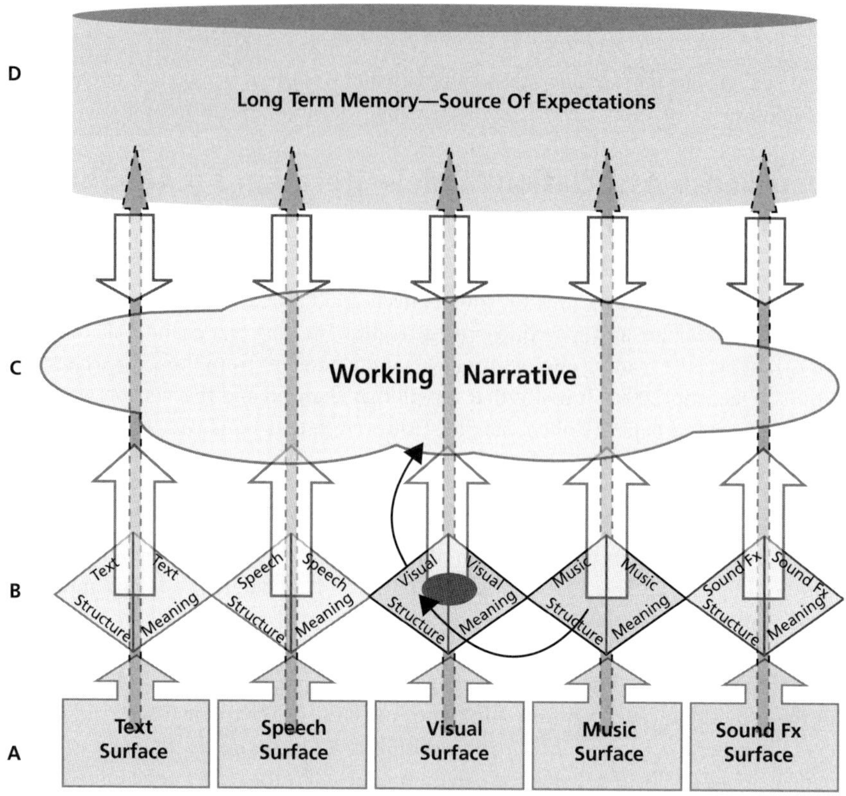

Figure 2.4 Congruence-Association Model—iteration 3. See text for explanation. Reproduced from Cohen, A. J., Music as a source of emotion in film. In Juslin, P. & Sloboda, J., *Handbook of music and emotion: Theory, research, application*, figure 31.3, p. 892 © 2010, Oxford University Press with permission.

Similarly, an associationist analysis of meaning applies to all channels of information, here referred to as *meaning* at level B. Music brings certain associations to mind, but so do sound effects, words as text or speech, and visual scenes. The brain does not necessarily care where the semantic information comes from. For example, Steinbeis and Koelsch (2008) have shown with electroencephalography and fMRI that 'meaning in music is represented in a very similar fashion to language meaning' (p. 1;. see also Steinbeis & Koelsch, 2010). So this parsimonious system in which all sensory input is analyzed for structure and for meaning helps to account for how the brain deals with this level of complexity arising from multiple sources of information.

Narrative

It is not sufficient to state that inferences based on experience are elicited as potential components of a story. We must consider another aspect, the ability to generate narrative. The word *narrative* had been used in the previous iteration, but the full implications had not been understood at the time. There has been recent interest among cognitive scientists in narrative ability. Cognitive scientist Mark Turner (1996) has noted that narrative imagination—comprehension and creation—is essential to human development and existence. While he and others (cf. Jaén & Simon, 2012) promote the idea of the natural and fundamental human ability, developmental psychologist Katherine Nelson (2005) has written that the narrative consciousness does not appear until a child is 3 or 4 years old, co-occurring with the 'newly emerging sense of self that is situated in time' (p. 134). Whether the ability to create stories is innate or is learned, it appears to be a very natural ability that is part of higher-order cognitive makeup. This story grammar may also play a role in our understanding of music. The story grammar includes the concept of beginning, middle, and end; of character; of what happens next; of causality; and of unity of time and place. It is a means of making sense out of complexity and may account for a large part of the appreciation of songs with lyrics (e.g., the Beatles' 'Yesterday,' and Schubert's *Wintereise*) and program music such as Tchaikovsky's *1812 Overture*. But the application of story grammar is not limited to music with either lyrics or a well-known context. Such narrative encoding may also underlie the appeal for a listener who traces a musical plot in which the characters (musical motifs) interact with each other and are transformed by the end of the piece.

Figure 2.4 presents the model expanded now to include the five channels of information identified by Metz and the story grammar in addition to LTM, the source of expectations. The term *working narrative* replaces the visual narrative of the former model, and it also replaces reference to STM. STM is subsumed as conscious activation (or partial regeneration) of representations in LTM that are matched by the outcome of bottom-up analysis. (For a dynamic version of this model showing the contribution to the working narrative from bottom-up and top-down processes, please visit <http://www.oup.co.uk/companion/tan>.)

Studies that are contrasting effects of diegetic and non-diegetic music

Recently, several researchers have begun to study empirically the role of film music in the diegetic and non-diegetic contexts. It is interesting to see how CAM-3 can help to interpret the results. Tan, Spackman, and Wakefield (2008) examined the effects of presenting the same piece of music diegetically or non-diegetically on viewers' interpretations of a film's narrative. They also explored the effects of non-diegetic music matching the mood of the scene (mood-congruent music) and non-diegetic music that was mood incongruent. A short (1min 25 sec) action sequence from *Minority Report* (2002) was paired with three soundtracks: (1) the original soundtrack, an orchestral rendition of the song 'Moon River' presented as if originating from within the environment of the characters (diegetic version); (2) the same recording of 'Moon River' presented louder and more clearly as if a dramatic score (non-diegetic version, mood incongruent), and (3) a third soundtrack, from a dramatic score accompanying a chase scene from *Empire of the Sun* (1987), serving as a mood-congruent condition to be compared with the mood-incongruent 'Moon River' soundtrack. In all versions, speech and sound effects remained intact, only the musical soundtrack was varied. Over 200 participants were asked to describe their interpretations of the film scene and to rate various aspects of the film and music. Ratings of the calmness of the scene and the degree of antagonism between key characters significantly differed under the three soundtracks. Ratings of the characters' emotions also varied with the musical soundtrack. For instance, with the non-diegetic version of 'Moon River' the male protagonist was seen as being less fearful, excited, and more romantically interested in the female character than with the diegetic presentation of the same song.

A similar manipulation was carried out by Fujiyama, Ema, and Iwamiya (2012) using music and an excerpt from a film by Akira Kurosawa in which the moods of the piano music and film were semantically incongruent. In one experimental condition, an image of a piano appeared in several shots, identifying the (diegetic) music source. The other non-diegetic condition, showed no piano source in the visual images. Presence as opposed to absence of the source of the piano sound led to higher ratings on a bad–good scale.

The CAM-3 model provides an explanation of the results of these two studies. In the Fujiyama et al. (2012) study, the music channel is the same in both diegetic and non-diegetic conditions, but the visual information differs, either including or excluding the source of the music. Bottom-up fast processing of the piano image from the visual channel serves to cue LTM and story grammar components to generate expectations of a piano that would also include the sound of piano music. This top-down expectation matches the piano sound ascending from bottom-up processing in the music channel. The match leads to conscious awareness of the music. Awareness of the piano as source of the music may help to explain the presence of music for which mood does not semantically fit the scene otherwise. Hence, viewer-listeners might evaluate the scene with diegetic incongruent music as better than when no source for the incongruent music appeared in the scene. In this latter case, the meaning of the music mismatched expectations generated by the top-down narrative inference processes. Fujiyama et al. (2012) together with the Tan et al. (2008) are the first to suggest that audience perceptions of the emotions of film characters and overall emotion of the scene can differ depending on whether the music is interpreted diegetically or non-diegetically, and the CAM model explains why. The specific set of bottom-up cues depends in part on whether the source of the music is known or not known. The specific cues lead to a particular set of top-down expectations. A unique working narrative is the outcome of the best match between expectations and the bottom-up analysis.

Engagement—transportation

In most movies, music adds to the compelling nature of the film. Anecdotally, we engage with the film as soon as the music starts, assuming the music is appropriate. In terms of CAM-3, appropriate music promotes the formation of a coherent working narrative. Inappropriate music would lead to an incoherent working narrative, while a condition of no music could be neutral with respect to the creation of the working narrative. The more coherent the working narrative, the more difficult it would be to detect information extraneous to the narrative due to the mismatch from the bottom-up processes. Therefore, in the presence of appropriate music, an item extraneous to the film could be more difficult to detect than in the presence of inappropriate music.

Examining this hypothesis, Cohen and Siau (2008) embedded extraneous X's into the corners of frames of a short silent film, *The Railrodder* (Potterdon & Biggs, 1965), starring Buster Keaton. Participants in the study viewed a 20-minute excerpt of the 24-minute film and were required to press a key as quickly as possible whenever they saw an X. There were 20 X's distributed across the film (see Figure 2.5). It was predicted that if participants were highly absorbed in the film (i.e., if their working narrative were cohesive), detection of X's would be slower and less accurate than if they were less absorbed in the film. The idea is similar to that of being so highly absorbed in a movie that one fails to notice a large spider that has lighted upon the corner of the screen. Under conditions of less absorption, the spider might be quickly detected. For the study, the prediction included the notion that if the music suits the film, absorption would be greater than if the music did not suit the film or if there were no music. It then followed that the music would influence whether or not the extraneous X was quickly or accurately detected. With appropriate music, response speed and accuracy were predicted to be slower and lower, respectively, than in the case of inappropriate or no music.

In the study, the film was presented twice, and, on the second viewing for all conditions, the researchers observed the expected effects. On this second viewing it took significantly longer to detect the X's under the appropriate music than under the no-music condition. As for the inappropriate music, it may have been appropriate for some of the film, and hence performance in this condition fell midway, and did not lead to any significant difference between either the original or no-music condition. The effect of slower responses under appropriate music was stronger for some of the 20 detection test locations in the film as compared to others, and begs for further exploration of visual and acoustic variables using this general experimental paradigm. That the original music led to a slower response time in the detection of the extraneous information was consistent with the hypothesis that the more coherent working narrative prevented

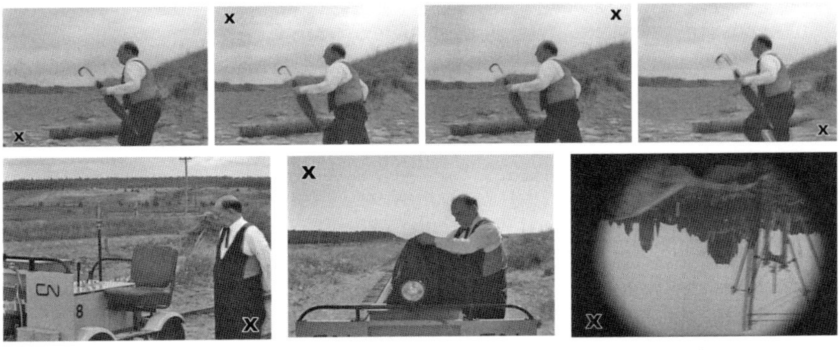

Figure 2.5 Film stills from *The Railrodder* that include the extraneous 'X.' The top row shows the same shot four times, each with the X in a different corner. Different participants received the X's in different locations to control for the potentially greater ease of detection provided by some locations or by some contrast levels between the X and the background in particular corners of the frame. The bottom row shows three additional frames of the total of 20 altered shots in the 20-minute presentation.

attention from wandering easily to information irrelevant to the story of the film. CAM allows the consideration of many variables including those of music and Cohen and Siau's (2008) study illustrates the predictive power of the CAM model, however, even more specific predictions could arise from stimuli in which associations and structures were carefully controlled and varied across modalities.

Congruence-Association Model—iteration 3: Diachronic considerations

Lifespan development and critical periods

Until now the model has focused on information that is presented in the film all at one time. In this sense the CAM model is *synchronic*, dealing with information presented simultaneously. However, the development of these processes for decoding film occurs over one's lifetime of exposure to film, video, computer games, and other electronic media. It is useful then to consider the model over time or, in other words, diachronically.

In line with this, the absorption study previously described also looked at some individual differences among participants, specifically the amount of time spent playing video games, and the susceptibility to absorption. We found that the number of X's detected increased with self-reported experience playing video games and decreased with increasing scores on the Tellegen test of openness to absorbing experiences (Tellegen & Atkinson, 1974). Bavelier, Green, Pouget, and Schrater (2012) reviewed effects of action video game playing in the context of complex training environments and suggested that action game play can facilitate a wide variety of learning by improving top-down allocation of resources, and ignoring sources of distraction (p. 408) (see also Chisholm, Hickey, Theeuwes, & Kingstone, 2010; and, see Grimshaw, Tan, & Lipscomb, Chapter 13, this volume specifically on sound and gaming). Bavelier et al. (2012) propose that action game play increases the ability to 'extract patterns or regularities in the environment... fostering learning to learn' (p. 410).

It is possible that early exposure to gaming or more generally, early immersion in electronic multimedia primes the efficiency of the cognitive processes represented in CAM, in the same way that exposure to a language or music practice early in life provides facility that cannot be easily duplicated later in life, a notion that has been referred to as *critical periods*. Based primarily on results of research on short-term recognition memory by different age cohorts for popular music excerpts, Cohen (2000) proposed a plasticity model of music grammar acquisition, suggested that during adolescence, some aspects of musical grammar are laid down. More recently, Cohen (2011) suggested that the ability to compose songs might have an earlier window of opportunity. Trainor (2005) has also argued that different aspects of music may have different critical periods. In any case, the notion of critical period can apply to the CAM model. Here, we can think of the processes underlying film and film music perception developing as a result of past experience (include any experience with video). Depending on the timing of the experience, the CAM model will take on various specific forms. If one is born into a movie-going environment or a video-gaming culture, then one's facility in interpreting moving images will differ from that of someone who has had no exposure to TV or movies or who never played video games.

To determine the extent to which experience with media plays a role in comprehension of film, Schwan and Ildirar (2010) compared adult viewers in Turkey, who had never before seen television, film, or video, with groups of adults from the same region who had either some or a lot of visual media experience. The naive viewers were able to follow discontinuities that preserved an action (e.g., consecutive cuts showing a continued action from a different perspective made sense to the naive viewers, but cuts that interposed a different activity or scene in the midst of an action presented interpretive difficulties). Thus, experience with some conventions used in electronic media plays a role in comprehending this media. This evidence of the role of experience on multimedia understanding is consistent with evidence above that experience playing computer games or of watching videos influences perception though the tasks are vastly different (Bavelier et al., 2012; Cohen & Siau, 2008). What remains to be discovered is the role of the specific onset and duration of exposure to and practice with electronic media. Analogous to the observation that those who begin language study or immersion after puberty (around 12 years of age) are unlikely to acquire a native accent, it has been suggested that children brought up with media experience are *digital natives* whose minds are primed for the 21st-century world of media (Prensky, 2001). According to this notion, unlike the younger digital natives, the elders (digital immigrants), who acquire experience with media later in life, may benefit from media experience but will still be left with an 'accent' (to apply this term in a different domain) and less flexibility, due to reduced brain plasticity associated with older ages.

Hence the CAM model, viewed comprehensively from the diachronic, developmental dimension (see Figure 2.6) suggests that, while the basic multimedia processing functions are common across all minds, experience plays a role, and moreover, the timing of this experience can be critical. Consequently, depending on their past years of experience, audience members may receive and interpret film and the effects of music on film differently.

Congruence-Association Model—iteration 4 (CAM-4)

The motor component

From the earliest days of film, the concept of motion has been connected with the moving image, with such enduring terms as *motion picture* and the *movies*. The picture on the screen depicts motion, and the celluloid film frames move across the projector beam 24 times per second (of course, this is now being simulated by digital technology). Human motion is also connected with music. Singing, for example, naturally entails motion of the entire body and is linked with dance in many cultures. Children's early singing on the playground and with friends is typically inseparable from clapping and movement games. Music psychologist Eric Clarke (2001) has considered music from the perspective of motion. As well, bodily kinesthetic information is available to film audiences who are always situated in the real world. Until recently, kinesthetic sensations arising from theater seats were irrelevant to the film or media experience, but recently certain movie theaters have outfitted seating that moves the audience member in a manner

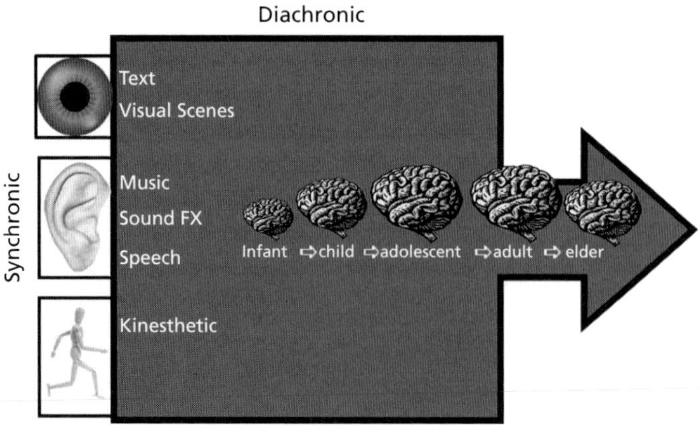

Figure 2.6 Congruence-Association Model in a developmental, diachronic context as depicted by the infancy to elderly continuum associated with images of the changing size of the brain (horizontal axis) and the separate domains of sensory experience on the vertical axis. An additional kinesthetic domain has been added to accommodate the motor component discussed in the 'CAM-4' section. Adapted from Cohen, A. J. Music in performance arts: Film, theatre and dance. In Hallam, S., Cross, I., & Thaut, M., *Oxford handbook of music psychology*, figure 41.3, p. 449 © 2010, Oxford University Press with permission.

corresponding to action in the film (e.g., X4D™ theater seats from MediaMation <http://www.mediamation.com>). Devices that provide kinesthetic feedback or which operate through such feedback are also associated with a number of videogames (e.g., vibrating controllers for Xbox 360™ or PlayStation® gaming consoles).

In the last 10 years, the notion of a mirror system in the brain has found support in primates (see Rizzolatti & Craighero, 2004, for review). In the famous initial study (as reported by Gallese, Fadiga, Fogassi, & Rizzolatti, 1996), electrodes had been inserted into over 500 neurons in the premotor cortex of the brain of two awake macaque monkeys. Amazingly, approximately 20 per cent of the neurons discharged on two different kinds of occasions: when the monkey performed an intended action (e.g., moved its own paw) or when the monkey observed the experimenter carry out the same action. The replicated finding suggested that such neurons (subsequently named 'mirror neurons') are activated when the organism carries out a particular activity or simply observes the action being carried out by some other being. An homologous system was proposed for humans, such that carrying out an activity engages neurons that would also be enabled if one viewed someone else carrying out the same activity. For humans, electrodes cannot be routinely inserted into the brain (with the exception of the very rare studies in which it is necessary prior to brain surgery, cf. Ojemann, 2010); however, human brain imaging studies have revealed certain neurological sites that are active when either an action is carried out or the same action is observed (Mukamel & Fried, 2012). Hence the notion of a human mirror neuron system homologous to that of the primate finds some support. Overy and Molnar-Szakacs (2009) suggested that music activates a human mirror neuron system in that, for example, listeners may imagine themselves creating the music they hear. The concept is connected also with empathy (Iacoboni, 2008). It is also possible that watching action in film engages audience members in imagining themselves enacting similar behaviors and engaging this mirror system.

As human motion (vicarious kinesthetic) information is prominent in film and media, it seems necessary to represent a kinesthetic channel in the CAM model. The channel would respond to the stimulation provided by the X4D™ theaters that offer kinesthetic feedback correlated with the film through the theater seats. However, the kinesthetic channel may be active at a higher level through the mirror neuron system stimulated indirectly by music or film stimuli. Thus, although quite speculative, this further addition to the CAM model captures the kinesthetic aspect in the diachronic (Figure 2.6) and synchronic (Figure 2.7) representations previously proposed. Hence, for greater completeness, the CAM model can incorporate an added kinesthetic dimension. To review, level A represents the physical surface features of each of six physical/sensory domains and is where the bottom-up processing begins. At B, the surfaces are similarly analyzed into structural and meaning components.

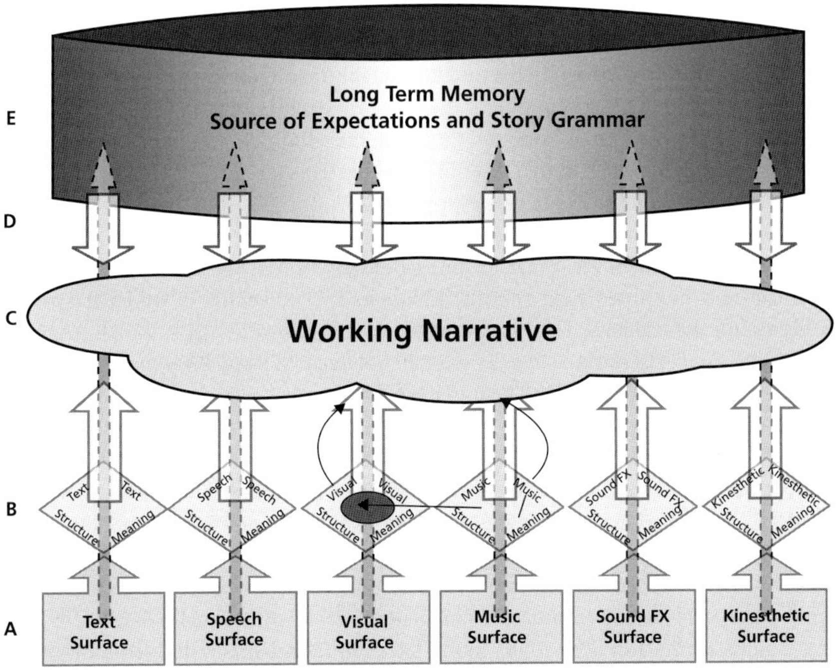

Figure 2.7 Congruence-Association Model—iteration 4: the CAM information flow diagram of mental activity underlying the joint processing of music and other continuous media. Reproduced from Cohen, A. J. Film music from the perspective of cognitive science. In Neumeyer, D. (Ed.), (2013). *Oxford handbook of music in film and visual media*, © Oxford University Press with permission.

Music structural information combines with similar (congruent) structural information from other domains (here visual scene domain similarity depicted by the arrow from music to visual) such that corresponding information patterns (here visual) receive priority for inclusion in the working narrative at C. Note that information from music associative meaning (at B) also travels directly to the working narrative at C. Fast preprocessing that starts at level A sensory surfaces leaks through (as on the dotted arrow ascending from A through to E) to the highest levels providing cues to the top-down processes at E. Hypotheses based on these cues drawing now on experience and story grammar at level E are generated at D to make sense of the six-channel information received at C reflecting the original sensory information at level A. Information selected for the working narrative at C is matched from LTM at level E through channels at level D. Some of this information admitted to the working narrative at level C may travel back to LTM (level E) to form new long-term memories.

Impact of CAM

The notion of CAM, first proposed in the paper by Marshall and Cohen (1988), has survived and expanded over the intervening 25 years. In 1998, the ICMPC invited a keynote address on psychology and film music at their bi-annual conference in Seoul (Cohen, 1999). That same year, musicologist Nicholas Cook asked if he could reprint the first published figure depicting the CAM model for his book on musical multimedia (Cook, 1998). In supporting his case for metaphor as a model of multimedia interaction he refers to the first proposal of the CAM model by saying that 'if the respective attributes of the two media intersect, then some or all of the remaining attributes of the one become available as attributes of the other' (p. 69). Cook's reference to CAM was followed by Boltz's (2004) suggestion of CAM as a possible theoretical account for effects of music on meaning and memory in film. Iben Have (2008, p. 124) in Denmark incorporated the image of the second iteration of the model into her book on music and multimedia (in Danish). Chapters I have written in which the model holds a central place have been used in courses at institutions across North America. Several doctoral dissertations (e.g., Force, 2008; Kulezic-Wilson, 2006) have also found explanatory value in the model. The impact of the work has further extended to invited contributions to various books on music psychology, music and emotion, film music, film, and discourse on language and music. None of this would have happened had a student with an interest in film music not knocked on my door, and if a band of dedicated colleagues had not realized that there was a buried treasure of knowledge about how the mind processes music in the context of film and other media.

In a sense, the CAM model applies to any multimedia situation, and it represents perceptual-cognitive processes in general. It is conceptually similar in several regards to the Kintsch (1998) model of comprehension, and it resembles early analysis-by-synthesis models and more recent predictive coding models that capture the top-down prediction procedures required to construct perception of the real world (e.g., Arnal, Wyart, & Giraud, 2011, p. 800). But what CAM does that is important and distinctive is to place music in a cognitive model of multimedia comprehension. CAM honors the fact that music in media is almost ubiquitous. Models of comprehension or cinema processing will only be complete and comprehensive themselves when they take into account music phenomena in the multimedia context. CAM provides some direction about how to do this.

In describing the perceptual cognitive information flow in the multimedia context, the CAM model has responded in its four iterations to new scientific information as it has become available. More modifications and refinements and neurophysiological instantiation are to come. Future research will determine the validity of the key concepts underlying CAM: the parsimonious analysis of all media types into structure (and the role of congruencies) and meaning (associations), the notion of the active perceiver, and the generation of the working narrative, which is the best match between the hypothesized bottom-up and top-down brain activity.

As described earlier, the CAM model provides some insights into several key psychological phenomena related to music in the multimedia context, for example, the 'unheard melody,' and the influence of music on interpretation. Today technology for conducting multimedia behavioral research is readily available on desktop and laptop computers and even in hand-held devices. Music, images, and videos can be exploited in brain imaging research. The stage is set for much future progress and the next iteration of CAM.

Acknowledgments

Key to the pursuit and continuation of the work was the support of the Social Sciences and Humanities Research Council of Canada. The SSHRC not only provided research grants but also a Canada Research Fellowship from 1987 to 1993. The Fellowship (held at Dalhousie University) enabled the early research on congruence and association, the results of which verified the proposed foundation for CAM. Though I have been gone from Dalhousie for almost two decades, it is heartening to see the work on film-music continued there with doctoral student Cindy Hamon-Hill. Gratitude is expressed to students and research assistants over the years and to the UPEI Psychology Department for its support including that of its technician, Robert Drew, for his expertise in music, video, and graphics.

Notes

1. An excellent example of this type of music is provided by a volume of music entitled *Sam Fox Moving Picture Music* composed by J. S. Zamecnik (1913). Volume 1 was directed to beginner and intermediate pianists, while other volumes were directed to more advanced performers. This can be found at <http://www.mont-alto.com/photoplaymusic/SamFoxMovingPictureVol1/SamFoxV1.html> along with MIDI renditions of the pieces.
2. The passage as translated by Benjamin Jowett is 'The second principle is that of division into species according to the natural formation, where the joint is, not breaking any part as a bad carver might.'
3. The term *congruence* also referred to another relation between the music and film, which focused on the overall music-visual compatibility on the semantic differential dimensions of activity and potency. The idea was that the rating on the evaluative dimension varied with the degree of congruence of ratings for the audio and visual materials: high congruence

leading to high evaluation. Both structural and semantic aspects of congruence are addressed by Bolivar, Cohen, and Fentress (1994) and by chapters in Part III of this volume.

4. The term *CAM model* is redundant as the 'M' in CAM refers to 'Model,' but has seemed more natural than 'the CAM' or the C-A Model.
5. Meaning in music is of course a very complex one (see also Chapter 3 on a semiotic approach by Kendall & Lipscomb, this volume). A debate began with Hanslick (1957), who emphasized the internal meaning of music and that one did not need to go beyond the musical domain to appreciate its essence. While much significance of music relies on the sensitivity of listeners to the patterning of sound, yet music does bring associations with it, whether due to universal factors (the relation between mood and the song one sings) or specific experiences related to cultural regularities or idiosyncratic uses of music in the life of an individual (the 'they're playing our song' phenomenon; Davies, 1978). The present discussion gains by accepting that music provides semantic context through association.
6. The term working narrative is a key component of CAM, and, to emphasize its significance, it has recently been referred to as CAM-WN (Arbib, 2013); however, for the present chapter, the simpler acronym CAM suffices given the historical context.

References

Arbib, M. A. (Ed.) (2013). *Language, music and the brain: A mysterious relationship.* Cambridge, MA: MIT Press.

Arnal, L. H., Wyart, V., & Giraud, A.-L. (2011). Transitions in neural oscillations reflect prediction errors generated in audiovisual speech. *Nature Neuroscience, 14,* 797–801.

Baddeley, A. D. (1986). *Working memory.* Oxford, UK: Oxford University Press.

Baumgartner, T., Lutz, K., Schmidt, C. F., & Jäncke, L. (2006). The emotional power of music: How music enhances the feeling of affective pictures. *Brain Research, 1075,* 151–164.

Bavelier, D., Green, C. S., Pouget, A., & Schrater, P. (2012). Brain plasticity through the life span: Learning to learn and action video games. *Annual Review of Neuroscience, 35,* 391–416.

Bolivar, V. J., Cohen, A. J., & Fentress, J. C. (1994). Semantic and formal congruency in music and motion pictures: Effects on the interpretation of visual action. *Psychomusicology, 13,* 28–59.

Boltz, M. G. (2001). Musical soundtracks as a schematic influence on the cognitive processing of filmed events. *Music Perception, 18,* 427–454.

Boltz, M. G. (2004). The cognitive processing of film and musical soundtracks. *Memory & Cognition, 32,* 1194–1205.

Boltz, M. G., Ebendorf, B., & Field, B. (2009). Audiovisual interactions: The impact of visual information on music perception and memory. *Music Perception, 27,* 43–59.

Boltz, M., Schulkind, M., & Kantra, S. (1991). Effects of background music on remembering of filmed events. *Memory and Cognition, 19,* 595–606.

Bregman, A. (1990). *Auditory scene analysis.* Cambridge, MA: MIT Press.

Bullerjahn, C., & Güldenring, M. (1994). An empirical investigation of effects of film music using qualitative content analysis. *Psychomusicology, 13,* 99–118.

Burkholder, P. (2006). A simple model for associative musical meaning. In B. Almen & E. Pearsall (Eds.), *Approaches to meaning in music* (pp. 76–107). Bloomington, IN: Indiana University Press.

Chisholm, J.D., Hickey, C., Theeuwes, J., & Kingstone, A. (2010). Reduced attentional capture: the case of action video game players. *Attention, Perception & Psychophysics, 74,* 257–262.

Clark, A. (in press). Whatever next? Predictive brains, situated agents, and the future of cognitive science. *Behavioral and Brain Sciences*.

Clarke, E. F. (2001). Meaning and the specification of motion in music. *Musicae Scientiae, 5*, 213–234.

Cohen, A. J. (1975). Perception of tone sequences from the Western-European chromatic scale: tonality, transposition, and the pitch set. (Unpublished PhD thesis.) Queen's University, Canada.

Cohen, A. J. (1993). Associationism and musical soundtrack phenomena. *Contemporary Music Review, 9*, 163–78.

Cohen, A. J. (1994). Introduction to the special volume on the psychology of film music. *Psychomusicology, 13*, 2–8.

Cohen, A. J. (1999). The functions of music in multimedia: A cognitive approach. In S. W. Yi (Ed.), *Music, mind, and science* (pp. 53–69). Seoul, Korea: Seoul National University Press.

Cohen, A. J. (2000). Film music: A cognitive perspective. In D. Neumeyer, C. Flinn, & J. Buhler (Eds.), *Music and cinema* (pp. 360–377). Middlebury, VT: Wesleyan University Press.

Cohen, A. J. (2005a). Music cognition: Defining constraints on musical communication. In D. Miell, R. MacDonald, & D. J. Hargreaves (Eds.), *Musical Communication* (pp. 61–84). Oxford, UK: Oxford University Press.

Cohen, A. J. (2005b). How music influences the interpretation of film and video: Approaches from experimental psychology. In R. A. Kendall & R. W. Savage (Eds.), *Reports in Ethnomusicology: Perspectives in Systematic Musicology, 12*, 15–36.

Cohen, A. J. (2006). How music influences absorption in film and video: The Congruence-Associationist Model. In M. Baroni, A. R. Addessi, R. Caterina, & M. Costa (Eds.), *Proceedings of the 9th International Conference on Music Perception & Cognition (ICMPC9)* (p. 1137). Bologna, Italy: ICMPC.

Cohen, A. J. (2009). Autobiography and psychomusicology: Introduction to the special issue 'A history of music psychology in autobiography.' *Psychomusicology: Music, Mind & Brain, 20*, 10–17.

Cohen, A. J. (2010). Music as a source of emotion in film. In P. Juslin & J. Sloboda (Eds.), *Handbook of music and emotion: Theory, research, applications* (pp. 879–908). Oxford, UK: Oxford University Press.

Cohen, A. J. (2011). Creativity in singing: Universality and the question of critical periods. In D. Hargreaves, D. Miell, & R. A. R. MacDonald (Eds.), *Musical imaginations: Multidisciplinary perspectives on creativity, performance, and perception* (pp. 173–189). Oxford, UK: Oxford University Press.

Cohen, A. J. (in press). Film music from the perspective of cognitive science. In D. Neumeyer (Ed.), *Oxford handbook of music in film and visual media*. New York, NY: Oxford University Press.

Cohen, A. J., Isaacs, P., Flores, S., Harrison, D., & Bradley, J. (1977). The computer as interdisciplinary catalyst. In S. Lusignan & J. North (Eds.), *Computing in the humanities* (pp. 197–208). Waterloo, Canada: University of Waterloo Press.

Cohen, A. J., MacMillan, K. A., & Drew, R. (2006). The role of music, sound effects & speech on absorption in a film: The congruence-associationist model of media cognition. *Canadian Acoustics, 34*, 40–41.

Cohen, A. J., & Siau, Y.-M. (2008). The narrative role of music in multimedia presentations: The Congruence-Association Model (CAM) of music and multimedia. In K. Miyazaki, Y. Hiraga, M. Adachi, Y. Nakajima, & M. Tsuzaki (Eds.), *Proceedings of the 10th International Conference* *on Music Perception and Cognition (ICMPC10) Sapporo, Japan* (pp. 77–82) [DVD]. Adelaide, Australia: Causal Productions.

Colavita, F. B. (1974). Human sensory dominance. *Perception & Psychophysics, 16*, 409–412.

Collier, W. G., & Hubbard, T. (2001). Judgments of happiness, brightness, speed and tempo change of auditory stimuli varying in pitch and tempo. *Psychomusicology, 17*, 36–55

Cook, N. (1998). *Analysing musical multimedia*. Oxford, UK: Clarendon Press.

Cuddy, L. L., & Cohen, A. J. (1976). Recognition of transposed melodic sequences. *Quarterly Journal of Experimental Psychology, 28*, 255–270.

Dehaene, S. (2009). *Reading in the brain*. New York, NY: Penguin, Viking.

Edelman, G., & Tononi, G. (2000). *A universe of consciousness: How matter becomes imagination*. New York, NY: Basic Books.

Eldar, E., Ganor, O., Admon, R., Bleich, A., & Hendler, T. (2007). Feeling the real world: Limbic responses to music depends on related content. *Cerebral Cortex, 17*, 2828–2840.

Ellis, R. J., & Simons, R. F. (2005). The impact of music on subjective and physiological indices of emotion while viewing films. *Psychomusicology, 19*, 15–40.

Foley, J. E., & Cohen, A. J. (1984). Working mental representations of the environment. *Environment and Behavior, 16*, 713–729.

Fujiyama, S., Ema, K., & Iwamiya, S. (2012). Effect of the technique of conflict between music and moving picture using Akira Kurosawa's movies. In *Proceedings of the Spring Meeting of Japanese Society of Music Perception and Cognition*, pp. 85–70. Tokyo, Japan: The Acoustical Society of Japan. (In Japanese.)

Force, K. A. (2008). *From Koyaanisqatsi (1982) to Undertow (2004): A systematic musicological examination of Philip Glass's film scores.* (Unpublished doctoral dissertation.) York University, North York, Canada.

Gallese, V., Fadiga L., Fogassi L., & Rizzolatti G. (1996). Action recognition in the premotor cortex. *Brain, 119*, 593–609.

Garner, W. (1962). *Uncertainty and structure as psychological concepts*. New York, NY: Wiley.

Garner, W. (1974). *Processing of information and structure*. New York, NY: Wiley.

Gibson, J. J. (1966). *The senses considered as perceptual systems*. Boston, MA: Houghton-Mifflin.

Gorbman, C. (1987). *Unheard melodies: Narrative film music*. Bloomington, IN: Indiana University Press.

Green, J. (2010). Understanding the score: Film music communicating to and influence the audience. *Journal of Aesthetic Education, 44*, 81–94.

Grossberg, S. (1995). The attentive brain. *American Scientist, 83*, 438–449.

Grossberg, S. (2007). Consciousness CLEARS the mind. *Neural Networks, 20*, 1040–1053.

Hamon-Hill, C., Cohen, A. J., & Klein, R. (in preparation). The role of music in parsing a short animation.

Hanslick, E. (1957). *The beautiful in music* (M. Weitz, Ed. & G. Cohen, Trans.). New York, NY: Liberal Arts Press. (Original work published in German in 1854.)

Have, I. (2008). *Lyt til tv: Underlægningsmusik i danske tv-dokumentarer* [Listening to TV: Background music in Danish television documentaries]. Aarhus, DE: Aarhus Universitetsforlag.

Heider, F., & Simmel, M. (1944). An experimental study of apparent behavior. *American Journal of Psychology, 57*, 243–259.

Hevner, K. (1935). The affective character of the major and minor modes in music. *American Journal of Psychology, 47*, 103–118.

Iacoboni, M. (2008). *Mirroring people.* New York, NY: Farrar, Straus & Giroux.

Iwamiya, S. (2008, August). *Subjective congruence between moving picture and sound.* Paper presented at the Tenth International Conference on Music Perception and Cognition, Hokkaido, Japan.

Jaén, I., & Simon, J. J. (2012). An overview of recent developments in cognitive literary studies. In I. Jaén and J. J. Simon (Eds.) *Cognitive literary studies: Current themes and new directions* (pp. 13–32). Austin, TX: University of Texas Press.

Jeong, J.-W., Diwadkar V. A., Chugani, C. D., Sinsoongsud, P., Muzik, O., Behenm M. E., Chugani, H. T., & Chugani, D. C. (2011). Congruence of happy and sad emotion in music and faces modifies cortical audiovisual activation. *Neuroimage, 54,* 2973–2982.

Kendall, R. A. (2005a). Music and video iconicity: Theory and experimental design. *Physiological Anthropology and Applied Human Science, 24,* 143–149.

Kendall, R. A. (2005b). Empirical approaches to musical meaning. In R. A. Kendall & R. W. H. Savage (Eds.), *Perspectives in Systematic Musicology, Selected reports in Ethnomusicology, 12,* 69–102.

Kendall, R. A. (2010). Music in film and animation: Experimental semiotics applied to visual, sound and musical structures. In B. E. Rogowitz & T. N . Pappas (Eds.), *Human Vision and Electronic Imaging XV* (Proceedings of SPIE-IS& T Electronic Imaging, SPIE, *Vol.* 7525) (pp. 1–13). Bellingham, WA: SPIE & The Society for Imaging Science and Technology.

Kim, K.-H., & Iwaymiya, S.-I. (2008). Formal congruency between Telop patterns and sounds effects. *Music Perception, 25,* 429–448.

Kintsch, W. (1998). *Comprehension: A paradigm for cognition.* Cambridge, UK: Cambridge University Press.

Koelsch, S. (2010). Towards a neural basis of music-evoked emotions. *Trends in Cognitive Sciences, 14,* 131–137.

Krumhansl, C. L. (1990). *Cognitive foundations of musical pitch.* New York, NY: Oxford.

Krumhansl, C. L., & Schenck, D. L. (1997). Can dance reflect the structural and expressive qualities of music? A perceptual experiment on Balanchine's choreography of Mozart's Divertimento No. 15. *Musicae Scientiae, 1,* 63–83.

Kubovy, M., & Yu, M. (2012). Multistability, cross-modal binding and the additivity of conjoined grouping principles. *Philosophical transactions of the Royal Society. B, 367,* 954–964.

Kulezic-Wilson, D. (2006). *Composing on Screen: The Musicality of Film.* (Unpublished doctoral dissertation.) University of Ulster, UK.

Langdale, A. (Ed.) (2002). *Hugo Münsterberg on Film. The Photoplay: A Psychological study and other writings.* New York, NY: Routledge.

Lerdahl, F., & Jackendoff, R. (1983). *A generative theory of tonal music.* Cambridge, MA: MIT Press

Lipscomb, S. D. (1999). Cross-modal integration: Synchronization of auditory and visual components in simple and complex media. In *Collected papers of the 137th Meeting of the Acoustical Society of America and the 2nd Convention of the European Acoustics Association* [CD-ROM]. New York, NY: The Acoustical Society of America.

Lipscomb, S. D. (2005). The perception of audio-visual composites: Accent structure alignment of simple stimuli. *Selected Reports in Ethnomusicology, 12,* 37–67.

Lipscomb, S. D., & Kendall, R. A. (1994). Perceptual judgment of the relationship between musical and visual components in film. *Psychomusicology, 13,* 60–98.

Marks, M. (1997). *Music and the silent film.* New York, NY: Oxford University Press.

Marshall, S. K., & Cohen, A. J. (1988). Effects of musical soundtracks on attitudes to geometric figures. *Music Perception, 6*, 95–112.

Metz, C. (1964). Le cinema: langue or langage? *Communications, 4*, 52–90.

Metz, C. (1974). *Film language: A semiotics of the cinema*. New York, NY: Oxford University Press.

Miller, G. A. (1956). The magical number seven plus or minus two: Some limits on our capacity for processing information. *Psychological Review, 63*, 81–97.

Mukamel, R., & Fried, I. (2012). Human intracranial recordings and cognitive neuroscience. *Annual Review of Psychology, 63*, 511–537.

Münsterberg, H. (1893). *Psychological laboratory of Harvard University.* [A catalogue of equipment and readings, prepared for the World's Columbian Exposition in Chicago.] In C. D. Green (Ed.), *Classics in the history of psychology. An Internet resourse.* Toronto, Canada: York University. Retrieved from <http://psychclassics.yorku.ca/Munster/Lab/>.

Münsterberg, H. (1970). *The photoplay: A psychological study*. New York, NY: Arno. (Original work published in 1916.)

Narmour, E. (1990*). The analysis and cognition of basic melodic structures*. Cambridge, MA: MIT Press.

Nelson, K. (2005). Emerging levels of consciousness in early human development. In H. S. Terrace & J. Metcalfe (Eds.), *The missing link in cognition: Origins of self-reflective consciousness* (pp. 116–141). New York, NY: Oxford University Press.

Ojemann, G. (2010). Cognitive mapping through electrophysiology. *Epilepsia, 51*, Suppl 1, 72–75.

Osgood, C. E., Suci, G. J., & Tannenbaum, P. H. (1957). *The measurement of meaning*. Urbana, IL: University of Illinois Press.

Overy, K., & Molnar-Szakacs, I. (2009). Being together in time: Musical experience and the mirror neuron system. *Music Perception, 5*, 489–504.

Plato. (2012). *Phaedrus* (B. Jowett, Trans.). Retrieved from <http://classics.mit.edu/Plato/phaedrus.html>. (Original work published 360 BCE.)

Potterton, G. (Director), & Biggs, J. (Producer). (1965). *The Railrodder* [Motion picture]. Ottawa, Canada: National Film Board.

Prensky, M. (2001). Digital natives, digital immigrants. *On the Horizon, 9*, 1–6.

Rigg, M. (1937). An experiment to determine how accurately college students can interpret the intended meanings of musical compositions. *Journal of Experimental Psychology, 21*, 223–229.

Rizzolatti, G., & Craighero, L. (2004). The mirror-neuron system. *Annual Review of Neuroscience, 27*, 169–192.

Schwan, S., & Ildirar, S. (2010). Watching film for the first time: How adult viewers interpret perceptual discontinuities in film. *Psychological Science, 21*, 970–976.

Shevy, M. (2007). The mood of rock music affects evaluation of video elements differing in valence and dominance. *Psychomusicology, 19*, 57–78.

Sirius, G., & Clarke, E. F. (1994). The perception of audiovisual relationships: A preliminary study. *Psychomusicology, 13*, 119–132.

Spelke, E. S. (1979). Exploring audible and visible events in infancy. In A. D. Pick (Ed.), *Perception and its development: A tribute to E. J. Gibson* (pp. 221–235). New York, NY: Wiley.

Spence, C. (2011). Crossmodal correspondences: A tutorial review. *Attention, Perception and Psychophysics, 73*, 971–995.

Spreckelmeyer, K. N., Kutas, M., Urbach, T. P., Altenmüller, E., & Münte, T. F. (2006). Combined perception of emotion in pictures and musical sounds. *Brain Research, 1070*, 160–170.

Steinbeis, N., & Koelsch, S. (2008). Comparing the processing of music and language meaning using EEG and fMRI. *PLoS ONE, 3*, e2226, 1–7.

Steinbeis, N., & Koelsch, S. (2010). Affective priming effects of musical sounds on the processing of word meaning. *Journal of Cognitive Neuroscience, 23*, 604–621.

Stam, R., Burgoyne, R., & Flitterman-Lewis, S. (1992). *New vocabularies in film semiotics*. New York, NY: Routledge.

Sundberg, J. (1983). Speech, song, and emotions. In M. Clynes (Ed.), *Music, mind, and brain: The neuropsychology of music* (pp. 137–149). New York, NY: Plenum.

Tan, S.-L., Spackman, M. P., & Bezdek, M. A. (2007). Viewers' interpretation of film characters' emotions: Effects of presenting film music before or after a character is shown. *Music Perception, 25*, 135–152.

Tan, S.-L., Spackman, M. P., & Wakefield, E. M. (2008). The effects of diegetic and non-diegetic music on viewers' interpretations of film. In K. Miyazaki, Y. Hiraga, M. Adachi, Y. Nakajima, and M. Tsuzaki (Eds.), *Proceedings of the 10th International Conference on Music Perception and Cognition (ICMPC10), Sapporo, Japan* (pp. 588–593). [DVD.] Adelaide, Australia: Causal Productions.

Tellegen, A., & Atkinson, G. (1974). Openness to absorbing and self-altering experiences ('absorption'), trait related to hypnotic susceptibility. *Journal of Abnormal Psychology, 83*, 268–277.

Thayer, J. F., & Levenson, R. W. (1983). Effects of music on psychophysiological responses to a stressful film. *Psychomusicology, 3*, 44–54.

Thompson, W. F., Russo, F. A., & Sinclair, D. (1994). Effects of underscoring on the perception of closure in filmed events. *Psychomusicology, 13*, 9–27.

Trainor, L. (2005). Are there critical periods for musical development? *Developmental Psychology, 46*, 262–278 .

Turner, M. (1996). *The literary mind: The origins of thought and language*. New York, NY: Oxford University Press.

Vines, B. W., Krumhansl, C. L., Wanderley, M. M., & Levitin, D. J. (2006). Cross-modal interactions in the perception of musical performance. *Cognition, 101*, 80–113.

Wertheimer, M. (1939). Laws of organization in perceptual forms. In W. D. Ellis (Ed.), *A source book of Gestalt psychology* (pp. 71–88). New York, NY: Harcourt Brace.

Zamecnik, J. S. (1913). *Sam Fox Moving Picture Music, Volume 1*. Cleveland, OH: Sam Fox.

Chapter 3

Experimental semiotics applied to visual, sound, and musical structures

Roger A. Kendall[a] and Scott D. Lipscomb[b]

[a]University of California, Los Angeles, USA
[b]University of Minnesota, USA

The ubiquity of multimedia at this point in intellectual history demands attention by experimental scientists; however, the majority of extant research is focused on static visuals and single tones or chords. Such stimuli are easily controlled in psychophysical experiments, and assumptions can be made about the orthogonality of variables. As the purview of experimental research has expanded into ecologically valid variables, temporality, particularly in music and visuals, has finally been acknowledged to be on at least equal footing with issues of tonality and melodic structure, which are often operationalized in experiments as an isochronous train of pitches. In fact, in a study investigating the perception of pitch patterns with various temporal structures, Monahan (1984) showed that rhythm can emerge as more influential than pitch in judgments of melodic similarity. The layering of temporally organized musical variables and visual variables in multimedia is an important area of study still in relative infancy.

The need for further study arises not only out of the need to address relations between psychophysical studies of static stimuli and those incorporating a temporal context, but also to move toward the ecological validity reflecting the temporally dynamic real world of sensory perception. A convergent approach comparing and contrasting data from natural contexts (e.g., film) and abstracted contexts (e.g., experimentally controlled animations) is useful in understanding the perception of the layering, or stratification, of musical and visual elements in multimedia. Studies of historical interest paved the way for the current research and are worth considering as background.

Empirical research of historical interest

Tannenbaum (1956) conducted an early study of a theatrical play performance that participants were asked to evaluate using semantic differential scales (e.g., good–bad, interesting–boring, active–passive). The performance conditions included a live performance, a recorded live performance, or a performance recorded in a studio. Phonograph recordings of music were played during these versions. Results indicated that the performance condition did not significantly change the ratings; however, the music selected altered the ratings, particularly for adjectives connected to potency (e.g., strong–weak) and activity (e.g., fast–slow). As in many early studies, the music was not edited to eliminate issues of temporal accent congruence (i.e., alignment of salient moments in the auditory and visual modalities) as a potential confounding variable. Results showed that the presence of music altered the meaning of the composite scene; that is, music tended to dominate the visual and other dramatic variables.

Marshall and Cohen (1988) constructed stimuli that used an animated film of abstract geometrical objects and composed music (consisting of two themes, considered 'strong' and 'weak') varying in tonality, texture, tempo, and pitch range/tessitura. Although music and visual alignment was the same across excerpts, accomplished through editing on videotape, no attempt was made to establish structural accent alignment within the movement of the film characters in the scene. Participants evaluated the animation without music, the music without animation, and composites using strong and weak music; respondents provided ratings on a series of semantic differential scales (as described earlier). Results demonstrated that music could influence the interpretation of a geometric figure's personality characteristics in terms of potency and activity, as Tannenbaum (1956) found previously. Music trumped visual elements in communicated meaning.

Lipscomb and Kendall (1994) conducted a study using excerpts from a Hollywood film. They set out to model film music in terms of communication, suggesting that a film composer and film editor have implicit schemata (knowledge structures) for combining visual and sonic elements. Therefore, the stimuli were drawn from a successful Hollywood film, *Star Trek IV* (1986; music by Leonard Rosenman, who received an Academy Award nomination for the score). Five scenes were selected via a pilot experiment to avoid redundancy of visual and musical elements. The music intended by the composer for each selected scene was then edited onto all other scenes, creating a composer-intended example with four foils or lures. These edits were made by a panel of film composition student experts so as to align the visual accents within a scene to the music with the best possible fit within scene. Participants were asked to rate the goodness of fit of music to the film scene for all 25 combinations.

Responses revealed that participants were able to determine the composer-intended match beyond chance. For example, even in the hospital scene in which the visual expressions and actions of the characters telegraphed tension and fear, the intended music in up-tempo major with its associations of comedy (a kind of 'keystone cops' musical excerpt) was selected as best fit by half the participants. To further explore these combinations, semantic differential ratings using evaluative, potency, and activity bipolar adjectives were collected for each audiovisual composite. Mean ratings varied significantly when different musical soundtracks were present. When visualizing the results, data were plotted in two forms: (1) keeping the visual component consistent across all audio components and (2) keeping the audio component consistent across all visual components.

The amount of change in ratings was clearly more dramatic when the musical aspect was the changing component, confirming again that the music can alter the 'meaning' defined in terms of these adjective pairs. In this empirical context, in fact, the researchers concluded that the musical component had exerted *more* influence on the ratings than the visual component. Cluster analysis resulted in branches representing the activity and potency components, as in the studies already described. As Marshall and Cohen (1988) suggested, the evaluation (i.e., goodness of fit) in this case can transcend these meaning changes as a composite rating that incorporates activity and potency dimensions. These results led both Lipscomb and Kendall (1994) and Marshall and Cohen (1988) to postulate a cognitive comparison involving associative as well as accent alignment congruence.

Theoretical considerations in musical semiotics

After completion of the aforementioned study by Lipscomb and Kendall (1994), one author (R.A.K.) noticed several aspects of the prevailing models. First, association, an apparently learned behavior and the foundation of much behavioral and cognitive theory, was at the heart of the tendency for music to change the meaning of a given visual scene. A common association was between music in major and minor keys and positive and negative events, respectively; this pairing has been studied and confirmed with children (e.g., Kastner & Crowder, 1990). Second, the congruence or alignment of accent structures, studied extensively by Lipscomb (1995; see also Lipscomb, Chapter 9, in this volume), was also perceptually important. Third, there is a comparative aspect linking relations between these variables in the temporally structured musical and visual domains resulting in a composite rating of goodness of fit or connected to aspects of attention. Studies of memory retention for visual and dramatic cues within film demonstrate the interaction of these components. Boltz (2001) states that: 'relative to a control group with no music, positive and negative music significantly biased viewers' interpretation and subsequent remembering of a film in mood-congruent fashion' (p. 427). An earlier experiment by Boltz (1991) also demonstrated that memory was enhanced for film music combinations in which the music foreshadowed incongruently, and in which music and visuals were mood congruent without foreshadowing.

Semiotics

Semiotics is often called the science, or study, of signs (for an analysis, see Nöth, 1990, p. 4). Ferdinand Saussure, one of the founders of modern semiotics, conceived of signs in a dyadic model consisting of a *signifier* (the form the sign takes, i.e., word), and a *signified* (the entity or concept it represents) (Saussure, 1998). Charles Peirce, another founder, forwarded a triadic model consisting of a *representatem* (similar but not identical to signifier), *interpretant* (the meaning of the sign), and *object* (the referent of the sign) (Buchler, 1955, pp. 98–203; Nöth, 1990, pp. 42–45 provides details and expansion). Implied in the details of these models are mental representations of signs and meanings, and this provides the catalyst to conceive of a process of communication using musical signs (motifs, patterns, rhythms, genres, instrumentation, etc.). Intended meanings are transmitted via recodings among composer, performer, and finally the listener/receiver who interprets the incoming musical message into either the intended meaning, or imposes another meaning (or none at all) (Kendall, 2005a, pp. 72–73).

A model incorporating issues of meaning via models in semiotics is hypothesized to be useful in extending and expanding research. Earlier approaches (Carterette & Kendall, 1996; Kendall, 1999, 2005a; Lipscomb & Kendall, 1994) based on a semiotic model are expanded and extended later in this chapter.

The concept of semiotics used in this paper is a broad one, including such experimental areas as the measurement of meaning (Osgood, Suci, & Tannenbaum, 1957) via bipolar semantic scales representing factors of meaning (e.g., evaluation, activity, and potency). The precursor of this approach is found in Hevner (1935a, 1935b, 1936, 1937) whose statistical analysis of participants' responses to music using adjectival checklists included not only musical segments, but responses recorded during the playing of extended music.

Dowling and Harwood (1986, chapter 8) approach music and emotion from a semiotical orientation, incorporating concepts from the writings of Leonard Meyer (1956) and Charles Peirce (1931–1932, Vol. 2). Each approach can be simplified into a three-part taxonomy. According to Meyer, meanings arise from *referentialism*, which is the associative aspect of music (a detailed explanation with examples is provided later; also see Cohen, Chapter 2, in the present volume). Another type of meaning, *formalism*, stems from a listener's explicit knowledge of facts about music, such as the formal structures (e.g., sonata form) or historical information (e.g., the year a piece was composed or first performed). A third, and essential, type of meaning is that which arises from within the music itself, which Meyer called *embodied meaning*. Embodied meaning results from expectations and their resolution (or lack thereof) generated by patterns within the music itself (for a recent expansive study of expectations in music, see Huron, 2006). The genesis of the source of meaning in music as within the music itself, *music qua music*, is well represented by the ideas of Hanslick (1854/1957).

Peirce may be credited with one of the first formal models of semiotics, which he called logic (Buchler, 1955, p. 98). His basic three-part taxonomy includes *index*, *icon*, and *symbol*. Although it is tempting to connect the concepts directly to Meyer, as described earlier, there are subtle differences that space precludes analyzing here (and both Peirce and Meyer expand concepts beyond the three incorporated here). Important in Peirce is the concept of *icon* (see Buchler, 1955, pp. 98–128), where a signifier has a pattern resemblance to the signified and, therefore, is partially referential. Thus, whereas the word *cat* denotes by an arbitrary association to the signified object, a smiley face with lines drawn away from its circumference to represent whiskers connotes its signified object; that is, it *suggests* a cat because of its form. Computer icons are thus formed similarly (for more on this topic, see Roginska, Chapter 15, in this volume).

A proposed continuum of referentiality

These useful taxonomic approaches can be cast in terms of a continuum of referentiality. Whereas referential elements, at their extreme, are completely arbitrary, there are patterns that connect to meaning that are partially referential, and meanings arising from the patterns themselves, without clear external reference. Thus, the Peirce and Meyer concepts were formulated into a continuum of referentiality (Carterette & Kendall, 1996; Kendall, 1999, 2005a; Lipscomb & Kendall, 1994)—from arbitrary reference (association) through partially referential (iconic) to areferential (embodied)—and are postulated to be of use in multimedia analysis and experimentation. However, this one-dimensional continuum of referentiality is the simplest representation of the fact that there are multidimensional spaces that layer on top of one another. In a more complex model, referential, iconic, and areferential elements would each exist as separate continua within a multivariate structure. The simple approximation used here is the least complicated, and most easily tested example (for a theoretical structure of multidimensional associative referentialism, see Kendall, 2005a, pp. 93–94). The power of music to have meanings that are, at times, simultaneously referential, iconic, and embodied is intimately related to its use with temporally organized visuals and can form a basis to understand the role of music in multimedia.

Referential meaning is associative, an example of which is found in the idea of the DTPOT ('Darling They're Playing Our Tune') phenomenon articulated by Davies (1978, pp. 69–70). A common associative meaning in music, whether in concert or on film, is a national anthem or patriotic tune. In the film *Footlight Parade*, for example, the musical score consists of arrangements of 'Yankee Doodle' and 'Anchors Aweigh' (among others), while the image in Figure 3.1 is created by the dancers. This can be called extra-referential in that the associative meaning is external to the film itself; those attending the movie are expected to already know the musical themes and their patriotic connections. In concert music, the musical quotation of 'La Marseillaise' (the French national anthem) in Tchaikovsky's *1812 Overture* is an example. Other film scores that extensively use extra-referential meanings within their structure include *Casablanca* and *Gone with the Wind*, both with music by Max Steiner. The use of major and minor tonality to associate with positive and negative events is also an example of extra-referentialism. There is no particular reason why major is positive; it is an arbitrary association. For example, in *Casablanca*, the French national anthem is associated with the French Resistance and is in major, while the German national anthem is associated with the occupation and is scored in minor.

Intra-referential meanings are associations within the film itself, a technique called *idée fixe* or *leitmotiv*, evolving out of compositional practice in 19th-century Romanticism of Hector Berlioz and Richard Wagner. Thus, there is the five-note theme

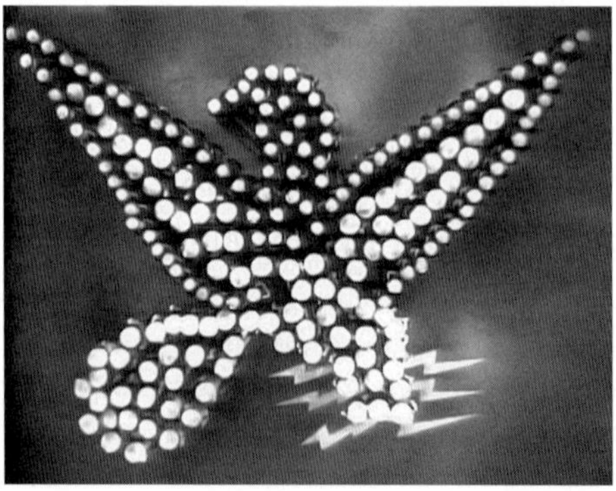

Figure 3.1 Still reproduced from *Footlight Parade* © Warner Brothers Pictures, 1933. Patriotic tunes elicit extra-referential meaning.

that is associated with the aliens in Williams' *Close Encounters of the Third Kind* score, or the simple minor-second motive representing the shark in *Jaws*, or the theme associated with the title character in *E.T.: the Extra-Terrestrial.*

Iconic meanings arise from pattern similarity and suggestion. Some writers (e.g., Jensenius, Wanderley, Godøy, & Leman, 2010; Leman, 2010; Nöth, 1990, pp. 392–401) use the word *gesture* to refer to aspects of these musical structures connected to visual structures. We identify several common icons, among others: *ramps*, which monotonically increase or decrease in a musical (loudness, texture, pitch, etc.) or visual (size, distance, height, etc.) variable; *arches*, which first increase and then decrease; and *bursts*, which are called 'stingers' in film composition parlance. Kendall (2005a) notes that the time versus magnitude relationship can involve 'any variable, such as pitch, loudness, timbre/texture or tempo. Various camera effects can be connected, including pan (left to right), zoom (front to back) and cut' (p. 93). Further, iconic meanings evolve from syntactical relations, but are partially referential (Kendall, 2005a, p. 93). For example, in the galley rowing scene in *Ben Hur* (1959), the rowing is not only temporally congruent (syntactical) with the musical score, but the upward and downward strokes of the oars are accompanied by a melodic line that ascends and descends in synchrony as well.

Tagg (2004) has written extensively about iconic elements in musicological semiotics, including film music. His concept of 'anaphone,' or analogous sound, is particularly applicable to the present model as a type of iconicity. He identifies sound anaphones, kinetic anaphones, and tactile anaphones, the last represented by harmonic textures. We can illustrate the concepts by considering the opening of the (silent) film *Metropolis* as accompanied by its original orchestral score. In the scene immediately following the titles, kinetic, temporally active anaphones are congruent with the montage of working machinery and the second hand of a clock. As the time for a worker shift change arrives, a sound anaphone is produced by the orchestra to accompany the visual of a steam whistle as it blows.

Many different sources of composer-intended meaning can be active simultaneously and can be dynamically changing during a given scene within a multimedia context. An audience's perception of the composer's and film-maker's/editor's intent will necessarily be varyingly veridical, not fixed in psychophysical isomorphism. Simply put, cultural understanding (e.g., shared explicit and implicit knowledge) is at work informing the communication process.

Film examples related to the proposed continuum of referentiality

E.T.: the Extra-Terrestrial (Kennedy, Mathison, Spielberg, & Spielberg, 1982), music by John Williams, provides an excellent example of referential, iconic, and areferential processes at work. The bicycle chase scene includes music that maintains syntactical congruence (with the use of an opening 3/4 + 3/8 meter to maintain connection to the pedaling of the cyclists) and also incorporates pitch contours that iconically follow the motion of the cyclists. Figure 3.2 is a still from this sequence; the music is a pitch arch that follows the cyclists over the hill, and is thus iconic relative to the visual motion. Such icons serve to reinforce and draw attention to the central activity. Although the

Figure 3.2 Pitch contour arch in the music follows the bicycle visual arch over the hill. Still reproduced from *E.T.: the Extra-Terrestrial* © Universal Pictures, 1982; musical score by John Williams © 1982.

character E.T. appears in this sequence, it is not until a close-up later in the sequence that the intra-referential theme associated with his character reappears.

A dissonance and loudness ramp appears before the cyclists visually ramp upward. The *E.T.* intra-referential theme appears and the accompanying music lines maintain the syntactical accent structure of the pedaling throughout. The intervals of the theme become greater (approaching and reaching an octave); the pitch height of the line iconically accompanies the rising of the cyclists. Thus, we have intra-referential, iconic, and congruent/syntactical meaning all at once (Figure 3.3).

As in *E.T.*, the orchestration of a melody can provide accompanying melodic and textural strata that emphasize visual motion. In the 'Scarecrow Dance' sequence from *The Wizard of Oz*, the orchestration provides an iconic descending pitch ramp as the dancing scarecrow falls into Dorothy's arms (Figure 3.4). The entire score is replete with such iconic elements and, of course, incorporates intra-referential themes such as that for the Wicked Witch of the West. In fact, the first appearance of Miss Gulch on the bicycle in Kansas incorporates congruent accent patterns

Figure 3.3 Flying, a still reproduced from *E.T.: the Extra-Terrestrial* © Universal Pictures, 1982.

Figure 3.4 Still reproduced from the 'Scarecrow Dance' scene from *The Wizard of Oz* © Metro-Goldwyn-Mayer, 1939. The orchestration includes an iconic descending pitch ramp as Ray Bolger's character falls.

(syntax) between the music and pedaling motion not dissimilar to that found in *E.T.*, as described earlier.

Syntactical relations refer to meanings embodied within the patterning among and within sound (e.g., music) and visuals (e.g., moving images), as represented by the musical alignment with the rowing motions in *Ben Hur* and the bicycle pedaling in *E.T.* or *The Wizard of Oz*. Other examples that exemplify this areferential (or self-referential) meaning include the relationship between sound and image represented in ice-skating

Figure 3.5 Still reproduced from the 'Cool Dance' sequence from *West Side Story* © The Mirisch Corporation, 1961.

routines, abstract animation and film, gymnastics, and various dance forms, as in *West Side Story* (1961) discussed later. The temporal congruence that is studied by Cohen and Iwamiya (see Chapters 3 and 7 in this volume) is, at its most fundamental level, an aspect of this syntactical/areferential meaning.

In the 'Cool Dance' sequence from *West Side Story*, soon after the statement of the main chorus, the music develops into polyphony based on a principal musical motif. At the same time, the dancers form independent groups that move congruently but are choreographed independently, creating what might be termed a polyvisual structure, responding to the increasingly layered melodic lines (Figure 3.5).

Empirical research

Kendall (2005a) set out to verify empirically the ability of musically-trained participants to use the continuum of referentiality delineated earlier in this chapter. Six graduate ethnomusicology students were given a handout that described the semiotical concepts of referentiality discussed earlier; the description was text only, including neither still images nor film excerpts. The experimenter chose audiovisual stimuli (five film excerpts and a television broadcast of an Olympic figure skating event) to span the continuum of referentiality, presenting these 30-second excerpts to each participant in a random order. Two excerpts were hypothesized to represent the extremes of the continuum: (1) *Footlight Parade* (the sequence described earlier) was designated referential (labeled REF1 in the results that follow) and (2) the 'Cool Dance' sequence from *West Side Story* was hypothesized to be syntactical (SYN1). The iconic center of the continuum of referentiality was represented by the galley rowing scene from *Ben Hur* (labeled ICON1). Other positions along the continuum were hypothesized to be represented by the 'inside the ship' sequence from *Close Encounters of the Third Kind* (ICREF1: iconic with referential elements) and two excerpts that included elements of syntax and iconicity (a figure skating sequence from the Albertville Olympics and the scene from *Fantasia* for which the Bach Toccata and Fugue in D minor serves as the musical score, labeled SYNIC1 and SYNIC2, respectively). Participants rated the stimuli on a continuous scale (see Figure 3.6).

Areferential/Syntax Icon Index/Referential

Figure 3.6 Response scale used in the experiment. The paper-based response line was 5 inches long and the 'X' representing the response was measured in centimeters from the left side.

Results are presented in Figure 3.7. A repeated measures ANOVA showed statistical significance for the referential main effect ($F(5,25) = 8.11, p < 0.001$). Post-hoc analysis of mean differences revealed that all of the means in Figure 3.7 were statistically different from one another ($p < 0.05$) except for the two SYNIC means and the SYNIC2 and ICON1 means. Although generalizability is limited by the highly-trained population of participants, this best-case scenario modestly confirms that the continuum is useable in experimental research to explore the communication of meaning in a commercial audiovisual context.

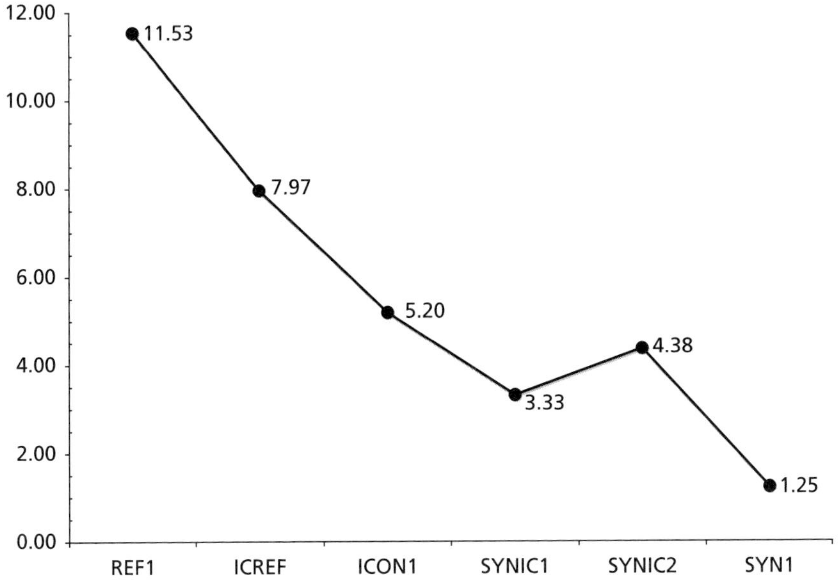

Figure 3.7 Mean ratings for six audiovisual stimuli along a continuum of referentiality (adapted from Kendall, 2005a, p. 97; used by permission).

Experiments in musical semiotics

Previous research has largely dealt with the associative aspects of music, identified as mood or affect, and its effects on subject perception of audiovisual composites. The area of iconicity is less thoroughly researched, although some efforts in domains outside of film are noteworthy. The concept of a musical gesture has been defined as 'human body movement that goes along with sounding music' (Jensenius et al., 2010, p. 13) and has been studied recently using new technologies in performance and conducting among other areas. This research, particularly that of Clynes' sentics (1986), often resembles the iconic aspects articulated earlier, representing a concept called physiognomics in which patterns suggest mood or affect, as in the naming of the 'weeping willow' (Davies, 1978, p. 104). The two experiments described in the following paragraphs (Kendall, 2010) employed animations to determine whether the hypothetical iconic archetypes are rated for best fit in the match between visual motion and melodic pitch pattern.

Monophonic icons

Kendall (2010) generated stimuli based on several iconic prototypes in both the auditory and visual modalities: ramp, arch, undulation, inward spin, and outward spin (Figures 3.8 and 3.9; to see examples of these stimuli, please visit

Figure 3.8 Pitch patterns generated with synthetic piano timbre with abbreviations used in the results. Note: The arch music visuals are different from the undulation as follows: Musically, the arch pattern starts and returns to the tonic and the visual pattern starts from the center of the figure and moves up and back to that origin. The undulation pattern moves up and down through these musical and visual points. Adapted from Kendall (2010, pp. 7–8).

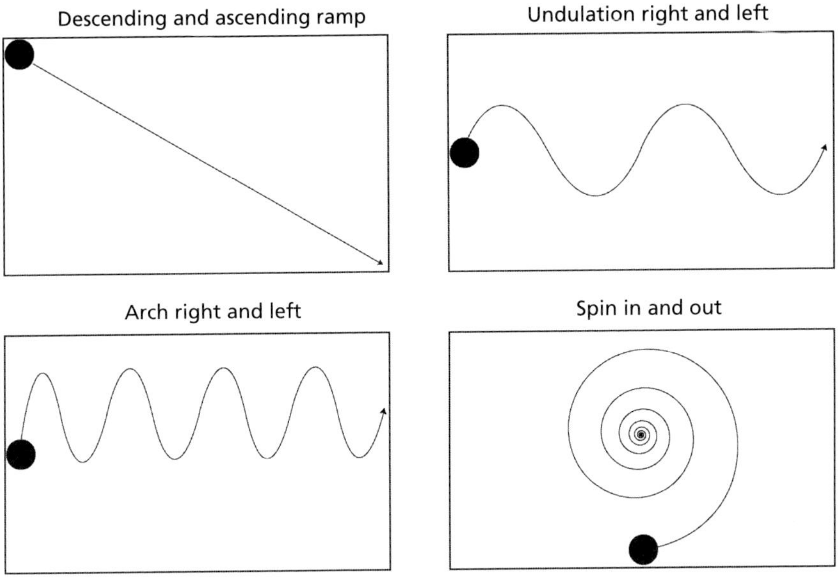

Figure 3.9 Animation patterns with labels (executed in both directions). See note included in caption for Figure 3.8. Adapted from Kendall (2010, p. 8).

<http://www.oup.co.uk/companion/tan>). The researcher then carried out two experiments, one focusing on combinations of icon types across modality and the other focusing on contours of auditory and visual motion across modalities.

In the first experiment, participants rated the stimuli on a visually continuous, 100-point scale of musical/visual fit. Stimuli were presented in two random orders of the 56 audiovisual composites (seven musical stimuli × eight visual stimuli (i.e., four patterns executed in two directions)). Figures 3.10 and 3.11 are example combinations of visual and music patterns. Each musical pattern was combined with every visual pattern, a crossed design.

A repeated measures ANOVA revealed significant differences for the main effects of visual animation pattern and melodic pattern. Of particular interest regarding the cross-modal model of multimedia semiotics presented earlier is the statistically significant interaction effect revealed visually in Figure 3.12. In general, the hypothesized combinations (arch with arch, ramp with ramp, etc.) resulted in the highest mean fitness scores across audiovisual composites. However, the spin-in and spin-out conditions did not match the intended musical patterns (increasing and decreasing inter-onset interval (IOI)) as well, nor did the visual undulation pattern moving toward the left side of the screen (perhaps suggesting a cultural bias for left-to-right spatial perception, a result worth additional attention) (see also Eitan, Chapter 8, in this volume). In this latter case, the hypothesized musical pattern 'match' would have been an undulation starting downward, since that is the initial visual motion, but this combination was rated no better than the upward pattern. This result is somewhat expected, since no direct pitch analog of leftward motion exists; clock time in music moves inexorably forward (perceived, in Western culture at least, as movement from left to right).

Descending ramp with descending ramp

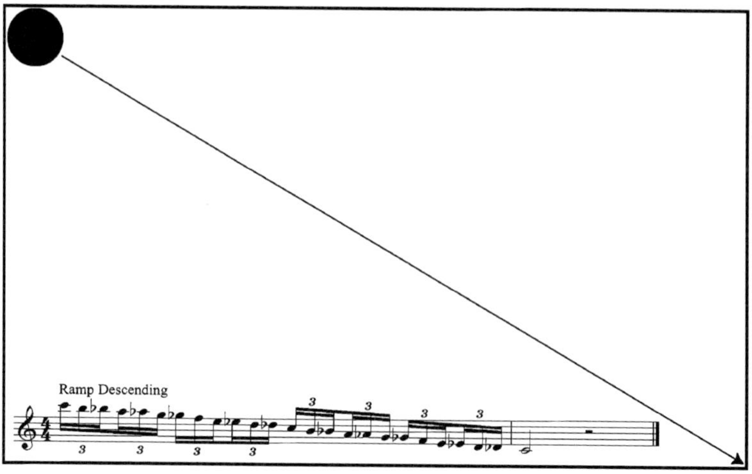

Figure 3.10 The descending ramp animation paired with the descending ramp music. Music notation is not to scale. Adapted from Kendall (2010, p. 8).

Descending ramp with undulation down

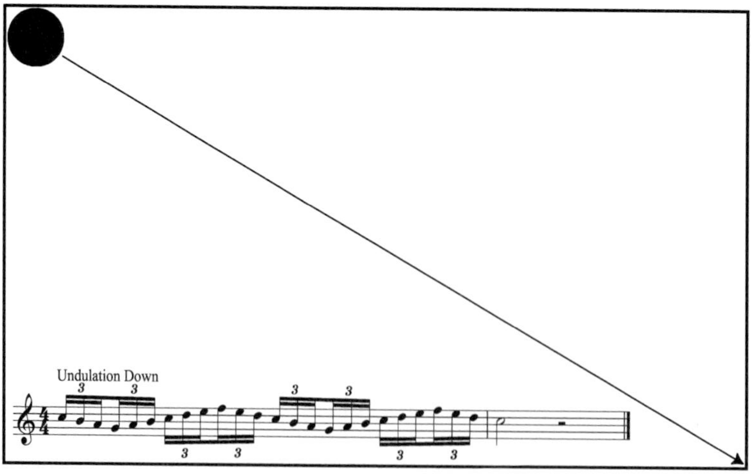

Figure 3.11 The descending ramp animation with the undulation down music. Music notation is not to scale. Adapted from Kendall (2010, p. 9).

The visual undulation moving from left to right, the last mean represented in Figure 3.12, matches well with the musical undulation up, again suggesting that left–right visual motion was more easily discerned relative to the musical undulation with these relatively rapidly changing shifts in visual and pitch contour through time. However, the arch patterns left and right are well matched since the musical pattern

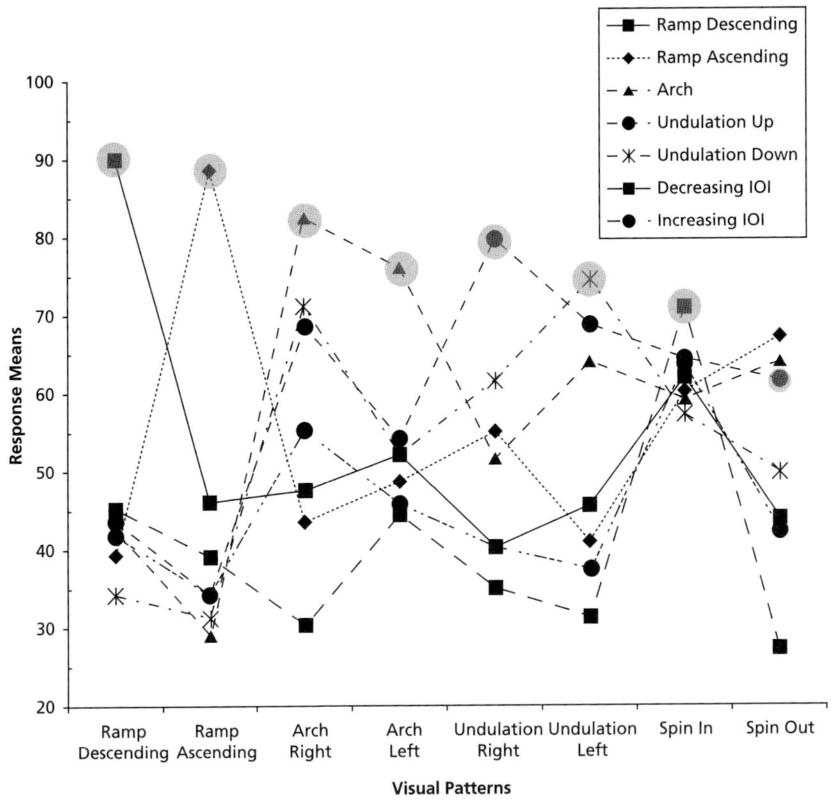

Figure 3.12 Interaction of visual and musical patterns. The experimental hypotheses of best fit are highlighted. The X-axis is the visual pattern and the legend refers to musical pattern. Adapted and re-arranged from Kendall (2010, p. 11).

is identical in both cases, starting from and returning to the tonic, thus not requiring a specific distinction regarding the initial direction. Future research should include visual and musical arch forms that start downward as well as upward.

Pilot study on musical and visual contours

The second experiment reported in Kendall (2010) dealt explicitly with the aspect of musical sound and visual motion known as *contour*. In a musical context, melodic contour is defined in terms of pitch inflection points, that is, changes of direction (up or down) in melodic motion. Previous research has demonstrated perceptual salience, or accent, at the point that a pitch pattern changes direction (see Lipscomb, Chapter 9, in this volume). The analog to these changes in melodic contour within the context of animation would be changes of direction in space through time. Kendall's pilot experiment paired a single monophonic pitch pattern, the arch (see Figure 3.8), with visual motion patterns: arch, circle, triangle, square, pentagon, hexagon, and a stair pattern (this last pattern constitutes a variation of the ramp with direction changes corresponding to pitch inflection points in the melody. To see examples of these stimuli, please visit <http://www.oup.co.uk/companion/tan>). The arch melodic pattern (at a tempo of 100 beats per minute) provides contour inflections at the eighth-note (eight total accents) before returning to the tonic on a half note.

Kendall (2010) hypothesized that visual and audio composites that align accent points would form good fits. Visual patterns with odd numbers of vertices, such as the triangle and pentagon, would be likely to result in a mismatch between contours. Of course, the circle has no physical inflection points at all. Empirical data (Monahan, Kendall, & Carterette, 1987) suggest that groups of temporal units that are bounded by the sound onset with groupings that favor even divisions of time are best remembered. Thus, this study hypothesized that visual motion patterns that fit or evenly subdivide this temporal interval (i.e., arch, square, hexagon, and stairs) would be rated as a better fit between modalities than those that are not congruent (i.e., triangle, pentagon, and circle).

Three undergraduate music majors participated in this pilot study, which included a total of seven audiovisual combinations (i.e., the seven shapes previously described combined with the auditory arch). Stimuli were presented in a unique random order to each participant, each of whom rated every audiovisual pair on the same continuous scale used in the previous experiment.

Mean responses are graphed in Figure 3.13. As hypothesized, the combination of the arch visual and arch musical patterns received the highest rating of fit. For this pattern, the inflection points as well as the contours were identical. The square animation has changes of direction that correspond to a melodic inflection point at the musical tonic; this was the combination receiving the next highest rating, though statistically the same as the circle. The circle animation has no inflections, except that implied by dividing it into four quadrants at ninety-degree intervals. Whether this was the implicit strategy used by participants in this study cannot be discerned from the data collected, but is worthy of further investigation. It is well known that, perceptually, pitch is (at least) two-dimensional and circular, with the scale wrapping back to the same pitch class, the tonic. As participants in this study were musically trained, perhaps pitch circularity trumped the lack of contour inflection correspondence, another topic for future research.

Also as hypothesized, the pentagon and triangle received the lowest ratings. The stairs and hexagon, with visual inflections at each melodic inflection point, were rated better in fit than the triangle and pentagon, but less so than the square, circle, and arch. The arch melodic pattern contains four equidistant tonic pitches (followed by a tonic half-note ending), but in the inflection point at the eighth note, a weaker fourth-scale degree is reached. This suggests that the concept of melodic contour theory coupled with melodic charge (position of a tone within the diatonic system) may provide a means to model the magnitude of inflection points in the musical domain, and this might be connected to magnitudes of visual motion contour.

Additional experiments have been conducted using polyphonic isochronous pitch patterns, timbral markers, and layered animations. The musical and visual patterns represented in Figures 3.8 and 3.9 were combined in pairs layered on top of one another in all possible combinations, resulting in two musical patterns using piano and oboe in

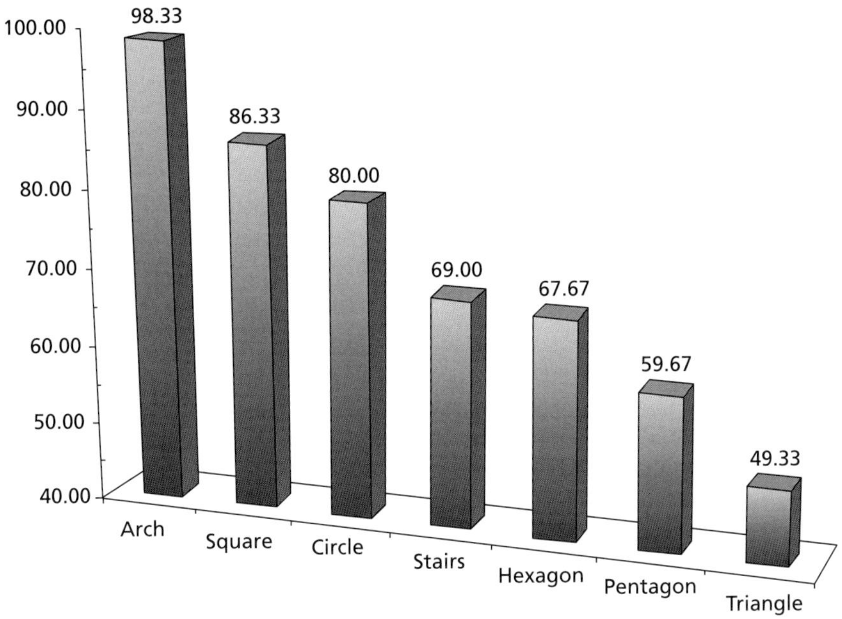

Figure 3.13 Results of the contour experiment. The X-axis is the visual pattern that was paired with the arch musical pattern. Adapted from Kendall (2010, p. 11).

polyphony and two animations using black and yellow circles moving polyvisually. (To see examples of these stimuli, please visit <http://www.oup.co.uk/companion/tan). Initial results suggest that stratification of patterns that have temporally rapid accent structures result in highly variable subject responses. Often, only combinations of musical and visual patterns with the least number of contour changes (i.e., the ramps) can be attached to timbre cues in music and color cues in the animations. Very quickly, there appears to be a cognitive overload using the types of patterns discussed here when they are polyphonically and multivisually stratified.

Conclusions and future directions

The studies described in this chapter have progressed from edited film excerpts, through semiotical theory for musicological analysis, to empirical experiments based on animations abstracted from patterns of sound and movement found in real film and animation. The convergence of results demonstrates that association, pattern similarity in iconicity, and temporal congruence all contribute to the establishment of a symbiotic relationship between musical and visual temporally organized structures.

Further investigations are needed to determine how the magnitudes of variables interact. For example, varying elements of distance in space, number of inflection points through time, and their interaction with association components such as major and minor tonalities would extend these studies. At this time, it is not possible, nor warranted, to accept one or another model of music and film as most useful. Taxonomic approaches, implying a magnitude threshold for the salience of one variable over another, have not been empirically tested to an adequate extent. The various experiments by Kendall (2010) suggest that elements of a multidimensional model based on continua may lead to a best-fit perceptual response. Further studies with real film, rather than abstractions in animation, need to converge on the extent to which different human populations, approaching film with different knowledge structures (schemata), employ distinct strategies in decoding the intended meaning of the film's creators. What is abundantly clear is that the interrelation of visual and musical variables in film is not arbitrary, but is purposeful, based on principles of communication, and thus amenable to study through both musicological and empirical theory and model building.

Acknowledgments

This chapter was adapted from the keynote presentation and proceedings document of the first author (Kendall, 2010) at the conference session 'Human Vision and Electronic Imaging XV,' San Jose, California, as part of IS&T/SPIE Electronic Imaging 2010. The original experiments described in this chapter were performed under the direction of Roger Kendall at the Music Perception and Cognition Laboratory at UCLA.

References

Boltz, M. G. (1991). Effects of background music on the remembering of filmed events. *Memory & Cognition, 19*(6), 593–606.

Boltz, M. G. (2001). Musical soundtracks as a schematic influence on the cognitive processing of filmed events. *Music Perception, 18*(4), 427–454.

Buchler, J. (Ed.) (1955). *Philosophical writings of Peirce*. New York, NY: Dover.

Carterette, E. C., & Kendall, R. A. (1996). Musical communication. In H. Fastl, S. Kuwano, & A. Schick (Eds.), *Recent trends in hearing research* (pp. 131–160). Oldenburg, Germany: Oldenburg University Press.

Clynes, M. (1986). *Sentics: The touch of the emotions*. New York, NY: Avery.

Davies, J. B. (1978). *Psychology of music*. Stanford, CA: Stanford University Press.

Dowling, W. J., & Harwood, D. L. (1986). *Music cognition*. Orlando, FL: Academic Press.

Hanslick, E. (1957). *The beautiful in music* (G. Cohen, Trans., & M. Weitz, Ed.). New York, NY: Liberal Arts Press. (Original work published 1854.)

Hevner, K. (1935a). The affective character of the major and minor modes in music. *American Journal of Psychology, 47*, 113–118.

Hevner, K. (1935b). Expression in music: A discussion of experimental studies and theories. *Psychological Review, 47*, 186–204.

Hevner, K. (1936). Experimental studies of the elements of expression in music. *American Journal of Psychology, 48*, 246–268.

Hevner, K. (1937). The affective value of pitch and tempo in music. *American Journal of Psychology, 49*, 621–630.

Huron, D. (2006). *Sweet anticipation: Music and the psychology of expectation*. Cambridge, MA: Bradford Books/MIT Press.

Jensenius, A. R., Wanderley, M. M., Godøy, R. I., & Leman, M. (2010). Musical gestures. In R. I. Godøy and M. Leman (Eds.), *Musical gestures: Sound, movement, and meaning* (pp. 12–35). New York, NY: Routledge.

Kastner, M. P., & Crowder, R. (1990). Perception of the major/minor distinction: iv. Emotional connotations in young children. *Music Perception*, *8*, 189–202.

Kennedy, K., Mathison, M., Spielberg, S. (Producers), & Spielberg, S. (Director). (1982). *E. T.: the Extra-terrestrial* [Motion picture]. United States: Universal Pictures.

Kendall, R. A. (1999, March). *A theory of meaning in film music.* Lecture presented at the Joint Meeting of the Acoustical Society of America and European Acoustics Association, Berlin, Germany.

Kendall, R. A. (2005a). Empirical approaches to musical meaning. *Selected Reports in Ethnomusicology*, *12*, 69–102.

Kendall, R. A. (2005b). Music and video iconicity: Theory and experimental design. *Journal of Physiological. Anthropology and Applied Human Science*, *24*(1), 143–149.

Kendall, R. A. (2010). Music in film and animation: Experimental semiotics applied to visual, sound and musical structures. In B. E. Rogowitz & T. N. Pappas (Eds.), *Human Vision and Electronic Imaging XV* (Proceedings of SPIE-IS&T Electronic Imaging, SPIE Vol. 7527) (pp. 1–13). Bellingham, WA: SPIE & The Society for Imaging Science and Technology.

Kendall, R. A., & Savage, R. W. H. (Eds.). (2005). Perspectives in systematic musicology [Special issue]. *Selected Reports in Ethnomusicology*, *12*.

Leman, M. (2010). Music, gesture, and the formation of embodied meaning. In Godøy and Leman (Eds.), *Musical gestures: Sound, movement, and meaning* (pp. 126–153). New York, NY: Routledge.

Lipscomb, S. D. (1995). *Cognition of musical and visual accent structure alignment in film and animation.* PhD dissertation, University of California, Los Angeles, CA.

Lipscomb, S. D., & Kendall, R. A. (1994). Perceptual judgment of the relationship between musical and visual components in film. *Psychomusicology*, *13*(1), 60–98.

Marshall, S. K., & Cohen, A. J. (1988). Effects of musical soundtracks on attitudes toward animated geometric figures. *Music Perception*, *6*, 85–112.

Meyer, L. B. (1956). *Emotion and meaning in music.* Chicago, IL: Chicago University Press.

Monahan, C. B. (1984). Parallels between pitch and time: The determinants of perceptual space. PhD dissertation, University of California, Los Angeles, CA.

Monahan, C. B., Kendall, R. A., & Carterette, E. C. (1987). The effect of melodic and temporal contour on recognition memory for pitch change. *Perception and Psychophysics*, *41*(6), 576–600.

Nöth, W. (1990). *Handbook of semiotics.* Bloomington, IN: Indiana University Press.

Osgood, C. E., Suci, G. J., & Tannenbaum, P. H. (1957). *The measurement of meaning.* Urbana, IL: University of Illinois Press.

Peirce, C. (1931–1932). *Collected papers of Charles Sanders Peirce* (Vols. 1 and 2) (C. Hartsborne & P. Weiss, Eds.). Cambridge, MA: Harvard University Press.

Tagg, P. (2004). *Gestural interconversion and connotative precision.* Université de Montreal. Retrieved from <http://www.tagg.org/articles/xpdfs/filminternat0412.pdf>.

Saussure, F. (1998). *Course in general linguistics* (R. Harris, Trans.) (Reprint ed.). Peru, IL: Open Court Publishing.

Tannenbaum, P. H. (1956). Music background in the judgment of stage and television drama. *Audio-Visual Communication Review*, *4*, 92–101.

Chapter 4

Integrating media effects research and music psychology

Mark Shevy

Northern Michigan University, USA

Public appetite for media seems insatiable. As shown by surveys and other research methods (e.g., Nielsen, 2012; Rideout, Foehr, & Roberts, 2010), audiovisual mass media—including film, television, video games, and the World Wide Web—occupy minds for a substantial portion of the day and potentially impact entire generations and societies. The potential for influencing such a large number of people raises important questions about the types of effects that media might have and when and how those effects can occur. Such questions may also be asked more specifically about the role of music in mass communication.

Although there is no comprehensive scientific analysis of the quantity or kind of music used in mass communication, anyone who watches television or movies is aware of the prevalence of music in traditional media. (The chapter on persuasive media in this volume provides some content analysis of music in advertising.) Music is also prevalent in new multimedia platforms. YouTube is the most-viewed video site on the Internet, providing almost 13.8 billion video streams to over 130 million unique audience members in the month of December, 2011, alone (Nielsenwire, 2012). In April 2012, 28 of the 30 most-viewed YouTube videos of all time featured music as a central component (e.g., professional music videos, or an animation of two children singing in the bathtub). Certain Web sites such as Internet radio stations and music video channels on MTV.com, Yahoo, and AOL, are devoted solely to music. Although their focus is music, their concurrent use of extramusical information (e.g., images, text, spoken or sung words) characterizes them as musical multimedia. Additionally, iTunes and video games supply musical multimedia both online and off-line, and mobile electronics allow musical multimedia to be present in nearly any location and situation.

Although music typically is integral to mass media productions, little research has been conducted on the psychological effects of music in mass communication. Such research is important given the potential power of mass media. The present chapter aims to inspire relevant research by developing a theoretical foundation that integrates media effects, psychology, and musical multimedia. The focus is on individual-level effects, which may occur in a single audience member, a subset of audience members within a larger audience, or plausibly within every individual consuming the content.

This chapter first directs attention to the prevalence of music in mass media, and then briefly describes the discipline of media effects research and its relationship with psychology and musical multimedia. Next, the nature of media effects is defined in more detail, and six antecedents of media effects are outlined. Finally, a selection of prominent theories of media effects illustrates how such theories may be integrated with music psychology to predict effects of music in mediated communication. Such predictions, if tested, could increase knowledge about the role of music in mass media.

Media effects research

Media effects research and mass communication

In their book *Perspectives on Media Effects*, Bryant and Zillmann (1986, p. xiii) refer to media effects as 'the social, cultural, and psychological impact of communicating via mass media.' Following the publication of *The Process and Effects of Mass Communication* (Schramm, 1954), the empirical, scientific study of media effects has been referred to as the 'media effects paradigm' or 'approach,' as distinguished from other approaches such as 'critical studies, cultural studies, and uses and gratifications approach' (Eveland, 2003, p. 395). Traditionally, the field is a discipline within the broader study of 'mass communication' or 'mass media.' Harkening back to concepts associated with the classic *The Mathematical Theory of Communication* (Shannon & Weaver, 1949), technically speaking, *mass communication* refers to the process by which a sender encodes meanings into symbols (words, sounds, images) within messages that are sent to large numbers of receivers (audience members) who construct meanings from the symbols. *Mass media* are the technological channels through which mass communication occurs (radio, television, etc.).

The convergence of traditional media, computers, and the Internet has created communication processes that sometimes challenge traditional definitions and models associated with these terms just referred to (Dominick, 2007; Li, 1998), while serving many of the same functions. For example, people turn to the Internet for entertainment or news about current events just as they turn to television for them. Websites, video games, and other newer media facilitate interaction, giving users more freedom to customize and contribute messages in contrast to the primarily one-way flow, one-size-fits-all nature of traditional mass media. In new media, people can fulfill the role of both receiver and sender, so the term 'user' regularly replaces the traditional term *audience member* found in much mass communication literature. As a convention, this chapter applies the term 'user' in reference both to those people who use new media and those who use traditional media. With further regard to terminology, sometimes scholars use the term 'media' rather than 'mass media' to include types of media that may not entirely fit traditional definitions. Regardless, 'mass communication,' 'mass media,' and 'media' are still all commonly used to refer to this overall field of research.

Mass communication research spans multiple levels of analysis, including analysis of individual people from a physiological and psychological standpoint, as well as analysis at the societal-level from a sociological or anthropological perspective (Paisley, 1972).

A substantial amount of mass communication research, particularly at the individual level, uses theories of psychology. A content analysis of three well-established mass communication journals (*Journalism & Mass Communication Quarterly*, *Journal of Communication*, and *Journal of Broadcasting & Electronic Media*) from the years 1956 to 2000 found that almost 60 percent of references to theories originated in the field of communication, while just over 12 percent originated in psychology, and 5 percent in sociology. However, further analysis of the communication theories revealed that approximately 30 percent of them were derived from psychology (e.g., social learning, cognitive dissonance, attribution theory, behaviorism, Piagetian, psychoanalytic theory), or sociology (e.g., social construction of reality, symbolic interactionism, Marxism, media hegemony) (Bryant & Miron, 2004). The area of mass communication research that draws the most heavily from psychology is that pertaining to media use and effects at the individual level.

Media effects research, as a dominant approach to mass communication studies (Eveland, 2003; McLeod, Kosicki, & Pan, 1991; Perse, 2008), has a variety of aims. Members of the public, the health industry, and government, aware of the pervasiveness of movies, radio, television, computer and mobile media, want to know what influence media have on individuals and society—how media use, for better or for worse, might impact thoughts and knowledge, might create or reinforce ideals and stereotypes, might alter views of reality, and might change or maintain emotions, moods, attitudes, and behaviors. Media producers and scholars are also interested in understanding how to harness multimedia for the purpose of entertaining, persuading, informing, and educating audiences. Media effects research aims to address these concerns.

Psychology has been integral to the development of the field of media effects research. Early media effects research through the 1930s was based on the stimulus-response model from psychology (Perse, 2001, p. 23). Cognition was given importance in mass communication research (e.g., Hawkins & Daly, 1988) when cognitive studies became a dominant paradigm within psychology. And when psychology made advances in the study of emotion, media effects research also experienced an increase in emotion-related studies (Döveling, von Scheve, & Konijn, 2011, p. 2). Although mass media research has traditionally been conducted by mass communication scholars, psychologists have also recently recognized the common interest in mass media and psychology through a proliferation of their own mass media research (Konijn & ten Holt, 2011).

Media effects research and musical multimedia

The close relationship between media effects research and psychology, and the presence of music in most media, raises expectations of an already developed psychological literature of musical multimedia within the field of mass communication. This expectation is further bolstered by similar categories of effects studied by both mass communication and music psychology: that is, cognitive, affective (mood and emotion), and behavioral effects (cf. North & Hargreaves, 2008; Tan, Pfordresher, & Harré, 2010; for media effects, Perse, 2001). Nevertheless, mass media effects research has paid little attention to music in media.

The few music research topics that do appear in mass communication journals and textbooks often fall into one of the following groups:

1. content analysis, such as the amount and type of sexual and violent content in songs and music videos (Conrad, Dixon, & Zhang, 2009)
2. correlations between preference and audience characteristics such as gender and personality (e.g., Hall, 2005; Hansen & Hansen, 1990)
3. rationales for consumption such as mood regulation (e.g., Knobloch & Zillmann, 2002)
4. impact—especially of music videos—on formation and activation of sexual or racial schemas and attitudes (Johnson, Trawalter, & Dovidio, 2000; Zhang, Miller, & Harrison, 2008), promoting body image ideals (Zhang, Dixon, & Conrad, 2009), or promoting other unhealthy behaviors such as cigarette use (Slater & Hayes, 2010).

In many of these studies, researchers test the combined effects of music, visuals, and words rather than their independent effects and their interactions. In one of the few summaries of music and media effects, Knobloch and Mundorf (2003) state that the presentation of their work does not distinguish between music and music videos. Some studies, however, do examine particular elements. Hansen and Hansen (1990) found that sexual visual imagery increased audience members' enjoyment of music videos, while imagery of violence decreased it. Their results also showed that increased arousal from the music increased the strength of the respective enjoyment or displeasure of the videos (see also Zillmann & Mundorf, 1987).

Effects of media

Effects of media may take many forms such as learning (antisocial or prosocial), alteration or reinforcement of social perceptions and beliefs, mood regulation, diversion from everyday life (e.g., entertainment), aggression, persuasion, and health behaviors. Media effects research must then measure a corresponding wide variety of dependent measures, and thus researchers have classified specific types of effects along the following dimensions (McLeod et al., 1991, p. 242; McLeod & Reeves, 1980, pp. 18–27; Perse, 2001, pp. 17–22):

1. cognitive, affective, or behavioral
2. alteration or reinforcement (e.g., of existing cognition, affect, or behavior)
3. short term or long term
4. intended or unintended by the message producer
5. occurring at an individual level (psychological) or at a societal level (e.g., political system)
6. based on media content or content irrelevant (e.g., media form)
7. based on a single media exposure or on cumulative multiple exposures.

This classification system of effects of media can in turn assist in determining what role music might contribute to the media effects, including the possibility that its role might be negligible.

Six antecedents of media effects

Antecedents are stimuli or conditions that cause, support, or influence psychological processes and their resulting effects. An antecedent may precede the effect, such as the existence of a user's happy mood before she laughs at a funny music video. An antecedent may also support or influence an effect concurrent with the effect. The happy mood may continue while she is laughing, facilitating the laughing as it occurs. In the following, I have organized antecedents into six types: user attributes, time, context, media content, media form, and interactivity.

User attributes

The user often selects the media forms, contents, and degree of technological interactivity that will ultimately lead to media effects. Media effects are universally constrained by the capabilities and limitations of the brain and are modulated by individual differences; psychological effects take the form of affective and cognitive processes, and behavioral effects fit the physical mechanics of individual kinesthetic capacities and limitations. The nature of an effect depends on the characteristics of the person in whom the effect occurs. Individual characteristics may lead one person to cry during a movie scene because of the impact of the musical score, yet another person may be distracted by the score. This does not preclude the possibility that some media can have the same effect on a great number of people.

Music media research indicates two ways in which user attributes influence effects. The first is the *selection* of music media. Two people may have different needs and expectations of media, causing them to make different choices of media or content. One might choose a music video to learn what a song is about (cf. Sun & Lull, 1986), while the other selects something with calming music in order to relax (cf. Knobloch & Zillmann, 2002). Furthermore, the same person can select different music media at different times to suit certain moods, situations, or goals. The *uses and gratifications* theoretical approach to media (Katz, Blumler, & Gurevitch, 1973) depicts the process of users selecting media to meet their needs. Although some researchers have considered media selection and use as a field of study distinct from media effects, research increasingly shows that selection and use can influence the effects of media (as will be discussed later).

The second influence of user attributes is known as the *conditional model* of effects (Perse, 2001, pp. 33–42), and it involves user attributes that alter or explain an effect of media. For example, the sex of a user can alter the appreciation of sexual imagery in a music video, such that certain imagery can increase males' appreciation and decrease females' appreciation (Zillmann & Mundorf, 1987). As another example, Tiggemann and Slater (2004) found that music videos emphasizing 'female thinness and attractiveness' (p. 51) caused female viewers to experience decreased satisfaction with their own bodies. This effect was dependent, however, on the amount of comparison each viewer made between herself and the video images. If a viewer made no comparison, the music videos had virtually no effect.

The concept of individual attributes is closely related to a psychological personality theory which distinguishes traits and states. *Traits* are dispositions such as aggressiveness, extraversion, neuroticism, psychoticism, and sensation seeking which are regarded as relatively stable over longer periods of time (Oliver & Krakowiak, 2009). Preference for particular musical styles has been shown to be related to traits (e.g., Rentfrow, Goldberg, & Levitin, 2011; Rentfrow & Gosling, 2003; Schuessler, 1948). Sensation seeking, a trait in which people seek 'varied, novel, complex, and intense sensations and experiences, and [have] the willingness to take physical, social, legal, and financial risks for the sake of such experience' (Zuckerman, 1994, p. 27), is considered to be important in music media selection. Users who are high in sensation seeking crave physiological arousal from media (Sparks & Sparks, 2000), which may lead them to choose novel, complex, and intense styles of music (Knobloch & Mundorf, 2003; Zuckerman, 2006). *States* are transient dispositions, such as mood or readiness to have an emotional response (Oliver & Krakowiak, 2009). Mood can guide music selection (Knobloch & Zillmann, 2002). While some research shows how states and traits motivate choice of music media, little is known about how these attributes subsequently alter or explain the effects of the musical media. For example, how might music in a message influence those who are high in sensation seeking differently than other people?

Some traits may influence musical multimedia effects more strongly than others. For example, 'psychoticism' (a tendency to be antisocial, aggressive, egocentric) and 'Machiavellianism' (a focus on selfish goals with lack of empathy for others) are associated with enjoyment of hard rock and heavy metal and violent content (e.g., Hansen & Hansen, 2000; Markey & Scherer, 2009; Rawlings & Leow, 2008; Tamborini, Stiff, & Zillman, 1987). Music may also interact with traits to influence states. For example, positive music has a greater ability to inspire a state of hope (transitory experience) in listeners who score high in the trait of dispositional hope (enduring attribute) (Ziv, Chaim, & Itamar, 2011). The variables mentioned so far are not an exhaustive account of user attributes that have the potential to alter the effects of music. Hargreaves, MacDonald, and Miell (2005) list the following as important considerations for music communication: individual differences such as gender, age, and personality; musical knowledge, including training, literacy, and experience; immediate and short-term preference patterns, medium- and long-term taste patterns; and self-theories such as musical identities. Additionally, physical and psychoauditory attributes may have unique interactions with musical multimedia. For example, how might musical multimedia experiences differ for people who have hearing or visual disabilities? How might differences in the duration of individuals' audio sensory stores (cf. Grossheinrich, Kademann, Bruder, Bartling, & Von Suchodoletz, 2010) impact the ability to perceive and encode complex or extended audio and music in multimedia?

User attributes can also prevent media from having an effect. The *minimal effects model* (Klapper, 1960, p. 8) early emphasized that mass communication is only one of many social and personal influences and is ordinarily not the sole cause of effects, most likely reinforcing rather than changing existing attitudes, and potentially causing change only if usual mediating factors are inoperative (e.g., there is no pre-existing attitude) or the user desires to change.

Time

Antecedents play out over time as do media effects themselves. Media effects can depend on the rate of information presented (amount/time); cumulative effects occur from repetition of content over time (e.g., Morgan, Shanahan, & Signorielli, 2009); and sleeper effects require a passage of time before they manifest (e.g., Zillmann, 2002). Effects of antecedents may differ depending on whether they occur simultaneously or sequentially with a target event. For example, Boltz, Schulkind and Kantra (1991) showed that music conveying a mood incongruent with the mood of a target film scene improved memory for the scene if the music was presented prior to the scene but not if it was presented simultaneously with the scene. Tan, Spackman, and Bezdek (2007) found that music presented *after* a target event (a character with neutral expression) nevertheless influenced interpretation of the emotion expressed by the character even though the music was not presented simultaneously with the character. Too much information from one or more antecedents can burden listeners' cognitive capabilities (Lang, 2000). Some formal features such as editing pace produce 'local' structures that have an immediate impact, whereas other structures such as narrative structure of a feature-length film may take the duration of the whole film before the full impact occurs (Detenber & Lang, 2011). Media can reinforce attitudes, making them stronger over time, and media can cause short-term fluctuation effects that appear for a period of time and then disappear (Potter, 2012).

Context

Media effects do not occur in a vacuum; situational, cultural, social, and historical factors may alter the way in which users perceive, interpret, and otherwise respond to musical media. *Context* refers to the environment, literally and metaphorically, in which media effects occur.

Perception of music in a movie might differ depending on whether the movie is in a living room, a theater, or an unconventional location available through mobile media. The interpretation of music in a television show scene may depend upon the context of previous scenes. While viewing a sexually explicit music video, a teenager's awareness of the presence of his parents may cause a more uncomfortable feeling than in the context of viewing alone or with friends. Listening to music with a group of people may reduce the emotional impact of the music (Egermann et al., 2011), although using media with companions who fit stereotypical gender roles or are a homogeneous group of friends might increase enjoyment (Denham, 2004; Zillmann, Weaver, Mundorf, & Aust, 1986). The situational context of a dance party may cause preference for styles of music that would not be preferred at a dinner party (cf. North & Hargreaves, 2008). The 9/11 terrorist attacks and ensuing political turmoil created a social-historical context within which people labeled certain songs and artists as inappropriate for broadcast in the United States (e.g., Rossman, 2004). Music video content that was condemned as controversial 20 years ago may be considered as tame by contemporary standards. North and Hargreaves (2008) state that music research often ignores the context in which music listening occurs, but context can make a crucial difference for music preference, selection, and perception, among other effects.

Media content and media form

Media content consists of images, text, dialogue, music, and sound effects (cf. Cohen, 2005; Metz, 1985). In practice, media researchers often treat meaning as content, too (e.g., the portrayal of a stereotype or description of a political issue). Each visual and audio element may convey meaning independently, and meanings can arise from the combination of elements (cf. Cohen, 2005). *Media form* refers to the structure of the presentation such as the pace of the editing, shot length, or tempo of the music. It also refers to perceptual qualities such as visual and audio modes and intensity of light or loudness (McLeod & Reeves, 1980; Perse, 2001). Studies with children show that slowing the pace and increasing the continuity of a message increases recall and recognition (Van Evra, 2004). Formal features are also known for eliciting orienting responses, such as when a startling sound causes attention to the television or radio (Anderson & Kirkorian, 2006; Potter, Lang, & Bolls, 2008). According to the *limited capacity model of motivated mediated message processing* (LC4MP) (Lang, 2006, 2009), formal features such as motion toward the camera and larger images should elicit 'motivational activation,' which may, in turn, result in arousal and allocation of cognitive resources for processing the information (Detenber & Lang, 2011). (Further description of the LC4MP is given later in this chapter.)

A number of scholars of musical multimedia acknowledge that music itself has both form and content. They have investigated properties of musical content and form (e.g., temporal structure, tempo, mode, etc.), music's meanings (e.g., happy versus sad, implied movie genre, etc.), and their interaction with such aspects of motion picture images (Boltz, 2001; Cohen, 2005; Lipscomb & Kendall, 1994; Shevy, 2007; Tan et al., 2007). Some researchers conceptualize music as a formal feature (e.g., Calvert, Huston, Watkins, & Wright, 1982) while others (e.g., Hoeckner & Nusbaum, Chapter 11, in this volume) treat it as content where it conveys meaning rather than merely being a structural or perceptual element in a larger message.

Interactivity

In traditional mass media such as movies and television, content flowed mainly one way, from the sender to the receivers (audience members). Contemporary media technology allows audience members to become users who contribute information, altering content and form on an ongoing basis. The result is *interactivity*, a communication process that resembles the reciprocal control of conversation found in two-way interpersonal communication (Rafaeli, 1988). In addition to being a *communication process*, media scholars have also defined interactivity as a *structural feature* of media technology that allows user interaction and as the *perception* that interactivity is available or occurring (cf. Kiousis, 2002; Sohn, 2011). Interactivity is important in effects research because it can moderate or mediate other effects such as gratification (Yoo, 2011), telepresence (Kiousis, 2002), learning (Rieber, 2005), and persuasion (Liu & Shrum, 2009).

Interactivity may be with a medium or with other people through the medium (Yoo, 2011) as occurs in multiplayer video games. A musical media example of interacting with a medium is the video game *Child of Eden* (Q Entertainment, 2011). The sound in the game consists of a musical soundtrack, and users' actions create sounds that fit the timbre, harmony, and timing of the sound track. Shooting at targets adds a snare-drum-like sound to the music; hitting certain targets contributes musical chords to the score, and the chord voicing changes with subsequent hits. By using a game system with motion detection (e.g., Xbox™ Kinect), users control the game by moving their arms and hands rather than a hand-held controller, and extra points are awarded when certain motions are in synch with the music. The overall experience of playing has led some to post comments on the Internet stating that the game creates a strong sense of immersion and emotion. Interacting with other people can occur in applications such as discussion boards and online games such as the *World of Warcraft* series (Blizzard Entertainment, 2004–2010).

Depending on the definition, interactivity can vary from being practically nonexistent to being a central, defining feature of a media experience. For example, one can walk into a movie theater and have no input or control over the delivery of the content. On the other hand, in some video games (e.g., *The Elder Scrolls V: Skyrim*, Bethesda Game Studios, 2011; *Star Wars: The Old Republic*, Bioware EA, 2011), the narrative content, the order in which it is presented, and formal features such as camera angles, are largely dependent on the game players' actions. In an even more extreme level of user input, the medium may merely provide tools and users generate nearly all of the content and structure (e.g., creating stories through animation websites or creating avatars and objects and living 'lives' in the virtual world of *Second Life*.) The amount and type of interactivity impacts message processing in a number of important ways. Four of them are: (1) control over content and form, (2) cognitive resource allocation, (3) community, and (4) creation of life-like experiences.

Control over content and delivery can help people use media to better achieve gratifications such as learning and entertainment. For example, repeating content could improve memory of information, and ability to skip through sections that are too familiar could improve arousal, engagement, and flow (cf. Cowley, Charles, Black, & Hickey, 2008; Kirkorian, Wartella, & Anderson, 2008; Roth, Vorderer, & Klimmt, 2009). Altering the content and form will likely change the mental representations and the extent to which information is processed. Musical multimedia research can extend knowledge in the area of interactivity by addressing questions such as: How can the musical element of interactive media help meet users' goals (e.g., arousal, learning, etc.)? Do the functions and effects of music change when moved from traditional movie screens to touch screen mobile devices or virtual reality technology? Are the psychological effects of musical soundtracks different in dynamic, interactive narratives than in the static story structures of television and film?

Cognitive resource allocation is a concern for interactive media because increased interactivity may leave fewer resources for other message processing. Working memory can only process a limited amount of information within a period of time (Lang, 2009). Making decisions and using interface controls may rob cognitive resources required by encoding, elaboration, and memory. For example, Southwell and Lee (2004) found that when a video presentation had complex formal features (e.g., types of edits), providing interactive controls for video playback significantly reduced recognition memory for the content. The level of music intensity (Chou, 2010), tempo, and familiarity (Hahn & Hwang, 1999) can vary the demand on cognitive resources. On the other hand, interaction and music may result in more engagement, arousal, or content structure that could result in more effective resource allocation for some types of learning. For example, Vogt, De Houwer, Koster, Van Damme, and Crombez (2008) showed participants images of faces that varied along the dimensions of valence and arousal. They found that presenting arousing images (facial expression) just before a spatial attention test increased allocation of spatial attention to a task. The valence, on the other hand, did not have an effect.

Finally, interaction with technology has the potential to change the way media are processed by providing a user with a *sense of community* and a *perception of life-like experience*. Some people use the Internet because they desire to engage in interpersonal communication with other people or they belong to a group in which they feel like they are members of a community (Smith, 2010; Yoo, 2011). The ability of music to facilitate social bonding (Boer et al., 2011) could play a role in enhancing the social dimension in this type of interactivity. Bolter and Grusin (2005) describe two ways in which media can make users feel like they are experiencing something akin to real life (i.e., immersion, transportation, or a similar sense). One way is through 'immediacy'—making the medium as transparent as possible so that users have a sense of 'being there' in the story. The second way is through 'hypermediacy,' where the medium itself presents so many stimuli, so many simultaneous streams of visual and audio information, that attending to them and interacting with the medium itself becomes the real-life event that people experience. Music could contribute to creating both immediacy and hypermediacy.

Theories and models

Theories explain relationships between antecedents and effects, often in terms of psychological processes, and over 150 theories have been used in the media effects literature (Potter, 2012). Theories that occur most frequently in the literature include cultivation, third-person perception, agenda setting, uses and gratifications, priming, cognitive capacity, framing, feminism, social learning, the elaboration likelihood model, schema, and diffusion of innovation (Potter, 2012, p. 73). The particular theories reviewed in this chapter are ones that frequently serve as foundations for media effects research or studies of entertainment effects. They are provided as examples to illustrate how media effects theories might advance the study of musical multimedia.

Social cognitive theory

Bandura (1986) explains how users not only imitate but also generate innovative new behaviors based on behaviors that are exemplified on television or other media. The theory is rooted in Bandura's well-known theory of observational learning. In application to the media effects context, behaviors performed by characters in media can influence audience members' behavior through four subfunctions of observational learning. The first subfunction, *attentional processes*, depends on content features such as the salience of an event, affective valence, complexity, accessibility, and functional value (how useful it is), as well as user attributes such as expectations and perceptual biases, cognitive capabilities, preconceptions, arousal level, and values. The model's next three processes, *retention*, *production*, and *motivation*, involve cognitive processes, physical capabilities, and the influence of context (e.g., social influence). *Retention processes* involve transforming and restructuring information for memory. *Behavioral production processes* occur when audience members use the learned information to generate their own conceptualization of an action that fits their personal abilities and circumstances. *Motivational processes* are means by which audience members decide whether to perform the behavior (e.g., deciding whether the benefits outweigh the consequences) (Bandura, 1986, 2009).

As stated by Wingood et al. (2003), in discussing their longitudinal study of the effects of rap music videos on African American female adolescents:

> A cornerstone of [social cognitive theory] states that modeling will occur more readily when the modeled behavior is salient, simple, and prevalent and has functional value. Thus, exposure to rap music videos, particularly gangsta rap (the most popular type of music video), which is explicit about sex and violence and rarely shows the potential long-term adverse effect of risky behaviors, may influence adolescents by modeling these unhealthy practices. (p. 438)

Wingood and colleagues also state that an alternative causal direction is possible, in which teens who already exhibit risky behaviors selectively expose themselves to rap videos. In this scenario, the videos would reinforce behavior rather than change it.

Media researchers use social cognitive theory (Bandura, 1986, 2009) frequently to explain effects (especially long-term effects of viewing violence). With reference to the terms used in the present chapter, the theory explicitly considers features from context, media content and form, user attributes (especially their ability to proactively reflect upon and regulate their own actions), and effects (e.g., behavior). The theory establishes the notion that people have agency (i.e., people can think about and control their actions). To do this, it defines a triadic reciprocal causal relationship between environmental determinants, personal determinants (e.g., cognitive, affective, biological), and behavioral determinants. What this means is that environmental factors (including media) influence people and their behavior. People have an impact on their environment and their own behavior. And finally, a person's behavior influences the person performing the behavior and the environment. Each determinant can gain dominance depending on the situation (Bandura, 1978). Bandura describes a musical situation to illustrate how behavior can be dominant:

> One example of this is persons who play familiar piano selections for themselves that create a pleasing sensory environment. The behavior is self-regulated over a long period by the sensory effects it produces, whereas cognitive activities and contextual environmental events are not much involved in the process. (1978, p. 346)

As another example of musical application, Hargreaves et al. (2005) extended the triadic reciprocal portion of Bandura's (1986, 1997) social cognitive theory to construct a model of musical communication where the composer, performer, performance context, and performance formed a tetrahedral (rather than triadic) set of relationships that are connected to another tetrahedral set consisting of the listener, listening context, music, and response.

Uses and gratifications model

The *uses and gratifications* model (Katz, Blumler, & Gurevitch, 1973; Rubin, 2009) grew out of the notion that audience members actively select media and content to meet their own needs. People have needs based on social and psychological factors, such as desiring to relate to other people, needing to know what is happening around them, or wanting to be entertained. They have expectations about what will fulfill those needs and choose their media and content consumption accordingly. This consumption may lead to gratification of the need or other consequences (Katz, Blumler, & Gurevitch, 1974; Krcmar & Strizhakova, 2009; Rubin, 2009). Uses and gratifications scholars have identified typical needs and their related uses of media. These can be *instrumental uses* that serve a purpose beyond the use of the medium such as getting information (surveillance), benefitting personal relationships with others, or supporting identity (Lull, 1980; McQuail, Blumler, & Brown, 1973) and *consummatory uses*, in which the use of the medium is an end in itself, such as relaxation, passing time, and entertainment (Ferguson & Perse, 2000). Researchers in music psychology have found these same types of motives and others for listening to music (e.g., MacDonald, Hargreaves, & Miell, 2002; North & Hargreaves, 2008; Russel, 1997; Tarrant, North, & Hargreaves, 2002; Zillmann & Gan, 1997). For example, listeners' social class, taste cultures (e.g., fans of certain types of music who share values, fashion, social class, etc.), massification (the notion that mass media create similar tastes in music or other media across diverse cultures), age, sex, personality, and musical training and ability can all influence music preference (North & Hargreaves, 2008).

The motives for choosing media and content and expectations about those choices can influence media effects. Research in this area is sometimes called *uses and effects* (Rubin, 2009). For example, Gantz (1978) surveyed television news viewers and found that those who watched with an intention to learn recalled more news stories than those who watched for other reasons. See, Petty, and Evans (2009) found that people with a higher 'need for cognition,' a personality trait that leads individuals to give more effort in processing messages, will think harder about messages that are labeled as complex. The uses and effects of music should be tested in multimedia contexts. Perhaps the inclusion of music in television news stories would divert cognitive resources and decrease recall for users who want to learn. On the other hand, maybe music could increase users' desire to learn. Might the presence of music create the expectation that a message will be more complex or less?

Although the uses and gratifications approach seems to imply conscious, logical choosing of media, this is not always the case. Research in mood management shows that people may choose media to optimize their mood or level of arousal without being cognizant of the role of mood in their decision (Knobloch-Westerwick, 2006; Oliver, 2009; Zillmann, 2003). For example, Knobloch and Zillmann (2002) induced experiment participants into a bad, good, or neutral mood by having a computer tell them that their performance on a facial expression recognition test was terrible, great, or neutral. Afterward, the respondents were told to listen to popular songs that appealed to them. Participants in a bad mood spent more time listening to energetic and joyful music than those in a good mood. They also switched songs less often. Music is also effective in regulating physiological arousal regardless of evaluative (positive–negative) properties. When explaining the emotional effects of music and music videos in mass communication, Knobloch and Zillmann state, 'Arousal plays a critical role in explaining the consumption, perception, and enjoyment of music—as it does with other media fare such as horror, suspense, and sexually explicit media' (2002, p. 498). Of course, not all selection of music for mood regulation is unconscious. Listeners frequently state that they intentionally choose music to regulate mood and emotion (e.g., Boer & Fischer, 2012; Greasley & Lamont, 2011; Saarikallio, 2011; Tarrant, North, & Hargreaves, 2000).

A current trend in media research examines how user attributes and motives influence cognitive processes used for selecting media (Hartmann, 2009). For example, Wang, Lang, and Busemeyer (2011) conducted an experiment where participants watched whatever television they wanted for 30 minutes from four available TV channels. The content on the channels varied in their levels of perceived emotional valence (positive, negative) and emotional arousal (arousing, moderately arousing, calm). As participants watched, the researchers measured physiological indicators and emotional responses, and noted when participants changed channels. As arousing content increased, so did cognitive effort, and once arousal reached a certain threshold, participants were more likely to change the channel if the valence of the message was unpleasant. Given musical multimedia's strength in manipulating arousal, such effects could be studied specifically with musical multimedia content. For example, how might music in a video game or movie help viewers achieve an optimal level of arousal? Under what circumstances might musically induced arousal cause users to stop using a medium?

Limited capacity model of motivated mediated message processing (LC4MP)

The LC4MP is a 'data-driven model developed to investigate the real-time processing of mediated messages' (Lang, 2009, p. 193). This model builds on the well-accepted notions that cognition systems work as limited capacity information processing systems with multiple processes simultaneously occurring (Lang, 2000; Miller, 1956). As Lang (2007) writes:

> Processing messages requires mental resources, and people have only a limited (and perhaps fixed) pool of mental resources. You can think about one thing, or two, or maybe seven, but eventually all your resources are being used, and the system cannot think yet another thing without letting a previous thought go. (p. 290)

The LC4MP provides explanations to how media messages are attended to, encoded, processed, stored, and recalled with respect to mental resource allocation (Lang, 2009). A significant question is how limited cognitive resources are allocated to certain stimuli and not others.

The LC4MP posits that resource allocation can occur under the control of the user (e.g., trying to pay attention or remember) or as an automatic process (Lang, 2009). In the case of automatic processing, media content and form (structure) may elicit an 'orienting response,' which is an automatic allocation of attention to new information such as the onset of music or camera changes (Lang, 2009, pp. 195–196). Automatic resource allocation can also occur if content or form activates appetitive and aversive motivational systems (Lang, 2009). Activation of the appetitive system, say, by food or a sexually provocative image, may elicit pleasant emotions and a motivation to select media content. Aversive system activation, perhaps by the image of a murdered body, may elicit unpleasant emotion and a motivation to avoid the content. Activation of either motivational system (or both simultaneously) can influence cognitive processes such as resource allocation, encoding, memory storage, and retrieval (Lang, 2006, 2009). As can be seen, the LC4MP can also help predict emotional responses in addition to cognitive responses.

Many aspects of the LC4MP are relevant to musical multimedia psychology. The model may be useful in helping to explain ways in which music draws attention to elements of a film scene or increases memory through an integration of cognitive and emotional processes. Music may help identify emotional and cognitive effects that fall outside the explanatory power of the LC4MP.

Entertainment theories

Music can impact arousal, emotion, and mood (Juslin & Sloboda, 2010). These same effects are often primary reasons that people turn to media for entertainment (Bryant & Miron, 2002). In media studies, users sometimes want to experience a state of hedonic pleasure through experiences such as an optimal physiological state or a positive emotion. Sometimes they desire satisfaction through a higher cognitive state of meta-emotions such as appreciation or eudaemonic well-being (i.e., a sense of meaningfulness or insightfulness) (Oliver & Bartsch, 2010; Schreier, 2006; Vorderer & Hartmann, 2009). As such, entertainment is an exceptional frame in which to study musical multimedia effects. The disposition (Zillmann & Cantor, 1977) and excitation transfer (Zillmann, 1983) theories described in the following sections are good examples for showing how music fits with multimedia entertainment.

Affective disposition theory

Affective disposition theory posits that individuals evaluate and form affiliations with media characters, and enjoyment is impacted by what happens with and to those characters (Raney, 2006, Zillmann & Cantor, 1977). 'Disposition' is the degree of positive or negative affect (e.g., like or dislike) that users develop toward characters (Raney, 2006). According to the theory, enjoyment increases when a character who is liked by the audience (e.g., a protagonist) receives deserved rewards. Enjoyment decreases with unjust punishment or failure. The same respective responses occur when despised characters receive just punishment or unjust rewards (Zillmann, 2006). Audience members' moral judgments and personal values play a primary role in this theory (Zillmann, 2003). Although it has not been tested empirically, music may contribute to the formation of dispositions, given that music can influence inferences about characters (Boltz, 2001). Raney (2006), a leading disposition theory scholar, states, 'it is reasonable to assume that various content features (e.g., camera movements, sound effects, music) would influence the formation and maintenance of dispositions toward characters' (p. 145).

Excitation-transfer theory

Excitation is conceived as a 'response-energizing mechanism' in emotion, involving heightened activity in the sympathetic nervous system, which is associated with fight or flight responses (Bunce, Larsen, & Cruz, 1993). The term 'excitation' is frequently used synonymously with 'arousal,' which is associated with the release of hormones and change in heart rate and blood pressure. The time to increase arousal may vary based on how arousal is achieved. In one study, for example, research participants rode a stationary bicycle for 1 minute to achieve arousal as measured by heart rate and blood pressure (Cantor, Zillmann, & Bryant, 1975). After participants felt that they had recovered from the bicycle ride, they misattributed the physiological arousal, which still persisted, to a film clip that they were shown, increasing their perception that the clip was arousing. After 30 years of subsequent research, Zillmann stated, 'It is established beyond doubt that excitation, once triggered, decays rather slowly. For all practical purposes, it takes at least three minutes, often 10 or more minutes, on occasion hours for excitation to return to normal levels' (Zillmann, 2006, p. 222).

Although physical arousal dissipates slowly, cognition is adept at switching focus to new situations much more quickly. This disparity between the speed of cognitive responses and the lingering state of arousal is what allows excitation transfer. Excitation transfer is thus the misattribution of physiological arousal from one stimulus to another, and is grounded in emotion research showing that cognitive information can influence the way in which a person labels or interprets her own feelings of arousal (e.g., Schachter & Singer, 1962). An initial scene such as a car chase can increase arousal. Then while the arousal lingers, the next scene might show a romantic encounter. As audience members cognitively comprehend the new situation, they may misattribute the lingering arousal as feelings about the romance. In addition, if the romantic scene is arousing in itself, there may be an additive effect of raising the elevated state of arousal to an even higher level (Zillmann, 2006). The fast pace of cinema and residual excitation can cause a more intense emotional reaction than would have been experienced otherwise. Excitation can intensify any number of emotions, so the enhanced reaction can occur when moving from a negative scene to a positive one just as it would if moving from negative to negative or any other potential sequence. Strategic construction of a cinematic narrative can take advantage of these effects to increase the pleasure audiences receive through emotional experiences (Zillmann, 2003). Note that for excitation transfer to occur, audience members must misattribute arousal to a person or event that is not the actual cause of the arousal. If they recognize the real source of the arousal, they can cognitively mitigate its effect (Cantor, Zillmann, & Bryant, 1975; Schacter & Singer, 1962).

Hansen and Hansen (1990) conducted an experiment that tested the effect of music arousal in rock music videos that contained sexually provocative or violent images. Participants rated the sexual images as appealing and the violent images as unappealing. Music that was high in arousal made the violent images even less appealing. The music did not influence the appeal of the sexually provocative images, though it did make the overall sexually provocative video more appealing. The authors concluded that, for the violent images, arousal from the music was misattributed to the imagery through excitation transfer. They also suggested that the lack of excitation transfer to the sexual images may indicate a 'possible boundary to excitation transfer' in which 'the physiological arousal state evoked by the sexual images was sufficiently different from that evoked by the arousing music that it did not transfer efficiently' (p. 231). Future research in musical multimedia should investigate how music might increase excitation over the duration of a piece and how it interacts with film narratives or other types of content for intensifying emotion, enjoyment, and other effects. Whether audience members consciously hear music and how they attribute arousal would also be a beneficial area to study. Additionally, music video research has shown the need for further refinement in excitation transfer theory to better determine possible boundaries and how arousal from music, lyrics, and images influences cognition (cf. Hansen & Hansen, 1990; Hansen & Krygowski, 1994; Zillmann & Mundorf, 1987).

Conclusion

In our media-saturated society, media effects research investigates ways in which the interaction between people and media produce both desirable and undesirable consequences in learning, persuasion, socialization, and entertainment. In spite of the prevalence of music in these contexts, most investigations neglect music. Mass communication researchers would do well to analyze musical content and form in more detail rather than only measuring the effects of a musical multimedia presentation as a whole. Music psychology researchers can also benefit from a stronger relationship with media effects research. As the previous review has illustrated, media effects research offers music psychology a plethora of everyday life situations and concerns as context for the study of musical multimedia.

Psychology-based media theories and models such as social cognitive theory (Bandura, 1986, 2009), the uses and gratifications model (Katz et al., 1973; Rubin, 2009), the LC4MP (Lang, 2009), affective disposition theory (Raney, 2006; Zillmann & Cantor, 1977), and excitation-transfer theory (Zillmann, 1971, 2006), provide exciting research opportunities for musical multimedia research. Dolf Zillmann, a renowned scholar of media effects and psychology, recognized the need for such research when he stated that ambiguities in the emotional impact of music and dramatic narrative 'call for the systematic empirical exploration of the relative degree of influence of dramatic components on music appreciation and of musical components on the enjoyment of drama' (Zillmann, 2011, p. 112). The call for systematic empirical exploration rings true not only for appreciation and enjoyment effects in drama, but also for the many other types of effects and media formats where music has a presence.

References

Anderson, D. R., & Kirkorian, H. L. (2006). Attention and television. In J. Bryant & P. Vorderer (Eds.), *Psychology of entertainment* (pp. 35–54). Mahwah, NJ: Lawrence Erlbaum Associates, Publishers.

Bandura, A. (1978). The self system in reciprocal determinism. *American Psychologist, 33*(4), 344–358.

Bandura, A. (1986). *Social foundations of thought and action: A social cognitive theory.* Englewood Cliffs, NJ: Prentice-Hall, Inc.

Bandura, A. (1997). *Self-efficacy: The exercise of control.* New York, NY: W.H. Freeman.

Bandura, A. (2009). Social cognitive theory of mass communication. In J. Bryant & M. B. Oliver (Eds.), *Media effects: Advances in theory and research* (3rd ed., pp. 94–124). New York, NY: Routledge.

Bethesda Game Studios. (2011). *The elder scrolls V: Skyrim* [Computer game]. United States: Bethesda Softworks.

Bioware EA. (2011). *Star wars: The old republic* [Computer game]. United States: Bioware EA.

Blizzard Entertainment. (2004–2010). *World of warcraft* [Computer game series]. United States: Blizzard Entertainment.

Boer, D., & Fischer, R. (2012). Towards a holistic model of functions of music listening across cultures: A culturally decentered qualitative approach. *Psychology of Music, 40*(2), 179–200.

Boer, D., Fischer, R., Strack, M., Bond, M. H., Lo, E., & Lam, J. (2011). How shared preferences in music create bonds between people. *Personality and Social Psychology Bulletin, 37*(9), 1159–1171.

Bolter, J. D., & Grusin, R. (2005). Remediation. In E. P. Bucy (Ed.), *Living in the information age: A new media reader* (2nd ed., pp. 50–58). Belmont, CA: Thomson Wadsworth.

Boltz, M. G. (2001). Musical soundtracks as a schematic influence on the cognitive processing of filmed events. *Music Perception, 18*(4), 427–454.

Boltz, M., Schulkind, M., & Kantra, S. (1991). Effects of background music on the remembering of filmed events. *Memory & Cognition, 19*(6), 593–606.

Bryant, J., & Miron, D. (2002). Entertainment as media effect. In B. Jennings & D. Zillmann (Eds.), *Media effects: Advances in theory and research* (2nd ed., pp. 549–582). Mahwah, NJ: Lawrence Erlbaum Associates.

Bryant, J., & Miron, D. (2004). Theory and research in mass communication. *Journal of Communication, 54*(4), 662–704.

Bryant, J., & Zillmann, D. (1986). *Perspectives on media effects.* Hillsdale, NJ: Erlbaum.

Bunce, S. C., Larsen, R. J., & Cruz, M. (1993). Individual differences in the excitation transfer effect. *Personality and Individual Differences, 15*(5), 507–514.

Calvert, S. L., Huston, A. C., Watkins, B. A., & Wright, J. C. (1982). The relation between selective attention to television forms and children's comprehension of content. *Child Development, 53*(3), 601–610.

Cantor J. R., Zillmann, D., & Bryant, J. (1975). Enhancement of experienced sexual arousal in response to erotic stimuli through misattribution of unrelated residual excitation. *Journal of Personality and Social Psychology, 32*(1), 69–75.

Chou, P. T. (2010). Attention drainage effect: How background music effects concentration in Taiwanese college students. *Journal of Scholarship of Teaching and Learning, 10*(1), 36–46.

Cohen, A. J. (2005). How music influences the interpretation of film and video: Approaches from experimental psychology. In R. Kendall & R. Savage (Eds.), *Selected reports in ethnomusicology: Perspectives in systematic musicology* (Vol. 12, pp. 15–36.). Los Angeles, CA: Ethnomusicology Publications, UCLA.

Conrad, K., Dixon, T. L., & Zhang, Y. (2009). Controversial rap themes, gender portrayals and skin tone distortion: A content analysis of rap music videos. *Journal of Broadcasting & Electronic Media, 53*(1), 134–156.

Cowley, B., Charles, D., Black, M., & Hickey, R. (2008). Toward an understanding of flow in video games. *ACM Computers in Entertainment, 6*(2). Retrieved from <http://doi.acm.org/10.1145/1371216.1371223>.

Denham, B. E. (2004). Toward an explication of media enjoyment: The synergy of social norms, viewing situation, and program content. *Communication Theory, 14*(4), 370–387.

Detenber, B. H., & Lang, A. (2011). The influence of form and presentation attributes of media on emotion. In K. Döveling, C. von Scheve, & E. Konijn (Eds.), *The Routledge handbook of emotions and mass media* (pp. 275–293). New York, NY: Routledge.

Dominick, J. R. (2007). *The dynamics of mass communication: Media in the digital age* (9th ed.). New York, NY: McGraw-Hill.

Döveling, K., von Scheve, C., & Konijn, E. (2011). Emotions and the mass media: An interdisciplinary approach. In K. Döveling, C. von Scheve, & E. Konijn (Eds.), *The Routledge handbook of emotions and mass media* (pp. 1–12). New York, NY: Routledge.

Egermann, H., Sutherland, M. E., Grewe, O., Nagel, F., Kopiez, R., & Altenmüller, E. (2011). Does music listening in a social context alter experience? A physiological and psychological perspective on emotion. *Musicae Scientiae, 15*(3), 307–323.

Eveland, W. P. (2003). A 'mix of attributes' approach to the study of media effects and new communication technologies. *Journal of Communication, 53*(3), 395–410.

Ferguson, D. A., & Perse, E. M. (2000). The world wide web as a functional alternative to television. *Journal of Broadcasting & Electronic Media, 44*(2), 153–174.

Gantz, W. (1978). How uses and gratifications affect recall of television news. *Journalism Quarterly, 55*, 664–672, 681.

Greasley, A. E., & Lamont, A. (2011). Exploring engagement with music in everyday life using experience sampling methodology. *Musicae Scientiae, 15*(1), 45–71.

Grossheinrich, N., Kademann, S., Bruder, J., Bartling, J., & Von Suchodoletz, W. (2010). Auditory sensory memory and language abilities in former late talkers: A mismatch negativity study. *Psychophysiology, 47*(5), 822–830.

Hahn, M., & Hwang, I. (1999). Effects of tempo and familiarity of background music on message processing in TV advertising: A resource-matching perspective. *Psychology & Marketing, 16*(8), 659–675.

Hall, A. (2005). Audience personality and the selection of media and media genres. *Media Psychology, 7*(4), 377–398.

Hansen, C. H., & Hansen, R. D. (1990). The influence of sex and violence on the appeal of rock music videos. *Communication Research, 17*(2), 212–234.

Hansen, C. H., & Hansen, R. D. (2000). Music and music videos. In D. Zillmann & P. Vorderer (Eds.), *Media entertainment: The psychology of its appeal* (pp. 175–196). Mahwah, NJ: Lawrence Erlbaum Associates.

Hansen, C. H., & Krygowski, W. (1994). Arousal-augmented priming effects: Rock music videos and sex object schemas. *Communication Research, 21*(1), 24–47.

Hargreaves, D. J., MacDonald, R., & Miell, D. (2005). How do people communicate using music? In D. Miell, R. MacDonald, & D. Hargreaves (Eds.), *Musical Communication* (pp. 1–25). New York, NY: Oxford University Press.

Hartmann, T. (Ed.) (2009). *Media choice: A theoretical and empirical overview*. New York, NY: Routledge.

Hawkins, R. P., & Daly, J. (1988). Cognition and communication. In R. P. Hawkins, J. Wiemann, & S. Pingree (Eds.), *Advancing communication science: Merging mass and interpersonal* (pp. 191–223). Newbury Park, CA: Sage Publications.

Johnson, J. D., Trawalter, S., & Dovidio, J. F. (2000). Converging interracial consequences of exposure to violent rap music on stereotypical attributions of blacks. *Journal of Experimental Social Psychology, 36*(3), 233–251.

Juslin, P. N., & Sloboda, J. A. (2010). Introduction: Aims, organization, and terminology. In P. N. Juslin & J. A. Sloboda (Eds.), *Handbook of music and emotion: Theory, research, applications* (pp. 3–12). New York, NY: Oxford University Press.

Katz, E., Blumler, J. G., & Gurevitch, M. (1973). Uses and gratifications research. *Public Opinion Quarterly, 37*(4), 509–523.

Katz, E., Blumler, J. G., & Gurevitch, M. (1974). Utilization of mass communication by the individual. In J. G. Blumler & E. Katz (Eds.), *The uses of mass communications: Current perspectives on gratifications research* (pp. 19–32). Beverly Hills, CA: Sage.

Kiousis, S. (2002). Interactivity: A concept explication. *New Media & Society*, *4*(3), 355–383.

Kirkorian, H. L., Wartella, E. A., & Anderson, D. R. (2008). Media and young children's learning. *The Future of Children*, *18*(1), 39–61.

Klapper, J. T. (1960). *The effects of mass communication*. New York, NY: Free Press.

Knobloch, S., & Mundorf, N. (2003). Communication and emotion in the context of music and music television. In J. Bryant, D. Roskos-Ewoldsen, & J. Cantor (Eds.), *Communication and emotion* (pp. 491–510). Mahwah, NJ: Lawrence Erlbaum Associates, Inc.

Knobloch, S., & Zillmann, D. (2002). Mood management via the digital jukebox. *Journal of Communication*, *52*, 351–366.

Knobloch-Westerwick, S. (2006). Mood management theory, evidence, and advancements. In J. Bryant & P. Vorderer (Eds.), *Psychology of entertainment* (pp. 239–254). Mahwah, NJ: Lawrence Erlbaum Associates.

Konijn, E., & ten Holt, J. (2011). From noise to nucleus: Emotion as a key construct in processing media messages. In K. Döveling, C. von Scheve, & E. Konijn (Eds.), *The Routledge handbook of emotions and mass media* (pp. 37–59). New York, NY: Routledge.

Krcmar, M., & Strizhakova, Y. (2009). Uses and gratifications as media choice. In T. Hartmann (Ed.), *Media choice: A theoretical and empirical overview* (pp. 53–69). New York, NY: Routledge.

Lang, A. (2000). The limited capacity model of mediated message processing. *Journal of Communication*, *50*(1), 46–70.

Lang, A. (2006). Using the limited capacity model of motivated media message processing to design effective cancer communication messages. *Journal of Communication*, *56*(s1), s57–s80.

Lang, A. (2007). The limited capacity model of mediated message processing. In R. T. Craig & H. L. Muller (Eds.), *Theorizing communication: Readings across traditions* (pp. 289–300). Thousand Oaks, CA: Sage Publications, Inc.

Lang, A. (2009). The limited capacity model of motivated mediated message processing. In R. L. Nabi & M. B. Oliver (Eds.), *The SAGE handbook of media processes and effects* (pp. 193–204). Thousand Oaks, CA: Sage Publications.

Li, X. (1998). Web design and graphic use of three U.S. newspapers. *Journalism and Mass Communication Quarterly*, *75*(2), 353–365.

Liu, Y., & Shrum, L. J. (2009). A dual-process model of interactivity effects. *Journal of Advertising*, *38*, 53–68.

Lipscomb, S. D., & Kendall, R. A. (1994). Perceptual judgment of the relationship between musical and visual components in film. *Psychomusicology*, *13*, 60–98.

Lull, J. (1980). The social uses of media. *Human Communication Research*, *6*(3), 197–209.

MacDonald, R. A. R., Hargreaves, D. J., & Miell, D. (Eds.) (2002). *Musical identities*. New York, NY: Oxford University Press.

Markey, P. M., & Scherer, K. (2009). An examination of psychoticism and motion capture controls as moderators of the effects of violent video games. *Computers in Human Behavior*, *25*(2), 407–411.

McLeod, J. M., Kosicki, G. M., & Pan, Z. (1991). On understanding and misunderstanding media effects. In J. Curran & M. Gurevitch (Eds.), *Mass media and society* (pp. 235–266). London, UK: Edward Arnold.

McLeod, J. M., & Reeves, B. (1980). On the nature of mass media effects. In S. Withey & R. Abeles (Eds.), *Television and Social Behavior: Beyond Violence and Children.* Hillsdale, NJ: Lawrence Erlbaum.

McQuail, D., Blumler, J. G., & Brown, J. R. (1973). The television audience: A revised perspective. In D. McQuail (Ed.), *Sociology of mass communications* (pp. 135–165). Middlesex, UK: Penguin.

Metz, C. (1985). Photography and fetish. *October, 34,* 81–90.

Miller, G. A. (1956). The magical number seven, plus or minus two: Some limits on our capacity for processing information. *Psychological Review, 63,* 81–97.

Morgan, M., Shanahan, J., & Signorielli, N. (2009). Growing up with television: Cultivation processes. In J. Bryant & M. B. Oliver (Eds.), *Media effects: Advances in theory and research* (3rd ed., pp. 34–49). New York, NY: Routledge.

Nielsen. (2012). *The crossplatform report: Quarter 3, 2011—U.S.* Retrieved from <http://www.nielsen.com/us/en/insights/reports-downloads/2012/cross-platform-report-q3–2011.html> (accessed April 20, 2012).

Nielsenwire. (2012). *December 2011: Top U.S. online video destinations.* Retrieved from <http://blog.nielsen.com/nielsenwire/online_mobile/december-2011-top-u-s-online-vide o-destinations/Acknowledgments> (accessed April 19, 2012).

North, A. C., & Hargreaves, D. J. (2008). *The social and applied psychology of music.* New York, NY: Oxford University Press.

Oliver, M. B. (2009). Affect as a predictor of entertainment choice: The utility of looking beyond pleasure. In T. Hartmann (Ed.), *Media choice: A theoretical and empirical overview* (pp. 167–184). New York, NY: Routledge.

Oliver, M. B., & Bartsch, A. (2010). Appreciation as audience response: Exploring entertainment gratifications beyond hedonism. *Human Communication Research, 36*(1), 53–81.

Oliver, M. B., & Krakowiak, K. M. (2009). Individual differences in media effects. In J. Bryant & M. B. Oliver (Eds.), *Media effects: Advances in theory and research* (3rd ed., pp. 517–531). New York, NY: Routledge.

Paisley, W. (1972). *Communication research as a behavioral discipline.* Palo Alto, CA: Institution for Communication Research, Stanford University.

Perse, E. M. (2001). *Media effects and society.* Mahwah, NJ: Lawrence Erlbaum Associates, Inc.

Perse, E. M. (2008). Media effects models: Elaborated models. In W. Donsbach (Ed.), *International Encyclopedia of Communication* (Vol. 1, pp. 2896–2900). Malden, MA: Blackwell Publishing.

Potter, R. F., Lang, A., & Bolls, P. D. (2008). Identifying structural features of audio: Orienting responses during radio messages and their impact on recognition. *Journal of Media Psychology: Theories, Methods, and Applications, 20*(4), 168–177.

Potter, W. J. (2012). *Media effects.* Los Angeles, CA: Sage.

Q Entertainment. (2011). *Child of Eden* [Computer game]. France: Ubisoft.

Rafaeli, S. (1988). Interactivity: From new media to communication. In R. P. Hawkins, J. M. Wiemann, & S. Pingree (Eds.), *Advancing communication science: Merging mass and interpersonal processes* (pp. 110–134). Newbury Park, CA: Sage.

Raney, A. A. (2006). The psychology of disposition-based theories of media enjoyment. In J. Bryant & P. Vorderer (Eds.), *Psychology of entertainment* (pp. 137–150). Mahwah, NJ: Lawrence Erlbaum Associates, Publishers.

Rawlings, D., & Leow, S. H. (2008). Investigating the role of psychoticism and sensation seeking in predicting emotional reactions to music. *Psychology of Music, 36*(3), 269–287.

Rentfrow, P. J., Goldberg, L. R., & Levitin, D. J. (2011). The structure of musical preferences: A five-factor model. *Journal of Personality and Social Psychology, 100*(6), 1139–1157.

Rentfrow, P. J., & Gosling, S. D. (2003). The do re mi's of everyday life: The structure and personality correlates of music preferences. *Journal of Personality and Social Psychology, 84*(6), 1236–1256.

Rideout, V. J., Foehr, U. G., & Roberts, D. F. (2010). *Generation M2: Media in the lives of 8- to 18-year-olds.* Retrieved from <http://www.kff.org/entmedia/upload/8010.pdf>.

Rieber, L. P. (2005). Multimedia learning in games, simulations, and microworlds. In R. E. Mayer (Ed.), *The Cambridge handbook of multimedia learning* (pp. 549–567). New York, NY: Cambridge University Press.

Rossman, G. (2004). Elites, masses, and media blacklists: The Dixie Chicks controversy. *Social Forces, 83*(1), 61–79.

Roth, C., Vorderer, P., & Klimmt, C. (2009). The motivational appeal of interactive storytelling: Towards a dimension model of the user experience. *Lecture Notes in Computer Science, 5915*, 38–43.

Rubin, A. M. (2009). Uses-and-gratifications perspectives on media effects. In J. Bryant & M. B. Oliver (Eds.), *Media effects: Advances in theory and research* (3rd ed., pp. 165–184). New York, NY: Routledge.

Russel, P. A. (1997). Musical tastes and society. In D. J. Hargreaves & A. C. North (Eds.), *The Social Psychology of Music* (pp. 141–158). New York, NY: Oxford University Press.

Saarikallio, S. (2011). Music as emotional self-regulation throughout adulthood. *Psychology of Music, 39*(3), 307–327.

Schachter, S., & Singer, J. (1962). Cognitive, social, and physiological determinants of emotional state. *Psychological Review, 69*(5), 379–399.

Schramm, W. (Ed.) (1954). *The process and effects of mass communication.* Urbana, IL: University of Illinois Press.

Schreier, M. (2006). (Subjective) well-being. In J. Bryant & P. Vorderer (Eds.), *Psychology of entertainment* (pp. 389–404). Mahwah, NJ: Lawrence Erlbaum Associates, Publishers.

Schuessler, K. F. (1948). Social background and musical taste. *American Sociological Review, 13*(3), 330–335.

See, Y. H. M., Petty, R. E., & Evans, L. M. (2009). The impact of perceived message complexity and need for cognition on information processing and attitudes. *Journal of Research in Personality, 43*(5), 880–889.

Shannon, C. E., & Weaver, W. (1949). *The mathematical theory of communication.* Urbana, IL: University of Illinois Press.

Shevy, M. (2007). The mood of rock music affects evaluation of video elements differing in valence and dominance. *Psychomusicology, 19*(2), 57–78.

Slater, M. D., & Hayes, A. F. (2010). The influence of youth music television viewership on changes in cigarette use and association with smoking peers: A social identity, reinforcing spirals perspective. *Communication Research, 37*(6), 751–773.

Smith, B. G. (2010). Socially distributing public relations: Twitter, Haiti, and interactivity in social media. *Public Relations Review, 36*(4), 329–335.

Sohn, D. (2011). Anatomy of interaction experience: Distinguishing sensory, semantic, and behavioral dimensions of interactivity. *New Media & Society, 13*(8), 1320–1335.

Southwell, B. G., & Lee, M. (2004). A pitfall of new media? User controls exacerbate editing effects on memory. *Journalism and Mass Communication Quarterly, 81*(3), 643–656.

Sparks, G. G., & Sparks, C. W. (2000). Violence, mayhem, and horror. In D. Zillmann & P. Vorderer (Eds.), *Media Entertainment: The psychology of its appeal* (pp. 73–91). Mahwah, NJ: Lawrence Erlbaum Associates.

Sun, S.-W., & Lull, J. (1986). The adolescent audience for music videos and why they watch. *Journal of Communication, 36*(1), 115–125.

Tamborini, R., Stiff, J., & Zillman, D. (1987). Preferences for graphic horror featuring male versus female victimization. *Human Communication Research, 13*(4), 529–552.

Tan, S.-L., Pfordresher, P., & Harré, R. (2010). *Psychology of music: From sound to significance.* New York, NY: Psychology Press.

Tan, S.-L., Spackman, M. P., & Bezdek, M. A. (2007). Viewers' interpretations of film characters' emotions: Effects of presenting film music before or after a character is shown. *Music Perception, 25*(2), 135–152.

Tarrant, M., North, A. C., & Hargreaves, D. J. (2000). English and American adolescents' reasons for listening to music. *Psychology of Music, 28*(2), 166–173.

Tarrant, M., North, A. C., & Hargreaves, D. J. (2002). Youth identity and music. In R. A. R. MacDonald, D. J. Hargreaves, & D. Miell (Eds.), *Musical Identities* (pp. 134–150). New York, NY: Oxford University Press.

Tiggemann, M., & Slater, A. (2004). Thin ideals in music television: A source of social comparison and body dissatisfaction. *International Journal of Eating Disorders, 35*(1), 48–58.

Van Evra, J. (2004). *Television and child development.* Mahwah, NJ: Lawrence Erlbaum Associates.

Vogt, J., De Houwer, J., Koster, E. H. W., Van Damme, S., & Crombez, G. (2008). Allocation of spatial attention to emotional stimuli depends upon arousal and not valence. *Emotion, 8*(6), 880–885.

Vorderer, P., & Hartmann, T. (Eds.). (2009). *Entertainment and enjoyment* (3rd ed.). New York, NY: Routledge.

Wang, Z., Lang, A., & Busemeyer, J. R. (2011). Motivational processing and choice behavior during television viewing: An integrative dynamic approach. *Journal of Communication, 61*(1), 71–93.

Wingood, G. M., DiClemente, R. J., Bernhardt, J. M., Harrington, K., Davies, S. L., Robillard, A., & Hook, E. W. (2003). A prospective study of exposure to rap music videos and African American female adolescents' health. *American Journal of Public Health, 93*(3), 437–439.

Yoo, C. Y. (2011). Modeling audience interactivity as the gratification-seeking process in online newspapers. *Communication Theory, 21*(1), 67–89.

Zhang, Y., Dixon, T. L., & Conrad, K. (2009). Rap music videos and African American women's body image: The moderating role of ethnic identity. *Journal of Communication, 59*(2), 262–278.

Zhang, Y., Miller, L. E., & Harrison, K. (2008). The relationship between exposure to sexual music videos and young adults' sexual attitudes. *Journal of Broadcasting & Electronic Media, 52*(3), 368–386.

Zillmann, D. (1971). Excitation transfer in communication-mediated aggressive behavior. *Journal of Experimental Social Psychology, 7*(4), 419–434.

Zillmann, D. (1983). Transfer of excitation in emotional behavior. In J. T. Cacioppo & R. E. Petty (Eds.), *Social psychophysiology: A sourcebook* (pp. 215–240). New York, NY: Guilford Press.

Zillmann, D. (2002). Exemplification theory of media influence. In B. Jennings & D. Zillmann (Eds.), *Media effects: advances in theory and research* (2nd ed., pp. 19–42). Mahwah, NJ: Lawrence Erlbaum Associates.

Zillmann, D. (2003). Theory of affective dynamics: Emotions and moods. In J. Bryant, D. Roskos-Ewoldsen, & J. Cantor (Eds.), *Communication and emotion: Essays in honor of Dolf Zillmann* (pp. 533–567). Mahwah, NJ: Lawrence Erlbaum Associates.

Zillmann, D. (2006). Dramaturgy for emotions from fictional narration. In J. Bryant & P. Vorderer (Eds.), *Psychology of entertainment* (pp. 215–238). Mahwah, NY: Lawrence Erlbaum Associates.

Zillmann, D. (2011). Mechanisms of emotional reactivity to media entertainments. In K. Döveling, C. von Scheve, & E. Konijn (Eds.), *The Routledge handbook of emotions and mass media* (pp. 101–115). New York, NY: Routledge.

Zillmann, D., & Cantor, J. R. (1977). Affective responses to the emotions of a protagonist. *Journal of Experimental Social Psychology, 13*(2), 155–165.

Zillmann, D., & Gan, S.-L. (1997). Musical taste in adolescence. In D. J. Hargreaves & A. C. North (Eds.), *The social psychology of music* (pp. 161–187). New York, NY: Oxford University Press.

Zillmann, D., & Mundorf, N. (1987). Image effects in the appreciation of video rock. *Communication Research, 14*(3), 316–334.

Zillmann, D., Weaver, J. B., Mundorf, N., & Aust, C. F. (1986). Effects of an opposite-gender companion's affect to horror on distress, delight, and attraction. *Journal of Personality and Social Psychology, 51*(3), 586–594.

Ziv, N., Chaim, A. B., & Itamar, O. (2011). The effect of positive music and dispositional hope on state hope and affect. *Psychology of Music, 39*(3), 3–17.

Zuckerman, M. (1994). *Behavioral expressions and biosocial bases of sensation seeking*. New York, NY: Cambridge University Press.

Zuckerman, M. (2006). Sensation seeking in entertainment. In J. Bryant & P. Vorderer (Eds.), *Psychology of entertainment* (pp. 367–388). Mahwah, NJ: Lawrence Erlbaum Associates.

Chapter 5

Musical analysis for multimedia: A perspective from music theory

David Bashwiner

University of New Mexico, USA

Multimedia psychology and music theory

The psychology of music in multimedia is a subject that is of interest to researchers in multiple fields, including both psychology and music theory. In a general sense, it can be said that psychologists and music theorists share a common goal with regard to multimedia: to understand how and why music functions the way it does when paired with other media. But the particulars of this goal can differ in important ways across the two disciplines.

Numerous writers have addressed these differences with respect to music and psychology generally (Clarke, 1989; Cook, 1994; Cross, 1998; Gjerdingen, 1999; Krumhansl, 1995; Walsh, 1984). While acknowledging that individual researchers are usually neither purely psychologists nor purely music theorists, a few differences between the two fields are worth noting.

First, music theory tends to be score-based, compared to music psychology, which 'is concerned with describing the processes underlying musical behaviors' (Krumhansl, 1995, p. 80). Eric Clarke (1989) elaborates upon this idea—criticizing some of his own publications—by pointing out the musical work's frequent 'absence' in psychologically based investigations:

> It is a characteristic of the psychology of music that it is primarily *not* concerned with individual pieces of music... It is perfectly reasonable within musical analysis to concentrate on a single movement of music, since the aim is to understand how particular pieces are constructed. In the psychology of music, however, as also in psychology more generally, the aim is virtually without exception to explore general processes that have a variety of manifestations and applications. (pp. 3–4)

Second, music psychology relies far more strongly upon empirical methodology than does mainstream music theory (although see Clarke & Cook, 2004, as well as articles in the journal *Empirical Musicology*). Stephen Walsh (1984) quips that musicians 'notoriously tend to talk about their subject in terms better adapted to the analyst's couch than the psychologist's laboratory' (p. 237). Cross (1998) goes so far as to draw a parallel between contemporary music-analytical practice and 'folk psychology,' or 'common-sense accounts of everyday life' (p. 5). Nevertheless, he allows the analogy to go only so far, given that folk psychology does not rely upon elaborate systems of scholarship, whereas 'the music analysts' folk psychology… is being used to articulate and impart highly particular insights within a community of experts' (p. 5).

An important by-product of this reliance on empirical methodology is the effect it yields in the complexity of materials dealt with and subsequent conclusions reached. Because music psychology is strongly wedded to empirical methods, the claims that psychologists draw tend to be more modest in scope than those drawn in music theory. As a result, music theorists not infrequently complain that the sorts of investigations conducted by music psychologists deal with such low-level constructs as to be inapplicable to the actual listening experience. Walsh (1984) writes, 'psychologists are apt to make prescriptions about the nature of music based on a narrow and often primitive understanding of the medium' (p. 237). Cook (1994), somewhat in contrast, complains that many so-called studies of music perception are in fact studies of 'ear training' as a result of relying too heavily (rather than too lightly, as with Walsh) upon the constructs of music theory. In both cases, there is dissatisfaction with the sophistication of the sorts of claims that tend to be tested in music psychology. Psychologists, in turn, have every right to question whether the majority of music theorists' claims are framed in a way that is testable and can be empirically supported.

A final point of difference concerns each field's relationship to the nature of perception. As pointed out by Cross (1998), the term 'perception' tends to be interpreted as 'involuntary and reflexive' for psychologists but 'conscious and volitional' for music theorists (p. 4). Moreover, as Walsh (1984) argues, many of the claims made by music analysts have to do simply with text-level structure and/or compositional method, rather than with perception. Not all music-theoretic claims, in other words, are intended to model perception directly. Nevertheless, there is much evidence that musicians and non-musicians hear music in similar ways, usually differing in gradation rather than typology (Cross, 1998, p. 5; see also Bigand, 1993; Koelsch, Gunter, Friederici, & Schröger, 2000). A possible interpretation of such findings is that the constructs music theorists use to describe music may indeed have some cognitive validity which simply remains to be empirically tested. This is a supposition many music theorists likely believe. A standard musical analysis of a piece may therefore be implicitly expected by a theorist to *somehow* model perception, even if the ways in which it does so have not been empirically demonstrated.

In sum, music theorists and music psychologists, despite having a common goal, seem to pursue that goal in highly divergent ways. Recognizing this difference is of value to the multimedia researcher. Because multimedia is such a variegated subject, productive scholarship in this area necessarily requires multiple perspectives. But generating knowledge that speaks across disciplines is not a trivial task. It is necessary, on occasion, for music theorists to remind themselves of the particular goals and *modi operandi* of psychologists, and for psychologists to do the same regarding music theorists.

The aim of this chapter is to discuss the function of music in multimedia from the music theorist's perspective. As such, its scales are tipped. The chapter takes as its main criterion the question of value to the music theorist: What is learned about music per se, rather than just about its perceivers? What is learned about specific pieces of music, even specific recordings or specific excerpts of those recordings? How do the particularities of musical structure—harmony, melody, rhythm, timbre, dynamics, and so on—contribute to any observed effects? To what extent is careful analysis of the music incorporated into the design of the experiment? Are the naive perceptions of non-expert listeners compared with in-depth analyses by experts? Is the music engaged with at sufficient depth to yield musically relevant observations?

Despite its music-theoretic orientation, however, this chapter is primarily intended to be of value to the psychologist. It is intended to speak to that portion of the researcher—from whatever field—that seeks to understand how and why music functions the way it does when paired with other media. Music theory can make a valuable contribution to this understanding, and this chapter aims to elucidate the nature of that contribution.

The complexity of dramatic potentiality: Barber's *Adagio for Strings*

The forte of the music theorist is to direct sustained attention to individual works with the aim of understanding their structure. In this chapter, I will argue that understanding the structure of a musical work profoundly benefits our understanding of how it functions in multimedia.

By way of first illustration, it will be useful to focus on a piece of music that has been employed as a stimulus in numerous psychological experiments: Samuel Barber's *Adagio for Strings* (Baumgartner, Esslen, & Jäncke, 2006; Boltz, 2001; Eich & Metcalf, 1989; Gomez & Danuser, 2004, 2007; Krumhansl, 1997; Morrow & Nolan-Hoeksema, 1990; Nawrot, 2003). In each case, the piece has been used to evoke emotions in listeners, sometimes in combination with pictures, a written narrative, or a film scene. But, quite interestingly, the emotions the piece is shown to evoke, and the interpretations to which it thus gives rise, differ across experiments. (On the importance of emotion in film music, see Cohen, 2010; and chapters by Cohen, and Hoeckner & Nusbaum, and Kuchinke, Kappelhoff, & Koelsch, in this volume; on emotions in music generally, see Juslin & Sloboda, 2010b.)

The opening measures of this familiar work are presented in Figure 5.1. Of the eight emotion and multimedia studies that use the piece, four assume a priori that the dominant emotion conveyed is sadness (Baumgartner et al., 2006; Eich & Metcalf, 1989; Krumhansl, 1997; Morrow & Nolan-Hoeksema, 1990). Boltz, in contrast, makes use of the *Adagio* because of its 'positive mood,' while Nawrot finds evidence for both negatively and positively valenced interpretations of the piece's emotional structure (as do both Krumhansl and Baumgartner et al. to some extent). Gomez and Danuser (2004), furthermore, find that the emotion expressed, though negative in valence, is high rather than low in arousal, suggesting something more like fear or anger than sadness (at least according to the dimensional or 'circumplex' model of emotion; see Russell, 1980).

There are modest limitations to drawing these comparisons. Only one of the eight studies indicates which recording of the *Adagio* was used (Krumhansl's). Furthermore, while some studies played the entire piece for participants, others played segments lasting 5 minutes, 3 minutes, 70 seconds, 30 seconds, or 20 seconds; only one of these studies specifies which portion of the piece was played (again Krumhansl's). On the

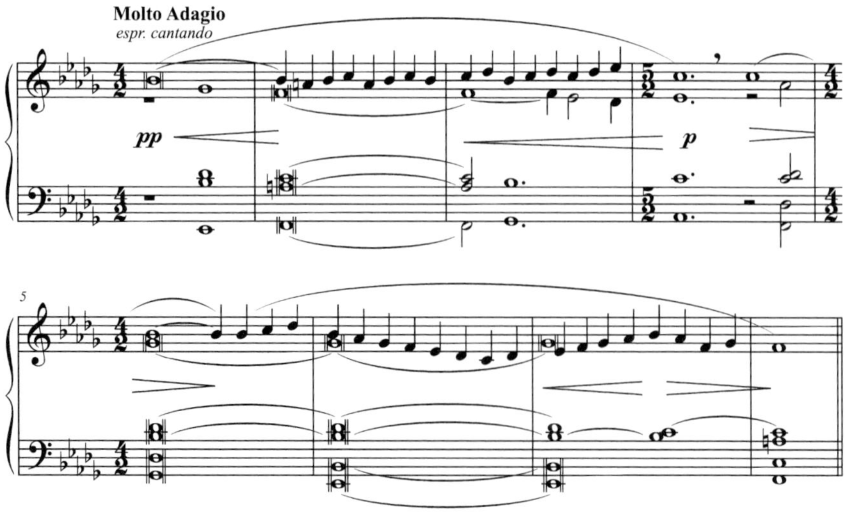

Figure 5.1 *Adagio for Strings*, measures 1–8, by Samuel Barber. Reduced for piano by the author from the orchestral score, G. Schirmer edition (1939).

one hand, this points out the importance of specifying precise excerpts used in any experiment. Are all possible excerpts of the *Adagio* equally sad? Probably not. On the other hand, the piece is homogeneous enough, and the theme quoted in Figure 5.1 recurs enough times throughout (in more or less varied form), that, for our purposes, a comparison is possible if not ideal. It will be assumed that the studies discussed here made use of a segment of the music including Figure 5.1 or a variant of it, although for the two shorter excerpts (20 seconds in Nawrot and 30 seconds in the two Gomez & Danuser studies), it is possible that this was not the case.

Happy or sad?

How can the same piece of music function to represent or evoke[1] both positive and negative affect[2]? Asking this question draws predominantly upon a comparison of how Barber's *Adagio for Strings* functions in the experiment by Boltz (2001) with how it functions in the remaining studies. Boltz writes that the *Adagio* was chosen to represent 'positive mood.... on the basis of structural parameters identified in the past literature as conveying positive versus negative music' (p. 434; references omitted). In an appendix, she describes the structural characteristics of the *Adagio* as follows: 'major mode; slow regular tempo; rhythm in a triple meter; wide pitch range with long melodic phrases' (p. 454). Based on this structural assessment, Boltz concludes that the *Adagio* is positive music, and she treats it as such in her experiment.

Importantly, beyond this a priori assumption that it *ought to* function as positive music, Boltz's results indicate that the *Adagio* in fact does. These results hinge upon participants' responses to a set of three stimuli, which were generated by pairing a 5-minute scene from the film *Vertigo* with either positive music (the *Adagio*), negative music (a selection from Tangerine Dream's *Rubycon*), or no music. Participants were shown one of these three versions and asked to describe the motives of the male protagonist, who is shown following a female throughout the scene's duration. Boltz reports that:

> in the no-music condition of *Vertigo*, the man was most often perceived as a private investigator who was intelligent, curious, and analytical. However, the same man was described as a sensitive, caring long-lost lover romantically infatuated with the woman when the accompanying soundtrack was positive in affect, but a cold, lonely hit man when the accompanying music was negative in affect. (2001, p. 440)

The *Adagio*, then, functioned as positive music when paired with a neutral film clip, shifting the interpretation of the protagonist's motives toward the positive side of the emotional spectrum.

Contrast this with the *Adagio's* function in the remainder of the studies cited. Both Eich and Metcalf (1989) and Morrow and Nolan-Hoeksema (1990) used the *Adagio* to elicit a depressed or melancholy mood (the latter in combination with a short story). Krumhansl (1997), Nawrot (2003), and Baumgartner et al. (2006) used it to represent or evoke sadness (the last in combination with pictures). Indeed, the *Adagio* did function to represent or evoke these negatively valenced states in these studies, as it did in the case of Gomez and Danuser (2004), in which no particular emotion was targeted.

The *Adagio* thus seems capable of representing/evoking both positive and negative emotions. Additional evidence presented by Krumhansl, Nawrot, and Baumgartner et al. supports this supposition. Krumhansl found that while the highest rated emotion for the *Adagio* was sadness, happiness and contentment were the next most highly rated emotions. Nawrot found that while 60 percent of adults paired the *Adagio* with a sad face, nearly 40 percent paired it with a neutral face; she also found that among 4-year-old children, only 22 percent paired it with a sad face, while over 40 percent paired it with a happy face. And Baumgartner et al. found that when the *Adagio* was presented alone (rather than with negative images), the emotions it conveyed were more ambiguous—favoring sadness but including happiness and fear. All of this evidence suggests that the emotional profile of the *Adagio* is complex—not simply happy or sad, but something like a mixture of the two. A closer look at how the piece is constructed will reveal why this is the case.

Major or minor?

Only two of the studies cited offer a rationale as to why the *Adagio* was chosen to represent or evoke the intended emotions. Krumhansl reports that her two sadness-eliciting stimuli were 'characterized by very slow tempos, minor harmonies, and fairly constant pitch ranges and dynamics' (1997, p. 350). Corroborating this sentiment, Boltz writes that, 'in general, the negative music displayed a minor mode, atonality, and an irregular rhythm. Conversely, the positive music displayed a major mode, a consistent tonality scheme, and a very predictable rhythm' (2001, p. 434).

Both writers invoke the long tradition in both the humanities and the sciences of examining the relationship between musical structure and musical emotion. As early as Zarlino (1558/1983), it was recognized that the modes with a minor third above the final were 'sad and languid,' in contrast to those with a major third above the final, which were 'lively and full of cheer' (pp. 21–22; see also Bashwiner, 2010, p. 22). Such statements began to be empirically tested as early as Heinlein (1928) for individual chords and Hevner (1935) for musical excerpts, revealing that (to Heinlein's dismay) listeners did tend to associate the major mode with positively valenced emotions and the minor mode with negatively valenced emotions (irrespective of register and dynamics). Two further experiments by Hevner (1936, 1937) examined the effects of figuration (firm versus flowing rhythms), harmonic complexity, direction of melodic line (ascending versus descending), tempo, and pitch height. Her findings, which have been confirmed and supplemented by numerous experiments since that time (see Gabrielsson & Lindström, 2010, for a review), indicated that the major mode most strongly correlated with adjectives of the 'happy-bright' type, while the minor mode most strongly correlated with adjectives of the 'sad-heavy' type.

Krumhansl and Boltz call upon this same tradition (both citing Hevner), but they arrive at different conclusions. Krumhansl takes the *Adagio* to be in the minor mode, while Boltz takes it to be in the major. As a result, Krumhansl deems the *Adagio* representative of sadness, while Boltz deems it representative of positive mood. Both find results consistent with their hypotheses. How can this be? Which interpretation is correct? Is the *Adagio* in major or in minor?

In some sense the answer to this question is an easy one: the key signature of the piece is five flats, and the first two chords are E-flat minor-seventh followed by F major—i.e., a iv^7 chord leading to a V chord. This unambiguously indicates that the tonic of the key is B-flat, and the mode is minor. If, following Hevner and related studies, the work is in minor, it should therefore be evocative/representative of sadness. Why, then, did it function to lighten the mood—to make the protagonist's intentions seem more romantic—in Boltz's experiment?

In the literal sense, the *Adagio* is in a minor key. But, fascinatingly, it has something like a major feel to it nonetheless. Of the nine chords in Figure 5.1, two are minor and one is half-diminished, but the remaining six are major; alternatively put, 18 of the excerpt's 31 beats (58 percent) are on major chords, while only 10 beats (32 percent) are on minor or diminished chords (the mode during the remaining 3 beats being ambiguous). As stated, following the opening B-flat and the E-flat minor seventh chord that eventually accompanies it, the F major chord of measure 2 signals that the tonic is B-flat minor and F is its dominant. But this dominant does not proceed to tonic as expected; it instead proceeds deceptively to G-flat major, the submediant (VI) of the key. This chord, in turn, continues to another major chord, A-flat major (VII), and after that to a major-major seventh chord in first inversion, D-flat major (III^6_5). G-flat major is then once again heard, and only after eight beats on it do the darker chords of the minor mode return: E-flat minor seventh (iv^7) followed by C half-diminished ($ii\o^6_5$). (Following the convention in harmonic analysis, uppercase Roman numerals are used to denote major triads and lowercase to denote minor triads). As these lead to the final dominant of the passage—which is major—the minor tonic is once again implied but not stated. Thus, though in a minor key, the first eight measures of the *Adagio*—which can be called the work's principal theme—predominantly stress the major sonorities of the mode.[3]

The music that immediately follows (not shown in Figure 5.1), furthermore, is a varied repeat of the first eight measures, but this time the phrase cadences in D-flat major rather than on the dominant of B-flat minor. Thus measures 1–15 not only have a lot of major chords in them, but they amount to a *trajectory* from minor to major. Of the 13 cadences in the piece (measures 8, 15, 19, 26, 28, 35, 42, 53, 57, 64, and 66), 11 are on major chords. Of these 11, two are on D-flat and one is on B-flat, but the remainder are on F, which is the dominant of—and hence implies—B-flat minor. Thus the statement made earlier about the first phrase applies roughly to the piece as a whole: though the mode is minor, there is nevertheless a sort of major feel throughout.[4]

Listeners' perceptions

Intrigued by the harmonic ambiguity of Barber's *Adagio for Strings*, and its multiple possibilities for affective interpretation, I asked my students in a freshman-year aural skills course (n=43) to listen to a recording of the excerpt in Figure 5.1 (played by the Philadelphia Orchestra with Klaus Tennstedt conducting, 1999) and then answer a few questions about it. The excerpt was played three times. When asked whether the excerpt was in major or minor, 88 percent said that it was in minor. When asked, however, to rate how major or minor the piece felt on a 7-point scale, with 1=very minor and 7=very major, the mean was 2.95. Gomez and Danuser (2007) asked a similar question of three 'experts' (a pianist, a singer, and a musicologist), and their ratings averaged out to 3.0. Both sets of ratings, in other words, yield results that somewhat resemble the claims made in the previous section: when judged along a continuum, the *Adagio* appears to display characteristics of both major and minor modes.

I also asked the students whether the piece felt as if it were 'in three' or 'in four,' since Boltz describes it as having 'rhythm in a triple meter,' whereas the score indicates a time signature of 4/2 (although Barber occasionally adds extra beats at cadences, as in measure 4). Somewhat surprisingly, the majority of respondents (65 percent) believed the piece to be 'in three,' with 6/8 being the most common time signature proposed. A glance at Figure 5.1 reveals why this might be the case. First of all, the lower-voice harmonies of measures 1–3 attack at irregular intervals, and they are held for long durations. Against this largely unpredictable background, the melodic motion in the top voice presents a stream of quarter notes, which are in fact grouped in threes (A-Bb-C, A-Bb-C, Bb-C-Db, Bb-C-Db, etc.). If the listener can establish a good sense of the 4/2 meter of the accompaniment, he/she can hear the top voice as syncopated against it. But because the excerpt heard was as brief as it was, establishing a firm sense of meter from the relatively ambiguous accompaniment may have proven difficult. Thus, in addition to being modally ambiguous, this excerpt appears to be metrically ambiguous as well.

A final question I asked my students concerned the emotional resonances of the excerpt: 'What sort of emotion words describe how you feel when you listen to this piece?' Interestingly enough, 51 percent of respondents used the term 'sad' or 'sadness' in their answer. When other words with negative connotations were included (e.g., pain, sorrow, turmoil, loss, terrible, hopeless, somber, cry), the number grew to 72 percent. Only 28 percent of respondents, in other words, did *not* use a negatively valenced word to describe the excerpt; these respondents used words such as delicate, tender, hope, pensive, nostalgic, thoughtful, peaceful, appreciative, and sweet. Notably, of those using no negatively valenced words, only one believed the piece to be in major. Thus, judgments of minor key and negative valence do not necessarily go hand in hand.

One of the more interesting trends in response to this final question was what I will call a dynamic-valence response (26 percent). To quote one participant, the piece is 'sad but hopeful.' To quote another, 'I feel like something terrible has happened, but it's already over, and there is now hope that things will get better.' Other words used (e.g., longing, anticipation, pleading) give a similarly dynamic sense of affect: of moving out of a current negative state toward a future positive state. While this was a sentiment voiced by only a quarter of students, it is one that captures both the positive and negative aspects of the *Adagio*'s affective profile. It is also one that has a parallel in the harmonic structure of the music, since the key is minor but it is the major harmonies within the minor mode that receive the most emphasis (conveying the sense, perhaps, of 'making the best of a bad situation'). The rising line in both the top and bottom voices of the first half of the excerpt may similarly bring out connotations of striving or enduring. Finally, the metric ambiguity of the passage could convey an uncertainty or timidity, or even a conflict of opposing forces. This complex set of affective resonances seems to me to be more representative of this work than are straight sadness or positive mood. (For more on the portrayal of complex emotions in music, see Karl & Robinson, 1995)

'From down here I can start up again': Endurance and empathy in *Platoon*

The value of thinking complexly about the *Adagio's* emotional profile is evident when considering its use in a film like *Platoon* (Kopelson & Stone, 1986/2006). In accord with the earlier discussed reasoning, the *Adagio* might be considered to convey something like 'endurance of hardship for the sake of personal growth' in this film—enduring a current negative state for the sake of emerging positively at a later time. Two voiceover narrations in the film give credence to this interpretation. The first of these occurs toward the beginning of the film, when, in a letter to his grandmother, protagonist Chris Taylor gives voice to a sense of finding the positive in the negative:

> Maybe I've finally found it, way down here in the mud. Maybe from down here, I can start up again. Be something I can be proud of without having to fake it… Maybe I can see something I don't yet see, or learn something I don't yet know. (0:17:19–0:17:35)

The second occurrence constitutes the final spoken lines of the script. Again writing to his grandmother, Chris says:

> I think now, looking back, we did not fight the enemy, we fought ourselves and the enemy was in us.… Be that as it may, those of us who did make it have an obligation to build again, to teach to others what we know, and to try with what's left of our lives to find a goodness and meaning to this life. (01:54:21–01:55:15)

Again, there is a sense of internal struggle, and of finding the positive in the negative. Even the imagery during the opening credits matches this trajectory: as the *Adagio* is heard (0:00:27–0:02:50), the viewer-listener encounters first the horrors of war—body bags, the noises of trucks and planes, aggressive behavior, wounds, and scars—but these are followed by eerily calm and beautiful images of the troops' natural surroundings as they head off into battle.

Figure 5.2 Protagonist Chris Taylor surveys the devastation his platoon has wreaked upon a peaceable Vietnamese village. Image from *Platoon* (1986/2006). Kopelson, A. (Producer) and Stone, O. (Director). 20th Anniversary Edition. Culver City, California: MGM. Publisher No. 14487. © 1986/2006, MGM.

There is yet another explanation for the *Adagio's* complex emotional effect in this film, as illustrated by its second appearance, when the platoon sets fire to a village of peaceable farmers in the Vietnamese jungle (0:55:26–0:57:18). The emotional profile of this sequence is strongly ambivalent. A number of the onscreen characters, such as Chris and Sgt. Elias, feel the pain of the villagers, and presumably much of the audience does as well. Chris's slumped posture as he views the devastation his platoon has wreaked (Figure 5.2) is expressive of his shared suffering. Juxtaposed against this is the relative nonchalance of the other platoon members in lighting fire to each hut, leading villagers away with ropes around their necks, and, at the sequence's climax, raping a young girl. The climactic moment in the *Adagio* (leading up to measure 53) accompanies this climactic moment in the sequence (as it does when Sgt. Elias is killed later in the film, 1:19:17–1:20:56).

The effect of the *Adagio* in this sequence seems not to be one of hope, but instead one of *empathy*. Fellow platoon member Big Harold encapsulates this idea a few minutes later in the film—after another brief appearance of the *Adagio* (0:57:55–0:58:45)—when he says about the village experience, 'I don't know, brothers, but I'm hurtin' real bad inside' (1:00:39–1:00:49). Similarly, Chris, upon breaking up the rape, yells, 'She's a fucking human being, man... You don't fucking get it, do you, man? You just don't fucking get it' (0:57:18–0:57:39). Both men express an empathetic connection with the villagers.

Music is often spoken of as being 'representative' of various emotions. However, it can also be thought of as being an *agent* of emotional change, or, in this case, of empathetic identification (Hoeckner, Wyatt, Decety, & Nusbaum, 2011; Overy & Molnar-Szakacs, 2009). It may be the case that the *Adagio* functions in this village sequence as an agent that brings about an empathetic connection between the sympathetic characters onscreen (Chris, Sgt. Elias, Big Harold) and the villagers. At the same time, it also seems to elicit an empathetic connection between these characters and the audience. It could be for this reason that the emotions in a mostly negative sequence such as this would be experienced as negative, whereas in a situation like that of Boltz's (2001) experiment (in which the emotional content of the scene was more neutral), the *Adagio*'s empathetic potential led participants to connect positively to the protagonist. The *Adagio* itself, in other words, may not so much have its own valence as bring about an empathetic connection between the audience and whatever is onscreen. This sort of logic posits music to be a *vehicle* for identification, rather than its object—a notion with interesting implications, for instance, for the philosophy of music.[5]

Summary

In sum, Samuel Barber's *Adagio for Strings* is a complex work, and its dramatic implications are equally complex. Researchers—whether psychologists or music theorists—must be sure to have at their disposal the requisite tools for understanding what makes a work complex and how these complexities give rise to dramatic potentialities. I have aimed to demonstrate here that the standard tools of music theory, though by no means sufficient, are nevertheless useful—and perhaps necessary—for achieving this goal.

A German accompaniment to an English declaration of war: Cross-domain interactions in *The King's Speech*

The second part of this chapter will address how music functions dramatically in a scene from the film *The King's Speech* (Canning, Sherman, Unwin, & Hooper, 2010; 1:42:30–1:47:30 on the DVD (Anchor Bay Entertainment WC23130)). As before, the aim will be to demonstrate the benefits of looking closely at the work's structure from the music theoretical perspective. I will argue that only by doing so does one become fully aware of the important parallels that emerge across the scene's three domains of activity—music, speech, and visuals. (For more on these domains, see Cohen, 2010.) The scene to be analyzed is the climactic speech of the film (for which the film was in fact named, at least according to one of the title's many meanings), in which Bertie, having just become King George VI of England, must declare war upon Germany in an international radio broadcast—a task that his debilitating stammer threatens to derail (Figure 5.3).

Music and drama: A hand-in-glove fit

Music and drama in this scene seem to fit hand-in-glove. The first chord of the music is heard just as Lionel, Bertie's speech therapist, counts down from four and gives the signal for the speech to commence. The music then continues through to the final words of the speech, itself cadencing as the speech, too, comes to a close. Despite the hand-in-glove fit, however, the piece is not underscore. It was written not by Desplat, the film's composer (who was nominated for an Academy Award for the music he did write), but by Beethoven (1811–1812/1989)—it is an excerpt from the *Allegretto* second movement of the Seventh Symphony (measures 1–100; see Figure 5.4). The pairing is

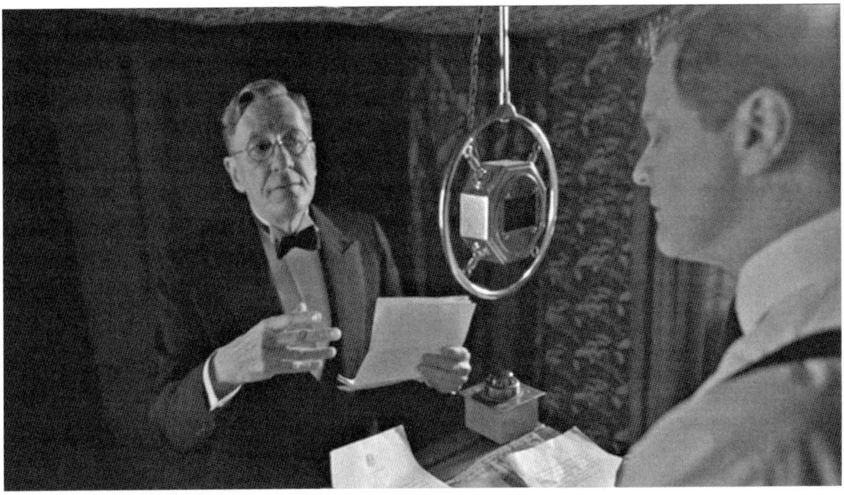

Figure 5.3 Lionel conducts along as both Bertie's performance and the camerawork capturing it become more fluid. Image from *The King's Speech* (2010). Canning, I., Sherman, E., and Unwin, G. (Producers), and Hooper, T. (Director). UK: See-Saw Films. © 2010, See-Saw Films.

nevertheless highly effective. This is due in part to chance, or at least good selection on the part of the film's editor, Tariq Anwar (whom director Tom Hooper credits with the aesthetic decision—see the DVD's 'Feature Commentary,' 1:42:45–1:43:31). Its effectiveness is also due to a modest amount of editing done to Beethoven's original score, which added length at three key moments—beginning, middle, and end.

At the beginning of the cue, the single introductory chord indicated in the original score is repeated a second time, seeming to give a sense of 'Okay, begin now… Okay, go ahead and begin now!' The music then goes ahead with its first phrase without Bertie, making it almost to the end of the phrase before Bertie has uttered a single word (see Figure 5.4, measures 1–10).

In the middle of the cue, an entire 24-measure section of the music is repeated verbatim. On the largest scale, the original score for the cue consists of a set of four continuous variations (with the actual theme arriving only in the second variation, the first variation functioning more like accompaniment *without* theme—an effective choice for underscoring a speaking voice). For the film version of the cue, the second of the four variations (measures 27–50) is repeated verbatim, yielding a structure of five variations (rather than the four presented by Beethoven), the second and third being identical. (These are labeled in Figures 5.4 and 5.5 as Variations I, IIa, IIb, III, and IV.) This repetition of a whole variation (three phrases) allows 24 measures (56 seconds) to be added to the music.

Finally, at the end of the original version of this music (as composed by Beethoven), measures 99–100 do not cadence with as much finality as they do in the film version of the cue. Instead, they transition to new material in the key of A major. To give finality to the film version of the cue, these final two bars are repeated three additional times, with the final iteration (measures 101–102) being transposed down an octave.

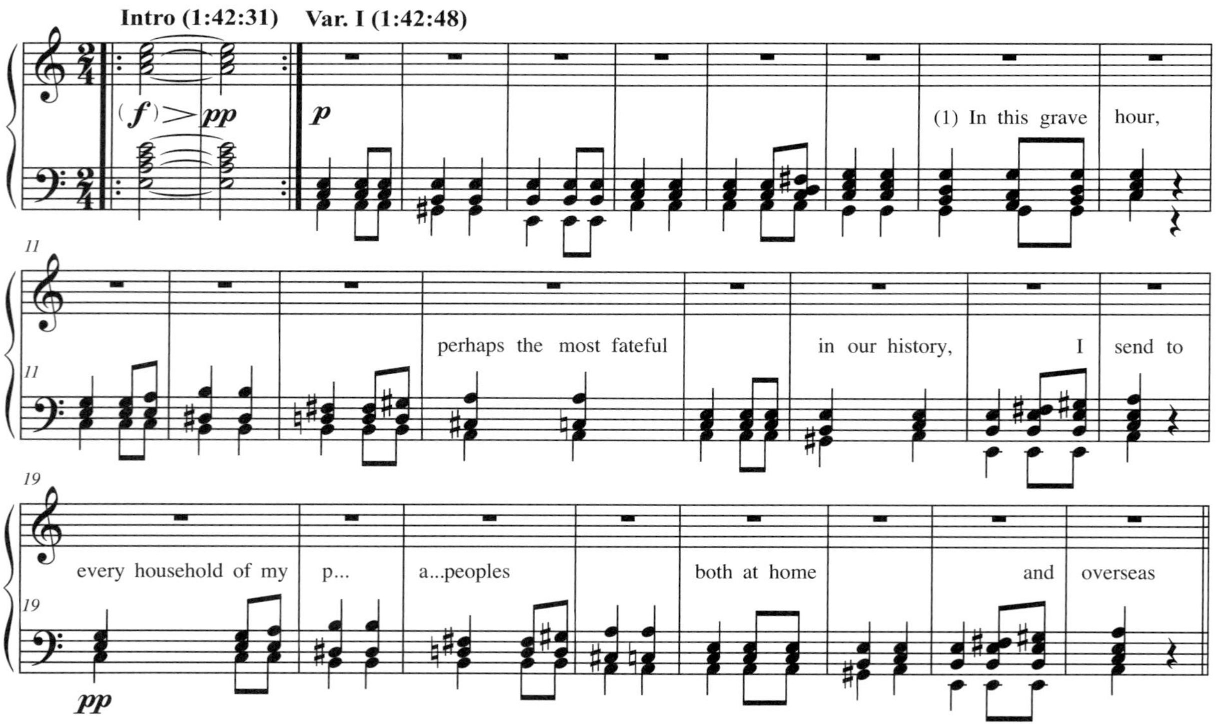

Intro (1:42:31)
Var. I (1:42:48)
(f) > pp
p
(1) In this grave hour,
11
perhaps the most fateful
in our history,
I send to
19
every household of my
p...
a...peoples
both at home
and overseas
pp

Figure 5.4 (Continued)

44
us we are at... at war. Over and over again
which, if it were to prevail, would be fatal to any civilized order in the world. Such a principle,
Var. III (1:45:29)
50
p cresc. poco a poco
we have tried disguise, is surely the mere primitive doc - trine that might
stripped of all
57
is right. For the sake of all that we ourselves hold dear, it is unthinkable that

Figure 5.4 *(Continued)*

80
in this time of trial. The task will be hard. There may be dark days ahead, and war
86
can no longer be confined to the battlefield. But we can only do the right as we

Figure 5.4 The *Allegretto* of Beethoven's Symphony No. 7, measures 1–100, as it appears in the film *The King's Speech* (1:42:30–1:47:30). All repeats are editorial alterations made to the film version of the cue, as are measures 101–102. Lyric underlay is approximate. Reduced for piano by the author from the orchestral score, Dover edition (1989). Excerpt from the screenplay of *The King's Speech* by David Seidler (copyright © 2010 by Speaking Films Ltd) quoted with permission of the publishers, Nick Hern Books: <http://www.nickhernbooks.co.uk>.

Why the pairing works

The pairing of music and drama in this all-important scene can be considered highly effective, as evidenced by the numerous reviews of the film that call attention to it (especially when compared with the minimal attention paid to Desplat's score; e.g., Schmidt, 2011; Schwarzbaum, 2011; Stabler, 2011). This no doubt has something to do with the piece's familiarity. As director Tom Hooper (2011) explains in the 'Feature Commentary' to *The King's Speech*, Desplat himself argued in support of using the Beethoven in part because of its familiarity, 'because Beethoven exists in our… public consciousness.' Hooper continues:

> We all have some memory, or most have some memory, of this music, and some of us know it very well, and it helps to elevate this scene to the space of a public event—whereas film score is always internal to the movie it's scored for and doesn't exist in our public consciousness in the same way. (1:42:45–1:43:31)

There must, however, be more to this piece's effectiveness than its familiarity. Countless familiar pieces would certainly not have worked as well (such as 'Happy Birthday' or 'Yellow Submarine'). The identity of Beethoven himself seems to some extent significant—it is curious in the least ('ironic' to quote Desplat (Holleran, 2012)) that a British declaration of war against Germany is accompanied by German rather than British music. Attention has also been called to the parallel between Beethoven's mounting deafness and the King's debilitating stammer—as well as the determination of each to persevere. These extramusical associations seem to lend depth and sophistication—even curiosity and conflict—to the pairing of music and narrative in this scene.

And yet again, there must be more to the *Allegretto's* effectiveness than its association with Beethoven, for other works by Beethoven—such as the slow movement of the *Pathétique*, or the fourth movement of the Ninth Symphony—would simply not have worked as well. Even substituting other movements of the Seventh Symphony provides a curiously poor accompaniment, as can be approximated by muting the sound on the film and listening to an audio recording simultaneously—which Buhler, Neumeyer, & Deemer (2009) call the 'commutation test' (pp. 110–113). Watching the scene accompanied by the fourth movement of the symphony—according to the present author's interpretation—yields a very different effect. With this musical accompaniment, Bertie appears to be giddily triumphant about being able to speak at all. In contrast, the third movement, with both its rapidity and its powerful but unpredictable accents, seems to intensify his stutter rather than smooth it out. When the second movement accompanies the speech, however (as it does in the film), the audiovisual juxtaposition is just right: the unevenness of Bertie's stammer is mollified, and his confidence grows over the course of the cue.

There must, then, be something particular about this musical passage—irrespective of its association with Beethoven's deafness or his Germanic heritage—that makes it as effective as it is. What is this effectiveness, and what is its cause? According to Desplat, the film's editor chose to use the *Allegretto* not so much because of any 'ironic' meanings, but because of its 'solemnity' (Holleran, 2012). Adjectives that reviewers have used to describe the piece (in combination with this dramatic scene) include: ominous, calm, gentle, pulsing, smooth, unruffled, sweet, melancholic, magnificent (Stabler, 2011); awesome, sad, solemn, majestic (Schwarzbaum, 2011); and haunting, dirge-like, painful, sad, and heartbreaking—yet joyful and triumphant (Schmidt, 2011). Hooper himself contributes additional nuance to the combination's interpretation, saying that an exchange between Bertie and Lionel immediately after the speech captures 'the complex emotion of the pleasure in the success of the speech, but also the awareness of the burden of the war to come' (1:48:47–1:49:17). The emotional tone of this music seems once again, as was the case with Barber's *Adagio for Strings*, complex—one not easily described with single adjectives or images, but rather emerging from conflicting interactions between multiple forces.

If the effectiveness of Beethoven's *Allegretto* in this scene can be called its 'solemnity,' its conveyance of both 'pleasure' and 'burden,' or its capacity to dramatically smooth the King's stammer while simultaneously building his confidence—what can be the cause of this effectiveness? Undoubtedly, since that cause cannot be *solely* extramusical (i.e., associations with Beethoven), it must lie somewhere in the music itself, and/or its cross-domain interaction. We will turn first to the musical structure of this cue and then to its interactions with spoken and visual aspects of the scene.

Musical structure: Stasis and crescendo

Perhaps the most powerful set of forces working dramatically in this cue are a pair of opposites: along one set of dimensions, the cue is static, repetitive, and predictable; yet along another, the dramatic arc is that of a large crescendo, climaxing and then diminishing again only in the final moments of the cue, as the speech too comes to a close. Figure 5.5 depicts this opposition graphically.

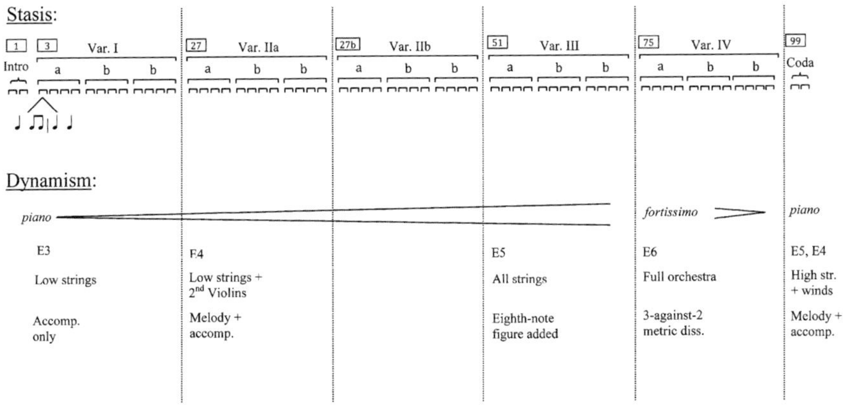

Figure 5.5 Aspects of stasis and dynamism in the *Allegretto* of Beethoven's Symphony No. 7, measures 1–100 (as it appears in *The King's Speech*). Original musical analysis by the author.

Stasis: Tempo, rhythmic patterning, and form

In at least three different musical dimensions, this cue can be considered 'static' (Figure 5.5, top). First, in terms of tempo, following the two opening sustained chords in the winds (measures 1–2), a slow but steady pulse settles in, varying little if at all until the final moments of the cue. The tempo employed by conductor Terry Davies for the film's rendition of the cue is slower than is typical for this work. Although Beethoven's choice of the word *Allegretto* implies a tempo of approximately 95 bpm (beats per minute), the actual bpm indication he gives is 75 (i.e., more like an *Andante*), and this appears to be observed fairly consistently by conductors today (e.g., Gardiner, 1994; von Karajan, 1960). Nevertheless, the tempo used for the film's cue is a significantly slower 55 bpm—i.e., more like an *Adagio*.

Despite this slow tempo, however, there is a persistence to the cue's motional qualities. This is due to at least two factors. First, though slow, the tempo is steady—it does not hesitate at the ends of phrases, for instance. Second, a single rhythmic pattern is maintained throughout (♩ ♫| ♩ ♩). Following the two introductory chords, this pattern persists throughout the cue (with the exception that, at the end of each phrase, the final quarter note is replaced by a rest; see, for example, measures 10, 18, and 26). While much slow music cannot be easily danced to (because slow music is often characterized by *rubato*, *fermatae*, and other sorts of temporal inconsistencies), this cue, though slow, is both steady and, thanks to the splitting of the second quarter into two eighths, consistently subdivided. As a result, it does seem to encourage movement—slow, steady, but energetic movement, perhaps something like a regal march.

A third dimension along which this musical cue is static, or at least repetitive, is its large-scale form. Setting aside the two introductory wind chords and the thrice-repeated, two-measure codetta, the form of the cue, as stated earlier, is a set of five continuous variations (the third being an exact repeat of the second). Each variation lasts 24 measures and consists of three phrases, the third of which is an exact repetition of the second (i.e., each variation is an asymmetrical period of the phrase structure *abb*). In sum, one can say that the cue is repetitive at the two-measure level (due to the rhythmic motif), the eight-measure level (every phrase being exactly eight measures long, and every *b* phrase repeating once immediately thereafter), and at the twenty-four-measure level (the opening variation being repeated four additional times).[6]

It is important to make note of the dramatic/semantic import of this repetitiveness. Repetition in a stimulus gives rise to predictability at the level of the perceiver, and perceivers that can entrain with a stimulus can as a result participate in it (Bispham, 2010; Clayton, Sager, & Will, 2004). To the extent that viewer-listeners feel that they are *with* the King in his performance, struggling just as much as he, but still confident and determined—i.e., to the extent that they identify with him—they may in part be doing so as a result of literally embodying the music that accompanies the scene, internally dancing to its lulling and predictable rhythms.

Crescendo: Dynamics, pitch height, instrumentation, and rhythmic complexity

Despite these elements of stasis and repetition, however, no listener would describe this cue as static. This is because, in dimensions not yet addressed, a sort of written-out crescendo[7] is achieved, climaxing at the beginning of the final variation and then tapering off into the denouement of the codetta. Dynamics, pitch height, instrumentation, and rhythmic complexity all participate to bring about this dramatic development (Figure 5.5, bottom).

With regard to dynamics, the cue begins *piano* in measure 3 (the introductory chords are marked *forte* by Beethoven but are played *piano* in the film's version of the cue); the music then begins to *crescendo poco a poco* in m. 51, rising to *forte* in m. 66, and reaching *fortissimo* in measure 75—declining again only in the last phrase before the codetta. Simultaneous with this rise in dynamic level, pitch height climbs in an almost directly parallel way: the most-repeated or 'modal' note of the first variation is E^3 (the E below middle C); in the second variation this note climbs to E^4, while in the third and fourth variations it climbs to E^5 and E^6, respectively. In instrumentation, a similar sort of 'crescendo' can be heard: the first variation involves only the lower strings; the second introduces the second violins; the third brings in the first violins to complete the string section; and the fourth brings in woodwinds, timpani, and brass to create a full orchestral *tutti*. Finally, with regard to rhythmic complexity, the first variation consists of a mere accompanimental pattern; the second introduces both a melody and rhythmic syncopation in the bass; in the third, the cellos and violas introduce an eighth-note arpeggiated figure to fill out the metrical space; and finally, in the fourth variation, the lower voices play triplet eighths against the duple eighths of the upper voices, creating a three-against-two metrical dissonance. As with volume, 'diminuendos' can also be heard in pitch height, instrumentation, and rhythmic complexity toward the end of the final variation and into the codetta: by the final bars of the cue, the dynamic is again *piano*, the highest note has dropped to A^4, the metrical dissonance has resolved, and the instrumental palette has been considerably reduced.

Harmony

To this point, little has been overtly stated concerning harmony. Nevertheless, harmonic logic is implicit in many of the previous observations. For instance, the 'continuous variations' nature of the movement is dependent upon both melodic *and* harmonic repetition. The opening wind sonority, furthermore, functions as introductory in part because it is unstable—though a tonic chord, it is in second inversion. Additionally, the codetta sounds final precisely because it reiterates, multiple times, a V^7 chord proceeding to a i chord—to borrow Lerdahl's (2001) terminology a more tense and highly attract*ed* sonority proceeding to a more relaxed and highly attract*ive* sonority. There is thus 'resolution' of a musico-dramatic sort in proceeding from V^7 to i, and this can be tangibly felt in the codetta to this cue—virtually irrespective of what occurs visually/narratively.[8]

Perhaps the most important observation to make about harmonic structure in this cue is that the reach of its tension and resolution arcs is limited to a middle level of scale. Every single variation of the *Allegretto* begins and ends in A minor. There is thus no large-scale sense of departure and return; like tempo, rhythmic patterning, and form, the large-scale harmonic structure of this cue is thus static. Nevertheless, within the span of the individual variation, harmony is indeed varied and exhibits a strong sense of departure and return: each *a* phrase begins on A minor and progresses to C major, while each *b* phrase does the reverse. At local levels, then, harmonic structure in this cue is dynamic (like loudness, pitch height, instrumentation, and rhythmic complexity), while at the most global level it is static (like tempo, rhythmic patterning, and form).

Dramatic interpretation

To summarize this excursion thus far, the climactic scene in *The King's Speech* is in part climactic because of its use of the *Allegretto* from Beethoven's Seventh Symphony, and this music must function climactically not solely because of its association with Beethoven, but also because of its musical structure. This structure demonstrates qualities of both stasis/repetition and growth/development, both of which are likely important in eliciting the intended dramatic effect in the context of the scene. The slow consistency of the temporal and formal properties of the music, for instance, likely contribute to the piece's soothing and 'solemn' quality, which in turn seems responsible for mollifying the King's stammer and reducing any anxieties that arise on account of it. The growth seen in the parameters of volume, pitch height, instrumentation, and complexity, on the other hand, seem to parallel the King's growing sense of confidence as well as the mounting passion experienced by his powerfully moved listeners.

It is instructive to look more closely at how musical, textual, and visual structure interact across domains to elicit these dramatic effects. We will turn first to spoken structure and then to visual structure.

Speech–music interactions

With regard to the actual speech's alignment and interaction with the music, a few points are relevant. First, the grammatical phrases of the spoken text do not align with the grammatical phrase and period structure of the music (refer again to Figure 5.4). There are effectively no synchronization points, in other words, between musical text and spoken text (save for the very beginning and end of the cue). This is all the more interesting given that, due to the King's halting delivery, the grammatical structure of his spoken text is itself not 'correctly' parsed by his own spoken performance. The first utterance of the speech begins in measures 7–8 of the music (at the tail end of the first musical phrase) with the words 'In this grave… hour.' The music then continues for three bars before the next utterance, 'perhaps the most faithful,' is finally spoken (measure 14), which is then followed two bars later by 'in our history.' By the end of the entire first variation, the King has managed to add onto this only 'I send… to every household… of my… a-peoples… both at home… and overseas'—in other words, he has not yet completed even a single sentence. The first sentence of the King's speech does not end until the middle of the second variation (measure 40a), and the second sentence starts shortly thereafter (measure 42a), still in the middle of the second variation. Spoken structure and musical structure, then, do not align. (This is not surprising, of course, given that the scene was not shot to the soundtrack, the latter having been added later by the film's editor.) Nevertheless, there seems to be a sense that, despite the unpredictability of the spoken words themselves, the King's determination (conveyed by the steady pulse of the music) is constant. Music and speech thus cooperate to deliver a complex effect that could not be brought about by either domain alone.

An additional point to be made about text–music interactions in this scene is that the King's rate of speech does become more fluid and efficient over the course of the performance, as is tangibly measurable against the steady metronomic pulse of the music. Over the course of the first variation, for instance, 24 words are spoken, while over the course of the final variation (excluding the coda), 67 are—nearly a threefold increase.

Visual–music interactions

A final layer of interest emerges when camera movement is considered. During the piece's introductory two chords, the camera is stationary, showing a close-up of Bertie from just behind the microphone (as well as one of Lionel from the opposite side). As the accompanimental pattern of the first variation then begins, the camera slowly dollies in toward various listeners (first Bertie's wife, then the sound engineer recording the speech, etc.). But as it returns to Bertie—who has not yet uttered a word—it is once again stationary and in close-up. A few words finally escape his lips, and the first musical phrase ends, creating a sort of dramatic pause, though an awkward one: the camera is still stationary, directed at Bertie in close-up with the microphone in between. The second musical phrase begins, a few more words are spoken, and the pattern continues: when focused upon Bertie and Lionel, the camera is stationary and in close-up, but when directed at listeners, it begins from farther away and dollies in slowly. The effect seems to be that what is a struggle for Bertie (and Lionel) is nevertheless sweeping listeners away—they are being drawn in, becoming more and more involved.[9]

The pattern shifts for the first time in the middle of the second variation (Var. IIa, measure 27, 1:43:38), at which point Bertie is shown from the side, with a subtly tracking camera. Upon his completion of the second sentence of the speech with the phrase 'we are... at... at war,' the camera for the first time slowly pulls inward toward Bertie—again from the side, but beginning with Lionel in the shot and eventually excluding him from it (the intended effect being, perhaps, that 'Bertie can do it on his own').[10] During the repeat of the second variation (Var. IIb, 1:44:33), the camera begins to be even more mobile in the studio, almost dancing—as if riding upon the wave of the melody emerging even more confidently this second time from the cellos and violas (as Lionel conducts along, as in Figure 5.3). More and more groups of listeners are shown now, and, each time, the camera draws slowly toward them, conveying their deep involvement in the speech. Occasional shots in the studio continue to capture Bertie from a stationary camera, and, in many of these shots, he continues to struggle with words; but his listeners are always being captured with a moving camera, and hence being 'swept away' and 'inwardly drawn' into the drama of the speech. In the final variation (Var. IV, measure 75, 1:46:22), the music is so overpowering that the King's words are almost difficult to make out, and nearly all of the camerawork involves movement inward. Thus, just as the music crescendos (in multiple parameters) across the entire cue, and as the rate of Bertie's speaking increases almost threefold, so too does camerawork progress from stasis to movement.

Summary: The indispensability of musical analysis

This emergence of dynamism from stasis, then, is a sort of meta-narrative that, although to some extent present in each domain of the stimulus individually (music, speech, and camerawork), most powerfully develops as a product of their complex interactions with one another. As should be readily apparent, illuminating the nature of these interactions to a satisfactory degree would not be possible without having analyzed carefully the musical aspect of the scene. Merely noting, as do the various reviews and blogs surveyed, that the piece is by Beethoven, or that it is by a German composer struggling with a physical infirmity, or that it is 'ominous' or 'solemn,' is not sufficient to arrive at more than a superficial understanding of how this piece of music functions in this film. A survey of listeners asking for ratings of either structural aspects ('how minor is the piece?') or emotion words ('how happy or sad is it?') would similarly do little better. With regard to understanding how this music works in this scene, musical analysis of the harmonic-melodic variety makes a unique and perhaps necessary contribution.

Conclusion: The empirical-analytical trade-off

As stated at the outset of this chapter, the perspective adopted in this chapter is in some sense a biased one. Both psychologists and music theorists are interested in research in music psychology, but they make different demands of that research, and they conduct that research in different ways. I have suggested that psychologists and music theorists will be most productive when they can learn from each other, and the aim of this chapter has been to present to the psychologist a view of multimedia research from the perspective of the music theorist.

Superficial engagement with musical stimuli seems—from the music theorist's perspective, at least—insufficient to yield the depth of insight required to understand how such stimuli function in multimedia. Observing that the *Adagio for Strings* is positive or negative in affect, that it is major or minor, or something of the sort, seems like it cannot yield the complexity necessary to appreciate its role in a film like *Platoon*. Observing that the *Allegretto* from Beethoven's *Seventh Symphony* was composed by a hard-of-hearing German, that it is 'ominous' or 'solemn,' or that it becomes more complex and exciting over time also seems insufficient to promote an understanding of how this work functions in *The King's Speech*. Simple observations of this sort may in the end be ultimately unrepresentative of the complex phenomena they are intended to explain.

No one analytical method will solve all analytical problems. What seems clear, however, is that the more closely one studies musical stimuli, the more complexity one finds. Such complexity is the lifeblood of art, including multimedia art. If it is true that 'he with only a hammer sees everything as a nail,' then it behooves the builder of complex mental representations to acquire as many tools as possible. While the analytical apparatus of standard music theory is only one perhaps limited and incomplete set of tools, it may nevertheless be an essential one for the multimedia researcher.

Music theorists, however, must also remember how essential to their own practices of analysis are the methods and findings of empirical psychology. To quote Richard Cohn (in a markedly different context), productive scholarship in music theory is necessarily 'a communal enterprise,' with the scholar's creativity being 'vitally inspired by field trips through the minds of others' (1992, p. 107). In addition to applying within the field of music theory, as originally intended, this statement also applies across fields: there are questions about music that cannot be answered by the study of music alone, and thus turning to psychology can be musically productive, if not essential. I hope to have demonstrated in this chapter that both psychologists and musicians can be 'vitally inspired' by 'field trips' through each other's minds. And I hope the reader will better appreciate the valuable contribution that music-analytical methods can make to the 'communal enterprise' of understanding the psychology of music in multimedia.

Acknowledgments

The author would like to thank Professor Heather Hoffmann of Knox College for reading early drafts of this manuscript and Professor Richard Hermann of the University of New Mexico for productive discussions on these and related matters.

Notes

1. The notion of representing emotion is distinguished in philosophical and musicological circles, as well as in the psychological literature, from the notion of evoking it (e.g., Kivy, 1980; Scherer & Zentner, 2001). A given piece could potentially represent one emotion while arousing another (e.g., 'the schmaltzy music made my stomach crawl'). Some studies discussed here speak of representing certain emotions, while others speak of evoking them (or arousing, producing, or eliciting them—all treated as synonymous with evocation). While the philosophical distinction is by all means important, the two types of study need not be deemed incomparable. Attention has been paid to accurately pairing correct terms with the authors who use them.
2. The terms 'affect,' 'emotion,' and 'feeling' are treated synonymously in this chapter. For disambiguation, see Scherer (2004) and Juslin and Sloboda (2010a).
3. It would be illuminating to empirically test these claims about the microstructure of affective valence by means of a probe-tone paradigm (Krumhansl & Shepard, 1979). The listener might, for instance, be first presented with the opening B-flat of Figure 5.1, and be asked to assign a 'happy/sad' rating to it. Next, the first two events, the B-flat followed by the E-flat minor seventh chord, would be presented, and again the listener would be asked to give a happy/sad rating. This would continue for at least each successive harmony of Figure 5.1, but could conceivably be used for longer passages. For an example of this method applied to the phenomenon of 'tonal tension,' see Lerdahl and Krumhansl (2007). For a more philosophical discussion of the changing implications of harmonies at different 'cursor points' in the music, see Lewin (1986).
4. The author notes that the focus in this context is on the listener's perception or experience of a piece of music, not on the analysis of the score. As researchers often select musical stimuli by piloting them on subjective judgments of undergraduate students, this may lead to varying or even opposing interpretations of musical works, leading them to be used toward different ends in research studies.
5. One of the great mysteries in the philosophy of music is why people choose to listen to 'sad' music if it makes them sad (Kivy, 1980; Levinson, 1997). The empathetic connection that music is capable of bringing about seems to provide a solution to this problem. In the amalgam of what we call 'sadness,' one can recognize there to be at least two types of affective state in dialogue with one another—a tonic negative feeling, and yet a desire for empathetic connection with others that will be experienced positively when fulfilled (Panksepp (1998) makes this argument from the neuroscientific perspective). Some sad music, rather than (or in addition to) inducing the tonic negative feeling, may instead (or

also) answer this yearning for communion by functioning as a 'prosthetic empathizer.' (On the related notion of prosthetic memory, see Landsberg, 2004.)

6. The melody itself is repetitive at the four-measure level as well, yielding what is called 'sentence structure' across the a and b phrases of each 24-bar period. This level of repetition is not indicated in Figure 5.5.
7. Ravel's Bolero is another familiar example of a 'written-out crescendo'—a musical texture that grows in apparent size not merely because of written indications (such as cresc.), but because of the addition of instruments, growth in pitch range, intensification of rhythmic patterning, and so on.
8. By way of comparison, consider the King's first speech, at the racetrack, which is led into by a very tangibly unresolved V chord (0:03:24–0:03:56 on the DVD). The irresolution at this moment heightens the sense of the audience's anticipation of a masterful performance. As it becomes clear that the speaker cannot in fact perform, a tonic chord does eventually arrive—but this time it is a rather disappointed minor tonic chord, rather than the anticipated, majestic major (0:04:11–0:05:17).
9. Director Tom Hooper corroborates this interpretation in the accompanying 'Feature Commentary' on the DVD: 'And here [*c.*1:43:34] the camera really starts to move for the first time consistently in the film. I wanted after all those shots where the camera is locked down, I wanted to give this flow, [to] put Bertie in the center of it. A lot of his close-ups are still static, because he's still in that struggle, but there's this fluidity when you go outside' (1:43:34–1:43:55).
10. Hooper's commentary again corroborates the interpretation: 'The whole idea of Geoffrey [i.e., Lionel] conducting and mouthing help to Colin [i.e., Bertie] really evolved like this, really evolved as we were shooting it… We didn't even find that idea in rehearsal… Geoffrey did a couple of things and I thought, 'Well that really helps,' and I really pushed him to do more, and the scene developed this wonderful shape of Geoffrey initially very involved in Colin's performance and then eventually just stopping to watch' ('Feature Commentary,' 1:44:13–1:44:41).

References

Barber, S. (1939). *Adagio for strings, op. 11.* New York, NY: G. Schirmer, Inc.

Bashwiner, D. M. (2010). *Musical emotion: Toward a biologically grounded theory.* (Doctoral dissertation.) Retrieved from ProQuest Dissertations and Theses A&I (Order No. 3408503).

Baumgartner, T., Esslen, M., and Jäncke, L. (2006). From emotion perception to emotion experience: Emotions evoked by pictures and classical music. *International Journal of Psychophysiology, 60*, 34–43.

Beethoven, L. v. (1811–1812/1989). Symphony no. 7 in A major, op. 92. *Allegretto*, pp. 198–201. In *Symphonies nos. 5, 6 and 7 in full score.* New York, NY: Dover Publications, Inc.

Bigand, E. (1993). The influence of implicit harmony, rhythm and musical training on the abstraction of 'tension-relaxation schemas' in tonal musical phrases. *Contemporary Music Review, 9*(1&2), 123–137.

Bispham, J. C. (2010). Music's 'design features': Musical motivation, musical pulse, and musical pitch. *Musicae Scientiae: Music and Evolution, (Special Issue 2009–2010)*, 41–62.

Boltz, M. G. (2001). Musical soundtracks as a schematic influence on the cognitive processing of filmed events. *Music Perception, 18*(4), 427–454.

Buhler, J., Neumeyer, D., & Deemer, R. (2009). *Hearing the movies: Music and sound in film history.* Oxford, UK: Oxford University Press.

Canning, I., Sherman, E., Unwin, G. (Producers), & Hooper, T. (Director). (2010). *The King's Speech* [Motion picture]. UK: See-Saw Films.

Clarke, E. (1989). Mind the gap: Formal structures and psychological processes in music. *Contemporary Music Review, 3*, 1–13.

Clarke, E., & Cook, N. (2004). *Empirical musicology: Aims, methods, prospects.* Oxford, UK: Oxford University Press.

Clayton, M., Sager, R., & Will, U. (2004). In time with the music: The concept of entrainment and its significance for ethnomusicology. *ESEM Counterpoint, 1*, 1–45.

Cohen, A. J. (2010). Music as a source of emotion in film. In P. N. Juslin & J. A. Sloboda (Eds.), *Handbook of music and emotion: Theory, research, applications* (pp. 879–908). Oxford, UK: Oxford University Press.

Cohn, R. (1992). Review: *The listening composer* by George Perle. *Music Theory Spectrum, 14*(1), 103–108.

Cook, N. (1994). Perception: A perspective from music theory. In R. Aiello with J. Sloboda (Eds.), *Musical Perceptions* (pp. 64–96). New York, NY: Oxford University Press.

Cross, I. (1998). Musical analysis and musical perception. *Music Analysis, 17*(1), 3–20.

Eich, E., & Metcalf, J. (1989). Mood dependent memory for internal versus external events. *Journal of Experimental Psychology: Learning, Memory, and Cognition, 15*(3), 443–455.

Gabrielsson, A., & Lindström, E. (2010). The role of structure in the musical expression of emotions. In P. N. Juslin & J. A. Sloboda (Eds.), *Handbook of music and emotion: Theory, research, applications* (pp. 367–400). Oxford, UK: Oxford University Press.

Gardiner, J. E. (1994). *Beethoven: 9 symphonies.* Performed with the Orchestre Révolutionnaire et Romantique. Hamburg: Deutsche Grammophon, GmbH.

Gerdingen, R. (1999). An experimental music theory? In N. Cook and M. Everest (Eds.), *Rethinking Music* (Vol. 2, pp. 161–170). Oxford, UK: Oxford University Press.

Gomez, P., & Danuser, B. (2004). Affective and physiological responses to environmental noises and music. *International Journal of Psychophysiology, 53*, 91–103.

Gomez, P., & Danuser, B. (2007). Relationships between musical structure and psychophysiological measures of emotion. *Emotion, 7*(2), 377–387.

Heinlein, C. P. (1928). The affective characters of the major and minor modes in music. *Journal of Comparative Psychology, 8*, 101–142.

Hevner. K. (1935). The affective character of the major and minor modes in music. *The American Journal of Psychology, 47*(1), 103–118.

Hevner, K. (1936). Experimental studies of the elements of expression in music. *American Journal of Psychology, 48*, 246–268.

Hevner, K. (1937). The affective value of pitch and tempo in music. *The American Journal of Psychology, 49*(4), 621–630.

Hoeckner, B., Wyatt, E. W., Decety, J., & Nusbaum, H. (2011). Film music influences how viewers relate to movie characters. *Psychology of Aesthetics, Creativity, and the Arts, 5*(2), 146–153.

Holleran, S. (2012, January 9). Interviews: Alexandre Desplat on *The King's Speech.* Retrieved from <http://www.scottholleran.com/writings/hello-world-2/>

Hooper, T. (2011). Feature commentary to *The King's Speech.* [DVD commentary]. UK: See-Saw Films.

Juslin, P. N., & Sloboda, J. A. (2010a). Introduction: Aims, organization, and terminology. In P. N. Juslin and J. A. Sloboda (Eds.), *Handbook of music and emotion: Theory, research, applications* (pp. 3–14). Oxford, UK: Oxford University Press.

Juslin, P. N. & Sloboda, J. A. (Eds.) (2010b). *Handbook of music and emotion: Theory, research, applications*. Oxford: Oxford University Press.

Karl, G., & Robinson, J. (1995). Shostakovich's Tenth Symphony and the musical expression of cognitively complex emotions. *Journal of Aesthetics and Art Criticism, 53*(4), 401–15.

Karajan, H. von. (1960). *Beethoven: Symphony no. 7 & Haydn: Symphony no. 104*. Performed with the Vienna Philharmonic. Decca Music Group Limited.

Kivy, P. (1980). *The corded shell: Reflections on musical expression*. Princeton, NJ: Princeton University Press.

Koelsch, S., Gunter, T., Friederici, A. D., & Schröger, E. (2000). Brain indices of musical processing: 'Nonmusicians' are musical. *Journal of Cognitive Neuroscience, 12*, 520–541.

Kopelson, A. (Producer) & Stone, O. (Director). (1986/2006). *Platoon* [Motion picture]. 20th Anniversary Edition. Culver City, CA: MGM. Publisher No. 14487.

Krumhansl, C. L. (1995). Music psychology and music theory: Problems and prospects. *Music Theory Spectrum, 17*(1), 53–80.

Krumhansl, C. L. (1997). An exploratory study of musical emotions and psychophysiology. *Canadian Journal of Experimental Psychology, 51*(4), 336–352.

Krumhansl, C. L., & Schenck, D. L. (1997). Can dance reflect the structural and expressive qualities of music? A perceptual experiment on Balanchine's choreography of Mozart's Divertimento No. 15. *Musicae Scientiae, 1*(1), 63–85.

Krumhansl, C. L., & Shepard, R. N. (1979). Quantification of the hierarchy of tonal functions within a diatonic context. *Journal of Experimental Psychology: Human Perception and Performance, 5*(4), 579–594.

Landsberg, A. (2004). Prosthetic memory. In *Prosthetic Memory* (pp. 25–48). New York, NY: Columbia University Press.

Lerdahl, F. (2001). *Tonal Pitch Space*. Oxford, UK: Oxford University Press.

Lerdahl, F. & Krumhansl, C. L. (2007). Modeling tonal tension. *Music Perception, 24*(4), 329–366.

Levinson, J. (1997). Music and negative emotion. In J. Robinson (Ed.), *Music and Meaning* (pp. 215–241). Ithaca, NY: Cornell University Press.

Lewin, D. (1986). Music theory, phenomenology, and modes of perception. *Music Perception, 3*(4), 327–392.

Morrow, J., & Nolan-Hoeksema, S. (1990). Effects of responses to depression on the remediation of repressive affect. *Journal of Personality and Social Psychology, 58*(3), 519–527.

Nawrot, E. S. (2003). The perception of emotional expression in music: Evidence from infants, children and adults. *Psychology of Music, 31*(1), 75–92.

Overy, K., & Molnar-Szakacs, I. (2009). Being together in time: Musical experience and the mirror neuron system. *Music Perception, 26*(5), 489–504.

Panksepp, J. (1998). *Affective neuroscience: The foundations of human and animal emotions*. Oxford, UK: Oxford University Press.

Russell, J. A. (1980). A circumplex model of affect. *Journal of Personality and Social Psychology, 39*, 1161–1178.

Scherer, K. (2004). Which emotions can be induced by music? What are the underlying mechanisms? And how can we measure them?' *Journal of New Music Research, 33*(3), 239–251.

Scherer, K., & Zentner, M. (2001). Emotional effects of music: Production rules. In P. N. Juslin & J. A. Sloboda (Eds.), *Music and Emotion: Theory and Research* (pp. 361–392). Oxford, UK: Oxford University Press.

Schmidt, E. M. (2011, January 30). Beethoven's Symphony no. 7 and 'The King's Speech.' *THOnline.com*. Retrieved from <http://www.thonline.com/article.cfm?id=310074> (accessed April 29, 2011).

Schwarzbaum, L. (2011, February 1). The director of 'The King's Speech' owes his DGA award to two other guys. *Inside Movies*. Retrieved from <http://insidemovies.ew.com/2011/02/01/kings-speech-tom-hooper-dga-award/> (accessed April 27, 2011).

Stabler, D. (2011, January 17). Beethoven's music in 'The King's Speech' a magical match. *OregonLive.com*. Retrieved from <http://www.oregonlive.com/performance/index.ssf/2011/01/beethovens_music_in_the_kings.html> (accessed April 29, 2011).

Tennstedt, K. (1999). *The Philadelphia Orchestra 1900–2000*. Philadelphia Orchestra Centennial Collection, POA100–4.

Walsh, S. (1984). Music analysis: Hearing is believing? *Music Perception*, *2*(2), 237–244.

Zarlino, G. (1558/1983). *On the modes: Part four of* Le istitutioni harmonische, 1558. (C. V. Palisca, Ed. & V. Cohen, trans.). New Haven, CT: Yale University Press.

Chapter 6

Emotion and music in narrative films: A neuroscientific perspective

Lars Kuchinke,[a,b] Hermann Kappelhoff,[a] and Stefan Koelsch[a]

[a]Freie Universität Berlin, Germany
[b]Ruhr-Universität Bochum, Germany

Reflecting on the role of music in film, composer Kurt Weill once said: 'The men who make our movies are well aware of…how much the score helps to "warm up" the action of the picture, to heighten the emotional impact …. They know that a good melody will move an audience when the words or the acting don't succeed' (1946, p. 257). Writing these sentences many decades ago, Weill remained skeptical about the working process and the pressure put on music composers in the film industry, but at the same time he admired the knowledge and work of the composers in developing and integrating an audiovisual composition that can stir an audience.

This chapter will explore our recent knowledge of how (film) music modulates affective responses to films and their most probable neural basis. Is there experimental and neuroscientific evidence for a proposed visual dominance in processing of multi-modal information, and how does the relationship between film and film music change when it comes to emotion-eliciting film scenes? We will explore neuroscientific studies on music, film, and film music based on recent developments in brain imaging methods and attempt to incorporate these findings in a coherent theoretical picture. A theoretical starting point is the question of the relationship between visual images and music in audiovisual communication of emotions.

The extent to which the proposition holds that sound and music properties are subordinate to visual aspects of film remains open to question. Although the development of synchronized sound-film opened the possibility for a composition of visual and sound images into an audiovisual unity, film-makers and theorists have mainly relied on the idea that sound helps to interpret the visual narrative, but the visual modality dominates in the reception of narrative structures (see Vitouch, 2001). In contrast, early Russian film director Sergei Eisenstein revealed, while experimenting with a montage of audio and visual aspects of film, that the 'two film pieces, of any kind, placed together, inevitably combine into a new concept, a new quality, arising out of that juxtaposition' (Eisenstein, 1947). Combining visual aspects and sound should according to Eisenstein lead to a common examination of audiovisual montages as unified entities that together modulate the perception and the feelings of the spectators. So what actually is the relationship between visual and sound images, and in particular between visual scenes and their underlying film music? Does one dominate the other in the perception of audiovisual narratives? And what can psychological and neuroscientific research tell us about the relationship?

Cognitive film theory and visual dominance

Over the past 25 years, cognitive film theory has been a dominant theoretical line in film analysis. It focuses on the narrative potential of feature films, examining the formal strategies by which feature films communicate plots. One of the central theoretical assumptions of cognitive film theory states that the essential structure of cinematic narration is the temporal distribution of plot-relevant cues (Bordwell, 1985). This theoretical approach led to the understanding that the perception of temporal coherence as well as temporal progress is shaped by the visual perception of continuity. Accordingly, the *temporal unfolding* of cinematic narration has been equated with continuity editing, i.e., the maintaining of movement directions over a series of shots. Only in relation to this temporal structure, all features of the audiovisual image (e.g., dialogue, facial expression, close ups, or sound events) serve as cues within the respective plot constellation.

Therefore, for a long time film analysis examined the different modalities separately, always starting with the visual features like cuts or camera angles, followed by an analysis of sound features and film music (Lissa, 1965). On the other hand, film theory includes several theoretical approaches that do not separate visual and sound features in regard to cinematic experience in general or the aesthetic organization of space, time or movement in particular (Deleuze 1985; Eisenstein 1947; Münsterberg, 1916/1996; also Kappelhoff, 2004). In this context Chion (1994) has provided a theory aiming explicitly at a holistic approach to the audiovisual image. He states that the analytical separation of image and sound is arbitrarily taking into consideration a unifying effect of audiovisual perception called synchresis. This theoretical assumption is supported by experimental studies within the field of psychology that hint at a respective salient feature matching mechanism (e.g., Fujisaki & Nishida, 2007). Nevertheless none of these holistic approaches has yet been elaborated into a model guiding film analytical research.

In film analysis the juxtaposition of the visual and the auditory image is sometimes solved by a common discussion of both aspects regarding the effects film has for the affective and aesthetic responses in the spectator/listener, and regarding an understanding of the dramatic and cinematic narrative (Lepa & Floto, 2005). This is counterintuitive, given that an ideal relationship between visual scenes and music may best be described as a symbiosis (Bullerjahn, 2001; Lipscomb & Kendall, 1994) or a synthesis (Lissa, 1965) of the two. Still, and in contrast to the empirical findings (e.g., Lipscomb & Kendall, 1994), in film analysis the dominance of all visual aspects over music is hardly questioned. Sometimes, this is discussed as being a remainder of silent film making (Lissa, 1965). Scholarly film analysis therefore mainly follows the guidelines of classical film-makers, in which the primary goal is the depiction of a visual story, along with textual elements like dialogue or voice-over (Boltz, 2004; Bordwell, 1985; Bordwell & Thompson, 1993).

Within film analytical approaches to the elicitation of emotions, the perspective on film music varies. One of the most influential concepts has been Tan's model of fiction emotions and artifact emotions (Tan, 1996), which we outline briefly. Adopting Frijda's object- and goal-related understanding of emotions (Frijda, 1986, 1987), Tan concludes that genuine emotional involvement in feature films derives from the spectator's sympathetic alignment with the goals of fictional characters. Thus he identifies dynamic appraisals of plot constellations as the spectator's main source of emotions, calling them fiction emotions. For Tan, formal and aesthetic aspects of the cinematic staging, the *mise-en-scène*, only evoke emotions as objects of aesthetic appraisals of the film as an artifact, hence calling them 'artifact emotions.'

Considering this, it is obvious that Tan's (1996) approach to film and emotions even strengthens the separation of image and sound and the corresponding accentuation of the visual. While film music can still provide a source of plot-relevant cues within the various theories of cinematic narration provided by cognitive film studies, the cognitive film studies approach to the cinematic elicitation of emotions mainly reduces film music to an object of emotions of its own that does not interfere with the emotions connected to the process of following an audiovisual narrative. In this regard, Tan's work can be seen as representative, and central works within this line of research adopt his focus on fictional characters as objects of spectator's emotions (Grodal, 1997, 2009; Plantinga 2009).

An alternative analytical perspective on film and emotions has been conceptualized by Smith (2003). His mood cue approach loosens the connection between fictional characters and spectator's emotions. According to Smith, feature films are able to elicit specific emotions across individuals highly varying in dispositions due to an orienting nature of moods. Thus, the redundant perception of emotionally coherent cues (e.g., vocalizations, facial expression, actions, sound events) leads to the emergence of a certain mood that, in return, reinforces the perception of cues coherent with that mood. Implicitly questioning the dominance of visual features, this approach offers a film theoretical perspective on how film music can modulate the emotional experience of audiovisual fiction.

On the other hand, it highlights the fact that an empirical approach to the relation of visual and sound processing in feature films is highly dependent on film analytical methods that do not only focus on the spectator's understanding of narratives, but instead aim at cinematic principles of organizing audiovisual perception (Kappelhoff & Müller, 2011). For example, the eMAEX (electronically based media analysis of expressional movement images) system has been developed recently as a holistic analytical tool that allows for exploring the audiovisual shaping of emotion in film and its temporal dynamics (Kappelhoff & Bakels, 2011). The system combines a standardized approach to film analysis with a Web-based infrastructure that aims at the systematic management of audiovisual data, analytical data and multimedia publishing (see Figure 6.1). Thus, eMAEX offers media scholars and fellow researchers a database on audiovisual media, including audiovisual material (clips taken from feature films, TV news, etc.), systematic descriptions of compositional features and strategies as well as

Figure 6.1 Screenshot of the eMAEX system. eMAEX is a standardized approach to film analysis built on a Web-based infrastructure to examine the dramaturgical and compositional bases of affective experience. The database, as it was developed for the war film genre, works on three interlinked levels of temporal organization: (1) the film defined as a temporal arrangement of genre-specific pathos scenes, (2) the pathos scene as a temporal dynamic of expressive movement units, (3) these expressive movement units as audiovisual patterns. Depicted is a screenshot of the Web-page presenting a film clip of an expressive movement unit together with its analytical description. The film used is *Gung Ho!* (1943) produced by Walter Wanger and directed by Ray Enright (Universal Pictures). (For more information on eMAEX see <http://www.empirische-medienaesthetik.fu-berlin.de/en/emaex-system/emaex_kurzversion>.)

meta data on the audiovisual material presented. With the help of eMAEX it is possible to examine the dramaturgical and compositional bases of affective experiences and their dynamic unfolding in the spectator at the different levels of temporal organization of film that can be taken as starting points for further examination or empirical studies.

On the relationship between visual and auditory information

On a theoretical level, visual dominance is supported by psychological principles of an attention and processing primacy of visual aspects. In psychology, for example, a juxtaposition of visual and auditory processing has been observed to modulate lower-level attentional processes, whereas interactions of both are discussed to occur at higher-order, meaning-related cognitive processing. On the basis of experimental data, Posner, Nissen, and Klein (1976) proposed that *visual dominance* arises from the weak capability of the visual system to both alert and sustain attention. Humans are visual animals in that our thinking, but also our expressions, mainly rely on the visual modality. Accordingly, visual dominance is usually the case in everyday life. This dominance of visual details to capture attention may therefore result in an overall perception and memory advantage for visual stimuli (Posner et al., 1976). Similarly, the McGurk effect shows that this visual dominance is also evident in the processing of bimodal audiovisual stimuli (McGurk & MacDonald, 1976). McGurk and MacDonald (1976) observed that the perception of faces in movement modulates speech perception dramatically. In the case that auditory and visual information do not match, the perception of such articulation can even change what we hear. (See Lipscomb, Chapter 9, in this volume for further discussion.)

A discrimination between the effects of visual and auditory processing is further supported by longstanding theories of working memory (Baddeley, 2003; Baddeley & Hitch, 1974) that distinguish between a visual-spatial and an auditory-verbal subsystem specialized for the respective type of input modality. This model of working memory has had huge influence in psychology, and it may have led to a further substantiation of the existence of a visual dominance in processing and the acceptance of this in film theorists. However, the theory itself has been challenged by newer proposals of multisensory working memories that do not overstress the separation of the two processing streams (e.g., Cowan, 1999). Accordingly, for example, Baddeley introduced an episodic buffer in his model (Baddeley, 2000, 2003) as a multisensory hub that integrates representations from the subsystems and operates as a global modality-independent workspace with close connections to long-term memory.

More recent developments have placed the verbal subsystem closer to auditory- and motor-based processing (Hickok & Poeppel, 2000, 2003). Hickok and Poeppel (2003) propose a dorsal (from the Latin for 'toward the back,' i.e., superior) auditory processing stream, which in a manner analogous to that of the dorsal visual processing stream is responsible for auditory-motor integration. The authors list music abilities as one major function of stream. Accordingly, this model of speech perception and related language functions was supported by a functional neuroimaging study that revealed common brain activations for music and language (Hickok, Buchsbaum, Humphries, & Muftuler, 2003; also Koelsch, 2011). The authors showed that speech and music, or in particular working memory for speech and music, share highly overlapping neural bases along the left planum temporale, the temporal-parietal boundary area in the brain in posterior regions of the *superior temporal sulcus* (STS, see Figure 6.2).

The notion of a general visual dominance in perception has recently been challenged by more recent examinations of the *Colavita effect* (Colavita, 1974). In the original study by Colavita, when presented with simple unimodal auditory (a tone), unimodal visual (a light), or bimodal audiovisual stimuli (light and tone together), participants fail to respond to the auditory stimulus under bimodal conditions where both stimuli have a comparable (subjective) intensity—but also if the tone is twice as loud as the intensity of the light. This effect has often been replicated and has also been extended

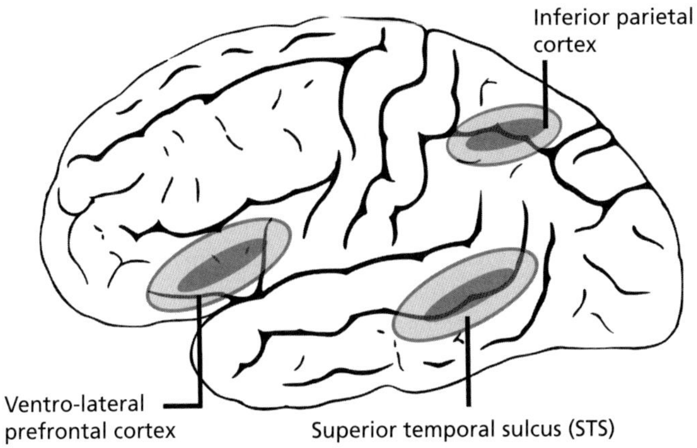

Figure 6.2 Multisensory regions in the human cortex. Appropriate location of the multisensory processing regions in the left hemisphere of the human cortex. Multisensory audiovisual regions have been identified in the ventrolateral prefrontal cortex, the inferior parietal cortex, and the posterior part of the superior temporal sulcus (STS) extending into the temporo-parietal boundary region. Reprinted from *Anatomy of the Human Body*, 20th U.S. edition, Gray, H., The brain or encephalon, pp. 766–819, © (1918), with permission from Elsevier.

to more complex stimulation conditions (Sinnett, Spence, & Soto-Faraco, 2007). It is therefore taken as strong evidence for the visual dominance. For example, Koppen and Spence (2007) were able to show that in a manner analogous to the Posner explanation given earlier, the Colavita effect is partially explained by the exogenous attention capturing qualities of the visual stimuli. In their study, the Colavita visual dominance effect was increased when a task-irrelevant and highly discriminable visual but not an auditory prime stimulus preceded the bimodal stimulus (experiment 4 in Koppen & Spence, 2007). Thus, attention directed to visual modality increased the Colavita effect for concurrently presented bimodal stimuli. Hence, visual primes seem to attract attention and to facilitate the processing of the visual aspects of the bimodal stimulus whereas auditory primes do not show such a processing advantage. But it is important to note that recent research also revealed that the Colavita effect is modulated by temporo-spatial congruency (see Spence, 2009) and by task effects. For example, Sinnett, Spence and Soto-Faraco (2007) show that when participants are forced to pay attention to the auditory stimulus modality, the visual dominance effect can be diminished. That is, the visual dominance effect was found to be enhanced when the authors reduced the perceptual load in the visual modality to free up available visual processing resources by simply reducing the number of unimodal visual distractor stimuli. The reverse effect was observed in a reduced auditory perceptual load condition. Again, these results support the assumption of attention capturing capabilities of the visual modality that are expected to be higher with fewer distracting visual stimuli.

A more recent functional neuroimaging study adds another piece to this puzzle: Schmid and colleagues revealed that the visual dominance in their study depended on whether participants focus on the competing modality (Schmid, Büchel, & Rose, 2011). Schmid et al. (2011) used neutral photographs and environmental sounds of 2 seconds' length in their study. Although visual dominance was expressed in a clear behavioral advantage for visual over auditory object memory, it originated only from conditions in which the attentional focus was located on the competing modality. Differences in brain activation were associated in this study with differences at encoding in auditory (STS) or visual (lateral occipital complex, LOC) processing regions in the brain. Importantly, these activations mirrored the behavioral effect in that auditory processing was susceptible to attention shifts in the case of a competing stimulus modality, but not that 'auditory processing is [...] generally inferior to visual processing' (Schmid et al., 2011, p. 309). It seems that, in the auditory processing regions, competition for attention was increased due to the parallel processing of a visual object. Accordingly, based on their functional neuroimaging results in a cross-modal auditory-visual processing study, Johnson and Zatorre (2006) propose that cross-modal attentional effects may simply reveal that the processing of one modality is enhanced at the expense of the other. This study revealed that while participants simultaneously processed visual shapes and unknown melodies, selective attention to one modality specifically enhanced activity in the sensory processing region of that modality to the expense of activity in the sensory processing regions of the other modality.

Given the nature of these experiments and the static visual stimuli used therein one has to note that the results are only generalizable for object recognition, a direct transfer to film and film music is speculative at this time (but see the McGurk effect, McGurk & MacDonald, 1976). While the research on visual dominance and the theoretical separation of the visual and the auditory processing streams might have substantiated the visual dominance hypothesis, other recent results strengthen the role of multisensory processing in which no one sense dominates. As explained earlier, the physiological separation of both modalities in different processing streams has mainly led to the suggestion that an interaction occurs at later meaning-related processing stages.

But an interaction between the visual and auditory modality has been observed at early pre-conscious processing stages too (Meredith & Stein, 1983; Musacchia, Sams, Skoe, & Kraus, 2006). Musacchia and colleagues (2006) measured electrophysiological brainstem potentials and revealed that the visual perception of an articulation of a syllable delays the brainstem response to the speech stimulus. The effect occurred as early as 11 milliseconds following the onset of the auditory stimulus. Similarly, in cats (Meredith & Stein, 1983) as well as in non-human primates (Wallace, Wilkinson, & Stein, 1996), cells in the *superior colliculus* (see Figure 6.3C) have been identified that respond to both modalities, suggesting a true integration of multisensory information at the neural level (Wallace, Wilkinson, & Stein, 1996; for a review see Stein & Standford, 2008). The superior colliculus is a midbrain structure which controls changes in orientation and eye movements and seems to act as one of the earliest integration mechanisms that sums activation from the different modalities located within the visual processing pathway but before object recognition takes place (Stein & Standford, 2008). It is notable here that the superior colliculus has also been indicated as implicated in the elicitation of emotions. Via its synaptic connections, the superior

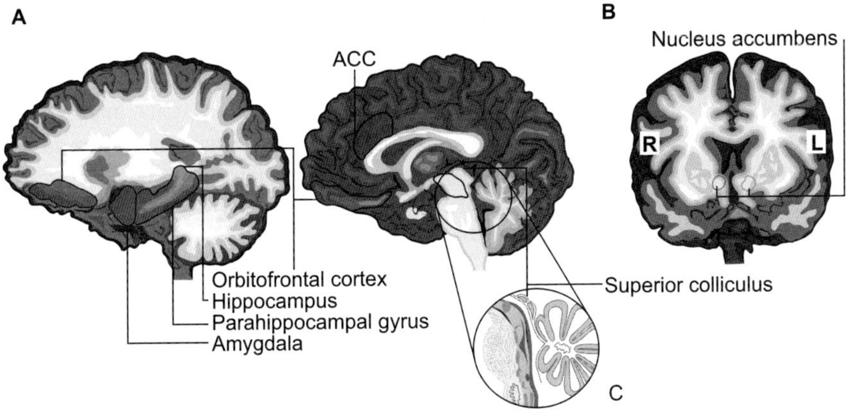

Figure 6.3 Limbic and paralimbic regions, and the superior colliculus. Illustration of brain regions belonging to the limbic/paralimbic emotion processing system. (A) lateral view of the right hemisphere; (B) anterior view; (C) location of the superior colliculus (SC) in the human mid-brain. The SC is a first hub in the visual processing stream and has interconnections to the primary visual areas in the occipital lobe, as well as connections to multisensory processing regions in the ventrolateral prefrontal cortex, the superior temporal sulcus, and the inferior parietal cortex (depicted in Figure 6.2). Part A and B are modified from a figure that was published in *Trends in Cognitive Sciences*, 14(3), Koelsch, S., Towards a neural basis of music-evoked emotions, pp. 131–137, © Elsevier (2010).

colliculus is directly linked to affective core regions in the brain, namely the amygdala and the limbic system (Linke, Lima, Schwegler, & Pape, 1999). Thus, the superior colliculus is seen as a pivotal part of the low route that supports fast and unconscious emotion processing (LeDoux, 1996; Morris, Öhmann, & Dolan, 1999).

Accordingly, further brain regions have been identified in non-human primates and humans to support multi-modal integration (Stein & Standford, 2008; see Figure 6.2) including the STS and inferior parietal and ventrolateral prefrontal cortices. These latter regions should be considered as supporting integration after stimulus identification and are therefore more closely related to semantic processing. The STS, for example, is also discussed to support cognitive empathy, that is, the following and understanding of the intentions of others (Frith & Frith, 2003; Hein & Singer, 2008). In sum, neuroscientific evidence exists for both early sensory integration and late meaning-related processing of (simple) audiovisual stimuli, which seems to indicate the existence of a highly interacting and overlapping processing network for complex, multi-modal stimuli.

Besides a visual dominance or a highly interacting processing system of audiovisual information, a third possibility shall be introduced shortly, which will enable us to examine the relationship between film and film music in more detail. As already explained, visual dominance may not hold for every processing situation. Accordingly, Collignon and colleagues have shown that, in emotional contexts, auditory information may be processed primarily (Collignon et al., 2008). In their study, participants were asked to judge the emotionality of short video clips portraying either unimodal fearful or disgusted faces or non-verbal voice sounds or displaying congruent or incongruent bimodal face-sound stimuli. As a second experimental factor, visual images were blurred and noise was added to the sound stimuli. For the evaluation of the bimodal stimuli, a visual dominance was only observable for the unblurred bimodal stimuli. In cases of blurred visual information participants favored the auditory modality. Thus, an *auditory dominance* was observed for the affective evaluation of difficult-to-process fearful and disgust stimuli.

Similar effects are also known from picture processing, where behavioral and functional neuroimaging data indicate an enhancement of emotional processing of affective pictures due to underlying classical music excerpts of sad and fearful music (e.g., Baumgartner, Lutz, Schmidt, & Jäncke, 2006). Correspondingly, brain activations in Baumgartner et al. (2006) were stronger during the combined presentation of affective pictures and music than during the presentation of the pictures alone in regions that are discussed to support affective processing, e.g., amygdala and the hippocampus (see Figure 6.3A). The fact that auditory information enhanced the emotional responses contradicts the context-independent assumption of a visual dominance.

Though not directly comparable, a study by Rickard (2004) may be taken as further evidence for this hypothesis: Herein, electrodermal responses that are highly linked to emotional arousal were greater for emotionally intense music compared to emotionally intense film clips. Furthermore, Eldar, Ganor, Admon, Bleich, and Hendler (2007) also showed in their functional neuroimaging study that activity changes in response to music in both the amygdala and the hippocampus are considerably stronger when the music is presented simultaneously with film clips (neutral scenes from commercials; positive music was also taken from commercials, and negative music mainly from soundtracks of horror movies). Activity changes in the amygdala and in areas of the ventrolateral frontal cortex (see Figure 6.2) were considerably larger for the combined (film and music) presentation than for the presentation of film clips alone or music alone. In the hippocampus, signal changes were stronger for negative music combined with the film clips. Notably, emotional music on its own did not elicit a differential response in these regions.

Subjective ratings in the study by Eldar et al. (2007) showed that the music plus film conditions were not perceived as significantly more positive or negative than when music was presented alone. Therefore, the functional significance of the increase in signal change (in the amygdala, the hippocampal formation, and the frontal cortex) remains unclear. Interestingly, the findings that the visual system modulates signal changes in the amygdala were corroborated by data showing that simply closing the eyes during listening to fearful music also leads to increased activity in the amygdala (Lerner, Papo, Zhdanov, Belozersky, & Hendler, 2009).

Effects of film music

These interesting results bring us back to the often-discussed proposition that music is a source of emotion in film (Bezdek & Gerrig, 2008; Bullerjahn, 2001; Cohen, 2001; Unz,

Schwab, & Mönch, 2008). Is it possible that sound and music are dominant over visual information in emotional contexts and, therefore, ground the interpretation of the narrative content in emotional circumstances? That is, a main function of film music is seen in the induction or elicitation of emotions (Bullerjahn, 2001, p. 188). Bullerjahn examined the basic principles of the effects of film music and revealed its dramatic, epic, structural, and persuasive functions (Bullerjahn, 2001). Dramatic function is understood as the mapping of emotions and the strengthening of an affective-aesthetic expression in the respective scenes. The epic or narrative function refers to the supporting of the narrative course by film music, when composers interpret and enhance the intention of the film-maker. Its structural function refers to the covering or emphasizing of particular film structures like cuts or single shots or movements. Finally, persuasive functions refer to all effects of film music where affective-empathic responses and the spectators' identification with a protagonist are enhanced.

It is obvious, that the proportion of these four functions of film music may vary depending on the genre (Bullerjahn, 2001, p. 69). Film music in a melodrama supports functions other than music in a horror movie, e.g., with regard to the identification with a protagonist. The effects of film music on the interpretation of narratives have been investigated by many researchers. For instance, in a study by Vitouch (2001), two different groups of participants watched the opening sequence of Billy Wilder's *The Lost Weekend* with either its original score or a fake score and afterward were asked to write down possible continuations of the plot. Quantitative analyses revealed that the continuations were systematically biased in their respective emotional content (Vitouch, 2001). Similarly, an earlier study by Bullerjahn, Braun, and Güldenring (1994) revealed that different film music elicits distinct judgments of genre membership and emotionality for the very same film scene. Effects of film music can thus be seen as resulting from a combination of the properties of film music and its relations to other film elements, and the expectations and needs of the film spectator (Bullerjahn, 2001). But film music itself may already elicit genre-specific emotions based on sound nonlinearities. Biologists Blumenstein, Davitian, and Kaye (2010) examined the hypothesis that film music contains specific non-linear features like noise and frequency transitions analogous to nonlinearities in the vocalization of vertebrates under duress (e.g., in fear screams). An examination of 102 films scores representing four different genres confirmed this hypothesis and revealed a genre-specific use of the different types of non-linearities in the film music.

Some empirical studies that examined the relationship between film music and affective responses mainly supported the idea of dominance of the auditory domain. Accordingly, media psychologists Unz, Schwab, and Mönch (2008) propose the following effects of film music on affective responses of the audience:

1. Polarization: genre-specific music moves the emotional perception of a neutral film scene in the emotional sphere of the film music.
2. Additive effect: a paraphrasing audiovisual relation increases the effect of music, both in the film context and in the context of pictures.
3. Auditory dominance: the perceived emotion of a film is more influenced by music than by the behavior of the protagonists.

4. Greater impact of negative emotions: the emotional effects of aggressive film content are less attenuated by positive film music than positive content by aggressive music.

It is suggested that people learn correlations between the frequency and the emotional connotation of musical excerpts and the particular situational narrative content in film (Bezdek & Gerrig, 2008; Boltz, 2004; Bullerjahn, 2001; Vitouch, 2001), and music becomes integrated in memory together with the visual information at a schema level (Cohen, 2005). In her *Congruence-Associationist Model*, Cohen (2001) describes how music, film, and speech are processed at four different levels, starting with unimodal processing at the sensory level, and further higher-order pre-conscious and conscious integrated audiovisual processing steps that provide a structuring of the multi-modal information. The basis of this model lies in the assumption that films generate their dynamic structure through repetition and variations of similar mental processes, such as in music (Cohen, 2005; see also Cohen, Chapter 2, in this volume). In support of this assumption, Goldin and colleagues discovered specific time courses of neural responses related to valence ratings in emotional scenes at different emotional qualities (Goldin et al., 2005).

Such correlations seem to affect the spectators' interpretation of the emotionality of the narrative content (Boltz, 2004; Bullerjahn, 2001; Cohen, 2005); and the characters' emotions, whether the music is presented before or after the film (Tan, Spackman, & Bezdek, 2007). Since the film scenes themselves are neutral in Tan et al.'s study, the music is most probably the only basis that guides spectators' interpretations of the character's emotion. Accordingly, these effects are observed when emotional music was combined with neutral film clips. This relationship reveals modulatory influences of music upon the cognitive processing of visual scenes (Boltz, 2001). Still, an examination of music effects on the interpretation of film scenes that explicitly addresses affective content is lacking.

A neuroscientific perspective on music, film, and film music

Functional neuroimaging and lesion studies have shown that music-evoked emotions can modulate activity in virtually all limbic and paralimbic brain structures, that is, in the core structures responsible for the generation of emotions (reviewed in Koelsch, 2010, see Figure 6.3A). With regard to the amygdala and the (anterior) hippocampal formation, functional neuroimaging has shown involvement of these structures in emotional responses to music, correlating with: (1) music-evoked chills (Blood & Zatorre, 2001), (2) pleasantness/unpleasantness (Koelsch, Fritz, von Cramon, Müller, & Friederici, 2006), (3) joy as well as fear (Eldar et al., 2007), and (4) sadness and fear (Baumgartner et al., 2006). Whereas these studies mainly use simple and short musical excerpts to examine the neural correlates of music and emotion, new technical advances in neuroscientific methods enable researchers to study the 'multitude of musical features' in more naturalistic pieces of music (Alluri et al., 2012). An advantage of this study is that the authors presented a piece of music of 8 minutes' length with a rich musical structure to examine the neural responses to music. The data analysis explored intersubject correlations in the neural activity, i.e., patterns of combined spatial and temporal similarities in the neural responses across different subjects. Furthermore, multivariate correlations were computed that revealed associations between automatically extracted perceivable features of music such as timbre and musical pulse and brain responses. The results clearly point to activations of the same cortical and subcortical cognitive, motor and emotion-related circuits being activated under such more naturalistic listening conditions.

Moreover, several studies (Blood & Zatorre, 2001; Brown, Martinez, & Parsons, 2004; Janata, 2009; Koelsch et al., 2006; Menon & Levitin, 2005; Salimpoor, Benovoy, Larcher, Dagher, & Zatorre, 2011) showed that listening to pleasant music activates brain structures implicated in reward and experiences of pleasure, particularly the ventral striatum (including the nucleus accumbens, see Figure 6.3B). One of these studies (Menon & Levitin, 2005) reported that activation of the ventral striatum was connected to activity in the ventral tegmental area and the hypothalamus. This suggests that the signal changes observed in the ventral striatum reflect the activity of the neurotransmitter dopamine, as part of the so-called 'reward circuit.' These results are consistent with findings from Salimpoor et al. (2011) showing decreased exogenous dopamine binding in the ventral striatum during music-evoked 'chills' as evidence of higher levels of endogenous dopamine transmission.

Importantly, activity in the nucleus accumbens correlates with motivation- and reward-related experiences of pleasure; for instance, during the process of obtaining a goal, when an unexpected reachable incentive is encountered, or when individuals are presented with a reward cue. In humans, nucleus accumbens activity has been reported, e.g., for sexual activity, intake of drugs, eating of chocolate, and drinking water when dehydrated (reviewed in Berridge, Robinson, & Aldridge, 2009; Nicola, 2007). It is interesting to note that in three of the mentioned studies (Brown et al., 2004; Koelsch et al., 2006; Menon & Levitin, 2005) participants did not report chill responses during music listening, suggesting that dopaminergic pathways including the nucleus accumbens can be activated by music as soon as it is perceived as pleasant (i.e., even in the absence of extreme emotional experiences involving chills).

As such, neuroscientific research on the interplay of film and emotion is still in its infancy. This should, in particular, be attributed to the fact that only in recent years were functional neuroimaging methods developed for the study of temporally extended stimulus events which has led to the foundation of *neurocinematics* (Hasson et al., 2008), an interdisciplinary study of cinema. Functional neuroimaging studies examine either blocks of stimulation as a whole or events of shorter durations of milliseconds up to a few seconds. Thus, due to the development of advanced analytical techniques for functional neuroimaging data and due to the fact that actual hardware has increasing computational power, functional neuroimaging studies have started to focus on the neural basis of watching films (see Spiers & Maguire, 2007, for a review of different analytical approaches).

Functional neuroimaging using film stimuli started with early examinations of neural responses under free viewing conditions that revealed functionally specialized processing in cortical and subcortical brain regions (Bartels & Zeki, 2004a, 2004b). Hasson and Malach (2005) found intersubjective correlations of spatial-temporal patterns of activation during the presentation of dynamic film scenes (for similar approaches see Jääskeläinen et al., 2008; Kauppi, Jääskeläinen, Sams, & Tohka, 2010). Wolf, Dziobek, and Heekeren (2010) monitored brain responses of participants while viewing film scenes, and were able to differentiate, by means of an independent component analysis, the neuronal activation patterns in independent, functionally connected components with differing courses of activation. With the use of these two techniques, independent component analysis and intersubject correlations, the parallel activation of independent brain networks during free viewing can be examined (Hasson, Malach, & Heeger, 2010). However, these earlier studies did not tell us much about specific relations to features of film and its narrative content.

Of note here are three studies that exemplify this new direction. A first study by Hasson and colleagues correlates cortical activation patterns with emotionally arousing scenes and regionally selective components (Hasson, Nir, Levy, Fuhrmann, & Malach, 2004). In doing so, they were able to show that, for example, the time course of intersubject correlation in a cortical face processing region, the fusiform face area, significantly varied depending on whether the stimulus film scene showed faces or not. In contrast to this, the intersubject correlation time course in a building-related cortical region, the parahippocampal place, was significantly higher when the film scene depicted places and buildings (Hasson et al., 2004). In the second study, Zacks, Speer, Swallow, and Maley (2010) let their participants identify fine and coarse segments in the event structure of a 10-minute film. Segment boundaries were defined by six types of situation changes in film, e.g., a spatial change was defined as a change in movement of a character or a change in the cameras' point of view (Zacks et al., 2010; see also Zacks et al., 2001). This event segmentation information was used in the following functional neuroimaging study to identify brain responses to such event boundaries. In the third study, Bartels and colleagues examined the neural responses of local and global motion changes that were mainly processed in early visual areas in the brain (Bartels, Zeki, & Logothetis, 2008). As such these three studies represent the current state of the art of functional neuroimaging studies of watching films and should be taken as first steps into a deeper examination of (internal) film structures. At the same time, these studies reveal that recent examinations rely on rather quantitative objective structures of films and that we are still quite far from an understanding of the unfolding of the narrative structure and its relation to emotional responses and their probable modulation by film music at a neural level.

Only a few functional neuroimaging studies have examined emotional aspects and still fewer have examined music. The earlier-mentioned study by Eldar et al. (2007) investigated the interplay of emotional music with neutral film scenes. When either positive (joyful) or negative (fearful) music was superimposed on short neutral film clips of 12 seconds each, stronger signal changes were observed in the amygdala, and in areas of the ventrolateral frontal cortex, compared to when music or film clips were presented alone. Film clips presented with negative (but not positive) music also elicited higher activations in the anterior hippocampus, a brain region discussed to support memory encoding and retrieval.

The time courses of emotion elicitation with film stimuli were examined by Goldin et al. (2005). In their study, online ratings of individual joy and sorrow time courses during the presentation of four short 2-minute film clips were included as predictors in their statistical model to predict brain responses. Of interest for the current analysis is that only the two sad film clips contained film music. This approach revealed the expected variations in emotion processing networks including insula and superior temporal regions. Furthermore, superior temporal and amygdala activation significantly covaried with subjective emotion-specific sadness time courses. In a follow-up study, Goldin, McRae, Ramel, and Gross (2008) found evidence for an influence of emotion regulation strategies on separate temporal components of the emotion-elicitation process examined by early, middle, and late components of neural activation during the presentation of emotion-eliciting film clips. Thus, strategy-dependent time courses were revealed in limbic regions, the amygdala, and the insula. These functional neuroimaging studies share the idea to use film stimuli to represent naturalistic settings of perception and of emotion induction. As a result it is shown that it is possible to examine emotional reactions in their dynamic course. But what is still missing are studies that examine the role of aesthetic and affective content, their dynamics, and the composition of an arc of tension of film stimuli. At present, there are no such studies which, for example, correlate micro structures of film and film music defined by the depicted content or based on film theoretical considerations of the emotional and aesthetic organization of space, time, or movement of the audiovisual image with the neural responses elicited.

This seems to result from a lack of interest in cognitive psychological research, where previous empirical studies of emotional films usually focused on the use of film material to induce emotions. There are different approaches to reliably induce emotions by the use of film scenes, and meta-analyses indicate that film scenes are one of the most effective methods to induce emotion (Westermann, Spies, Stahl, & Hesse, 1996). Gross and Levenson (1995) have created a standardized film stimulus database composed of 16 clips that reliably elicits eight discrete emotions (see also Hewig et al., 2005; Rottenberg, Ray, & Gross, 2007). Of these clips only six contained music or tone, the two sadness-inducing film clips and the two fear-inducing film clips as well as one surprise clip. Another disgust-inducing clip used a nursery rhyme as a counterpoint. This low proportion of film music in the database is surprising given the earlier discussion on the role of film music. And it would be interesting to see whether the use of film music would increase the reliability of emotion induction and whether such effects occur in a genre-specific manner.

The majority of the published physiological studies on the affect of film also focus on emotion induction and the differentiation of physiological response patterns of the different affective conditions (see Christie & Friedman, 2004; Hagemann et al., 1999; Kreibig, Wilhelm, Roth, & Gross, 2007; Palomba, Sarlo, Angrilli, Mini, & Stegagno, 2000; Montoya, Campos, & Schandry, 2005). Such studies refer to the relevance of physiological responses as a component of emotional reactions, but again tell only a little about the specific characteristics of film that lead to these emotional responses and even less, so far, about the role of music.

Some theoretical notes

While these studies present a clear indication of the appropriateness of film and audiovisual material in emotion induction and the differentiation between specific emotional conditions, there are no further behavioral or neuroscientific studies that address specifically the question of the aesthetic and emotional effects of cinematic material, and the dynamics of their narrative processes.

Scherer (2005) introduced a useful model that established the currently popular view of emotions as a hierarchy of processes or components involved. Emotions here are characterized as 'as an episode of interrelated, synchronized changes in the states of all or most of the five organismic subsystems in response to the evaluation of an external or internal stimulus event as relevant to major concerns of the organism' (Scherer, 2005, p. 697). The five organismic subsystems are information processing, support, executive, action, and monitoring and are highly linked to emotional functions and associated emotional components (Scherer, 2005, table 1). Scherer sets focuses on cognitive appraisal processes, and thus the *Scherer model* sets the stage for a multi-modal examination of emotion production. In particular, emotion in a strict sense is defined by a high 'synchronization of all organismic subsystems, including cognition, during the emotion episode' (Scherer & Zentner, 2001, p. 384).

Moreover, Scherer and Zentner (2001) suggest that, at least in the case of musical emotions (but see Scherer, 1998, for a discussion of other kinds of audiovisual media) empathy may be the relevant precursor for emotional responses to media. In particular, the authors revealed that a main function of music is the production of emotion, rather than its experience. i.e., music does not only trigger emotional experiences itself but it is necessary for producing affective responses via appraisal processes that are related to the music. Appraisal processes, together with motivational aspects and action tendencies (Frijda, 1986) seem an appropriate level of description for an analysis of musical emotions and an analysis of the integration of visual and auditory aspects of film at the level of memory and cognition. But more concrete research is needed. Still the earlier-mentioned functional neuroimaging studies that revealed a synchronized neural network may already point to a strong presence of emotional processes when viewing dynamic audiovisual film scenes.

Affective and aesthetic responses to film as an aesthetic artifact can be determined within the model of aesthetic appreciation and aesthetic judgments (Leder, Belke, Oeberst, & Augustin, 2004). The model evaluates aesthetic judgments and affective-aesthetic responses along five cognitive processing stages: (1) perception, (2) implicit and (3) explicit classification, (4) cognitive mastering, and (5) evaluation. Most importantly, the early mainly automatic processing stages contain novelty checks and familiarity processing that may lead to an initial aesthetic experience, whereas later stages again strengthen the role of (conscious) appraisal processes and evaluations based on meaning-related classifications and cognitive (top-down) mastering to elicit an aesthetic judgment and an aesthetic emotion. Multi-modal integration may be incorporated into this model at the stage of implicit memory integration and at the conscious cognitive mastering processing stages, but no particular view on audiovisual aesthetic artifacts is included yet. Both the Scherer and the Leder model, thus, cover the range of possible audiovisual interactions and have their strengths in the description of a parallel and nested processing along a hierarchy of stages or components.

We would like to shift the theoretical focus somewhat more. To explain the elicitation of emotions by film stimuli, one should further consider psychological concepts of empathy and embodiment, because it seems highly plausible that empathic processes are involved in elicitation of emotions by dynamic and figurative stimuli. Affective empathy is the ability to share the feelings of others, together with the cognitive ability to understand the feelings of others and the ability to sympathetically respond to the feelings of others (Decety & Jackson, 2004). Current theories of empathetic processes emphasize a role of frontal and posterior temporal areas (along the posterior superior temporal sulcus into the plenum temporale) and the insula (Decety, 2011; Hein & Singer, 2008). Embodiment theories, on the other hand, support neuroscientific findings, which show that the same neural structures are involved in the representation of one's own body, as in the perception and representation of other bodies that are perceived. It is assumed that such physical and subjective (experience-based) information facilitates the decoding of emotions and feelings of others (Gallese, 2005). On a cortical level, empathy and embodiment are discussed to rely on simulation processes, like the recruitment of networks that support similar processes as in self-experienced emotions. Thus, internal simulations may be a good starting point for the examination of film-based experiences and the way they are modulated by music. Again, as introduced earlier, this seems to be a functional role of the posterior temporal regions including the STS, which have been discussed as being both a neural basis of simulation (Hein & Singer, 2008) and a multi-modal hub and multi-modal convergence zone, in particular for audiovisual integration (Hickok & Poeppel, 2003).

The focus on empathic processes is also an integral part of current film theories (Smith, 2003) that assume a direct link to the aesthetic quality of expression and the emotional reaction of the audience. Common to both the neophenomenologic film theory (Sobchack, 1992) and the cognitive film theory (Smith, 2003) is the assumption that film scenes impact the audience as a result of their compositions, their montage of auditory and visual aspects, and an emotional arc of tension that develops over time to unfold emotional reactions in the spectators. Given the overlapping neural networks for the processing of multi-modal information and simulation processes previously described and the overall close relationship between film, film music, and emotion, it will be interesting to see how these film theoretical models are developed further and integrated into neuropsychological theories of empathic responding and the appraisal of emotions—specifically focusing on the narration and the affective responses to film and film music.

References

Alluri, V., Toiviainen, P., Jääskeläinen, I. P., Glerean, E., Sams, M., & Brattico, E. (2012). Large-scale brain networks emerge from dynamic processing of musical timbre, key and rhythm. *NeuroImage*, *59*, 3677–3689.

Baddeley, A. D. (2000). The episodic buffer: A new component of working memory? *Trends in Cognitive Sciences*, *4*, 417–423.

Baddeley, A. D. (2003). Working memory: Looking back and looking forward. *Nature Reviews Neuroscience*, *4*, 829–839.

Baddeley, A. D., & Hitch, G. J. (1974). Working memory. In G. Bower (Ed.), *Recent advances in learning and motivation* (Vol. 8, pp. 47–90). New York, NY: Academic Press.

Bartels, A., & Zeki, S. (2004a). The chronoarchitecture of the human brain in natural viewing conditions reveal a time-based anatomy of the brain. *NeuroImage, 22*(1), 419–433.

Bartels, A., & Zeki, S. (2004b). Functional brain mapping during free viewing of natural scenes. *Human Brain Mapping, 21*, 75–83.

Bartels, A., Zeki, S., & Logothetis, N. K. (2008). Natural vision reveals regional specialization to local motion and to contrast-invariant, global flow in the human brain. *Cerebral Cortex, 18*, 705–717.

Baumgartner, T., Lutz, K., Schmidt, C. F., & Jäncke, L. (2006). The emotional power of music: How music enhances the feeling of affective pictures. *Brain Research, 1075*, 151–164.

Berridge, K. C., Robinson, T. E., & Aldridge, J. W. (2009). Dissecting components of reward: "Liking," "wanting," and learning. *Current Opinion in Pharmacology, 9*, 65–73.

Bezdek, M. A., & Gerrig, R. J. (2008). Musical emotions in the context of narrative film. *Behavioral and Brain Sciences, 31*, 578.

Blood, A., & Zatorre, R. J. (2001). Intensely pleasurable responses to music correlate with activity in brain regions implicated in reward and emotion. *Proceedings of the National Academy of Sciences of the United States of America, 98*, 11818–11823.

Blumenstein, D. T., Davitian, R., & Kaye, R. D. (2010). Do film soundtracks contain nonlinear analogues to influence emotion? *Biology Letters, 23*, 751–754.

Boltz, M. G. (2001). Musical soundtracks as a schematic influence on the cognitive processing of filmed events. *Music Perception, 18*, 427–454.

Boltz, M. G. (2004). The cognitive processing of film and musical soundtracks. *Memory & Cognition, 32*, 1194–1205.

Bordwell, D. (1985). *Narration in the fiction film*. Madison, WI: University of Wisconsin Press.

Bordwell, D., & Thompson, K. (1993). *An introduction to film art* (4th ed.). New York, NY: McGraw-Hill.

Brown, S., Martinez, M. J., & Parsons, L. M. (2004). Passive music listening spontaneously engages limbic and paralimbic systems. *NeuroReport, 15*, 2033–2037.

Bullerjahn, C. (2001). *Grundlagen der Wirkung von Filmmusik* [Basics in the effects of film music]. Augsburg, Germany: Wißner-Verlag.

Bullerjahn, C., Braun, U., & Güldenring, M. (1994). *Wie haben Sie den Film gehört? Über Filmmusik als Bedeutungsträger—eine empirische Untersuchung* [How did you hear the movie? About film music as carriers of meaning]. *Musikpsychologie, 10*, 140–158.

Chion, M. (1994). *Audiovision. Sound On Screen.* New York, NY: Columbia University Press.

Christie, I., & Friedman, B. (2004). Autonomic specificity of discrete emotion and dimensions of affective space: A multivariate approach. *International Journal of Psychophysiology, 51*, 143–153.

Cohen, A. J. (2001) Music as a source of emotion in film. In P. N. Juslin and J. A. Sloboda (Eds.), *Music and emotion: Theory and research* (pp. 249–272). New York, NY: Oxford University Press.

Cohen, A. J. (2005). How music influences the interpretation of film and video. Approaches from experimental psychology. In R. A. Kendall & R. W. H. Savage (Eds.), *Selected reports in ethnomusicology: Perspectives in Systematic Musicology, 12*, 15–36.

Colavita, F. B. (1974). Human sensory dominance. *Perception & Psychophysics, 16*, 409–412.

Collignon, O., Girard, S., Gosselin, F., Roy, S., Saint-Amour, D., Lassonde, M., & Lepore, F. (2008). Audio-visual integration of emotion expression. *Brain Research, 1242*, 126–135.

Cowan, N. (1999). An embedded-processes model of working memory. In A. Miyake and P. Shahs (Eds.), *Models of working memory* (pp. 62–101). Cambridge, UK: Cambridge University Press.

Decety, J. (2011). Dissecting the neural mechanisms mediating empathy. *Emotion Review, 3*, 92–108.

Decety, J., & Jackson, P. L. (2004). The functional architecture of human empathy. *Behavioral and Cognitive Neuroscience Reviews, 3*(2), 71–100.

Deleuze, G. (1985). *Das Zeit-Bild. Kino 2* [The time-picture. Cinema 2]. Frankfurt/Main, Germany: Suhrkamp Verlag.

Eisenstein, S. M. (1947). *The film sense*. New York, NY: Harcourt Brace Jovanovich, Publishers.

Eldar, E., Ganor, O., Admon, R., Bleich, A., & Hendler, T. (2007). Feeling the real world: Limbic response to music depends on related content. *Cerebral Cortex, 17*, 2828–2840.

Frijda, N. H. (1986). *The emotions*. Cambridge, UK: Cambridge University Press.

Frijda, N. H. (1987). Emotion, cognitive structure, and action tendency. *Cognition and Emotion, 1*, 115–143.

Frith, U., & Frith, C. D. (2003). Development and neurophysiology of mentalizing. *Philosophical Transactions of the Royal Society London, Series B, 358*, 459–473.

Fujisaki, W., & Nishida, S. (2007). Feature-based processing of audio-visual synchrony perception revealed by random pulse trains. *Vision Research, 47*, 1075–1093.

Gallese, V. (2005). Embodied simulation: From neurons to phenomenal experience. *Phenomenology and the Cognitive Sciences, 4*, 23–48.

Goldin, P. R., Hutscherson C. A. C., Ochsner, K. N., Glover, G. H., Gabrieli J. D., &, Gross, J. J. (2005). The neural bases of amusement and sadness: A comparison of block contrast and subject-specific emotion intensity regression approaches. *Neuroimage, 27*, 26–36.

Goldin, P. R., McRae, K., Ramel W., &, Gross, J. J. (2008). The neural bases of emotion regulation: Reappraisal and suppression of negative emotion. *Biological Psychiatry, 63*, 577–586.

Grodal, T. K. (1997). *Moving pictures. A new theory of film genres, feelings and cognition*. Oxford, UK: Oxford University Press.

Grodal, T. K. (2009). *Embodied visions. evolution, emotion, culture and film*. Oxford, UK: Oxford University Press.

Gross, J. J., & Levenson, R. W. (1995). Emotion elicitation using films. *Cognition & Emotion, 9*, 87–108.

Hagemann, D., Naumann, E., Maier, S., Becker, G., Lurken, A., & Bartussek, D. (1999). The assessment of affective reactivity using films: Validity, reliability and sex differences. *Personality and Individual Differences, 26*, 627–639.

Hasson, U., Landesman, O., Knappmeyer, B., Vallines, I., Rubin, N., & Heeger, D. J. (2008). Neurocinematics: The neuroscience of film. *Projections, 2*, 1–26.

Hasson, U., & Malach, R. (2005). Human brain activation during viewing of dynamic natural scenes. *Novartis Foundation Symposium, 270*, 203–212.

Hasson, U., Malach, R., & Heeger, D.J. (2010). Reliability of cortical activity during natural stimulation. *Trends in Cognitive Sciences, 14*, 1364–1366.

Hasson, U., Nir, Y., Levy, I., Fuhrmann, G., & Malach, R. (2004). Intersubject synchronization of cortical activity during natural vision. *Science, 303*, 1634–1640.

Hein, G., & Singer, T. (2008). I feel how you feel but not always: the empathic brain and its modulation. *Current Opinion in Neurobiology, 18*, 153–158.

Hewig, J., Hagemann, D., Seifert, J., Gollwitzer, M., Naumann, E., & Bartussek, D. (2005). A revised film set for the induction of basic emotions. *Cognition and Emotion, 19*, 1095–1109.

Hickok, G., Buchsbaum, B., Humphries, C., & Muftuler, T. (2003). Auditory-motor interaction revealed by fMRI: speech, music, and working memory in area Spt. *Journal of Cognitive Neuroscience, 15*, 673–682.

Hickok, G., & Poeppel, D. (2000). Towards a functional neuroanatomy of speech perception. *Trends in Cognitive Sciences, 4*, 131–138.

Hickok, G., & Poeppel, D. (2003). Dorsal and ventral streams: a framework for understanding aspects of the functional anatomy of language. *Cognition, 92*, 67–99.

Jääskeläinen, I. P., Koskentalo, K., Balk, M. H., Autti, T., Kauramäki, J., Pomren, C., & Sams, M. (2008). Inter-subject synchronization of prefrontal cortex hemodynamic activity during natural viewing. *Open Neuroimaging Journal, 2*, 14–19.

Janata, P. (2009). The neural architecture of music-evoked autobiographical memories. *Cerebral Cortex, 19*, 2579–2594.

Johnson, J. A., & Zatorre, R. J. (2006). Neural substrates for dividing and focusing attention between simultaneous auditory and visual events. *Neuroimage, 31*, 1673–1681.

Kappelhoff, H. (2004). *Matrix der Gefühle: Das Kino, das Melodrama und das Theater der Empfindsamkeit* [Matrix of emotion: The cinema, the melodrama and the theater of sensitivity]. Berlin, Germany: Vorwerk 8.

Kappelhoff, H., & Bakels, J.-H. (2011). Das Zuschauergefühl: Möglichkeiten empirisch orientierter Filmanalyse [The feeling of viewing: Possibilities for empirically oriented analysis of movies]. *Zeitschrift für Medienwissenschaft, 5*, 2.

Kappelhoff, H., & Müller, C. (2011). Embodied meaning construction: Multimodal metaphor and expressive movement in speech, gesture, and in feature film. *Metaphor and the social world, 1*(2), 121–153.

Kauppi, J.-P., Jääskeläinen, I. P., Sams, M., & Tohka, J. (2010). Inter-subject correlation of brain hemodynamic responses during watching a movie: localization in space and frequency. *Frontiers in Neuroinfromatics, 4*, 5.

Koelsch, S. (2010). Towards a neural basis of music-evoked emotions. *Trends in Cognitive Sciences, 14*, 131–137.

Koelsch, S. (2011). Toward a neural basis of music perception—a review and updated model. *Frontiers in Psychology, 2*, 110.

Koelsch, S., Fritz, T., von Cramon, D. Y., Müller, K., & Friederici, A. D. (2006). Investigating emotion with music: An fMRI study. *Human Brain Mapping, 27*, 239–250.

Koppen, C., & Spence, C. (2007). Seeing the light: exploring the Colavita visual dominance effect. *Experimental Brain Research, 180*, 737–754.

Kreibig, S. D., Wilhelm, F. H., Roth, W. T., & Gross, J. J. (2007). Cardiovascular, electrodermal, and respiratory response patterns to fear- and sadness-inducing films. *Psychophysiology, 44*, 787–806.

Leder, H., Belke, B., Oeberst, A., & Augustin, D. (2004). A model of aesthetic appreciation and aesthetic judgments. *British Journal of Psychology, 95*, 489–508.

LeDoux, J. (1996). *The emotional brain: The mysterious underpinnings of emotional life.* New York, NY: Simon and Schuster, Inc.

Lepa, S., & Floto, C. (2005). Audio-Vision als Konstruktion. Grundzüge einer funktionalistischen Audioanalyse von Multimedia und Film [Audio-vision as construction. Basics of a functional audioanalysis of multimedia and film]. In H. Segeberg & F. Schätzlein (Eds.), *Sound. Zur Technologie und Ästhetik des Akustischen in den Medien* [Sound: About the technology and aesthetic of acoustics in media] (pp. 347–365). Marburg, Germany: Schüren.

Lerner, Y., Papo, D., Zhdanov, A., Belozersky, L., & Hendler, T. (2009). Eyes wide shut. Amygdala mediates eyes-closed effect on emotional experience with music. *PLoS ONE, 4*, e6230.

Linke, R., De Lima, A. D., Schwegler, H., & Pape, H. C. (1999). Direct synaptic connections of axons from superior colliculus with identified thalamoamygdaloid projection neurons in the rat: Possible substrates of a subcortical visual pathway to the amygdala. *Journal of Comparative Neurology, 403*, 158–170.

Lipscomb, S. D., & Kendall, R. A. (1994). Perceptual judgment of the relationship between music and visual components in film. *Psychomusicology, 13*, 60–98.

Lissa, Z. (1965). *Ästhetik der Filmmusik* [Aesthetics of film music]. Berlin, Germany: Henschel.

McGurk, H., & MacDonald, J. (1976). Hearing lips and seeing voices. *Nature, 264*, 746–748.

Menon, V., & Levitin, D. J. (2005). The rewards of music listening: Response and physiological connectivity of the mesolimbic system. *NeuroImage, 28*, 175–184.

Meredith, M. A., & Stein, B. E. (1983). Interactions among converging sensory inputs in the superior colliculus. *Science, 221*, 389–391.

Montoya, P., Campos, J. J., & Schandry, R. (2005). See red? Turn pale? Unveiling emotions through cardiovascular and hemodynamic changes. *Spanish Journal of Psychology, 8*, 79–85.

Morris, J. S., Öhman, A., & Dolan, R. J. (1999). A subcortical pathway to the right amygdala mediating 'unseen' fear. *Proceedings of the National Academy of Sciences of the United States of America, 96*, 1680–1685.

Münsterberg, H. (1916). *Das Lichtspiel—eine psychologische Studie* [The photoplay: A psychological study]. Vienna, Austria: Synema.

Musacchia, G., Sams, M., Skoe, T., & Kraus, N. (2006). Seeing speech affects acoustic information processing in the human brainstem. *Experimental Brain Research, 168*, 1–10.

Nicola, S. M. (2007). The nucleus accumbens as part of a basal ganglia action selection circuit. *Psychopharmacology, 191*, 521–550.

Palomba, D., Sarlo, M., Angrilli, A., Mini, A., & Stegagno, L. (2000). Cardiac responses associated with affective processing of unpleasant film stimuli. *International Journal of Psychophysiology, 36*, 45–57.

Plantinga, C. (2009). *Moving viewers. American film and the spectator's experience.* Berkeley, CA: University of California Press.

Posner, M. I., Nissen, M. J., & Klein, R. M. (1976). Visual dominance: an information-processing account of its origins and significance. *Psychological Review, 83*, 157–171.

Rickard, N. S. (2004). Intense emotional responses to music: a test of the physiological arousal hypothesis. *Psychology of Music, 32*, 371–388.

Rottenberg, J., Ray, R. D., & Groos, J. J. (2007). Emotion elicitation using films. In J. A. Coan & J. J. B. Allen (Eds.), *Handbook of emotion elicitation and assessment, Series in affective science.* New York, NY: Oxford University Press.

Salimpoor, V. N., Benovoy, M., Larcher, K., Dagher, A., & Zatorre, R. J. (2011). Anatomically distinct dopamine release during anticipation and experience of peak emotion to music. *Nature Neuroscience, 14* (2), 257–262.

Scherer, K. R. (1998). Emotionsprozesse im Medienkontext: Forschungsillustrationen und Zukunftsperspektiven [Emotional processes in the context of media: Research illustrations and future perspectives]. *Medienpsychologie, 10*, 276–293.

Scherer, K. R. (2005). What are emotions? And how can they be measured? *Social Science Information, 44*(4), 695–729.

Scherer, K. R., & Zentner, M. (2001). Emotional effects of music: Production rules. In P. N. Juslin & J. A. Sloboda (Eds.), *Music and emotion: theory and research* (pp. 361–392). New York, NY: Oxford University Press.

Schmid, C., Büchel, C., & Rose, M. (2011). The neural basis of visual dominance in the context of audio-visual object processing. *NeuroImage, 55*, 304–311.

Sinnett, S., Spence, C., & Soto-Faraco, S. (2007). Visual dominance and attention: The Colavita effect revisited. *Perception & Psychophysics, 69*, 673–686.

Smith, G. M. (2003). *Film structure and the emotion system.* Cambridge, UK: Cambridge University Press.

Sobchack, V. (1992). *The Address of the Eye. A Phenomenology of Film Experience.* Princeton, NJ: Princeton University Press.

Spence, C. (2009). Explaining the Colavita visual dominance effect. *Progress in Brain Research, 176*, 245–258.

Spiers, H. J., & Maguire, E. A. (2007). Decoding human brain activity during real-world experiences. *Trends in Cognitive Sciences, 11*, 356–365.

Stein, B. E., & Stanford, T. R. (2008). Multisensory integration: Current issues from the perspective of the single neuron. *Nature Reviews Neuroscience, 9*, 255–266.

Tan, E. S. (1996). *Emotion and the structure of narrative film. Film as an emotion machine.* Mahwah, NJ: Lawrence Erlbaum Associates, Inc.

Tan, E. S., Spackman, M. P., & Bezdek, M. A. (2007). Viewers' interpretations of film characters' emotions. *Music Perception, 25*, 135–152.

Unz, D., Schwab, F., & Mönch, J. (2008). Filmmusik und Emotionen [Movie soundtracks and emotion]. In S. Weinacht & H. Scherer (Eds.), *Wissenschaftliche Perspektiven auf Musik und Medien* [Scientific perspectives on music and media] (pp. 177–193). Wiesbaden, Germany: VS Verlag für Sozialwissenschaften.

Vitouch, O. (2001). When your ear sets the stage: Musical context effects in film perception. *Psychology of Music, 29*(1), 70–83.

Wallace, M. T., Wilkinson, L. K., & Stein, B. E. (1996). Representation and integration of multiple sensory inputs in primate superior colliculus. *Journal of Neurophysiology, 76*, 1246–1266.

Weill, K. (1946). Music in the movies. *Harper's Bazaar, 80*, 257–259.

Westermann, R., Spies, K., Stahl, G., & Hesse, F. W. (1996). Relative effectiveness and validity of mood induction procedures: a meta-analysis. *European Journal of Social Psychology, 26*, 557–580.

Wolf, I., Dziobek, I., & Heekeren, H.R. (2010). Neural correlates of social cognition in naturalistic settings: A model-free analysis approach. *NeuroImage, 49*(1), 894–904.

Zacks, J. M., Braver, T. S., Sheridan, M. A., Donaldson, D. I., Snyder, A. Z., Ollinger, J. M., Buckner, R. L., *et al.* (2001). Human brain activity time-locked to perceptual event boundaries. *Nature Neuroscience, 4*, 651–655.

Zacks, J. M., Speer, N. K., Swallow, K. M., & Maley, C. J. (2010). The brain's cutting-room floor: segmentation of narrative cinema. *Frontiers in Human Neuroscience, 4*, 168.

Part II

Cross-Modal Relations in Multimedia

Chapter 7

Perceived congruence between auditory and visual elements in multimedia

Shin-ichiro Iwamiya

Kyushu University, Japan

Visual media productions, such as movies and television programs, are rarely composed purely of motion pictures. They are a combination of motion pictures and sound. Sound plays an integral part in visual media productions and gives them life. A vital element in making visual media presentations more impressive is 'perceived congruence' between sound and moving pictures. Perceived congruence reportedly contributes to improvement in visual media productions (Iwamiya, 1994). Visual media production companies are particularly concerned with the matching of sound and moving pictures, and empirical researchers have tried to clarify the factors that create this perceived congruence (see also Cohen, Chapter 2, in this volume).

According to past studies (Bolivar, Cohen, & Fentress, 1994; Cohen, 2001; Iwamiya, 2002), perceived congruence between sound and moving pictures has two aspects. One is *formal congruency*: the matching of auditory and visual temporal structures. The other is *semantic congruency*: the similarity between auditory and visual affective impressions. Formal congruency provides a united perceptual form to auditory and visual information, whereas semantic congruency helps to communicate the meaning of audiovisual content to the perceiver. Both types of congruency play important roles in the cross-modal interaction of disparate events in auditory and visual domains.

The synchronization of auditory and visual accents, as the temporal structure, creates formal congruency. In the discourse of film production, this synchronization technique has been called 'Mickey Mousing.' Lipscomb (2005) investigated the effect of synchronization between musical and visual accent structure alignment. Indeed, perceived congruence was found to be higher when the accent structures between sounds and visual images were synchronized than when accent structures occurred at different rates. This study showed the effect of formal congruency (see also Lipscomb, Chapter 9, in this volume).

Bolivar et al. (1994) indicated that affective congruency of musical and visual elements contributed to creating perceptual congruence, in addition to the contribution of temporal congruency. The visual stimulus was the documentary footage of social interactions between pairs of wolves. They showed that the combination of friendly video and music or that of aggressive video and music created higher perceived congruence than the combination of friendly video and aggressive music or that of aggressive video and friendly music. When the affective impression of video was similar to that of music, the perceived congruence was higher than when the impression was opposite. This study showed the effect of semantic congruency.

Furthermore, there is another factor that creates perceived congruence between sound and moving pictures: the similarity, correspondence, or matching of imagery between changing patterns of auditory and visual signals. The relation between the transformation of a visual image and the changing pattern of sound can also create perceived congruence between sound and moving pictures. Lipscomb and Kim (2004) pointed out that the highest ratings for a perceived congruence between auditory and visual components were obtained from the combinations of vertical location with pitch, size with loudness, and shape with timbre. Eitan and Granot (2006) conducted an empirical investigation of the ways in which listeners associate changes in musical parameters with physical space and bodily motion. In their experiments, participants were asked to associate melodic stimuli with imagined motions of a human character and to specify the type, direction, and pace change of these motions, as well as the forces affecting them. Results indicated that most musical parameters were significantly associated with several aspects of motion imagery: in particular, musical tempo with speed, pitch contour with verticality, and dynamics with distance. For instance, pitch contour affected imagined motion along verticality, velocity, and energy.

Perceived congruence between sound and moving pictures in commercial visual media productions

In this chapter, the author introduces a series of empirical studies on perceived congruence between sound and moving pictures and discusses how to make congruent audiovisual combinations. Before systematically discussing the factors that create this congruence, this section describes empirical approaches using actual commercial visual media productions.

Lipscomb and Kendall (1994) examined transmission to the audience of the producer's intention to match sound and moving pictures. They asked participants to select a 'best fit' musical score for five visual scenes of a movie (*Star Trek IV: The Voyage Home*, Paramount Pictures, 1986). The original musical score for each of the five scenes was paired with all five scenes. Of the 25 combinations, the most frequently selected musical scores were those originally intended for the scenes. This study showed that the producer's selections were generally appropriate and created perceived congruence between sound and moving pictures.

Iwamiya (1994) conducted a rating experiment on perceived congruence between sound and moving pictures selected from commercial visual productions. In this study, half of the audiovisual stimuli were 20 excerpts of laserdiscs on the market. The sound and motion pictures of these 'original stimuli' were intentionally matched by professionals. The other half were 'recombined stimuli' from the original audiovisual stimuli. The 20 'recombined stimuli' were created by combining original videos with 'wrong' audio tracks (for 16 stimuli) or by delaying the original sounds (for four stimuli). If the intention of the producers was communicated to the audience, the perceived congruence between sound and image of the original stimuli might be higher than that of recombined stimuli. Perceived congruence between sound and image was rated on a 7-point scale of the degree of matching, with 1 being the lowest and 7 being the highest rating. As expected, the average score for the original stimuli (6.1) was significantly larger than that for the recombined stimuli (3.9).

Furthermore, for the original stimuli, the subjective evaluation of the quality (good or bad) of both sound and image increased when they were combined, compared to when presented alone. It appears that the accompanying sound raised the evaluation of the visual material, and vice versa. This kind of interaction, in which each modality contributes to the effect of the other, is referred to as *cooperative interaction*, in this case between auditory and visual processing. Thus, in audiovisual communication, both modalities work together to make products more effective. This effect, however, was not shown for the recombined stimuli (i.e., arbitrary combinations), indicating that the matching of sound and image is important for cooperative interaction. As the matching of sound and image improves, cooperative interaction is more prominent, that is, the degree of matching correlates with the strength of cooperative interaction. The matching of sound and image depends on integration in the processing of auditory and visual information. Cooperative interaction is thus based on a function of the integration process.

In television, film, and other electronic multimedia, 'telop' characters (captions) are often used to convey linguistic information to the audience. For example, when you watch a television news program, sometimes you may see texts of important words superimposed on the screen; they are telops. *Telop* is the abbreviation for *television opaque projector*. It is a transmitting device used to broadcast characters, images, and other visual information onto television screens directly without the use of a camera. Most current telops use a computer system. In general, sound effects are combined with telops to make the presentation more impressive. Thus, a vital element in making telop patterns more effective is perceived congruence between auditory and visual information.

Kim and Iwamiya (2008) conducted a rating experiment on perceived congruence between sound and original as well as recombined telop patterns. The original telop patterns and sounds were extracted from TV programs. Examples of the patterns are shown in Figure 7.1. The recombined telop patterns were combinations of sounds and telops from the different original telop patterns. Similar to Iwamiya (1994), they found that perceived congruence of the original telop patterns was generally higher than that of the recombined telop patterns. They also found that cooperative interaction functioned in this case. That is, the evaluation of the quality of telop patterns was proportional to the perceived congruence between sound and telops.

In commercial visual media productions, such as television programs or movies, producers sometimes intentionally break congruence between sound and moving pictures. Thus, perceived congruence might change as a function of time. Fujiyama, Oonishi, and Iwamiya (2010) continuously measured the perceived congruence between sound and moving pictures of commercial products. The participants' task was to continuously grade the perceived congruence of sound and moving pictures for 160 seconds in two

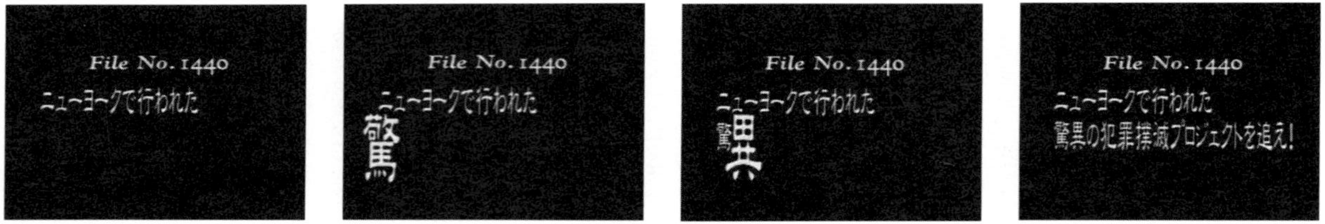

(0 ms)..................(99 ms)..........................(231 ms)........................(2264 ms)................(2433 ms)

Telop A: Seventeen characters appeared one by one from the bottom. Synchronized intermittent sound bursts (■ ■ ■ ■ ■) were combined with the characters.

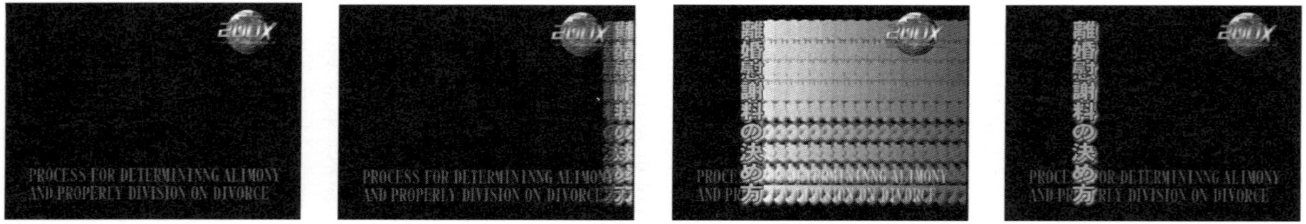

(33 ms)....................(594 ms)......................(924 ms)........................(1594 ms)................(3933 ms)

Telop B: The characters moved in from the right side and stopped. A single sound burst (■) was combined with the characters.

Figure 7.1 Examples of telop patterns. Telop A: Seventeen characters appeared one by one from the bottom. Synchronized intermittent sound bursts (■ ■ ■ ■ ■) were combined with the characters. Telop B: The characters moved in from the right side and stopped. A single sound burst (■) was combined with the characters. Originally published as figure 1, in Ki-Hong Kim & Shin-ichiro Iwamiya, 'Formal Congruency between Telop Patterns and Sound Effects,' in *Music Perception* vol. 25, no. 5 (January, 2008): 429–448. © 2008 by The Regents of the University of California. Reprinted with permission from the University of California Press.

excerpts from *Fantasia* (Disney, 1940). The two original programs and two recombined programs in which sounds and images were interchanged were used. As expected, the perceived congruence of the original programs was generally higher than that of the recombined stimuli. Furthermore, the level of perceived congruence of the original stimuli changed as a function of time. The resultant variation in the perceived congruence in the stimuli suggested that producers generally maintain high congruency in audiovisual content, but sometimes intentionally degrade perceived congruence to give variation to products.

Formal congruency

This section introduces empirical approaches to clarify the effect of formal congruency between auditory and visual elements; the matching of auditory and visual temporal structure. Iwamiya, Sugano, and Kouda (2000) examined the effect of audiovisual synchronization in an experiment on perceived congruence between sound and moving pictures. In this experiment, the visual stimulus was a ball on a grid surface, as shown in Figure 7.2. The viewpoint moved successively, and visual accents were created by discontinuous changes in the visual scene. Auditory accents were based on the rhythmic structure of the music stimulus. The auditory stimulus was a short and simple melody played on a bass and drums.

Scores of perceived congruence between sound and moving pictures are shown in Figure 7.2. When the musical accents synchronized with the visual accents, formal congruency was created. As a result, the perceived congruence between sound and moving pictures was higher. In contrast, when the musical and visual accents were not synchronized, the perceived congruence was lower. This result demonstrated the effectiveness of formal congruency in raising perceived congruence. Furthermore, when the perceived congruence was higher, the rating value for impressiveness was also higher. Formal congruency contributed to the creation of a single perceptual unit of auditory and visual information. The sense of unification of the auditory and visual events raised not only the audiovisual congruence, but also the impressiveness of the audiovisual stimuli. (To hear and see the audiovisual stimuli used in the eight conditions in this experiment, please visit <http://www.oup.co.uk/companion/tan>.)

Sugano and Iwamiya (2000) also examined the effect of synchronization between auditory and visual accents. In this study, in addition to synchronized and asynchronized conditions, there was a temporal phase-shift condition in which auditory and visual accents occurred during the same period, but there was a constant time difference between them. In the asynchronized condition, the time difference was not constant. As shown in Figure 7.3, perceived congruence was highest for the synchronized condition and lowest for the asynchronized condition, with the congruence of the temporal phase-shift condition in between, as shown by Lipscomb (2005). The relatively higher congruence of the phase-shift condition indicated the importance of corresponding periods between auditory and visual periodical events.

Despite synchronization of auditory and visual events, perceived congruence was created when the periods of auditory and visual accents corresponded or had integer ratios, such as 1 to1, 2 to 1, 3 to 1, or 4 to 1 (Sugano & Iwamiya, 1998). In this

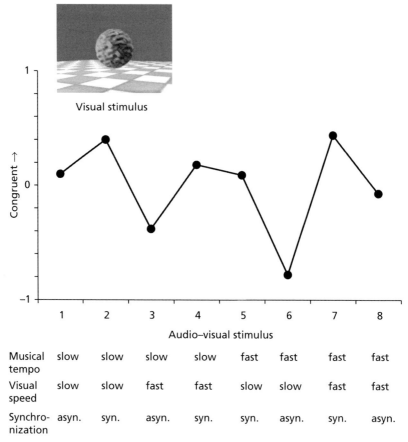

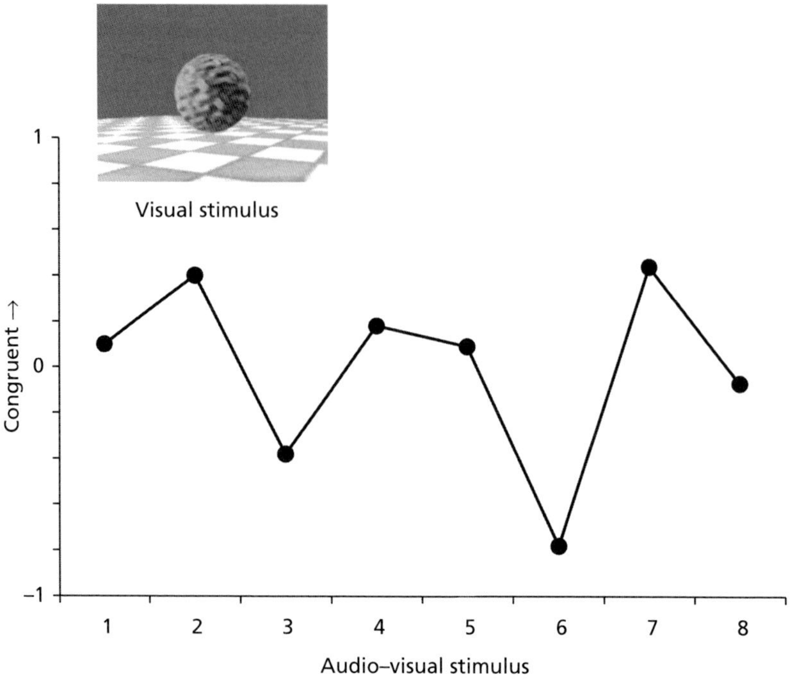

	1	2	3	4	5	6	7	8
Musical tempo	slow	slow	slow	slow	fast	fast	fast	fast
Visual speed	slow	slow	fast	fast	slow	slow	fast	fast
Synchro-nization	asyn.	syn.	asyn.	syn.	syn.	asyn.	syn.	asyn.

Figure 7.2 Average ratings of perceived congruence of audiovisual stimuli in synchronized and asynchronized conditions. Originally published as figure 3, in Shin-ichiro Iwamiya, Yoshimori Sugano, & Keisuke Kouda, 'The effects of synchronization of temporal structures of sound and motion picture on the impression of audio-visual contents,' in *Proceedings of the 2000 IEEE International Conference on Systems, Man, and Cybernetics*, 1222–1225. © Shin-ichiro Iwamiya, reproduced here with permission.

experiment, participants were asked to adjust the speed of a visual object moving periodically on the screen to match music presented at a constant tempo. The participants tended to match the visual speed to make the auditory and visual accents an integer ratio, so that the accents were synchronized or shifted by a constant time difference. When the periods of visual accents and auditory accents corresponded or there was an integer ratio, formal congruency was created.

Formal congruency based on the synchronization of auditory and visual elements is also used for telop patterns. The effect of formal congruency has been examined using telop patterns and sound effects (Kim & Iwamiya, 2008). For telop pattern A in Figure 7.1, in which letters successively appeared with synchronized intermittent

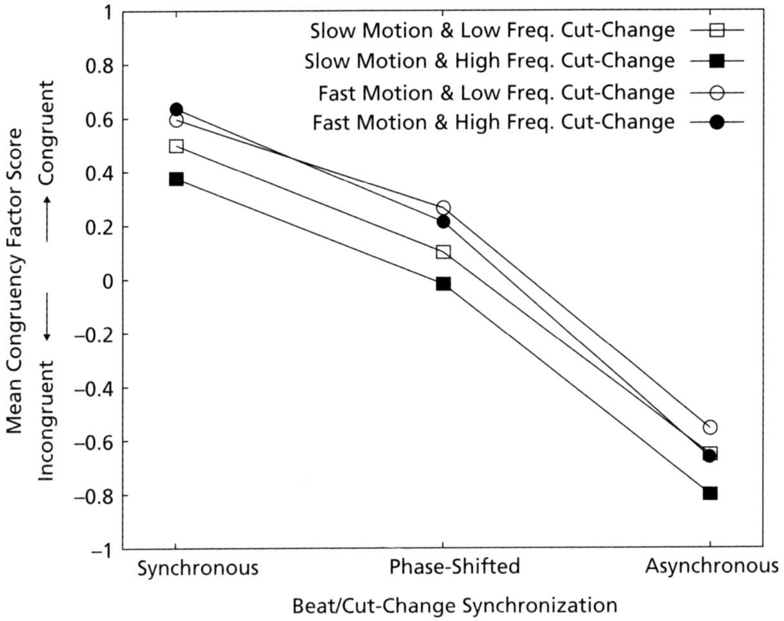

Figure 7.3 Average ratings of perceived congruence of audiovisual stimuli in synchronized, asynchronized, and phase-shift conditions. Originally published as figure 5, in Yoshimori Sugano & Shin-ichiro Iwamiya, 'The effects of the synchronization between auditory and visual accents and those of matching between musical tempo and visual speed on the emotional impression of combinations of motion picture and music,' in *The Journal of the Acoustical Society of Japan* vol. 56, no. 10 (October, 2000): 695–704. © 2000 by The Acoustical Society of Japan.

sound bursts, the rating experiment showed that the perceived congruence between the moving picture and sound was higher. However, when a single sound burst was combined with the same telop pattern, the perceived congruence was lower. This type of single sound burst was matched with simple telop pattern B in Figure 7.1, with letters appearing together on the right side of the display and moving to the center.

Semantic congruency

We now turn to empirical approaches to clarify the effect of semantic congruency between auditory and visual elements: the similarity between auditory and visual affective impressions. The effect of semantic congruency was examined by a rating experiment for various audiovisual combinations (Iwamiya, Jogetsu, Sugano, & Takada, 2002). The variables for this experiment were the number (density) of visual objects and their speeds, and the tempo and tonality of the music. The audiovisual stimuli consisted of a computer-generated moving picture and a short piece of music. The moving picture was a simplified image of human beings on a grid surface. They moved constantly from the right to the left side of the screen. The object density was set for two conditions. Figure 7.4 shows the visual stimuli for the low-density and high-density conditions. In the high-density condition, there were eight to ten objects in one scene. In the low-density condition, there were one to two objects. Their speed was set under two conditions. In the fast-motion condition, 1 second elapsed for the movement of an object from right to left. Under the slow-motion condition, 10 seconds was set for the movement. The auditory stimulus was simple music consisting of synthesized brass, drums, and bass. The tempo of the auditory stimulus was 60, 90, 120, 180, 240, and 300 beats per minute (bpm). The original melody was composed using a major scale.

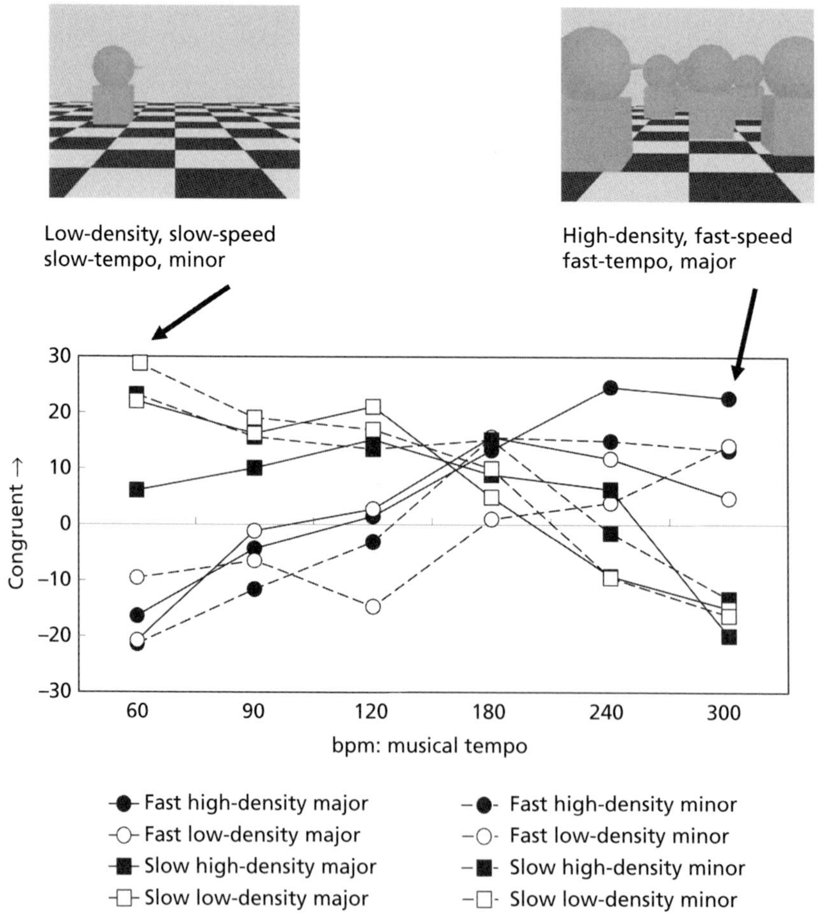

Figure 7.4 Average ratings of perceived congruence of various audiovisual combinations as a function of musical tempo. Originally published as figure 3, in Shin-ichiro Iwamiya, Yutaka Jogetsu, Yoshimori Sugano, & Masayuki Takada, 'The effects of musical tempo and tonality and visual speed and density on perception of audiovisual content,' in *Journal of Music Perception and Cognition* vol. 8, no. 2 (2002): 53–64. © 2002 by The Japanese Society for Music Perception and Cognition.

A modulated version based on a minor scale was also used. The visual stimuli were presented on a 17-inch computer display.

The experimental results of rating experiments on semantic differential scales showed that the speed of the moving visual objects affected the participants' assessment of speed and crowdedness: the faster the speed of the visual objects, the faster and more crowded the affective impression. The density of the visual objects also affected the subjective crowdedness: the higher the density, the more crowded the affective impression. Musical tempo affected the subjective speed, brightness, and crowdedness: the faster the musical tempo, the faster, brighter, and more crowded the affective impression. Tonality affected the subjective brightness: a major key increased subjective brightness, and a minor key increased subjective darkness.

Figure 7.4 shows scores for the degree of perceived congruence obtained by the rating experiment for each audiovisual stimulus. Speed matching was found to be the dominant factor in ratings of perceived congruence between sound and moving pictures. Fast visual object speed was found to match fast musical tempo, and slow speed was found to match slow tempo. Furthermore, high visual array density was found to match fast musical tempo, and low density matched slow tempo. Moreover, fast visual object speed matched a major key, and slow visual object speed matched a minor key.

Results revealed two types of highly congruent audiovisual combinations: One was the combination of high-density, fast-speed image and major-key, fast-tempo music. The other was the combination of low-density, slow-speed image and minor-key, slow-tempo music. In these combinations, auditory and visual elements had similar effects on affective impressions of audiovisual stimuli. Both the visual object speed and the musical tempo affected subjective speed, while visual object density and musical tempo affected subjective crowdedness. Finally, the visual object speed and tonality of the music affected subjective brightness. Therefore, this type of congruence between auditory and visual elements was considered to be created by semantic congruency based on the similarity of auditory and visual effects.

As shown in Figure 7.4, when the auditory and visual elements of two types of congruent stimuli were interchanged, the congruence scores were lowest. In these incongruent stimuli, auditory and visual elements had opposite effects on the affective impressions of audiovisual stimuli. Thus, semantic congruency was not created. (To hear and see the congruent and incongruent audiovisual stimuli employed in this experiment, please visit <http://www.oup.co.uk/companion/tan>.)

The effect of semantic congruency was examined in another experiment using piano music and computer graphics of a piano performance under various colors of lighting (Iwamiya & Hayashi, 1999). The lighting colors used were red, yellow, yellowish green, green, cyan, blue, violet, and purple, which are equally spaced on the Munsell hue circle. The musical stimuli were eight short musical passages from popular piano tunes produced by a MIDI synthesizer. The degree of matching between color of lighting and music and the affective impression of music with various colors of lighting were measured by rating experiments.

Figure 7.5 shows scores for the degree of perceived congruence of each audiovisual combination obtained by the rating experiment. Blue, violet, purple, and red were highly matched with music in a minor key played at a fast tempo. The results of the

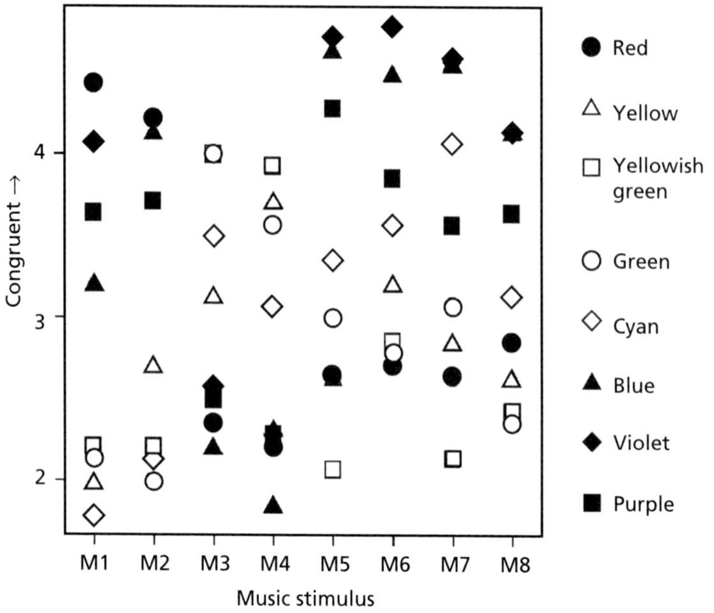

Music stimulus (tempo, tonality)

M1 Chopin: Revolutionary (fast, minor)
M2 Brahms: Hungarian Dances No. 1 (fast, minor)
M3 Chopin: Black Key (fast, minor)
M4 Mozart: Pinao Sonata (fast, minor)
M5 Erroll Garner: Misty (slow, major)
M6 Carmichael: Skylark (slow, major)
M7 Ravel: Pavance for a Dead Princess (slow, major)
M8 Satie: Gnossienne No. 1 (slow, minor)

Visual stimulus

Figure 7.5 Average ratings of perceived congruence of various combinations of music and color. Originally published as figure 5, in Shin-ichiro Iwamiya & Katsuaki Hayashi, 'The effects of color on the impression of music,' in *Design issue of Kyushu Institute of Design*, vol. 1 (1999): 63–68. © Shin-ichiro Iwamiya, reproduced here with permission.

rating experiment on the affective impression of the music showed that this kind of music created a powerful and dark impression. When these colors were combined with this type of music, the affective impression of the music was more powerful than when the other colors, such as cyan, yellowish green, yellow, and green, were combined. Bright music in a major key and at a fast tempo was matched with green, yellowish green, yellow, and cyan. The results of the rating experiment on the affective impression of the music showed that these colors made the music seem brighter.

In general, music matched with colors enhanced the affective impression created by the music itself. Powerful music was matched with colors that made the music more powerful, and bright music was matched with colors that made the music brighter. This type matching was shown to be created by a type of semantic congruency. However, in this experiment, the psychophysical properties of color, such as chroma, saturation, and brightness, were not systematically controlled. Further research is necessary to confirm this finding.

As previously described, telop patterns are used to convey linguistic information to the television audience. In general, sound effects are combined with telop patterns to make telop presentations more effective. Semantic congruency of audiovisual content is another important factor related to making effective telop patterns.

The effect of the similarity of affective impressions between sound effects and type styles of telop characters on perceived congruence between sounds and images and the subjective evaluation of telop patterns have been examined (Kim, Iwamiya, & Fujimaru, 2005). In this experiment, a telop pattern simply appeared and disappeared. The timing of appearance of sound and telop pattern was synchronized for all the stimuli, so that the level of formal congruency was kept constant. The telop pattern (directly projected characters on a television display) was a meaningless combination of letters, 'gksnzdq,' to avoid the effect of meaning on subjective impression. When the affective impression of the sound effects and that of the style of telop characters were similar, the perceived congruence between the sound and image tended to be higher than when the auditory and visual impressions were opposite. The effect of similarity of affective impression was the most prominent between auditory and visual brightness among the various psychological attributes. In contrast, it was not as prominent between auditory and visual beauty. The psychological property and physiological process related to perceiving auditory and visual brightness are relatively clear and simple. Those for beauty are complex, because the meaning of beauty is more ambiguous. The effect of semantic congruency was more prominent when the psychological property was clear, and the physiological process was simple. The meaning of brightness was clear, while that of beauty was ambiguous. The effect of similarity between auditory and visual affective impressions was more prominent for simpler auditory and visual processes. Furthermore, when auditory and visual affective impressions were similar, the subjective evaluation of the quality of telop patterns was also better.

Linguistic information from telops was a more essential factor. Thus, the effects of semantic congruency between the affective impression of words used as telop characters and sound effects were examined by a rating experiment (Kim, Iwasaki, & Iwamiya, 2007). In this experiment, the same type style was used for each telop to avoid the effect of type style on affective impression. The temporal structure of the telop stimuli was simply a pattern that appeared and disappeared. The semantic congruency between sounds and images based on the correspondence of the affective impression of words and sound effects, such as the combination of a word and a sound eliciting a bright affect, contributed to increasing the perceived congruence of the sound and image. For example, the word 'marriage' elicited bright affect and matched bright sounds. When the affective impression of the words were opposite to those of the sound effects, such as the combination of a 'bright' word and a 'dark' sound, the perceived congruence between sound and image was much lower. Further, the subjective evaluation of the quality of telop patterns was found to be proportional to the perceived congruence between sound and image. The semantic congruency between words and sound effects also contributed to creating an effective telop pattern.

When the meaning of letters and affect elicited by type style was similar to the affective impression for accompanying sounds, perceived congruence was higher. Semantic congruency is an effective way to make impressive telop patterns. More broadly speaking, semantic congruency is a basic way to make congruent and high-quality audiovisual content for sound effects and music in multimedia.

Similarity between changing patterns of visual image and sound

Combination of simple visual movement and unidirectional pitch shift

In addition to formal and semantic congruency, the similarity, correspondence, or matching of imagery between the changing patterns of a visual image and sound can also create perceived congruence between sound and moving pictures. To examine this effect, switching patterns of images were used (Arita & Iwamiya, 2004; Arita, Su, Kawakami, Ueda, & Iwamiya, 2005). Switching patterns are used when a visual image changes to another image in television programs or movies. When an image is switched, a sound effect is usually added. In these studies, rating experiments using various types of switching patterns and ascending and descending pitch scales were conducted. In each switching pattern, the image simply changed from a green board to a blue board to avoid the effect of visual content. Each switching pattern was combined with an ascending or descending pitch scale.

In the experiments, a pair of congruent patterns of combinations of switching and pitch scale patterns was shown. One was a combination of an ascending pitch scale and enlarging image pattern. The other was a combination of descending pitch scale and diminishing image pattern. Figure 7.6 shows an example of the experimental results (Arita & Iwamiya, 2004). In this condition, the pitch changed continuously between C3 and C6. Furthermore, when the pitch change was instead a series of discrete tones in other experimental conditions, such as C3–E3–G3–C4–E4–G4–C5 or C5–G4–E4–C4–G3–E3–C3, a similar tendency was observed. Direction of pitch shift is the dominant factor in this tendency, while the pattern of pitch shift might not be an essential factor.

These forms of matching might be associated with the Doppler illusion, which refers to the auditory effect that occurs when an object producing a sound at a stable pitch approaches an observer, and the observer perceives the pitch as ascending (Neuhoff & McBeath, 1996). Enlarging the image pattern elicits the perception of the sound approaching, while reducing the image pattern elicits the perception of the sound receding. These combinations could therefore be perceived as being very natural, similar to the Doppler illusion in daily life, so that the perceptual connection between moving picture and sound was created. Thus, perceived congruence was high when ascending pitch and enlarging image or descending pitch and diminishing image were combined.

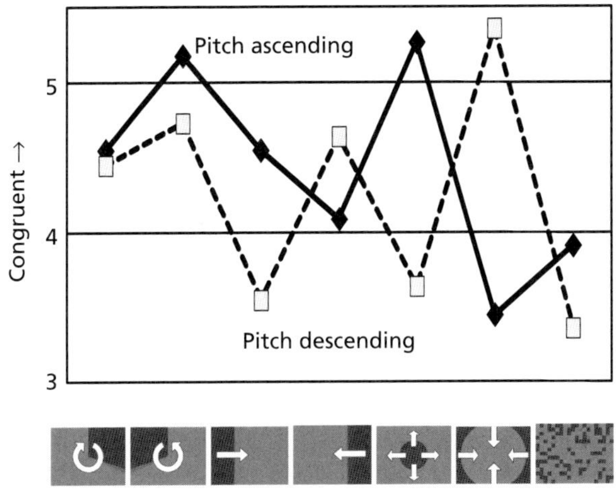

Figure 7.6 Average ratings of perceived congruence between various switching patterns and ascending or descending pitch scales. Originally published as figure 3, in Motonori Arita & Shin-ichiro Iwamiya, 'The effects of structural characteristic of switching patterns and pitch patterns of sound on the subjective congruency of sound and moving picture,' in *Proceedings of the Autumn Meeting of Japanese Society of Music Perception and Cognition* (2004): 71–76. © Shin-ichiro Iwamiya, reproduced here with permission.

Furthermore, another pair of congruent patterns for combinations of switching and pitch patterns is shown in Figure 7.6. One was a combination of an ascending pitch scale and a sliding movement from left to right. The other was a combination of a descending pitch scale and a sliding movement from right to left. The pitch patterns of this pair were also set as a continuous pitch shift between C3 and C6.

This relationship between horizontal direction and pitch direction can be seen in keyboard instruments, such as pianos, organs, and musical synthesizers. Thus, the matching between horizontal movement and pitch shift could be based on an association with musical keyboards. Arita et al. (2005) examined the perceived congruence between horizontal movement of the image and unidirectional pitch shift of a sound. Participants were students majoring in piano and non-musician students. The non-musicians did not have formal musical training. Both groups showed a similar tendency, which reflected the previously shown congruent audiovisual combinations: an ascending pitch scale matched a sliding movement from left to right, and a descending pitch scale matched a sliding movement from right to left. Therefore, this tendency is not clearly explained by an association with musical keyboards. Furthermore, handedness of the participants did not affect this tendency.

This tendency might be explained by an association with a feeling of power. People associate a feeling of powerfulness or a higher level of potency with ascending pitch (Eitan & Granot, 2006). Furthermore, in many tuning meters, higher level is indicated by right-direction movement. Old-fashioned sound level meters are typical examples. When the sound is louder, the indicator moves from left to right. Even when LED indicators are used, higher level is assigned to right direction movement. When the energy level is higher, LEDs successively turn on from left to right. People may associate a feeling of powerfulness or higher level of potency with right-direction movement and ascending pitch. People may associate a feeling of powerlessness or lower level of potency with left-direction movement and descending pitch. Therefore, it is likely that participants would perceive relatively high congruence from these combinations of horizontal movement and pitch shift. (To hear and see examples of the audiovisual stimuli employed in this experiment, please visit <http://www.oup.co.uk/companion/tan>.)

An association between pitch and horizontal direction was also indicated by Rusconi, Kwan, Giordano, Umiltà, and Butterworth (2006). They measured reaction time of pitch discrimination using right and left keys. The reaction time was shorter when the right key was assigned to a higher pitch and the left key was assigned to a lower pitch than when the key assignment was altered. Results also supported the association of right direction and higher pitch, and that of left direction and lower pitch.

Vertical correspondence of direction between movement of a visual image and pitch shift is assumed to have a strong effect on congruence between the switching pattern of an image and sound. From our daily experiences, the combination of rising and ascending pitch, and that of falling and descending pitch have spontaneous associations. We can find applications of this association all around us. For example, there is auditory notification when an elevator stops, distinguished by a rise and fall in pitch based on passengers' ascending or descending, respectively.

As expected, the combination of a rising image and an ascending pitch scale, and that of a falling image and a descending pitch scale did indeed create higher perceived congruence than the alternative combinations (Arita et al., 2005). This experiment confirmed that the vertical correspondence of direction between visual movement and pitch shift was effective in creating perceived congruence.

In many languages, such as English, Spanish, French, German, Italian, Japanese, Chinese, and Korean, the same expressions are used for vertical direction and pitch shift direction. The words 'high, low, up, down, raise, lower, ascend, descend' are used for both pitch shift and vertical movement. People strongly associate pitch directions and vertical directions in space. For example, higher pitch is associated with higher position, and vice versa. Therefore, we might feel a strong congruence between moving pictures and sound if the visual image and pitch of a sound moved in the direction represented by the same verbal expression. Lipscomb and Kim (2004) showed that the highest ratings for perceived match between auditory and visual components were obtained from the vertical correspondence of direction between visual movement and pitch shift.

The effect of this correspondence between visual movement and pitch shift has been shown in a different context. Maeda, Kanai, and Shimojo (2004) indicated that gratings with ambiguous motion accompanied by ascending pitch were more likely to be perceived as an upward motion, those accompanied by descending pitch as a downward motion, whereas noise caused no directional bias. The ambiguous motion of this experiment was created by upward and downward luminance gratings presented simultaneously.

Combination of complex visual movement and unidirectional pitch shift

To examine the matching pitch pattern for the combination of horizontal and vertical movement, a rating experiment using diagonal switching patterns, as described previously, was conducted (Arita et al., 2005). The visual stimuli for this experiment were four switching patterns. The direction of their switching movement was upper-right, lower-right, upper-left, and lower-left. These switching patterns were combined with continuously ascending and descending pitch scales between 125 Hz and 2 kHz.

We can estimate the congruent pitch scale for these switching patterns based on vertical or horizontal movements. If vertical correspondence was the dominant factor in determining perceived congruence between sound and a moving picture, the vertical direction of an orthogonal movement might decide the congruent pitch pattern. Upper-right and upper-left movements might match an ascending pitch scale, while lower-right and lower-left movement might match a descending pitch scale. If the congruence of a horizontal movement and pitch shift was the dominant factor, upper-right and lower-right movements might match an ascending pitch scale, while upper-left and lower-left movements might match a descending pitch scale.

Figure 7.7 shows the experimental results. Upper-right and upper-left movements matched an ascending pitch scale, and lower-right and lower-left movements matched a descending pitch scale. When an opposite-direction pitch scale was combined with these visual stimuli, the perceived congruence was lower. The experimental results

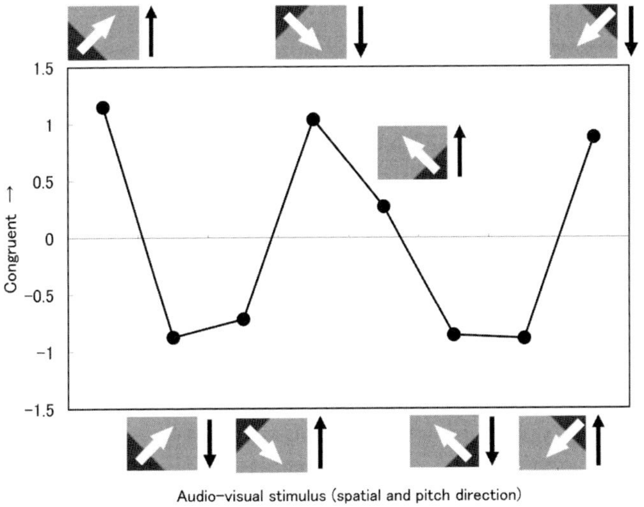

Figure 7.7 Average ratings of perceived congruence between diagonal switching patterns and ascending or descending pitch scales. Originally published as figure 8, in Motonori Arita, Xun Su, Hiroshi Kawakami, Mari Ueda, & Shin-ichiro Iwamiya, 'The subjective congruency between direction of pitch movement and direction of switching pattern movement,' in *Proceedings of the Autumn Meeting of Japanese Society of Music Perception and Cognition* (2005): 31–36. © Shin-ichiro Iwamiya, reproduced here with permission.

demonstrated that the correspondence between the vertical direction of a diagonal switching movement and the pitch shift direction was the determinant factor in creating a congruent audiovisual combination. (To hear and see examples of the audiovisual stimuli used in the eight conditions in this experiment, please visit <http://www.oup.co.uk/companion/tan>.)

Rotation is another combination of vertical and horizontal movement. Perceived congruence between the rotating movement of a visual image and the pitch shift of a sound was also examined (Kim, Iwamiya, & Kitano, 2008). The visual stimuli used were rotating switching patterns. Switching patterns were used when a visual image changed to another image. A green board was changed to a blue board using a rotating line from the center of the display. In this experiment, up-and-down (or down-and-up) bending pitch patterns were combined in addition to unidirectional ascending or descending pitch patterns. These four pitch patterns are schematically shown in Figure 7.8. The extent of frequency shift was between 125 Hz and 2 kHz. Pitch shift synchronized rotation switching, and the duration of rotation and pitch shift was 1 second. (To hear and see examples of the audiovisual stimuli employed in this experiment, please visit <http://www.oup.co.uk/companion/tan>.)

As shown in Figure 7.8, when the rotation switching of the image started from the top of the display, a descending then ascending pitch pattern matched the rotating switching pattern. When the rotation switching started from the bottom of the display, an ascending then descending pitch pattern matched. This type of congruence was based on the matching of the vertical movement of rotation and the pitch change. Spatial rising matched ascending pitch and spatial falling matched descending pitch. These results also showed that vertical movement of rotation was the dominant factor in determining the match with pitch movement. However, horizontal movement did not affect the matching pitch pattern. Furthermore, congruence of the audiovisual combinations also had the effect of raising the level of their evaluation of the quality.

Effect of loudness patterns

Iwamiya and Ozaki (2004) conducted a rating experiment on perceived congruence between various transformation patterns of image and various kinds of loudness patterns, in addition to pitch patterns. The extent of frequency shift was between 131 Hz and 880 Hz. The presented sound pressure level changed from 70 dB to 95 dB for the crescendo pattern, and from 95 dB to 70 dB for the decrescendo pattern. When the size of the image monotonously changed, the moving picture matched a continuous and unidirectional pitch pattern. In particular, similar to previous studies, the ascending pitch pattern matched the enlarging image, and the descending pitch matched the diminishing image. Furthermore, as shown in Figure 7.9, their study also demonstrated that a crescendo pattern of loudness enhanced the perceived congruence between ascending pitch scale and enlarging image, and a decrescendo pattern of loudness enhanced perceived congruence between descending pitch scale and diminishing image. A random or zigzag pitch pattern did not create perceived congruence with monotonous enlarging or diminishing image and decreased congruence between sound and moving pictures.

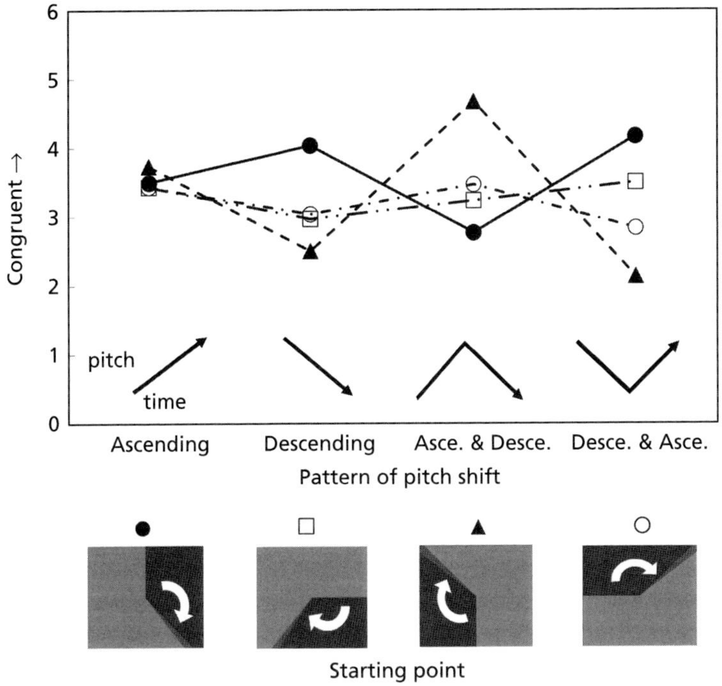

Figure 7.8 Average ratings of perceived congruence between rotating switching patterns and ascending or descending pitch scales or their combinations. Originally published as figure 2, in Ki-Hong Kim, Shin-ichiro Iwamiya, & Hiroyuki Kitano, 'Subjective congruence between rotating transition of moving picture and pitch shift pattern of a sound,' in *Journal of Music Perception and Cognition*, vol. 14, nos. 1&2 (2008): 29–36. © 2008 by The Japanese Society for Music Perception and Cognition.

Cultural differences in perceived congruence based on the similarity between the changing patterns of a visual image and sound

Su, Kim, and Iwamiya (2009) confirmed, using a paired comparison task, that three pairs of audiovisual combinations created high congruence for Japanese, Korean, and Chinese participants, as shown in the following. The experiment was conducted in Japan. Vertical correspondence of direction between the movement of an image and the pitch shift of a sound had a strong effect on perceived congruence. The combination of a rising image and an ascending pitch, and that of a falling image and a descending pitch created a higher perceived congruence than the alternative combinations. The combination of an enlarging image and an ascending pitch, and that of a diminishing image and a descending pitch created a higher perceived congruence. Furthermore, the combination of a movement sliding from left to right and an ascending pitch, and that of a movement sliding from right to left and a descending pitch created higher perceived congruence. For these simple visual movements, participants from all three

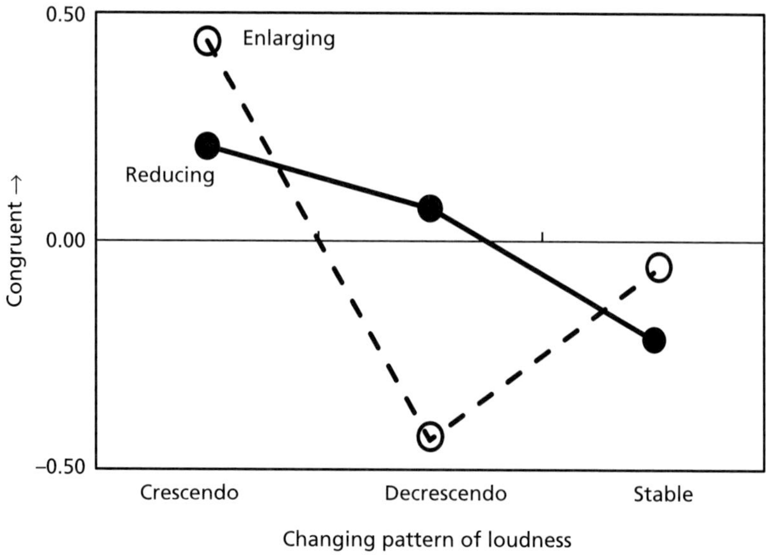

Figure 7.9 Average ratings of perceived congruence between enlarging or reducing of image and increasing or decreasing loudness (crescendo or decrescendo) of a sound. Originally published as figure 6, in Shin-ichiro Iwamiya, Hanako Ozaki, & Masayuki Takada, 'The effects of various pitch patterns and transformed simple figures on the impression of audio-visual contents,' in *The Journal of the Acoustical Society of Japan* vol. 61, no. 5 (May, 2005): 250–259. © 2005 by The Acoustical Society of Japan.

countries showed similar tendencies. In these experiments, the pitch patterns were continuous pitch shifts between 250 Hz and 4 kHz. The switching patterns used were similar to those used in previous studies (Arita & Iwamiya, 2004; Arita et al., 2005). Among them, the switching patterns of enlarging and diminishing, and those of sliding movements are shown in Figure 7.6.

Su, Kim, and Iwamiya (2010) examined the perceived congruence between various complex transformation patterns of an image and pitch shift patterns of a sound by rating experiments using a paired comparison method for Japanese, Korean, and Chinese participants. The visual transformation patterns were the combinations of two patterns among three types of transformation: rising or falling, enlarging or diminishing, and right or left direction movement. The combined pitch patterns were continuously ascending and descending pitch shifts between 250 Hz and 4 kHz.

The rising and falling transformation was the most effective factor in determining congruent pitch shift for participants from all three countries. A spatially rising element matched pitch ascending, and a spatially falling element matched pitch descending. This factor was effective when the other visual transformations were combined. The next most effective transformation factor was the enlarging and reducing. As shown in the case of single transformation patterns (Su et al., 2009), the combination of an enlarging image and an ascending pitch, and that of a diminishing image and a descending pitch created higher perceived congruence. This factor was effective when the horizontal movement was combined for the three countries' participants, but not effective for Korean and Chinese participants when the vertical movement was combined. The transformation of right and left direction movement was not strongly effective in determining the perceived congruence for any of the participants.

Furthermore, when enlarging or reducing was combined with vertical movement, mainly for Japanese participants, perceived congruence created by the combination of diminishing image and descending pitch was found to be higher than that of enlarging image and ascending pitch. Also, mainly for Japanese participants, when horizontal movement was combined with enlarging or reducing, or vertical movement, the effect of the combination of right direction movement and ascending pitch on perceived congruence was stronger than that of left direction movement and descending pitch.

As a more complex condition, perceived congruence between pitch shift of a sound and moving pictures consisting of vertical, horizontal, and size transformations was examined by rating experiments with Japanese, Korean, and Chinese participants (Iwamiya, Su, Koyama, & Kim, 2010). As expected from previous studies, the combinations of a rising image and an ascending pitch, a falling image and a descending pitch, an enlarging image and an ascending pitch, and a diminishing image and a descending pitch created higher congruence between moving pictures and sounds. Vertical movement and size transformation were effective in creating perceived congruence with unidirectional pitch shift, while horizontal transformation was less effective in creating congruence.

For Japanese and Chinese participants, the effect of the combination of rising image and ascending pitch on perceived congruence was found to be stronger than that of falling image and descending pitch. For Japanese participants, similar to the tendencies obtained when two types of transformations were combined, perceived congruence created by the combination of diminishing image and descending pitch was found to be higher than that of enlarging image and ascending pitch. Also, the effect of the combination of right direction movement and ascending pitch on perceived congruence was stronger than that of left direction movement and descending pitch.

Combining formal and semantic congruency

In commercial visual media productions, the effects of formal congruency, semantic congruency, and matching (similarity) between changing patterns of visual image and sound are often combined in complex ways. Combinations of these effects have also been empirically examined. These approaches are the most holistic and connected to real world experiences.

As shown in the earlier section on formal congruency, Iwamiya et al. (2000) and Sugano and Iwamiya (2000) examined the effect of audiovisual synchronization in experiments on perceived congruence between sound and moving pictures. In these experiments, the musical tempo and visual speed of the object were the experimental variables, in addition to audiovisual synchronization. When musical tempo and visual speed were balanced, the perceived congruence was found to be higher than when they were not balanced. These effects were based on semantic congruency: matching of auditory and visual perception of the speed. Furthermore, these studies demonstrated the effect of synchronization and that speed matching independently affected perceived congruence. In this case, semantic and formal congruency independently functioned to create perceived congruence.

Using telop patterns, Kim and Iwamiya (2008) showed that the relationship between transformation patterns of image and pitch and loudness patterns of sound created perceived congruence. In this study, they examined the effect of formal congruency and that of similarity between changing patterns of visual image and sound. Both effects were found to be effective in creating perceived congruence. They also discussed the difference in quality between formal congruency and similarity between changing patterns.

In the case of formal congruency, synchronization of the onsets of telop and sound patterns was found to be more important than synchronization of the offsets. When the onsets were synchronized, perceived congruence was created regardless of temporal relationships between auditory and visual offsets. When the auditory and visual onsets of telop patterns were not synchronized, the perceived congruence remarkably decreased. Formal congruency was exclusively determined by the synchronization of the auditory and visual onsets.

Contrary to formal congruency, the matching between changing patterns of auditory and visual information could be created between various types of patterns. Namely, one visual changing pattern matched several types of auditory changing patterns, and vice versa. For example, in the case of a zooming-in (expanding) type of telop pattern, not only the increasing loudness but also the ascending pitch of the auditory stimulus created perceived congruence. Furthermore, the increasing loudness of sound created perceived congruence with the increasing brightness. The gradually brighter or brighter then darker telop pattern matched the gradually increasing or increasing then decreasing loudness of sound. Brightness reflects the intensity of the visual stimulus, while loudness reflects the intensity of the auditory stimulus. The brightness of the visual domain is closely related to the loudness of the auditory domain (e.g., Marks, 1989; Stevens, 1957). Thus, this similarity between variations in energy level of auditory and visual signals created perceived congruence.

Furthermore, Arita and Iwamiya (2004) examined the effect of continuity of pitch shift on perceived congruence between image movement and pitch shift. When the image movement was continuous and the direction of pitch shift was the same, the congruence was higher when the pitch shift was also continuous than when the pitch shift pattern was intermittent. This congruence was created by a kind of formal congruency. The previously shown effect of similarity between changing pattern of image and sound is effective when formal congruency is created.

The relationship between the rotating movement of a visual image and the periodic pitch modulation of a sound in creating perceived congruence was examined in a rating experiment (Kim, Iwamiya, & Kitano, 2009). The visual stimulus of this study was a ball continuously rotating along a circular track, as shown in Figure 7.10. The period of ball rotation was 2 seconds, and the ball rotated five times. The sound stimulus was a periodically ascending and descending pitch modulation of a pure tone (frequency modulation). The extent of frequency modulation was between 125 Hz and 2 kHz. The highest congruence between a moving picture and a sound was obtained when the

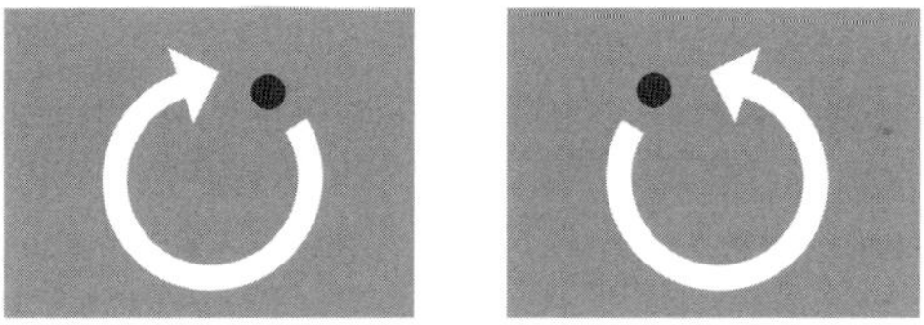

Figure 7.10 Track of a rotating ball as an experimental stimulus. Originally published as figure 1, in Ki-Hong Kim, Shin-ichiro Iwamiya, & Hiroyuki Kitano, 'Subjective congruence between rotating movement of a visual image and pitch modulation of a sound,' in *Ergonomics*, vol. 45, no. 6 (December, 2009): 336–343. © 2009 by Japan Ergonomics Society.

period of pitch modulation corresponded, or almost corresponded to that of the rotation of the ball. When the periods were obviously different, the degree of congruence remarkably decreased. When pitch modulation preceded ball rotation, the congruence was more degraded than when pitch modulation was delayed. Studies on sensitivity to synchronization of auditory and visual events have indicated that human beings are less sensitive to the delay of sound than the precedence of sound (Dixon & Spitz, 1980).

In the case of periodic variation, similar to previous studies on the combination of vertical and horizontal movements, the vertical correspondence of visual movement and pitch shift was an effective factor in creating perceived congruence between ball rotation and pitch modulation. When the directions of the pitch shift and visual movement were opposite, the perceived congruence was lower than when they were the same. The difference between clockwise and counterclockwise rotations of a ball did not affect perceived congruence. The effect of horizontal movement was negligible. In this case, the perceived congruence of audiovisual combinations also raised the level of their evaluation. For periodic rotation, both the matching of periods of auditory and visual variation as a kind of formal congruency, and the vertical correspondence of visual movement and pitch shift as a kind of similarity between changing patterns of visual image and sound, contributed to creating perceived congruence.

The effect of the combination of semantic and formal congruency was examined using telop patterns (Kim et al., 2006). As described before, the similarity of affective impression between sound effects and type styles of telop characters contributed to creating perceived congruence between sounds and telops. The highly congruent audiovisual stimuli of this study were used to examine the combination effect of semantic and formal congruency. In these stimuli, sounds and telop patterns were synchronized. To discuss the combination effect of semantic and formal congruency, the synchronization of sounds and telops was intentionally degraded. The onset of sounds was preceded or delayed 1.8 seconds from the onset of telop patterns.

Generally, when sounds and telops were not synchronized, the perceived congruence of the audiovisual stimuli was degraded. However, when the effect of similarity of auditory and visual affects was very prominent, the effect of degradation of formal congruency caused by damage of the synchronization between the sounds and images was slight. Although sounds and telops were not synchronized, the congruence of such stimuli was kept at a high level.

To increase perceived congruence based on formal congruency, synchronization of auditory and visual elements seems to be crucial. However, there might be a temporal margin associated with the perception of synchronization. In the real world, the transmitted speeds of sound and light are not equal; the speed of light is much faster than that of sound. Furthermore, auditory and visual information is independently transmitted from peripheral organs to the central nervous system of human beings, and transmitted speeds in the auditory and visual nervous system are reportedly different (Stein & Stanford, 2008). Related to synchronization judgment, the temporal gap between auditory and visual information is corrected in the brain. Therefore, human beings can adapt to small time gaps between auditory and visual information (Nishida, Fujisaki, Kashino, & Shimojo, 2004). When the effect of semantic congruency is very prominent, sensitivity to synchronization of auditory and visual events might be reduced.

Conclusion

In this chapter, various findings from empirical studies on perceived congruence between sound and moving pictures have been discussed. These findings enhance our understanding of how people process audiovisual materials in everyday life, including television programs, movies, and other electronic multimedia such as video games or online videos. Furthermore, they provide various suggestions relevant for producers, sound designers, and film-music composers of visual media productions to assist in creating impressive and effective audiovisual works.

Acknowledgments

This work was partially supported by the Ministry of Education, Culture, Sports in Japan, Science and Technology, Grant-in-Aid for Scientific Research (C), 22615027, 2010–2012. The original sources of Figures 7.6 and 7.7 of this chapter are provided in the captions, and were subsequently included in somewhat altered form in Shin-ichiro Iwamiya, 'Subjective congruence between moving picture and sound,' in *Proceedings of the 10th International Conference on Music Perception and Cognition* (2008): 83–87.

References

Arita, M., & Iwamiya, S. (2004). The effects of structural characteristic of switching patterns and pitch patterns of sound on the subjective congruency of sound and moving picture. In *Proceedings of the Autumn Meeting of Japanese Society of Music Perception and Cognition* (pp. 71–76). Kyoto, Japan: Japanese Society of Music Perception and Cognition. (In Japanese.)

Arita, M., Su, X., Kawakami H., Ueda, M., & Iwamiya, S. (2005). The subjective congruency between direction of pitch movement and direction of switching pattern movement. In *Proceedings of the Autumn Meeting of Japanese Society of Music Perception and Cognition* (pp. 31–36). Kyoto, Japan: Japanese Society of Music Perception and Cognition. (In Japanese.)

Bolivar, V. J., Cohen, A. J., & Fentress, J. C. (1994). Semantic and formal congruency in music and motion pictures: Effect on the interpretation of visual action. *Psychomusicology, 13*, 28–59.

Cohen, A. J. (2001). Music as a source of emotion in film. In P. N. Juslin & J. A. Sloboda (Eds.), *Music and emotion: Theory and research* (pp. 249–272). New York, NY: Oxford University Press.

Dixon, N. F., & Spitz, L. (1980). The detection of auditory visual desynchrony. *Perception, 9*, 719–721.

Eitan, Z., & Granot, R. Y. (2006). How music moves: Musical parameters and images of motion. *Music Perception, 23*, 221–248.

Fujiyama, S., Oonishi, E., & Iwamiya, S. (2010). Continuous measurement of emotion caused by music and moving picture. *Proceedings of the Auditory Research Meeting, The Acoustical Society of Japan, 40*, 833–837. (In Japanese.)

Iwamiya, S. (1994). Interactions between auditory and visual processing when listening to music in an audiovisual context: 1. Matching 2. Audio quality. *Psychomusicology, 13*, 133–154.

Iwamiya, S. (2002). Multimodal communication by music and motion picture. In *Proceedings of the 7th International Conference on Music Perception and Cognition* (pp. 3–8). Rundle Mall, Australia: Causal Productions.

Iwamiya, S. & Hayashi, K. (1999). The effects of color on the impression of music. *Design issue of Kyushu Institute of Design, 1*, 63–68. (In Japanese.)

Iwamiya, S., Jogetsu, Y., Sugano, Y., & Takada, M. (2002). The effects of musical tempo and tonality and visual speed and density on perception of audiovisual content. *Journal of Music Perception and Cognition, 8*, 53–64. (In Japanese.)

Iwamiya, S., & Ozaki, H. (2004). Formal congruency between image patterns and pitch patterns, In *Proceedings of the 8th International Conference on Music Perception and Cognition* (pp. 145–148). Rundle Mall, Australia: Causal Productions.

Iwamiya, S., Su. X., Koyama, M., & Kim, K. H. (2010). Subjective congruence between complex transformation patterns of moving pictures and pitch shift of a sound: rating experiments for Japanese, Korean and Chinese participants. *Japanese Journal of Physiological Anthropology, 15*, 105–113. (In Japanese.)

Iwamiya, S., Sugano, Y., & Kouda, K. (2000). The effects of synchronization of temporal structures of sound and motion picture on the impression of audio-visual contents. In *Proceedings of the 2000 IEEE International Conference on Systems, Man, and Cybernetics* (pp. 1222–1225). (CD-ROM; IEEE Catalog Number 00CH37166C, ISBN 0-7803-6586-0.)

Kim, K. H., & Iwamiya, S (2008). Formal congruency between telop patterns and sound effects. *Music Perception, 25(5)*, 429–448.

Kim, K. H., Iwamiya, S., & Fujimaru, S. (2005). Effects of similarity of impressions between sound effects and shapes of telop characters. *Journal of Music Perception and Cognition, 11*, 73–90. (In Japanese.)

Kim, K. H., Iwasaki, K., & Iwamiya, S. (2007). Effects of semantic congruency between impressions of words in telops and sound effects in telop presentation. *The Journal of the Acoustical Society of Japan, 63*, 121–129. (In Japanese.)

Kim, K. H., Iwamiya, S., & Kitano, H. (2008). Subjective congruence between rotating transition of moving picture and pitch shift pattern of a sound. *Journal of Music Perception and Cognition, 14*, 29–36. (In Japanese.)

Kim, K. H., Iwamiya, S., & Kitano, H. (2009). Subjective congruence between rotating movement of a visual image and pitch modulation of a sound. *Ergonomics, 45*, 336–343. (In Japanese.)

Lipscomb, S. D. (2005). The perception of audio-visual composites: Accent structure alignment of simple stimuli. *Selected Reports in Ethnomusicology, 12*, 37–67.

Lipscomb, S. D., & Kendall, R. A. (1994). Perceptual judgement of the relationship between musical and visual components in film. *Psychomusicology, 13*, 60–98.

Lipscomb, S. D., & Kim, E. M. (2004). Perceived match between visual parameters and auditory correlates: An experimental multimedia investigation. In S. D. Lipscomb, R. Ashley, R. O. Gjerdingen, & P. Webster (Eds.), *Proceedings of the 8th International Conference on Music Perception and Cognition* (pp. 72–75). Evanston, IL: Society for Music Perception & Cognition.

Maeda, F., Kanai, R., and Shimojo, S. (2004). Changing pitch induced visual motion illusion, *Current Biology, 14*, 990–991.

Marks, L. E. (1989). On cross-modal similarity: The perceptual structure of pitch, loudness, and brightness. *Journal of Experimental Psychology: Human Perception and Performance, 15*, 586–602.

Neuhoff, J. G., & McBeath, M. K. (1996). The Doppler illusion: The influence of dynamic intensity change on perceived pitch. *Journal of Experimental Psychology: Human Perception and Performance, 22*, 970–985.

Nishida, S., Fujisaki, W., Kashino, M., & Shimojo, S. (2004). Reaction of audio-visual simultaneity: Where does it occur? In *Proceedings of 18th International Congress on Acoustics*, We2.X2.5. (CD-ROM; ISBN 4-9901915-6-0.)

Rusconi, E., Kwan, B., Giordano, B. L., Umiltà, C., & Butterworth, B. (2006). Spatial representation of pitch height: The SMARC effect. *Cognition, 99*, 113–129.

Stein, B. E., and Stanford, T. R. (2008). Multisensory integration: Current issues from the perspective of the single neuron, *Neuroscience, 9*, 255–267.

Stevens, S. S. (1957). On the psychophysical law. *Psychological Review, 64*, 153–181.

Su, X., Kim, K. H., & Iwamiya, S. (2009). Subjective congruence between switching patterns of moving pictures and pitch shift of sound. *The Journal of the Acoustical Society of Japan, 65*, 555–562. (In Japanese.)

Su, X., Kim, K. H., & Iwamiya, S. (2010). Subjective congruence between complex transformation patterns of an image and monotonous pitch shift patterns of a sound. *The Journal of the Acoustical Society of Japan, 66*, 497–505. (In Japanese.)

Sugano, Y., & Iwamiya, S. (1998). On the matching of music and motion picture using computer graphics and computer music. In *Proceedings of the 5th International Conference on Music Perception and Cognition* (pp. 465–468). Seoul, Korea: Western Music Research Institute, Seoul National University.

Sugano, Y., & Iwamiya, S. (2000). The effects of the synchronization between auditory and visual accents and those of matching between musical tempo and visual speed on the emotional impression of combinations of motion picture and music. *The Journal of the Acoustical Society of Japan, 56*, 695–704. (In Japanese.)

Chapter 8

How pitch and loudness shape musical space and motion

Zohar Eitan

Tel Aviv University, Israel

For the listener-viewer, the musical and visual aspects of multimedia can relate in diverse ways, each of which may affect the perceived meaning of the conjoined artifact (see Cohen, 2005, for a review). For instance, music and visuals can be temporally congruent or incongruent, as their points of accentuation synchronize or desynchronize (Kendall, 2005a; Lipscomb, 1995; Lipscomb & Kendall, 1994); the emotions they express or evoke may appear similar or contrasting (and the entire gamut between these poles); and music may evoke specific objects or events that may or may not concur with those presented visually.

This chapter presents a different, and seemingly simpler, type of audiovisual correlation, one which nevertheless may itself affect the complex relationships just mentioned: associations between basic auditory features, particularly pitch and loudness, and aspects of physical space and motion, such as spatial location and direction, speed, or physical size. Pitch, for instance, is referred to in diverse languages as 'high' and 'low.' Is pitch 'height' indeed consistently related, in perceptual or cognitive processes, with spatial height? Is pitch also associated with other attributes of space and motion, not necessarily codified in language, like distance, object size, or speed?

This chapter surveys empirical research pertaining to perceptual and cognitive associations of auditory pitch and loudness with spatial or spatio-kinetic features, emphasizing studies investigating these relationships in a musical context. Notably, most relevant psychological research—psychophysical, perceptual, or cognitive—did not examine music or musical multimedia, but simple auditory and visual stimuli like single pitches and points of light. While variables in such stimuli can be easily controlled, they are far removed from the complex, dynamic experience of music and of music-related multimedia, such as films, operas, or computer games. Here, I review some of that basic cross-modal research (also surveyed in Marks, 2000, 2004; Spence, 2011), then proceed to report in more detail several recent studies examining such interactions using music or music-like stimuli. Finally, I will discuss an insufficiently explored issue particularly relevant to the perception and cognition of cross-modal interactions in music and music-related multimedia: how auditory-spatial interactions function when stimuli are *dynamic* (time-varying). For instance, how would the association of pitch change (pitch 'rise' or 'fall') with physical size compare with that of 'static' pitch values ('high' versus 'low' pitch). The few studies that have examined dynamic audio-spatial interactions suggest that they differ from static ones in important ways.

Cross-domain feature correspondence

The relationships discussed in this chapter, as well as other associations of auditory features, demonstrate *cross-domain feature correspondence.*[1] In cross-domain correspondence, values of a feature in one domain of perception or cognition (e.g., high spatial location, visually perceived) are associated in a consistent way with values in another (e.g., 'high' auditory pitch). This association may affect perception, cognition, or action related to one or both domains. The associated domains may demonstrate *cross-modal* correspondence when they belong to different sense modalities, as in the given example; they may also be *intramodal*—belong to the same modality (e.g., auditory pitch and auditory-perceived spatial height). Feature correspondences may also extend beyond sensory relationships per se, linking sensory features to diverse domains of human experience, through experiential associations or abstract 'conceptual metaphors' (Lakoff & Johnson, 1980). For instance, higher pitch has been shown to associate, in musical contexts, with positive emotional valence, femininity, and younger age (Eitan & Timmers, 2010; Gabrielsson & Lindström, 2010). Here, the general term cross-domain (rather than cross-modal) feature correspondence, which includes such relationships, is used, though this chapter mainly discusses correspondence of features between and within sensory modalities. Note also that feature correspondences may occur when the same feature can be perceived by different sense modalities (e.g., spatial location, which can be traced by sight, hearing, and touch; or shape, which may be perceived visually or tactilely). This chapter, however, mainly discusses correspondences between different, and often apparently unrelated, features, such as pitch and spatial height or loudness and size (see also Marks, 1978; Spence, 2011).

The psychological effects of cross-domain feature correspondence, as well as the types and levels of mental processing they involve, may vary considerably. Feature correspondence may directly affect stimulus perception; for example, perceiving higher pitches as actually stemming from a higher spatio-visual source (Pratt, 1930; Roffler & Butler, 1968). It may affect our ability to selectively attend to one modality or the other, and thus facilitate or inhibit tasks like stimulus detection or discrimination. For instance, people classify high and low pitch faster when the higher pitch is accompanied by a spatially higher visual stimulus, as compared to trials in which the higher pitch is accompanied by a spatially lower visual stimulus (see Marks, 2004, for a research review). It may facilitate or inhibit motor responses whose features are congruent or incongruent with those of a stimulus (e.g., pressing a lower or higher key when detecting a high or low pitch; see Lidji, Kolinsky, Lochy, Karnas, & Morais, 2007; Rusconi, Kwan, Giordano, Umiltà, & Butterworth, 2006). It may evoke a sense of compatibility or incompatibility between two features—imagine, for instance, a sunrise film scene whose soundtrack features music gradually descending to the lowest pitch register, in diminuendo—without necessarily affecting their perception (Eitan & Timmers, 2010). Cross-modal correspondence is also often expressed in the language used to describe perceived musical and auditory features, teeming with synesthetic and kinesthetic metaphors (high pitch, bright sound, small voice, rough dissonance, etc.; see Zbikowski, 2008).

Feature correspondences may also differ in their origins and in their development throughout the lifetime. Some, such as loudness and brightness (Lewkowicz & Turkewitz, 1980), or pitch and spatial elevation (Jeschonek, Pauen, & Babocsai, 2012; Wagner, Winner, Cicchetti, & Gardner, 1981; Walker et al., 2010), may be inborn, or at least originate in very early development, since they affect behavior and even physiological response (e.g., heart rate habituation; Lewkowicz & Turkewitz, 1980) in early infancy. Indeed, some correspondences (pitch and visual lightness; Ludwig, Adachi, & Matsuzawa, 2011) were also reported for non-human primates. Such presumably innate correspondences may stem from structural similarities in the neural processing of both features (e.g., accelerated firing rate for both increased auditory and visual intensity, i.e., loudness and brightness) or from a shared or nearby brain areas (Spence, 2011). Other correspondences (e.g., between pitch and size; Marks, Hammeal, & Bornstein, 1987; Mondloch & Maurer, 2004) mature later, and may reflect statistical learning of naturally occurring correlations or effects of a linguistic lexicon in which the same terms (e.g., high/low, bright/dim) are used for features in different modalities.

In short, cross-modal (and more generally, cross-domain) correspondences do not seem to present a single phenomenon. They are *not* all based on a single type of mental processing, associated with the same processing level or sharing the same brain structures. Rather, the term may be used as an umbrella term, relating phenomena with different origins, which may affect perception, cognition, or action in many different ways and at different processing levels. In the following sections I will survey some of these phenomena, in so far as they relate to correspondences between pitch or loudness and aspects of space and motion.

Pitch height, space, and motion

What this section discusses and what it does not

Pitch perception is multidimensional. The scaling of pitch from 'high' to 'low' is only one—and seemingly the simplest—of several structures delineating this basic auditory parameter. These include, for instance, octave-equivalence and its concomitant pitch-chroma (pitch-class) relationships, and fifth-related pitch-classes, which generate the circle of fifths and the parameter of key distance stemming from it (see Krumhansl, 1990, for related cognitive research). Here, however, I deal only with the ways *pitch height* (generally associated with the fundamental frequencies of harmonic tones), and *pitch directions* (ascent, descent) are associated with space and motion, putting aside other important structures involving pitch.

Sound sources may be projected from different spatial locations and move from one point in space to another, and thus directly relate to perceived physical space and motion. Here, however, I will only marginally discuss auditory *localization*—how we actually perceive the location and movement of sound sources. Rather, I will present research indicating that non-spatial attributes of perceived sound (pitch in this section, loudness in the next) are associated by listeners with aspects of space and motion, associations that do not necessarily reflect the acoustics of sound localization. In other words: sounds do not need to actually move, or to stem from different spatial locations, to evoke associations with motion and space. In this section, I will survey studies examining how pitch associates with location and motion in the three spatial axes (vertical, lateral, and sagittal), speed, and physical size. While the relationship of pitch and spatial height, embedded in language and music notation, may be the first that comes to mind, pitch has been shown to associate perceptually with other spatial and spatio-kinetic domains, including lateral location and motion, distance, and perhaps most important, physical size.

Pitch and spatial height

A variety of languages (including English, German, Japanese, and Hebrew), as well as Western musical notation, associate pitch polarities ('high' versus 'low' pitch) with the vertical spatial plane, and pitch change (e.g., 'rise' and 'fall') with motion up or down, respectively.[2] While pitch height is not literally associated with spatial height—higher pitch does not necessarily stem from an elevated location—diverse empirical findings suggest that the mapping of pitch onto spatial height does not merely reflect a convenient figure of speech, but may affect perception, cognition, and action in a variety of ways. For instance, 'higher' pitch is actually perceived as being emitted from a higher location in space: listeners who were asked to detect the apparent locations from which tones varying in pitch were emitted, associated higher-pitched sounds with higher locations, regardless of the actual source location (Cabrera, Ferguson, Tilley, & Morimoto, 2005; Pratt, 1930; Roffler & Butler, 1968). The association of pitch and height also affects perception and action in a variety of implicit ways, independent of conscious reflection or awareness. Thus, in speeded discrimination experiments (Ben-Artzi & Marks, 1995; Bernstein & Edelstein, 1971; Melara & O'Brien, 1987) participants are presented with higher or lower pitch simultaneously with visual stimuli (dots on a computer screen) higher and lower in space. They are asked to rapidly discriminate (by pressing a pre-designated key) each auditory stimulus as high or low pitch, while ignoring concurrent visual stimuli; in a complementary task, participants discriminate visual stimuli, ignoring auditory stimuli. Despite instructions, however, participants cannot ignore the 'irrelevant' stimuli. Rather, their performance is better (i.e., faster and more accurate) when visual and auditory stimuli are congruent (high pitch and high spatial location, low pitch and low spatial location). Correspondingly, congruence of pitch and height is also revealed via stimulus-response compatibility effects (the SMARC effect; see Lidji et al., 2007; Rusconi et al., 2006): when asked to respond to high and low pitch by pressing a spatially high and low key, respectively, participants' performance is considerably better than when response keys are reversed (high pitch/low key, low pitch/high key).

While these experiments suggest that the congruence of pitch and spatial height can be automatically activated and does not necessarily rely on conscious reflection, this association may still be semantically mediated. Martino and Marks (1999, 2001) distinguish between two hypotheses concerning the source of cross-modal congruence effects. The *sensory hypothesis* suggests that 'congruence effects involve absolute correspondences processed within low-level sensory mechanisms' (Martino & Marks,

2001, p. 64), which may stem from shared neural codes or resources. In contrast, the *semantic-coding hypothesis* suggests that cross-modal congruence is meaning-based, and mediated by experience (e.g., frequent correlation between values in two modalities, as with loud sound and large objects) or language (e.g., by the shared tags high/low for pitch and spatial elevation), producing abstract representations based on an 'abstract semantic network that captures synesthetic correspondence' (p. 64).

Several lines of research, however, suggest that the correspondence of pitch and spatial height may have a perceptual basis. First, the direction of pitch change has been shown to affect the attention of infants (less than 6 months of age) to corresponding visual stimuli, indicating that this cross-modal analogy is inborn or at least learned very early in life, when language and cultural knowledge are not yet available (Jeschonek et al., 2012; Wagner et al., 1981; Walker et al., 2010).

Furthermore, recent experiments with adult participants demonstrate effects of pitch direction on visual perception, while controlling for semantic influences. For instance, Maeda, Kanai, and Shimojo (2004) presented two horizontal gratings (parallel bars) moving simultaneously in contrasting directions (up and down), such that the resulting overall motion was ambiguous, together with ascending or descending pitch glides. Participants, asked to judge whether visual motion was ascending or descending, tended to judge motion as ascending when accompanied by an ascending pitch, and as descending—when accompanied by a descending pitch. Replacing actual ascending and descending pitch with the words 'up' and 'down' did not produce this effect, supporting the hypothesis that the effect is primarily perceptual, rather than semantic in origin.

Importantly, effects of pitch/height correspondences were also found by way of indirect measures, i.e., where the experimental tasks did not demand attending to either pitch height or elevation. Evans and Treisman (2010, experiment 2) presented to participants high and low piano and violin sounds simultaneously with parallel gratings on the computer screen. The gratings pointed to the right or left, and appeared above or below a fixation point. The participants' task did not directly involve pitch or spatial height. Rather, they were asked to rapidly indicate whether they heard a violin or piano sound (indirect auditory task) or whether the gratings viewed pointed to the right or to the left (indirect visual task). Though tasks did not involve attending to pitch height or to visual elevation, pitch/elevation congruence significantly improved performance. Participants discriminated instrumental timbres, as well as lateral visual orientation, better when pitch and height were congruent (higher pitch/higher position; lower pitch/lower position). In a different indirect task, using the oddball paradigm, Raphaeli (2011) presented to participants ascending or descending pitch glides simultaneously with dots moving up or down on a computer screen. A gap (a brief silence and/or brief disappearance of the dot) appeared in a minority (15%) of the visual or auditory stimuli (the 'oddball' condition). Participants were asked to detect gaps 'as rapidly and accurately as possible,' by pressing a computer keyboard key. Detection was better (lower error rate) and faster when pitch and visual direction were congruent (ascending glides and ascending dots or descending glides and descending dots), though the task had nothing to do with either pitch direction or spatial direction. The significant effects of pitch/height congruence in such indirect tasks, where attention is directed away from both attributes, suggest a perceptual source, automatic and independent of attention, for pitch/height correspondences.

Pitch height and lateral position

A number of experiments, using different methods, have indicated that pitch height is associated with *lateral position*: higher pitch is related to right-side position, and lower pitch—to left-side position. Mudd (1963) presented children with pairs of sounds, and asked them to place a peg representing each sound on a pegboard. Children tended to place pegs representing higher pitches not only above, but also to the right of those representing lower pitches. Using the very different paradigm of speeded detection with adult participants, Stevens and Arieh (2005) asked participants to respond rapidly when they detected a visual target in either the right or left side of the computer screen, while trying to ignore a tone (high or low) preceding the target by 400 milliseconds. Reaction time was significantly faster when pitch and lateral position were congruent (high-right, low-left). Deutsch, Hamaoui, and Henthorn (2007) show that pitch-laterality mapping may generate an actual perceptual illusion. They presented to participants a constant oboe-like tone together with a sine tone glide. The glide and the constant tone alternated between the loudspeakers: when one emanated from the left, the other emanated from the right. While the constant tone was perceived correctly as switching between right and left, the glide was heard as a continuous sound, moving either from right to left or from left to right. The perceived lateral direction of the sound depended on pitch contour: in 'ascending' glides, the sound was perceived as moving from left to right, while in 'descending' glides it was perceived as moving from right to left. Notably, this illusion was consistent in right-handed participants only.

A source of such pitch-laterality associations may be the spatial association of the lateral and vertical axes: when up–down stimuli were mapped to left–right responses in stimulus-response compatibility (SRC) experiments, an up-right/down-left mapping advantage was found (Cho & Proctor, 2005; Weeks & Proctor, 1990). Since pitch is mapped onto spatial verticality (higher pitch/higher position), and spatial verticality is mapped onto laterality (high/right, low/left positions), mapping of pitch into the lateral dimension may indirectly result. Interestingly, however, mappings of the vertical to the horizontal dimension were stronger—not only in auditory tasks—for musicians, particularly pianists. This suggests that for musicians this mapping may also stem from the structure of the musical keyboard, where higher pitches are to the right of lower ones (Stewart, Walsh, & Frith, 2004). Indeed, some experiments suggest that the pitch-laterality mapping affects mainly musically trained participants. In a study by Rusconi and associates (2006), already mentioned, an association of stimulus (pitch height) and response (spatial position of response key) was found for the vertical dimension, regardless of musical training, but when lateral position was involved, the formation of an association differed for musically trained and untrained participants. Training-based differences emerged in particular for 'indirect tasks,' in which task requirements neither attracted attention to pitch height nor referred to this dimension explicitly; rather, participants were asked to discriminate the instrumental timbres (woodwind versus percussion) of both high- and low-pitched tones. For musically trained participants, a significant interaction of pitch height and the lateral position of response keys nevertheless emerged: when pitch was high, timbres were discriminated better (faster and with less errors) given a right-side response key, while when pitch was low, timbres were discriminated better given a left-side response key. Importantly, this effect was not found for the musically untrained, suggesting that musicians may develop a stronger and more automatic association of pitch and lateral direction, which does not rely on explicit labeling or on allocating attentional resources to pitch height (see also Lidji et al., 2007, for comparable results).

Pitch height and distance

There seems to be an acoustical basis for perceptual correspondences of pitch height, as well as pitch direction, with spatial distance: the Doppler effect in which frequency is shifted down for a receding source. For instance, a continuous sound of a train horn would be heard as a downward glide when the train steadily moves away. Thus, a lower or descending pitch would be associated with greater or increasing distance. However, in apparent contrast to the Doppler effect, participants in a music-induced imagery experiment associated pitch *rises* with increasing distance (Eitan & Granot, 2006). In a rating task, in which participants rated high and low pitch, as well as music with high or low overall pitch register, on a number of polar adjective scales, no significant correspondence was found between pitch height and distance ratings: higher pitch (or music in a higher pitch register) was not significantly associated with either 'near' or 'far,' as compared to lower pitch or register (Eitan & Timmers, 2010). Thus, while (unlike the case with the correspondence between pitch and height) a natural acoustic correlation between pitch height and distance exists, this correlation does not, rather surprisingly, seem to be reflected in our associations of the two dimensions, at least within musical contexts.

In accounting for these equivocal results, and for the apparent contrast between them and implications of the Doppler effect, two issues may be mentioned. First, to an observer situated on a relatively flat surface in a three-dimensional space (probably our most frequent point of view in daily experience), height would naturally correlate with distance, such that higher objects would be more distant than lower ones. Possibly relevant is also the association of higher pitch with smaller size and the apparent smaller size of distant objects (discussed later). Since higher pitch is 'small,' and distant objects are also subjectively smaller than proximate objects, higher pitch and greater distance may be associated.

Interestingly, however, an association between pitch rise and looming (rapidly approaching) motion was found for rhesus monkeys (Ghazanfar & Meier, 2009). Indirectly, such association may be reflected in humans by a tendency to hear rising pitch with unchanging intensity as increasing in loudness (Neuhoff, McBeath, & Wanzie, 1999),[3] and thus presumably as approaching (loudness increase is an important auditory cue for approaching motion; see later).

Pitch height and speed

Pitch height has also been associated, through several experimental paradigms, with the speed of motion: higher pitch is perceived as moving faster than lower pitch. Using a Stroop-like paradigm, Walker and Smith (1984, 1986) show that discrimination of the words 'fast' and 'slow' is quicker when the words are accompanied by high (5500 Hz) and low (50 Hz) tones, respectively, than when 'fast' is accompanied by the low-pitched tone, and 'slow'—by the high-pitched tone (Walker & Smith, 1984, 1986). In an adjective rating experiment, participants rated the metaphor 'fast' as more appropriate to a high-register musical segment, and 'slow' as more appropriate to a low-register segment, though the two did not differ in tempo or attack rate (Eitan & Timmers, 2010). Notably, the associations of static and dynamic pitch with speed seem to contrast: though lower register music is perceived as 'slower' than higher register (Boltz, 2011), and participants (musicians and non-musicians alike) prefer faster tempi for higher-pitched music (Tamir & Eitan, submitted), descent in pitch is associated with accelerating, rather than decelerating motion (Eitan & Granot, 2006).

Pitch height and physical size

In a variety of experimental paradigms involving both children and adults, larger physical size was consistently associated with lower pitch. Three-year-old children matched larger objects with lower pitch (Mondloch & Maurer, 2004), though Marks et al. (1987) found a similar tendency only at or above 9 years of age. For adults, the pitch/size correspondence is reflected also in implicit tasks. When adult participants were asked to rapidly judge whether a visual stimulus was larger or smaller than a standard stimulus preceding it (Gallace & Spence, 2006), responses were faster when the comparison stimulus was accompanied by a sound congruent to it in pitch (larger stimuli with lower pitch, smaller stimuli with higher pitch) than for incongruent stimuli (larger stimuli with higher pitch, smaller stimuli with lower pitch). Similarly, when smaller or larger visual stimuli were presented with high or low pitch, participants discriminated both visual and auditory stimuli faster when stimuli were congruent. A congruence effect similar in magnitude was also observed in an indirect task (similar to that described earlier for pitch and height), in which participants were not required to attend to either pitch or visual size (Evans & Treisman, 2010). This suggests that the pitch/size correspondence is based on perceptual processing and does not require attention, let alone conscious reflection. Comparable results were reported when the words 'large' and 'small,' rather than actual objects, were matched with high and low pitch in a Stroop-like task (Walker & Smith, 1984, 1986). In musical contexts, participants rated the metaphor 'small' as more appropriate for high-register music, and 'large' as more appropriate for lower-register music (Eitan & Timmers, 2010).

The association of pitch and size may stem from our life-long experience of correlation between an object's size and the pitch it would produce. In particular, pitch height is correlated across animal species with body size, as larger species tend to produce lower-pitched sounds. This correlation may have important behavioral ramifications for a variety of species, including humans. Ethologist Eugene S. Morton observed a widespread tendency among both mammals and birds to use lower-pitched, rough voice in confrontational situations, when the expression of aggression or hostility is called for, and higher-pitched, tone-like voice as an expression of submission or friendliness. Morton (1977, 1982, 1994) suggests that since larger body size is advantageous in a physical conflict, animals in an aggressive stance would try to appear larger both visually (e.g., erecting their feathers, raising their tail) and vocally, by producing lower-pitched sounds, associated with larger, stronger animals (see also Ohala, 1994; Scherer, 2003). Correspondingly, an expression of submission would entail appearing small and hence unthreatening, and would thus be related to higher pitch. Associations of lower pitch with dominance and threat, possibly stemming from the pitch/size correspondence, are also effective for humans (Puts, Gaulin, & Verdolini, 2006). The pitch/size association seems to effect emotional expression in music as well, as average pitch height affects the characterization of music as more or less threatening (Huron, Kinney, & Precoda, 2006).

Note, however, that studies relating higher pitch and smaller size have mostly used static auditory stimuli (a stationary pitch or a steady pitch range). Importantly, when dynamic stimuli (ascending or descending pitch) were mapped into size, ascent was associated with increase, rather than decrease in size (Antovic, 2009; Eitan, Schupak, Gotler, & Marks, in press; Kim & Iwamiya, 2008). I will return to this important incongruity between static and dynamic stimuli later.

Pitch height, then, interacts not only with spatial height (a relationship shown to be perceptual and possibly inborn), but also with laterality, depth, speed, and size. A one-to-many relationship associates pitch space with multiple dimensions of physical space and motion.

Loudness, space, and motion

Loudness becomes associated with different aspects of physical space and motion in diverse ways. Some associations (e.g., loudness and distance) clearly derive from acoustical correlations between sound intensity and spatial location or motion, while others (e.g., loudness and spatial height) may be based on abstract cross-domain mappings or on language, having less to do with actual acoustical relationships. Here, I focus on perceptual and cognitive correspondences between loudness and several attributes of space and motion—distance, spatial height, speed, and physical size—some of which have only recently been studied empirically.

Loudness and distance

Loudness change is the main (though not the only) auditory cue for distance change, as sound pressure level (SPL), the main determinant of auditory loudness, drops (given little or no reflections or reverberations) by approximately 6 dB per doubling of distance, according to the inverse square law (Blauert, 1997; see Zahorik, Brungart, & Bronkhorst, 2005, for a review of recent research).

When visual information is lacking (e.g., at night, inside a thick forest) loudness increase may be the main cue that an object is rapidly approaching. Rapid and reliable perception of such looming loudness change, and preparation for immediate action thereafter, may thus have an important survival value, because in natural environments the approaching object may present an immediate threat or, alternatively, provide a welcome but fleeting food source. Recent behavioral and neurophysiological research indeed suggests that increase in loudness serves as a basic, low-level alert signal. Listeners overestimate increasing loudness change, as compared to decreasing change of an equal intensity (Neuhoff, 1998). Correspondingly, listeners underestimate arrival time (Gordon & Rosenblum, 2005) and distance (Neuhoff, 2001) of approaching sound sources, increasing in loudness. Attentional bias toward increasing loudness has been observed even in 6-month-old infants (Morrongiello, Hewitt, & Gotowiec, 1991) and in non-human primates (Rhesus monkeys; Ghazanfar, Neuhoff, & Logothetis, 2002), comparably to findings concerning visual looming (e.g., Schiff, 1965). Physiological and neurophysiological research, however, suggests that the source of this bias is pre-attentive, and even pre-perceptual. Bach et al. (2008) found that sound stimuli increasing in loudness (as compared to decreasing and unchanging ones) facilitate an autonomic orienting reflex. Using event-related functional magnetic resonance imaging, they also found that stimuli increasing in loudness strongly activate the amygdala (associated with early processing of arousing signals), as well as the left temporal plane, associated with auditory spatial analysis, and the superior temporal sulcus, related to cross-modal interaction and integration. Correspondingly, using transcranial magnetic stimulation, Romei, Murray, Cappe, and Thut (2009) found that sounds increasing in intensity heightened *visual* cortex excitability. Importantly, the onset of this effect occurred a mere 80 milliseconds following stimulus onset, about 35 milliseconds prior to psychophysical discrimination threshold. As the authors propose, these results are 'strongly suggestive of a mechanism that allows for auditory-driven modulation of visual cortex at pre-perceptual processing stages' (Romei et al., 2009, p. 4). Thus, complementary evidence suggests that increase in loudness, due to its association with decreasing distance from the sound source, serves as a primeval signal of impending danger. This signal may automatically activate a multi-modal brain network, aimed at immediately dealing with the incoming sound source.[4]

A recent study of musical tension (Granot & Eitan, 2011) reveals that increasing loudness (*crescendo*) serves as a key determinant of tension in musical contexts. Regardless of the values of other musical parameters manipulated (pitch direction, pitch register, and tempo change), listeners perceived musical segments increasing in loudness as increasing in tension. Loudness change also had the strongest effect on the perception of the overall tension level of a musical phrase. Notably, listeners' ratings of tension in this study were conscious, language-mediated cognitive responses, far removed from the low-level neurophysiological and perceptual effects described earlier. Yet, results suggest that the spatio-kinetic correspondences of increasing loudness, and their primeval implications of tension and threat, may importantly affect listeners' emotional responses to music.

Loudness and spatial height

Loudness and spatial height, unlike loudness and distance, do not seem to correlate physically or perceptually in a direct way.[5] Yet, diverse languages associate loudness levels with elevation-related terms. *Alto* (from the Latin *altus*) denotes both (spatially) high and loud in Italian, Spanish, and Portuguese. In English, the loud speaker is urged 'don't raise your voice,' while in Hebrew *kol ram* (literally 'high voice') or *kol nisa* (literally, 'a raised voice') both denote 'loud voice' (e.g., Deuteronomy 27:14).[6] Do loudness and height, like pitch and height, associate cognitively or interact perceptually? Several recent studies suggest that they do. In a music-induced imagery task, diminuendi were significantly associated with falling or descending motion—indeed, as strong an association as that with descents in pitch. This association was found for adult musicians and non-musicians (Eitan & Granot, 2006), children aged 6 and 11 (Eitan & Tubul, 2010), as well as congenitally blind adults (Eitan, Ornoy, & Granot, 2012). In a movement task, in which children (aged 4 to 10) were asked to move in a manner that would 'depict to a friend what the music is like,' crescendo and diminuendo were associated with motion up and down, respectively (Kohn & Eitan, 2009). Experiments using Garner's speeded classification paradigm (Eitan, Schupak, Gotler, & Marks, submitted) suggest that the congruence relationship between loudness and height may be automatic and does not necessarily rely on conscious reflection. In these experiments, participants were presented with sine tones increasing or decreasing in loudness simultaneously with dots ascending or descending on a computer screen. Participants performed two tasks: in the auditory task, they rapidly discriminated sounds changing in loudness, by pressing one pre-assigned key for crescendo, and another for diminuendo, while attempting to ignore visual stimuli. In the visual task, they discriminated rises and falling dots, attempting to ignore the concurrent sounds. Congruent audiovisual combinations (crescendo and rising dots, diminuendo and falling dots) resulted in faster, more accurate responses than incongruent ones (crescendo and falling dots, diminuendo and rising dots) in both auditory and visual tasks.

Research investigating loudness-height correspondences, however, is still in its infancy, and the sources, processing levels, or the specific effects of this relationship are far from completely understood. Furthermore, current studies of this correspondence all involve dynamic stimuli (crescendo and diminuendo, moving dots) or responses (bodily motion). We do not know whether the loudness-height correspondence they indicate generalizes to static stimuli (steady loud and soft sounds) as well. Nevertheless, findings to date do suggest that the association between loudness and height is not merely lexical and may affect both the perception of music and that of music-related multimedia.

Loudness and speed

While sound perception associates loudness and distance, sound production may associate loudness and speed, since increased impact velocity would produce louder impact sound. Lifetime exposure to such naturally occurring correlations (particularly through self-motion, as in tapping, hand clapping, or playing a percussion instrument) may result in generalized associations between increased speed or velocity and increased loudness.

Loudness-speed correspondences were investigated in experiments involving imagery, adjective ratings, and motion tasks. In music-related imagery tasks adults and children associated stimuli in crescendi with accelerating physical motion, though no actual acceleration occurred in the stimuli, composed of equi-durational sounds (Eitan & Granot, 2006; Eitan & Tubul, 2010; Eitan et al., 2012). Interestingly, the loudness-speed relationship was asymmetrical: crescendi evoked images of acceleration, but diminuendi did not evoke images of deceleration. A comparable result for static loudness was obtained when children rated musical stimuli, in which loudness, pitch height, and tempo were systematically varied, on various bipolar adjective scales, including fast–slow (Eitan, Katz & Shen, 2010; Katz, 2011). Louder music was rated as 'faster' than softer music with the same tempo. The loudness-speed correspondence was also revealed in actual motion tasks, in which children tended to react to crescendi and diminuendi with accelerating and decelerating motion, respectively (Kohn & Eitan, 2009; Kohn, 2011).

Loudness and physical size

Children 3 years of age and older, asked to match sounds differing in pitch and loudness to objects of different sizes, matched larger objects with louder sounds (Smith & Sera, 1992). Similar associations of louder sound with larger physical size were found for participants varying in cultural and linguistic background, age, and musical training (Lipscomb & Kim, 2004; Walker, 1987). The loudness-size association may be based on experiential correlations between the size of objects (including humans and other animals) and the loudness of the sounds they tend to produce. Indeed, in everyday experience loudness serves a prominent role in the auditory discrimination of objects' length and overall size (Burro & Grassi, 2001; Carello, Anderson, & Kunkler-Peck, 1998).

A more direct perceptual relationship of loudness, as well as pitch, with phenomenal size or 'volume' was proposed by eminent psychophysicist S.S. Stevens. Stevens (1934) suggested that volume is a basic phenomenal attribute of sound; that is, we perceive sounds as occupying more or less space. Stevens shows that sounds' 'phenomenal volume' increases as their intensity increases and as frequency decreases. When presented with two sine tones differing in frequency and asked to change the intensity of one tone until it appeared equal in volume to the other, participants increased the intensity of higher tones, and decreased the intensity of lower tones. A larger, or more 'voluminous' pure sound, then, is higher in intensity but lower in frequency; and this relationship generally holds, in complex sounds, for the auditory attributes of loudness and pitch: to increase a sound's 'volume' one should reduce its pitch and increase its loudness.

Mapping music onto space and motion

Cross-domain correspondences found for simple stimuli like single tones do not necessarily apply to music or musical multimedia; likewise, the latter may reveal correspondences not found for simple stimuli. One reason for such possible discrepancy is that even the simplest music involves a continuous, dynamic interaction of many parameters at various levels of mental processing, from basic acoustical attributes to high-level, culture-specific aspects of harmonic and melodic structure. These diverse features do not necessarily interact in an additive way, and not enough is known concerning how they may conjoin in delineating cross-domain correspondences. Hence, a prerequisite for a study of cross-domain correspondences in music is being able, at least in part, to tell effects of different parameters apart.

A modest step toward understanding auditory-spatial and auditory-kinetic correspondences in musical contexts, while controlling for the interaction of musical parameters, is exemplified in several recent studies conducted by Eitan and associates. Here some of this research, still underway, is briefly presented, and its main findings so far are discussed.

Experiments using music-related imagery

In a series of studies involving diverse population groups (adults and children, both musically trained and untrained, as well as a group of congenitally blind participants), Eitan and associates asked participants to associate melodic stimuli with imagined motions of a human character, and to specify the type (e.g., walking, running), directions in the three spatial axes, and pace-change (acceleration, deceleration) of these imagined motions (Eitan & Granot, 2006, 2011; Eitan & Tubul, 2010; Eitan et al., 2012). The stimuli in these experiments consisted of pairs of brief melodic figures (with pair members presented to participants in random order), each pair presenting contrasting changes in a single musical parameter, while other parameters are kept constant between pair members. For instance, one stimulus presented a musical motive ascending sequentially in pitch, while a contrasting stimulus presented the same motive descending sequentially (Figure 8.1A); another pair of stimuli presented repeated equi-durational tones, either increasing or decreasing in loudness (crescendo versus diminuendo; Figure 8.1B). Other stimulus pairs presented contrasting changes in additional musical parameters, including tempo, the size of melodic intervals, or articulation (*staccato*, *legato*). These stimuli, while short, simple, and controllable, are more music-like than stimuli used in many psychophysical and perceptual experiments involving cross-domain correspondence, regarding both the sound used (sampled piano) and structure. (To hear some of the stimuli employed in this study, please visit <http://www.oup.co.uk/companion/tan>.)

Eitan and Granot (2006) used this task and stimuli in two experiments (differing in the overall tempo of stimuli) involving 173 adult participants. While corroborating some of the cross-domain correspondences found in previous studies using simpler stimuli, results suggest a more complex relationship between musical and spatio-kinetic parameters than previously realized in empirical research. Most musical parameters investigated, primarily pitch direction and loudness change, significantly affected several dimensions of motion imagery. Pitch direction was associated with

Figure 8.1 (A) Pitch direction: stimuli from Eitan and Granot (2006). (B) Loudness change: stimuli from Eitan and Granot (2006). (A) and (B) reprinted from figure 1 in Zohar Eitan and Roni Y. Granot, 'How Music Moves,' in *Music Perception* vol. 23, no. 3 (February 2006), pp. 221–248. © 2006 by the Regents of the University of California. Published by the University of California Press.

imagined motion along all three spatial axes (vertical, horizontal, and sagittal), as well as speed and the 'energy' participants ascribed to the imagined motion. Loudness change affected imagined motion in the vertical and sagittal (distance change) axes, speed change, and energy. Importantly, beyond expected music/motion correspondences, such as those between pitch direction and vertical direction, or loudness and distance change, results present some surprising mappings. Thus (as mentioned), pitch rise, rather than fall, was associated with motion away, in contrast to implications of the Doppler effect. Rising pitch patterns were associated with speeding up as well, though they involved equi-durational tones and no change of tempo. Crescendo[7] was related to accelerated motion (though, again, no change in tones' duration or overall tempo was actually involved) and diminuendo over a repeated tone was strongly associated with spatial descent.

A surprising finding of the study (Eitan & Granot, 2006), not reported in previous research, is that musical-spatial analogies are often directionally asymmetrical: a musical change in one direction evokes a significantly stronger spatial analogy than its opposite. Loudness changes (crescendi and diminuendi) are directionally asymmetrical with regard to vertical direction, as well as speed: while diminuendi are strongly associated with spatial descents, crescendi are not significantly associated with ascents; and while crescendi evoke speeding up, diminuendi do not evoke slowing down. The associations of pitch direction with space and motion are asymmetrical with regard to several dimensions: speed change, distance change, horizontal direction, and perhaps most importantly, vertical direction. Thus, though pitch descents (as might have been expected) strongly evoke spatial descents, pitch rises are associated with spatial ascents to a considerably lesser degree, and only for musically trained participants. In addition, pitch rise is associated with speeding up and approaching, while pitch fall is not associated with slowing down or moving away. Pitch rise, however, is significantly related to motion leftward, while falls do not significantly suggest rightward motion. In general, 'decreases' or abatements in a musical parameter, such as diminuendi or pitch descents, tended to be associated with spatial descents, while intensifications (pitch rises, crescendi, as well as accelerandi) were associated with increasing speed, rather than ascent.

Eitan and Tubul (2010) replicated this study with 60 school children, aged 6 and 11 years. They corroborated the major findings of the earlier study, including some of the asymmetries already noted. However, unlike adults, for which whom pitch direction seems to be the most important generator of virtual musical space, children related sound and motion primarily through changes in *loudness*. Loudness was significantly associated not only with distance, but with vertical direction (as strongly or more strongly than pitch), speed, and energy. In contrast, pitch contour evoked fewer and weaker spatio-kinetic associations in children, as compared to adults.

Eitan and associates (2012) also replicated in part Eitan and Granot's (2006) study, examining 26 congenitally blind adults, devoid of any visual percepts or experience. Significant differences between sighted and the congenitally blind were found in associating pitch direction with motion in the vertical and sagittal directions. These differences included the most entrenched pitch mapping: the congenitally blind, unlike the sighted, did not associate pitch rise and fall with rise and fall in physical space. This finding suggests that the correspondence of auditory pitch and spatial height may be inherently associated with sight and could stem from early audiovisual experience, rather than language.

While these experiments all involved stimuli in which one musical parameter changed while others remained constant, Eitan and Granot (2011) examined systematically the effects of *interactions* between musical parameters on music-motion mappings. We presented to participants (78 adults, 35 music-trained) brief melodic stimuli, based on stimuli in Eitan and Granot (2006), which systematically combined changes in loudness (crescendo or diminuendo), pitch direction (up or down), tempo change (accelerando or ritardando), and changes in melodic interval size. For instance, the stimuli in Figure 8.2 present the four combinations of increase and decrease in loudness with pitch rise and fall, using the same melodic pattern.[8] (To hear the stimuli in Figure 8.2, please visit <http://www.oup.co.uk/companion/tan>.) Results corroborate that, in addition to the traditionally recognized correspondences of musical parameters and spatio-kinetic dimensions (pitch direction/vertical direction, loudness change/distance change, tempo/speed), each dimension of motion imagery is associated with several musical parameters and their interactions. Speed change associates not only with tempo, but (often as strongly) with changes in loudness and with pitch direction. Thus, participants did not associate accelerated stimuli with increased speed when loudness was concurrently reduced. This suggests that loudness change may even override the expected impact of tempo change on perceived musical motion. Similarly, vertical direction (rise/fall) is associated not only with pitch direction but with loudness. Accordingly, pitch rises in diminuendo were associated with spatial fall, rather than rise, again suggesting that loudness change may dominate the enshrined spatial associations of pitch height and pitch direction. Moreover, significant interactions (non-additive relationships) among musical parameters suggest that effects of single musical parameters (as revealed, e.g., in Eitan & Granot, 2006) cannot wholly predict

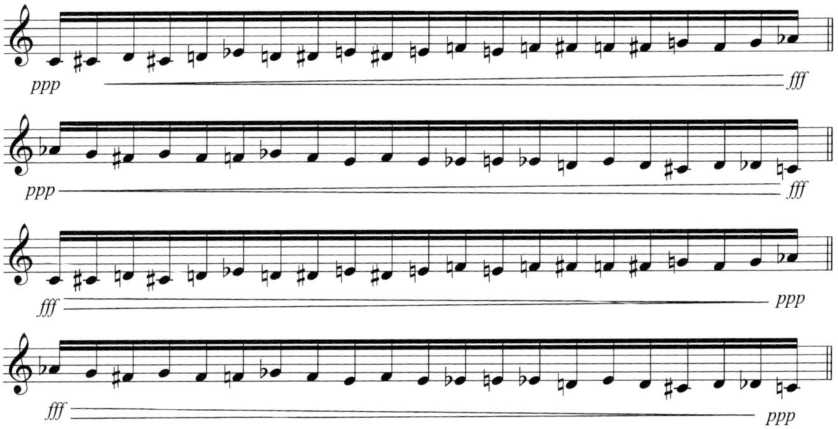

Figure 8.2 Stimuli combining changes in pitch and loudness. Reproduced from material presented in Zohar Eitan and Roni Y. Granot, 'Listeners' images of motion and the interaction of musical parameters,' Paper presented to the 10th Conference of the Society for Music Perception and Cognition (SMPC), Rochester, NY, August, 2011.

music-motion mappings. For instance, both loudness and pitch and pitch and tempo significantly interact in conveying distance change.

Adjective ratings

Eitan, Katz, and Shen (2010; also see Katz, 2011) systematically manipulated pitch register, loudness, and tempo in two phrases of Varèse's *Density 21.5* for flute, creating a matrix of 8 versions of each phrase (three musical parameters × two values of each parameter), and asked 137 participants of three age groups (children 8 and 11 years old and adults) to rate each stimulus on 15 bipolar adjective scales, including several attributes of space and motion: high/low, fast/slow, big/small, and jumpy/wavy. (To listen to some of the stimuli used in this study, please visit <http://www.oup.co.uk/companion/tan>.) As in the imagery experiments described earlier, most ratings were significantly associated with more than one musical parameter. Spatial height was associated with both pitch and loudness, such that a stimulus was rated as spatially higher not only when its pitch register was higher, but also when it was louder. In addition to tempo, speed was associated with both pitch and loudness: stimuli higher in pitch and louder were rated as 'faster.' Size was also associated with all three manipulated parameters, such that stimuli lower in pitch, louder, and slower were rated as 'larger.' Notably, loudness associated with ratings (including high/low) in the strongest way, corroborating other findings (e.g., Eitan & Tubul, 2010) suggesting that loudness, rather than pitch or tempo, is the most effective musical parameter in delineating spatial and spatio-kinetic associations of music. Age groups differed mainly in the effect of pitch register on ratings, which was weaker for the younger children. Notably, there were no significant age-related differences in responses to loudness, suggesting that these mature at a relatively early age.

Motion responses

The earlier described experiments, applying imagery and ratings tasks, all involved verbal responses. Kohn and Eitan (2009; see also Kohn, 2011) examined how actual bodily movement responses to music are associated with musical parameters (pitch direction, loudness change, and tempo change) and compared results with those obtained via verbal responses. We presented 104 children, aged 4 to 5 and 8, with nine short musical stimuli. Five stimuli were excerpts from commercial recordings of actual 18th- to 20th-century music. Four others were created specifically for the experiment, enabling tighter control of musical parameters. In all stimuli either pitch direction, loudness, or tempo changed bi-directionally (e.g., crescendo followed by diminuendo, pitch rise and fall). Participants were asked to move in a manner that would 'depict to a friend what the music is like,' and their motion responses were videotaped and analyzed according to categories of Laban Motion Analysis (Laban, 1971) by three referees, who watched the videos with sound muted. (For video examples of participants' responses, please visit <http://www.oup.co.uk/companion/tan>.)

While the studies described in previous sections might have represented conceptual, language-based associations, Kohn and Eitan's (2009) study investigated how musical parameters are mapped onto actual motor responses, with no explicit verbal mediation. Importantly, results of this motion-based study often paralleled the verbal responses reported in previous experiments. Thus, while specific musical parameters were primarily associated with specific motion dimensions—pitch with vertical motion, loudness change with both muscular energy and vertical motion, and tempo change with speed and muscular energy—the direction of change in each musical parameter was significantly associated with the direction of change in several motion dimensions: increase in loudness, for instance, was associated with increasing speed, increasing in muscular energy, spatial rise, and forward motion. As in other experiments involving children (and in some involving adults), loudness, rather than pitch or tempo, seems to be the strongest link between music and motion, as changes in loudness were significantly associated with changes in most movement dimensions investigated.

Beyond specific music-motion analogies, Kohn and Eitan's (2009) results indicate a general tendency to associate musical and motional growth and abatement. Thus, 'growth' or increase in musical parameters (pitch rise, crescendo, accelerando) was associated with 'growing' motions, such as increasing muscular energy, speeding up, rise, opening motions (e.g., spreading hands) and motion forward, and abating musical changes (pitch fall, diminuendo, ritardando)—with abating or decreasing motion.

A notable finding of Kohn and Eitan (2009) suggests a top-down effect of overall structure on music-related motion. While stimuli presenting pitch rises followed by falls tended to engender analogous rise–fall movements, stimuli presenting pitch falls followed by rises were *not* associated with fall–rise movements. A possible explanation for this discrepancy is an interaction between preferences for convex (inverted U) contours—'growth' followed by 'decline'—in movement (Kestenberg-Amighi, Loman, Lewis, & Sossin, 1999) and the implications of pitch contour. Thus, when pitch fall preceded pitch rise, the interaction of two opposing tendencies—the bodily tendency to move first up, then down, and pitch contour, suggesting moving down, then up—have possibly annulled any effects, resulting in movements whose vertical directions were not significantly associated with pitch contour.

Tentative insights: Sound space/musical space

What do experiments examining the spatial and kinesthetic associations of music indicate that experiments using simple audiovisual stimuli have not? Most generally, they depict an image of musical space and motion that is far more complex than previously determined, based on experiments using simpler stimuli. First, the experiments reveal one-to-many and many-to-one correspondences between musical parameters and aspects of space and motion. Rather than associating each musical parameter with a single feature of space or motion (e.g., pitch to height, loudness to distance, tempo to speed), the experiments indicate that each of the musical parameters associates with several spatio-kinetic attributes. For instance, pitch direction was shown to be associated with motion in all three spatial axes, as well as size, speed, and energy. Complementarily, each of the investigated attributes of space or motion was associated with several musical parameters. Thus, spatial height and motion in the vertical axis were associated with pitch, loudness, and tempo, rather than with pitch alone. The complexity of musical space and motion is revealed in other ways as well. Musical space presents directional asymmetry, such that pitch direction, for instance, is strongly associated with motion in the vertical axis when pitch descends, but not when it rises. Findings of Eitan & Granot (2011) also suggest interactive, rather than additive relationships between musical parameters in delineating aspects of space and motion; and Kohn and Eitan's (2009) bodily motion tasks also indicate that the overall contour of a musical phrase, rather than local pitch direction alone, may affect the spatio-kinetic associations of pitch height.

As noted, some of the music/space and music/motion correspondences indicated by the experiments were also found for simpler stimuli. Importantly, however, other relationships, such as the correspondence of loudness and height (or loudness change and vertical direction) had been hardly investigated elsewhere, and may be chiefly related to musical contexts. Moreover, the direction of the auditory-spatial correspondence in music may even reverse that suggested by non-musical sound, as seems to be the case with pitch direction and distance (whose correspondence in musical contexts contrasted with that suggested by the Doppler effect).

Finally, results suggest that the hierarchy of musical parameters delineating musical space and motion may conflict with the parametric hierarchy assumed by many music theorists. Loudness, traditionally regarded as a 'secondary' parameter of musical structure (subservient to the primary parameters: pitch and duration; see Meyer, 1989), was shown to be the parameter most strongly and ubiquitously associated with spatial and spatio-kinetic attributes. While the preeminence of loudness is particularly robust for children, where it often exceeds pitch even with regard to the latter's mapping with spatial height, the effect of loudness on adults' mappings is robust as well, applying to dimensions of motion and space that have rarely been associated by music scholars with this auditory parameter.

The music/motion studies just described leave an important open question unanswered: Do the complexities of musical space and motion they reveal typify music in particular, perhaps stemming from its specific cognitive and cultural connotations, or can they be found in other auditory contexts, such as speech, expressive vocalizations, and commonly experienced environmental sounds? One factor to be taken into account in approaching this issue is the dynamic nature of music. Music involves *changes* in auditory parameters. It is far from evident that the spatial correspondences found for static auditory parameters (e.g., stationary high or low pitch) would be similar to those of dynamic, time-varying auditory parameters (e.g., ascending and descending pitch). Investigating how dynamic auditory parameters associate with spatio-kinetic features is particularly important for music-related multimedia, in which changes in musical parameters are presented concurrently with visually perceived motion (see Kendall, 2005b; Kim & Iwamiya, 2008 for relevant empirical studies). In the last section of this chapter, a few experimental findings concerning this issue are presented.

Examining dynamic auditory stimuli

Diverse studies indicate that, in dynamic stimuli, the perception and mental representation of values such as stimulus magnitude or position are strongly affected by inherently dynamic qualities such as the direction of change. For instance, magnitude estimation for loudness is more variable in dynamic conditions and affected asymmetrically by the direction of change: when equal increase and decrease in sound intensity are presented, increases would be evaluated as greater than comparable decreases (Canévet & Scharf, 1990; Neuhoff, 1998). In response time and stimulus-response compatibility experiments, spatial direction interferes with the perception of spatial position (Bosbach, Prinz, & Kerzel, 2005; Michaels, 1988). In the auditory domain, perceiving pitch position comparably interacts with the direction of pitch change (Walker & Ehrenstein, 2000). The direction of change affects not only perception, but mental representation of spatial position as well, as memory for the final position of a moving object is distorted in ways consistent with its path of motion. Analogies of this 'directional momentum' effect (Freyd & Finke, 1984) were also found for auditory pitch (Freyd, Kelly, & DeKay, 1990; Kelly & Freyd, 1987). Together, such effects strongly suggest that static and dynamic auditory parameters may differ in their spatial and spatio-kinetic associations.

A case in point is the relationship between pitch and physical size. As noted earlier, research involving both diverse human populations and studies of animal behavior suggests that higher pitch is associated in perception, cognition, and behavior with smaller size. However, when participants (of different cultures and age groups) associate *dynamic* pitch patterns—ascending or descending melodies or pitch glides, rather than high and low pitch—with visual stimuli, they map pitch rise into *growing* size and pitch fall into *shrinking* size—just the opposite of what correspondences of static pitch and size would predict. Thus, Japanese participants judged rising pitch patterns as congruent with expanding (rather than shrinking) animated visual shapes (Kim & Iwamiya, 2008). Similarly, Serbian and Romanian 11-year-old children, presented with an octave leap, tended to term the higher pitch 'big' and the lower pitch 'small,' in contrast with results for isolated pitches, where lower-pitched sounds were associated with large size (Antovic, 2009). In another experiment, utilizing implicit measures (Garner's speeded classification paradigm; see partial description of procedure for comparable experiments involving loudness and vertical direction, mentioned earlier) rather than ratings, participants classified rising and falling pitch glides faster when rising pitch was accompanied by growing animated figures and falling pitch by shrinking figures, as compared to trials in which rising pitch was accompanied with shrinking figures and falling pitch with growing figures (Eitan et al., in press). Note that in an experiment using a similar design but *static* visual and auditory stimuli (large and small visual figures, high and low pitch) contrasting results were demonstrated: co-occurrence of high pitch with *small* size and of low pitch with *large* size improved performance (Gallace & Spence, 2006).

Paradoxically, pitch is perceived as growing in size as it rises (as experiments using dynamic stimuli suggest), yet high pitch is perceived as smaller, rather than larger than low pitch (as experiments using static stimuli suggest). This apparent paradox suggests that different mental processes are at work when mapping static and dynamic pitch onto other domains. For the pitch/size relationship, this difference may stem from different bases for mappings: while for static stimuli the experiential correlation between the physical size of objects and the sound they tend to produce (larger size→lower pitch) possibly serves as a basis for association, for dynamic stimuli the more abstract (and perhaps language-based) analogy between two types of increase—pitch 'rise' and physical growth—may take hold.

Static and dynamic pitch differ also in their association with speed. As noted earlier, while lower register music is perceived as 'slower' than higher register music (Boltz, 2011), and faster tempi are preferred for higher register music (Tamir & Eitan, submitted), descent in pitch was associated with accelerating, rather than decelerating motion (Eitan & Granot, 2006). Again, the association of static (high versus low) pitch and speed (fast versus slow) may stem from different experiential sources than that of dynamic (ascending and descending) pitch. A possible account (completely speculative as yet) may suggest that lower pitch, as already noted, correlates with larger, heavier, and often slower sound sources. Descending pitch, in contrast, would be associated (as studies surveyed above indicate) with falling and, hence, accelerating motion.

Finally, and perhaps most interestingly, the most entrenched auditory-spatial relationship, that of pitch and height, seems to be essentially dynamic, rather than static. Jeschonek and associates (2012) presented to 7- to 12-month-old infants upward or downward moving circles, followed by ascending or descending pitch. When an ascending pitch was presented, infants tended to look longer at the location in which the upward moving visual stimulus had appeared; when presented with a descending pitch, they looked longer at the previous location of the descending visual stimuli. However, when static tones were similarly combined with static visual stimuli, no audiovisual association was found. This suggests that preverbal infants, while systematically associating the direction of pitch change with vertical motion, do not associate static pitch and height. Thus, pitches may not inherently be 'high' and 'low,' but they do move up and down: the pitch-height association is basically, and perhaps innately, dynamic.

At least for pitch, then, 'location' (high and low) and 'direction' (rise and fall) differ, and even paradoxically contrast, in their spatial connotations. These differences, which are as yet neither completely mapped nor fully understood, present a challenge to research of musical space and motion, in particular within the dynamic, multi-modal environment of multimedia.

Conclusion: Sound and music as multimedia

This chapter has only implicitly referred to music in multimedia; it has, however, discussed music *as* multimedia. Empirical work discussed here suggests that even apparently 'abstract' music, devoid of any explicit associations to visual images, bodily motion, or narrative, inherently transcends its own auditory medium, carrying connotations of bodily motion in physical space. These connotations emerge even when sound sources are stationary, as they are embodied in the basic dimensions of musical sound: duration, pitch and loudness. Musical sounds and sound patterns may accordingly be perceived as virtual objects moving in a virtual space—not an abstract mathematical or music-theoretical space, but one analogous in important ways to the physical space we experience through bodily action and movement. Thus, sound objects may be smaller or larger, lighter or heavier, move in specific directions—up or down, approaching or moving away, right or left—at faster or slower speed, and endowed with higher or lesser kinetic energy. As perceptual and cognitive studies indicate, pitch and loudness, basic parameters of sound, delineate such perceived spatial and kinetic attributes in consistent, yet often surprisingly complex ways. Thus, musical sounds or sound patterns differing in pitch or loudness would correspondingly differ in their perceived spatial and kinetic features.

Music, then, does not require actual visual images to suggest space and motion—it produces its own. Music-related multimedia thus combine two different spatio-kinetic configurations: the implied space and motion evoked by musical parameters, and actual movement in the visually-perceived space on the stage, screen, or computer display. This duality, of course, is not new to multimedia practitioners and theorists. Opera composers from Monteverdi to Verdi, Wagner, and Alban Berg, film creators and composers, and composers of music for computer and video games, have all used, and sometimes theorized about, the intricate relationships between these two spaces.[9] Indeed, Nicholas Cook's pioneering book on the analysis of musical multimedia (1998), drawing upon such creative and speculative endeavors (as well as on cross-modal and metaphor research), arrives at a conclusion which parallels that suggested by the research surveyed here, though referring to a very different realm of multi-medial relationship: 'even "music alone" should properly be seen a form of multimedia in which all the components except one have been forced to run underground, sublimated or otherwise marginalized' (1998, p. 270).

The empirical studies surveyed here, however, may inform the theory and practice of musical multimedia—and of music *as* multimedia—in several important and novel ways. First, they provide ample evidence that musical space and motion are not only psychologically real, but are often perceived or reacted to automatically and even pre-attentively. We simply cannot help but perceive sound objects, and hence musical objects, in terms of physical space and movement. Second, they indicate that the supposedly 'non-temporal' dimensions of pitch and loudness shape perceived musical motion no less, and sometimes even more strongly than rhythm and tempo. Third, these studies start to chart the actual terrain and 'physics' of that novel space, revealing the complex web of correspondences and interactions among the auditory and spatio-kinetic features that shape it. These interactions are often different from—and more complex than—what music and multimedia theorists and critics had imagined. It is this gradually revealed complexity that may provide new insights, new tools, and new challenges for those creators and researchers of musical multimedia aiming to associate music's apparently disembodied 'tonally moving forms' (Hanslick, 1891/1986) with the real space and actual motion we all experience.

Acknowledgments

Research for this chapter was supported by an Israel–USA Binational Science Foundation (BSF) Grant No. 2005-524 to Zohar Eitan and Lawrence E. Marks.

Notes

1. Diverse terms have been used to describe the variety of cross-modal associations (e.g., synesthetic correspondence, synesthetic similarity, cross-modal similarity). See Spence (2011) for a discussion of relevant terminology.
2. Spatial directions and positions, height included, are defined here in relation to an observer in a three-dimensional spherical space (our normal point of view in daily experience). Note

that such an observation point may suggest some experiential correlations between spatial dimensions. For instance, for an observer situated on relatively flat ground, increased height would suggest increased distance (though the relationship is not symmetrical, as increased distance would not suggest increased height).

3. Note that this relationship does not simply stem from differences in sensitivity to sound intensity at different frequencies. Indeed, static frequency and intensity have been shown to interact perceptually, such that for different frequencies the same sound intensity would produce different levels of subjective loudness (as described by 'equal loudness contours,' e.g., Suzuki, 2003). However, the increase in loudness associated with pitch rise is not predicted by such equal loudness contours, generated by static tones. For instance, while (given unchanging intensity) listeners perceived a rise in pitch from 1047 Hz to 1108 Hz as increasing in loudness, a static 1108 Hz tone was perceived (given the same level of intensity) as *softer* than a 1047 Hz tone (Neuhoff, McBeath, & Wanzie, 1999).
4. The survey in this paragraph is indebted to Granot & Eitan (2011).
5. Auditory localization in the vertical plane is primarily affected by the pinnae, which distorts high-frequency spectral components, thus creating spectral-shape filters associated with different vertical locations (Blauert, 1997). These elevation-related filters (which vary among individuals) do not indicate correlation of spatial height with loudness.
6. Such up–down mappings are not limited to the earlier-mentioned auditory dimensions, but apply to many polar attributes involving magnitude (both sensory and abstract), such as ones of sensory intensity (brightness), spatial extent (length, volume), and emotional or moral valence (happy/sad, good/bad; see also Lakoff & Johnson, 1980).
7. Due to the large number of musical terms in Italian and other foreign languages in this chapter (as they are often used as variable labels), they do not appear consistently in italics as in most other chapters.
8. Because the present chapter deals only with pitch and loudness, tempo change examples will not be discussed.
9. For analyses of interactions of musical and visual space and movement in multimedia, see, for instance, Clarke (2005), Cook (1998), and Godøy (2010).

References

Antovic, M. (2009). Musical metaphors in Serbian and Romani children: An empirical study. *Metaphor and Symbol, 24*, 184–202.

Bach, D. R., Schächinger, H., Neuhoff, J. G., Esposito, F., Di Salle, F., Lehmann, C., *et al.* (2008). Rising sound intensity: An intrinsic warning cue activating the amygdala. *Cerebral Cortex, 18*, 145–150.

Ben-Artzi, E., & Marks, L. E. (1995). Visual-auditory interaction in speeded classification: Role of stimulus difference. *Perception & Psychophysics, 57*, 1151–1162.

Bernstein, I. H., & Edelstein, B. A. (1971). Effects of some variations in auditory input upon visual choice reaction time. *Journal of Experimental Psychology, 87*, 241–246.

Blauert, J. (1997). *Spatial hearing: The psychophysics of human sound localization.* Cambridge, MA: MIT Press.

Boltz, M. G. (2011). Illusory tempo changes due to musical characteristics. *Music Perception, 28*, 367–386.

Bosbach, S., Prinz, W., & Kerzel, D. (2005). Is direction position? Position-and direction-based correspondence effects in tasks with moving stimuli. *The Quarterly Journal of Experimental Psychology, 58a*(3), 467–506.

Burro, R., & Grassi, M. (2001). Experiments on size and height of falling objects. In *Phenomenology of sounds events, Report No. 1* (pp. 31–39). The Sounding Object, IST project no. IST-2000-25287.

Cabrera, D., Ferguson, S., Tilley, S., & Morimoto, M. (2005). Recent studies on the effect of signal frequency on auditory vertical localization. In E. Brazil (Ed.), *Proceedings of ICAD 05—Eleventh meeting of the international conference on auditory display* (pp. 1–8). Limerick, Ireland: ICAD.

Canévet, G. & Scharf, B. (1990). The loudness of sounds that increase and decrease continuously in level. *The Journal of the Acoustical Society of America, 88*, 2136–2142.

Carello, C., Anderson, K. L., & Kunkler-Peck, A. J. (1998). Perception of object length by sound. *Psychological Science, 9*, 211–214.

Cho, Y., & Proctor, R. (2005). Representing response positionrelative to display location: Influence on orthogonal stimulus response compatibility. *Quarterly Journal of Experimental Psychology, A, 58*, 839–864.

Clarke, E. (2005). *Ways of Listening: An ecological approach to the perception of musical meaning.* New York, NY: Oxford University Press.

Cohen, A. J. (2005). How music influences the interpretation of film and video: Approaches from experimental psychology. In R. A. Kendall & R. W. Savage (Eds.), *Selected Reports in Ethnomusicology: Perspectives in Systematic Musicology, 12*, 15–36.

Cook, N. (1998). *Analysing musical multimedia.* Oxford, UK: Clarendon Press.

Cytowic, R. E. (1989). *Synesthesia: A union of the senses.* New York, NY: Springer-Verlag.

Deutsch, D., Hamaoui, K., & Henthorn, T. (2007). The Glissando illusion and handedness. *Neuropsychologia, 45*, 2981–2988.

Eitan, Z., & Granot, R. Y. (2006). How music moves: musical parameters and images of motion. *Music Perception, 23*, 221–247.

Eitan, Z., & Granot, R. Y. (2011, August). *Listeners' images of motion and the interaction of musical parameters.* Paper presented to the 10th Conference of the Society for Music Perception and Cognition (SMPC). Rochester, NY.

Eitan, Z. Katz, A. & Shen, Y. (2010, August). *Effects of pitch register, loudness and tempo on children's use of metaphors for music.* Poster presentation, 11th International Conference on Music Perception & Cognition (ICMPC11). Seattle, WA.

Eitan, Z., Ornoy, E., & Granot, R. Y. (2012). Listening in the dark: congenital and early blindness and cross-domain mappings in music. *Psychomusicology: Music, Mind, and Brain, 22*, 33–45.

Eitan, Z. Schupak, A., Gotler, A., & Marks, L. E. (in press). Lower pitch is larger, yet falling pitches shrink: Interaction of pitch change and size change in speeded discrimination. *Experimental Psychology.*

Eitan, Z. Schupak, A., Gotler, A., & Marks, L. E. (submitted). *Louder is higher: Loudness change and visual vertical motion interact in speeded classification.* Manuscript submitted for publication.

Eitan, Z., & Timmers, R. (2010). Beethoven's last piano sonata and those who follow crocodiles: Cross-domain mappings of auditory pitch in a musical context. *Cognition, 114*, 405–422.

Eitan Z., & Tubul, N. (2010). Musical parameters and children's images of motion. *Musicae Scientiae, (Special Issue)*, 89–111.

Evans, K., & Treisman, A. (2010). Natural cross-modal mappings between visual and auditory features. *Journal of Vision, 10*, 1–12.

Freyd, J. J., & Finke, R. A. (1984). Representational momentum. *Journal of Experimental Psychology: Learning, Memory, and Cognition, 10*, 126–132.

Freyd, J. J., Kelly, M. H., & DeKay, M. (1990). Representational momentum in memory for pitch. *Journal of Experimental Psychology: Learning, Memory, and Cognition, 16,* 1107–1117.

Gabrielsson, A., & Lindström, E. (2010). The role of structure in the musical expression of emotions. In J. A. Sloboda & P. N. Juslin (Eds.), *Handbook of music and emotion: theory, research, applications* (pp. 367–400). New York, NY: Oxford University Press.

Gallace, A., & Spence, C. (2006). Multisensory synesthetic interactions in the speeded classification of visual size. *Perception & Psychophysics, 68,* 1191–1203.

Ghazanfar, A. A., & Maier, J. X. (2009). Monkeys hear rising frequency sounds as looming. *Behavioral Neuroscience, 123,* 822–827.

Ghazanfar, A. A., Neuhoff, J. G., & Logothetis, N. K. (2002). Auditory looming perception in rhesus monkeys. *Proceedings of the National Academy of Sciences of the United States of America, 99,* 15755–15757.

Godøy, R. I. (2010). Gestural affordances of musical sound. In R. I. Godøy and M. Leman (Eds.), *Musical gestures: Sound, movement, and meaning* (pp. 105–127). New York, NY: Routledge.

Gordon, M. S., & Rosenblum, L. D. (2005). Effects of intra-stimulus modality change on audiovisual time-to-arrival judgments. *Perception and Psychophysics, 67,* 580–594.

Granot, R. Y., & Eitan, Z. (2011). Musical tension and the interaction of dynamic auditory parameters. *Music Perception, 28,* 219–245.

Hanslick, E. (1986). *On the musically beautiful.* (G. Payzant, Trans. and Ed.). Indianapolis, IN: Hackett. (Original work published 1891.)

Huron, D., Kinney, D., & Precoda, K. (2006). Influence of pitch height on the perception of submissiveness and threat in musical passages. *Empirical Musicology Review, 1,* 178–179.

Jeschonek, S., Pauen, S., & Babocsai, L. (2012). Cross-modal mapping of visual and acoustic displays in infants: The effect of dynamic and static components. *European Journal of Developmental Psychology.* (First published online May 3, 2012.)

Katz, A. (2011). Metaphor as representation of children's musical thought: Metaphorical mapping and musical parameters. (Doctoral dissertation, in Hebrew.) Tel Aviv University, Israel.

Kelly, M. H., & Freyd, J. J. (1987). Explorations of representational momentum. *Cognitive Psychology, 19,* 369–401.

Kendall, R. A. (2005a). Empirical approaches to musical meaning. *Selected Reports in Ethnomusicology, 12,* 69–102.

Kendall, R. A. (2005b). Music and video iconicity: Theory and experimental design. *Journal of Physiological Anthropology and Applied Human Science, 24,* 143–149.

Kestenberg-Amighi, J., Loman, S, Lewis, P., & Sossin, K. M. (1999). *The meaning of movement. Developmental and clinical perspectives of the Kestenberg movement Profile.* Amsterdam, the Netherlands: Gordon and Breach.

Kim, K.-H., & Iwamiya, S. (2008). Formal congruency between telop patterns and sound effects. *Music Perception, 25,* 429–448.

Kohn, D. (2011). Music and movement: Musical parameters, bodily movement responses, and children's images of motion. (Doctoral dissertation, in Hebrew.) Tel Aviv University, Israel.

Kohn, D., & Eitan, Z. Musical parameters and children's movement responses. In J. Louhivuori, T. Eerola, S. Saarikallio, T. Himberg, & P. S. Eerola (Eds.), *Proceedings of the 7th Triennial Conference of European Society for the Cognitive Sciences of Music (ESCOM 2009)* (pp. 233–241). Jyväskylä, Finland: ESCOM.

Krumhansl, C. L. (1990). *Cognitive foundations of musical pitch.* New York, NY: Oxford University Press.

Laban, R. (1971). *The mastery of movement.* (Revised and enlarged by L. Ullmann.) Boston, MA: Plays, Inc.

Lakoff, G., & Johnson, M. (1980). *Metaphors we live by.* Chicago, IL: University of Chicago Press.

Lidji, P., Kolinsky, R., Lochy, A. Karnas, D. and Morais, J. (2007). Spatial associations for musical stimuli: A piano in the head? *Journal of Experimental Psychology: Human Perception and Performance, 33,* 1189–1207.

Lipscomb, S. D. (1995). *Cognition of musical and visual accent structure alignment in film and animation* (Doctoral dissertation). University of California, Los Angeles, CA.

Lipscomb, S. D., and Kendall, R. (1994). Perceptual judgment of the relationship between musical and visual components in film. *Psychomusicology, 13,* 60–98.

Lipscomb, S. D., & Kim, E. M. (2004, August). *Perceived match between visual parameters and auditory correlates: an experimental multimedia investigation.* Paper presented at the 8th International Conference on Music Perception and Cognition. Northwestern University in Evanston, IL.

Lewkowicz, D. J., & Turkewitz, G. (1980). Cross-modal equivalence in early infancy: Auditory-visual intensity matching. *Developmental Psychology, 16,* 597–607.

Ludwig, V. U., Adachi, I., & Matsuzawa, T. (2011). Visuoauditory mappings between high luminance and high pitch are shared by chimpanzees (Pan troglodytes) and humans. *Proceedings of the National Academy of Sciences of the United States of America, 108*(51), 20661–20665.

Maeda, F., Kanai, R., & Shimojo, S. (2004). Changing pitch induced visual motion illusion. *Current Biology, 19,* R990–R991.

Marks, L. (1978). *The unity of the senses: Interrelations among the modalities.* New York, NY: Academic Press.

Marks, L. E. (2000). Synesthesia. In E. A. Cardea, S. J. Lynn, & S. C. Krippner (Eds.), *Varieties of anomalous experience: Phenomenological and scientific foundations* (pp. 121–149). Washington, DC: American Psychological Association.

Marks, L. E. (2004). Cross-modal interactions in speeded classification. In G. Calvert, C. Spence, C., & B. E. Stein (Eds.), *Handbook of multisensory processes* (pp. 85–106). Cambridge, MA: MIT Press.

Marks, L. E., Hammeal, R. J., & Bornstein, M. H. (1987). Perceiving similarity and comprehending metaphor. *Monographs of the Society for Research in Child Development, 52* (Serial no. 215).

Martino, G., & Marks, L. E. (1999). Perceptual and linguistic interactions in speeded classification: Tests of the semantic coding hypothesis. *Perception, 28,* 903–923.

Martino, G., & Marks, L. E. (2001). Synesthesia: strong and weak. *Current Directions in Psychological Science, 10,* 61–65.

Melara, R. D., & O'Brien, T. P. (1987). Interaction between synesthetically corresponding dimensions. *Journal of Experimental Psychology: General, 116,* 323–336.

Meyer, L. B. (1989). *Style and music: Theory, history, and ideology.* Philadelphia, PA: University of Pennsylvania Press.

Michaels, C.F. (1988). S-R compatibility between response position and destination of apparent motion. *Journal of Experimental Psychology: Human Perception and Performance, 14,* 231–240.

Mondloch, C. J., & Maurer, D. (2004). Do small white balls squeak? Pitch-object correspondences in young children. *Cognitive, Affective, & Behavioral Neuroscience, 4,* 133–136.

Morrongiello, B. A., Hewitt, K. L., & Gotowiec, A. (1991). Infants' discrimination of relative distance in the auditory modality: Approaching versus receding sound sources. *Infant Behavior and Development, 14,* 187–208.

Morton, E. S. (1977). On the occurrence and significance of motivation-structural rules in some bird and mammal sounds. *American Naturalist, 111,* 855–869.

Morton, E. S. (1982). Grading, discreteness, redundancy, and motivation-structural rules. In D. E. Kroodsma, E. H. Miller, & H. Ouellet (Eds.), *Acoustic communication in birds* (pp. 182–212). New York, NY: Academic Press.

Morton, E. (1994). Sound symbolism and its role in non-human vertebrate communication. In L. Hinton, J. Nichols, & J. Ohala (Eds.), *Sound symbolism* (pp. 348–365). Cambridge, UK: Cambridge University Press.

Mudd, S. A. (1963). Spatial stereotypes of four dimensions of pure tone. *Journal of Experimental Psychology, 66,* 347–352.

Neuhoff, J. G. (1998). Perceptual bias for rising tones. *Nature, 395,* 123–124.

Neuhoff, J. G. (2001). An adaptive bias in the perception of looming auditory motion. *Ecological Psychology, 13,* 87–110.

Neuhoff, J. G., McBeath, M. K., & Wanzie, W. C. (1999). Dynamic frequency change influences loudness perception: A central, analytic process. *Journal of Experimental Psychology: Human Perception and Performance, 25,* 1050–1059.

Ohala, J. (1994). The frequency code underlies the sound-symbolic use of voice pitch. In L. Hinton, J. Nichols, & J. J. Ohala (Eds.), *Sound symbolism* (pp. 325–347). Cambridge, UK: Cambridge University Press.

Pratt, C. C. (1930). The spatial character of high and low tones. *Journal of Experimental Psychology, 13,* 278–285.

Puts, D., Gaulin, S., & Verdolini, K. (2006). Dominance and the evolution of sexual dimorphism in human voice pitch. *Evolution and Human Behavior, 27,* 283–296.

Raphaeli, M. (2011). Investigating dynamic crossmodal interactions using the oddball paradigm: Congruency effects between pitch direction and vertical motion. (Unpublished MA Thesis.) Tel Aviv University, Israel.

Roffler, S. K. & Butler, R. A. (1968). Localization of tonal stimuli in the vertical plane. *Journal of the Acoustical Society of America, 43,* 1260–1265.

Romei, V. B., Murray, M. M., Cappe, C., & Thut, G. (2009). Perceptual and stimulus-selective enhancement of low-level human visual cortex excitability by sounds. *Current Biology, 19,* 1799–1805.

Rusconi, E., Kwan, B., Giordano, B. L., Umiltà, C., & Butterworth, B. (2006). Spatial representation of pitch height: The SMARC effect. *Cognition, 99(2),* 113–129.

Scherer, K. R. (2003). Vocal communication of emotion: A review of research paradigms. *Speech Communication, 40,* 227–256.

Schiff, W. (1965). Perception of impending collision—a study of visually directed avoidant behavior. *Psychological Monographs, 79,* 1–26.

Smith, L. B., & Sera, M. D. (1992). A developmental analysis of the polar structure of dimensions. *Cognitive Psychology, 24,* 99–142.

Spence, C. (2011). Crossmodal correspondences: A tutorial review. *Attention, Perception & Psychophysics, 73*, 971–995.

Stevens, S., S. (1934). The volume and intensity of tones. *American Journal of Psychology, 46*, 397–408.

Stevens, S. T., & Arieh, Y. (2005). *What you see is what you hear: The effect of auditory pitch on the detection of visual targets.* Poster presented at the 76th annual meeting of the Eastern Psychological Society, Boston, MA.

Stewart, L., Walsh, V., & Frith, U. (2004). Reading music modifies spatial mapping in pianists. *Perception & Psychophysics, 66*, 183–195.

Suzuki, Y. (2003). *Precise and full-range determination of two-dimensional equal loudness contours.* Geneva, Switzerland: International Organization for Standardization (ISO).

Tamir, H., & Eitan, Z. (under revision). *Tempo preferences and melodic features.* Manuscript submitted for publication.

Wagner, S., Winner E., Cicchetti, D., & Gardner, H. (1981). Metaphorical mapping in human infants. *Child Development, 52*, 728–731.

Walker, B. N., & Ehrenstein, A. (2000). Pitch and pitch change interact in auditory displays. *Journal of Experimental Psychology: Applied, 6*, 15–30.

Walker, R. (1987). The effects of culture, environment, age, and musical training on choices of visual metaphors for sound. *Perception & Psychophysics, 42*, 491–502.

Walker, P., Gravin Brenmer, J., Mason, U., Spring, J., Mattock, K., Slater, A., & Johnson, S.P. (2010). Preverbal infants' sensitivity to syneasthetic cross-modality correspondences. *Psychological Science, 21*, 21–25.

Walker, P., & Smith, S. (1984). Stroop interference based on the synaesthetic qualities of auditory pitch. *Perception, 13*, 75–81.

Walker, P., & Smith, S. (1986). The basis of Stroop interference involving the multimodal correlates of auditory pitch. *Perception, 15*, 491–496.

Weeks, D. J., & Proctor, R. W. (1990). Salient-features coding in the translation between orthogonal stimulus and response dimensions. *Journal of Experimental Psychology: General, 119*, 355–366.

Zahorik, P., Brungart, D. S., & Bronkhorst, A.W. (2005). Auditory distance perception in humans: A summary of past and present research. *Acta Acustica united with Acustica, 91*, 409–420.

Zbikowski, L. (2008). Metaphor and music. In R. W. Gibbs, Jr. (Ed.), *The Cambridge handbook of metaphor and thought* (pp. 502–524). Cambridge, UK: Cambridge University Press.

Chapter 9

Cross-modal alignment of accent structures in multimedia

Scott D. Lipscomb
University of Minnesota, USA

In contemporary Western society, sounds and visual images assail us constantly; many were created and carefully placed specifically to attract attention, manipulate mood, or influence behavior. Though we are not (yet) as intrusively imposed upon by these stimuli as presented in futuristic fictional accounts like *Blade Runner* (1982) or *Minority Report* (2002), we are certainly stimulated to a greater degree than was the case for previous generations. The world of multimedia exemplifies yet another arena within which the role of music is frequently intended to manipulate perceptual and emotional responses and/or alter behavior.

The specific purpose of the present chapter is to investigate the relationship between events within multimedia contexts perceived as salient (i.e., accented) in the aural and visual modalities. While numerous studies—many cited in other chapters of this volume—address associational and referential aspects inherent in multimedia, this chapter will begin to establish a current state of understanding about the stratification of accent structures across modalities, their alignment, and the impact of this alignment on the perceiver-audience.

To establish a foundation for this work, I will first enumerate the determinants of *accent*, i.e., salient moments or what Lipscomb (2005) referred to as 'points of emphasis' within the aural and visual sensory fields (p. 38). While primary focus will remain on the auditory and visual fields, cross-modal influence of tactile stimuli will also be mentioned, given the relevance of this modality in some cinematic and gaming contexts. The topic of multi-modal integration will then be addressed from a number of perspectives. The psychophysical approach to empirical research has been used to inform us about multi-modal integration, the threshold for asynchrony, adaptation to multi-modal stimuli, and the 'ventriloquism effect' (e.g., McGurk & MacDonald, 1976). Two models of multimedia perception (Cohen, 2010; Lipscomb, 2005) will be presented to establish the need for an understanding of the manner in which stimuli arriving at the listener's spatial location via different sensory modalities are judged to be synchronous (or not). Finally, though the empirical literature is limited at present, studies directly investigating the synchronization of accent structures across modalities in the context of multimedia will be reviewed.

Determinants of accent

In order to establish the degree of accent structure alignment (i.e., perceived synchronization) across modalities, it is first essential to determine contributing factors to the perception of salience. What is it that makes one moment in the auditory or visual field more or less significant than surrounding moments?

A review of literature related to the concept of accent in the auditory field revealed several allusions to the perceptual identification of accented events. In an examination of musical sound, Huron and Royal (1996) identified moments of 'increased prominence, noticeability, or salience ascribed to a given sound event' as musical *accents* (p. 489). Fraisse (1982) explained that an accent occurs 'as soon as a difference is introduced into an isochronous sequence' (p. 157).[1] Deliège (1987) stated that 'in perceiving a difference in the field of sounds, one experiences a sensation of *accent*' (p. 326). Boltz and Jones (1986) proposed that 'accents can arise from any deviation in pattern context' (p. 428), and Jones (1987) provided examples of ways in which musical accents can occur specifically as a result of both pitch and temporal relationships (pp. 622–625). The notion of difference or deviation in comparison to surrounding events in the referenced modality is a central point of agreement among these authors as they each provide a general explanation for this phenomenon. Cooper and Meyer (1960) described an accented event as 'a stimulus which is *marked for consciousness*' (cited in Huron & Royal, 1996, p. 489), identifying three major sources of accent: dynamic accent (stress), agogic accent (duration), and tonic accent (melodic). A fourth potential source was added by Monahan and Carterette (1985): pitch level or 'the absolute value of pitch changes' (p. 2). For the purpose of this paper, in the context of multimedia, the manner in which cross-modal moments of salience are synchronized over time will be referred to as *accent structure alignment*.

Concerning the visual modality, Hutchinson and Kuhn (1992) stated that the visual components of early film, like those of the later video, evinced a link with music through temporality; their utilization of discreet frame and sequenced visual composition create dynamic rhythmic and harmonic visual structures easily analogous to music (p. 545). The creation of such perceived rhythms stimulated within the visual domain are readily evident in the hand-drawn, experimental animations of Norman McLaren (e.g., *Dots*, 1940; *Canon*, 1964; and *Synchromy*, 1971); the digital, computer-based creations of John Whitney (1980); and the *Animusic* series (2004, 2005) of music-based animations.

In previous publications, the present author set out to determine specific parameters that could be varied in both the auditory and visual domains, providing potential sources of perceived accent (Lipscomb, 1995, 2005). That review resulted in a list of specific potential determinants of accent within the auditory field (pitch, loudness, and timbre) and within the visual field (location, shape, and color); these parameters were then manipulated in a set of experiments to investigate the relationship between auditory and visual accent structure alignment; results of these studies are reported later in this chapter. These short lists are not intended to provide an exhaustive set of potential sources of accent in the auditory and visual fields, but merely to enumerate representative parameters—from among others that might have been chosen—that are likely to be perceived as salient when changing dynamically within a musical or visual context.

Multi-modal integration

In order to address the manner in which accent structures align across modalities, it will be useful to have a model upon which to base comparisons of the various accent structure strata (i.e., auditory, visual, etc.). Yeston's (1976) innovative approach to considering musical rhythm provides an exemplary model for this purpose. Yeston categorized metrical structure into three types: consonant, dissonant, or out-of-phase (what he referred to as 'a displaced consonant stratum,' p. 113). Within a musical context, *consonant* metrical structures consist of layers of musical sound that are perfectly nested (e.g., eighth notes within quarter notes, quarter notes within half notes, etc.). An *out-of-phase* structure results when these nested structures still retain their isochronously temporal relationships, but are shifted temporally so that they either precede or follow the primary beat pattern, resulting in a slight anticipation or delay of what would have constituted a consonant relationship. The *dissonant* structure is represented by examples within which subdivisions of the beat pattern do not resolve to integer multiples of the underlying beat. (For a more detailed explanation of Yeston's (1976) theory, including many excellent examples, see Monahan and Carterette (1985).)

If, instead of layers of musical sound, we assess the relationships between stimuli impinging upon various sensory modalities, Yeston's (1976) model can be directly applied to multimedia (Lipscomb, 1995, 2005; Lipscomb & Kendall, 1994). If the pair of constituent elements in each item contained in Figure 9.1 were considered to be musical sound (on the top) and visual images (on the bottom), then we could describe the alignment of cross-modal accent structures using Yeston's terminology: consonant (Figure 9.1A), out-of-phase (Figure 9.1B), and dissonant (Figure 9.1C). It is quite rare, however, for such a predicable rate of periodicity to occur in real-world multimedia contexts, which tend to involve much greater levels of complexity in inter-modal

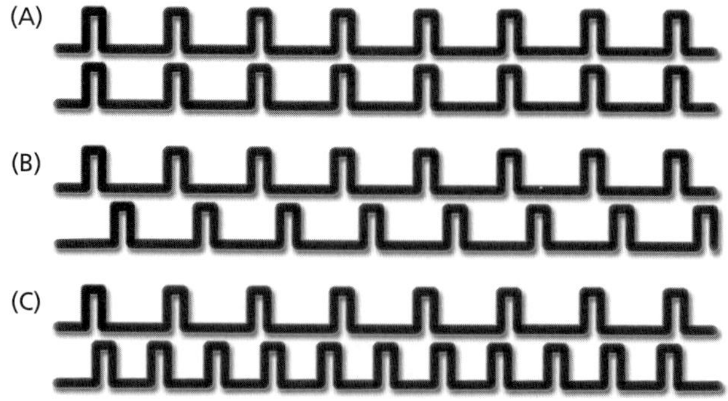

Figure 9.1 Three levels of accent structure alignment: (A) consonant, (B), out-of-phase, and (C) dissonant. Adapted from Lipscomb (1995, 2005) and Lipscomb and Kendall (1994); used with permission.

interactions. For example, in the common 'Mickey-mousing' relationship between audio and visual components of animated sequences, many visual accents are reinforced by accents in the musical soundtrack, though—in this real-world multimedia context—the accents do not occur isochronously; see the opening segment of *Who Framed Roger Rabbit?* (1988). In addition to the alignment of accent structures across modalities, a careful analysis of this cinematic scene will reveal many other methods of correlation between the audio and visual signals (as explained by both Eitan, Chapter 8, and Kendall & Lipscomb, Chapter 3, in the present volume). As a result, in many complex multimedia contexts, it will be necessary to consider the relationship simply in terms of whether the salient moments—periodic or aperiodic in recurrence—are aligned (consonant) or not (dissonant or out-of-phase), keeping in mind that nested accent structures are still possible within even an extremely complex multimedia context.

Cross-modal influence on perception and cognitive processing: Psychophysical literature

By far, the majority of extant research related to cross-modal influence in audiovisual (AV) stimuli involves low-level psychophysical studies, observing change in one modality as a result of a stimulus presented to another. For example, early work in this area utilized light flashes and sine tones emitted from a carefully arranged configuration of speakers (Bermant & Welch, 1976; Massaro & Warner, 1977; Mershon, Desaulniers, Amerson, & Kiefer, 1980; Regan & Spekreijse, 1977; Ruff & Perret, 1976; Staal & Donderi, 1983). While such research studies provided information about cross-modal processing of AV stimuli, the ability to generalize these results to real-world, multimedia experiences is limited due to the lack of ecological validity.

One of the initial challenges to a theory of cross-modal accent structures is the level of incongruity between the aural and visual modalities in our experience of the physical world; for example, the fact that sound and light energy travel at radically different speeds. While the speed of light is 186,282 miles per second, the speed of sound energy propagation is much slower (only about 1,130 *feet* per second[2]). As a result, a real-world event that occurs at some distance will involve a significant lag of the auditory signal behind the visual information arriving at our perceptual organs. For example, consider the experience of watching an individual bounce a basketball 300 feet away or watching fireworks explode in the sky, both clear examples in which the visual stimulus reaches the eye significantly earlier than the auditory signal reaches the ear. In a specifically musical context, the difference in speed between light and sound transmission becomes readily apparent when watching a marching band perform in a large football stadium, where the visual image of the band (watching the timing of their footsteps and synchronized turns) is perceived much sooner than the auditory sound (the music); the latter can take close to a second to travel from one end of the stadium to the other, arriving at the perceiver well after the visual data have already been processed.

The discrepancy in the time required to process this information adds another layer of complexity to AV perception in multimedia. In contrast to the physical propagation temporal discrepancy described earlier, in the act of processing perceptual information, the auditory system assumes the advantage. According to Fain (2003, cited in Heron, Whitaker, McGraw, & Horoshenkov, 2007, p. 1), the biochemical process of transduction for visual signals takes approximately 50 milliseconds (ms) longer than the process for transducing auditory signals. At a certain distance (just over 50 feet), the physical characteristics of energy propagation and the temporal duration of perceptual processing effectively cancel one another out; at all other distances, however, our minds must determine the synchronization of events that are non-congruent, as determined by physical measurement.

Colonius and Diedrich (2010) refer to a *spatiotemporal window of integration*, stating that 'crossmodal information falling within this window is highly likely to be integrated, whereas information falling outside is not' (p. 1). In order to be perceived as temporally aligned, some research has revealed that auditory signals must typically lag behind visual signals by between 40 and 50 ms, though judgments of synchronous AV events can range widely. According to van Eijk, Kohlrausch, Juola, and van de Par (2009), such cross-modal events can be perceived as simultaneous when the audio component precedes the video by about 50 ms to a situation in which the video precedes the audio by as much as 150 ms; these authors refer to the center of this range as the 'point of subjective simultaneity (PSS)' (p. 1254) as opposed to the physically precise alignment, which they refer to as the 'point of objective simultaneity (POS)' (p. 1255). In a series of experiments, Alais and Carlile (2005) determined that, as the distance from an auditory source increases, the lag time required for the audio signal to be perceived as synchronous with the visual component also increases, concluding that 'the capacity to align external auditory and visual signals is important functionally as it ties them to the environmental event that caused them' (p. 2247). Thus, responses of participants in this study appeared to model their real-world experience (i.e., the greater the distance from the source, the greater the auditory delay).

One of the primary empirical means of determining the perception of synchrony is a finger-tapping task in which 'an action is temporally coordinated with a predictable external event' (Repp, 2005, p. 969). To further complicate the challenge of determining temporal alignment across modalities, research studies have revealed that finger taps precede the auditory referent by between 20 and 60 ms and, for musicians, the accuracy of tapping and cross-modal discrimination ability vary on the basis of musical specialization, in essence, the primary musical instrument played by the musician-participant (Krause, Pollok, & Schnitzler, 2010). Specifically, Krause et al. revealed that drummers have superior synchronization and discrimination abilities when compared to pianists, singers, and non-musicians. In a comparison of adults and 2- to 8-month-old infants, Lewkowicz (1996) determined that the temporal separation at which participants perceive asynchrony between a computer-generated bouncing disk and a complex tone varied, determined by whether the sound preceded or followed the visual event. When the sound preceded the visual bounce, the threshold at which adult participants perceived asynchrony was 65 ms, while the infants required 350 ms. When the sound followed the visible event—as would occur in a distant, real-world experience—the threshold was even larger (112 ms for adults and 450 ms for infants).

Audiovisual integration

In an effort to make sense out of the world, humans are constantly attempting to seek meaningful and relevant patterns within the surrounding environment. In the context of multisensory stimuli, at times, this can result in the perception of events that are correlated or synchronized, despite clear discrepancies between temporal congruency when measured physically, a cognitive manipulation referred to as *adaptation* (Radeau, 1973; Radeau & Bertelson, 1978) or *recalibration* (Di Luca, Machulla, & Ernst, 2009; Roseboom, Nishida, & Arnold, 2009)

Numerous studies have revealed that information across perceptual modalities can exert significant influence on the perception of cross-modal stimuli. As the name suggests, the *ventriloquism effect* occurs when an individual's perception of such stimuli is different than what is physically presented. For example, if sound and image are presented simultaneously but from different locations, a viewer-listener will often perceive the sound source to be identical to that of the visual source, similar to what happens when the sound of a ventriloquist's voice seems to be coming from the mouth of the dummy on her lap. A related phenomenon associated with speech perception was discovered by McGurk and MacDonald (1976) and is thus known as the *McGurk effect*. In this experiment, the researchers replicated an earlier finding that, when a visual image of repeated lip movements for the sound 'ga' are combined with dubbed utterances of the syllable 'ba,' the vast majority of listeners (98 percent of adults) perceive the sound as 'da,' a fusion of the auditory and visual inputs.[3] As a result, the authors conclude that 'auditory-based theories of speech perception are inadequate to accommodate' these findings (p. 747), requiring consideration of the role of *vision* in the perception of speech sounds. Furthermore, McGurk and MacDonald assert—as confirmed anecdotally by my own demonstrations to hundreds of students over the past two decades—that this perceptual fusion does not habituate over time, even when participants are explicitly made aware of the specific content of the auditory and visual components and are provided a full understanding of the perceptual fusion that occurs. It can, in fact, be quite astonishing to have students watch the video, close their eyes for a few seconds, then reopen them. The auditory perception during the period when their eyes are closed accurately reflects the actual auditory stimulus ('ba'), yet when they open their eyes to reintroduce the visual component—knowing that nothing has changed in the auditory track—the perceived syllable returns to 'da.'

Extending the concept of ventriloquism between the auditory and visual modalities, Rahne, Böchmann, Von Specht, and Sussman (2007) presented participants with ambiguous auditory stimuli: a series of three high tones separated by a semitone and three low frequency tones with a four semitone distance between the high and low tone groups, the musical interval at which 'listeners perceive one integrated stream of sounds 50 percent of the time' (p. 132). These sets of tones were selected to induce an ambiguous auditory effect when isochronous sequences of these tones alternated between the high and low pitch groups; the consecutive pitches could either be perceived as a single integrated melody or as two segregated melodic lines, according to the principals of streaming proposed in Bregman's (1990) theory of *auditory scene analysis*. The visual stimuli consisted of computer-generated white circles and squares on a black background; the circles were two sizes (large and small) and the squares were three sizes (small, medium, and large). Stimuli were presented in five conditions, including an audio-only condition and a visual-only condition. The three multi-modal conditions were intended to produce two segregated streams, two integrated streams, or a single stream and were produced by aligning sizes and shapes of the visual objects with selected tones within the auditory stream. Rahne et al. (2007) determined that this synchronous presentation of visual stimuli served to resolve the ambiguity inherent in the audio-only stimulus, because added salience was provided to those tones aligned with the visual stimuli.

Moving into the realm of detecting motion and its direction, Kim, Peters, and Shams (2011) exposed participants to a visual motion detection task that consisted of a series of trials involving pairs of AV stimuli. The visual stimuli were dynamic dot patterns, and the procedure consisted of exposure to one interval (either the first or second, randomly determined) containing coherent visual motion and the other interval containing only random visual motion. The auditory component varied according to three conditions: (1) informative-congruent presentation (sound was present for both stimuli, but moved only in the interval with coherent visual motion, moving in the same direction as the visual motion), (2) non-informative-congruent presentation (the sound moved in the same direction as coherent visual motion in *both* intervals, providing no distinguishing information to assist in the discrimination task), and (3) non-informative-incongruent presentation (sound moved during both intervals, but in the direction opposite from that of the coherent visual motion). Results of two experiments were reported, the first using independent groups for each of the auditory conditions and the second employing a within-participants design allowing each participant to respond to stimulus pairs representing all three of the auditory conditions. Results were consistent across both experiments, revealing that adding sound improved response accuracy in the discrimination task, but that this improvement occurred only when the sounds moved in the same direction as the coherent visual motion.

In the cognitive attempt to merge stimuli arriving at different perceptual modalities, human perception sometimes causes events in our surrounding world that are not physically simultaneous to be perceived as coincident. In a series of three experiments, Cook and Van Valkenburg (2009) found that participants consistently identified events in the auditory and visual domains as synchronous when they were temporally incongruent by up to 240 ms (temporal ventriloquism). Mozolic, Hugenschmidt, Peiffer, and Laurienti (2008) revealed the importance of attentional focus to cross-modal perception. In this study, the researchers asked participants to attend to a single modality (selective attention) and discovered that the enhanced performance observed in previous studies as the result of redundant information presented to multiple sensory modalities was eliminated. Those previous studies had not incorporated an attentional factor into their research design.

The ventriloquist effect has proven extremely robust and has been confirmed by numerous empirical investigations during the past several decades (Bertelson & Aschersleben, 2003; Bertelson, Vroomen, de Gelder, & Driver, 2000; Fowler & Dekle, 1991; Kitajima & Yamashita, 1999; Radeau, 1973, 1992; Radeau & Bertelson, 1987; Shi, Chen, & Muller, 2010; Vroomen & de Gelder, 2004). In a musical context, Schutz and

Lipscomb (2007) demonstrated that the perceived duration of musical tones produced by a master marimba player can be influenced by a video presentation communicating either the performance of a 'long' or 'short' tone. These researchers recorded the percussionist playing three marimba tones across the range of the instrument: E1 (~82 Hz), D4 (~587 Hz), and G5 (~1568 Hz); each tone was recorded using three stroke types: long, short, and damped (i.e., physically touching the bar with a hand after playing the note to shorten the tone duration). For the visual stimuli, the percussionist was videotaped from the waist upward, providing a view of his full range of mallet motion; he was asked to perform two stroke types: long and short. After peak-normalizing the audio stimuli, six AV combinations (three audio stroke types × two visual stroke types) were created for each of the three pitch levels (E1, D4, and G5). Participants provided responses via a computer interface, using a slider object representing a 101-point scale anchored by the terms 'short' and 'long.' Results revealed that identical auditory recordings were consistently perceived as 'longer' when paired with the video showing a stroke commonly associated with long tones and 'shorter' when paired with a staccato stroke. Schutz (2009) and Schutz and Kubovy (2009) confirm this result, but determined the importance of tone envelope, clarifying that the visual influence on auditory sound is robust for percussive sounds but does not significantly influence the perception of sustained tones. (See also Chapter 10 by Boltz in this volume for other examples of visual influence on music perception.)

Further experimentation has revealed that human perception of spatially incongruent events can be influenced through a process of *adaptation* or *recalibration*. By implementing a pre-experimental period of participant exposure to incongruent stimuli, the perceived location of auditory test sounds can be displaced perceptually (e.g., Bertelson, Frissen, Vroomen, & de Gelder, 2006; Lewald, 2002; Lewald & Guski, 2003; Navarra, Hartcher-O'Brien, Piazza, & Spence, 2009; Radeau & Bertelson, 1974, 1977, 1978; Velasco, Spence, & Navarra, 2011). Tactile stimulation has also been shown to influence or be influenced by auditory and visual stimuli (e.g., Bruns, Spence, & Roder, 2011; Fujisaki & Nishida, 2009; Marks, 1987).

Models of multimedia addressing synchronization

One of the main purposes of empirical work is to enhance understanding of human experience by developing theories within a given discipline concerning the relationship of relevant variables one to another. The following section of this chapter will describe two extant models of multimedia cognition. During recent decades, there have been a number of eloquent theoretical treatises that address the AV relationship (e.g., Chion, 1994; Cook, 1998), though the models proposed are rarely based primarily on experimental investigations. The most complete model of this experience to date was proposed and continues to be developed by Annabel Cohen (e.g., Cohen, 2001, 2010; Marshall & Cohen, 1988). Identified as the 'Congruence-Association Model' (CAM) and focused primarily on the cognition of film music, it has evolved significantly over the course of the past two and a half decades and can be applied effectively to a wide variety of multimedia contexts, as readers will note from its reference throughout the present volume. Though a much more detailed accounting of this evolution can be found in Cohen's chapter in the present volume, the fundamental aspects of her model are important to the following discussion, so will be delineated here. Of particular relevance to the present chapter is the notion of congruence, especially as it relates to temporal aspects of cross-modal multimedia content.

Marshall and Cohen (1988) performed an experiment using abstract animations in which 'characters' included a large triangle, a small triangle, and a small circle moving on-screen in the vicinity of a rectangular enclosure that opens and closes. These images were accompanied by primarily monophonic (sometimes doubled at the octave) melodies composed by one of the researchers. According to the CAM, based on the results of the experiments presented by Marshall and Cohen, a cross-modal comparison is made between the visual and musical components of the film stimulus. Results of their experiments revealed a direct influence of the music on the interpretation of the visual content in both the Potency and Activity dimensions (see Osgood, Suci, & Tannenbaum, 1957 for a discussion of the Evaluative, Potency, and Activity dimensions). Judgments of the Evaluative dimension in Marshall and Cohen (1988) appeared to rely on a more complex AV comparison between the values on the three separate Potency, Activity, and Evaluative dimensions and will not be discussed further here. Of most importance to the present chapter is a congruence aspect of the CAM, which includes a 'temporal component' (Marshall & Cohen, 1988, p. 109). The authors proposed that:

> congruence between internal structure of film and music alters the attentional strategy to and subsequent encoding of information in the film. That is, the pattern of attention to music alone or to film alone is altered under conjoint presentation. (p. 110)

A recent revision of the model (Cohen, 2010) included five channels, adding 'text' and 'sound effects' to the three channels previously represented in the model; the internal structural congruence is represented by an arrow connecting the 'music structure' to the 'visual structure' elements. (For a more detailed discussion of this model and its evolution, see Cohen, Chapter 2, in the present volume.)

To determine the impact of music on visual images in a more ecologically valid context, Lipscomb and Kendall (1994) performed a pair of experiments using excerpts from *Star Trek IV: The Voyage Home* (1986), a mainstream Hollywood film. As a result of the experience of matching musical excerpts to visual excerpts not intended by the composer (a preliminary study leading to the main experiment), the model of film music perception proposed by the authors included an explicit 'accent structure alignment' component. Focusing specifically on this temporal congruence aspect of viewer-listener perception, Lipscomb (1995, 2005) investigated the role of aligning audio and visual components in a multimedia context. Through a series of three experiments utilizing increasingly complex stimuli, this research determined that, with simple and moderately simple stimuli, alignment of accent structures across modalities is very influential upon verbal responses received from experimental participants. However, as the audio and visual stimuli reach the level of complexity inherent in actual Hollywood films, the alignment appears to become less important, being overridden by the associative aspects of the musical sound and imagery. The revised model (Lipscomb, 2005) will be presented later in this chapter.

Accent structure alignment in multimedia

While cross-modal influence has been well documented in reductionist experiments using simple stimuli (e.g., flashes of light and single tones), there is a paucity of research investigating accent structure alignment specifically in the context of multimedia; descriptions of several of those few studies that do exist will be provided in the following paragraphs. One point of clarification is essential to this discussion, providing a philosophical basis for such perceptual-cognitive research. The position adopted here concerning the determination of 'congruence' is that the human perception of events must be used as the primary basis for such comparisons. Though temporal and spatial measures of physical aspects of stimuli are highly relevant and provide useful information in discussions of the multimedia experience, because the focus of this chapter is on the *perceived* alignment of stimuli across modalities, veridical measures of human experience must be based on the perceptions of these events rather than the measurements of the physical events that lead to them. This distinction has been referred to in past literature as the Humean and Cartesian frames of reference, perspectives considering reality on the basis of perceptual versus physical attributes, respectively (Campbell & Heller, 1980; Hodges & Sebald, 2011, chapter 2; Kendall & Carterette, 1990)

Distinguished from Lewkowicz's investigation of sounds aligned with points of apparent impact of an animated disk (1996; discussed previously), Namba, Hayashi, and Wako (2003) observed the perceived congruence between an animated disk (with consistent start and end points in the animation sequence) and the duration of pure tones, the latter serving as an experimentally manipulated variable. While the visual stimulus was held to a constant duration of 1000 ms, the duration of the auditory stimuli ranged from 500 to 1500 ms in increments of 100 ms. There were two AV conditions: one in which the cross-modal stimuli were physically synchronized at the beginning of the tone ('S,' synchrony at Starting point) and one in which the AV stimuli were synchronized at the end of the tone ('E,' synchrony at Ending point). Participants were required to respond using a two-item, forced-choice procedure, choosing between 'the duration of disk is identical with that of sound' or 'the duration of disk is not identical with that of sound' (p. 179).

The three experiments revealed a clear normal distribution of participant responses in terms of the percentage of those who heard the various components of the AV stimuli as 'identical' (perfectly aligned) across the various durations of auditory stimuli with the mode response (i.e., the response that occurred most frequently) representing the AV combination including the 1000 ms auditory stimulus; this was true in both the S and E conditions, whether the apparent motion was vertical or horizontal, whether the speed of apparent motion was constant or linearly increased, and whether the tone was fixed at 300 Hz or started at that frequency and decreased using a pitch bend function to create a descending glide for the full duration of the tone (this last manipulation of the auditory stimulus was used in association with the vertical apparent motion stimulus only). However, the spread of responses was much greater for the E condition (mode percentage approximately 67 percent) than the S condition (mode percentage approximately 91 percent), suggesting that there is more tolerance for variation in the start time within these simple AV stimuli (condition E, when the endings are aligned but start times staggered) than in the end time (condition S, when start times are aligned, but end times staggered). Though the authors do not speculate, this outcome may result from our real-world experience in which auditory and visual stimuli do not arrive at our sensory organs in perfect physical alignment, yet we maintain a *perception* of congruence over a wide range of asynchronies as discussed earlier (Bertelson & Aschersleben, 2003; Bertelson et al., 2000; Fowler & Dekle, 1991; Kitajima & Yamashita, 1999; Radeau, 1973, 1992; Radeau & Bertelson, 1987; Shi et al., 2010; Vroomen & de Gelder, 2004).

In a study that more closely represents the real-world, AV experience of watching a film, Baggett (1984) presented an instructional film with voice-over narration to 14 independent groups of participants (n=24 for each group), considering two independent variables: a recall test (given immediately after viewing the film or 7 days later) and AV synchronization (seven conditions: audio preceding video by 21, 14, or 7 seconds; in synchrony; audio delayed by 7, 14, or 21 seconds). The recall test was based solely on associations made between audio and visual content, specifically 'the association of an object with its name' (p. 408). The film was about Fischer Technik 50, a Lego™-like assembly kit, including 48 different pieces that were named during the film, which lasted just over 30 minutes. Included in the film narration were a description of each piece shown, its name and features, and a description of some of its uses. The two groups scoring highest on recall were those participants who viewed the film in synchrony or with visuals occurring 7 seconds *before* the intended narration. In a statement of the practical application of these findings, the author concludes:

> In a dual-media presentation, the narration should shortly follow, or be in synchrony with, the visual image and should not precede it.... If one's objective is associative recall of names of objects, one should present the visual part early or simultaneously with the text. (pp. 415–416)

While Baggett's study addresses the auditory narration component of a film and the impact of altering the cross-modal synchronization upon associative recall, the relevance of this finding may not be readily apparent with respect to the focus of the present volume: *music* in multimedia. That specific problem (i.e., the synchronization of music and image) was addressed in a series of studies that will be described in the following sections.

Accent structure alignment in animation and mainstream motion pictures

In a series of three experiments, Lipscomb (1995) investigated accent structure alignment between audio and visual components in multimedia at three different levels of stimulus complexity (single-object animations, excerpts from experimental animations, and excerpts from a mainstream motion picture). In the first experiment, researcher-created, single-object animations and accompanying monophonic MIDI music tracks (consisting of isochronous pitch sequences) were used to create periodically spaced moments of salience (i.e., accents) in the perception of both auditory and visual stimuli. Following an extensive literature review, potential sources of accent were determined in both the *auditory domain*—melodic (position in tonal system, pitch height, serial position, articulation, contour (interval size, direction)), dynamic (loudness), qualitative (timbre), and temporal (duration) (1995, p. 36)—and in the *visual domain*—spatial (shape/form, size, orientation, location), spectral (color, lighting, pattern, texture), and temporal (motion (horizontal, vertical), rotations in depth, rotations in the plane, translations in depth, translations in the plane) (p. 39).

Experimental stimuli

Lipscomb selected three of the potential variables in each domain for use in creating perceived accents in the experimental stimuli. In the musical stimuli, this included changes in pitch, loudness, and timbre; in the visual domain, location, shape, and color were used. Animations and musical stimuli were created to induce three different temporal periodicities in the perception of accent: 500 ms, 800 ms, and 1000 ms; two periodicities were intentionally chosen to provide a nesting of accent structures: 500 ms and 1000 ms. The AV stimuli were created based on Yeston's (1976; discussed previously) three types of accent structure strata: consonant, out-of-phase, and dissonant. This was the only experiment within the study in which such controlled manipulation of accent structures was possible, since stimuli for the other two experiments were taken from extant multimedia.

For the second experiment, AV stimuli were extracted from experimental animations by Canadian animator Norman McLaren (*Dots*, 1940; *Canon*, 1964; and *Synchromy*, 1971). For the third experiment, excerpts from a mainstream Hollywood film (*Obsession*, 1975; directed by Brian DePalma with a musical score by Bernard Herrmann) were selected. For experiments two and three, the periodicities inherent in the animations or film excerpts were used to create AV combinations representing each of Yeston's categories. For all experiments, a series of preliminary studies was carried out in order to determine which audio and visual stimuli 'produced the most reliable sense of accent periodicity' (Lipscomb, 1995, p. 152) and—for experiments two and three—which combinations incorporating intended audio and visual components and which combinations incorporating one of several musical tracks other than the intended soundtrack were considered the 'least synchronized' (p. 96). These determinations were made empirically, based on participant responses on a verbal rating scale (not synchronized—synchronized). The least synchronized version of the intended soundtrack was used as the out-of-phase composite, while the least synchronized version of the unintended soundtrack was used as the dissonant composite.

Method

The method for all three experiments differed only in the stimulus materials used. Two independent groups performed separate tasks. One group watched each AV composite and responded on two verbal scales (synchronization and effectiveness). These two terms were differentiated for participants as follows: 'The rating of 'synchronization' refers to how often important events in the music coincide with important events in the visual scene. The rating of 'effectiveness' simply concerns your subjective evaluation of how well the two go together' (Lipscomb, 1995, p. 51). The second group performed a paired comparisons task, experiencing every possible pair of AV stimuli (including identities) and responding on a single scale labeled at opposite ends as 'not same' and 'same.' The following explicit distinction was provided: 'throughout the experiment, 'same' will be defined as 'identical' and 'not same' will be defined as 'maximally different' (p. 52).

Results

Results of the first experiment clearly revealed that the alignment of audio and visual components in the researcher-created animations was a determining factor in participant responses; verbal responses to both verbal scales (synchronization and effectiveness) changed significantly as a function of this alignment. The highest ratings were in response to the consonant combinations, while the lowest ratings were associated with the dissonant pairs. The out-of-phase combinations filled an intermediate space. Considering the nested pairs (stimuli incorporating 500 ms accents in one modality and 1000 ms accents in the other), ratings for the nested consonant stimuli approached the high ratings given for consonant pairs with identical periodicities and the out-of-phase nested combinations were rated in the low range of the dissonant composites. Though ratings for synchronization and effectiveness were highly correlated ($r = 0.96$, 0.94, and 0.74 across the three experiments, respectively), participant ratings of synchronization were consistently more extreme than those for effectiveness, suggesting that ratings of effectiveness reveal a slightly higher degree of tolerance for misalignment than do the synchronization ratings.

Based on similarity judgment data collected from the second group of participants, multidimensional scaling (MDS) and cluster analysis also clearly differentiated the three alignment conditions, revealing three criteria by which participants determined similarity among AV composites: the visual component, the audio component, and alignment condition (Figure 9.2). In a discussion of these results, Lipscomb (2005) concluded that a model of film music perception must account for these accent structure relationships (p. 59).

Discussion

Based on participant ratings of effectiveness and synchronization, results of the second and third experiments (using excerpts from experimental animations and a mainstream motion picture, respectively) confirmed the descending pattern of mean ratings (highest for consonant, intermediate for out-of-phase, and lowest for dissonant) across AV stimuli, regardless of level of complexity (see Figure 9.3). Analysis of the similarity judgment data also confirmed the three criteria used in these responses across levels of complexity: visual, audio, and alignment.

Three important points of divergence were apparent in the results of the third experiment using mainstream motion picture excerpts. First, in the verbal ratings of synchronization and effectiveness, the former reveal the consistent descending pattern of mean ratings observed in the previous two experiments—though response ranges for mean ratings across conditions were smaller—while, in the latter, the statistically significant difference between the consonant and out-of-phase conditions disappears. Second, of particular interest (and contrary to the researcher's hypothesis), on the effectiveness scale, participants rated the consonant and out-of-phase combinations similarly (sometimes the out-of-phase combination was actually rated *higher* than the

```
                                      DISTANCES
     0.000                                                          100.000
V1A1_C    ---
               +-------
V1A1_O    ---      |       Audio 1
                   +-------------------
V1A1_D    ----------                 |              Visual 1
                                     +-------------------------------
V1A2_D    ------------     Audio 2   |                              |
                     +---------------                               |
V1A2_C    -----      |                                              |
              +-------                                              |
V1A2_O    -----                                                     |
                                                                    +------
V2A2_O    ---                                                       |
            +----------                                             |
V2A2_C    ---         |    Audio 2                                  |
                      +-------------------------                    |
V2A2_D    -------------                        |    Visual 2        |
                                               +---------------------
V2A1_D    -----------      Audio 1             |
                    +---------------------------
V2A1_C    -----     |
              +------
V2A1_O    -----
```

Figure 9.2 Cluster analysis tree diagram (complete linkage, farthest neighbor) for similarity ratings provided by participants in experiment one of Lipscomb (1995). The naming convention for plotted points is: visual identifier/audio identifier/underscore ('_')/alignment condition (e.g., V2A1_D represents visual two combined with audio one to create a dissonant alignment condition). Adapted from Lipscomb (1995); used with permission.

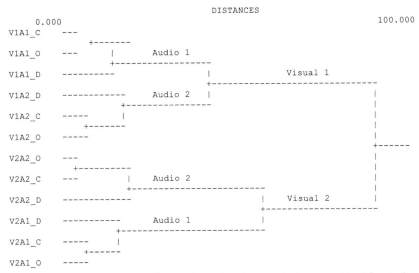

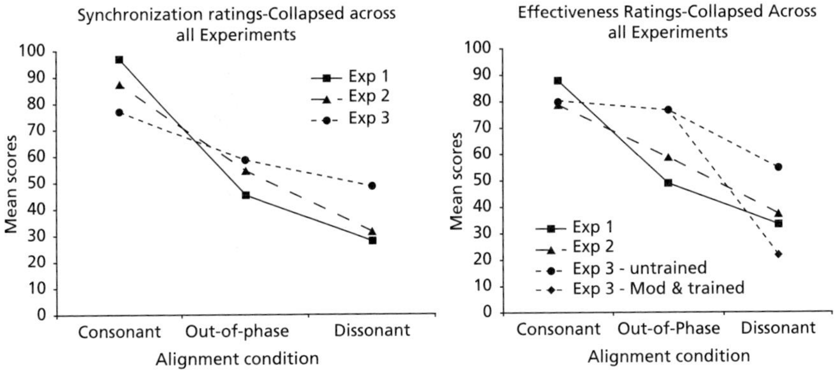

Figure 9.3 Response means for the verbal response scales across all three experiments in Lipscomb (1995); including the separation of levels of musical training. Adapted from Lipscomb (1995); used with permission.

consonant combination). Third, the clear role of alignment condition also disappeared from the MDS solution based on participant responses in the third experiment (using motion picture excerpts). Two of the factors apparent in previous experiments were clearly present (visual component and audio component), but the impact of alignment condition was absent. In their ratings of similarity, participants appeared to be 'judging the 'consonant to out-of-phase' comparisons (i.e., comparing a consonant alignment condition to the composite with the same audio & visual components, but incorporating an out-of-phase alignment condition) as identical' (Lipscomb, 1995, p. 159). The third dimension of the MDS solution, which had in the previous two experiments been confidently interpreted as representing alignment condition, appeared instead to relate to 'general AV congruency (i.e., appropriateness)' (p. 159).

Participants in each of these experiments represented three levels of musical training. This independent variable had no effect on the results of the first two experiments; however, in the third experiment, higher levels of training were associated with greater sensitivity to the mismatch represented by dissonant combinations. Post-hoc analyses confirmed that, for the dissonant combinations of these film excerpts only, there was a statistically significant difference between the 'effectiveness' responses of the musically untrained participants and the moderately and highly trained participants. Those individuals with some level of musical training proved more sensitive to this mismatch, providing substantially lower ratings on the scale of effectiveness (Figure 9.3).

Results of Lipscomb's (1995) three experiments reveal a changing level of significance in the accent structure alignment as a result of the complexity of the auditory and visual components of the multimedia experience. Revising a model originally presented by Lipscomb and Kendall (1994), the researcher proposed:

> a weighted relationship between the factors of accent structure alignment and association judgment, both of which are subcomponents of an individual's overall determination of AV congruency. In this model, the importance of accent alignment is considered appropriately high at low levels of stimulus complexity, but decreases in salience as AV complexity increases. (Lipscomb, 1995, p. 143)

For simpler stimuli (e.g., single-object animations and AV combinations that exemplify the relationship referred to as 'Mickey-mousing'), the alignment of sound and audio appears to be a primary perceptual factor in the experience. However, as the complexity of the auditory and visual stimuli increases (as in most mainstream Hollywood films), the alignment between film and soundtrack can be shifted quite a bit—as illustrated by responses to the consonant and out-of-phase composites in the third experiment—without having a significant impact upon the perception of effectiveness of the AV combination. Lipscomb (1995) concluded that:

> when the audio and visual components were simple or moderately complex, accent structure alignment did appear to be a necessary condition in order for an AV combination to be considered effective. However, when the audio and visual stimuli attained the complexity of a typical motion picture, accent alignment was no longer a necessary condition. (p. 166)

With the more complex AV stimuli, the judgment of congruity between the associative content of the audio and visual stimuli appeared to override the crucial role of alignment condition evidenced in simpler stimuli. The dotted boxes in Figure 9.4 are intended to represent this dynamic aspect of the model. When perceiving more complex stimuli, rather than being perceived as clearly out of synchronization, it is possible that the shifted musical accent structure simply aligned with other salient moments in the visual scene. As has been demonstrated by Marilyn Boltz, varying a musical score

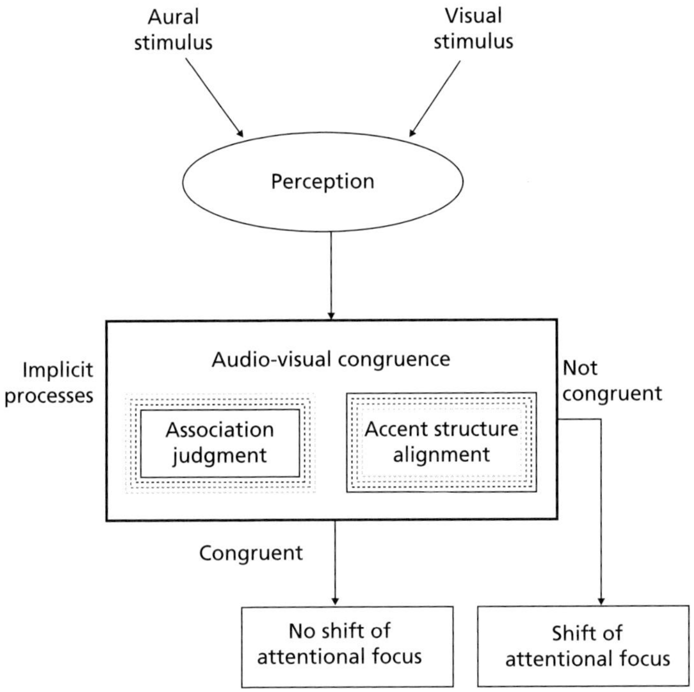

Figure 9.4 Revised model of film music perception. Adapted from Lipscomb (1995) and Lipscomb and Kendall (1994; used with permission).

results in the memory of different objects in the visual scene, revealing that 'positive and negative music significantly biased viewers' interpretation and subsequent remembering of a film in a mood-congruent fashion' (Boltz, 2001, p. 427). She also determined that the interpretation of a musical score can be altered by the interpretation of a visual component (Boltz, Ebendorf, & Field, 2009). Though neither of Boltz's studies described here directly addressed accent structure alignment, focusing instead on 'mood-congruence' (i.e., association), inherent in each of the various musical components was an associated accent structure that varied as the result of the changing audio and may have played a role in focusing attention on specific aspects of the visual scene, a result that remains open to future investigation. In their original formulation of the Congruence-Associationist Model (CAM), Marshall and Cohen (1988) address the matters of temporal congruence and the importance of accented events. Focusing specifically on the relevance of participant responses related to one of the shapes in their animated AV stimuli, the authors suggested that:

> a temporal congruence between the music and the activity of the small triangle may have drawn attention to or accented the behavior of the small triangle, making the information available for processing and memory.... The temporal component of music may then affect interpretation of a film through congruence with the action or pattern of motion of the film at least at an initial level of analysis. (pp. 108–109)

As a result, the findings of Lipscomb (1995, 2005) may be seen to expand the congruence component of the CAM.

Conclusion

While the purpose of this chapter has been to address cross-modal accent structures and the manner in which their alignment impacts the multimedia experience, it is important to blend this systematic viewpoint with the perceptual reality discussed early in this chapter, revealing that items occurring across a fairly broad range of physical incongruency between modalities—up to 240 ms apart (Cook & Van Valkenburg, 2009)—are perceived as synchronous. In the following excerpt, Zettl (1990) makes a case, if only anecdotal, for the ability of music to meld with a variety of visual stimuli:

> To witness the structural power of music take any video sequence you have at hand and run some arbitrarily selected music with it. You will be amazed how frequently the video and audio seem to match structurally. You simply expect the visual and aural beats to coincide. If they do not, you apply psychological closure and make them fit. Only if the video and audio beats are, or drift, too far apart, do we concede a structural mismatch—but then only temporarily. (p. 380)

In the broad sense of the word (Lefrancois, 1982, p. 144), the psychological principle of closure is important in the context of Zettl's statement above, providing a foundation upon which to base an explanation of the results of the studies of congruity referenced earlier in this chapter. One well-known example of the type of arbitrary combination referenced by Zettl can be experienced by viewing the *Wizard of Oz* (1939) while listening to Pink Floyd's *Dark Side of the Moon* (1973);[4] at the risk of minimizing the feature of 'arbitrariness' touted by Zettl, the effect seems to be particularly striking if you initiate playback of the CD recording of Pink Floyd's album at the beginning of the third roar of the MGM lion in the video.

Confirming this same experience in an empirical context, individuals who participated in preliminary studies for Lipscomb and Kendall (1994) experienced this by watching numerous AV combinations and directly manipulating the alignment of sound and image. As mentioned in an earlier discussion, the stimuli for that particular study consisted of excerpts from *Star Trek IV: The Voyage Home* (1986). In addition to AV composites that used the composer-intended music for every selected scene, each film excerpt was combined with music from other sections of the film. Given the experimental context, however, the authors did not believe a simple 'needle-drop' technique (i.e., a completely arbitrary means of superimposing music on a visual scene) was appropriate. Instead, graduate student composers watched multiple alignment possibilities for each musical and visual combination and were assigned the task of selecting the alignment that created the best match possible, despite the fact that the music was not originally intended to align with that particular visual scene. Through this process, participants (including one author; SL) learned that shifting the musical soundtrack temporally did not always create a more- or less-synchronized alignment; rather, as proposed in the discussion found in Lipscomb and Kendall (1994), the musical accents sometimes simply aligned with different events in the visual scene. This was a primary rationale for carrying out the series of experiments reported by Lipscomb (1995, 2005).

Future research directions

Much future work is needed to enhance our understanding about the role of the alignment of accent structures in multimedia. As evident from the content of the present chapter, the vast majority of past work has employed highly reductionist stimuli (tone sequences and single-object animations) rather than more ecologically valid films and animations. As evident from Lipscomb (1995), the use of such complex stimuli presents a number of challenges. Only by addressing these challenges and carrying out systematic investigations incorporating such stimuli will future researchers be able to confidently generalize experimental results to real-world multimedia experiences.

Research is needed specifically to determine the relative importance of the associational and accent structure components proposed in Lipscomb's (1995) model of film music perception. The dynamic nature of these components of the model must be subjected to systematic testing for verification or reconsideration. The use of a more comprehensive set of alignment conditions (rather than just the three used in Lipscomb's study) would also be a welcome addition to the literature. The rhythmic patterns incorporated by Cooper and Meyer (1960) and supplemented by Monahan and Carterette (1985) could serve as an interesting possibility in this regard, if applied to a cross-modal context.

The establishment of reliable metrics to assess the multimedia experience is crucial. Numerous innovative approaches have been employed in the studies cited throughout this chapter, but much more effort will be required to ensure that the results of future experiments will be both reliable and valid and will be meaningfully generalizable to real-world multimedia experiences. Given the sociological significance of these art forms and the multi-billion dollar industries behind them, it is surprising that so little empirical work is available to enhance our understanding of the multimedia experience. Of particular note is the paucity of research specifically addressing accent structure alignment within the multimedia context. Finally, now that some forms of multimedia include tactile information in addition to the auditory and visual accent structures (e.g., D-Box film presentation or video games with vibrating controllers), investigations of the experience moving beyond merely auditory and visual components must be carried out. Very little ecologically valid research exists at present that addresses accent structures across three or more concurrent perceptual modalities.

While the immediate goal of this chapter was to determine the impact of alignment condition on the multimedia experience, the long-term, overarching goal of this line of research is to facilitate a greater understanding of general human cognitive processing.

Notes

1. An isochronous sequence is one in which events occur at regular intervals, with an equal temporal duration between each event.
2. Because the speed of propagation is influenced by the density of a propagating medium and its temperature, it is important to note that the speed for sound transmission provided here is based on an environment with dry air at a temperature of 70°F (Roederer, 1979, p. 68).
3. Many versions of this illusion are available online and are readily accessible to the interested reader, e.g., <http://www.youtube.com/watch?v=aFPtc8BVdJk>.
4. Because the movie (*Wizard of Oz*) lasts substantially longer than the musical recording (*Dark Side of the Moon*), the music will conclude long before the movie comes to an end. Regardless, during the approximately 50 minutes of music, this combination provides an interesting example of the 'structural match' referred to by Zettl (1990).

References

Alais, D., & Carlile, S. (2005). Synchronizing to real events: Subjective audiovisual alignment scales with perceived auditory depth and speed of sound. *PNAS Proceedings of the National Academy of Sciences of the United States of America, 102*(6), 2244–2247.

Baggett, P. (1984). Role of temporal overlap of visual and auditory material in forming dual media associations. *Journal of Educational Psychology, 76*(3), 408–417.

Bermant, R. I., & Welch, R. B. (1976). Effect of degree of separation of visual-auditory stimulus and eye position upon spatial interaction of vision and audition. *Perceptual and Motor Skills, 43*(2), 487–493.

Bertelson, P., & Aschersleben, G. (2003). Temporal ventriloquism: Crossmodal interaction on the time dimension: 1. Evidence from auditory-visual temporal order judgment. *International Journal of Psychophysiology, 50*(1-2), 147–155.

Bertelson, P., Frissen, I., Vroomen, J., & de Gelder, B. (2006). The aftereffects of ventriloquism: Patterns of spatial generalization. *Perception & Psychophysics, 68*(3), 428–436.

Bertelson, P., Vroomen, J., de Gelder, B., & Driver, J. (2000). The ventriloquist effect does not depend on the direction of deliberate visual attention. *Perception & Psychophysics, 62*(2), 321–332.

Boltz, M. G. (2001). Musical soundtracks as a schematic influence on the cognitive processing of filmed events. *Music Perception, 18*(4), 427–454.

Boltz, M. G., Ebendorf, B., & Field, B. (2009). Audiovisual interactions: The impact of visual information on music perception and memory. *Music Perception, 27*(1), 43–59.

Boltz, M. G., & Jones, M. R. (1986). Does rule recursion make melodies easier to reproduce? If not, what does? *Cognitive Psychology, 18*(4), 389–431.

Bregman, A. S. (1990). *Auditory scene analysis: The perceptual organization of sound.* Cambridge, MA: MIT Press.

Bruns, P., Spence, C., & Roder, B. (2011). Tactile recalibration of auditory spatial representations. *Experimental Brain Research, 209*(3), 333–344.

Campbell, W., & Heller, J. (1980). An orientation for considering models of musical behavior. In D. A. Hodges (Ed.), *Handbook of music psychology* (pp. 29–36). Lawrence, KS: National Association for Music Therapy.

Chion, M. (1994). *Audio-vision: Sound on screen.* New York, NY: Columbia University Press.

Cohen, A. J. (2001). *Music as a source of emotion in film Music and emotion: Theory and research* (pp. 249–272). New York, NY: Oxford University Press.

Cohen, A. J. (2010). *Music as a source of emotion in film Handbook of music and emotion: Theory, research, applications* (pp. 879–908). New York, NY: Oxford University Press; US.

Colonius, H., & Diederich, A. (2010). The optimal time window of visual-auditory integration: A reaction time analysis. *Frontiers in Integrative Neuroscience, 4*, 11.

Cook, L. A., & Van Valkenburg, D. L. (2009). Audio-visual organisation and the temporal ventriloquism effect between grouped sequences: Evidence that unimodal grouping precedes cross-modal integration. *Perception, 38*(8), 1220–1233.

Cook, N. (1998). *Analysing musical multimedia.* New York, NY: Oxford University Press.

Cooper, G., & Meyer, L. B. (1960). *The rhythmic structure of music.* Chicago, IL: University of Chicago Press.

Deliège, I. (1987). Grouping conditions in listening to music: An approach to Lerdahl & Jackendoff's grouping preference rules. *Music Perception, 4*(4), 325–359.

Di Luca, M., Machulla, T.-K., & Ernst, M. O. (2009). Recalibration of multisensory simultaneity: Cross-modal transfer coincides with a change in perceptual latency. *Journal of Vision, 9*(12), 7.

Fowler, C. A., & Dekle, D. J. (1991). Listening with eye and hand: Cross-modal contributions to speech perception. *Journal of Experimental Psychology: Human Perception and Performance, 17*(3), 816–828.

Fraisse, P. (1982). Rhythm and tempo. In D. Deutsch (Ed.), *The psychology of music* (pp. 149–180). New York, NY: Academic Press.

Fujisaki, W., & Nishida, S. y. (2009). Audio-tactile superiority over visuo-tactile and audio-visual combinations in the temporal resolution of synchrony perception. *Experimental Brain Research, 198*(2-3), 245–259.

Heron, J., Whitaker, D., McGraw, P. V., & Horoshenkov, K. V. (2007). Adaptation minimizes distance-related audiovisual delays. *Journal of Vision, 7*(13), 1–8.

Hodges, D. A., & Sebald, D. C. (2011). *Music in the human experience: An introduction to music psychology.* New York, NY: Routledge.

Huron, D., & Royal, M. (1996). What is melodic accent? Converging evidence from musical practice. *Music Perception, 13*(4), 489–516.

Hutchinson, W., & Kuhn, L. (1992). I musernas sällskap [The complementarity of music and the visual arts]. In *Festschrift für Ulla-Britta Legeroth* (pp. 534–564). Sweden: Wiken.

Jones, M. R. (1987). Dynamic pattern structure in music: Recent theory and research. *Perception & Psychophysics, 41*(6), 621–634.

Kendall, R. A., & Carterette, E. C. (1990). The communication of musical expression. *Music Perception: An Interdisciplinary Journal, 8*(2), 129–163.

Kim, R., Peters, M. A. K., & Shams, L. (2011). 0 + 1 > 1: How adding noninformative sound improves performance on a visual task. *Psychological Science, 10*(10), 1–7.

Kitajima, N., & Yamashita, Y. (1999). Influence of visual attention upon sound localization. *Japanese Journal of Psychology, 69*(6), 459–467.

Krause, V., Pollok, B., & Schnitzler, A. (2010). Perception in action: The impact of sensory information on sensorimotor synchronization in musicians and non-musicians. *Acta Psychologica, 133*(1), 28–37.

Lefrancois, G. R. (1982). *Psychological theories and human learning* (2nd ed.). Monterey, CA: Brooks/Cole Publishing Company.

Lewald, J. (2002). Rapid adaptation to auditory-visual spatial disparity. *Learning & Memory, 9*(5), 268–278.

Lewald, J., & Guski, R. (2003). Cross-modal perceptual integration of spatially and temporally disparate auditory and visual stimuli. *Cognitive Brain Research, 16*(3), 468–478.

Lewkowicz, D. J. (1996). Perception of auditory-visual temporal synchrony in human infants. *Journal of Experimental Psychology: Human Perception and Performance, 22*(5), 1094–1106.

Lipscomb, S. D. (1995). *Cognition of musical and visual accent structure alignment in film and animation.* (Unpublished doctoral dissertation.) University of California, Los Angeles, CA.

Lipscomb, S. D. (2005). The perception of audio-visual composites: Accent structure alignment of simple stimuli. *Selected Reports in Ethnomusicology, 12*, 37–67.

Lipscomb, S. D., & Kendall, R. A. (1994). Perceptual judgment of the relationship between musical and visual components in film. *Psychomusicology, 13*(1), 60–98.

Marks, L. E. (1987). On cross-modal similarity: Perceiving temporal patterns by hearing, touch, and vision. *Perception & Psychophysics, 42*(3), 250–256.

Marshall, S. K., & Cohen, A. J. (1988). Effects of musical soundtracks on attitudes toward animated geometric figures. *Music Perception, 6*(1), 95–112.

Massaro, D. W., & Warner, D. S. (1977). Dividing attention between auditory and visual perception. *Perception & Psychophysics, 21*(6), 569–574.

McGurk, H., & MacDonald, J. (1976). Hearing lips and seeing voices. *Nature, 264*, 746–748.

Mershon, D. H., Desaulniers, D. H., Amerson, T. L., & Kiefer, S. A. (1980). Visual capture in auditory distance perception: Proximity image effect reconsidered. *Journal of Auditory Research, 20*(2), 129–136.

Monahan, C. B., & Carterette, E. C. (1985). Pitch and duration as determinants of musical space. *Music Perception, 3*(1), 1–32.

Mozolic, J. L., Hugenschmidt, C. E., Peiffer, A. M., & Laurienti, P. J. (2008). Modality-specific selective attention attenuates multisensory integration. *Experimental Brain Research, 184*(1), 39–52.

Namba, S., Hayashi, Y., & Wako, S. (2003). On the synchrony between figure movement and sound change. *Empirical Studies of the Arts, 21*(2), 177–184.

Navarra, J., Hartcher-O'Brien, J., Piazza, E., & Spence, C. (2009). Adaptation to audiovisual asynchrony modulates the speeded detection of sound. *Proceedings of the National Academy of Sciences of the United States of America, 106*(23), 9169–9173.

Osgood, C. E., Suci, G. J., & Tannenbaum, P. H. (1957). *The measurement of meaning.* Urbana, IL: University of Illinois Press.

Radeau, M. (1973). The locus of adaptation to auditory-visual conflict. *Perception, 2*(3), 327–332.

Radeau, M. (1992). Cognitive impenetrability in auditory-visual interaction. In J. Alegria, D. Holender, J. Morais, and M. Radeau (Eds.), *Analytic approaches to human cognition* (pp. 41–55). Oxford, UK: Elsevier.

Radeau, M., & Bertelson, P. (1974). The after-effects of ventriloquism. *Quarterly Journal of Experimental Psychology, 26*, 63–71.

Radeau, M., & Bertelson, P. (1977). Adaptation to auditory-visual discordance and ventriloquism in semirealistic situations. *Perception & Psychophysics, 22*(2), 137–146.

Radeau, M., & Bertelson, P. (1978). Cognitive factors and adaptation to auditory-visual discordance. *Perception & Psychophysics, 23*(4), 341–343.

Radeau, M., & Bertelson, P. (1987). Auditory-visual interaction and the timing of inputs: Thomas (1941) revisited. *Psychological Research, 49*(1), 17–22.

Rahne, T., Böckmann, M., Von Specht, H., & Sussman, E. S. (2007). Visual cues can modulate integration and segregation of objects in auditory scene analysis. *Brain Research, 1144*, 127–135.

Regan, D., & Spekreijse, H. (1977). Auditory-visual interactions and the correspondence between perceived auditory space and perceived visual space. *Perception, 6*(2), 133–138.

Repp, B. H. (2005). Sensorimotor synchronization: A review of the tapping literature. *Psychonomic Bulletin & Review, 12*(6), 969–992.

Roederer, J. G. (1979). *Introduction to the physics and psychophysics of music* (2nd ed.). New York, NY: Springer-Verlag.

Roseboom, W., Nishida, S. y., & Arnold, D. H. (2009). The sliding window of audio-visual simultaneity. *Journal of Vision, 9*(12), 4.

Ruff, R. M., & Perret, E. (1976). Auditory spatial pattern perception aided by visual choices. *Psychological Research, 38*(4), 369–377.

Schutz, M. R. (2009). Crossmodal integration: The search for unity. (Dissertation.) *Dissertation Abstracts International: Section B: The Sciences and Engineering, 70*(6-B), 3816.

Schutz, M. R., & Kubovy, M. (2009). Causality and cross-modal integration. *Journal of Experimental Psychology: Human Perception and Performance, 35*(6), 1791–1810.

Schutz, M. R., & Lipscomb, S. D. (2007). Hearing gestures, seeing music: Vision influences perceived tone duration. *Perception, 36*(6), 888–897.

Shi, Z., Chen, L., & Muller, H. J. (2010). Auditory temporal modulation of the visual Ternus effect: The influence of time interval. *Experimental Brain Research, 203*(4), 723–735.

Staal, H. E., & Donderi, D. (1983). The effect of sound on visual apparent movement. *The American Journal of Psychology, 96*(1), 95–105.

van Eijk, R. L., Kohlrausch, A., Juola, J. F., & van de Par, S. (2009). Temporal interval discrimination thresholds depend on perceived synchrony for audio-visual stimulus pairs. *Journal of Experimental Psychology: Human Perception and Performance, 35*(4), 1254–1263.

Velasco, I., Spence, C., & Navarra, J. (2011). The perceptual system: That little time-machine. *Anales de Psicologia, 27*(1), 195–201.

Vroomen, J., & de Gelder, B. (2004). Temporal ventriloquism: Sound modulates the flash-lag effect. *Journal of Experimental Psychology: Human Perception and Performance, 30*(3), 513–518.

Whitney, J. (1980). *Digital harmony: On the complementarity of music and visual art.* Peterborough, NH: Byte Books.

Yeston, M. (1976). *The stratification of musical rhythm.* New Haven, CT: Yale University Press.

Zettl, H. (1990). *Sight, sound, motion: Applied media aesthetics* (2nd ed.). Belmont, CA: Wadsworth Publishing Co.

Part III

Interpretation and Meaning

Chapter 10

Music videos and visual influences on music perception and appreciation: Should you want your MTV?

Marilyn G. Boltz

Haverford College, USA

Given the technology of today's society, an individual has a variety of options through which to experience music. On the one hand, one may listen to a performance via the radio, an iPod, MP3 player, or CD recording—all of which allow one to listen to a song exclusively in its auditory form. Alternatively, one can view a music video while listening to a song and see the performance as it is being produced.

From a cognitive perspective, this raises an interesting question. Does the presence of visual information enhance or impair apprehension of the accompanying music? Despite the impressive abilities of the human mind, people are nonetheless limited in the amount of information they can effectively process. Numerous studies have consistently shown that situations requiring divided attention among two or more events typically result in poorer cognitive performance than situations in which attention is directed toward a single event alone (Driver, 2001; Kahneman, 1973; Pashler, 1994). In the context of music videos, this suggests that videos may have a distracting influence and may interfere with the processing of musical information. However, it is possible that the opposite effect occurs such that videos actually enhance music cognition. As many contributions within this volume attest, a substantial amount of research has shown that music can exert a variety of effects upon the movie-viewing experience by accentuating or attenuating the emotional impact of a scene (Bolivar, Cohen, & Fentress, 1994), influencing the types of inferences about characters' motivations and actions (Boltz, 2001; Bullerjahn & Güldenring, 1994), directing attention toward some information and away from others, and thereby influencing how much is remembered, what is remembered, and what is confabulated (Boltz, 2001, 2003; Boltz, Schulkind, & Kantra, 1991). Overall, these findings suggest that music is integrated with film information to aid both the understanding and appreciation of a visual story.

Given the effects of music on film, it may be the case that a reciprocal effect occurs such that audiovisual productions are more informative and have a greater impact upon listeners than do audio productions alone. Although the literature addressing this question is relatively sparse, the existing research has primarily been directed toward issues involving music education and performance. More recently, the popularity of music videos as an art form has motivated psychomusicologists to examine ways in which videos may influence the perception and memory of a musical selection. The following sections discuss these respective bodies of literature and then attempt to make sense of the observed results by appealing to certain theoretical constructs within the more general field of cross-modal perception.

Music instruction and evaluation

Suppose that one is a music professor who instructs students to play various instruments and that the students, on occasion, perform in various ensembles. What is the best way to evaluate student performances? Should one rely on an audio recording and simply listen to a performance for its different acoustical qualities? Or, is it better to rely on an audiovisual recording so that one can both see and listen to the performance as it is being produced? Similar questions arise when auditioning for a professional gig. Again, one must decide whether to submit material in an audio or audiovisual format. Over the past several years, a number of studies have addressed these sorts of questions and yielded a fairly consistent pattern of results that, in turn, offer some practical recommendations for music educators.

Linklater (1997) considered the issue of learning in musical instruction. Especially during the early stages of instrumental study, performance is likely to improve through observational learning and emulating an appropriate role model. By experiencing musical compositions performed by expert musicians, students are able to observe how these pieces should be played and thereby enhance their musical instruction. In his study, Linklater examined *what kind* of model is most effective during this learning process. A sample of 5th and 6th graders, all learning to play the clarinet, were each given one of three types of material to study during home practice: an audiotape of a solo clarinetist accompanied by other instruments; a videotape providing both a visual and aural presentation of the same performances; or, as a control condition, a non-modeling audiotape of instrumental performances with no clarinetists. After studying this material over an 8-week period, each group of students was evaluated by two experienced judges on several visual criteria (e.g., posture, lip movements, body positioning relative to the instrument) as well as auditory criteria (e.g., tone quality, intonation, melodic and timing accuracy). To assess the long-term effectiveness of each instructional mode, the students were also tested again both 3 and 5 months later. The results showed a clear audiovisual advantage. Relative to the two audio-alone conditions those students who had studied the videotape were judged significantly higher on the visual criteria of posture and body movements and, in the longitudinal assessments, higher on tone quality and intonation. In addition, this group spent more time practicing each week. The advantage of videotapes is that they relate *what* movements are required to produce different effects and a high sound quality, and *how* these movements should be performed, both of which enhance instrumental instruction and serve as a motivating influence. Although Linklater (1997) is one of the few studies to date that has examined the learning process as a function of mode of instruction, his results suggest that audiovisual presentations should be particularly effective for instruments that require large body movements during performance, which can be more easily communicated.

A substantially larger body of literature has addressed the set of questions raised earlier, namely, what is the optimal means through which to evaluate musical performance? The typical methodological strategy is to present judges with either an audio or audiovisual recording of a performance and ask them to rate both the overall quality of musicianship as well as those acoustical qualities appropriate to a given instrument. The results of such studies consistently show that judgments are markedly higher when evaluators can both see and hear a performance, an effect observed with male and female vocalists (Cassidy & Sims, 1991; Wapnick, Darrow, Kovacs, & Dalrymple, 1997), violinists (Gillespie, 1997; Wapnick, Mazza, & Darrow, 1998), and pianists (Ryan & Costa-Giomi, 2004; Wapnick, Ryan, Lacaille, & Darrow, 2004), and especially when these performers are highly accomplished in their abilities.

So why does this effect occur? In contrast to an aural-alone format, the added presence of the visual modality allows one to see the performer who is producing the music. At least two aspects of this visual information have been argued to influence evaluative judgments. The first involves physical appearance while the second concerns the affordant value of musical gestures.

Physical appearance

Within the fields of social and personality psychology, a plethora of studies has demonstrated that attractive individuals are ascribed a number of positive traits in that they are assumed to be more competent, sociable, warm, kind, sensitive, trustworthy, and successful. This belief, referred to as the *halo effect* (Dion, Berscheid, & Walster, 1972), is a ubiquitous one found across different cultures and demographic variables including age, sex, and race (Eagly, Ashmore, Makhijani, & Longo, 1991; Feingold, 1992). As one might expect, the halo effect has a number of social consequences. Relative to those who are less attractive, more attractive individuals have greater occupational success and are more likely to be hired (Bull & Rumsey, 1988); are less likely to be convicted of a crime and, if so, receive lighter sentences (Stewart, 1980; Zebrowitz & McDonald, 1991); are more likely to receive aid from both strangers and acquaintances (Barocas & Vance, 1974; Patzer, 1985); and are more successful at influencing others such as in advertising situations (Eagly & Chaiken, 1984).

Wapnick and colleagues have argued that the halo effect also influences evaluative judgments of musical ability and contributes to the modality effect. Several studies, in fact, support this claim. In the first demonstration of this phenomenon, Wapnick et al. (1997) videotaped several male and female vocalists performing a classical piece that was approximately 90 seconds in duration. The first half of the video showed close-up views of a singer's face while the remaining half presented full-body views. A sample of judges, who were all musically experienced, were then randomly assigned to one of three groups and asked to rate either the attractiveness of the performer based on visual information alone or several performance qualities based on aural versus audiovisual information. These performance qualities included intonation accuracy, musical phrasing, diction, efficient breath management, and color/warmth as well as overall performance quality. Consistent with the halo effect, more attractive performers received higher performance ratings than those who were less attractive, but the surprising finding is that this occurred in *both* the aural and audiovisual presentation modes. In the aural condition, judges were not able to see the performers and so ratings were based exclusively on acoustical qualities alone. Nonetheless, more attractive performers were considered more proficient in their abilities.

Subsequent research has examined whether this latter finding is a reliable one that is not simply due to sampling error and, in addition, has attempted to more clearly define the general concept of attractiveness assessed in this earlier study. Perhaps most commonly, attractiveness refers to the physiognomy and physique of an individual. However, it can also include the manner and appropriateness of dress as well as stage behaviors such as smiling, animation, and projected enthusiasm. The question is, which of these various dimensions influence evaluative judgments? Wapnick et al. (1998) investigated this issue in a research design that was very similar to that of the 1997 study described earlier. Here, however, a group of experienced violinists was evaluated by 72 expert judges who, in one condition, rated the physical attractiveness, attire, and stage presence of each performer based on visual information alone. Two other groups received audio or audiovisual recordings of these same performances and for each, assessed the qualities of phrasing, dynamic range, intonation, overall sound, and performance ability. The results revealed that all three components of attractiveness influenced musical evaluation. Those performers rated higher on stage presence and manner of dress benefited from a videotaped presentation, especially on the qualities of dynamic range, overall sound, and performing ability. On the other hand, those violinists rated lower on dress and stage manner were not penalized for their judged musical ability. Evaluations in the audiovisual condition, in fact, were equivalent to those in the audio-alone condition. The dimension of physical attractiveness once again yielded the more interesting result. As in the earlier study (Wapnick et al., 1997), those performers considered high in physical attractiveness were judged more musically proficient on all performance criteria in both the audiovisual and audio-alone presentations. This suggests that the attractiveness bias in music evaluation may actually arise during musical instruction and training. During the period when one is first learning to play an instrument, it may be the case that more attractive individuals are given more encouragement and individualized attention such that they subsequently become better musicians. Parallel findings have been reported in elementary and secondary schools wherein more attractive children are expected to achieve greater academic success (e.g., Adams, 1978; Adams & LaVoie, 1974; Clifford & Walster, 1973) and, in fact, do attain higher grades (e.g., Felson, 1980; Lerner & Lerner, 1977; Salvia, Algozzine, & Scheare, 1977) and are considered to be more qualified applicants for college admissions (Shahani, Dipboye, & Gehrlein, 1993). Given these types of findings, it may not be surprising that the attractiveness bias extends to music education and performance ability.

Musical gestures

The visual modality, of course, offers other information beyond the attractiveness and appeal of a performing musician; even more importantly, it allows one to see the body movements and gestures required to produce music. In addition to aiding the learning of a musical instrument (Linklater, 1997), body movements also facilitate music perception—much in the same way that access to lip movements aids speech perception (e.g., Summerfield, 1979). Production and perception are inextricably entwined such that music often reflects the body movements used to produce sound, and vice versa (Godøy & Leman, 2010). For example, the height at which a drumstick is raised is directly correlated with percussive striking velocity (Dahl, 2000, 2004), and both the velocity and pressure of a bow gesture is reflected in the amplitude envelope and spectrum change produced on a violin (Askenfelt, 1989).

This type of interrelationship between sound and gesture confers a number of benefits to cognitive behavior. First, relative to audio information alone, access to visual body movements helps to clarify the perception of musical structure and increases a listener's confidence in what they have heard. Some support for this idea comes from the work of Vines and colleagues (e.g., Vines, Krumhansl, Wanderly, & Levitin, 2006). Participants in these studies are typically asked to watch and/or listen to a musical performance and as they do so, to indicate the location of all musical phrase boundaries through the use of a sliding potentiometer. The results consistently show that phrase structure is more clearly communicated, and hence more easily perceived, in an audiovisual versus audio-alone presentation. Musicians' movements serve to cue new phrase boundaries and not only enable an audience to perceive their presence but anticipate when in time phrase onsets will occur. Another methodological strategy has been to display a performer's body movements and determine whether viewers can accurately perceive the corresponding sound that *would* occur if sound were actually present. Thompson and Russo (2007), for example, presented visual recordings of vocalists and asked participants to rate the size of the tonal intervals they imagined the singers were producing. It was found that viewers could do so quite accurately and primarily relied on movements of the lips, head, and eyebrows to make their judgments.

Lastly, Schutz and Lipscomb (2007) found that the arm movements of marimba performers affected perceived tone duration and, in fact, can lead to an auditory illusion such that notes produced with a long gesture are heard as longer than those produced by a short gesture—even when no actual acoustical difference exists between the two audio stimuli. (see Figure 10.1 and accompanying caption. For an audiovisual version of this phenomenon and to see the original stimuli used in this study, please visit <http://www.oup.co.uk/companion/tan>.) A follow-up study by Armontrout, Schutz, and Kubovy (2009) employing point-light representations of the marimbist determined that the illusion is driven primarily by the duration of the post-impact motion. (Please visit <http://www.oup.co.uk/companion/tan> for an audiovisual illustration of this effect.)

In addition to highlighting the underlying structure of a musical composition, gestures aid music perception in another way: they more clearly communicate the underlying intent of the performer. Davidson (1993) was perhaps the first to demonstrate this phenomenon with the use of Johansson's (1973) point-light display. Reflective tape was attached to all joints (i.e., head, shoulders, elbows, wrists, hips, knees, ankles) of a group of violinists and pianists that, in a darkened room, allows one to monitor the performers' movements over time. Each musician was instructed to play a selection of their choice in a particular expressive style (i.e., deadpan, projected, exaggerated), and

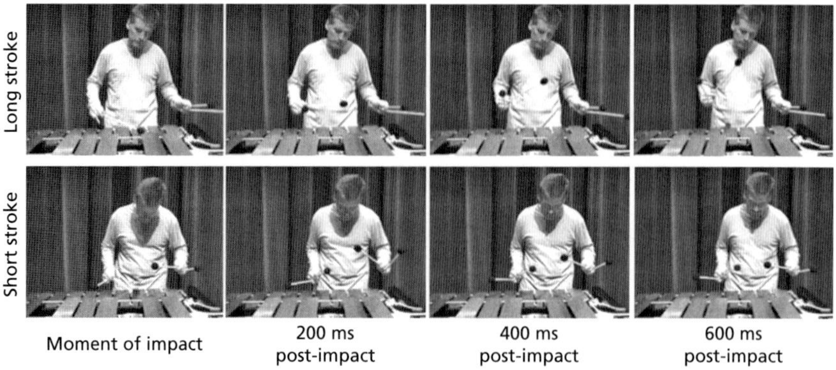

Figure 10.1 Time-elapsed images of the videos used in Schutz and Lipscomb's (2007) study. Captured 200 milliseconds apart, they show that acclaimed percussionist Michael Burritt's striking mallet (held in his right hand) continues moving for a longer time after impact for the 'long' stroke (top row) versus the 'short' stroke (bottom row). Although the difference in post-impact motion does not affect the tone's acoustic duration, it often affects *perception* of the duration of the tone—leading to the perceptual illusion of long strokes generating tones of longer duration than short strokes. © Michael Schutz and Scott Lipscomb. This figure appeared previously in *Psychology of Music: From Sound to Significance* (Tan, Pfordresher, & Harré, 2010), p. 37. (For an audiovisual version of this figure, please visit <http://www.oup.co.uk/companion/tan>.)

participants were asked to rate the expressivity of this performance on a scale ranging from deadpan to exaggerated. The results showed that the ability to perceive the performers' intent was best when viewing a video and more difficult when simply listening to performances. This finding was even more apparent for musically untrained individuals (Davidson, 1995), suggesting that many concert-goers rely more on the artists' gestures than the music to infer the level of expressiveness within a performance.

Similar findings have been reported for the perceived emotionality of music. Dahl and Friberg (2007), for example, presented silent videos of both marimba and woodwind performers that were intended to communicate different emotions. Based on the particular type of movements produced by the musicians, participants were able to accurately identify, at above chance levels, the intended emotions of sadness, happiness, and anger but had more difficulty in discerning fear—which Dahl and Friberg argue is less commonly expressed in music unless it is in a narrative context. More interestingly, there was a close correspondence between musical structure and the nature of the gestures used to express a given emotion. The fast *tempi* and large melodic intervals characteristic of happy melodies were accompanied by fast, large body movements; the slow *tempi* and tonal attacks of sad music were produced by slow movements; and the *staccato* articulation and irregular rhythm of angry melodies corresponded to jerky body movements. These findings reinforce the idea that gesture and sound are inextricably entwined which, in the context of music listening, suggests that the intended emotion of a composition should be more clearly and unambiguously communicated to an audience via an audiovisual versus audio- or visual-alone presentation. This, in fact, has been found by both Marolt (2006) and Vines and colleagues (Vines et al., 2006; Vines, Krumhansl, Wanderley, Dalca, & Levitin, 2011) and, as in the case of expressive style (Davidson, 1995), the added presence of visual information is more important for non-musicians than musicians.

In sum, the literature is quite consistent in showing that evaluative judgments of musical performances are markedly higher in an audiovisual format that affords a view of those musicians producing the music. The magnitude of this effect was recently quantified through a meta-analysis by Platz and Kopiez (2012) who focused on a set of 15 studies published between 1940 and 2011 as peer-reviewed articles in English or German, dissertations, or conference proceedings. Each had assessed evaluative ratings (i.e., of liking, expressiveness, or the overall quality of musicianship) in response to performances with no accompanying artifice (e.g., animations, film sequences, point-light displays). When ratings from the audio-alone condition were subtracted from those in the audiovisual condition, an average effect size of 0.51 standard deviations was observed. Platz and Kopiez conclude that 'the visual component is not a marginal phenomenon in music perception, but an important factor in the communication of meaning. This process of cross-modal integration exists for classical as well as pop and rock music' (p. 75). On a behavioral level, the literature indicates that the communicative meaning of audiovisual information stems from several different sources. Body movements and gestures can clarify the perception of musical structure and the performers' intent. In addition, the visual modality benefits those musicians who are physically attractive and/or are well-dressed and project an appealing stage presence.

To return to a question posed at the beginning of this section, what then is the optimal means by which to evaluate students or to submit material for a preliminary 'audition?' With respect to the former, Gillespie (1997) recommends that instructors whose job is to critically judge a performance should rely on audio information alone, because the added presence of the visual modality may lead one to believe that a student's musicianship is better than what it actually is. On the other hand, those musicians auditioning for a professional gig may want to submit an audiovisual recording, such as a DVD, in order to capitalize on the benefits that the visual modality confers. Lastly, from the perspective of an audience, this research suggests that, when given the choice, one may want to experience a musical artist through both sight and sound. Visual information will reinforce and highlight the intended meaning of a performance as well as one's level of appreciation and enjoyment—which, after all, is the end goal that is sought.

The coordination of musical performance

The relationship between music and gesture has implications for another group of individuals, namely, the members of a performing group (e.g., band, ensemble, orchestra) who play together. In order to produce a unified stream of textured sound, performers must be able to anticipate one another and synchronize the onsets and offsets of individual instruments. One might ask, is the ability to perform as a coordinated unit influenced by the ability to see one's fellow performers, or is it enough to be able to simply hear one another? Although this issue has not yet been well investigated, preliminary research suggests that visual access to one another's gestures enhances coordinated performance.

Davidson, once again, is one of the pioneers in this field (Davidson & Good, 2002) and has relied on case studies of ensembles who are videotaped during a performance or rehearsal and then analyzed for their pattern of body movements relative to the unfolding sequence of sound. In general, these types of analyses indicate that there are different types of gestures that serve different functions. One category acts to mark the entrances and exits of a given instrument. For example, a violinist may precede his or her entrance with a large upward gesture of the bowing arm that better enables the other performers to synchronize the onsets of their own instruments. Secondly, gestures are commonly used to mark dynamics and changes in amplitude. This primarily occurs by varying the size of movement in the head, arms, or shoulders such that smaller movements correspond to softer phrases, while larger movements correspond to a louder dynamics. Lastly, Davidson and Good have noted a third category of gestures termed 'circular body sways' that are used more explicitly for timing coordination and expressiveness. In this case, the body moves in a rotational manner, much like ripples in a pond, to highlight the directional flow of a musical phrase and moment-to-moment changes in tempo and rhythm.

More recently, others have adopted an empirical approach to investigate the influence of the visual modality on performance coordination. In one such study by Levine and Schober (2008), saxophone and jazz piano duos (who had never before played with one another) were compared across three different contexts: in the same physical space with visual access to one another, in separate physical spaces but able to hear one another via headphones, or in separate physical spaces but able to see one another via a live video. Timing analyses of these performances revealed that synchronization was markedly higher when performers were able to see one another, either face-to-face or through live video, and this was especially true for the coordination of entrances at phrase transitions. These results, then, converge with the qualitative data reported by Davidson, and, as a set, indicate that performers' body movements aid *both* production and perception. This research also explains those findings from the earlier section showing that perception of musical structure and intent is facilitated by visual access. The coordination of instrumental performance is more challenging at points of phrase onsets and dynamic/expressive change, and the gestures used to highlight these locations benefit both other performers and a perceiving audience, albeit for different reasons.

The experience of music videos as an art form

The literature addressed thus far has highlighted the benefits of an audiovisual versus audio presentation of music in order to aid the instruction, evaluation, and coordination of musical performances. However, another line of research has investigated the behavioral consequences of using music videos for a second purpose, namely, as a form of artistic expression.

When silent films were first introduced in the early 1900s, orchestras often played in the background in order to mask the noise of the film projector. Although advances in technology quickly resolved the noise problem, music continued to be used as an accompaniment to film which, in turn, led to a debate among film theorists. Some argued that music was a distraction that interfered with the visual narrative, and that its use should, therefore, be abandoned to achieve a more 'pure' cinematic art form (e.g., Arnheim, 1957; Clair, 1972). Others, however, acknowledged the psychological functions of music and argued that in the context of film, sound and image merge into a single entity to offer an audience a more enriched experience (e.g., Bazin, 1967).

It is interesting that this very same debate reappeared several decades later with the introduction of the music video format that later became so popular through venues such as MTV. In contrast to a depiction of the musicians performing a given composition, which Finnas (2001) has referred to as a documentary style video, these videos have perhaps more commonly adopted a non-documentary style which relies on images unrelated to the musical performance (e.g., nature scenes, narrative image sequences). When this new art genre first emerged in the early 1980s, the debate centered on the predicted effectiveness of video as a means through which to promote musical artists and their songs. Some, such as Zorn (1984), argued that videos would decrease the appeal of a song by imposing a given interpretation that, thereby, limits a listener's imagination and cognitive involvement. Others, however, claimed that videos would enhance the aesthetic appeal of music by clarifying a song's intended meaning (e.g., Sun & Lull, 1986).

One means by which to address this controversy is to simply ask the primary audience of this media what they think. Of these endeavors, one of the most ambitious was conducted by Sun and Lull (1986) who surveyed 587 high school students. Participants were given a set of statements to indicate their degree of agreement/disagreement as well as a set of open-ended questions concerning their reasons for watching MTV and what they liked about this medium. As one might imagine, the results were varied, but overall, 80 percent of all students surveyed watched music videos, on average, for 2 hours per day and cited the main reasons as one of entertainment and social learning—learning about one's self and others; the future and relevant social issues in the world; and how to act, dress, and relate to others. Of more interest here are their comments concerning what they liked about MTV. Many mentioned that the video made the music better, helped them 'get' what the artists were attempting to communicate, and served to pictorially represent the song's meaning. Overall, most respondents expressed a very positive attitude toward MTV and claimed it was more profound and relevant than most other television programs.

A very different approach was adopted by Goldberg, Chattopadhyay, Gorn, and Rosenblatt (1993) who investigated whether 'wear out'—becoming tired of a song due to excessive exposure—was more likely to occur when the song recurred by itself or in the context of a video. This study relied on an experimental design in which the number of exposures to a given song ('Slow Dancing' by Lindsay Buckingham) was varied as well as the presentation format (audio alone, the original video, or an edited video that lacked closure). When participants were asked to indicate how much they liked the song on successive occasions, the results showed that ratings did not change for the original video but decreased in the audio-alone condition and increased for the edited version. These authors concluded that videos are more likely to maintain a listener's interest in a song over time, especially when they are relatively ambiguous and open to multiple interpretations.

From a cognitive perspective, music videos raise a more general question, that is, in what ways does visual information influence the perception, appreciation, and remembering of music? This question is worth considering from several viewpoints. On an academic level, such research will further illuminate the nature of cross-modal perception and the underlying mechanisms at play. For example, is the influence of visuals on music analogous to the influence of music on film that has been so well documented? Does visual information interfere with the processing of music, or are the two modalities integrated to provide a more enriched cognitive representation as claimed by the respondents in Sun and Lull (1986)? On a more practical level, this type of research may better inform musical artists about whether videos should be used to promote a song and, if so, the behavioral consequences of different techniques.

Surprisingly, very few studies to date have empirically assessed these sorts of issues. One, performed by Geringer, Cassidy, and Byo (1996, 1997), presented participants with certain musical selections either alone or as an accompaniment to film excerpts from the Walt Disney classic, *Fantasia*. Immediately after each selection, participants described their emotional reactions to the music and those qualities that most held their attention. The results showed that, relative to the music-alone condition, the music videos evoked greater emotional engagement that primarily was attributed to a composition's tempo, instrumentation, and dynamics. (See also Keown [2013] on the perspective of performers).

Additional research by Boltz, Ebendorf, and Field (2009) asked whether visuals extend their influence by altering the perceived acoustical qualities that typically convey emotion within music. For example, suppose that a tune with a neutral affect is accompanied by a video that is clearly negative (sad) in its content. Relative to an audio-alone format, is this tune perceived to have a slower tempo, softer amplitude, and a lower pitch—qualities that all convey sadness in the auditory modality (Gabrielsson & Lindstrom, 2001; Scherer, 1979)? Conversely, is this same tune perceived to be faster, louder, and higher in pitch when accompanied by a positive video? These questions were addressed in a set of two experiments that acted as converging operations to one another.

The methodological strategy of both was to present participants with a set of 'ambiguous' melodies defined as those displaying a neutral affect and intermediate degree of activity (e.g., Russell, 1980). As a control condition, one melody was presented by itself, but the four remaining were paired with visual displays that varied in both their affect (positive, negative) and format (a montage or slideshow of still photos versus a video of thematic scenes that smoothly transitioned from one to another). In the first experiment, participants were asked to rate each stimulus on a variety of dimensions; of most interest were a set of musical qualities that included tempo, amplitude, rhythm, tonality, harmony, flow, and overall affect.

The results showed that visual displays influenced melody perception in a variety of ways. First, the mere presence of *any* visual information, regardless of its affect or format, enhanced certain musical dimensions: melodies were heard as faster, more rhythmic, louder, more active, more tonal, and more harmonious than the same melodies heard alone. Some insight into this finding comes from ratings of the visual displays, which indicated they were perceived high in meaningfulness. Hence, an overgeneralization effect may have occurred to render accompanying melodies more interesting and more meaningful, which in turn biased the perception of these particular acoustical qualities. Second, visual affect influenced music perception in a mood-congruent fashion. Melodies pre-rated as neutral in affect were judged to have a positive affect in the presence of positive scenes but a negative affect in the presence of negative scenes. More interestingly, the acoustical qualities of these tunes were influenced in a corresponding manner. Melodies in a positive visual context seemed louder, faster, more rhythmic, and more active than those in a negative context. The mood of the film, then, not only biased the affective interpretation of an accompanying tune but, once this interpretation was adopted, changed the way the tune was heard in a mood-congruent manner.

Lastly, visual format also influenced perceptual ratings. In contrast to the videos that were judged smoother and more passive, visual montages seemed more active and *staccato* in nature. These terms, in fact, aptly describe the structure of each format. The videos used in this research displayed a relatively slow rate of action in which thematically related scenes gradually transitioned from one to the other. The montages, on the other hand, contained a large set of discrete photos that shared the same affect but were thematically unrelated to one another and changed every 700 milliseconds. In this sense, then, the montage format was, in fact, more active and less smooth than the video one.

This overall pattern of results was corroborated in a second experiment that relied on a more implicit task. After encountering each of the five melodies in an initial phase, participants were then given a surprise recognition memory task in which they were required to discriminate each old melody from a transformed version that had been increased or decreased in tempo, pitch, or both together to reflect a more positive or negative affect, respectively. The results revealed memory distortions such that melodies were falsely recognized as faster or slower than their actual *tempi* in the presence of positive and negative displays, respectively.

As a set, this research, along with that of Geringer et al. (1996, 1997), indicates that the effects of visuals on music perception and remembering are parallel to the effects of musical soundtracks on film. (See also Chapter 11 by Hoeckner and Nusbaum, in this volume.) In the context of film, music with a clear positive or negative affect within the background of an ambiguous scene biases inferences about a character's motivations, dispositional nature, and actual behavior in a positive or negative manner. Memory is also influenced, not only in terms of which particular objects are remembered but also what is confabulated (Boltz, 2001). When one examines the reverse relationship and the effects of visuals on music, an analogous phenomenon occurs: visual affect leads to a general emotive interpretation that then biases the perception and remembering of a melody and its corresponding acoustical qualities in a mood-congruent fashion.

Theoretical bases of audiovisual interactions

In the earlier section addressing musical evaluation and performance, it was found that music and gestures were inextricably entwined such that one reflects the other in documentary performance videos. Similarly, within the context of non-documentary videos, music and visuals are also reciprocally related. The fact that one modality influences and biases the other suggests that both are integrated in a single unified percept that is then used to guide behavior. Parallel ideas are encountered in the discipline of film studies. Theorists such as Michel Chion (1994) and Kathryn Kalinak (1992) have noted that, historically, many film courses have addressed sound on the one hand and film on the other. More recently, music and film have been argued to display a more intimate relationship of interdependence, a phenomenon that Chion (1994) terms 'audio-vision.' Kalinak (1992) expresses this position well when she claims that:

> while certainly music affects the image, it is likewise the case that the image affects the music. In fact, the relationship between them is so interdependent that when one cannot be 'squared' with the other, credibility itself is threatened, however momentarily, and the suspension of disbelief necessary to maintaining a fiction becomes potentially disruptible. (pp. 29–30)

The research described in this chapter provides empirical evidence for this argument by demonstrating that characteristics of a visual display (e.g., body movements, affect, structural format) are attributed to their accompanying melodies, and vice versa, such that, cognitively, they are perceived and remembered as congruent with one another. In a theory of cross-modal perception, Welch (1999) has claimed that this phenomenon is inherent to the cognitive system and reflects the 'unity assumption' (p. 373). The basic idea of the *unity assumption* is that humans are motivated to maintain congruence in their perceptual world such that any physical discrepancies, of a reasonable magnitude, are reduced in order to attain an integrated and unitary percept. On a behavioral level, unity presumably provides individuals with a sense of orderliness and well-being and, importantly, ensures a more efficient use of cognitive resources. In lieu of dividing one's attention among separate sources of information, perceptual unification allows one to direct attention toward a single event that entails less effort (Kahneman, 1973). Welch (1999) has primarily discussed the unity assumption relative to intersensory conflicts such as the 'ventriloquism effect' in which listeners perceive sound emanating from the moving lips of a dummy versus a human actually producing sound through non-moving lips. Relative to these types of situations, an ambiguous event (music or visual scene) accompanied by another event with a clear, unambiguous meaning is even more likely to result in unification.

On a more analytical level, Cohen (1999, 2009) has offered a *Congruence-Association Model* (CAM) which outlines the mediational mechanisms involved in audiovisual processing. (See also Chapter 2 by Cohen on this model, in this volume.) Although this model was originally developed to address the effects of music on film, it can also accommodate the reverse relationship and the effects of visuals on music. In general, CAM envisions a set of hierarchical stages that operate in both a top-down and bottom-up fashion in order to generate an interpretation (i.e., narrative construction) of a given audiovisual event.

At the lowest level of the model (identified as level A), independent sources of information (e.g., music, visual scenes, dialog, sound effects) are each processed for their physical features (e.g., rhythm and tempo; pitch height and contour; spatial motion; accents or natural breakpoints). These features are then compared at level B for any cross-modal structural congruencies—which, if present, will lead to what Welch (1999) has termed perceptual unification. Within this stage, greater attention may be directed toward the visual or auditory modality depending on the intended purpose of the art form (i.e., cinematic art to depict a visual story or a music video to portray a song). At level C, information enters short-term, working memory (i.e., consciousness) where people attempt to construct and make sense of the working narrative. This interpretative process is based on two sources of information. The first is the structurally integrated (bottom-up) information from level B. The second is relevant (i.e., top-down) information retrieved from long-term memory at level D. Long-term memory is a product of one's life experiences and consists of knowledge of how people typically behave in different situations, and how this behavior may vary according to different social roles and dispositions. Hence, this type of experiential knowledge will contribute to the interpretative process within working memory, and that knowledge which best matches the lower-level structural information will emerge as the working narrative that people consciously adopt.

The types of visual influences on music that have been discussed in this chapter are all consistent with CAM. In the case of documentary videos depicting performing musicians, visual body movements often reflect the sound they produce (e.g., Godøy & Leman, 2010). This, in turn, readily promotes an audiovisual integration of structural features at the pre-attentivc level (level B), even before the narrative meaning of the video is consciously constructed in working memory (level C). However, pre-stored knowledge (from level D) will also contribute to narrative construction. Repeated listening and viewing experience will eventually create a learned association between music and body gestures such that the two are expected to co-occur. When both modalities are in fact present, visual information can enhance the clarity of music perception and increase the confidence of what one has heard (e.g., Krumhansl & Schenk, 1997; Vines et al., 2006, 2011). Alternatively, an audience who has visual access to a performer's movements in situations in which sound is momentarily obscured or absent can nonetheless 'hear' the missing music and discern features such as tonal duration (Schutz & Lipscomb, 2007) and the size of sung intervals (Thompson & Russo, 2007).

A similar process applies to non-documentary music videos. Again, structural parallels between the auditory and visual modalities will be evaluated and lead to the integration of any congruent information. This integration, for example, may occur on the basis of the video's format (e.g., montage of discrete scenes versus those that smoothly transition from one to another) and musical activity (e.g., rhythm, tempo). Perhaps more importantly, the auditory and visual correlates of emotional affect, which have been so well documented in the literature (e.g., Dahl & Friberg, 2007; DeMeijer, 1989), will be structurally integrated to form a lower-level narrative interpretation within working memory. This interpretation will then be matched to that derived from relevant long-term knowledge. As the literature has shown, mood-congruent information from the audio and visual modalities acts to enhance the emotional impact of the listening and viewing experience (Boltz et al., 2009; Geringer et al., 1996, 1997). Alternatively, if one modality is mood ambiguous while the other is mood unambiguous, then the latter can bias the interpretation of the former and change the way that a melody is heard (Boltz et al., 2009) or a film is viewed (Boltz, 2001) in a mood-congruent fashion. As is true of music and gestures within documentary music videos, learned cross-modal associations enable one to 'fill in' missing affective information in one modality (i.e., tunes or scenes with a neutral affect) when the other modality conveys a clear and unambiguous affect.

Future directions

In addition to providing an explanatory framework for the types of music-visual interactions observed in the past literature, the theoretical constructs of perceptual unity (Welch, 1999) and congruence-association (Cohen, 1999, 2009) have the added advantage of generating additional avenues of future research. This is very useful because, as noted earlier, relative to research investigating the effects of music on the processing of film, much less attention has been directed toward the reverse relationship and, especially, ways in which visual displays might influence the perception, interpretation, and remembering of music.

One issue concerns the debate that arose shortly after music videos were popularized by MTV and other media, namely, whether videos exert a distracting or enhancing influence on music. The research by Sun and Lull (1986), Geringer et al., (1996, 1997), and Boltz et al. (2009) all suggest the latter, but there very well may be instances in which videos interfere with music perception and appreciation. From the perspective of CAM, one way in which this might occur is if there is very little or no structural congruence between the two modalities at level B. For example, video sequences of musical artists engaged in activities other than music performance or, more generally, body movements that do not correspond to the accompanying song may be difficult to unify into a single percept. Perhaps a more interesting situation is one in which visual displays and music independently convey strong and unambiguous emotions but ones that conflict with one another. This technique, known as 'ironic contrast,' is commonly used in film-making to convey a more subtle meaning to the visual narrative. However, it is not yet clear whether a reciprocal effect applies such that videos confer ironic contrast to a song. If not, then this may result in two independent percepts that distract from one another and interfere with cognitive processing.

A second issue concerns songs containing lyrics that must be processed relative to the accompanying acoustical and visual information. In this case, there are three sources of information that must be assessed for shared commonalities. Must congruence among all three levels be present for unification to occur, are certain combinations more important than others, and what are the behavioral consequences of incongruence at one level or another? As a related question, in what ways might audiovisual qualities influence the interpretation of lyrics and a song's meaning? These issues, as a set, highlight the fact that, although past research has addressed the interrelationship between music and visual information, there are additional levels of structure that contribute to perceptual integration and certainly merit investigation.

A third and final issue that has been relatively neglected in the literature concerns level D in CAM and top-down contributions from pre-stored knowledge. Many individuals have certain stereotypes or cultural associations (Rentfrow & Gosling, 2007) for different genres of music (i.e., rap, country, jazz, rock, etc.) that may influence evaluations of an accompanying video and its content. On the reverse side, there are many different film genres (i.e., romance, adventure, comedy, horror, mystery, etc.) with their own sets of associations (Grant, 2007), and it is quite possible that this sort of pre-knowledge will influence the audience's perception and memory of the accompanying soundtrack. In short, research is needed to clarify the ways in which bottom-up *and* top-down processing operate in tandem to influence the experience of 'audio-vision.'

In closing, the art genre of music videos raises a host of interesting questions that have yet to be investigated, and, as this work progresses, it promises to better illuminate the nature of the genre itself, *how* it influences an audience's experience of music, and *why* this is so. More importantly, the reciprocal relationship between music and visuals and their mutual influence upon one another reflects the oneness, the unity of the two sources of information that Chion (1994) has referred to as 'audio-vision.' Visuals and music often reflect one another and, regardless of the genre (i.e., cinematic film versus music video), the unified representation of audiovisual information provides a framework to guide the perception, interpretation, and remembering of the event of interest. At the most general level, investigations of the effects of visuals on music and vice versa will enhance our understanding of those processes mediating intersensory perception that is so typical of everyday cognition.

References

Adams, G. (1978). Racial membership and physical attractiveness effects on preschool teachers' expectations. *Child Study Journal, 8*, 29–41.

Adams, G., & LaVoie, J. C. (1974). The effect of student's sex, conduct, and facial attractiveness on teacher expectancy. *Education, 95*, 76–83.

Armontrout, J. A., Schutz, M., & Kubovy, M. (2009). Visual determinants of a cross-modal illusion. *Attention, Perception, & Psychophysics, 71*, 1617–1627.

Arnheim, R. (1957). *Film as art.* Berkeley, CA: University of California Press.

Askenfelt, A. (1989). Measurement of the bowing parameters in violin playing II: Bow bridge distance, dynamic range, and limits of the bow force. *Journal of the Acoustic Society of America, 86*, 503–516.

Barocas, R., & Vance, F. L. (1974). Physical appearance and personal adjustment counseling. *Journal of Consulting Psychology, 21*, 96–100.

Bazin, A. (1967). *What is cinema? (Vol. 1).* Berkeley, CA: University of California Press.

Bolivar, V.J., Cohen, A.J., & Fentress, J.C. (1994). Semantic and formal congruency in music and motion pictures: Effects on the interpretation of visual action. *Psychomusicology, 13*, 28–59.

Boltz, M. G. (2001). Musical soundtracks as a schematic influence on the cognitive processing of filmed events. *Music Perception, 18*, 427–454.

Boltz, M. G. (2003). The cognitive processing of film and musical soundtracks. *Memory & Cognition, 32*, 1194–1205.

Boltz, M. G., Ebendorf, B., & Field, B. (2009). Audiovisual interactions: The impact of visual information on music perception and memory. *Music Perception, 27*, 43–59.

Boltz, M. G., Schulkind, M., & Kantra, S. (1991). Effects of background music on the remembering of filmed events. *Memory & Cognition, 19*, 593–606.

Bull, R., & Rumsey, N. (1988). *The social psychology of facial appearance.* New York, NY: Springer-Verlag.

Bullerjahn, C., & Güldenring, M. (1994). An empirical investigation of effects of film music using qualitative content analysis. *Psychomusicology, 13*, 99–118.

Cassidy, J. W., & Sims, W. L. (1991). Effects of special education labels on peers' and adults' evaluations of a handicapped youth choir. *Journal of Research in Music Education, 39*, 23–34.

Chion, M. (1994). *Audio-vision: Sound on screen*. New York, NY: Columbia University Press.

Clair, R. (1972). *Cinema yesterday and today*. New York, NY: Dover.

Clifford, M., & Walster, E. (1973). The effects of physical attractiveness on teacher expectations. *Sociology of Education, 46*, 248–258.

Cohen, A. J. (1999). The functions of music in multimedia: A cognitive approach. In S. W. Yi (Ed.), *Music, mind, and science* (pp. 53–69). Seoul, Korea: Seoul National University Press.

Cohen, A. J. (2009). Music in performance arts: film, theatre, and dance. In S. Hallam, I. Cross, & M. Thaut (Eds.), *Oxford handbook of music psychology* (pp. 441–451). New York, NY: Oxford University Press.

Dahl, S. (2000). The playing of an accent—preliminary observations from temporal and kinematic analysis of percussionists. *Journal of New Music Research, 29*, 225–233.

Dahl, S. (2004). Playing the accent—comparing striking velocity and timing in an ostinato rhythm performed by four drummers. *Acta Acustica united with Acustica, 90*, 762–776.

Dahl, S., & Friberg, A. (2007). Visual perception of expressiveness in musicians' body movements. *Music Perception, 24*(5), 433–454.

Davidson, J. W. (1993). Visual perceptions of performance manner in the movements of solo musicians. *Psychology of Music, 21*, 103–113.

Davidson, J. W. (1995). What does the visual information contained in music performances offer the observer? Some preliminary thoughts. In R. Steinberg (Ed.), *Music and the mind machine: Psychophysiology and psychopathology of the sense of music* (pp. 105–114). Heidelberg, Germany: Springer.

Davidson, J. W., & Good, J. M. (2002). Social and musical coordination between members of a string quartet: An exploratory study. *Psychology of Music, 30*, 186–201.

DeMeijer, M. (1989). The contribution of general features of body movement to the attribution of emotions. *Journal of Nonverbal Behavior, 13*, 247–268.

Dion, K.K., Berscheid, E., & Walster, E. (1972). What is beautiful is good. *Journal of Personality and Social Psychology, 24*, 285–290.

Driver, J. (2001). A selective review of selective attention research from the past century. *British Journal of Psychology, 92*, 53–78.

Eagly, A. H., Ashmore, R. D., Makhijani, M. G., & Longo, L. C. (1991). What is beautiful is good, but… : A meta-analytic review of research on the physical attractiveness stereotype. *Psychological Bulletin, 110*, 109–128.

Eagly, A. H., & Chaiken, S. (1984). Cognitive theories of persuasion. In L. Berkowitz (Ed.), *Advances in experimental social psychology* (Vol. 17, pp. 267–359). New York, NY: Academic Press.

Feingold, A. (1992). Good-looking people are not what we think. *Psychological Bulletin, 111*, 304–341.

Felson, R. (1980). Physical attractiveness, grade, and teachers' attributions of ability. *Representative Research in Social Psychology, 11*, 64–71.

Finnas, L. (2001). Presenting music live, audio-visually or aurally—does it affect listeners' experiences differently? *British Journal of Music Education, 18*, 55–78.

Gabrielsson, A., & Lindstrom, E. (2001). The influence of musical structure on emotional expression. In P. Juslin & J. Sloboda (Eds.), *Music and emotion* (pp. 223–248). Oxford, UK: Oxford University Press.

Geringer, J., Cassidy, J. W., & Byo, J. (1996). Effects of music with video on responses of nonmusic majors: An exploratory study. *Journal of Research in Music Education, 44*, 240–251.

Geringer, J., Cassidy, J. W., & Byo, J. (1997). Nonmusic majors' cognitive and affective responses to performance and programmatic music videos. *Journal of Research in Music Education, 45*, 221–233.

Gillespie, R. (1997). Ratings of violin and viola vibrato performance in audio-only and audiovisual presentations. *Journal of Research in Music Education, 45*, 212–220.

Godøy, R. I., & Leman, M. (2010). *Musical gestures: Sound, movement, and meaning.* New York, NY: Routledge.

Goldberg, M. E., Chattopadhyay, A., Gorn, G. J., & Rosenblatt, J. (1993). Music, music videos, and wear out. *Psychology & Marketing, 10*, 1–13.

Grant, B. K. (2007). *Film genre: From iconography to ideology.* London, UK: Wallflower Press.

Johansson, G. (1973). Visual perception of biological motion and a model for its analysis. *Perception and Psychophysics, 14*, 201–211.

Kahneman, D. (1973). *Attention and effort.* Englewood Cliffs, NJ: Prentice Hall.

Kalinak, K. (1992). *Settling the score.* Madison, WI: University of Wisconsin Press.

Keown, D. J. (2013). *The effects of projected films on singers' expressivity in choral performance.* (Unpublished doctoral dissertation). University of Missouri-Kansas City, Kansas City, MO.

Krumhansl, C. L., & Schenk, D. L. (1997). Can dance reflect expressive qualities of music? A perceptual experiment on Balachine's choreography of Mozart's Divertimento No. 15. *Musicae Scientiae, 1*, 63–85.

Lerner, R., & Lerner, J. (1977). Effects of age, sex, and physical attractiveness on child-peer relations, academic performance, and elementary school adjustment. *Developmental Psychology, 13*, 585–590.

Levine, M., & Schober, M. (2008, November). *How physical co-presence affects jazz musicians' coordination.* Paper presented at the 49th Meeting of the Psychonomic Society, Chicago, IL.

Linklater, F. (1997). Effects of audio- and videotape models on performance achievement of beginning clarinetists. *Journal of Research in Music Education, 45*, 401–414.

Marolt, M. (2006). Listeners' emotional engagement with performances of a Scriabin Etude: An explorative case study. *Psychology of Music, 34*(4), 481–510.

Pashler, H. (1994). Dual-task interference in simple tasks: Data and theory. *Psychological Bulletin, 116*, 220–244.

Patzer, G. L. (1985). *The attractiveness phenomenon.* New York, NY: Plenum Press.

Platz, R., & Kopiez, R. (2012). When the eye listens: A meta-analysis of how audio-visual presentation enhances the appreciation of music performance. *Music Perception, 30*, 71–83.

Rentfrow, P. J., & Gosling, S. D. (2007). The content and validity of music-genre stereotypes among college students. *Psychology of Music, 35*, 306–326.

Russell, J. A. (1980). A circumplex model of affect. *Journal of Personality and Social Psychology, 39*, 1161–1178.

Ryan, C., & Costa-Giomi, E. (2004). Attractiveness bias in the evaluation of young pianists' performances. *Journal of Research in Music Education, 52*(2), 141–154.

Salvia, J., Algozzine, R., & Scheare, J. (1977). Attractiveness and school achievement. *Journal of School Psychology, 15*, 60–67.

Scherer, K. (1979). Acoustical concomitants of emotional dimensions: Judging affect from synthesized tone sequences. In S. Weitz (Ed.), *Nonverbal communication* (pp. 249–253). New York, NY: Oxford University Press.

Schutz, M. R., & Lipscomb, S. D. (2007). Hearing gestures, seeing music: Vision influences perceived tone duration. *Perception, 36*, 888–897.

Shahani, C., Dipboye, R., & Gehrlein, T. (1993). Attractiveness bias in the interview: Exploring the boundaries of an effect. *Basic and Applied Social Psychology, 14*, 317–328.

Stewart, J. E. (1980). Defendant's attractiveness as a factor in the outcome of criminal trials. *Journal of Applied Social Psychology, 10*, 348–361.

Summerfield, Q. (1979). Use of visual information for phonetic perception. *Phonetica, 36*, 314–331.

Sun, S.-W., & Lull, J. (1986). The adolescent audience for music videos and why they watch. *Journal of Communication, 36*, 115–125.

Tan, S.-L., Pfordresher, P., & Harré, R. (2010). *Psychology of music: From sound to significance.* New York, NY: Psychology Press.

Thompson, W. F., & Russo, F. A. (2007). Facing the music. *Psychological Science, 18*(9), 756–757.

Vines, B. W., Krumhansl, C. L., Wanderley, M. M., Dalca, I. M., & Levitin, D. J. (2011). Music to my eyes: Cross-modal interactions in the perception of emotions in music performance. *Cognition, 118*, 157–170.

Vines, B. W., Krumhansl, C. L., Wanderley, M. M., & Levitin, D. J. (2006). Cross-modal interactions in the perception of musical performance. *Cognition, 101*, 80–113.

Wapnick, J., Darrow, A., Kovacs, J., & Dalrymple, L. (1997). Effects of physical attractiveness on evaluation of vocal performance. (I) *Journal of Research in Music Education, 45*(3), 470–479.

Wapnick, J., Mazza, J. K., & Darrow, A. (1998). Effects of performer attractiveness, stage behavior, and dress on violin performance evaluation. (II). *Journal of Research in Music Education, 46*(4), 510–521.

Wapnick, J., Ryan, C., Lacaille, N., & Darrow, A. (2004). Effects of selected variables on musicians' ratings of high-level piano performances. *International Journal of Music Education, 22*(1), 7–20.

Welch, R. B. (1999). Meaning, attention, and the "unity assumption" in the intersensory bias of spatial and temporal perceptions. In G. Aschersleben, T. Bachmann, & J. Musseler (Eds.), *Cognitive contributions to the perception of spatial and temporal events* (pp. 371–387). New York, NY: Elsevier Press.

Zebrowitz, L. A., & McDonald, S. M. (1991). Impact of litigants' babyfacedness and attractiveness on judicial decisions in small claims court. *Law and Human Behavior, 15*, 603–623.

Zorn, E. (1984, February 13). Memories aren't made of this. *Newsweek, p.* 6.

Chapter 11

Music and memory in film and other multimedia: The Casablanca effect

Berthold Hoeckner and Howard C. Nusbaum

University of Chicago, USA

'Play it, Sam!'

Consider two scenes from the famous romance-drama *Casablanca* (Wallis & Curtiz, 1942), which was ranked the third best movie of all times (after *Citizen Kane* and *The Godfather*) by the American Film Institute (2007). In the first scene, Ilsa (Ingrid Bergman) visits 'Rick's American Café' with her husband, a political refugee from the Nazis. When she recognizes the pianist Sam (Dooley Wilson), she urges him to play the song 'As Time Goes By.' At first Sam refuses, but when Ilsa hums the melody for him, he begins to sing. While Sam is playing, Ilse's beautiful face appears lost in thought (see Figure 11.1). We do not see what she is seeing, but we know that the song reminds her of something. At the end of the chorus, Rick (Humphrey Bogart) bursts into his café from the backroom reprimanding Sam: 'I told you never to play this song again.' When his eyes meet Ilsa's we sense why: this was 'their' song, now bringing up beautiful and painful memories. In the second scene, later that night, Rick tries to drown his heartache in gin, while Sam is improvising at the piano. Now it is Rick's turn to ask for the song. When the camera zooms in on his face, Sam's piano changes to full orchestra in the underscore (see Figure 11.2). And when the close-up of Rick's face has dissolved into an image of the Arc de Triomphe in Paris, 'As Time Goes By' is replaced by before the song beginning of the 'Marseillaise.' This cuts to Rick and Ilsa driving through the French countryside, scored with an orchestral variant of the song. Thus, after the dissolve, we see what Rick is seeing and presumably what Ilsa saw earlier: pictures of the time in France when they had been in love.

Of course, these scenes should not be taken as an accurate representation of our actual memory system, as if memories are projected like a film on a mental screen. Moreover, if couples sometimes associate the time of their courtship with a song—a phenomenon that has been called 'Darling, they are playing our tune' (Davies, 1978)—such associations may be no different than those formed at other emotionally intense experiences involving music, such as religious services or a rock concert. Nor can we assume that a movie with a memorable score is perceived and remembered differently than an opera, operetta, or stage musical. At the same time, the proliferation of multimedia as a fixed

Figure 11.1 Ilsa (Ingrid Bergman) listening to 'As Time Goes By' in *Casablanca*, being reminded of her romance with Rick (Humphrey Bogart) in Paris. Reproduced from *Casablanca* © 1942, Warner Bros.

Figure 11.2 Rick (Humphrey Bogart) listening to 'As Time Goes By' in *Casablanca*, dissolving to an image of Paris. Reproduced from *Casablanca* © 1942, Warner Bros.

combination of music and image has definitely changed our exposure to multi-modal experiences and raises questions about how they affect us and our memory of them. One such question is whether music and sound are more successful in conjuring up images than images are in calling up music or sound. It is surely striking that soundtracks without film footage are big business, while nobody sells image-tracks without sound or music. This is not to say that film music is primarily created and consumed to recollect visual content (there may also be books, posters, and other merchandise to serve as mementos of a film), yet memories of the movie's narrative are certainly a significant by-product of listening to its soundtrack album. Hence one may ask whether there exists what we call hypothetically a Casablanca effect: Is music a better vehicle, and thus a better cue, for recalling visual content than images are for music?

We will return to this question later by reporting on a study in progress that explores whether there is indeed a measurable asymmetry tilted toward music in cross-modal memory. For now, we will first consider this issue in a broader cultural, aesthetic, and psychological context. While music has long been part of multisensory events that can be remembered by the music, the 20th century has seen a proliferation of mechanically produced and reproduced multimedia content, which has resulted in a massive increase of audiovisual stimuli in everyday life, many of these associated with the sound of music. With the invention of sound cinema and television, sound and image became firmly attached to each other. At the same time, the growing mobility of sound-producing devices—from portable radios and cassette players to the Discman and from the iPod to the iCloud—has made it possible to associate music with many different experiences and life situations. Today, the relationship between music and image has become even more malleable, as affordable and easy-to-use software has made it possible for users to become producers of multimedia content that can be distributed through Internet venues such as YouTube and social networks such as Facebook. Thus the evolution of multimedia has made music an ever more wide-ranging cue for visual memories, making an important contribution to the way individuals and societies remember. As a result, the psychological investigation of music-evoked memory in multimedia intersects with empirical research ranging from the role of music in autobiographical memory to its function in commercials. While the psychology of advertisement is a well-established field with an important focus on electronic media as well as the effects of music, empirical research about autobiographical memory has begun to pay attention to both music and film. In turn, many films are about memory, while film scholarship has taken note of empirical research on the perception and understanding of multimedia.

In light of all this, what follows is organized in three parts. We begin by reviewing some trends in films representing memory and discuss them in conjunction with early psychological ideas about film's contribution to understanding memory processes. We then consider the relationship between music-evoked memory and different types of memory studied in memory research. Finally, we discuss specific research on the cognitive processes involved in the perception and understanding of audiovisual media, in so far as they are pertinent to memory.

Memory films and psychology

While the *artistic representation* of memory in film and television is a typical concern in the humanities, its *empirical study* constitutes a common task in the social and biological sciences. This suggests a broader distinction between the depiction of memory psychology in multimedia and the psychology of multimedia itself. Interestingly, movies made about the subject of memory have often responded to new developments in technology or advances in memory science (Kelley & Calkins, 2006; Vidal, 2011). The growing popularity of psychoanalysis in the 1940s and 1950s resulted in a rise of films about repressed and traumatic memories, including not only such largely forgotten

B-movies as John Brahm's 1946 *The Locket* and Curtis Bernhardt's 1947 *Possessed*, but also the well-known Hitchcock classics *Spellbound*, *Vertigo*, and *Marnie*. Auteur directors around the world have been preoccupied with individual memory as well as memory shared by smaller or larger groups, for which Maurice Halbwachs coined the expression 'collective memory' (Halbwachs, 1992): Akira Kurosawa (*Rashōmon*), Ingmar Bergman (*Wild Strawberries*), Alain Resnais (*Hiroshima mon amour*), Andrej Tarkovsky (*The Mirror* and *Solaris*), Woody Allen (*Radio Days*), and Wong Kar Wai (*In the Mood for Love* and *2046*), to name just a few.

Mainstream films, too, have often taken up the topic of memory to experiment with new forms of cinematic narration. A successful example is Christopher Nolan's *Memento* (2000) whose protagonist has anterograde amnesia and whose plot alternates between black-and-white scenes shown chronologically and a series of color sequences shown in reverse order (Vidal, 2011). More recently, greater awareness of mental illness has inspired such films as Lodge Kerrigan's *Clean Shaven* (1993) and Richard Eyre's *Iris* (2001), which deal with memory problems in schizophrenia and dementia respectively. Developments in digital technology and neuroscience have been taken up in Kathryn Bigelow's *Strange Days* (1995), Omar Naim's *The Final Cut* (2004), and Michel Gondry's *Eternal Sunshine of the Spotless Mind* (2004), which deal with prosthetic memory (devices attached to the body to store memory) as well as fanciful depictions of memory storage and erasure in the brain. None of these films should be taken as an accurate picture of memory processes or memory science, though some try to be quite realistic in their portrayal.

Memory and remembrance have been central for the cinema in different ways as well. Early on, documentary film was touted as an ideal visual archive because moving pictures appeared to audiences as an exact rendition of the world. Film seemed ideal as a new and effective medium for recording history and for preserving a slice of cultural, ethnic, and autobiographical reality—with greater fidelity than painting, printing, and photography; and more life-like than written chronicles and historical narratives (Amad, 2010). Yet there were also problems with such a view. Inasmuch as the cinema seemed to preserve an accurate record of events, films could use new techniques, such as close-ups or slow motion, to present hitherto unseen aspects of already existing reality or put newly constructed realities before its audiences' eyes. These two views of cinema—as a reproduction of the existing world and a creation of new worlds—seem to align with the distinction between documentary and fictional genres. But the difference is not hard and fast and is complicated by overlapping modes of narrative construction and editing. In the early days of cinema, single-take and single-frame shorts offered merely a slice of a remembered or imagined reality, but film-makers soon put these slices together to create longer features by developing editing techniques that seemed to resemble human memory and imagination.

In 1916, the Harvard psychologist Hugo Münsterberg published a ground-breaking study of the cinema which laid a foundation for the perception and understanding of film and its effects. In his chapter on 'Memory and Imagination,' Münsterberg examined a central element of the representational technique that was new to the cinema: the cut allowed the photoplay to 'overcome the interval of the future as well as the interval of the past' (Langdale, 2002, p. 91). Although theater had already made use of scene breaks and off-stage narration, cinematic technology enabled spectators to see not only earlier and future scenes or events, but also to witness what went on in a character's mind: foremost dreams, hallucinations, and memories. Flashbacks soon became a staple of cinematic presentation of character and narrator memory (Turim, 1989). Yet for Münsterberg the cut was not just a narrative device, but an actual representation of mental activity. Because cinema has 'the mobility of our ideas which are not controlled by the physical necessity of outer events,' he believed that it 'obeys the laws of the mind rather than those of the outer world' (Langdale, 2002, p. 91). For example, Münsterberg noted that in movies physically distant events '*are fusing in our field of vision, just as they are brought together in our own consciousness*' (Langdale, 2002, p. 96, emphasis in original). Not surprisingly, film and television have come to use modes of presentation that idealize cultural notions of spontaneous and voluntary recollection and imagination: just as a movie cuts from one scene to another, human memory and imagination often seem to jump freely across time and space, whereas in outer reality time is linear and space is contiguous. Such observations resonate with studies showing that people tend to restructure much narrative into a temporally and causally coherent form rather than the experienced form (Baker, 1978; Pennington & Hastie, 1988).

Münsterberg also felt that the cinema had the power to put audiences in 'a state of heightened suggestibility' by exerting control over the play of associations. While outer impressions given on stage, a screen, or in life might provide a cue 'which stirs up in our memory or imagination any fitting ideas,' he noted that the mind knew that these ideas were not part of objectively reality. At the same time, Münsterberg argued, the presentation of outer perceptions attained such a 'controlling influence' in the cinema that any 'associated idea is not felt as our creation but as something to which we have to submit': film thus worked like the 'hypnotizer whose word awakens in the mind of the hypnotized person ideas which he cannot resist' and therefore 'accept as real' (Langdale, 2002, p. 97). This view of cinema as hypnosis is certainly incorrect, since it is not a state of the external control of consciousness as might have been derived from Franz Mesmer's ideas (Spiegel, 2002). Yet when hypnosis is seen as a state of focused attention (Raz, Fan, & Posner, 2006a; Raz, Kirsch, Pollard, & Nitkin-Kaner, 2006b), there may be some merit in Münsterberg's claim, if not its specifics. The structure of each frame and the movement from frame to frame focuses the trajectory of attention to the unfolding of a movie, especially in terms of the choreography of action.

This directorial control of the viewer's attention is important because that is the way in which film gets encoded into memory (e.g., Wimber, Heinze, & Richardson-Klavehn, 2010). On the one hand, attention seems necessary for explicitly encoding information into memory—it is unlikely for us to remember something that we did not attend to. On the other hand, directing attention to an event is no guarantee that it will be remembered. Even if our attention is directed to an event, cuts and the structure of scenes serve to organize the accessibility of memories once encoded. Research has shown that our memory for movies has a narrative structure much as we have for discourse (Baker, 1978; Kurby & Zacks, 2008; Radvansky & Copeland, 2006). We do not treat a sequence of events as an undifferentiated stream, but remember the organization of meaningful groups of events, and our memory within such chunks (Miller, 1956) is largely dictated by narrative relevance (Trabasso 1985). From Bartlett (1932) on, we have known that narrative coherence that fits with cultural knowledge and daily reality is understood and remembered better than exotic and foreign stories. Bartlett showed that while people forget many details not clear to a particular cultural audience, narratives that instantiate idealized cultural themes and forms should be much easier to understand and remember correctly. Film provides a means to create such idealizations in a very concrete and salient form and thus represents a way of constructing powerful memories.

What fascinated Münsterberg was how easily film could cut from the present to an event that seemed to have taken place in the past. While films themselves may serve as a medium for individual and collective remembrance, flashbacks did the same within a movie itself. But since a cut might mean a change of place or a change of place and time, directors needed to develop cinematic conventions that enabled viewers to understand a cut as a flashback that filled in backstory or represented a character's memory. Early on, silent films used intertitles to signal changes of scene and time, but directors soon developed non-verbal conventions for introducing the memory flashback of a character, for example, the camera zooming on a face followed by a cut or dissolve. Musical conventions for flashbacks have varied. During the silent era, accompanists were advised not to change the music as to signal that a flashback belonged to the consciousness of a character merely thinking about the past. After the advent of mechanically reproduced sound, flashbacks were often introduced by a sound bridge, which could be used in two ways: either sound or music in the present appeared to trigger a character's memory (as for Rick in *Casablanca*); or a sound advance preceded the visual cut or dissolve, thereby suggesting that the character internally remembers sounds or music from the past, which then call up the visual memory (this happens in *Possessed* where Joan Crawford's character hears a piece from Schumann's *Carnaval*, which takes her back to her piano-playing lover).

Flashback montages and flashback narrations were used as early as Paul Fejos's *The Last Moment* (1928, now lost) or Mervyn Leroy's *Two Seconds* (1932), where the protagonist sees his life flit by in the seconds before drowning or being electrocuted (Turim, 1989). Such experiences seemed to be rooted in reality, yet they were also shaping reality. Once cinema had naturalized the flashback as a representation of memory, the term started to be widely used to describe certain memory experiences in the real world. The psychologist Douwe Draaisma has shown, for example, that after the invention of film, people who had been in near-death situations reported their experiences by borrowing from the movies. Although language describing the visual character of such experiences can be found in accounts from before the advent of photography, 'by far the most common metaphor in recent descriptions of panoramic memory is *film* and its associated terms like flashback, replay and slow motion' (Draaisma, 2004, p. 255). As end-of-life montages have now become a narrative convention, they are often accompanied by music as, for example, in *American Beauty* (1999), which is narrated by the central character from beyond the grave, suggesting that a complete life is remembered at the moment of death. It is of course unlikely that experiences of panoramic memory in near-death-situations would be accompanied with an inner hearing of music. But music is often used by directors to capture a dying character's sense of an altered state, which has often been reported to involve a feeling of tranquility and serenity.

In sum, then, film has become a medium to represent memory because it is a real form of externalized memory as with any kind of narrative form. Unlike other narrative forms, however, the development of cinematic technique and technology have made possible representations that accord more with our experience of using memory. As film became more characteristic of ways we think memory operates, it has become a medium that both creates and represents memories. While film-makers manipulate aspects of narrative structure and event presentation to depict memory on the screen, such manipulations can also emphasize or diminish the memories an audience carries away from seeing a film.

Musical cues and types of memory

The memorable nature of the movies has been noted, eloquently, by Stanley Cavell, whose reflections on film opened with a chapter entitled 'An Autobiography of Companions.' Cavell wrote that these films created 'hours and days of awe; momentous, but only for the moment; unrecapturable fully except in memory and evocation' (Cavell, 1979, p. 10). If life holds in store many memorable events, cinema adds powerful experiences to these events. Their memorability stems from the sustained attention to a story created by a powerful combination of sound and images in a darkened theater. The vivid memories of going to 'the pictures' as part of everyday life has found its way into films themselves, such as Giuseppe Tornatore's *Cinema Paradiso* (1988), Terence Davies's *The Long Day Closes* (1992), or Stanley Kwan's *Centre Stage* (1992). Therefore it is not surprising that psychologists have used films to test how cinema's powerful simulation of real life affects people, including their memory. In a study by Furman and colleagues (2007), a narrative movie was used to test real-life learning and memory, because movies were seen to be approximations of real-life-like events in that they simulate aspects of real-life experience and thus can provide a controlled condition for measuring short-term and long-term memory through cued recall and recognition. An important finding of this study is that specific, visually cued, event memory for seeing a film without memory instructions was robust up to 3 weeks of retention, suggesting that ecologically coherent event information can be retained for a long time even without explicit instructions to remember or rehearse.

Since films are well suited to simulate real-life situations, researchers began in the 1960s to test the intrusive memory by using films depicting stressful or traumatic events (see Holmes & Bourne, 2008, for an overview). Another cluster of studies, using retrospective self-reports, has examined the memory of scary or romantic movies during childhood and adolescence. Harrison and Cantor (1999) showed that people remember details of scary movies that contain stimulus types leading to phobic reactions. Memories of these films can lead to disturbances in sleep and eating patterns and may cause residual anxiety years later. Hoekstra, Harris, and Helmick (1999) found that fantasy empathy (the ability to become empathetically involved with fictional presentations) and perspective taking played some role in experiencing movies negatively. Autobiographical memories of watching frightening or romantic movies on a date were the object of two studies (Harris et al., 2000; Harris et al., 2004) finding that the dating context provided occasion for gender-stereotypical behavior in reacting toward the film. At its most basic, then, films as well as filmic content constitute events that can become part of autobiographical memory.

Given that many films and multimedia make prominent use of music, the question arises whether and what role this music might play in our memory of film. Music has been deployed in the movies for various purposes that range from expressing a character's emotion to heightening dramatic effect or from suggesting narrative outcomes to providing ironic commentary. Many film scores make use of recurring themes or so-called *leitmotifs* which become associated with a character, event, or idea and connect different moments in the story. Furthermore, films often include memorable songs and instrumental music to highlight a particular moment in the story. In certain films (especially in music-based genres such as musicals), music takes on a central role through musical *performances*. While a powerful number in a musical or the striking use of a characteristic piece in a non-musical film can become a cue that enables viewers to recall a particular scene or the film as whole, repeated use of themes and motifs are also likely to facilitate recall. Thus theme music playing during the opening credits and returning at various junctures of the film not only can give a film a sonic signature but also can capture its overall atmosphere and mood: the famous theme for the James Bond movies is just one example that has been imitated by similar genre films, such as the *Mission Impossible* series. The practice of using music as a sonic signature of a film is widespread and can be easily observed in the choice of cues used for the DVD menu of a movie. Similarly, *leitmotifs* that frequently recur in symphonic scores—such as the melody of the Shire in *The Lord of the Rings* trilogy or 'The Imperial March' in *Star Wars*—are not only associated with a plot element but can also become part of the memory of the film as a whole. Moreover, such music may become even more memorable when it occurs both as source music, which is the so-called 'diegetic music' that originates in and belongs to the world of the story (*diēgēsis* is the Greek word for 'narrative'); and as the 'non-diegetic' music which resounds from the underscore. A famous example is David Raskin's music for *Laura* (1944) whose theme not only dominates the score, but also pipes from the radio or is played by a salon orchestra. Finally, a special case of music drawing attention to itself in such a way is when music triggers a character's memory shown in a flashback: *Casablanca* is of course one of the most famous examples.

Let us return now to the two scenes from *Casablanca* mentioned earlier, because they can serve as a basic model of how music becomes a vehicle for our memories by distinguishing between *transport* and *transportation* (Hoeckner, 2007; see also Franklin, 2011). On one hand, music transports us into an emotional state; on the other hand, music also serves as means of transportation by invoking specific associations. Musical transport and transportation are two components of audiovisual memory, highlighted in the film in different ways. We observe first how Ilsa is transported into a heightened emotional state of sadness, but what she is remembering is not specified. It is only later that we can see the transportation of specific events when the music calls up images on Rick's inner eye.

In what follows, we will connect the distinction between musical transport and transportation to two types of memory—episodic and semantic memory—as well as the relationship between these two types (Tulving, 1983). *Episodic memory* is a type of long-term memory that involves the recollection of specific events and experiences. While episodic memory can be cued in many different ways, one of the most famous examples is the taste of the Madeleine cookie which initiates a rush of remembrance for the narrator in Proust's novel *In Search of Lost Time.* Similarly, a song can call back a specific time of our life, which is why *autobiographical memory* is one of the forms of episodic memory. By contrast, *semantic memory* is a memory of meanings, concepts, and world knowledge not directly related to such events and experiences. Thus, in *Casablanca*, we immediately get a general sense of Ilsa's sadness, perhaps nostalgia, triggered by the music, but we are not given any specifics. Similarly, for someone not familiar with James Bond movies, the theme music will not call up a particular film from the franchise, but merely a broad knowledge of the genre of the spy thriller, which comes from having watched similar films or television programs. Indeed, given the enormous increase of our exposure to multimedia, we need to consider also how semantic memory relates to *implicit memory*, a type of non-declarative memory where previous experiences help us carrying out a task without our awareness of these experiences.

Episodic memory

In a review article on emotional responses to music, Juslin and Västfjäll (2008) put forward six mechanisms underlying the musical induction of emotion. Two of these mechanisms are episodic memory and visual imagery: while visual images are self-conjured or the product of our imagination (Kosslyn, 1980), the focus of episodic memory is on personal events in particular places and at particular times (Tulving, 2002). The other four mechanisms proposed by Juslin and Västfjäll (2008) include the brainstem reflex or orienting response (focusing attention on 'potentially important changes or events in the close environment'); evaluative conditioning or attitudes (enabling the 'association of objects or events with positive and negative outcomes'); emotional contagion (enhancing group cohesion and social interaction); and musical expectancy (facilitating symbolic language with a complex semantics; Juslin and Västfjäll, 2008, p. 570). The authors note that investigation into the precise interaction among the different mechanisms is a task for future research. Although they concede that visual imagery may occur with episodic memory, they advocate distinguishing between the two mechanisms

> because a musical experience may evoke emotions when a listener conjures up images of things and events that have never occurred, in the absence of any episodic memory from a previous event in time. Moreover, visual imagery is more strongly influenced or shaped by the unfolding structure of the music than is episodic memory, for which the music mainly serves as a retrieval cue. (Juslin & Västfjäll 2008, p. 567)

The distinction between music serving to construct images or recalling previously perceived images is a good starting point for understanding the nature of image-based episodic memory as evoked by music. The role of music as a retrieval cue for autobiographical memory has been the subject of only a few studies, of which two are relevant in the present context. The first is the study of long-term memory of popular music by Schulkind, Hennis, and Rubin (1999). The researchers used 60 commercially successful songs released between 1935 and 1994, asking younger and older adult participants whether they recognized the songs, had specific knowledge of them (year, performer, title), how much they liked the song, and what emotions and autobiographical memories the songs elicited. They found that memory of song attributes (such as texts, title, and artist) degraded over time and that the recollection of specific events from their lives varied with the age. Two specific findings of their study are particularly important. First, while songs were better at cueing the general memory of life-time periods than autobiographical memories of specific events in older adults, the opposite was true in younger adults. The authors suggest that this result may not only be attributed to 'increased forgetting due to the longer retention interval for the older adults or to age-related declines of the recall ability,' but could also suggest that music was more deeply embedded in the lives of younger adults (Schulkind et al., 1999, p. 952). Second, emotionality ratings of the songs correlated significantly with several dependent measures, showing that both younger and older adults 'were more likely to recall information or retrieve an autobiographical memory when they were cued by a song that moved them emotionally' (Schulkind et al., 1999, p. 952). In light of our model, this suggests that transport facilitates transportation.

In a more recent study, Janata, Tomic, and Rakowski (2007) investigated the actual content of music-evoked autobiographical memories in young adults by evaluating their responses to a sample of top Billboard-ranked pop and R&B songs. Participants were asked about their familiarity with the songs, their affective response, and a song's autobiographical salience (i.e., whether it reminded them of a specific person, place, life event, life period), and the image vividness of the memory. Several of their findings are relevant in the present context: (1) autobiographical salience was strongly correlated with image vividness; (2) the likelihood of providing a written description with details of a memory was positively correlated with the emotional salience of a song; (3) memory creation was tied to certain listening preferences and behaviors (especially dancing and driving) as well as being with friends, boyfriends, and girlfriends; and (4) the recognition of a song's genre could suffice as a trigger of autobiographical memories. Important questions are raised by this study. The authors note that while reports on image vividness are striking, it is unclear whether image vividness results from better encoding or is prompted by greater motivation to go into detail at the moment of recall. The propensity for detailed description was also correlated with the emotional salience of the music, confirming similar findings of enhanced recall for positively valenced and arousing events.

Although Eschrich, Münte, and Altenmüller (2008) have shown that emotional valence modulates episodic memory for music alone, we do not know whether emotionally salient (what we would call transport-producing) music creates an association at the moment of encoding or whether this association is merely the result of emotional conditioning or affective learning (see Juslin & Västfjäll, 2008). In the case of the latter, *any* piece of music that is paired with another stimulus could become a means of 'transportation' for that other stimulus. Anecdotal evidence suggests that such accidental pairings take place in different ways. During the occurrence of traumatic or happy events—similar to the claims about experience of flashbulb memories (see McCloskey et al., 1988; Weaver, 1993)—emotional salience may not be evoked by the music that happens to be present at the time of the event, but by another stimulus, that is, the event itself. In the context of multimedia, this suggests that we need to take into account that music and image can make separate contributions to the formation of a memory (see Bezdek & Gerrig, 2008). This also raises the issue of accidental conditioning: happy music may be associated with a sad event (or vice versa). In films, such combinations are often used for ironic effect, and they may enhance memory simply because they draw attention to the situation.

These considerations raise another important aspect in music-evoked autobiographical memory: the relationship between past experience and present experience at the moment of recall. Janata et al. (2007) report that the complex emotion of nostalgia was identified most frequently after the attributions of 'happy' and 'youthful' to autobiographically salient songs. They asserted that 'temporal separation' is a 'defining characteristic' of nostalgia, because it is 'unlikely to have been experienced at the time of encoding' (Janata et al. 2007, p. 858). In other words, Rick and Ilsa were happy in Paris, but later in Casablanca Rick forbids Sam to play the song 'As Time Goes By' because it makes him sad. Thus the emotional effect of 'Darling, they are playing our tune' can have either of two valences, depending on whether the couple is still together or not. The situation becomes more complex, when taking into account why the entertainment industry thrives on producing prospective nostalgia. The song 'As Time Goes By' exhorts lovers to enjoy the present so that it can be remembered. Thus individuals, couples, or groups are drawn to evocations of nostalgic remembrance because they simulate now how we will feel about the present in the future. Hence people may feel nostalgic when hearing a nostalgic song, but when hearing the song later their sense of nostalgia evoked by the song may be confounded by feeling nostalgic for the time they initially heard the song.

These may be complex cases, but it is important to realize that media culture capitalizes on selling music during the life periods of youth and adolescence—music that can be marketed as a memory-carrier to the same demographic a generation (or less) later. Music heard during our youth tends to shape taste preferences. Janata et al. (2007) point out that listening preferences and listening behavior are also conducive to the formation of episodic memory. This is hardly surprising: certain life situations and environments (such as dancing or driving) are or have been (re)configured for the experience and consumption of music, just as dating and friendships provide occasions for shared listening (Juslin & Laukka, 2004; Sloboda, O'Neill, & Ivaldi, 2001). Thus Holbrook and Schindler (1989) demonstrated that listeners prefer music which was popular during their youth. A study of musically-cued autobiographical memories in young adults showed that memories formed during high school and college not only are recalled with greater vividness and specificity than childhood and middle school memories but also brought back the intensity of the emotions felt at the time (Cady, Harris, & Knappenberger, 2008). Not surprisingly, young adults have long constituted a core group for the consumption of popular music and have also been targeted as a primary audience for cinematic blockbusters and television series—which have put into circulation an ever-widening stock of visual imagery associated with music—often popular hits—that are sold as soundtracks.

The film-music scholar, composer, and cultural theorist Michel Chion (1994) created the term *synchresis* for the phenomenon that any image and any music can fuse into a meaningful audiovisual unit in the cinema. Indeed, powerful combinations of music and image, especially when viewed for the first time, tend to form a lasting impression and create persistent associations for music. Famous examples are the opening of Stanley Kubrick's *2001: A Space Odyssey*, using the Strauss's tone poem *Also Sprach Zarathustra* for a sunrise, or the helicopter attack on a Vietnamese village in Francis Coppola's *Apocalypse Now*, using Wagner's 'The Ride of the Valkyries.' While these films deploy famous and memorable pieces of classical music, popular songs (e.g., 'The Sound of Silence' for *The Graduate*), and original film scores (e.g., John Williams's music for *Indiana Jones* or *Jaws*) have been equally successful in creating such firm associations, so that the memory of films is cued by music in the same way as music cues events in episodic memory. To be sure, there are different types of image–music relationships that shape the formation of memories. Diegetic performances in films (Rachmaninoff's Third Piano Concerto in *Shine*) or song and dance numbers in film musicals ('I'm Singin' in the Rain' in the musical *Singin' in the Rain*) draw attention to themselves and thus may be more likely to create memorable episodes. A first step toward empirically testing the recall and recognition of a film as cued by original score or original song would establish a corpus of successful films seen by audiences in the last years. One example for establishing such a corpus was provided in a survey of feature-length narrative movies by Simonton (2007). The author showed that award-winning or award-nominated original scores more likely than songs correlated with the artistic and commercial success of a film, as measured by award nominations, wins, box office gross, and critical evaluations.

Given that circulation of music in multimedia contexts has increased over the course of the last century, we also need to consider the phenomenon of re-association, whereby music already serving as a cue for one cinematic memory, may also become the cue for another one formed later. Compilers and composers of film music realized early on that using well-known musical works and popular songs could be assembled in mood music collections (Rapée, 1924). As the use of such music brought up pre-existing associations, these could either enhance or detract from the understanding of screen content (Altman, 2004). During the rapid growth of the film industry, such recycling had advantages and disadvantages. Powerful pieces such as the 'Ride of the Valkyries' from Wagner's *Ring* tetralogy proved to be particularly effective, because audiences were swept along with its distinct rhythm and orchestration to sense the underlying martial character of the Valkyries. (In Norse mythology the immortal Valkyries fly their horses over the battlefields to collect the souls of dead heroes.) A famous example is the ending of D.W. Griffith's *The Birth of a Nation* (1915). Carl Breil, who created the score for Griffith, chose Wagner's 'Ride' to accompany the climatic scene during which a coalition of carpetbaggers and emancipated slaves are driven out by the Ku Klux Klan. Francis Coppola clearly alluded to this controversial scene during one of the most notorious sequences of postwar American cinema from his 1979 film *Apocalypse Now* (shown in Figure 11.3). As a US helicopter squadron attacks a Vietnamese village, the commanding Colonel engages in a sinister and cynical attempt of psychological warfare by blasting Wagner's 'Ride' from the gunships.

Although associations from pre-existing music could provide useful commentary for a scene, early compilers of music for films already observed that audiences watching a

Figure 11.3 Helicopter attack on a Vietnamese village from Francis Coppola's *Apocalypse Now* where Wagner's 'Ride of the Valkyries' is played from the gunships. Reproduced from *Apocalypse Now* © 1979, United Artists.

film with music they knew from another context (including other films) experienced distracting 'phenomena of interference and association' (Erdmann & Becce, 1927, vol. 1, p. 4). Thus George Beynon, an early practitioner and writer on movie music, noted that music from well-known operas such as Bizet's *Carmen* could bring up associations that could hamper the audience's enjoyment or understanding of a film:

> If a tense dramatic situation must receive a fitting accompaniment, it would be the height of folly to use the death music from "Carmen". The minds of the patrons would revert at once to the scene outside the bullring. They would see again the blade driven into Carmen's bosom, while her lover falls despairingly across her outstretched body. In the mean time the Hero on the screen sits bound in the chair, straining to break the ropes that bind him, in order that he can rush to the Maiden that is being spirited away by the wily Villain. Imagine the contradiction of the two ideas, and the incongruity of the attempt to blend them into one. (Beynon, 1921, p. 36)

Thus the use of well-known music can lead to what may be called *double projections*: memories projected on a mental screen compete with the film shown in the theater.

These interferences, however, also brought new aesthetic possibilities. Pre-existent image–music combinations that are particularly salient and memorable are often intentionally referenced in later films by the music alone. Music, in turn, accumulates new associations and may do so in different ways. At the end of Pixar's hugely successful *Finding Nemo* (2003), a scene where a child wants to play rough with the little fish is scored with Bernard Herrmann's famous murder cue from Hitchcock's *Psycho* (1960). The reference surely understood by adults familiar with Hitchcock's classic, but for children the association with Nemo is formed first. Both the global expansion and the longer history of the entertainment industry have resulted in ever-richer and more sophisticated forms of such intertextuality. Just as pre-existing music and songs are well-known to audiences, newly composed songs may circulate even before the film is released. This is standard procedure in Bollywood cinema where film music is synonymous with popular music, so that song and dance numbers from a film are independently distributed as music videos. Finally, Web sites such as YouTube and other providers have become highly frequented venues where film excerpts, music videos, or music (sometimes with new, user-assembled images or footage) have become widely available in ways that are likely to change not only the formation and recall, but also the content, of the episodic memory of multimedia.

Semantic memory

Since semantic memory is knowledge of the world that involves learning without a specific autobiographical index, music-evoked semantic memory in the context of multimedia presupposes prior exposure to such media, as well as other cultural associations established with music. It involves what is sometimes called media literacy: the learning of how to listen to and watch multimedia to understand its specific audiovisual codes. Over the course of the last century, the creation of films and television for mass consumption has greatly augmented the number of people exposed to multimedia products worldwide. Tagg (1979) has estimated that by the mid 1970s the title theme of the *Kojak* television series had been heard by at least 100 million people in at least 70 countries worldwide. Mainstream media consumers thus constitute a subject pool that can be sampled for the empirical investigation of multimedia memory. In a ground-breaking study, Tagg and Clarida (2003) had listeners respond to ten title tunes of film and television music by asking them to write down whatever they thought 'could be happening on an imaginary film TV screen along with the tune' (Tagg & Clarida, 2003, p. 118). They coded these responses as 'visual-verbal associations' according to functions of film music (such as emphasizing movement or representing time and location), categories of library music (ranging from emotions and moods to genres and recurring events), and more complex meanings in which respondents inferred from music more circumscribed cultural connotations (small town versus large city or male versus female, etc.). The authors argued that film and television music uses a well-established stock of musical stereotypes that evoke more or less well-defined sets of verbal and visual associations. As these associations shape the understanding of visual content, the continuing circulation of musical stereotypes in multimedia reinforce not only a broad network of existing associations, but also form new ones.

Coding rich datasets of visual-verbal responses is related to the corpus analyses undertaken by compilers of film and production music libraries. From the silent era until today, music for film, television, and (more recently) for Internet Web sites and other multimedia content has been classified systematically according to such categories as mood, dramatic situation, and specific pre-existent associations, for example, national anthems, folksongs, or religious holidays. Additional classifications have included the distinction between song and instrumental music, tempo, and genre. Although the repertory of music for film has changed over time—now including a large variety of popular music as well as world and ethnic music—the basic principle behind these classifications has stayed the same. The most thorough early taxonomy, devised at the end of the silent era by Erdmann and Becce (1927), relied on the compilers' expert knowledge of mostly classical repertory—ranging from opera to program music and from non-programmatic symphonies to dances and hymns. A frequent method for their classification of excerpts was a reverse musical hermeneutics, whereby the original context in which a passage or piece had occurred (for example, in an opera or programmatic work) was used to determine for which kind of movie scene it might be suitable. Similar sounding passages from other works were then categorized accordingly—a procedure that goes back to 17th-century catalogues of rhetorical figures (such as a repetition of a musical passage to express amplification) and musical topoi (such as a funeral march to illustrate solemnity) that were to be deployed in text settings. One of the leading distributors of library music today is DeWolfe Music (2012)—a company that has been in business since the silent era.

The practice of composing film and television music is thus rooted in a rich tradition of musical semiotics (see Kendall & Lipscomb, Chapter 3, in this volume) whose application in the various contexts of multimedia relies on a system of expressive devices and codes that evolved in the history of Western music, and have been variously called musemes (Tagg & Clarida, 2003) or musical memes (Walker, 2004). This system of musical signs has acquired broad currency because it has been developed to serve overlapping narrative, affective, and informational purposes in modern multimedia on a global scale. It includes music denoting such basic emotions as happy and sad or stock figures that mimic onscreen action (so-called hurries and chases), conventional genre schemas (such as thriller and melodrama), and specific symbolic connotations for particular contests and occasions ranging from Christmas to Independence Day, or from birthdays to funerals. While this system of musical signs predated film and television, it continued to develop alongside the proliferation of movies, contributing to the creation of specific musical styles associated with film genres: westerns, melodrama, comedy, thriller, horror, adventure, science fiction, and others. A much-noted study on popular music by Gjerdingen and Perrott (2008) found that listeners presented with excerpts as short as 250 milliseconds were able to reliably identify genre from a list of ten categories ranging from country to classical, rap to rock, and jazz to Latin. The authors suggest that the salience of timbre may be an important factor in genre recognition. While a similar study for film and television music is a desideratum for future research, some film music genres and timbres—such as westerns and cartoons—are easier to recognize than others, since not all genres have an unequivocal set of characteristics, making it more difficult for audiences to distinguish, for example, thriller from adventure music or scores for horror films from those for science fiction movies. Despite such confounds as well as the fact that music can take on different meanings (a dissonant chord can denote something fearful or funny), it will be useful to design and conduct experiments that would show whether genre recognition enhances theme music recall and whether genre aids in the musical recall of films.

Of course, film and television scores consist of more than generic film music, making use also of musical schemas drawn from popular songs, concert music, and, increasingly, non-Western music (Donnelly, 2002). Indeed, due to constant demand for a fresh sound, genre characteristics in film music have evolved historically, so that film music and film sound have become an important part of media memory. Today producers pressure film composers to explore new sounds, styles, and timbres, even as radical deviations from genre conventions are not encouraged. Scores by the Canadian film composer Michael Danna, for example, make use of medieval or ethnic idioms and instruments, which are idiosyncratic yet effective (*The Sweet Hereafter* or *The Ice Storm*); Thomas Newman's score for *American Beauty* (1999) was inspired by gamelan. Film scores continue to rely on other pre-existing music to identify time and place which has become particularly common in period movies: surf songs call up California in the early 1960s; a Renaissance string consort brings us to the court of Elizabeth I; or the shakuhachi (a bamboo flute) captures Japanese culture. As film scores make heavy use of iconic songs or well-known music as to evoke period (such as *Forest Gump* and *The Big Chill*) or place (*The Last Samurai* or *Crouching Tiger, Hidden Dragon*), the learning of generic characteristics and musical schemas depends not on the establishment and dissemination of cultural stereotypes alone. While these can vary greatly with the cultural context of the country in which they are produced or with audience background and demographic, video and computer games contribute to learning and memory across increasingly globalized user communities. In a study by Wingstedt, Brändström, and Berg (2008), young adolescents were asked to adapt musical parameters to visual scenes on a computer scene, including urban, pastoral, and science fiction environments, showing that participants had a shared knowledge of the musical narrative codes and conventions learned through films, computer games, and other narrative multimedia. The authors suggest that by learning 'not only *through* the multimodal text', but also *about* the modes themselves,' we become 'multimodally literate,' which includes a competency in the narrative functions of music in multimedia (Wingstedt et al., 2008, p. 212).

In the context of music-evoked memory in multimedia, the line between semantic and episodic memory is of course not hard and fast. This can be illustrated through their relation to transport and transportation. If transport is the invoking of a emotional experience from music without the explicit retrieval of some particular memory, this kind of emotional experience may come from several different sources, including fundamental psychoacoustic consequences of acoustic properties such as chills (Halpern et al., 1986), direct episodic associative implicit memory retrieval (see Schacter, 1987), and cultural/semantic knowledge that maps musical patterns onto emotional states. Musical transport through semantic memory can be 'diffusely' associative because it is built up across experiences of musical transportation evoking the memory of similar visual content, but leaving only the average for types of music and emotional states portrayed. Thus melodramatic music is associated with specific kinds of scenes with certain emotional outcomes so that the general features of the music (in this case: surging strings in the mid to low register, a sweeping melodic line, poignant harmonies, etc.) map to the general features of the experience (e.g., McClelland & Rumelhart, 1985). This is culturally mediated because cultural practices have dictated the correspondences exploited when making movies. Hence semantic memory need not be formed on the basis of one particular event but may be constituted by repeated episodes. For many Americans, the sound of cartoon music may bring back the cartoon hour on Saturday mornings, but not a particular day of their life. In turn, specific episodes from the *Looney Tunes* or *Silly Symphonies* are called up by pieces from the classical repertory used in them, but the music does not trigger recollection of the circumstances when the cartoons were first seen.

Thus some semantic memory of film music is derived from personal experience; some is learned by cultural transmission: when watching a movie we may not experience the emotion of melodrama ourselves, but over time learn the correspondence.

Episodic and semantic memory are the two basic categories of so-called *declarative memory* or *explicit memory* which involves conscious recall of facts or events. But learning through exposure also involves implicit memory which is non-declarative and reflects previous experiences that are not consciously recollected. An important paradigm in testing implicit memory has been to measure whether people respond faster to words they have recently been exposed to, showing that unconscious priming makes it more likely that information is used later on (Meyer & Schvaneveldt, 1971). As Tillman, Peretz, and Samson (2011) point out, research in the dissociation between explicit and implicit memory in music is still in its infancy, despite several studies showing exposure effects on pleasantness ratings in people with or without memory disorders, such as Alzheimer patients (Peretz, Gaudreau, & Bonnel, 1998; Halpern & O'Connor, 2000, Schellenberg, Peretz, & Vieillard, 2008). A useful paradigm for research on remembering bimodal stimuli is the recognition of song versus spoken song texts, though results so far have been not consistent. Several studies have shown both enhanced and reduced recall for texts when sung (Calvert, Chapter 12, this volume; Calvert & Tart, 1993; Racette & Peretz, 2007; Rainey & Larsen, 2002), while more recent testing of musical memory for songs and lyrics demonstrated increased recognition accuracy for sung over spoken song texts only in patients with Alzheimer's disease, suggesting more diversified encoding in standard episodic learning, not needed by healthy adults (Simmons-Stern, Budson, & Ally, 2010).

Such bimodal studies indicate that certain kinds of film music lend themselves well to measuring learning and exposure effects. This applies especially to music used in the narrative cinema of classical Hollywood (and films in that tradition) which film scholar Claudia Gorbman (1987) has called 'unheard melodies.' Gorbman's claim that musical underscoring is 'unheard' rests on the assumption that so-called non-diegetic film music (whose invisible source is lodged outside of the world of the filmic narration) is not consciously attended to, or at least perceived at a lower level of attention than the pictures or other elements of filmic narration, especially dialogue. We will see later that, when reviewing paradigms for the psychological study of film music, movies provide researchers with stimuli where the audience's foremost attention to the visual portion of the stimulus makes it easier to test the effects of the auditory component. Studying children's recall of television advertisements, Maher, Hu and Kolbe (2006) have shown that visual information is not only more memorable and retrievable than audio information, but that the former can also hinder the processing of the latter.

The effect of selective attention in bimodal stimuli was tested in a combined behavioral and functional magnetic resonance imaging (fMRI) study by Johnson and Zatorre (2005). The researchers presented participants simultaneously with visual and auditory stimuli (simple melodies and geometrical shapes). When instructed to direct their attention to one modality, participants' memory was better for the attended information than the unattended information. The fMRI portion of the study demonstrated that these instructions increased the recruitment of the sensory cortices that subserve the attended modality. Not surprisingly, while unattended listening has been an important condition in the empirical study of film music, only a few of these studies have been concerned with measuring memory effects, including memory effects that result from music (as one modality) *directing* our attention to the other modality, and vice versa.

Finally, since emotions play an important role in memory formation in general, emotional memory can serve as a link between declarative and non-declarative memory. Baumgartner, Lutz, Schmidt, and Jäncke (2006) have shown that music enhances the emotional experience of affective pictures. Noting the much-observed phenomenon that the emotional experience of horror movies is much reduced when watched without music, they demonstrate that pictures shown with music result in the activation of brain areas known to participate in emotion processing, while pictures alone mainly increased brain activity in the cognitive dorsal system for emotion perception in the prefrontal cortex. However, because the researchers did not include a music-only condition, further research will be needed to determine what part of the neural responses could have been activated by music alone. (See also Chapter 6, which takes a neuroscientific perspective on emotion and film, by Kuchinke, Kappelhoff, and Koelsch, in this volume.) Thus the study of the specific contribution of emotions to music-evoked memory of visual content from exposure to multimedia awaits a more targeted investigation. Future studies on memory effects of music in multimedia should not only distinguish between emotion representation and induction, but also try to measure exposure effects across modalities. For example, since music often sets the 'tone' of a film or multimedia product, it can influence likability judgments of visual content. Thus it is not uncommon that the reception of a B movie is given a lift by a good score from an A-level composer. An example is the prolific output by Jerry Goldsmith, who wrote not only music for such acclaimed classics as *Planet of the Apes* and *Patton Medicine Man* but also scored such films as *Hollow Man* or *The Challenge*. Another issue is whether cultural and stylistic differences lead to different exposure effects, making it possible, for example, to judge films by style period or provenance. Scores for classical Hollywood melodrama such as *Dark Victory* or *Now Voyager* (music by Max Steiner) have a lush orchestral sound that is heavy on strings, allowing musical emotions to change much more quickly in response to dramatic situations. By contrast, the composer Nino Rota (who worked much with Federico Fellini) often wrote as cues little pieces that served as a stable accompaniment for a scene creating a popular idiom now associated with a post-neo-realist Italian cinema of the 1960s and 1970s.

In sum, different types of memory provide a good starting point for measuring the effect of music on how we remember specific films, gain a knowledge of cinematic genres and narrative conventions, and respond to the exposure of movies with changing perception and understanding of multimedia. Amid the autobiographical memory evoked by film music and the presence of film music schemas, however, there are relatively few empirical studies that have researched the perceptual and cognitive properties of music-evoked memory in a multimedia context. In the next section we will review some of these studies in more detail.

Some music-evoked memory effects in multimedia

Given Gorbman's claim that the music in classical Hollywood cinema film is 'unheard' the question arises: Is there empirical evidence that audiences attend to and remember visual content, narrative, and dialogue better than the music? The sense of graded attention to auditory and visual information appears to favor a particular design in experimental studies of musical effects in multimedia. Here music comes with a cover story to the laboratory: as part of an audiovisual stimulus, the nature of the musical underscoring is often not disclosed to participants, allowing researchers to vary the kind of music presented in different conditions for the same visual content (see, for example, the ground-breaking study by Marshall & Cohen, 1988, who scored the 1944 animated film by Heider and Simmel of moving geometric shapes with allegro or adagio music, as well as the studies by Boltz, 2001; Boltz, Schulkind, & Kantra,1991; Bullerjahn & Güldenring, 1994; Shevy, 2007; and those by Hoeckner, Wyatt, Decety, & Nusbaum, 2011; Tan, Spackman, & Bezdek, 2007, discussed later in this chapter).

Before looking at film music experiments that involve memory measures, we need to consider briefly two important phenomena that have been studied in advertisements: the role of music in product recall and music's congruence with other components of an advertisement (for an in-depth treatment of music and advertisement see Chapter 14 by Shevy and Hung, in the present volume). While many commercials use music as part of the sales strategy, an important element is the association between a product and a specific piece of music (Gorn, 1982). Gershwin's *Rhapsody in Blue* in advertisements for United Airlines is a famous example, yet unknown or newly composed music can also become associated with a brand. In a series of experiments Yalch (1991) tested whether in songs and jingles (i.e., slogans set to a memorable melody), music enhances product recall. While music served as a mnemonic aid in creating a network of associations and information otherwise not available, after repeated exposure music lost its advantage as a mnemonic device compared with slogans without music. As the use of jingles and songs in advertisement is a form of episodic memory, different types of music are often deployed in advertisements to bring up stereotypical associations in the manner of semantic memory. Thus classical music is associated with higher education and social distinction while hip-hop stands for a youthful urban environment (Cook, 1998).

Although these stereotypes may not be compatible across cultures (Murray & Murray, 1996), we should note that the use of music in advertisement contributes to the formation of stereotypes in ways that are similar in film. Useful in this respect are two concepts proposed in a study by MacInnis and Park (1991): *indexicality* (the 'extent to which music arouses emotion-laden memories' (p. 162)) and *fit* (the 'relevance of appropriateness to the central ad message' (p. 162)). The researchers showed that both musical indexicality and fit play an important role in the processing of advertisements by 'high-involvement' and 'low-involvement' consumers (which refers to the degree of personal relevance for the product, which will in turn affect consumers' level of 'involvement' in the persuasive message). Specifically, indexicality enhanced message processing of low-involvement consumers, but distracted high-involvement consumers from message processing, suggesting that emotion-laden memories can modulate understanding of advertisement messages.

Since music moves the meaning of a product toward specific associations by directing attention to aspects of the advertisement that are congruent with the music, advertisements are read differently when combined with different music: images of stylish design gain a sense of sophistication and high culture when combined with baroque music and a sense of hipness when combined with a rock song (Hung, 2001). While congruence between music and other components of an advertisement remains tantamount to advertising strategies, incongruence challenges listener-viewers to resolve differences between music and other components into a coherent message (Hung, 2000). In audiovisual advertisements that use only non-verbal cues, carefully chosen non-congruent music can be effective in getting the audience's attention for 'high-involvement' products, such as a car or a large sofa, which requires a lot of effort and time to select, in comparison with 'low-involvement' products, such as a sausage or other mundane purchase (Lalwani, Lwin, & Ling, 2009). In a study of recognition accuracy for music video, Cupchik and Saltzman (1999) found that videos with a serious content (judged as socially relevant and pleasing) were recognized more accurately than light videos. In addition, recognition for light videos improved when the video image fit the music, but the lyrics did not fit the melody.

Congruence and incongruence between music and image have been the subject of several related studies on film music that are relevant for our understanding of memory cued by music. Cohen (2001 and 2005) developed the Congruence-Associationist Model, according to which music directs attention to visual elements, whose surface properties (along with speech) are temporally and structurally congruent. The processing of this information is then compared with inferences from long-term memory (based in past experience, including emotion) which allows the audience to create a 'working narrative' of the film. Audiovisual congruence can be temporal (Marshall & Cohen, 1988), semantic (Bolivar, Cohen, & Fentress, 1994; Cupchik & Saltzman, 1999), or mood-based (Boltz, 2001; Shevy, 2007). Music thus activates schemas that create an interpretive framework for understanding visual content (Boltz 2004). For example, Bullerjahn and Güldenring (1994) and Vitouch (2001) tested the influence of music on the understanding of narrative by asking participants who watched differently scored episodes of a narrative film about the continuation of a scene. The authors could show that different music (such as melodrama and thriller) led participants to project different outcomes that were in line with the generic meaning of the music. Given such effects of film-musical schemas on our perception and understanding of visual content the question arises how film music impacts our memory of such content.

In regard to this question, the most comprehensive study with the most far-reaching results to date was conducted by Boltz, Schulkind, and Kantra, (1991). To provide evidence for the cognitive processing of film music and its influence on remembering film events, the authors tested how positive and negative background music (placed to accompany or foreshadow the events of a scene) affected the recall of visual content as well as the accuracy of music-cued recognition of these scenes. They showed that visual content was better remembered when the musical underscore accompanying a scene was congruent with its outcome (positive and negative music with positive and negative outcomes, respectively), suggesting that congruent music directs attention to corresponding elements of the scene. Since incongruent music accompanying a scene did not hinder memory performance relative to the no-music condition, the authors suggested that incongruent music was simply not used in the encoding of the audiovisual event. However, incongruent music in the foreshadowing condition did significantly enhance the memorability of visual content, more so if the outcome of the scene was negative than positive. The researchers proposed that expectation violations (sometimes deployed by directors as 'ironic contrast' or 'audiovisual counterpoint') can lead to an increase of attention and thus improve memorability. In the music-cued recognition task, both mood-congruent and incongruent music increased accuracy in the foreshadowing condition, suggesting that music in this condition contributes to retrieval regardless of congruence.

In a more recent study, Boltz, Ebendorf, and Field (2009) have looked at the reverse effect, asking whether visual information influences the perception and memory of music. Previous research has shown, for example, that visual information contributes to the perception and understanding of musical performance and may create greater emotional involvement and appreciation of the music, compared to listening to music alone (Geringer, Cassidy, & Byo, 1996, 1997). Departing from a much-used paradigm in film music studies, where the video remains unchanged and music is used as the variable, Boltz et al. kept the music constant but varied the video. The authors hypothesized that if the video altered the perceived emotional and acoustic qualities of the music, these effects should result in memory distortions. During a later recognition test, participants were asked to discriminate the original melody from systematically transformed versions, showing a pattern of false recognitions that reflected a bias due to the visual information. Visual affect did indeed distort the recognition of memory, reflecting a mood-congruent bias: melodies were falsely recognized to be slower or faster than the tempi heard in the original audiovisual stimulus. In short, the qualities of the visuals were attributed to the accompanying music. As Boltz et al. put it for film music: in the processing of visual and musical information, music and visual displays provide 'an interpretive framework that then biases the nature of perception and memory. In the context of film, the mood of music influences inferences about why people are exhibiting the behaviors they are, what items from a scene are best remembered and what's likely to be confabulated, and how well the film persists in long-term memory' (Boltz et al., 2009, p. 55; see also Cohen, 2001).

These two studies conducted by Boltz and her colleagues confirm not only that film music contributes to the encoding of audiovisual events in cinema and television, but also that it is part of a changing interpretive framework which can influence what is being remembered. Especially interesting in this regard are the different results for congruent and incongruent music, suggesting that congruent music can rely more easily on semantic memory, while expectancy violations, by drawing attention to themselves, are likely to enter into episodic memory. Finally, the fact that Boltz et al. (1991) also tested the effect of music on a scene *after* the music had ended suggests that it would be useful to measure the implicit memory of film music, specifically the influence of priming effects (see also Bullerjahn & Güldenring, 1994; Vitouch, 2001). For example, does a clip heard with thriller music and seen later without such music make the clip more suspenseful?

One study exploring this line of inquiry is by Tan, Spackman, and Bezdek (2007). Noting that film music schemas had previously been shown to be active when music accompanies a scene, the authors wanted to know whether music played before and after a scene provided evidence for forward and backward affective priming, asking whether music would influence participants' interpretation of character's emotions. While many studies of film music use bipolar types of music, Tan et al. also broadened the range of emotions to happiness, sadness, anger, and fear. In another important variation from studies measuring music's congruence or incongruence with visual content, they kept the visual content neutral. Their results confirmed that film music has a forward and backward priming effect in that the music influences participants' attribution of emotions to the characters shown in the clip (more strongly when played before the target than after). The implications of this study are manifold: it not only extends our understanding of musical effects in cinematic narration and characterization, but also suggests that these effects, starting as early as the title sequence, may aggregate over the course of a film and thus shape our memory of the entire film, especially when composers choose to endow the score with a coherent character. A famous example for this is the music for *Psycho*, which was written for strings only and described by the composer Bernard Herrmann as being in 'black and white.'

The use of covert listening tasks for the study of implicit effects in Tan et al. (2007) is also part of a related study by Hoeckner, Wyatt, Decety, and Nusbaum (2011) demonstrating that melodrama and thriller music can modulate likeability of movie characters. In this study, characters where presented to participants in clips ending with a close-up reaction shot of a neutral facial expression, scored with either melodrama or thriller music. Asked to rate the character's likeability as well as their certainty about the character's thoughts, participants found characters more likeable in the melodrama condition and less likeable in the thriller condition while expressing more and less certainty about the character's thoughts in the respective conditions. During subsequent cued recall of screen content using a still shot, participants attributed emotions to characters in a manner congruent with the music (i.e., sadness for melodrama and fear and anger for thriller). Moreover, in a follow-up experiment by our research group, schema-congruent likeability ratings remained in effect (although weakened) one week after the original task. This study shows not only that the effects of film music on likeability and theory-of-mind judgments can provide antecedents for empathic concern and empathic accuracy, but also that music creates a lasting effect by moving the judgment of neutral visual content into the direction of attributes congruent with film music schemas.

'Play it, *again*, Sam!'

Let us return, in conclusion, to the Casablanca effect. While the studies discussed so far in this chapter contribute to an increasingly sophisticated framework for our understanding of film music and memory, they do not directly address the seeming asymmetry between music-cued recall of images and image-cued recall of music in modern multimedia. A first approach to testing such asymmetry in cross-modal recall has been undertaken in a study by our research group. A first experiment measured first whether music-cued recall of visuals from film clips is more accurate than image-cued recall of music. Twenty-four clips each of 30 seconds' length were created from 24 films with characteristic classic scores, including *The Magnificent Seven*, *Chinatown*, *The Godfather*, *Doctor Zhivago*, *Laura*, and *Spellbound*. After watching all clips in randomized order, participants were given either 15 seconds from the audio clip or from the video clip as cue for recognizing 15 seconds of video or audio respectively. Participants were tested in two groups to counterbalance the clips, so that each audio and video clip could be paired with both a correct and incorrect target. Half of the trials were matches, the other half mismatches. Strikingly, results showed that recognition was significantly more accurate when prompted with visuals than with music, but participants were *faster* when cued by the music. A speed/accuracy trade-off could be ruled out, as error disparity remained when video and audio recall groups were matched in response times. While there was a significant difference in recognition sensitivity between the audio and video, audio recognition sensitivity was still significantly above chance, suggesting that while video might be a better cue, participants performed above chance with the audio recall cues. Moreover, since there were four specific clips in which music was a stronger cue than the visuals, these clips showed indeed a Casablanca effect.

In a follow-up experiment (currently underway) these clips will be tested for cue or stimulus salience. In other words, for these four clips the music or the video could be a much more memorable stimulus simply on its own merits (stimulus salience) thereby leading to better memory performance (akin to 'transport'). On the other hand, the relationship between the music and video could be stronger such that music is more effective in eliciting the video ('transportation'). Indeed, a related study on two-way interactions between music and language based on priming recognition of tune and lyrics suggests that the asymmetrical relation between the two components of a song (lyrics priming melody more effectively than vise versa) is no longer present when both lyrics and melody are equally recognizable (Peretz, Radeau, & Arguin, 2004).

Of course, memory for any experience integrates the sensory elements of that experience including, in the case of movies, the sights and the sounds that are particularly relevant. Yet beyond the associative structures derived from patterns of stimulation across modalities, our understandings, attitudes, and construals become bound into these sensory patterns, sometimes even changing the shape of what we remember. This is the import of the now-classic work by Bartlett (1932) on the way knowledge and schemata change memories. Cultural experience, which is today increasingly shaped by multimedia, has a strong hand in revising our memories of sensory experiences as well as of narrative experiences. As mainstream movies bring together high-impact sensory experiences in the context of a rich narrative, they create some of the most powerful memorable stimuli we are exposed to today. While this speaks to the potential for remembering information and sensory experiences from movies, one should take a broader view to understand the possible asymmetry of recall in the Casablanca effect.

This effect is most likely to be obtained in movies where music and visuals were particularly distinctive and charged with emotional content. In order to recall a visual sequence from the music, we must recognize the music and associate it with the video it accompanied. When particularly distinctive pairings in classic scenes are repeated again and again in popular culture, these associations are rehearsed and their meanings elaborated and enriched. In such exceptional cases it remains a relatively common experience that the music is more effective in recalling the visual experience than vice versa. The challenge for future researchers will be to test the dependence of the effect on sufficient exposure to audiovisual pairings from movies where the complexity of the stimuli appears to be richly encoded into memory. When such encoding nears asymptotic levels of salient representation—as in the case demonstrated by Kraemer, Macrae, Green, and Kelley (2005) when a highly familiar song (in a kind of imagined replay) continues to produce neural activity similar to actually hearing the song—the asymmetry in cueing effectiveness between music and visual images may be revealed more clearly. On one hand, the robust representation of music may be more effective in cueing the retrieval of highly associated visual images. On the other hand, the richness of music from full orchestration to smoothed-over elevator music, rather than our generative ability, may promote the asymmetry given the power of enriched retrieval cues to aid recall. In either case, the common experience of the Casablanca effect suggests that important aspects of our memory system remain to be understood and can be revealed in the complexities of multimedia experience.

Amid the proliferation of film, video, and Internet content, more research is necessary to understand the perceptual, cognitive, and neurological mechanisms of music-evoked memory: ranging from image vividness in long-term autobiographical memory to the semantic, implicit, and emotional memory effects that contribute to the way music cues episodic memory of visual content. Many questions about music-induced memory effects in multimedia remain to be answered. Are multimedia experiences involving music more memorable than non-mediated—live—events or vice versa? How easily can music be re-associated with new memories in a multimedia context? What is the effect of long-term exposure through new platforms and venues (mobile phones versus IMAX theaters) on remembering the experience of a multimedia product and how does the historical change in such exposure affect the music-evoked memory? Although we have come a long way from Curtiz's classic film, the direct and indirect effects of music on the memory of multimedia have, if anything, only become more pervasive.

Acknowledgments

Writing of this chapter was supported by a New Directions Fellowship from the Andrew W. Mellon Foundation. The authors would like to thank Marilyn Boltz at Haverford College for valuable suggestions and constructive comments to an earlier version of this chapter.

References

Altman, R. (2004). *Silent film sound.* New York, NY: Columbia University Press.

Amad, P. (2010). *Counter-archive: film, the everyday, and Albert Kahn's Archives de la Planète.* New York, NY: Columbia University Press.

American Film Institute. (2007). *AFI's 100 Years... 100 Movies, 10th Anniversary Edition.* Retrieved from <http://www.afi.com/100years/movies10.aspx>.

Baker, L. (1978). Processing temporal relationships in simple stories: Effects of input sequence: *Journal of Verbal Learning and Verbal Behavior, 17*, 559–572.

Bartlett, F. C. (1932). *Remembering: a study in experimental and social psychology.* Cambridge, UK: Cambridge University Press.

Baumgartner, T., Lutz, K., Schmidt, C. F., & Jäncke, L. (2006). The emotional power of music: How music enhances the feeling of affective pictures. *Brain Research, 1075*, 151–164.

Beynon, G. W. (1921). *Musical presentation of motion pictures.* New York, NY: G. Schirmer.

Bezdek, M. A., & Gerrig, R. J. (2008). Musical emotions in the context of narrative film. *Behavioral and Brain Sciences, 31*(5), 578–578.

Bolivar, V. J., Cohen, A. J., & Fentress, J. C. (1994). Semantic and formal congruency in music and motion pictures: Effects on the interpretation of visual action. *Psychomusicology, 13*(1–2), 28–59.

Boltz, M. G. (2001). Musical soundtracks as a schematic influence on the cognitive processing of filmed events. *Music Perception, 18*(4), 427–454.

Boltz, M. G. (2004). The cognitive processing of film and musical soundtracks. *Memory & Cognition, 32*(7), 1194–1205.

Boltz, M. G., Ebendorf, B., & Field, B. (2009). Audiovisual interactions: The impact of visual information on music perception and memory. *Music Perception, 27*(1), 43–59.

Boltz, M. G., Schulkind, M., & Kantra, S. (1991). Effects of background music on the remembering of filmed events. *Memory & Cognition, 19*(6), 593–606.

Bullerjahn, C., & Güldenring, M. (1994). An empirical investigation of effects of film music using qualitative content analysis. *Psychomusicology, 13*(1–2), 99–118.

Cady, E. T., Harris, R. J., & Knappenberger, J. B. (2008). Using music to cue autobiographical memories of different lifetime periods. *Psychology of Music, 36*(2), 157–178.

Calvert, S. L., & Tart, M. (1993). Song versus verbal forms for very-long-term, long-term, and short-term verbatim recall. *Journal of Applied Developmental Psychology, 14*(2), 245–260.

Cavell, S. (1979). *The world viewed: reflections on the ontology of film.* Cambridge, MA: Harvard University Press.

Chion, M. (1994). *Audio-vision: sound on screen* (C. Gorbman, Trans.). New York, NY: Columbia University Press.

Cohen, A. J. (2001). Music as a source of emotion in film. In P. N. Juslin & J. A. Sloboda (Eds.), *Music and emotion: Theory and research* (pp. 249–272). Oxford, UK: Oxford University Press.

Cohen, A. J. (2005). How music influences the interpretation of film and video: Approaches from experimental psychology. In R. A. Kendall & R. W. Savage (Ed.), *Selected Reports in Ethnomusicology: Perspectives in Systematic Musicology* (pp. 15–36). Los Angeles, CA: Dept. of Ethnomusicology, University of California.

Cook, N. (1998). *Analyzing musical multimedia.* Oxford, UK: Oxford University Press.

Cupchik, G. C., & Saltzman, M. (1999). Reception and memory for serious and light rock music videos. *Empirical Studies of the Arts, 17*(1), 59–72.

Davies, J. B. (1978). *The psychology of music.* Stanford, CA: Stanford University Press.

DeWolfe Music (2012). *DeWolfe music catalog online.* Retrieved from <http://www.dewolfemusic.com/home/default.asp>.

Donnelly, K. J. (2002). Tracking British television: Pop music as stock soundtrack to the small screen. *Popular music, 21*(3), 331–343.

Draaisma, D. (2004). *Why life speeds up as you get older: How memory shapes our past.* Cambridge, UK: Cambridge University Press.

Erdmann, H., & Becce, G. (1927). *Allgemeines Handbuch der Film-Musik* (Vols. 1–2). Berlin, Germany: Schlesinger and Lienau.

Eschrich, S., Münte, T. F., & Altenmüller, E. O. (2008). Unforgettable film music: The role of emotion in episodic long-term memory for music. *BMC Neuroscience, 9*, 48.

Franklin, P. (2011). *Seeing through music: Gender and modernism in classic Hollywood film scores.* New York, NY: Oxford University Press.

Furman, O., Dorfman, N., Hasson, U., Davachi, L., & Dudai, Y. (2007). They saw a movie: Long-term memory for an extended audiovisual narrative. *Learning & Memory, 14*(6), 457–467.

Geringer, J., Cassidy, J. W., & Byo, J. L. (1996). Effects of music with video on responses of nonmusic majors: An exploratory study. *Journal of Research in Music Education, 44*(3), 240–251.

Geringer, J., Cassidy, J. W., & Byo, J. L. (1997). Nonmusic majors' cognitive and affective responses to performance and programmatic music videos. *Journal of Research in Music Education, 45*(2), 221–233.

Gjerdingen, R. O., & Perrott, D. (2008). Scanning the dial: The rapid recognition of music genres. *Journal of New Music Research, 37*(2), 93–100.

Gorbman, C. (1987). *Unheard melodies: Narrative film music.* Bloomington, IN: Indiana University Press.

Gorn, G. J. (1982). The effects of music in advertising on choice behavior: A classical conditioning approach. *Journal of Marketing, 46*(1), 94–101.

Halbwachs, M. (1992). *On collective memory* (L. A. Coser, Trans.). Chicago, IL: University of Chicago Press.

Halpern, L., Blake, R., & Hillenbrand, J. M. (1986). The psychoacoustics of a chilling sound. *Perception and Psychophysics, 39*, 77–80.

Halpern, A. R., & O'Connor, M. G. (2000). Implicit memory for music in Alzheimer's disease. *Neuropsychology, 14*(3), 391–397.

Harris, R. J., Hoekstra, S. J., Scott, C. L., Sanborn, F. W., Dodds, L. A., & Brandenburg, J. D. (2004). Autobiographical memories for seeing romantic movies on a date: Romance is not just for women. *Media Psychology, 6*(3), 257–284.

Harris, R. J., Hoekstra, S. J., Scott, C. L., Sanborn, F. W., Karafa, J. A., & Brandenburg, J. D. (2000). Young men's and women's different autobiographical memories of the experience of seeing frightening movies on a date. *Media Psychology, 2*(3), 245–268.

Harrison, K., & Cantor, J. (1999). Tales from the screen: Enduring fright reactions to scary media. *Media Psychology, 1*(2), 97–116.

Hoeckner, B. (2007). Audiovisual memory: Transport and transportation. In D. Goldmark, L. Kramer, & R. D. Leppert (Eds.), *Beyond the soundtrack: representing music in cinema* (pp. 163–183). Berkeley, CA: University of California Press.

Hoeckner, B., Wyatt, E. W., Decety, J., & Nusbaum, H. (2011). Film music influences how viewers relate to movie characters. *Psychology of Aesthetics, Creativity, and the Arts*, 5, 146–153.

Hoekstra, S. J., Harris, R. J., & Helmick, A. L. (1999). Autobiographical memories about the experience of seeing frightening movies in childhood. *Media Psychology, 1*(2), 117–140.

Holbrook, M. B., & Schindler, R. M. (1989). Some exploratory findings on the development of musical tastes. *Journal of Consumer Research, 16*(1), 119–124.

Holmes, E. A., & Bourne, C. (2008). Inducing and modulating intrusive emotional memories: A review of the trauma film paradigm. *Acta Psychologica, 127*(3), 553–566.

Hung, K. (2000). Narrative music in congruent and incongruent TV advertising. *Journal of Advertising, 29*(1), 25–34.

Hung, K. (2001). Framing meaning perceptions with music: The case of teaser ads. *Journal of Advertising, 30*(3), 39–49.

Janata, P., Tomic, S. T., & Rakowski, S. K. (2007). Characterisation of music-evoked autobiographical memories. *Memory, 15*(8), 845–860.

Johnson, J. A., & Zatorre, R. J. (2005). Attention to simultaneous unrelated auditory and visual events: Behavioral and neural correlates. *Cerebral Cortex, 15*(10), 1609–1620.

Juslin, P. N., & Laukka, P. (2004). Expression, perception, and induction of musical emotions: A review and a questionnaire study of everyday listening. *Journal of New Music Research, 33*(3), 217–238.

Juslin, P. N., & Västfjäll, D. (2008). Emotional responses to music: The need to consider underlying mechanisms. *Behavioral and Brain Sciences, 31*, 559–575.

Kelley, S., & Calkins, S. (2006). Evaluating popular portrayals of memory in film. *Teaching of Psychology, 33*(3), 191–194.

Kosslyn, S. M. (1980). *Image and mind.* Cambridge, MA: Harvard University Press.

Kraemer, D. J. M., Macrae, C. N., Green, A. E., & Kelley, W. M. (2005). Musical imagery: Sound of silence activates auditory cortex. *Nature, 434*(7030), 158–158.

Kurby, C. A., & Zacks, J. M. (2008). *Segmentation in the perception and memory of events. Trends in Cognitive Sciences, 12*, 72–79.

Lalwani, A. K., Lwin, M. O., & Ling, P. B. (2009). Does audiovisual congruency in advertisements increase persuasion? The role of cultural music and products. *Journal of Global Marketing, 22*(2), 139–153.

Langdale, A. (2002). *Hugo Münsterberg on film: The photoplay: a psychological study and other writings.* New York, NY: Routledge.

MacInnis, D. J., & Park, C. W. (1991). The differential role of characteristics of music on high- and low-involvement consumers' processing of ads. *Journal of Consumer Research, 18*(2), 161–173.

Maher, J. K., Hu, M. Y., & Kolbe, R. H. (2006). Children's recall of television ad elements. *Journal of Advertising, 35*(1), 23–33.

Marshall, S. K., & Cohen, A. J. (1988). Effects of musical soundtracks on attitudes toward animated geometric figures. *Music Perception, 6*(1), 95–112.

McClelland, J. L., & Rumelhart, D. E. (1985). Distributed memory and the representation of general and specific information. *Journal of Experimental Psychology: General, 114*, 159–197.

McCloskey, M., Wible, C. G., & Cohen, N. J. (1988). Is there a special flashbulb-memory mechanism? *Journal of Experimental Psychology: General, 117*, 171–181.

Meyer, D. E., & Schvaneveldt, R. W. (1971). Facilitation in recognizing pairs of words: Evidence of a dependence between retrieval operations. *Journal of Experimental Psychology, 90*(2), 227–234.

Miller, G. A. (1956). The magical number seven, plus or minus two: Some limits on our capacity for processing information. *Psychological Review 63* (2), 81–97.

Murray, N. M., & Murray, S. B. (1996). Music and lyrics in commercials: A cross-cultural comparison between commercials run in the Dominican Republic and in the United States. *Journal of Advertising, 25*(2), 51–63.

Pennington, N., & Hastie, R. (1988). Explanation-based decision making: Effects of memory structure on judgment. *Journal of Experimental Psychology: Learning, Memory, and Cognition, 14*, 512–533.

Peretz, I., Gaudreau, D., & Bonnel, A.-M. (1998). Exposure effects on music preference and recognition. *Memory & Cognition, 26*(5), 884–902.

Peretz, I., Radeau, M., & Arguin, M. (2004). Two-way interactions between music and language: Evidence from priming recognition of tune and lyrics in familiar songs. *Memory & Cognition, 32*(1), 142–152.

Racette, A., & Peretz, I. (2007). Learning lyrics: To sing or not to sing? *Memory & Cognition, 35*(2), 242–253.

Radvansky, G. A., & Copeland, D. E. (2006). Walking through doorways causes forgetting. *Memory & Cognition, 34*, 1150–1156.

Rainey, D. W., & Larsen, J. D. (2002). The effects of familiar melodies on initial learning and long-term memory for unconnected text. *Music Perception, 20*(2), 173–186.

Rapée, E. (1924). *Motion picture moods, for pianists and organists; a rapid-reference collection of selected pieces, adapted to fifty-two moods and situations.* New York, NY: Schirmer.

Raz, A., Fan, J., & Posner, M. I. (2006a). Neuroimaging and genetic associations of attentional and hypnotic processes. *Journal of Physiology, Paris, 99*(4–6), 483–491.

Raz, A., Kirsch, I., Pollard, J., & Nitkin-Kaner, Y. (2006b). Suggestion reduces the Stroop effect. *Psychological Science, 17*(2), 91–95.

Schacter, D. L. (1987).Implicit memory: history and current status. *Journal of Experimental Psychology: Learning, Memory, and Cognition, 13*, 501–518.

Schellenberg, E. G., Peretz, I., & Vieillard, S. (2008). Liking for happy- and sad-sounding music: Effects of exposure. *Cognition and Emotion, 22*(2), 218–237.

Schulkind, M. D., Hennis, L. K., & Rubin, D. C. (1999). Music, emotion, and autobiographical memory: They're playing your song. *Memory & Cognition, 27*(6), 948–955.

Shevy, M. (2007). The mood of rock music affects evaluation of video elements differing in valence and dominance. *Psychomusicology, 19*(2), 57–78.

Simmons-Stern, N. R., Budson, A. E., & Ally, B. A. (2010). Music as a memory enhancer in patients with Alzheimer's disease. *Neuropsychologia, 48*(10), 3164–3167.

Simonton, D. K. (2007). Film music: Are award-winning scores and songs heard in successful motion pictures? *Psychology of Aesthetics, Creativity, and the Arts, 1*(2), 53–60.

Sloboda, J. A., O'Neill, S. A., & Ivaldi, A. (2001). Functions of music in everyday life: An exploratory study using the experience sampling method. *Musicae Scientiae, 5*(1), 9–32.

Spiegel, D. (2002). Mesmer minus magic: Hypnosis and modern medicine. *International Journal of Clinical and Experimental Hypnosis, 50*(4), 397–406.

Tagg, P. (1979). *Kojak-50 seconds of television music: toward the analysis of affect in popular music.* Göteborg, Sweden: Musikvetenskapliga Institut Göteborg University.

Tagg, P., & Clarida, R. (2003). *Ten little title tunes: Towards a musicology of the mass media.* New York, NY: Mass Media Music Scholars' Press.

Tan, S.-L., Spackman, M. P., & Bezdek, M. A. (2007). Viewers' interpretations of film characters' emotions: Effects of presenting film music before or after a character is shown. *Music Perception, 25*(2), 135–152.

Tillmann, B., Peretz, I., & Samson, S. V. (2011). Neurocognitive approaches to memory in music: Music is memory. In S. Nalbantian, P. Matthews, & J. McClelland (Eds.), *The memory process: Neuroscientific and humanistic perspectives* (pp. 377–394). Cambridge, MA: MIT Press.

Trabasso, T., & Sperry, L. L. (1985). Causal relatedness and importance of story events. *Journal of Memory and Language, 24*, 595–611.

Tulving, E. (1983). *Elements of episodic memory.* Oxford, UK: Oxford University Press.

Tulving, E. (2002). Episodic memory: From mind to brain. *Annual Review of Psychology, 53*(1), 1–25.

Turim, M. C. (1989). *Flashbacks in film: Memory and history.* New York, NY: Routledge.

Vidal, F. (2011). Memory, movies, and the brain. In S. Nalbantian, P. Matthews, & J. McClelland (Eds.), *The memory process: Neuroscientific and humanistic perspectives* (pp. 395–415). Cambridge, MA: MIT Press.

Vitouch, O. (2001). When your ear sets the stage: Musical context effects in film perception. *Psychology of Music, 29*(1), 70–83.

Wallis, H. B. (Producer), & Curtiz, M. (Director). (1942). *Casablanca* [Motion picture]. United States: Warner Bros.

Walker, R. (2004). Cultural memes, innate proclivities and musical behaviour: a case study of the western traditions. *Psychology of Music, 32*(2), 153–190.

Weaver, C. A. (1993). Do you need a 'flash' to form a flashbulb memory? *Journal of Experimental Psychology: General, 122*, 39–46.

Wimber, M., Heinze, H.-J., & Richardson-Klavehn, A. (2010). Distinct frontoparietal networks set the stage for later perceptual identification priming and episodic recognition memory. *Journal of Neuroscience, 30*(40), 13272–13280.

Wingstedt, J., Brändström, S., & Berg, J. (2008). Young adolescents' usage of narrative functions of media music by manipulation of musical expression. *Psychology of Music, 36*(2), 193–214.

Yalch, R. F. (1991). Memory in a jingle jungle: Music as a mnemonic device in communicating advertising slogans. *Journal of Applied Psychology, 76*(2), 268–275.

Part IV

Applications: Music and Sound in Multimedia

Chapter 12

Children's media: The role of music and audio features

Sandra L. Calvert

Georgetown University, USA

In days gone by, bards sang tales as they traveled from village to village, carrying their messages in a melodic form that was often memorable to listeners (Calvert & Tart, 1993). In the 21st century, contemporary 'bards' typically travel to listeners electronically through digital media, providing instantaneous global access to their music. How does exposure to electronically generated music through multimedia, as well as to other perceptually salient audio techniques like sound effects, affect moods, attention, and learning from infancy through early adulthood? And how do older youth use the symbolic systems of audiovisual media to create their own multimedia?

This chapter explores the effects of infants', children's, and adolescents' exposure to music presented in multimedia. The role of music on the moods and feelings of youth, including the link to learning, is examined. Auditory formal production features (i.e., sound effects, non-speech vocalizations, music, and singing, that are used to present multimedia content) are considered in relation to children's attention and learning of content. These non-content auditory features serve to influence children's attention to content by eliciting orienting responses—as well as by providing modes that children can use to think about and represent the visual and verbal content by, for instance, presenting language with melodies to make the words more memorable. The ways that older youth are now creating their own digital stories, using the same production techniques that they often enjoy viewing, are also considered. Finally, promising research directions for the field are advanced.

Exposure to music and song

Listening to music and songs is an activity that frames human interactions from the beginnings of life. Using a nationally representative survey in which parents were randomly called by land-line phones, the Kaiser Family Foundation reported on the media use patterns of children who were in the first 6 years of life (Rideout & Hamel, 2006). On a typical day, 82 percent of children under age 6 years spend some time listening to music. Slightly more infants aged 6 months to 1 year old listen to music (88 percent) than 2- to 3-year-old (84 percent) or 4- to 6-year-old children (78 percent). For those who listen to music, the average amount of time invested per day is 58 minutes, with

6-month- to 1-year-olds listening to music for slightly more time (74 minutes per day) than 2- to 3-year-old (60 minutes per day) or 4- to 6-year-old children (53 minutes per day). The overall picture that emerges, then, is that very young children are consistently exposed to a considerable amount of music each and every day from the beginnings of life. In addition, all 6 month- to 6-year-old US children are exposed to an average of about 1.5 hours of screen media a day. For the youngest children, that exposure often involves infant videos that use heavy concentrations of background music, and to a lesser extent foreground music and singing (Goodrich, Pempek, & Calvert, 2009).

Listening to music and songs continues to occupy a considerable amount of time by 8- to 18-year-olds. According to the most recent nationally representative Kaiser Family Foundation survey of media use (Rideout, Foehr, & Roberts, 2010), 8- to 18-year-old youth spend an average of 2 hours, 31 minutes per day with music and other audio media, an increase in time spent with media when compared to their earlier studies. Overall, there has been an increase of 47 minutes per day in listening to music among 8- to 18-year-olds from the 2004 to the 2010 surveys, the heaviest increase in exposure to any category of media (Roberts, Foehr, & Rideout 2005; Roberts, Foehr, Rideout, & Brodie, 1999). Mobile devices designed for listening to music contribute to this pattern. During 2008 and 2009, for instance, 79 percent of a nationally representative sample of 12- to 17-year-old US teens reported owning an iPod or other digital musical device which are used almost exclusively to listen to music (Lenhart, Ling, Campbell, & Purcell, 2010).

In the most recent Kaiser Family Foundation survey (Rideout et al., 2010), the amount of time spent listening to music increases with age, with 8- to 10-year-olds listening to only about 1 hour of music and other audio media per day, but 18-year-olds investing an average of 3 hours per day. Girls listen to more music than boys (Rideout et al., 2010). However the gender gap in listening to music is beginning to disappear according to the most recent Kaiser survey due to the introduction and concentration of iPods, MP3 players, cell phones, and computers in the hands of preadolescent and adolescent youth. Minority youth are especially heavy users of music. Eight- to 18-year-old Hispanic youth listen to music an average of 2 hours, 52 minutes per day, African American youth listen to music an average of 2 hours 42 minutes per day, and Caucasian youth listen to music approximately 1 hour 48 minutes daily (Rideout et al., 2010).

Exposure to music is also probably much higher for this age group than reported by the Kaiser Family Foundation because 8- to 18-year-old youth invest heavily in viewing television content, playing video games, and interacting on the computer in which there is a heavy concentration of music that accompanies the video features. Specifically, the average US 8- to 18-year-old is now exposed to 7.5 hours of screen media per day, and much of that exposure to television, games, and movies includes music and singing (Rideout et al., 2010). For instance, African American youth spend approximately 3 hours each day watching televised music videos, a format that combines music with video content (Ward, Hansbrough, & Walker, 2009). Music videos transmit cultural information and provide visual imagery consistent with the message of the song (Sun & Lull, 1986), perhaps making them a source of cultural pride for minority youth.

Listening to music often occurs during multitasking, in which multiple activities are done simultaneously; multitasking often involves more than one media platform at a time, such as listening to music as youth write a paper on their computer for a homework assignment (Rideout et al., 2010; Roberts et al., 2005). In fact, 73 percent of 7th to 12th graders reporting multitasking while listening to music (Rideout et al., 2010). Thus, how children perform at other tasks while listening to music, particularly their homework assignments, is of considerable importance for understanding what US children take away from their everyday experiences. This topic will be discussed in more detail later in the chapter.

In summary, music is a favored activity of infants, children, and adolescents throughout their development. Very young children make up a captive audience, listening to the music that their parents or other adults choose for them, whereas older youth select their own tunes. Listening to music has increased over time for older youth, in part due to increased access to mobile devices that allow youth to listen to music wherever they are. Minority youth and girls are particularly likely to listen to music, though boys are increasingly choosing to listen to music as well. Overall, music and singing provide a backdrop for many everyday activities as well as take center stage at times. How do these extensive experiences that children and youth spend with audio and audiovisual media influence developmental outcomes? Why do youth choose to spend so much of their time listening to songs and musical tracks? We turn now to the important role that music plays in mood regulation.

Music, mood, and emotions

Music often elicits emotions and arousal from listeners. Indeed, one of the more widely-cited studies that presumably linked listening to specific kinds of music to spatial learning may actually be caused by mood changes. In their initial study, Rauscher, Shaw, and Ky (1993) found that college students increased on a combined score measuring performance on three spatial tasks after listening to a Mozart tape for 10 minutes. The comparison groups were students who listened to a relaxation tape or who sat in silence. Although spatial skills were higher immediately after exposure for those who had listened to Mozart music than for the other two groups, the effects wore off after 10 to 15 minutes. These results suggested an acute short-term improvement for spatial skills after listening to Mozart music, a finding that came to be dubbed by the media as 'the Mozart Effect.'

The Mozart Effect, however, was not replicated in subsequent research with adults. For example, when Steele, Bass, and Crook (1999) attempted to replicate the findings of the original Rauscher et al. (1993) study, they found no increases in spatial skills after listening to Mozart music. They did find an increase in mood. They argued that the Mozart Effect might be caused by mood elevation prior to testing which then boosted spatial performance in the original Rauscher et al. (1993) study.

Evidence to support mood changes by listening to Mozart music was further supported by a study of college students (Husain, Thompson, & Schellenberg, 2002). The tempo (fast or slow) and the mode (major or minor) of a Mozart sonata were manipulated. After listening to one of these four tapes, participants took a spatial task, an arousal measure, and a mood scale. Those who listened to the Mozart tapes that had faster tempos were more aroused than those who listened to Mozart tapes with slower tempos. Moods were best after listening to the major mode. Performance on spatial tasks was better after hearing the Mozart music that was fast paced and after hearing Mozart music in a major mode. Thus, Husain and colleagues (2002) proposed that the improved spatial skills attributed to the Mozart Effect appeared to be mediated by feelings and arousal levels induced by the music.

Given the equivocal results from numerous studies about the potential beneficial outcomes of listening to music on spatial skills, Rauscher and Shaw (1998) subsequently argued that the effect was limited to the spatial-temporal task of their measure. Although there are discrepancies in the findings and the interpretations about how adults who listen to Mozart subsequently perform on tasks assessing spatial-temporal performance, nonetheless considerable enthusiasm was generated for the potential of music to enhance spatial as well as other kinds of cognitive skills, including those of the very youngest children. Indeed, interest in the Mozart Effect became pronounced when it was described in relation to children's learning from media, even though youngsters had not been studied at that point in time (see Bangerter & Heath, 2004; Rauscher, 2009). Rauscher (2009) also argued that her research had been misinterpreted, and that discussions about the beneficial effects of music on infants and children's brain function and general intelligence were beyond the scope of her original research.

As beliefs about the beneficial influences of early exposure to music ensued, videos with titles such as *Baby Mozart* and the *Mozart Effect for Babies* entered the infant and toddler marketplace. Although improvements in spatial skills after listening to Mozart music has not been empirically documented for infants, 5- to 9-month-olds do demonstrate musical preferences. Specifically, infants prefer happy to sad music, suggesting that certain emotional responses to music are innate or are at least apparent within the first year (Nawrot, 2003). The mood regulation facets of music may well be overlooked as a reason for why parents show baby videos to their very young children. Music may have a calming effect that could be accentuated by other kinds of formal features that are slow as well as by content that is familiar and soothing. During infancy, music is played to put infants to sleep as well as to engage them during their daily activities. Indeed, 6-month-old infants sustain their attention better when they view tapes of their mothers singing to them than when they view tapes of their mothers speaking to them, perhaps because singing is more repetitive than speaking, thereby helping infants to modulate their arousal levels (Nakata & Trehub, 2004; see also Shenfield, Trehub, & Nakata, 2003). Or music may be played to induce happy moods. Although older children do not select the same exact emotions, such as happy, sad, fearful, angry, or neutral, that adults do to describe the music they are listening to, children do select similar facial expressions and provide similar verbal descriptions to music as adults do, suggesting that they too sense the emotions of music (Nawrot, 2003).

One important factor in the identification of moods associated with music is the use of musical modes (e.g., major and minor). For example, Kastner and Crowder (1990) played musical pieces in major and minor modes to preschool and grade school children. Children then selected pictures that conveyed the feelings in the music. Although there were age-related improvements in matching moods to pictures connoting feelings, even 3-year-old children performed above chance level in mapping happy or contented pictures to major modes, and sad or angry feelings to minor modes. Using

Zajonc's (1968) theory of mere exposure, the authors argued that mere exposure leads to familiarity and then to liking of musical pieces. Since major modes are heard more often than minor modes, even children, they argued, come to associate the familiar major modes with happiness and the less familiar minor modes with sadness or anger.

The uses of music and the needs filled by listening to music are many and varied. When played in social settings, music can be used for courtship rituals, for the creation and maintenance of friendships, as a topic of conversation, and as a way to encourage dancing (Roberts & Christenson, 2001). Females are more likely to use music for social reasons than males are (Carroll et al., 1993). By adolescence, mood regulation is the major reason reported for listening to music (Christenson & Roberts, 1998). Listening to music is typically a solitary rather than a social activity, and hence, mood regulation via music is typically experienced in private settings, such as one's bedroom (Christenson, 1994). Females are more likely to listen to music to improve their moods or to dwell on melancholy moods, whereas males are more likely to use music to increase their arousal levels and to get excited (Larson, Kubey, & Colletti, 1989). Females also report listening to music to relieve feelings of loneliness more than males do (Roberts & Christenson, 2001). The sad feelings that adolescents feel after a relationship ends is one reason that adolescents may listen to sad and melancholy music (Zillmann & Gan, 1997).

Music videos, in which songs and visual images are combined, fill the needs of listener-viewers as well as influence their arousal level. High school students, for example, reported that they used music videos in part because they were bored (Sun & Lull, 1986). Music videos clearly have the potential to excite. When sexual and violent visual images were inserted into rock-music, college students reported more excitement, enjoyment, and appreciation of that video (Zillmann & Mundorf, 1987). College students also reported more emotional involvement when they heard an animated vignette with music than when the same music was heard without visual images, though their judgments about the music (e.g., tempo, melody, harmony) varied depending on the animated vignette that they viewed (Geringer, Cassidy, & Byo, 1996; Geringer, Cassidy, & Byo, 1997). Chapter 10 in this volume by Boltz reviews the literature about music videos in more depth.

Formal features of media

Entertainment media are presented through visual and auditory production techniques, known as *formal features* (Huston & Wright, 1983). Just as language is a symbol system that must be learned, so too are the formal features that are used to present content via electronic media. Although many believe that visual features are the reason that people watch television and other visual media, *auditory* features play an extremely important role as they tell us when to look.

Berlyne (1960) argued that attention is initially influenced by perceptually salient features that embody movement, contrast, incongruity, surprise, and complexity followed by habituation to salience per se as attention shifts towards a search for meaningful content. Using Berlyne's theory of perceptual salience, Huston and Wright (1983) theorized that attention is initially influenced by perceptually salient television production features. Such features include action in which characters move through space, sound effects that include the 'booms' of explosions and the high-pitched whirring sounds of grinding engines in car races, rapid pace where there are frequent changes in location and characters, loud foreground music, and vocalizations, i.e., non-speech utterances such as the character Scooby Doo saying 'Scooby Dooby Doo!' or the character Fred Flintstone saying 'Yabba Dabba Doo!' With developmental change and experience with the media, Huston and Wright (1983) predicted that attention comes under the strategic control of the viewer-listener who is increasingly in search of meaningful content, at which time non-salient features, such as child, female, and male dialogue and background music that occurs during speech, increasingly influence attention. Put another way, this change from exploration as a function of perceptual salience to a search for meaningful content reflects a change from attention being controlled by *exogenous* external events, in which attention is controlled more by external stimuli per se—to *endogenous* control of attention, in which attention is increasingly under the volitional control of children.

This section of the chapter will explore the role of auditory features in multimedia designed for infants and children. The discussion will be divided into two parts, focusing first on (1) sound effects and vocalizations; and then shifting to the topic of (2) music and singing.

Sound effects and vocalizations: Effects on children's attention and learning in multimedia experiences

When children view media, they do not sit and stare at the content. Rather, they play with toys and look at the television content periodically. In addition to music, auditory features such as sound effects and vocalizations play an important role in children's attention to, as well as their learning from, audiovisual media.

In an early study that involved the children's television cartoon, *Fat Albert and the Cosby Kids*, Calvert and colleagues (1982) advanced two ways that formal features may influence children's attention to content. One pathway to attention was due to the *perceptual salience* of the features per se. Thus, when a striking sound effect such as a slide whistle occurs, children should look at the screen due to a *primitive attentional orienting response*. The second pathway to attention, known as the *marker function*, occurs when children *learn to associate* certain auditory features with important story information. For example, in this production, Fat Albert would say the vocalization 'Hey, Hey, Hey,' followed by important dialogue that was essential for understanding the plot. That vocalization was a marker for children who were familiar with this production and who were in search of the important story content. In essence, the vocalization tells them when to look. These two pathways represent the developmental change described earlier in which infants and very young children shift from exogenous to endogenous control of attention.

Once visual attention is gained through either the salience or the marker functions of features, Calvert and colleagues (1982) expected that contiguous presentation between the salient auditory feature and the story content would provide one pathway to comprehension. That is, temporal proximity between the salient feature and story content would enhance the probability of children learning whatever followed the perceptually salient auditory feature.

Perceptually salient auditory features for attention and early learning from video during infancy

In a study of 6-, 9-, and 12-month-olds, Gola and her colleagues examined infant attention to both auditory and visual formal features for four different infant video programs, two of which were high in pace and two of which were low in pace (i.e., the rate of scene and character change). For auditory formal features, the researchers found that character vocalizations, foreground music, and background music were more likely to elicit attention when each of these features was present rather than absent for all age groups (Gola, Kirkorian, Perez, Anderson, & Calvert, 2011). Similarly, 12-, 15-, and 18-month-olds reliably oriented to vignettes from the *Baby Mozart* series when sound effects, such as a metronome or a ticking sound, were presented on the audio track, regardless of prior exposure (Barr et al., 2008). Taken together, the results suggest that perceptually salient audio features reliably elicit infant attentional orienting responses to the screen.

The shift to an understanding of the marker functions of perceptually salient auditory features appears to emerge in the first year of life, at least for very short video vignettes that are made just for experiments. Barr, Wyss, and Somander (2009) exposed 6-, 12-, and 18-month-olds to a 1-minute video in which sound effects were either matched or mismatched to the target actions, such as taking a mitten off a puppet. Four different sound effects were used. In the matched condition, the sound effects were a 'popping' noise when a mitten was taken off of a puppet, a 'swooshing' noise when the puppet moved, a ringing bell as the mitten was shaken, and a 'squelching' sound as the mitten was put back on the puppet. The same sound effects were used in the mismatched condition, but the sounds were out of synch with the puppet actions. Infants viewed the video six times. After a 24-hour delay, deferred imitation was assessed to measure memory of the task. Six-month-old infants imitated the task whether the sound effects matched the presentation or not, but 12- and 18-month-old infants imitated more target behaviors correctly when sound effects were matched rather than mismatched with target actions. These results also suggest a shift from exogenous control of attention by external stimuli to endogenous volitional control of attention at about age 1 year. Put another way, infants learn to discriminate and can use sound effects that are synchronized with targeted actions to improve their learning between the ages of 6 and 12 months.

Perceptually salient auditory features for attention and learning from television during early childhood

In a study of the cartoon, *Fat Albert and the Cosby Kids*, Calvert et al. (1982) examined the naturally occurring formal features of the program in relation to preschoolers' and kindergarteners' versus 3rd and 4th grade children's learning of important plot-relevant content. The formal features were first scored, and questions that assessed comprehension of the central plot-relevant and the incidental content were generated. Then children viewed the program and answered the multiple-choice questions that assessed their understanding of the program content. The central story plot was about children who liked doing non-traditional activities, in this case Penny who was a talented athlete who could kick a football out of sight, and Fat Albert who liked to cook.

By contrast, incidental content involved humorous events such as the rather robust Fat Albert character jumping behind a rather thin Native American statue that fully hid him, an event accentuated by a sound effect that went 'zip!'; this event did not advance the plot.

A consistent vocalization used in the program by Fat Albert, the main character, was 'Hey, Hey, Hey' followed by the words, 'I've got something to say.' Important plot-relevant content typically followed that vocalization. Children of both age groups were more attentive when sound effects and vocalizations were present rather than absent. As predicted, attention during the presence of character vocalizations improved both age groups' recognition of central television content. More specifically, children who paid attention when the character vocalizations occurred remembered more of the central plot-relevant content than did the children who were less attentive during these vocalizations. Put another way, by eliciting young children's visual attention at key program points, the character vocalizations increased children's comprehension of the contiguously presented content. Attention during vocalizations and sound effects also predicted comprehension of incidental content for the preschoolers and kindergarteners, but not for the 3rd and 4th graders, which suggests that the older children were better able to use features as markers of important content than were the younger children. Thus, there appears to be a shift from using the salience, attention-getting role of features that is based on primitive orienting responses to changes in the environment to the marker function of audio features in which children understand the meaning of features sometime between early and middle childhood for programs designed for a middle-childhood audience.

The role of auditory features for attention and comprehension using experimentally inserted sounds at key program points was the next research direction. Scene transitions, for example, are a critical time for children to attend to a program. If children attend during these transitions, they are more likely to see important story content that needs to be linked across program boundaries in order for them to understand the story narrative. To illustrate, for instance, in an episode of the children's program *Spanky and our Gang* called 'Mama's Little Pirates,' the scene shifts from Spanky being asleep in his bedroom to a new scene in which he is going to search for pirate treasure as part of a dream sequence. A giant eventually chases Spanky in this dream for stealing his gold, at which point the scene shifts again and Spanky wakes up in his bed. If children are not looking during those transitions, they may experience more difficulty with story comprehension.

In an experimental study using this episode from *Spanky and our Gang*, Calvert and Gersh (1987) inserted three sound effects of a slide whistle at the important scene transitions where Spanky goes from being awake to going to sleep to being awake again. In the sound effect condition, each of these three transitions was highlighted with a 1-second sound effect. The control group viewed the same story, but without the sound effects. Kindergartners' recognition of the most difficult plot-relevant content was improved when they heard sound effects during these three scene transitions when compared to the kindergarteners who did not hear these sound effects. By contrast, older 5th graders did not need sound effects to understand the story plot. These results suggest that sound effects can improve comprehension for young children if they are used selectively to highlight important scene changes that need to be processed for mature story comprehension.

Rapidly paced programs, in which there are frequent changes of scenes and characters, place particularly heavy demands on children's ability to integrate key program information (Wright et al., 1984). Think of pace as being part of a play, with the curtain going up and down, sometimes to a new place (which would be a new scene) and sometimes to a familiar place (which would be a familiar scene). Characters also come and go from each stage setting, just as they do in television, film, and video scenes. When those changes occur rapidly, they place demands on the audience to integrate changes in time and place that are necessary to understand the story.

To assist children with these information processing demands, Calvert and Scott (1989) inserted five sound effects of a slide whistle into two live-format commercial children's television programs that were either high or low in program pace (i.e., the rate of scene and character change). The control versions of these programs had no sound effects. The rapidly paced program, titled *Search and Rescue*, involved trained animals who rescued a father and son who were in a car accident. In the slowly paced program, titled *Thunder, the Adventures of a Superhorse*, Thunder helps save a dog that drank poisoned water from a mine. Preschoolers and 4th-grade children viewed one of these four versions of these programs and then completed sequencing tasks where they put pictures in order that came from the central story scenes. Children of both age groups were more likely to attend to the key program transitions in the rapidly paced program when sound effects were present rather than absent. Selective attention at these key story transitions also predicted comprehension of the rapidly paced program. By contrast, attention during the slowly paced program did not vary by sound effect condition, presumably because it was already easy to follow the flow of action of the slowly paced television program.

Summary

Taken together, the results suggest the value of sound effects and character vocalizations as a way to draw attention to key program content, thereby leading to temporal integration of key program events and comprehension of central story content. That is, sound effects and character vocalizations can help young children link and integrate important program content across transitions, fill in knowledge gaps, and understand central program content when they are viewing television programs. The effectiveness of these salient features to guide attention occurs very early in development when used with simple experimentally made video presentations. Perceptually salient audio features such as sound effects and vocalizations initially draw attention and influence learning because they elicit primitive orienting responses that later shift to purposeful attention and learning, with these same kinds of audio features now serving as a marker of important content. This salience function is especially useful for children who are age 5 or younger who have difficulty determining which content is important, particularly when viewing a dynamic story presentation. Perceptually salient audio features are also easily integrated into existing programs, making them a very cost-effective way to improve children's comprehension of televised stories.

Music and singing: Effects on children's attention and learning in multimedia experiences

As discussed earlier, Calvert and colleagues (1982) identified two ways that formal features can influence children's attention to content: through perceptually salient features (such as a high-pitched whistle) that elicit a primitive attentional orienting response; and through the *marker function*, which occurs when children associate specific auditory features with important story information—for example, learning that a recurring harp *glissando* indicates that a character has transformed into a superhero.

In an analysis of television programs designed for a preschool and grade school audience, Huston and colleagues (1981) examined the use of perceptually salient and non-salient features. Based on their analyses, they created a third cluster of features, known as *reflective*, because it provides children with opportunities to rehearse content. Singing, for example, was classified as a reflective feature because it combines repetition with language that is presented melodically rather than spoken, thereby providing opportunities to *rehearse* the content (Huston et al., 1981). Rap music, though, is an exception to this definition as it uses rhythmic language in ways that can potentially be very catchy and attention getting to audiences.

In a more recent analysis of the formal production features used in infant videos, Goodrich and colleagues (2009) found that no singing occurred in almost one-third of the productions and 60 percent had no rhyming. This finding was surprising given that reflective features such as singing were expected to be prevalent in videos designed for very young children as they provide an opportunity for repetition and rehearsal of content. The authors also expected to find perceptually salient techniques like sound effects and character vocalizations to be used just before dialogue occurred as these sounds can create attentional orienting responses to language. Indeed, sound effects often occurred when both child and male dialogue were onscreen, and character vocalizations often occurred when females were speaking to another character. Because foreground music is perceptually salient, foreground music was expected to occur more than background music that contains speech. Surprisingly, contrary to prediction, non-salient background music that contained speech was twice as prevalent as perceptually salient foreground music that had no speech. In other words, music with characters speaking in the background were found to be more prevalent in the infant videos reviewed by Goodrich and colleagues than music with no speech.

The previous discussion on the role of sound effects and vocalizations identified two ways that formal features can direct children's attention to content: (1) perceptually salient features eliciting a primitive attentional orienting response and (2) the 'marker function' described earlier. The following discussion shifts to a focus on music and singing, which will address both of these functions as well as highlight (3) 'reflective' features particularly where singing is used to support memorization and learning. As we shall see, the role of music and singing in children's engagement with multimedia is somewhat complex; the following discussion encompasses both attention and distraction effects of music, as well as the benefits and limitations of incorporating songs and singing in children's learning.

Attention and distraction effects of music for imitation tasks on video during infancy

Infants and preschoolers are more likely to look at television content when lively music is present rather than absent (Anderson & Levin, 1976), particularly when they are familiar with the music (Barr, Zack, Garcia, & Muentener, 2008). For example, Barr and colleagues (2008) showed 12-, 15-, and 18-month-old infants a portion of an episode of *Baby Mozart* from the *Baby Einstein* series or *Kids Favorite Songs 2* by Sesame Workshop and recorded their visual attention to the videos. Infants who had viewed *Baby Mozart* before looked more during musical segments than those who had no prior exposure to this series.

Audio features have been used to help call attention to the content, sometimes with disruptive outcomes. For instance, Barr and colleagues (Barr, Shuck, Salerno, Atkinson, & Linebarger, 2010) conducted an experimental study in which 6-, 12-, and 18-month-olds were exposed to a 1-minute video in which the auditory track included background music or no music. The background music was 'Clubhouse Capers.' The visual track depicted a puppet with a televised adult demonstrating key actions, such as pulling a mitten off a puppet's hand and then shaking it. Infants viewed the vignette six times. Deferred imitation was then assessed 24 hours after exposure. Infants who heard the musical track play in the background during the video presentation performed no better than the infants who had no exposure to the task at all. In other words, hearing the musical track reduced infant performance to baseline levels. When a live adult exposed infants to this same task three times with the same music in the background, infants were able to demonstrate the imitation task.

The results suggest that there was a cognitive overload when music was added to the video presentation, forcing infants to allocate scarce attentional resources to multiple tracks simultaneously without a clear signal about which content was most important. If, as Goodrich et al. (2009) found, background music is often presented with characters also speaking in the background, this may be particularly challenging for infants. The implication is that background music on videos can overload infants' and toddlers' developing cognitive systems by requiring them to simultaneously process language, music, and video images, thereby disrupting infants' skills to detect what they should be attending to. In a second related study (Barr et al., 2010), an additional vignette was created that added sound effects to accompany the music. When sound effects were added to mark the targeted actions on the musical video presentation, performance improved, but it still did not surpass a condition in which there was no music. (These challenges of cognitive load are not limited to infants and children's engagement with multimedia. See also chapters by Grimshaw, Tan, and Lipscomb; Shevy and Hung; and Roginska, in this volume, for similar implications for cognitive load in the context of video games, television advertisements, and auditory displays.)

Memorization and recitation of sequentially presented information during the preschool years

One important consideration in processing musical tracks may involve the novelty of the tune. If the music is novel, it may place more demands on memory than a familiar tune. For example, Calvert and Billingsley (1998) taught kindergarten-aged children their phone numbers by either singing or speaking the numbers in a short song. A novel tune was selected for the singing condition. Although we predicted that information that is organized sequentially, in this case a series of numbers, would be better recalled when presented in a song, we found the opposite effect. That is, young children recalled their phone numbers from a spoken presentation better than from a sung presentation. The novelty of the tune apparently impeded learning, an interpretation that is consistent with the demands placed on memory when there are multiple tracks to be processed simultaneously. That is, children had to think about the novel music as well as their phone numbers. Perhaps initially familiarizing children as well as infants with a melody may lead to better learning from music.

In another study, Calvert and Billingsley (1998) also examined how well preschoolers could recite the lyrics, recognize the central plot-relevant content, and sequence visual items after one or multiple exposures to an animated French or English version of the song 'Frère Jacques.' After multiple exposures, English-speaking preschoolers could actually recite the French version of the song better than the English version. However, only age predicted better recognition of the central content or sequencing of the visual story content with older children outperforming the younger ones on both tasks. Taken together, these experiments indicated that singing improves verbatim memory of information, but that a deeper understanding of the verbal messages presented in songs is problematic for preschoolers. Our findings support the educational practice of repeatedly exposing very young children to songs that teach verbatim memories of sequentially presented material, such as the 'ABC' song, but it calls into question the use of songs to help children understand the actual content of vignettes.

Why, though, do preschool teachers so often use songs to teach young children if the children are not really learning much beyond a rote recitation of the lyrics? Surely the teachers would have noticed? Perhaps the motor rehearsal that accompanies songs in preschools, in which children enact key actions, can help toddlers understand the meaning of a song. To test this hypothesis, Calvert and Goodman (1999) had toddlers sing several songs with an adult who either played a guitar while singing or who sang the lyrics while displaying actions that conveyed the song meaning. For instance, toddlers either sang 'I'm a Little Teapot' and tipped their bodies over as they and the adult 'poured out' the tea, or they just sang the song as an adult played it on a guitar and sang it with them. The toddlers who used enactive, body movements as ways of rehearsing the song lyrics subsequently understood the meaning of the songs better than those who simply sang them without the aid of motor rehearsal. Interestingly, one of the groups of children made up their own tea party when motor aids were not part of their condition. The implication is that the motor behaviors provided an additional modality to think about and to encode the content, which, in turn, enhanced children's understanding of the song lyrics.

Superficial processing of educational messages of sung videos from middle childhood through early adulthood

As mentioned earlier, singing is a 'reflective' feature because it allows children to rehearse the same content when the chorus is sung repeatedly (Calvert & Tart, 1993).

Singing also combines the two symbol systems of language and music (Huston et al., 1981), thereby providing dual modes to represent content. Although educators have often thought that singing is a useful way to improve learning, singing typically provides a bridge to verbatim memory, rather than to comprehension of content, even at older ages. Much of the research on this question involves a series called *Schoolhouse Rock!*, an instructional video series designed to teach children history, science, mathematics, and English. In this series, short video vignettes of approximately 3 minutes presented animated bits with singing to accentuate the message. Does exposure to these video vignettes improve children's or adults' learning?

In one of the first studies of *Schoolhouse Rock!*, Calvert and Tart (1993) examined the Preamble to the Constitution, a part of the history rock vignettes that were originally televised and later presented as videos. Two versions of the video were created: one involved the original video, and the other involved a spoken rather than a sung version that was dubbed onto the original video track. College students then heard the Preamble several times in either spoken or sung conditions. After exposure was completed, immediate and then very long-term recall of the words to the Preamble was assessed. Verbatim memory of the exact temporal order of the Preamble was better for those who had been exposed repeatedly to the sung rather than to the spoken version of the vignette. The results linked repeated exposure to a sung vignette to both very good short-term and long-term memory of words, implicating singing as a way to improve verbatim memory of scholastic tasks. Even so, students at times mixed up the words, and hence the meanings, of the passages. For instance, one college student wrote 'to ensure the blessings of liberty to ourselves and our *prosperity*' instead of '... our *posterity*.' Thus, it was unclear if processing of songs was any deeper than a rote recitation of the content. This finding is consistent with Craik and Lockhart's (1972) levels of processing theory in which they argue that some information is processed at a relatively superficial level at the expense of a deeper integration of the content with existing information in memory. In our case, students may have been processing songs at a relatively superficial phonic level without thinking about the meaning of the lyrics that they were hearing.

In two subsequent experiments (Calvert, 2001), the role of two additional *Schoolhouse Rock!* videos on children's memory was examined. The first involved 'The Shot Heard Round the World,' a *Schoolhouse Rock!* history vignette about the start of the American Revolution, to shed light on whether children actually understand the information embedded in songs. In this study, the use of a visual or a nonvisual track was manipulated with an audio track that was sung or spoken. Second grade children and college students were exposed to the vignette one time. Contrary to prediction, children recognized information, as assessed by multiple-choice items, better when it was presented as a spoken track rather than as the original sung track.

'I'm Just a Bill,' another *Schoolhouse Rock!* video vignette, depicted the process of how a bill becomes a law in the United States. Using a narrative, the bill, who is depicted as an animated piece of paper with writing on it, tells his story to a young animated boy. In the second experiment, this vignette was shown in its original form to 3rd graders and college students and manipulated whether students viewed the vignette repeatedly (four exposures over a period of 2 weeks) or viewed it only once (Calvert, 2001). Verbatim word-for-word recall, verbal sequencing of how a bill becomes a law, and assessment for recognition of important educational content (as indexed by a multiple-choice recognition test), took place immediately after the last exposure. Repeated exposure increased children's and adults' verbatim recall of the sung material and their verbal sequencing of the steps required for a bill to become a law. Thus, songs improved memory of material that follows a sequential pattern. However, repetition did not improve children's or adults' recognition of multiple choice items that assessed their memory of important story content. When asked what a bill was, one child said that a bill was 'something that you pay' and another said that a bill was 'a piece of paper with writing on it.'

Repetition again emerged as a key reason that 2nd graders learned science information from a *Schoolhouse Rock!* video episode about 'Interplanet Janet,' a vignette that conveyed information about the solar system. Kotler and Wright (1998) exposed groups of children to a spoken or a sung version of this video either two or four times and compared their performance to a control group. Those who viewed the video four times in either the spoken or sung conditions remembered more conceptual information about the solar system than those who saw the video only twice, who in turn, remembered more information than those who had no exposure to the video at all. Thus, spoken and sung exposures had similar effects on memory in this study.

Morton and Trehub (2007) found support for both content and form when interpreting the emotional connotations of songs. Children who were ages 5 and 10 years and adults listened to music that conveyed emotion through cues such as tempo and vocal tone. Some of the music had lyrics that were consistent with the emotions of the song whereas others had nonsense lyrics. Songs were then judged as being happy or sad based on the feelings expressed by the singer's voice. Emotions were judged correctly when they were conveyed by nonsense lyrics, suggesting that children and adults alike understand performance cues. These findings are consistent with a 'level of processing' framework in which lyrics are processed at a superficial phonic level rather than at a deeper level of understanding (Craik & Lockhart, 1972). However, when real lyrics were part of the audio track, children relied more on the lyrics for judging emotion, but adults continued to rely on cues such as tempo and vocal tone for judging emotion. Because children and adults had been asked to make judgments about emotional feelings based on the sound of the singer's voice, adults' decisions were in keeping with directions.

However, these findings do not mean that listeners do not attend to the meaning of any of the lyrics that they hear. Although adolescents say that they choose their favorite songs based on the sound, the lyrics are also an important reason that many of them report liking certain songs (Roberts & Christenson, 2001). For example, approximately 17 percent of 12- to 18-year-old males and almost 25 percent of females report that their favorite song has lyrics that express how they feel (Rosenbaum & Prinsky, 1987). Youth who listen to the musical lyrics the closest report that they tend to do so because music is important to them, or because the lyrics are controversial (Christenson & Roberts, 1998).

Distraction effects of multitasking on middle-aged adults memory and high school students' homework performance

Basic research about the role of listening to music on short-term memory sheds light on the role that music may play on multitasking, such as studying while listening to music or completing homework assignments in front of the television. As mentioned earlier, almost three-quarters of 7th to 12th graders reported multitasking while listening to music (Rideout et al., 2010). In a series of experiments that used a variety of musical excerpts on memory, researchers Salamé and Baddeley (1989) examined the role of vocal music, instrumental music, silence, and 'pink' noise on college students' through middle-aged people's immediate memory of nine visually presented digits. Overall, vocal music impaired short-term memory the most. Instrumental music also disrupted short-term memory, but not as much as vocal music did. Silence and 'pink' noise, the latter being non-speech sounds presented at the same amplitude, were least disruptive to short-term memory. The authors argued that working memory involves a detection system that could involve positive or negative filters. In the case of a negative filter, the acoustic system may allow certain sounds to pass through while screening out others, much like a coffee filter stops the coffee grinds from passing through the filter, but not the actual liquid. Thus, speech passes through the filtering system more readily than uninformative noises. Alternatively, in the case of a positive filter, the acoustic system could privilege certain information over others, such that it is sensitive to language. In either case, memory would involve a detection and storage system that is preferentially responsive to speech or speech-like sounds.

When background television programs are played while 8th graders are doing their homework, performance is disrupted on memorization tasks as well as on paper and pencil assignments, but audio presentations did not disrupt performance (Pool, Koolstra, & van der Voort, 2003a; Pool, Koolstra, & van der Voort, 2003b). The implication of this research is that watching television programs disrupts homework assignments, in part because youth watch the programs instead of concentrating on the homework task. However, music appears to have differential effects, with background music often yielding no disruptive effect, but with vocal music interfering with homework performance, perhaps because listeners may be distracted when the music and the homework assignment require verbal processing of language, thereby creating an interference effect.

Summary

Taken together, the findings suggest that singing provides an excellent and durable way to rehearse and remember content in a verbatim form and is also an important vehicle for conveying mood. However, if the goal is to improve comprehension of the message, speaking the same content instead of singing it is the most consistent approach for improving comprehension. These findings support Craik and Lockhart's (1972) levels of processing theory in which content can be processed at a superficial level without a deeper understanding of the meaning of that content. It appears that singing, unless accompanied by enactive rehearsal techniques where children act out the meaning of the content of songs, such as 'I'm a Little Teapot,' tends to be a superficial learning technique, whereas the use of language without singing is more likely to receive deeper processing.

Singing, then, can enhance learning, but it is best suited for tasks that involve verbatim memory or sequencing that is sensitive to the order of material. Although songs are very durable memories, a challenge for learning from songs is to get children and even adults to go beyond the surface and dig deeper for meaning. Because songs provide such an efficient structure for remembering the associated linguistic content, it is possible for youth to process the content at any time, given that the specific words, of course, were coded accurately in the first place. There is also a substantial minority of youth who do pay close attention to musical lyrics. Because vocal music and television content can disrupt short-term memory of verbal content as well as homework performance during multitasking, listening to vocal music or watching television should be minimized when doing homework assignments, particularly for complex tasks. Consistent with this thesis, background music played during a video also disrupts relatively simple imitation tasks by overloading the limited cognitive resources that infants bring to a viewing situation.

Youth, digital communications, and digital creations

The 21st century increasingly offers youth opportunities to navigate the Internet and to make digital productions rather than just consume the productions of others. Most youth are now 'digital natives,' a term coined to reflect the ease with which they traverse and understand the digital landscape because they have used digital media throughout much of their development (Prensky, 2001). For instance, youth often send information to one another through the Internet. Among teens who use instant messaging, 31 percent reported sending music or video files (Lenhart, Madden, & Hitlin, 2005). Forty-three percent of online teens also make purchases online, such as music (Lenhart et al., 2005), though many youth also go to sites where they can download music for free, violating copyright laws in the process.

Certain kinds of music are integral to adolescent identity expression, reflecting the broader cultural influences in which they live. In a study of the social networking site Facebook conducted by Pempek, Yermolayeva, and Calvert (2009), more than 64 percent of college students included their favorite music in their profile information, which is the place where people share personal information about themselves. Of the sixty-four percent of students who included their favorite music in their profile information, 65 percent of those students indicated that they did so because it was important information that expressed 'who I am.' In fact, media preferences were more likely to be reported in user profile information and to be selected as integral to identity than were traditional identity markers such as religion or political views (Erikson, 1963).

Technological advances offer youth opportunities to be more than just consumers of multimedia but to also take part as producers of their own digital creations. The multimedia creations of 'digital natives' reflect a remarkable level of 'multimodal literacy.' In an innovative study, Wingstedt, Brändström, and Berg (2008) gave young adolescents (aged 12 to 13 years) some pieces of music and asked them to shape the music to fit three short three-dimensional animated films in real time, as they viewed the animations. The seven musical parameters the participants were able to control and adapt (using REMUPP software) were instrumentation, tempo, harmonic complexity, rhythmic complexity, register, articulation, and reverberation level. A high level of agreement was found among 23 young adolescents' creations in their use of these parameters to fit the visual scenes, reflecting a shared knowledge of musical narrative codes and conventions most likely absorbed through exposure to films, music videos, computer games, and other narrative multimedia.

Rap music is a preferred genre among African American adolescents (Roberts et al., 2005) that reflects a larger hip-hop culture. Since African American youth often listen to rap music and view music videos (Ward et al., 2009), music may be a major focus of the media content that these adolescents not only view, but also create. Do the production features of music videos also find their way into digital productions made by minority youth?

To answer this question, Baker, Staiano, and Calvert (2011) examined the digital creations made by twenty-four African American adolescents who were attending a college preparatory summer program at Georgetown University, which is located in Washington, DC. This procedure allowed adolescents even more creative freedom than in the Wingstedt et al. (2008) study. Students were taught basic film editing techniques and then given a camera to take pictures about their summer experiences on campus. The students then edited and integrated those pictures into a visual narrative that included audio material. Because adolescents spend a considerable amount of time watching music videos (Ward et al., 2009), students were expected to use formal features such as songs and foreground music with no background dialogue in their digital productions. Students' digital productions included one to four songs, averaging 1.5 songs per production. Consistent with previous literature (Roberts et al., 2005), African American youth included rap music the most in their productions (37.5 percent), but there was considerable musical variety. Specifically, about 29 percent of these students used pop, 21 percent used rock, and 13 percent used rhythm and blues music in their productions. Perceptually salient foreground music, in which there was no accompanying speech, was used more than non-salient background music that included speech on top of the musical track. These findings suggest that African American students copy the popular music video formats that they listen to and watch, integrating that style into their own digital productions to make original content. The implication is that the forms that are viewed of others' lives can become an integral part of creative expression when applied to one's own life experiences.

Future research directions

Over 20 years ago, Kastner and Crowder (1990) argued that developmental and cross-cultural research were key areas to explore in order to unravel the genetic and environmental contributions between certain musical tones and feelings. Nevertheless, the extant literature on a variety of developmental and cultural issues about music remain somewhat of a mystery. One promising research area involves when and how children begin to interpret different kinds of music, and how that understanding changes with age. The use of multiple symbol systems can either enhance, or detract from, learning the content embedded in multimedia presentations that involve singing, foreground music, background music, language, visual images, sound effects, text, and non-speech vocalizations. When do overlapping symbol systems assist learning, and when do they create an overload in information processing activities? Why do children and adults so often stay on the surface when listening to the lyrics of a song, and what prompts them to dig deeper for meaning? How does using media with different kinds of music affect academic performance, such as homework assignments, and does performance vary depending on the kind and the complexity of the task?

It may also be the case that older children could benefit from interventions used with younger children when the content is more complex. For instance, could sound effects assist comprehension during middle childhood if children are watching a program intended for an adult audience? Cross-cultural research of children at different points in development could also be a promising research direction to unravel universal relations of music and other auditory attributes on developmental outcomes.

Another promising research direction involves an examination of the kinds of digital products children and youth make, and how those products reflect important parts of their lives. Although media interfaces have rapidly evolved, the developmental needs of children are much more stable. For instance, children create identities that are reflected in their digital products (e.g., as reviewed earlier in the study by Baker et al., 2011). Do different age groups create other products that reflect who they are and what their needs are, using the rich symbol systems of media to convey that sense of self?

Better understanding is needed about why some children and youth listen to certain kinds of songs and music to alter depressed moods, and why others listen to music to sustain depressed moods. According to mood-management theory, individuals organize their environments to diminish bad moods, to change bad moods to good ones, and to sustain and accentuate good moods (Zillmann & Gan, 1997). Therefore, if music can be used to change a mood when a teen feels unhappy, is it functional to accentuate and sustain an unhappy mood? If so, why? What are the underlying motivations that lead different youth to use music in disparate ways?

Finally, what role does silence play in the 21st century? Youth are constantly wired to electronic media, often listening to music during their adolescent years (Rideout et al., 2010). Is quiet time when reflection takes place being lost in the process, and if so, what else is being lost—perhaps the imaginative activity that flourishes during times of reflection (Valkenburg & Calvert, 2012)?

Conclusions

Audiovisual media now permeate the landscape of symbolic communication, with rich musical and other attention-getting audio features accompanying and accentuating the visual images, and shaping their understanding of the unfolding story. While music and songs provide an additional structure and modality for thinking about and rehearsing television and video content, they can also overload infants', children's, and even adolescents' information processing systems if they do not tightly overlap with and map onto the visual and thematic messages that they are meant to convey. Music also sets the stage for interpreting character feelings, and for thinking about the underlying motives that inspire and that motivate characters to act. These important functions make it important for educators, film-makers, and musicians alike to employ production practices that enhance learning by linking the emotions and the arousal that are elicited by auditory features to the messages that listener-viewers are meant to take away. Twenty-first century youth may not wait for adults to implement these practices, instead creating their own digital creations to represent their realities.

Acknowledgments

Support for this project was provided by Grant #0126014 from the National Science Foundation to Sandra L. Calvert. I also thank Brian Borromeo and Margaret Girard for their assistance.

References

Anderson, D. R., & Levin, S. R. (1976). Young children's attention to 'Sesame Street.' *Child Development, 47*, 806–811.

Baker, C. M., Staiano, A. E., & Calvert, S. L. (2011). Digital expression among urban, low-income African American adolescents. *Journal of Black Studies, 42*, 530–547.

Bangerter, A., & Heath, C. (2004). The Mozart effect: Tracking the evolution of a scientific legend. *British Journal of Social Psychology, 43*, 605–623.

Barr, R. F., Shuck, L., Salerno, K., Atkinson, E., & Linebarger, D. L. (2010). Music interferes with learning during infancy. *Infant and Child Development, 19*, 313–331.

Barr, R. F., Wyss, N., & Somander, M. (2009). The influence of electronic sound effects on learning from televised and live models. *Journal of Experimental Child Psychology, 103*, 1–16.

Barr, R. F., Zack, E., Garcia, A., & Muentener, P. (2008). Infants' attention and responsiveness to television increases with prior exposure and parental interaction. *Infancy, 13*, 30–56.

Berlyne, D. E. (1960). *Conflict, arousal, and curiosity*. New York, NY: McGraw Hill.

Calvert, S. L. (2001). Impact of televised songs on children's and young adults' memory of educational content. *Media Psychology, 3*, 325–342.

Calvert, S. L., & Billingsley, R. L. (1998) Young children's recitation and comprehension of information presented by songs. *Journal of Applied Developmental Psychology, 19*, 97–108.

Calvert, S. L., & Gersh, T. L. (1987). The selective use of sound effects and visual inserts for children's television story comprehension. *Journal of Applied Developmental Psychology, 8*, 363–375.

Calvert, S. L., & Goodman, T. (1999, April). *Enactive rehearsal for young children's comprehension of songs*. Poster presented at the biennial meeting of the Society for Research in Child Development, Albuquerque, NM.

Calvert, S. L., Huston, A. C., Watkins, B. A., & Wright, J. C. (1982). The relation between selective attention to television forms and children's comprehension of content. *Child Development, 53*, 601–610.

Calvert, S. L., & Scott, M. C. (1989). Sound effects for children's temporal integration of fast-paced television content. *Journal of Broadcasting and Electronic Media, 33*, 233–246.

Calvert, S. L. & Tart, M. (1993). Song versus verbal forms for very long-term, long-term, and short-term verbatim recall. *Journal of Applied Developmental Psychology, 14*, 245–260.

Carroll, R., Silbergleid, M., Beachum, C., Perry, S., Pluscht, P., & Pescatore, M. (1993). Meanings of radio to teenagers in a niche-programming era. *Journal of Broadcasting and Electronic Media, 37*, 159–176.

Christenson, P. G. (1994). Childhood patterns of music use and preferences. *Communication Reports, 7*, 136–144.

Christenson, P. G., & Roberts, D. F. (1998). *It's not only rock and roll: Popular music in the lives of adolescents*. Cresskill, NY: Hampton Press.

Craik, F., & Lockhart, R. S. (1972). Levels of processing: A framework for memory research. *Journal of Verbal Learning and Verbal Behavior, 11*, 521–533.

Erikson, E. H. (1963). *Childhood and society.* New York, NY: Norton.

Geringer, J., Cassidy, J., & Byo, J. (1996). Effects of music with video on responses of nonmusic majors: An exploratory study. *Journal of Research in Music Education, 44*, 240–251.

Geringer, J., Cassidy, J., & Byo, J. (1997). Nonmusic majors' cognitive and affective responses to performance and programmatic music videos. *Journal of Research in Music Education, 45*, 221–233.

Gola, A. A., Kirkorian, H. L., Perez, M., Anderson, D. R., & Calvert, S. L. (2011, May). *Attention-eliciting versus attention-maintaining formal features of infant DVDs.* Virtual presentation at the International Communication Association, Boston, MA.

Goodrich, S., Pempek, T., & Calvert, S. L. (2009). Formal production features in infant programming. *Archives of Pediatrics and Adolescent Medicine, 163*(12), 1151–1156.

Husain, G., Thompson, W. F., & Schellenberg, E. G. (2002). Effects of musical tempo and mode on arousal, mood, and spatial abilities. *Music Perception, 20*, 151–171.

Huston, A. C., & Wright, J. C. (1983). Children's processing of television: The informative functions of formal features. In J. Bryant & D. R. Anderson (Eds.), *Children's understanding of television: Research on attention and comprehension* (pp. 35–68). New York, NY: Academic.

Huston, A. C., Wright J. C., Wartella, E. A., Rice, M. L., Watkins, B. A., Campbell, T., ***et al.*** (1981). Communication more that content: Formal features of children's television programs. *Journal of Communication, 31*, 32–48.

Kastner, M. P., & Crowder, R. G. (1990). Perception of the major/minor distinction: IV, emotional connotations in young children. *Music perception: An Interdisciplinary Journal, 8*, 189–201.

Kotler, J. A., & Wright, J. C. (1998, March). *Effects of song versus prose on verbatim and conceptual recall: Does schoolhouse need to rock?* Poster presented at the biennial meeting of the Southwestern Society for Research in Human Development, Galveston, TX.

Larson, R., Kubey, R., & Colletti, J. (1989). Changing channels: early adolescent media choices and shifting investments in family and friends. *Journal of Youth and Adolescence, 18*, 583–589.

Lenhart, A., Ling, R., Campbell, S., & Purcell, K. (2010). *Teens and mobile phones.* Washington, DC: Pew Internet and American Life Project.

Lenhart, A., Madden, M., & Hitlin, P. (2005). *Teens and technology.* Washington, DC: Pew Internet and American Life Project.

Morton, J. B., & Trehub, S.E. (2007). Children's judgements of emotion in song. *Psychology of Music.* Retrieved from <http://www.sagepub.com/evansmprstudy/articles/Chapter04_Article01.pdf> (accessed March 7, 2011).

Nakata, T., & Trehub, S. (2004). Infants' responsiveness to maternal speech and singing. *Infant Behavior and Development, 27*, 455–464.

Nawrot, E. S. (2003). The perception of emotional expression in music: evidence from infants, children, and adults. *Psychology of Music, 31*, 75–92.

Pempek, T., Yermolayeva, Y., & Calvert, S. L. (2009). College students social networking experiences on Facebook. *Journal of Applied Developmental Psychology, 30*, 227–238.

Pool, M., Koolstra, C., & van der Voort, T. (2003a). Distraction effects of background soap operas on homework performance: An experimental study enriched with observational data. *Educational Psychology, 23*, 361–380.

Pool, M., Koolstra, C., & van der Voort, T. (2003b). The impact of background radio and television on high school students' homework performance. *Journal of Communication*, *53*, 74–87.

Prensky, M. (2001). Digital natives, digital immigrants. *On the Horizon*, *9*, 1–6.

Rauscher, F. H. (2009). The impact of music instruction on other skills. In S. Hallam, I. Cross, & M. Thaut (Eds). *The Oxford handbook of music psychology* (pp. 244–252). New York, NY: Oxford University Press.

Rauscher, F. H., & Shaw, G. L. (1998). Key components of the 'Mozart effect.' *Perceptual and Motor Skills*, *86*, 835–841.

Rauscher, F. H., Shaw, G. L., & Ky, K. N. (1993). Music and spatial task performance. *Nature*, *365*, 611.

Rideout, V. J., Foehr, U. G., & Roberts, D. F. (2010). *Generation M2: Media in the lives of 8–18 year-olds.* Menlo Park, CA: The Henry J. Kaiser Family Foundation.

Rideout, V., & Hamel, E. (2006). *The media family: Electronic media in the lives of infants, toddlers, preschoolers and their parents.* Menlo Park, CA: The Henry J. Kaiser Family Foundation.

Roberts, D. F., & Christenson, P. G. (2001). Popular music in childhood and adolescence. In D. Singer & J. Singer (Eds.), *Handbook of children and the media* (pp. 395–413). Thousand Oaks, CA: Sage.

Roberts, D. F., Foehr, U. G., & Rideout, V. (2005). *Generation M: Media in the lives of 8–18 year-olds.* Menlo Park, CA: The Henry J. Kaiser Family Foundation. Retrieved from <http://kff.org/entmedia/7251.cfm>.

Roberts, D. F., Foehr, U. G., Rideout, V., & Brodie, M. (1999). *Kids and media at the new millennium.* Menlo Park, CA: The Henry J. Kaiser Family Foundation.

Rosenbaum, J., & Prinsky, L. (1987). Sex, violence, and rock 'n' roll: Youths' perception of popular music. *Popular Music and Society*, *11*, 79–89.

Salamé, P., & Baddeley, A. D. (1989). Effects of background music on phonological short-term memory. *Quarterly Journal of Experimental Psychology A: Human Experimental Psychology*, *41*, 107–122.

Shenfeld, T., Trehub, S. E., & Nakata, T. (2003). Maternal singing modulates infant arousal. *Psychology of Music*, *31*, 365–375.

Steele, K. M., Bass, K. E., & Crook, M. D. (1999). The mystery of the Mozart effect: failure to replicate. *Psychological Science*, *10*, 366–369.

Sun, S., & Lull, J. (1986). The adolescent audience for music videos and why they watch. *Journal of Communication*, *36*, 115–125.

Valkenburg, P. M., & Calvert, S. L. (2012). Television and the child's developing imagination. In D. Singer & J. Singer (Eds.), *Handbook of children and the media* (2nd ed., pp. 157–170). Thousand Oaks, CA: Sage.

Ward, L. M., Hansbrough, E., & Walker, E. (2009). Contributions of music video exposure to Black adolescents gender and sexual schemas. *Journal of Adolescent Research*, *20*, 143–166.

Wingstedt, J., Brändström, S., & Berg, J. (2008). Young adolescents' usage of narrative functions of media music by manipulation of musical expression. *Psychology of Music*, *36*(2), 193–214.

Wright, J. C., Huston, A. C., Ross, R. P., Calvert, S. L., Rollandeli, D., Weeks, L. A., *et al.* (1984). Pace and continuity of television programs: Effects on children's attention and comprehension. *Developmental Psychology*, *20*, 653–666.

Zajonc, R. B. (1968). Attitudinal effects of mere exposure. *Journal of Personality and Social Psychology Monograph Supplement*, *9*(2, Part 2), 1–27.

Zillmann, D., & Gan, S. -L. (1997). Musical taste in adolescence. In D. J. Hargreaves & A. C. North (Eds.), *The social psychology of music* (pp. 161–187). Oxford, UK: Oxford University Press.

Zillmann, D., & Mundorf, N. (1987). Image effects in the appreciation of video rock. *Communication Research*, *14*, 316–334.

Chapter 13

Playing with sound: The role of music and sound effects in gaming

Mark Grimshaw,[a] Siu-Lan Tan,[b] and Scott D. Lipscomb[c]

[a]Aalborg University, Denmark; [b]Kalamazoo College, USA; [c]University of Minnesota, USA

The role of sound in gaming has evolved since the early 1970s, heavily influenced by developing technologies associated with audio, video, and data storage. Until 1971, early computer games had no sound. *Tennis for Two* (Higinbotham, 1958) and *Spacewar!* (Russell, Graetz, & Witaenem, 1962)—both contenders for the title of the world's first computer game—were silent, as was the first home gaming console, the Magnavox Odyssey (1972). Nutting Associates' *Computer Space* (Bushnell & Dabney, 1971) and Atari's *Pong* (Alcorn, 1972), both arcade games, were the first to feature sound—*Pong*'s synthesized beep when ball meets paddle rapidly became iconic. Looking back on almost 40 years of development in music and sound in gaming, one can closely match the style, density, and richness of the music and sound to the development of faster computer chips, larger amounts of random access memory (RAM), and the increasing capacity of digital storage media. Equally, throughout that period, players have been enjoying—and demanding—more emotive musical scores and realistic and/or immersive sound environments, and much of the empirical work that we detail in this chapter is directed toward understanding, and therefore potentially improving, the player's engagement with game sound and interaction with the gaming experience.

This chapter examines the wide variety of roles for sound and music in computer games. The first section provides the context for empirical research in the field through an exploration of game sound technology and theory. The development of game sound technology is discussed in the context of player interaction with the gameworld; the technology dictates what can be achieved, and what is achieved has significance for the player's relationship to the gameworld. We then focus on the role of sound in the game as analyzed or proposed by various game sound theorists; the empirical researcher should have knowledge of the function and practice of game sound, since the ideas emerging from theoretical exploration very often provide the impetus for empirical studies. The second section provides an overview of the empirical studies at the heart of the chapter. We first outline studies on the effects of game sound on player performance before looking at physiological effects and subjective measures as they relate to player experience.

Throughout the chapter, the terms 'game' and 'gaming' refer to computer games and the act of playing them and, by 'computer games' we include all forms of digital games or video games running on platforms from arcade, casino video lottery terminals, and virtual reality machines to desktop and laptop computers to video consoles and handheld devices. However, where necessary to indicate the precise game system used in various empirical studies, we have incorporated the terms used by those studies. We employ the term 'gameworld' to limit our discussion to game sound deriving from 'the contained universe or environment designed for play in which actions and events take place' (Jørgensen, 2011, p. 89) rather than the wider palette of sounds (e.g., chat during gameplay) sometimes present in the gamespace (Droumeva, 2011). The term 'game sound' should be taken to include sound effects (e.g. gunshots, footsteps, and ambient sounds) and music but, where the distinction is required, this is explicitly made.

Evolving technologies associated with game sound

The developmental trajectory of audio technology and consequent improved quality and inherent potential of game sound parallel that for game graphics. Technological advances have allowed graphics to progress from two-dimensional, static vector graphics (still useful for some platforms and game types) to the inclusion of full-motion video (FMV), the illusion of three-dimensional (3D) spaces and character animation approaching the quality of that found in modern blockbuster animated films like *Toy Story 3* (Unkrich, 2010) or *How to Train Your Dragon* (Sanders & DeBlois, 2010). Similarly, game sound has progressed from simple, synthesized beeps and one- or two-line melodies utilizing a low-level, hardware-based sound generation process, to stored MIDI tracks incorporating richer, multilayer polyphony, then to the use of actual digital recordings of sound effects and music (audio samples).

At the time of this chapter's publication, many computer games employ composers who produce high-quality, lavishly arranged, and impeccably recorded compositions. In the 1990s, in addition to sound effects and specially-composed MIDI tracks, game music could present the latest chart hits. For example, *Wipeout* (Psygnosis, 1995/1996) included tracks from a range of electronica artists. Other games such as the *Final Fantasy* series (Square Enix, 1987–2010) include thematically rich scores that, as technology improved, have been composed, arranged, and recorded to meet the same exacting standards as film scores for mainstream cinema.

In terms of interaction—a notion highly relevant to any discussion of the role of music and sound in games—it is important to note the role of rapidly advancing technology in promoting different levels of player engagement. The beeps of *Pong* were produced by real-time synthesis; that is, the game's video hardware included a sync generator that provided the required frequency and loudness of the beep each time it was required. As game hardware developed, dedicated tone generators were added, allowing for more complex tones and greater polyphony in both music and sound effects. Although audio samples had been utilized alongside real-time synthesis as MIDI soundcards became a standard part of PCs in the late 1980s, from the early 1990s, the use of audio samples for gaming dramatically increased, to the detriment of synthesis, thanks in large part to the development of the compact disc (CD) and its relatively large storage capacity. This resulted in a significant shift, not only in the technological basis of sound and music, but also in the relationship between sound and player.

Prior to the inclusion of audio samples, game developers had realized that the player develops an interactive relationship with both sound effects and music. An early example, as Collins (2005) points out, was *Space Invaders* (Taito, 1978), with its rhythmically driving, repetitive background score, increasing in tempo the longer gameplay continues uninterrupted. Such a close tracking of the gamer's performance by the music became more tenuous once music of greater complexity and length was recorded onto and played from large capacity storage media such as CD. The genre of music games retains this intimate and reactive musical bond (e.g., *Rez* (United Game Artists, 2001) and *Aurifi* (Four Door Lemon, 2010)); but other genres, following the trend of increasing differentiation between music soundtrack and sound effects, have largely relegated music to background accompaniment that can often be turned off by the player (*Quake III Arena* (id Software, 1999) or *Lord of the Rings: The Two Towers* (Stormfront Studios & Hypnos Entertainment, 2002), for example).

Current immersive games utilize a palette of hundreds, if not thousands, of audio samples, often using digital processing in real time (such as reverberation, echo, filtering) to match the acoustical properties of the visual space displayed on screen. This audio manipulation results in rich and immersive soundscapes of a variety and complexity well beyond that accessible to early game sound pioneers.

CDs—and, more recently, DVDs and Blu-ray[1]—have limited storage capacity, only a portion of which can be devoted to audio samples. Thus, the game sound designer is required to provide just a few audio samples of each sound effect (e.g., footsteps or gunshots). Since the mid-2000s, computer processing power has allowed such samples to be further processed in real time to provide greater variety. The *Source* audio engine (Valve, 2004a), incorporated into several first-person shooter games, including *Half-Life 2* (Valve, 2004b), processes audio samples according to the spaces and materials depicted on screen. Indeed, both controlled studies and surveys show that realistic sound effects and high sound quality are very important to the enjoyment of a game (Skalski & Whitbred, 2010; Wood, Griffiths, Chappell, & Davies, 2004).

Increased computer processing power has the potential to end the dominance of audio samples within the genres relying upon them, allowing their replacement by a return to real-time sound synthesis, albeit a more advanced form of this sound generation process than was previously possible. Computationally intensive procedural audio techniques, for example, provide a form of sound synthesis that has the potential to produce more authentic sounds than traditional analogue or digital forms of synthesis (see Farnell, 2011). The precision accorded to each footstep can be synthesized quite precisely according to specific characteristics of the game character (e.g., weight, gait, and clothing), the ground surface, and acoustic space. This recent form of sound synthesis requires only a fraction of the storage space associated with a single audio sample file, let alone the hundreds or thousands of files typically required to produce the same variety and intimacy with the character and associated behaviors.

Of equal interest are the possibilities offered by current consumer biofeedback devices such as the Emotiv Epoc headset. Such devices monitor the player's physiological responses through methods such as electroencephalography or electromyography, although they have yet to achieve widespread use in gaming. Their potential lies in the possibility to combine the data they generate with the real-time sound synthesis and processing techniques outlined earlier in order to create sounds that more immediately impact the player's responses and emotions or to increase the perceived level of immersion. For instance, the tempo (pace) and loudness of music may accelerate with increasing heart rate or tightened grip on the remote. Empirical research directed toward this topic is at an early stage and must deal with problems such as how to map sound parameters to physiological data or how to assess biofeedback data as representative of a range of affect beyond mere arousal and valence. (Readers are referred to Garner, Grimshaw, & Abdel Nabi, 2010 and Garner & Grimshaw, 2011, for preliminary studies and a mapping strategy.)

In the following section, we briefly analyze the role of sound in computer games dealing first with sound effects, then music. The relationship between sound and player action is discussed as is the role of sound in contributing to player immersion in the gameworld. Approaches to the composition of computer game music are explored as well as the role of music in the special case of music games.

Sound design for computer games

Much of the theorizing about the role of sound and consequent practice of sound design in games derives from theory and practice in cinema. Typically, however, cinema is not an interactive medium in the way that games are at their very essence; the auditory component of gaming constitutes an important aspect of the interactivity established between player and game. Our discussion will begin with a focus on modern *first-person shooter* (FPS) games, but we will also expand the scope to music games (where the explicit purpose of the game is music-making), racing games, *role playing games* (RPGs), and other game genres.

Sound effects

FPS games are replete with human or humanoid characters and other beings, sophisticated weaponry and vehicles, and a visual premise that presents the player with a first-person perspective on the gameworld. Consequently, the player's action in firing a rifle, clutched in the character's hands that recede into the game's 3D perspective, produces not only the visual effect of the gun firing and the projectile hitting the target, but also a variety of sound effects. The number and nature of such sounds are dependent upon the strictures of the game system's software and hardware and on the choices of the sound designer(s). They might include the explosion of the projectile as it leaves the barrel, the impact sound (often accompanied by cries of pain from the target), the sound of empty cartridges clattering on the ground, and the sound of the gun's mechanism loading another round. Similarly, the opening and shutting of doors, smashing of windows by the player, and movement across various ground surfaces are all examples of player initiated actions in which the sound effects produced are appropriate to the visual depiction of action. In the context of the FPS gameworld, such sounds are indexed directly to the player's actions, resulting in a raw interactivity that is at the heart of the relationship between player and game sound.

Sound also supports and is part of the *mise-en-scène*[2] of the gameworld. In *Medal of Honor: Operation Anaconda* (Danger Close, 2010), an Afghanistan-based FPS, visual artifacts such as weapons and vehicles are modeled according to the game's historical premise. The sounds accompanying such artifacts tend to be authentic recordings of the real-world objects in use. In games like the *Quake* and *Doom* series, sound designers must use their imaginations to create sound effects associated with futuristic weaponry and teleporters that, like the technique used in science fiction films, retain a level of indexicality to the source or activity. Sound effects also greatly facilitate the realistic representation of the visual spaces through which the player navigates. Visual three-dimensionality is an illusion on the two-dimensional screen, and sound reverberation of the appropriate decay and timbral quality can serve to position the player in a resonant, cavernous space or a small, metallic chamber to provide a couple of specific examples.

The activity of other inhabitants of the gameworld—either automated, non-player characters, or characters controlled by other players in a multiplayer game—is signified by sound. As part of the 'hunter and the hunted' premise of the FPS game, this indication of activity is of particular importance. Whether playing as part of a team or as an individual fighting alone, the player must be attentive to sounds cueing the presence of friend or foe and to sounds marking the effects of their actions. Close temporal coupling between a character's action and sound effects is, therefore, very important to gameplay. Young and Nguyen (2009) showed that delaying the time between seeing an enemy firing a weapon and the resulting sound of an explosion decreased participants' accuracy in identifying which of three enemies had caused the explosion. For delays of 2 seconds, players' accuracy often fell below chance level. Interestingly, performance was not diminished when delay intervals varied with respect to duration and, sometimes, even improved when the delay intervals were irregular. Gamers seem to respond to events in virtual worlds more like they do in the unpredictable 'real world' than in the structured context of a laboratory where variables can be uniformly manipulated.

Equally important is the location of the sound. Whereas the visual gameworld exists only directly in front of the player—presented on the screen that itself occupies only a small part of the player's visual field—FPS game sound is designed to be omnipresent, enveloping the player and providing locational cues not only to activities that take place on the screen but also to the side and behind the player.[3] This is particularly the case when the player is using stereo headphones at a sound level of sufficient intensity to monopolize the sense of hearing. Even when simply watching a short video clip, participants report having a greater sense of being 'present' in the virtual world when the sound is presented through headphones rather than via loudspeakers (Bracken, Pettey, Guha, & Rubenking, 2010). Further, playing a video game with the sound played on a 5.1 surround sound system heightens a player's sense of presence in the 'world' created by the game more than sound directed through stereo loudspeakers (Skalski & Whitbred, 2010).

Sound also represents an avenue for making interactive games more inclusive and accessible by enabling the creation of sound-based versions of popular games such as *AudioBattleship* (Sánchez, 2005) and *AudioDoom* (Merabet & Sánchez, 2009), that can be played without visual feedback, or 'hands-free' computer games using a 'camera-mouse' controlled by head movements and guided by verbal and nonverbal sound cues (Evreinova, Evreinov, & Raisamo, 2008). For instance, *AudioDoom* (loosely based on the popular FPS *DOOM* (id Software, 1993) employs sound cues—such as continuous footsteps and knocking—to provide contextual spatial information to navigate a virtual space, enabling blind or sighted individuals to play this FPS game without visual cues.[4]

A significant amount of research has focused on player immersion in virtual worlds, and FPS games—in which the player is first-person auditor—are particularly fertile ground for such study. Immersion is an elusive concept with a number of competing models and frameworks concerning how to define it and how it occurs. For a more complete discussion of this topic, the reader is directed to Calleja (2007) and Jennett (2010); for an empirical study of immersion in games, Jennett et al. (2008); for an analysis of immersion and game sound, Grimshaw (2012) or Huiberts (2010); or, for an analysis of immersion and in-game voice, Ward (2010). In Zehnder, Igoe, and Lipscomb (2003)—a preliminary study leading to Lipscomb and Zehnder (2005) and Zehnder and Lipscomb (2006), both discussed later in this chapter—the researchers defined immersion as the strength of a rendered experience in constructing a perceptually salient imaginary or virtual reality. From a visual perspective, enhancement of the player's immersion in the virtual gameworld is accomplished through design elements, including: realistic visuals, a compelling interface perspective, convincingly rendered worlds, multiple layers and extensibility, well-differentiated levels and settings, attention to the context of the game as a whole, and attention to the user interface.

Although theories and models of immersion abound, there is a paucity of empirical studies assessing immersive states or processes. Several investigations have used subjective responses (e.g., semantic differential scales), physiological measurements (e.g., electromyography or galvanic skin response), or combinations of these methods. Psychophysiological methods employed tend to be minimally invasive and allow the collection of data during gameplay; however, the degree to which these measures correspond to the player's actual mental or immersive state has not yet been determined. For instance, Nacke and Grimshaw (2011) have provided an overview of such methods in the context of game sound and the role of emotion and affect in immersion. Questionnaires collect subjective responses after the fact, bringing into question both their reliability and validity. To give some examples of the range of measures used in recent studies: Jennett (2010) equates immersion with dissociation from the real world; Kearney and Pivec (2007) use eye movement and blink rate as their criteria; and Grimshaw, Lindley, and Nacke (2008) and Nacke, Grimshaw, and Lindley (2010) employ psychophysiological measures in their investigations of immersion due to game sound in the context of FPS games.

Grimshaw (2008) takes the view that the player and FPS acoustic environment together form an acoustic ecology within which the player and game engine are contributing components. This notion is a development of Schafer's (1994) soundscape theories and Truax's (2001) ideas concerning acoustic communication in which the relationship between listener and sound and the role of sound in societal formation were expounded upon. In these latter cases, the acoustic ecologies defined and studied are those present in the real world. Applying the same concept to virtual worlds presupposes the immersion of the player in the game's acoustic environment and makes explicit the participation of the player, as described earlier, in the creation of that soundscape.

Music

As previously stated, *Space Invaders* (Taito, 1978) was the first computer game to introduce continuous music; that is, an underscore playing throughout the game above which various sound effects are heard. This music, a primitive and highly repetitive, rhythmic 'march of the aliens' (see Figure 13.1), was an important, though simple, early example of music taking its cue from the actions of the player; the longer the gameplay and the more successful the defense of the player's bases, the faster the tempo of the music. The musical sound was, therefore, closely related to the game's narrative and fictional world and an early indicator of the potential for musical interactivity in computer games. As we shall describe later, this potential was not greatly explored until the advent of music games. Game composers have seemed generally content to follow the example of Hollywood film composers.

The music of early arcade and gambling machines served primarily to attract prospective players' attention in a crowded and noisy arena (Collins 2008). This is a point Granner (1999) makes with regard to arcade machine sound, while also stating that the sound of such machines must additionally, upon insertion of a coin, provide an 'amusement dividend' of approximately 3 minutes. Such a requirement, led by the direct and explicit short-term monetary cost to the player, dictates that any music must be instantly accessible, while also being recognizable and familiar.

These musical necessities, combined with computer storage limitations, led to the use of looping. An innovative technological solution, looping required that short musical fragments be stored in the machine's memory and repeated throughout the game, becoming imprinted upon the player's own memory and providing a recognizable and familiar sound amid the hubbub of other arcade machines. Many early arcade machines made use of musical genres appropriate to the game's historical premise or integrated well-known baroque or classical themes, such as the use of Bach's *Toccata and Fugue in B Minor* in *Gyruss* (Okamoto, 1983), presaging a future reliance upon established Hollywood film music practices, merely one mode in which gaming is converging with the mainstream film industry.

Figure 13.1 Music notation for the *Space Invaders* 'march of the aliens' music (transcribed by S. Lipscomb).

In the early 2000s, game development costs approached the multimillion dollar range of a typical, low-budget feature film of the period.[5] This meant that game development also relied on investors who were willing to take a financial risk in the hopes of receiving a large return on this investment if the game was a success. One proven way to mitigate potential losses was to associate with already-popular franchises, including associations with films (such as *James Bond*, *Toy Story*, *Lord of the Rings*, etc.). In other cases, games might associate with a successful popular music act. An early example of such a game is *Journey's Escape* (Data Age, 1982), featuring both the rock band's members as characters in the game and their music as an important component of the soundtrack (Collins 2008). This practice has been developed further with games such as *Guitar Hero* (RedOctane & Harmonix Music Systems, 2005–2010), including a specialized guitar-like interface enabling the player to jam along to well-known rock tracks; later versions also included a drum set, bass guitar, and microphone interfaces, allowing multiple players to perform collectively as a 'band.'

Games such as *Guitar Hero*, *Rock Band* (Harmonix Music Systems, 2007), and *SingStar* (London Studio 2007) were, at the time, unusual in the computer game industry in that their *raison d'être* was the 'performance' of extant examples of popular music. The more successful the player is at performing the prescribed sequence of button presses, drum hits, vocal melodies, or key presses (recent versions of *Rock Band* added a keyboard interface), the closer the music will sound to the actual recordings by the featured artists. Such overriding, musically consequential interactivity is also found in *PaRappa the Rapper* (NanaOn-Sha, 1996), in which the player is required to press button sequences on the game's controller in order to join in with the accompaniment, *DJ Hero* (FreeStyleGames, 2009), in which the player 'scratches' pre-existing recordings on a virtual turntable, and *Rez*, in which the completion of tasks and other forms of player activity builds up a complex, layered musical soundtrack, not to mention other games that expand the definition of what constitutes musicianship. A recent addition to these music-based games is *Rocksmith* (UbiSoft, 2011), which—along with the game disc—includes a special cable with a ¼-inch guitar plug on one end and a USB plug on the other that allows the player to connect any electric guitar to the game system. Using a visual representation very similar to *Guitar Hero* and *Rock Band*, the player learns to play the electric guitar through a series of rehearsals and performances that gradually increase in complexity based on the player's developing performance ability on the instrument.

As interactive music video games have gained popularity, one question is whether skills learned from these games may facilitate (or perhaps even hinder) formal music training. To what extent might skills learned from hours spent perfecting *Guitar Hero*, *Rock Band*, or *SingStar* transfer to real musical skills for playing instruments and singing? Although we are not aware of any empirical work that has addressed this question directly, Gower and McDowall (2012) conducted an exploratory study employing semi-structured interviews with children (aged 9 to 11 years) and music teachers to address the potential link between music video games and music teaching and learning. One teacher argued that most important musical skills are not transferable, such as note-reading (as most games scroll performance cues vertically while music notation is oriented horizontally), and that creative musicianship such as composition and expressive playing are not sufficiently emphasized in most games. Another teacher believed that many skills are transferable, such as keeping a steady beat and learning to play on time. Most students thought they were developing relevant skills, such as hand–eye coordination, rhythm, and dexterity from *Guitar Hero* and improved pitch from *SingStar*. The largely positive views are in line with a growing interest among music educators to incorporate multimedia as informal tools for music education. These tools include music video games to incorporate students' interests into the curriculum (Goble, 2009), and the use of other multimedia including film and animation, music videos, YouTube, and television commercials in music listening and analysis courses (Webb, 2007). These approaches expand on the premise that video games (not just educational games) can serve as positive contexts for learning (e.g., see Gee, 2007), although the specific benefits of interactive music games have yet to be empirically validated.

The influence of film

Aside from genres such as music games, the majority of music in computer games, is pre-composed and serves a role similar to that of film music, constituting a crucial component, but often not the primary focus of attention. Music, often in combination with video, can be used in 'cut-scenes' that help to move the game along by masking the technical process of loading the next game level into digital memory, but it is often used as an underscore throughout gameplay. Parallel to discussions of film music, such a musical soundtrack is often referred to as 'non-diegetic,' contrasting with the 'diegetic' sound effects that arise directly from the logic of the gameworld and the actions of the player in that gameworld. Non-diegetic music closely mimics the film music practice of underscoring, using music to convey general mood (scope, placement in time, level of energy); the internal life, thoughts, and feelings of characters through the use of *leitmotifs* (musical themes associated with a character, event, object, or emotion); and narrative structure (to focus attention, set pace, facilitate continuity, or provide background filler) (Lipscomb & Tolchinsky, 2005). The terms 'diegetic' and 'non-diegetic' are applied slightly differently by computer game theorists compared to their application by film scholars, and this reflects the functional nature of much of game sound being driven by the need for physical interaction with the gameworld. Game sound theorists (Grimshaw, 2008, and Jørgensen, 2011, for example) have devised variations of the terms non-diegetic and diegetic in order to account for an expanded number of functions of game sound compared to film sound, due to the requirements of, and the possibilities engendered by, the highly interactive nature of computer games. (For brief descriptions of the terms diegetic and non-diegetic as applied to film, see Chapters 3 and 11 in this volume.)

Zehnder and Lipscomb (2006) state that game music often forms a dramatic arc within scenes, especially in games with a clear narrative. The 'arc' consists of a building of tension as the player succeeds in making progress toward a goal, finally reaching a climax. At the point of climax, there is an abrupt change in the soundtrack, marking the climactic arrival and proceeding to a denouement. With regard to the structure of game music, the authors find elements of Western musical structures (e.g., the exposition, development, and recapitulation/resolution of classical sonata form) intermingled with the use of other music compositional devices such as leitmotifs. They also use Chion's (1994) terminology of listening (i.e., reduced listening, semantic listening, and causal listening), which was developed in Pierre Schaeffer's writings about electro-acoustic music. They apply Chion's terms to film sound and find examples of each in game music and specify that:

> *Reduced* listening emphasizes the sound itself and the source of meaning of the audio. *Causal* listening refers to listening to a sound to be able to identify its cause, while *semantic* listening focuses on code systems in audio (i.e., spoken language) that symbolize ideas, actions, or things. In the case of video game music, reduced listening would emphasize the mood of the music, causal [listening] would highlight the actions that trigger certain sounds/loops, and semantic listening would focus on the lyrical or genre-related (i.e., hip-hop vs. symphonic classical) connotations of the audio. (p. 244)

Zehnder and Lipscomb further suggest that music also provides a sense of presence and immersion to signify emotional states (that the player should adopt), signaling narrative and plot changes, and providing aesthetic and thematic unity. They too address the issue of diegesis by stating that diegetic music 'refers to the world of the characters and story within the film; everything that happens to the characters and in the environment portrayed on screen,' while nondiegetic music 'functions as an interpretive element, guiding the listener toward a certain feeling, subjectively beyond the visual elements' (p. 249, citing Sonnenschein, 2001; see also Tan, Spackman, & Wakefield, 2008). They also suggest that Peirce's sign classification—index, icon, and symbol—provides a means to understand the modes of communication that game music can use. (For a detailed discussion of this topic, see Kendall & Lipscomb, Chapter 3, in the present volume.)

Just as the influence of film is apparent in the structure and sound design of computer games, however, it is possible that games can also influence films. Grieb (2002) proposes that the wide-ranging appeal of the popular German film *Run Lola Run* (see Figure 13.2) can be explained in part by its ability to strongly reference the video game, 'a form [director] Tykwer uses as a stylistic template to structure *Run Lola Run*' (p. 158). This is apparent in the repetition of three segments that tell the same story line with minor variations and different endings, a story that is 'driven by the navigation of space' (p. 163) more so than character or plot development, the unnatural camera angles, and point-of-view shots. These are reflected in the unrelenting non-diegetic techno music that also resembles the character of some computer or video game music more closely than a conventional film score. Thus, although the influence is strongest in the direction of film to interactive games, some films have also come to emulate certain aspects of the medium of the computer or video game, down to the musical scoring.

There is often a fine line between sound effects and sound effects functioning as music. Of particular interest on this topic is Cook's (2006) analysis of sound effects in *Mario and Luigi: Partners in Time* (AlphaDream, 2005). Noting the music-like nature of the composite soundscape (that is, the soundscape that arises from the player's actions), the author devised a notation system analyzing rhythm and points of sound intensity. His suggestion that player experiences can be interchangeably represented by a pseudo-musical notation has been used by Cook as an aid to the design of games.

Figure 13.2 Scene from Tykwer's (1998) *Run Lola Run*, a film that emulates the computer or video game in many ways including structure and music track. Reproduced from *Run Lola Run* © 1998 Sony Pictures Home Entertainment.

This is an interesting inversion of the usual game design method (design gameplay, then add sounds), and Cook claims that, as an *ab initio* game design technique, it has the potential to lead to new game designs that provide for a greater positive relationship between the psychological rewards a player receives in the form of sonic events and the successful completion of game objectives.

Empirical investigations of the effects of computer game sound

In spite of the significant advances and increasing sophistication of game sound and the wealth of information that audio cues can convey, few empirical studies have focused on the role of sound on players' performance or on the subjective aspects of the gaming experience. This is particularly surprising in light of research showing that sound is often rated as one of the most important features of video games by adolescents (Griffiths & Hunt, 1995) and by adults (Wood, Griffiths, Chappell, & Davies, 2004) and both male and female players (Wood et al., 2004). In particular, the category of 'realistic sound effects' was rated as 'very important' or 'extremely important' to the enjoyment of a game by two-thirds of a sample of 382 male and female university students, among the most highly rated items from a list of general characteristics of video games that cut across different game genres (Wood et al., 2004). In fact, 'realistic sound effects' received higher ratings for importance than a host of other features, including presence of a story line, humorous elements, options to customize characters, different ending options, and inclusion of 'Easter eggs'[6] or cheats. Presence of background music and characters that speak were rated as somewhat less important, and inclusion of narration was rated as the least important audio feature with respect to enjoyment of a game.

This section provides an overview of empirical studies examining the relationship between player and game sound. We review current research investigating the effects of game sound on players' performance, physiological arousal, and subjective aspects of the gaming experience as conveyed by players' self-reports. This provides not only an empirical basis for the previous discussion but lays the groundwork for future study and for game music composition and sound design in expectation of the continuing development of game technology.

Effects on performance

The growing body of literature addressing the effects of game sound on player's performance has yielded mixed findings. In some instances, the presence of game audio seems to improve gameplay whereas other studies suggest that sound has no effect or may even interfere with performance. For instance, Tafalla (2007) designed an experiment to determine the impact of a soundtrack consisting of chilling music and sounds of weapons, screams, and heavy breathing on performance while playing the FPS game *DOOM* (id Software, 1993). Male participants scored almost twice as many points in the condition with sound compared to those playing in silence (without music or sound effects). In contrast, Yamada, Fujisawa, and Komori (2001) found that participants playing the racing game *Ridge Racer V* (Namco, 2000) scored the fastest lap times when playing without music. In this experimental context, the presence of nine of ten music tracks of different genres had a negative effect on performance compared to engine and tire sounds alone; 'new age' music was the only genre for which this negative effect was not observed. It was interesting to note that scores were lowest when playing with Boom Boom Satellite's 'Fogbound,' the intended soundtrack for the game.

Cassidy and MacDonald (2009) also found that music diminished performance in a driving game, with respect to speed and driving accuracy. They asked participants to play a driving video game (a modified driving simulation game) in one of the following sound conditions: (1) car sounds only, (2) car sounds and a 'high arousal' music track, (3) car sounds and a 'low arousal' music track, or (4) car sounds plus a music CD chosen by the participant. The researchers selected popular music tracks for the high and low arousal soundtracks based on previous studies showing that highly arousing music tends to be fast in tempo (North, Hargreaves, & Heath, 1998), loud (Belojevic, Slepcevic, & Jakovljevic, 2001), exciting (Hallam & Price, 1998), and more complex—for instance, less repetitive, less predictable melodic lines, and more instrumental layering (Furnham & Allass, 1999). Although scores for both lap time and lap speed were fastest when playing with either the high arousal music or the self-selected music, the highest number of errors (as measured by hitting road cones or barriers) was yielded when driving with high arousal music selected by the experimenter. In other words, driving with highly arousing music increased the speed of driving but also seemed to make drivers less careful or less precise. Low arousal music selected by the experimenter had detrimental effects on all measures of performance, leading to the lowest scores on accuracy, slowest lap times, and slowest lap speed. (See also Cassidy & MacDonald, 2010, for similar findings yielded by a separate study.)

When it comes to game sound, it seems 'more is not always better.' In fact, soundtracks with complex music and a rich variety of auditory and musical cues built into the game can pose a challenge to the novice. Tan, Baxa, and Spackman (2010) tracked the progress of 20 participants during four sessions as they were learning to play *The Legend of Zelda: Twilight Princess* (Nintendo EAD, 2006), an adventure role-playing game on the Nintendo Wii console. The study employed a within-participants design with sound conditions distributed over the four experimental sessions according to a Latin square. This ensured that each individual was assigned to play in a different sound condition on each of 4 days in a systematically randomized order. The four sound conditions were: (1) silence (both screen and remote control turned off), (2) partial sound (sounds emitted by the Wiimote (remote control) only), (3) full sound (sounds emitted by the Wiimote and the television screen), and (4) a musical soundtrack CD of *LoZ: Twilight Princess* playing in the background. In this last condition, musical soundtracks were selected that were unrelated to the game levels the participants were playing at the time.

Tan et al. (2010) found that the presence of sound facilitated performance to some degree; performance was weakest when playing in the 'silent' condition and was increasingly stronger when enhanced by 'partial sound' and by 'full sound,' respectively. This is to be expected, as *Twilight Princess* employs a rich musical soundtrack and a host of sound effects and audio cues, many of which may help the player successfully navigate the virtual environment and complete tasks. For instance, a monkey claps or squeaks when the avatar nears a correct path, Midna (an avatar who accompanies the protagonist on certain parts of the journey) giggles to alert the player to access important areas, sounds of enemies warn of their approach, some enemies emit noises before attacking, and successful attacks on enemies sound different than unsuccessful attempts. Surprisingly, however, participants earned their highest scores when playing with the *unrelated* background music CD that was not intended to accompany the player's specific actions and was therefore irrelevant to the onscreen events in the game. Specifically, when playing with this background music, players completed the greatest number of tasks and played significantly longer before having to use a 'continue' to extend their play after running out of life. The researchers found this to be surprising, as all of the rich audio cues embedded in the game were unavailable to the player when playing with unrelated background music.

Cognitive load and performance

What is one to make of these mixed findings? Does game sound help or hinder gameplay? Researchers have pointed to several explanations for the mixed findings in this area, but most are linked to the idea of competition for limited cognitive resources. The presence of auditory stimuli competes for limited processing resources when performing a complex task such as engaging in a challenging video game (North & Hargreaves, 1999) requiring 'rapid processing of sensory information and prompt action [and] constant switching of processing priorities and continual adjustments to new task demands' (Dye, Green, & Bavelier, 2009, p. 321). This may explain why performance was best in the self-selected music condition in Cassidy and MacDonald's (2009) driving simulation study. These participants supplied an audio CD containing music they usually play when driving in the real world. As a result, the self-selected music would have been very familiar and predictable, with little or no cognitive load implications. On the other hand, playing while listening to a new piece of music selected by the experimenter may have placed extra cognitive demands on players, interfering with performance requiring moment-to-moment decisions, such as avoiding tricky obstacles while driving.

Further, although many auditory events within a game serve as helpful audio cues to guide players in accomplishing a variety of tasks, some musical features and sound effects do not directly affect a player's ability to complete tasks. Atmospheric music swelling and fading, the sounds of waterfalls or rustling leaves, or an intermittent owl's screech may simply add interest or deepen the sense of immersion in a virtual world. Forms of information that add enjoyment or appeal—but are irrelevant to learning—have been referred to as 'seductive details' in the learning literature (Garner, Brown, Sanders, & Menke, 1992, p. 239). As seductive details increase cognitive load and compete for limited cognitive resources in working memory, while not adding information directly helpful to task completion, they can detrimentally affect learning and performance—especially when complex information is presented in multisensory formats (Mayer, 2009; Sweller, 1999). Complex music and a rich variety of sound effects may even distract players or lead them off track, as they attempt to decipher a sound that turns out to be extraneous.

A 'redundancy effect' may also be at play, as some audio cues simply double or reinforce information that is already available on the screen. For example, successful hits are usually apparent from their consequences on screen (e.g., explosions or injuries to enemies) in addition to associated sound effects. Redundant information may add extraneous cognitive load to working memory without accumulating benefits, thereby diminishing performance (see Leahy, Chandler, & Sweller, 2003, for similar findings concerning learning in multimedia contexts). In other words, some salient audio cues may help guide players, perhaps explaining why the presence of sound effects and music may enhance performance in a FPS game like *DOOM* (Tafalla, 2007). On the other hand, some auditory information may reinforce visual cues and provide a more appealing or immersive experience, but may also interfere with optimal performance by adding cognitive load (North & Hargreaves, 1999).

The fact that game sound often provides information that is both relevant *and irrelevant* to the completion of tasks is pertinent to the potential load on the player's cognitive processing. For instance, Brünken, Plass, and Leutner (2004) showed that performance suffers when participants are asked to process visual information accompanied by both task-relevant narration and task-irrelevant background music, but not when accompanied by wholly irrelevant background music (see also Moreno & Mayer, 2000). This is because attention must be split between dual sensory modes in the first condition whereas the participant can simply tune out the auditory events and focus on visual information alone when auditory input is completely irrelevant to the task. As game sound usually includes task-relevant and task-irrelevant information, players cannot simply block out one sensory channel but must alternate their attention between sources or integrate multisensory information to advance in the task. Therefore, attending to auditory input for potentially helpful cues may add a burden to players working at the limits of their cognitive capacities while figuring out a challenging new game. This may explain why the majority of participants played most successfully when accompanied by music that was entirely task-irrelevant in the *Twilight Princess* study by Tan et al. (2010).

As players get used to a game, however, the cognitive load required to play should be reduced, freeing attentional resources to allocate to audio cues. Therefore, contingent sound may be increasingly helpful to players as they advance in the game. This was hinted at in some trends identified in the data collected by Tan et al. (2010). Specifically, participants who reported having played several previous *Legend of Zelda* games seemed to benefit most from the presence of 'full sound' (Wiimote and screen sound) when playing a new game (*LoZ: Twilight Princess*). Members of this group typically earned their top or second best scores when playing with full sound provided by the television and remote control. On the other hand, the presence of rich audio seemed to diminish performance for the rest of the participants, who earned the lowest or second lowest scores out of four sessions when playing with full sound.

Other studies also suggest that the effects of game sound interact with the level of the participant's previous experience with a certain genre or game series (e.g. Tafalla, 2007, discussed earlier) and with one's familiarity with the technology employed (e.g., see Fassbender, Richards, Bilgin, Thompson, & Heiden, 2012, for an educational application). Overall, these findings point to the challenges of processing multisensory cues while playing elaborate video games and suggest that the most successful players swiftly develop strategies incorporating task-relevant information conveyed by *both* sounds and images when learning a new game or tackling a new level in a familiar game.

3D sound

Recent studies have explored the effects of 3D sound on performance. 3D sound brings externalization and directionality to a game's audio by giving the impression that sounds are coming from the three-dimensional space around the player. It may be achieved through the use of hardware, such as a surround sound system, or through the use of digital processing before audio is reproduced through a pair of speakers or stereo headphones. The presence of 3D sound may reduce time taken to find objects in a virtual space (Gunther, Kaman, & MacGregor, 2004), improve the ability to find the right timing to cross an intersection in a virtual traffic gap-crossing task (Bernhard, Grosse, & Wimmer, 2011), enhance performance in a collaborative game in an augmented reality environment (Zhou, Cheok, Yang, & Qui, 2004), improve cognitive skills of blind children playing a sound-based computer game (Sánchez & Lumbreras, 1999), and assist blind adults in navigating real environments after exploring virtual models (Merabet & Sánchez, 2009).

In Zhou et al.'s (2004) study, for instance, two players teamed up to battle a virtual witch and fly to a castle to rescue a princess. Partners who played in silence took about one and a half times as long (133 seconds versus 88 seconds) to complete the task, compared to those who played with 3D sound. The presence of 3D sound aided depth perception, task efficiency, and facilitated collaboration between players. Sánchez and Lumbreras (1999) also found that blind children who played a computer game with 3D sound were subsequently able to build accurate 3D models of the route they navigated using LEGO® blocks. Visually impaired adults who explore sound-based virtual representations of real environments can even transfer their learning by subsequently navigating a real city subway system and real indoor environments (Merabet & Sánchez, 2009).

However, 3D sound does not always enhance performance. For instance, Gunther et al. (2004) found that while 3D sound helped participants locate specific objects quickly, it hindered their ability to acquire an overall spatial knowledge of the virtual environment. As with non-3D sound, the effects of 3D sound are not simple and may be mediated by many other factors. Further, many studies that have focused on the effects of 3D sound have not included a non-3D sound condition as a comparison (e.g., Gunther et al., 2004; Sánchez & Lumbreras, 1999; Zhou et al., 2004) so the extent to which the findings in this section are specific to 3D sound (as opposed to the presence of any sound) is not clear.

Physiological measures

The physiological effects associated with gaming have been demonstrated in many studies, providing evidence of arousal, indicated by increased heart rate, breathing, oxygen consumption, and elevated blood pressure; stress reactions, indicated by increases in cortisol secretion; and neurological effects, such as seizures induced by flashing lights (see Anderson & Bushman, 2001 for a review). Further, studies have shown that it is not primarily the physical movements or physical exertions accompanying gameplay that lead to these physiological changes, but involvement in the gaming experience itself. For instance, Calvert and Tan (1994) showed that an elevated pulse rate after playing a 4-minute aggressive virtual reality (VR) arcade game (*Dactyl Nightmare* (W Industries, 1991)) could not be attributed simply to the physical movements involved in the VR game (e.g., raising the arms to hold a gun or moving from side to side to search for targets in the virtual environment). This study included a control group that mirrored the head, arm, and full-body movements of the players without the gaming component. Participants who played the VR game showed a significantly greater increase in pulse rate (+11.33 beats per minute (bpm)) compared to the control group (+5.00 bpm) or those who had merely been observing the game (+2.33 bpm), compared to baseline measures. Calvert and Tan (1994) concluded that physiological arousal was not merely the result of physical exertion of movements performed by those playing the game, but was more likely a function of being immersed in the VR experience.

The presence of game sound has been shown in some studies to intensify physiological responses. For instance, Hébert, Béland, Dionne-Fournelle, Crête, and Lupien (2005) examined the effects of the presence of music on stress (assessed by monitoring cortisol levels) while playing a computer game. The music consisted of the (built-in) soundtrack for the game, which can be described as relatively fast in tempo, very repetitive, and without chord changes as the bass repeats a single pitch). The researchers asked 52 participants to play the FPS game *Quake III Arena* either with the music playing fairly loudly at 70 dBA to 85 dBA or with the music turned off. In both conditions, the sound effects were switched off so that any differences found could be attributed to the presence or absence of music alone. Analysis revealed that those who played the game accompanied by music experienced higher cortisol levels (indicating more stress) than those who played without music when cortisol readings were taken 15 minutes after playing, the time at which cortisol is expected to reach maximum level following a triggering event.

Similarly, in the same study that revealed a performance enhancement as described earlier, Tafalla (2007) found that heart rate accelerated significantly in male participants when playing the FPS game *DOOM* with music and sound effects in comparison to a condition in which both were switched off (10.78 bpm increase versus 7.09 bpm increase from baseline measures). Female participants, on the other hand, showed a significant increase in systolic and diastolic blood pressure when playing with the music and sound effects when compared to measurements taken after playing with music and sound effects switched off. Tafalla concluded that the presence of sound, while playing this violent game, elicited greater physiological arousal in men (as indicated by increased heart rate) and greater stress in women (as indicated by elevated blood pressure) in comparison to the results when playing in silence.

Beyond the realm of research investigating computer games, auditory/computer interface studies have also shown that arousal is enhanced by the presence of sound—especially when urgency is conveyed through increasing pitch, loudness, and speed of sounds in a pulsating manner (Edworthy, Loxley, & Dennis, 1991; Haas & Edworthy, 1996). Indeed, sensory arousal and reinforcement for winning moves provided by sounds and music (such as beeps, chimes, catchy jingles) may be among the structural features of computer games and slot machines that make them highly addictive, both psychologically and physiologically (Griffiths, 2002; Hébert et al., 2005).

Physiological responses to short episodes of gameplay can be difficult to track, however, and not all studies have yielded clear results. For instance, Wolfson and Case (2000) did not find significant differences in pulse rate as measured by a pulse oximeter, while manipulating the loudness of upbeat dance music (loud versus soft) when playing a simple ball-and-paddle game created by the researchers. Similarly, the investigations of Grimshaw et al. (2008) and Nacke et al. (2010), yielded no significant physiological effects for presence of music or sound effects while playing a FPS game, as discussed further in the following section.

Participant verbal reports

While successful performance and physiological measures lend themselves to quantifiable (though not wholly unproblematic) measures, personal and subjective aspects of the gaming experience are more difficult to measure. Aside from the problems that arise when relying on self-report and issues regarding reliability and validity, these measures are usually obtained retrospectively and not 'in the heat of the game.' Whether participants can accurately report on experiences that often involve a lack of self-awareness (e.g., flow, immersion, presence, and time distortion) is a matter of debate. Further, the degree to which participants' reports of their physical or psychological states are isomorphic with their physiological responses is also open to question. For instance, while Hébert et al. (2005) found that playing a game accompanied by a musical soundtrack led to significantly higher levels of cortisol secretion, the participants did not report higher levels of perceived stress when compared to a silent condition. Nonetheless, verbal reports offer some valuable insights into subjective aspects of gaming.

Researchers have focused on the effects of sound on a variety of aspects of the gaming experience including immersion, presence, flow, perceived passage of time, focused attention, sense of control and effectance (i.e., one's influence on the environment), subjective sense of how well one is performing, and enjoyment. Two of the most commonly examined aspects of the gaming experience are enjoyment and 'presence' (a feeling of 'being there' in the virtual environment and an accompanying loss of awareness of one's real physical setting; Barfield, Zeltzer, Sheridan, & Slater, 1995). Skalski and Whitbred (2010) examined the relative influence of image quality and sound quality on players' sense of presence and enjoyment of the FPS game *Ghost Recon: Advanced Warfighter* (Ubisoft, 2001). Whereas manipulating the quality of the image (1080i high definition versus standard definition) had no effect, improving sound quality (Dolby 5.1 surround sound versus Dolby stereo) positively affected the players' sense of presence and enjoyment of the game. Specifically, participants playing the game with surround sound reported feeling greater engagement, experienced a greater sense of being 'present' in the action of the game world, described the experience as more socially intimate and more perceptually real, and rated the game as more enjoyable than those playing with stereo sound. (See also Chapter 16 by Kerins on the impact of surround sound, in this volume.) However, few studies have focused on the role of sound and music in this area, so many other aspects of game audio on 'presence' have yet to be explored.

Sound may also affect the perceived pace and duration of playing time. A study focusing on addictive behaviors in video lottery terminals (such as those found in casinos) showed that turning off the sounds created by the machine and decreasing the speed of play led to lower ratings of enjoyment, excitement, and tension-reduction in pathological gamblers compared to controls (Loba, Stewart, Klein, & Blackburn, 2001). Interestingly, pathological gamblers also had more difficulty stopping play than controls—but only when playing at fast speed with the sound on. As Parke and Griffiths (2006) have stated, the frequent and continuous sounds of slot machines may suggest to players that 'winning is more common than losing' (p. 171). The effects of background music playing in the casino may have more complex effects. Dixon, Trigg, and Griffiths (2007) found that speed of betting was influenced by the tempo of background music; faster betting occurred when faster music was played—though it did not affect the size of the bet. Both frequent sounds of slot machines and fast background music seem to incite casino players to keep playing.

On the other hand, the presence of music may also make players less susceptible to time distortion. When small groups of participants played slot machines in a dimly-lit room with no windows or clocks, while hearing the recorded sounds of typical casino noise (jackpot bells, coins, people talking), they tended to underestimate the amount of time they spent playing (Noseworthy & Finlay, 2009). However, when music was added to the typical casino sounds, participants more accurately estimated their playing time—especially when the music was slow in tempo and loud (90 dB). The authors concluded that music 'provides a cue of interval from which players can more accurately reconstruct their elapsed duration of play' (p. 340). Loud music may also direct players' attention away from slot machine play so they may not be as absorbed in their game. (For a fuller review of the literature on sound in electronic gambling machines, see Collins et al., 2011.)

The musical soundtrack can also affect players' perception of the game. Not surprisingly, for instance, in Tafalla's (2007) study mentioned previously, both males and females judged the game *DOOM* to be significantly more violent when playing with the built-in suspenseful music and sound effects of weapons and screams than when playing the game without sound. Lipscomb and Zehnder (2005) investigated the impact of music in the RPG *The Lord of the Rings: The Two Towers* (Stormfront Studios & Hypnos Entertainment, 2002). Participants were randomly assigned to one of three groups: music-only (no gameplay involved, listening task only), game without music, or game with music. Based on responses to 21 verbal scales, significant differences were observed for four of the verbal scales: (1) the music-only and game with music conditions were considered more 'dangerous' than the game without music condition, (2) the game with music condition was considered more 'colorful' than the music-only condition, which was considered more so than the game without music, (3) the game with music condition was considered less 'simple' than either the music-only or game without music conditions, and (4) the game with music condition was considered less 'relaxed' than the music-only condition, which was less relaxed than the game without music condition. Though a significant difference in participant responses was not revealed for all 21 of the verbal response scales, the four that were significant revealed a clear influence of musical condition.

Studying the impact of music and sound effects on immersion in the context of a FPS game, researchers have attempted to correlate questionnaire-based data with physiological measurements (Grimshaw et al., 2008; Nacke et al., 2010). Specifically, the investigators employed electroencephalography, electrocardiography, electromyography, galvanic skin response, and eye tracking equipment as participants played *Half-Life 2* in each of four conditions in a counterbalanced order: (1) music on/sound effects on, (2) music on/sound effects off, (3) music off/sound effects on, and (4) music off/sound effects off. This was combined with a Game Experience Questionnaire (GEQ) to examine whether physiological data can be correlated with participant reports of immersion. While the study found a significant main effect for sound on/off leading to higher positive ratings of GEQ dimensions (immersion, tension, competence, flow, negative affect, positive affect, and challenge—in particular between sound FX and immersion and flow), no systematic relationship was found between the physiological measures and subjective GEQ ratings. The researchers suggest that physiological data needs to be more accurately tracked for a closer examination of the possible interrelationships between the various physiological and self-report measures.

Nacke, Lindley, and Stellmach (2008) present a potential solution to this in logging game events with the same temporal accuracy of physiological events but this method has yet to be fully implemented. The system they propose would allow for phasic correlation of physiological data to specific game events (i.e., including game events initiated by the player in response to previous stimuli) and to game experience analysis data generated by tools such as eye-tracking equipment.

Summary

The complexity and density of sound effects and music have developed concurrently with developments in audio and storage technology and with improvements in game graphics; concurrently, the player's engagement with sound has become more complex, demanding more of the player's attention. The simple, monophonic beeps of *Pong* have given way in many modern games to multichannel, real-time processed 3D audio and lavish orchestral arrangements of a fidelity rivaling any hi-fi recording. With this increasing engagement comes a reliance on sound to complete various game tasks and to improve one's performance, whether the goal is to operate the game, to navigate a course faster, to attain a higher score, or to be part of a victorious team. In some audio-only or music games, player performance relies almost solely upon the ability to recognize the sound effect source and/or to locate it in the soundfield or upon the player's musical skills. In others, such as FPS and survival horror games, apprehension of the sound source and its location is combined with visual information to aid the player's performance. The sound of tires crunching through gravel or sand in *Gran Turismo 5* (Polyphony Digital, 2010) is often the first indicator of the detrimental effects on player performance of straying into one of the numerous speed traps on the racing tracks.

As we have presented in our review of empirical investigations into music and sound effects in gaming, the effects of sound conditions on game performance and on subjective aspects of the experience may depend on many variables including the particular features of the game, the audio presentation mode and loudness, the relationship between the events in the game and the player's actions, and the player's level of expertise and experience, to name just a few of the potential parameters. Results from some of the empirical studies are inconclusive or mixed; throughout the chapter, we have suggested reasons for this as well as noting proposals to improve the quality and reliability of data collection or the more temporally accurate correlation of physiological and psychological states with game events.

As technology continues to develop, player and gameworld will become more closely integrated and the game system itself finer and more detailed in its affect tracking and in its responses to the player's physiological and psychological states. Much more empirical work must be conducted before, for example, the game system is able to sense that the player is unfazed in the face of zombies and, thus, can respond by synthesizing even more unnerving sounds and eerie music. While this chapter has concentrated on empirical studies of the auditory component of the gaming experience, such studies can only follow the *design* of that auditory component. This design is moving toward more personalization of the immediate player experience, an evolution that has implications for the player relationship to the game and, thus, for the direction of future studies of that experience.

Acknowledgments

The authors would like to thank their colleagues and the following institutions for the generous support and use of facilities that made many of the referenced projects possible: the University of Wolverhampton and the Blekinge Tekniska Högskola (Grimshaw), Kalamazoo College and Brigham Young University (Tan), Northwestern University and the University of Minnesota (Lipscomb). We would also be remiss were we not to thank the many participants who willingly played an essential role in these studies.

Notes

1. From CD to Blu-ray, storage capacity has risen from 650 MB to over 50 GB. It is difficult to specify how many audio, graphic, or video files such a medium will hold as the compression of files and their format will affect their size. Typically, though, videos require more storage than audio of the same length.
2. The term *mise-en-scène* refers to the design of visual aspects of the scene and its representation of the space, which can greatly impact the interpretation of viewers concerning the general mood and relationships between objects within the scene.
3. It is important to note that hearing these surround sound aspects of games requires the appropriate equipment. Not all players have their systems configured or own high-quality headphones to allow them to experience the true surround sound auditory experience as intended by the sound designers.
4. A range of audio-only games may be found at <http://audiogames.net>.
5. The BBC reports that Namco's PacMan was developed for $100,000 in 1982 whilst the typical Sony Playstation PS3 game in 2007 cost $15,000,000 to develop and Microsoft's 2007 title Halo3 reportedly cost $30,000,000 (Takatsuki, 2007).
6. An 'Easter egg' is a surprise in-game gift from the designers that, typically, can only be received if the correct sequence of player actions has occurred. Arriving at this sequence is often serendipitous and the unexpected Easter egg may take the form of a joke or message, some music, or a video clip—it is usually unconnected to the gameplay.

References

Alcorn, A. (1972). *Pong* [Computer game]. United States: Atari.

AlphaDream. (2005). *Mario and Luigi: Partners in time* [Computer game]. Japan: Nintendo.

Anderson, C. A., & Bushman, B. J. (2001). Effects of violent games on aggressive behavior, aggressive cognition, aggressive affect, physiological arousal, and prosocial behavior: A meta-analytic review of the scientific literature. *Psychological Science, 12,* 353–359.

Barfield, W., Zeltzer, D., Sheridan, T. B., & Slater, M. (1995). Presence and performance within virtual environments. In W. Barfield & T. A. Furness, III (Eds.), *Virtual environments and advanced interface design* (pp. 473–513). Oxford, UK: Oxford University Press.

Belojevic, G., Slepcevic, V., & Jakovljevic, B. (2001). Mental performance in noise: The role of introversion. *Journal of Environmental Psychology, 21,* 209–213.

Bernhard, M., Grosse, K., & Wimmer, M. (2011). Bimodal task-facilitation in a virtual traffic scenario through spatialized sound rendering. *Association for Computing Machinery (ACM) Transactions on Applied Perception, 8,* 1–22.

Bracken, C. C., Pettey, G., Guha, T., & Rubenking, B. E. (2010). Sounding out small screens and telepresence: The impact of audio, screen size, and pace. *Journal of Media Psychology: Theories, Methods, and Applications, 22,* 125–137.

Brünken, R., Plass, J. L., & Leutner, D. (2004). Assessment of cognitive load in multimedia learning with dual-task methodology: Auditory load and modality effects. *Instructional Science, 32,* 115–132.

Bushnell, N., & Dabney, T. (1971). *Computer space* [Computer game]. United States: Nutting Associates.

Calleja, G. (2007). *Digital games as designed experience: Reframing the concept of immersion.* (Unpublished PhD thesis.) Victoria University, Wellington, New Zealand.

Calvert, S. L., & Tan, S. -L. (1994). Impact of virtual reality on young adults' physiological arousal and aggressive thoughts: Interaction versus observation. *Journal of Applied Developmental Psychology, 15,* 125–139.

Cassidy, G. G., & MacDonald, R. A. R. (2009). The effects of music choice on task performance: A study of the impact of self-selected and experimenter-selected music on driving game performance and experience. *Musicae Scientiae, 13,* 357–386.

Cassidy, G. G., & MacDonald, R. A. R. (2010). The effect of music on time perception and performance of a driving game. *Scandinavian Journal of Psychology, 51,* 455–464.

Collins, K. (2005). From bits to hits: Video games music changes its tune. *Film International, 12,* 4–19.

Collins, K. (2008). *Game sound: An introduction to the history, theory, and practice of video game music and sound design.* Cambridge, MA: MIT Press.

Collins, K., Tessler, H., Harrigan, K., Dixon, M. J., & Fugelsang, J. (2011). Sound in electronic gambling machines: A review of the literature and its relevance to game sound. In M. Grimshaw (Ed.), *Game sound technology and player interaction: Concepts and developments.* (pp. 1–21). Hershey, PA: IGI Global.

Cook, D. (2006). *Creating a system of game play notation.* Retrieved from <http://lostgarden.com/2006/01/creating-system-of-game-play-notation.html> (accessed February 21, 2006).

Danger Close. (2010). *Medal of honor. Operation anaconda* [Computer game]. United States: Electronic Arts.

Data Age. (1982). *Journey's escape* [Computer game]. United States: Atari.

Dixon, L., Trigg, R., & Griffiths, M. (2007). An empirical investigation of music and gambling behavior. *International Gambling Studies, 7,* 315–326.

Droumeva, M. (2011). An acoustic communication framework for game sound: Fidelity, verisimilitude, ecology. In M. Grimshaw (Ed.), *Game sound technology and player interaction: Concepts and developments* (pp. 131–152). Hershey, PA: IGI Global.

Dye, M.W.G., Green, C. S., & Bavelier, D. (2009). Increasing speed of processing with action video games. *Current Directions in Psychological Science, 18,* 321–326.

Edworthy, J., Loxley, S., & Dennis, I. (1991). Improving auditory warning design: Relationship between warning sound parameters and perceived urgency. *Human Factors, 33,* 205–231.

Evreinova, T. V., Evreinov, G., & Raisamo, R. (2008). Non-visual game design and training in gameplay skill acquisition: A puzzle game case study. *Interacting with Computers, 20,* 386–405.

Farnell, A. (2011). Behaviour, structure and causality in procedural audio. In M. Grimshaw (Ed.), *Game sound technology and player interaction: Concepts and developments* (pp. 313–339). Hershey, PA: IGI Global.

Fassbender, E., Richards, D., Bilgin, A., Thompson, W. F., & Heiden, W. (2012). Virschool: The effect of background music and immersive display systems on memory for facts learned in an educational virtual environment. *Computers and Education, 58,* 490–500.

FreeStyleGames. (2009). *DJ hero* [Computer game]. United States: Activision.

Furnham, A., & Allass, K. (1999). The influence of musical distraction of varying complexity on the cognitive performance of extraverts and introverts. *European Journal of Personality, 13*, 27–38.

Four Door Lemon. (2010). *Aurifi* [Computer game]. United Kingdom: Punk Pie.

Garner, R., Brown, R., Sanders, S., & Menke, D. (1992). 'Seductive details' and learning from text. In K. A. Renninger, S. Hidi & A. Krapp (Eds.), *The role of interest in learning and development* (pp. 239–254). Hillsdale, NJ: Erlbaum.

Garner, T., & Grimshaw, M. (2011, September 7–9). A climate of fear: Considerations for designing an acoustic ecology for fear. In *Proceedings of Audio Mostly 2011*, Coimbra, Portugal. Retrieved from <http://www.audiomostly.com/index.php?option=com_content&view=article&id=9:proceedings&catid=7:amc&Itemid=14>.

Garner, T., Grimshaw, M., & Abdel Nabi, D. (2010, September 14–16). A preliminary experiment to assess the fear value of preselected sound parameters in a survival horror game. In *Proceedings of Audio Mostly 2010*, Piteå, Sweden. Retrieved from <http://www.audiomostly.com/index.php?option=com_content&view=article&id=9:proceedings&catid=7:amc&Itemid=14>.

Gee, J. P. (2007). *Good video games and good learning: Collected essays on video games, learning, and literacy*. New York, NY: Peter Lang.

Goble, J. S. (2009). Pragmatism, music's import, and music teachers as change agents. In T. Regelski & J. T. Gates (Eds.), *Music education for changing times: Guiding visions for practice* (pp. 73–84). Dordrecht, the Netherlands: Springer.

Gower, L., & McDowall, J. (2012). Interactive music video games and children's musical development. *British Journal of Music Education, 29*, 91–105.

Granner, C. (1999) Tales from the trenches of coin-op audio. Retrieved from Gamasutra on January15,2007, http://www.gamasutra.com/features/19991118/Granner_01.htm [page no longer available]

Grieb, M. (2002). Run, Lara run. In G. King & T. Krzywinska (Eds.), *Screenplay: Cinema, videogames, interfaces* (pp. 157–170). London, UK: Wallflower.

Griffiths, M. D. (2002). *Gambling and gaming addictions*. Leicester, UK: British Psychological Society/Blackwells.

Griffiths, M. D., & Hunt, N. (1995). Computer game playing in adolescence: Prevalence and demographic indicators. *Journal of Community and Applied Social Psychology, 5*, 189–194.

Grimshaw, M. (2008). *The acoustic ecology of the first-person shooter: The player experience of sound in the first-person shooter computer game*. Saarbrücken, Germany: VDM Verlag Dr. Mueller.

Grimshaw, M. (2012). Sound and player immersion in digital games. In K. Bijsterveld & T. Pinch (Eds.), *Oxford handbook of sound studies* (pp. 347–366). New York, NY: Oxford University Press.

Grimshaw, M., Lindley, C. A., & Nacke, L. (2008, October 22–23). Sound and immersion in the first-person shooter: Mixed measurement of the player's sonic experience. In *Proceedings of Audio Mostly 2008*, Piteå, Sweden. Retrieved from <http://www.audiomostly.com/index.php?option=com_content&view=article&id=9:proceedings&catid=7:amc&Itemid=14>.

Gunther, R., Kazman, R., & MacGregor, C. (2004). Using 3D sound as a navigational aid in virtual environments. *Behaviour & Information Technology, 23*, 435–446.

Haas, E. C., & Edworthy, J. (1996). Designing urgency into auditory warnings using pitch, speed and loudness. *Computing and Control Engineering Journal, 7*, 193–198.

Hallam, S., & Price, J. (1998). Can the use of background music improve the behaviour and academic performance of children with emotional and behavioural difficulties? *British Journal of Special Education*, *25*, 88–91.

Harmonix Music Systems. (2007). *Rock band* [Computer game]. United States: Electronic Arts.

Hébert, S., Béland R., Dionne-Fournelle, O., Crête M., & Lupien S. J. (2005). Physiological stress response to video-game playing: The contribution of built-in music. *Life Sciences*, *76*, 2371–2380.

Higinbotham, W. (1958). *Tennis for two* [Computer game]. (Unpublished.)

Huiberts, S. (2010). *Captivating sound: The role of audio for immersion in games.* (Unpublished PhD thesis.) University of Portsmouth, UK and Utrecht School of the Arts, the Netherlands.

id Software. (1993). *DOOM* [Computer game]. United States: id Software

id Software. (1999). *Quake III arena* [Computer game]. United States: id Software.

Jennett, C. I. (2010). *Is game immersion just another form of selective attention? An empirical investigation of real world dissociation in computer game immersion.* (Unpublished PhD thesis.) University College London, UK.

Jennett, C., Cox, A. L., Cairns, P., Dhopare, S., Epps, A., Tijs, T., & Walton, A. (2008). Measuring and defining the experience of immersion in games. *International Journal of Human-Computer Studies*, *66*, 641–661.

Jørgensen, K. (2011). Time for new terminology? Diegetic and non-diegetic sounds in computer games revisited. In M. Grimshaw (Ed.), *Game sound technology and player interaction: Concepts and developments* (pp. 78–97). Hershey, PA: IGI Global.

Kearney, P. R., & Pivec, M. (2007, June 13–15). *Immersed and how? That is the question.* Unpublished paper presented at Game in' Action, Göteborg University, Sweden.

Leahy, W., Chandler, P., & Sweller, J. (2003). When auditory presentations should and should not be a component of multimedia instruction. *Applied Cognitive Psychology*, *17*, 401–418.

Lipscomb, S. D., & Tolchinsky, D. E. (2005). The role of music communication in cinema. In D. Miell, R. MacDonald, & D. Hargreaves (Eds.), *Musical communication* (pp. 383–404). Oxford, UK: Oxford University Press.

Lipscomb, S. D., & Zehnder, S. M. (2005). Immersion in the virtual environment: The effect of a musical score on the video gaming experience. *Journal of Physiological Anthropology and Applied Human Science*, *23*, 337–343.

Loba, P., Stewart, S. H., Klein, R. M., & Blackburn, J. R. (2001). Manipulations of the features of standard video lottery terminal (VLT) games: Effects in pathological and non-pathological gamblers. *Journal of Gambling Studies*, *17*, 297–320.

London Studio. (2007). *SingStar* [Computer game]. Europe: Sony Computer Entertainment Europe.

Mayer, R. E. (2009). *Multimedia learning* (2nd ed.). New York, NY: Cambridge University Press.

Merabet, L. B., & Sánchez, J. (2009). Audio-based navigation using virtual environments: Combining technology and neuroscience. *Association for Education and Rehabilitation (AER) Journal: Research and Practice in Visual Impairment and Blindness*, *2*, 128–137.

Moreno, R., & Mayer, R. E. (2000). A coherence effect in multimedia learning: The case for minimizing irrelevant sounds in the design of multimedia instructional messages. *Journal of Educational Psychology*, *92*, 117–320.

Nacke, L., Grimshaw, M., & Lindley, C. A. (2010). More than a feeling: Measurement of sonic user experience and psychophysiology in a first-person shooter game. *Interacting with Computers*, *22*(5), 336–343.

Nacke, L., & Grimshaw, M. (2011). Player-game interaction through affective sound. In M. Grimshaw (Ed.), *Game sound technology and player interaction: Concepts and developments* (pp. 264–285). Hershey, PA: IGI Global.

Nacke, L., Lindley, C. A., & Stellmach, S. (2008). Log who's playing: Psychophysiological game analysis made easy through event logging. *Fun and Games, Lecture Notes in Computer Science, 5294*, 150–157.

Namco. (2000). *Ridge Racer V* [Video game]. Tokyo, Japan: Namco.

NanaOn-Sha. (1996). *PaRappa the rapper* [Computer game]. Japan: Sony Computer Entertainment.

Nintendo EAD. (2006). *The legend of Zelda: Twilight princess* [Computer game]. Japan: Nintendo.

North, A. C., & Hargreaves, D. J. (1999). Music and driving game performance. *Scandinavian Journal of Psychology, 40*, 285–292.

North, A. C., Hargreaves, D. J., & Heath, S. (1998). Musical tempo and time perception in a gymnasium. *Psychology of Music, 26*, 78–88.

Noseworthy, T. J., & Finlay, K. (2009). A comparison of ambient casino sound and music: Effects on dissociation and on perceptions of elapsed time while playing slot machines. *Journal of Gaming Studies, 25*, 331–342.

Okamoto, Y. (1983). *Gyruss* [Computer game]. Japan: Konami.

Parke, J., & Griffiths, M. (2006). The psychology of the fruit machine: The role of structural characteristics (revisited). *International Journal of Mental Health Addiction, 4*, 151–179.

Psygnosis. (1995/1996). *Wipeout* [Computer game]. Japan: Sony/Sega.

RedOctane, & Harmonix Music Systems. (2005–2010). *Guitar hero* [Computer game series]. United States: Activision.

Russell, S., Graetz, M., & Witaenem, W. (1962). *Spacewar!* [Computer game].

Sánchez, J., & Lumbreras, M. (1999). Virtual environment interaction through 3D audio by blind children. *CyberPsychology & Behavior, 2*, 101–111.

Sánchez, J. (2005). AudioBattleship: Blind learners develop cognition through sound. *International Journal on Disability and Human Development, 4*, 303–309.

Sanders, C., & DeBlois, D. (Directors). (2010). *How to train your dragon* [Motion picture]. United States: Dreamworks.

Schafer, R. M. (1994). *The soundscape: Our sonic environment and the tuning of the world.* Rochester, VT: Destiny Books.

Skalski, P., & Whitbred, R. (2010). Image versus sound: A comparison of formal feature effects on presence and video game enjoyment. *PsychNology Journal, 8*, 67–84.

Sonnenschein, D. (2001). *Sound design: The expressive power of music, voice, and sound effects in cinema.* Studio City, CA: Michael Wiese Productions.

Square Enix. (1987–2010). *Final fantasy* [Computer game series]. Japan: Nintendo.

Stormfront Studios, & Hypnos Entertainment. (2002). *The lord of the rings: The two towers* [Computer game]. United States: Electronic Arts.

Sweller, J. (1999). *Instructional design in technical areas.* Camberwell, Australia: ACER Press.

Tafalla, R. J. (2007). Gender differences in cardiovascular reactivity and game performance related to sensory modality in violent video game play. *Journal of Applied Social Psychology, 37*, 2008–2023.

Taito. (1978). *Space invaders* [Computer game]. Japan: Taito.

Takatsuki, Y. (2007, December 27). Cost headache for game developers. *BBC News*. Retrieved from <http://news.bbc.co.uk/1/hi/business/7151961.stm> (accessed November 3, 2010).

Tan, S. -L., & Spackman, M. P., & Wakefield, E. M. (August, 2008). Effects of diegetic and non-diegetic presentation of film music on viewers' interpretation of film narrative. In *Conference Proceedings for the 2008 International Conference of Music Perception and Cognition*, pp. 588–593. Hokkaido University, Japan. Australia: Causal Productions.

Tan, S. -L., Baxa, J., & Spackman, M. P. (2010). Effects of built-in audio versus unrelated background music on performance in an adventure role-playing game. *International Journal of Gaming and Computer-Mediated Simulations*, *2*(3), 1–23.

Truax, B. (2001). *Acoustic communication* (2nd ed.). Westport, CN: Ablex.

Tykwer, T., Potente, F., Bleibtreu, M., Knaup, H., Petri, N., Sony Pictures Classics, *et al.* (1998). *Run Lola run: Lola rennt*. Culver City, CA: Sony Pictures Home Entertainment.

Ubisoft. (2001). *Ghost recon: Advanced warfighter* [Computer game]. France: Ubisoft.

Ubisoft. (2011). *Rocksmith* [Computer game]. France: Ubisoft.

United Game Artists. (2001). *Rez* [Computer game]. Japan: Sega.

Unkrich, L. (Director). (2010). *Toy story 3* [Motion picture]. United States: Walt Disney Pictures.

Valve. (2004a). *Source* [Game audio engine]. United States: Valve.

Valve. (2004b). *Half-life 2* [Computer game]. United States: Electronic Arts.

Ward, M. (2010). Voice, videogames, and the technologies of immersion. In N. Neumark, R. Gibson & T. van Leeuwen (Eds.), *VOICE Vocal Aesthetics in Digital Arts and Media* (pp. 265–277). Cambridge, MA: MIT Press.

Webb, M. (2007). Music analysis down the (You) Tube?: An exploration of the potential of cross-media listening for the music classroom. *British Journal of Music Education*, *24*, 147–164.

W Industries. (1991). *Dactyl Nightmare* [Virtual reality game].

Wolfson, S., & Case, G. (2000). The effects of sound and colour on responses to a computer game. *Interacting with Computers*, *13*, 183–192.

Wood, R. T. A., Griffiths, M., Chappell, D., & Davies, M. N. O. (2004). The structural characteristics of video games: A psycho-structural analysis. *CyberPsychology*, *7*, 1–10.

Yamada, M., Fujisawa, N., & Komori, S. (2001). The effect of music on the performance and impression in a racing game. *Journal of Music Perception and Cognition*, *7*, 65–76.

Young, M. E., & Nguyen, N. (2009). The problem of delayed causation in a video game: Constant, varied, and filled delays. *Learning and Motivation*, *40*, 298–312.

Zehnder, S. M., Igoe, L., & Lipscomb, S. D. (2003, June). *Immersion-sound: A study of the influence of sound on the perceptual salience of interactive games*. Paper presented at the conference of the Society for Music Perception & Cognition. Las Vegas, NV.

Zehnder, S. M., & Lipscomb, S. D. (2006). The role of music in video games. In P. Vorderer & J. Bryant (Eds.), *Playing Video Games: Motives, Responses, and Consequences* (pp. 241–258). Mahwah, NJ: Lawrence Erlbaum Associates.

Zhou, Z., Cheok, A. D., Yang, X., & Qui, Y. (2004). An experimental study on the role of 3D sound in augmented reality environment. *Interacting with Computers*, *16*, 1043–1068.

Chapter 14

Music in television advertising and other persuasive media

Mark Shevy[a] and Kineta Hung[b]

[a]Northern Michigan University, USA

[b]Hong Kong Baptist University, Hong Kong

In Greek mythology, mariners had more to worry about than just the wind, waves, and other natural hazards of the sea. If they ventured too close to a particular island, they would hear the enchanting songs of sirens. Those who heard the music were unable to resist, following it to their deaths as their boats crashed into the island's rocky shores. Although few would argue nowadays that music is strong enough to render listeners as helpless as the ill-fated Greek adventurers, studies show that music does have the power to sway people navigating the waters of today's media-saturated society (Allan, 2008; Bruner, 1990; North & Hargreaves, 2008). Music is used as a means of persuasion in love, political messages, and commercial advertising. Empirical research in media persuasion suggests that music, in conjunction with extra-musical information (e.g., visual images, words, narrative structure), exerts a persuasive influence through cognitive and affective processes. Alexomanolaki, Loveday, and Kennett (2007) state that 'Music may play several roles and have many effects in advertising; it may attract attention, carry the product message, act as a mnemonic device, and create excitement or a state of relaxation' (p. 51).

This chapter presents an overview of theories and research on the role of music in advertising and other persuasive media. Most of the work in music and mediated persuasion has been conducted in the field of advertising, but the concepts should be beneficial for other contexts that use persuasion, such as public service announcements, edutainment, and online shopping sites. The discussion begins with a brief consideration of the prevalence of music in advertising. Next, the Elaboration Likelihood Model of media persuasion is introduced, which provides a conceptual framework for explaining how music can persuade people through a variety of psychological processes. The chapter then addresses specific effects of music on message processing, mood, attention, attitude, memory, musical fit, meaning construction, priming, and conditioning, followed by a consideration of the psychological functions of music in the commercial use of branding, jingles, and virtual atmospheres. Finally, the chapter explores the idea that persuasion is not merely a function of media. Moderating variables such as music preference and familiarity, and sex and culture of the audience can also have a bearing on how consumers are influenced by musical messages.

The prevalence of music in advertising

Advertising is pervasive in everyday life. Through television, an average American aged 18 or above is exposed to close to 150 commercials (or just over 60 minutes of advertising) every day (Holt, Ippolito, Desrochers, & Kelley, 2007). The number would be even higher if radio and internet advertising were included. These advertising messages often include music. Over 80 percent of television advertisements in the United States contain music (Allan, 2008; Furnham, Abramsky, & Gunter, 1997), and the percentage may be even higher in other countries (Murray & Murray, 1996). Content analyses of television and radio advertisements provide information such as whether an advertisement contains any music and whether the music is a jingle, contains lyrics, or is easily identifiable (Stewart and Furse, 1986). Allan (2008) conducted an analysis of 3,456 US prime-time television commercials aired on ABC, CBS, FOX, and NBC. Results revealed that 14 percent contained popular music, 5 percent used jingles, and 81 percent used generic, prefabricated, multipurpose musical beds.

Other studies have examined specific attributes of the music itself. For example, Hung and Rice's (1992) content analysis used a typology that followed Bruner's (1990) discussion of musical elements, including time- (e.g., tempo), texture- (e.g., volume), and pitch-related (e.g., modality) structural elements of music. It also included consideration of musical style (e.g., easy listening, jazz, fanfare/march) and mnemonic devices (e.g., theme song, jingle) to account for musical elements that could potentially contribute to consumer affect and recall of the content of advertisements. This typology was tested on 292 advertisements aired on three US networks (ABC, NBC, and CBS) on a weekday at different times: 9–10 a.m., 1–2 p.m., and 8–9 p.m. Selecting all the commercials during these time periods allowed for a broad representation of commercials aired on each network over the course of a normal programming day. Repeats were excluded so that each commercial was counted only once. The analysis revealed that 80 percent of the music in the sampled commercials was instrumental (no lyrics). There was a variety of musical styles, including adult contemporary (29.1 percent), classical (20.1 percent), easy listening (13.1 percent), jazz (12.7 percent), rap/dance (6.1 percent), fanfare/march (5.7 percent), atmospheric (5.7 percent), and hard rock/metal (5.7 percent). The music was likely to be in a major mode (72 percent), soft (62 percent), and have a moderate tempo (49 percent). Most had a distinct melody (52 percent), but only 10 percent used a jingle (defined as 'an identifiable musical or otherwise audio fragment which is associated with a brand name across different ads of the same brand'; Hung & Rice, 1992, p. 225).

Theoretical foundations: The Elaboration Likelihood Model

In most cases, the ultimate goal of persuasive messages is to produce an intended behavior, such as voting for a candidate, buckling seatbelts, donating to a cause, or buying a product (Petty, Briñol, & Priester, 2009). Social psychologists and media scholars have considered how *input variables* such as the message, message source (e.g., spokesperson), and the recipient might each influence persuasion through a hierarchy of psychological processes (*output variables*), including exposure to the message, attention, comprehension, yielding to a new attitude, and action based on the attitude (McGuire, 1985). Music constitutes one input variable that interacts with other input variables to influence output variables in the persuasion process.

Allan (2007) reviewed 28 studies from 1982 to 2006 investigating the effects of music in advertising and found that musical properties such as tempo (i.e., speed or pace of the music), mode (major or minor), and fit with extra-musical elements may have a positive, a negative, or no influence on a variety of psychological variables (e.g., attitude toward an advertisement, perception of advertisement time, brand recall, message processing, pleasure, arousal, mood, product preference, and purchase intention). Factors that may interact with music include audience characteristics (e.g., familiarity with the music), the type of product, imagery, or other extra-musical meanings in the message. For example, Allan reported studies indicating that attitude toward a brand can become more positive if the meanings of the music and the rest of the advertisement fit well together from the listener's perspective (North, MacKenzie, Law, & Hargreaves, 2004) but attitude may become more negative if they do not (Shen & Chen, 2006). Allan summarized the review by saying that the influence of music in advertising can be effective, but it is 'complicated' (Allan, 2007, p. 28). For reviews of the literature on musical persuasion, see Allan (2008), Bruner (1990), Hahn & Hwang (1999), and North & Hargreaves (2008).

Attitude change and the Elaboration Likelihood Model

Many scholars view attitudes as cognitive structures that lead to the favorable or unfavorable evaluation of some entity such as a person, activity, idea, or product (Eagly & Chaiken, 1993). Attitudes can consist of both cognitive and affective elements. That is, people may associate an entity with positive or negative thoughts and feelings (Eagly & Chaiken, 1993). Over the past few decades, researchers have used the *Elaboration Likelihood Model* or ELM (Petty & Cacioppo, 1986) to explain attitude change through mass media (e.g., Allan, 2007; Petty, Briñol, & Priester, 2009; North & Hargreaves, 2008; Trampe, Stapel, Siero, & Mulder, 2010).

The ELM is a 'dual-route' model depicting how a message may change one's attitude through either a peripheral or central route. The basic elements of the model are depicted in Figure 14.1 (slightly adapted to consider the possible role of music). People are more likely to give greater cognitive effort ('elaboration') to the central argument (a logical, persuasive appeal) of a message if they have the motivation and ability to do so. This is called *central route processing*, in which a person is highly involved with the message and critically evaluates the argument. According to the ELM, if the central argument of the message is strong, containing relevant, logical facts, the individual will develop a more favorable attitude toward a product. If the argument is weak, the individual is likely to develop a less favorable attitude. If the motivation or ability to elaborate is lacking, the model predicts that a person will give less cognitive effort to the central argument, and the argument quality will have less impact. This is called *peripheral route processing*. In this instance, the individual does not or cannot give the argument much thought. Yet, people may still be persuaded by cues that require little thought, such as whether the message source is an attractive person or whether they like the background music.

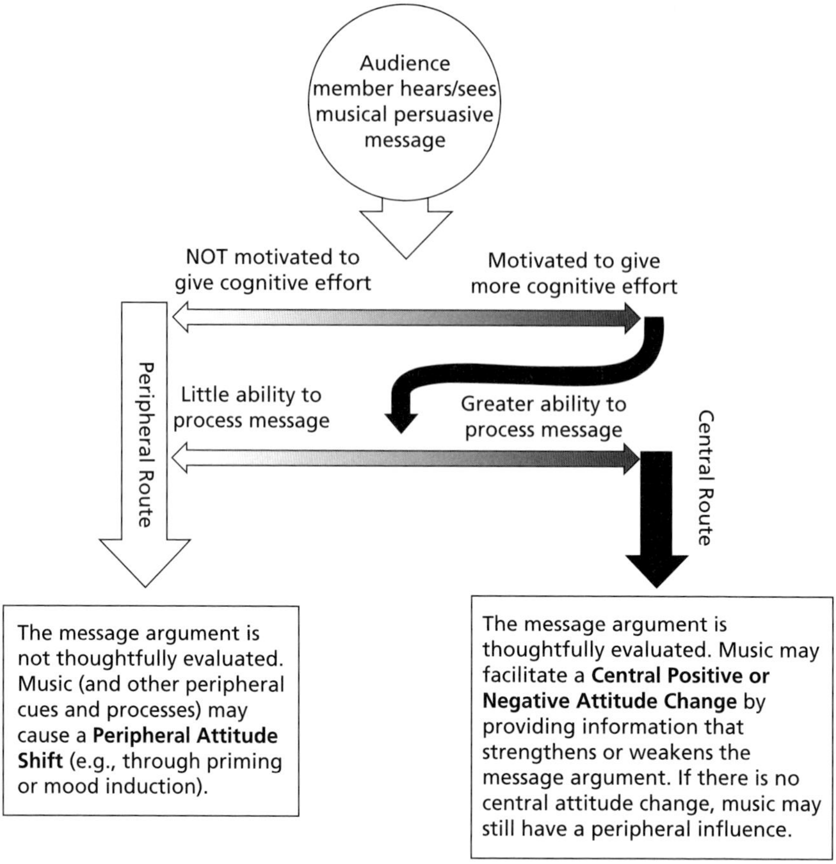

Figure 14.1 Proposed Elaboration Likelihood Model for music persuasion. Music may increase or decrease the listener's motivation and ability to process the persuasive message. It can also provide information within peripheral- and central-route processing. The ELM terminology and general concepts are adapted from Petty and Cacioppo (1986) and Petty, Briñol, and Priester (2009).

The two routes are distinguished by the amount of elaboration given to a message. Elaboration is the extent to which cognitive effort is expended to understand issue-relevant arguments and contemplate main points, logic, and counter-arguments in order to form an attitude or judgment. Empirically, elaboration has been measured by participants' self-reports of the level of effort expended, thought-listing measures (participants write down their thoughts about a message, and the thoughts are analyzed to indicate the amount of elaboration), psychophysiological measures (e.g., electromyographic activity), and participant responses to message argument quality. There is greater differentiation between strong and weak arguments when participants expend more cognitive effort (Petty & Cacioppo, 1986).

In past empirical work, researchers have manipulated ability and motivation to elaborate in a number of ways. For example, they may decrease a participant's level of ability to process information by presenting distractions that disrupt participants' ability to think or they may improve the ability to scrutinize arguments by repeating messages (Petty & Cacioppo, 1986). Motivation can be raised by increasing the relevance of a message to participants, heightening their level of involvement (Petty & Cacioppo, 1986). When MacInnis and Park (1991) wanted to induce high involvement in order to study the effect of music in a TV shampoo commercial, they told participants that the brand of shampoo would be available locally. Trampe et al. (2010) manipulated the level of relevance by telling participants they would have to write a review about an advertised product. Petty & Cacioppo (1979) told participants that a policy would alter their own graduation requirements rather than those at a distant university. Motivation can also be increased through a heightened sense of personal responsibility. If participants think they are part of a smaller group (e.g., four participants) and their responses are important, they tend to expend more effort than if they think they are part of a larger group (e.g., 16 participants; Tormala, Briñol, & Petty, 2007).

Further, some participants may be more naturally motivated to process messages more thoughtfully than others, a trait that Cacioppo and Petty (1982) and others refer to as the 'need for cognition.' Need for cognition (NFC) refers to the extent to which a person engages in and enjoys effortful cognitive processing, and was first identified by Cohen, Stotland, and Wolfe (1955). People who are driven to understand the nature of things and enjoy engaging in intellectual activities are high in NFC, whereas those who tend to avoid tasks requiring a lot of mental effort and do not find much intrinsic pleasure in such activities are low in NFC. In general, individuals with a low need for cognition are more likely to engage in peripheral processing of persuasive messages—for instance, focusing on the physical attractiveness of the product endorser—whereas those with a high need for cognition are more likely to attend to the quality of the message or the strength of the argument (Haugtvedt, Petty, Cacioppo, & Steidley, 1988).

In general, attitudes and learning produced through the central route of the ELM model are more enduring, more resistant to counter-persuasion, and more predictive of behavior than those produced through the peripheral route (Petty, Briñol, & Priester, 2009; Petty & Cacioppo, 1986). The price for trying to achieve a high-quality central-route attitude in advertising, though, is that it requires a strong argument that can withstand the scrutiny of potential consumers.

Elements of a message are not intrinsically central or peripheral. For example, the attractiveness of a beautiful model in a TV commercial is usually considered a peripheral cue, because it is not part of the central argument. However, according to the 'match-up hypothesis' (e.g., Kahle & Homer, 1985; Trampe et al., 2010), the model's appearance could support the central argument if attractiveness is relevant to the product being sold (e.g., beauty products). Likewise, music could have an influence in either the peripheral or central route, depending upon the degree of elaboration, the music's relation to the central message, and other factors such as the structural qualities of the music and their relation to other elements of the advertisement (e.g., images, editing pace). This will become more apparent in the following sections. Similarly, it is important to note that 'peripheral' and 'central' are not enduring audience member traits. Each individual may process messages with more central processing at one time and more peripheral processing at another time, depending on the message relevance and the person's ability afforded by the context of a specific instance.

The Elaboration Likelihood Model, music, and mood

There are two main ways music may function within the ELM. First, music may increase or decrease motivation or ability to elaborate, guiding a person toward central or peripheral route processing. Second, music can provide information that is processed within a particular route. Some of the psychological processes discussed later in this chapter illustrate how music can fulfill these functions.

In the first function or role of music within the ELM, mood induced by music (e.g., Gorn, Pham, & Sin, 2001) may increase the motivation or ability to think about the argument by increasing arousal (Kellaris, Cox, & Cox, 1993). On the other hand, music may also increase cognitive load, reducing one's ability for central processing. For example, if sad music were used in an otherwise cheerful commercial, people might miss the central argument, because they are busy wondering what the incongruous music is supposed to mean (cf. Oakes and North, 2006; Park & Young, 1986). As another example, a favorite or emotionally moving tune could increase one's motivation to attend to the music itself but not to the central argument. This type of value-expressive motive is called 'affective involvement' and may be an instance in which attitudes are formed based on peripheral cues despite a higher level of cognitive effort (Park & Young, 1986).

In addition to guiding potential consumers to use the central or peripheral route in an advertising context, music may provide information that is processed within the route. (This is the second possible function or role that music may play in the ELM). For instance, the 'affect-as-information' model of cognition and emotion suggests that people may consider their own feelings during decision-making. When they do, the valence dimension (positive or negative affect) provides evaluative information (positive or negative appraisal), and the arousal dimension indicates urgency or importance (Gorn, Pham, & Sin, 2001; Storbeck & Clore, 2008). Gorn, Pham, and Sin (2001) found that positive or negative mood induced by music directed participants' liking for an ambiguous print advertisement in a mood-congruent direction. The valence of the mood did not influence liking for advertisements that already had a clear positive or negative affective tone. However, arousal induced by the music strengthened the effect of the advertisement, causing the positive advertisement to seem more favorable and the negative ad to seem less favorable. The authors concluded that the results were consistent with the affect-as-information model. If the advertisement was ambiguous, participants considered the valence of their own feelings (positive or negative) when making an evaluation. If the advertisement had an affective tone, participants' level of arousal determined how strongly they felt about the advertisement. The authors further stated that the results could also be consistent with the ELM, but were inconclusive whether attitude formation based on one's own feelings was a peripheral-route heuristic or a type of central-route processing.

MacInnis and Park (1991) found an example in which music clearly had an effect by providing information within the peripheral route. The authors elicited high or low involvement for a television shampoo commercial by telling participants whether the brand of shampoo would be locally available. Those who believed that the shampoo would be locally available were more highly involved with the commercial, which increased central-route processing. Participants in the low-involvement condition (peripheral-route processing) experienced negative emotions (e.g., disgust, annoyance, and boredom) when the music (e.g., 'Stop in the Name of Love' by Diana Ross & the Supremes) did not fit the commercial's primary message that the shampoo was closely associated with nature. A lack of musical fit did not cause negative emotions for high-involvement participants. The authors determined that emotion caused by perception of musical fit was a peripheral cue. In support of their findings, MacInnis and Park stated that 'Previous research suggests that executional cues (e.g., music) in an ad exert their influence primarily under conditions of low involvement in the form of peripheral processing' (1991, p. 161).

Other areas of mood and ELM research allow inferences about the effects of music, though research that specifically addresses the role of music is still needed. One such area is the awareness of manipulation. A person who becomes aware of attention-getting tactics and emotionally manipulative content (both of which plausibly include music) can become more critical toward an advertisement and form a negative attitude toward it (Campbell, 1995; Cotte, Coulter, & Moore, 2005). Researchers should investigate whether music can cause awareness of manipulation and whether such awareness influences the level of elaboration (first function) or provides information within a route (second function).

Another area for research is the influence of mood valence on elaboration. Bless, Bohner, Schwarz, and Strack (1990) found that German university students who were induced into a negative mood by recalling an unpleasant life event gave more elaboration to an audio announcement than those who were induced into a positive mood by recalling a pleasant event. Researchers should determine whether musically induced mood can have the same effect. More recently, studies have indicated that negative mood can enhance attention and memory for central, episodic details of an object or event by creating a 'narrowing effect' that reduces attention to contextual or peripheral information (Avramova, Stapel, & Lerouge, 2010). In contrast, positive mood can enhance the use of contextual information and conceptual processes, which could increase the use of peripheral cues in message processing (Kensinger, 2009).

Factors affecting the impact of advertisements

Attention, memory, and cognitive load

Before a message can persuade, it must attract a person's attention. In media research, attention is a state of focus on a particular stimulus, such as a television advertisement, and is often, but not always, accompanied by the orientation of sensory organs (e.g., eyes and ears) toward the stimulus and its message (Shevy & Hawkins, 2008). Sometimes media content can elicit an automatic reaction such as an orienting response in which a sound in a television show causes audience members to reflexively look at the source. Other times, people have a more voluntary response, such as consciously deciding to look at the television to determine the cause for an onset of musical sound. Research investigating automatic and controlled attention generally falls into two categories: (1) what increases attention to a message and (2) how the stimulus-induced attention impacts message processing, such as the construction of comprehension and memory.

Media researchers have studied music as a means of attracting children's attention to educational shows to facilitate learning. (See also Chapter 12 by Calvert, in this volume.) Observing kindergarten, 3rd-, and 4th-graders, Calvert, Huston, Watkins, and Wright (1982) measured how the formal features of the show (e.g., movement of objects within a shot, camera zooms, sound effects, and music) affected children's visual attention and comprehension of a television cartoon. Although some formal features increased selective attention to visual content, the presence of music had the opposite effect. The older children (3rd- and 4th-graders) who did pay attention during the music learned more incidental, non-essential story content. Recall of incidental information is typically associated with younger children, who have less ability to filter and comprehend the central, important elements of a story. Wakshlag, Reitz, and Zillmann (1982) conducted a similar experiment and found that children were more likely to tune into a television show (selective exposure) that had fast, appealing background music. However, once a show was selected, the fast-tempo music reduced children's visual attention, especially if the music was appealing. Furthermore, the fast-tempo music reduced the amount that children learned.

Other studies suggest that music can enhance attention and facilitate memory. In an experiment with background music in radio advertisements, participants reported paying more attention to a commercial when it contained popular music (e.g., Eminem's 'Without Me'), especially if the original lyrics or lyrics altered to promote the sponsor were included, compared to no-music versions (Allan, 2006). Versions of the music with altered lyrics also consistently increased brand recall. Kellaris, Cox, and Cox (1993) proposed that, as certain properties of the music increase arousal in listeners, attention increases, which results in better memory for the persuasive message.

The mixed results in the attention and memory research reviewed here point to the challenge of incorporating attention-getting devices in advertisements without overburdening limited cognitive capacity. Cognitive resources can be allocated toward some stimuli and processes to the detriment of others (Lang, 2009). Thus, music with arousing properties, such as a fast tempo, may attract attention to an advertisement, but it may also draw the allocation of cognitive resources toward the music, leaving fewer resources for encoding the persuasive message into memory. A goal for message producers, then, is to find ways of using music in a manner that maximizes memory by heightening attention while minimizing detriment to memory caused by resource reallocation.

Day, Lin, and Huang (2009) refer to this as 'background music as the arousal inducer versus the distractor' (p. 130). They proposed that the effect of background music may be contingent upon the type of music, the task the person is attempting to perform, listener differences, and 'other contextual factors' (p. 130). Day et al. asked undergraduate students to complete easy and difficult problem-solving tasks while either a faster or slower version of a new-age piano piece ('In the Enchanted Garden' by Kevin Kern) played in the background. The results showed that the faster-tempo music improved accuracy in the difficult task, which supports the idea of 'background music as arousal inducer.' (The easier task had relatively high accuracy scores regardless of music tempo.)

Hahn and Hwang (1999) found that there is an optimal range for the tempo of background music for effective message processing and that listeners' familiarity with the music also played a role in attention and cognitive load. They conducted two experiments involving college students in Korea, one in which they added slow versus fast and familiar versus unfamiliar music (Western classical style) to a fictional TV soap commercial, and a similar second experiment in which they added music to a TV car commercial, using three *tempi*: 60, 90, and 120 beats per minute (bpm). The first study revealed that unfamiliar music increased cognitive load, reducing message recall, while familiar music improved cognitive efficiency as determined by improved recall scores. The slower of the two *tempi* in the first study resulted in marginally better recall than higher tempo, but only if the music was familiar. The familiarity results were not replicated in their second study. However, the second study showed that recall was better at 90 bpm than at the slowest or highest *tempi*. The authors suggested that there may be an optimal range for increasing cognitive resource allocation without creating an overload, and that range may follow the 'inverted U' pattern found in other studies of cognitive efficiency, emotion, and aesthetics (e.g., Anand & Sternthal, 1990).

Salient changes in stimulus parameters have also been associated with attracting attention and increasing recall. Olsen (2002) found that stopping background music during a radio advertisement—using silence to highlight a piece of spoken information—increased recall for that information. This effect was most pronounced for the first one or two pieces of information highlighted and when the silence lasted no longer than 3 seconds. Olsen concluded that the increase in attention was due to an orienting response causing increased attention and greater salience of the highlighted information. In a previous study, Olsen (1997) found that too much silence between pieces of information in an advertisement would lead to lower recall for low-involvement listeners. This was apparently because their minds would start to wander. Olsen's study indicated that light classical music in the background during these times helped keep listeners' attention on the message by delaying interfering thoughts.

In summary, certain properties of music may increase attention and impact the allocation of cognitive resources to persuasive messages. Yet, music can also draw attention away from the important information or overload cognition, leaving fewer resources for encoding messages into memory. Music tempo seems to influence attention and memory, as do listeners' familiarity with the music, the amount of cognitive effort required to process a message (or perform a task), and dramatic changes in the audio stimulus (e.g., insertion of silence). Another variable that may impact cognitive load is the degree to which the audiovisual stimuli match (referred to here as 'musical fit'), discussed in the 'Musical fit' section.

Musical fit

Musical fit refers to the subjective perception that the music in an advertisement is relevant or appropriate to an extra-musical attribute of the advertisement, such as the central message (MacInnis & Park, 1986). For example, if a television advertisement for a luxury car presents words and images that portray the car as sophisticated and high class, most people would probably say that classical background music fits the commercial better than bluegrass music. The amount of musical fit is based upon 'pattern activation' as described by Gawronski and Bodenhausen (2006, pp. 693, 698–700). In pattern activation, the pairing of two stimuli activates memories common to both, making their shared attributes more salient. An example can be drawn from Nicholas Cook's (1998) analysis of a television car commercial in his book *Analysing Musical Multimedia*. Visually, the commercial presents scenes of artistic painters in the countryside interjected with images of a car 'racing along a country lane' (p. 6). The opening of Mozart's overture to the *Marriage of Figaro* initially occurs only when the car is shown, but it later accompanies the images of both the painters and the car.

Cook (1998) explains that, separately, the music could have a broad range of meanings and the visuals might not make much sense. Within the context of one another, however, the visuals give meaning to the music, and the music gives meaning to the visuals through the salience of shared attributes. The overture and car each possess attributes of 'liveliness and precision' (Cook, 1998, p. 6). Thus, the combined music and images communicate that the car has a lively engine and precise road-holding. The music and painters both have associations with high art and prestige. Cook states that meanings emerge from these attributes to communicate that the car 'represents an ideal synthesis of art and technology' (p. 6). In terms of musical fit, we can say that the classical music fits with both the technological features of car and the painters, allowing the audience to associate the car with a favorable meaning constructed from the music and painters.

The example drawn from Cook (1998) considers the musical fit of the meaning of images, but the principles presented by MacInnis and Park (1991) and Gawronski and Bodenhausen (2006) suggest that musical fit could result from matching patterns between music and many other variables, including words, emotion, product and spokesperson traits, the overall tone or style of an advertisement, or the emotional state of an audience member.

Kellaris, Cox, and Cox (1993) conducted an experiment that showed how musical fit and the attention-gaining properties of music could interact to influence memory for information in a radio advertisement. Selecting pieces of music that were determined to have high or low attention-gaining value and evoked imagery (e.g., sounding like an 'adventure movie'), the researchers used these auditory stimuli as background music in advertisements that promoted products that either fit (e.g., adventure music with an adventure movie advertisement) or were incongruent with the music (e.g., adventure music with a restaurant). In general, the results showed that high attention-gaining music with good fit (message congruent) led to better memory of advertisement information than the low-fit and low-attention music combinations. However, memory in the high-attention, good-fit condition was only about the same as that for advertisements without music. In other words, the best music condition did not improve memory, but the other conditions decreased memory, probably due to increased cognitive load. Kellaris et al. (1993) encouragingly stated, however, that although some music might interfere with cognitive processes, it might benefit persuasion in other ways, such as mood elevation and affect transfer.

North et al. (2004) not only found that good fit of background musical style (instrumental easy listening, jazz, new age, etc.) in a radio advertisement increased recall above that of no-musical advertisements, but that it also led to a positive attitude toward the advertisement and increased the likelihood that a participant would purchase the advertised brand. The authors suggested that the good-fitting music primed brand-relevant concepts that improved cognitive processing, while poor-fitting music diverted attention away from the advertisement messages. (This is an example of how musical fit and priming can influence elaboration in the ELM.)

Oakes and North (2006) raised the possibility that music tempo could be a matter of musical fit leading to reduction of memory for advertising content. They speculated that the 'fast-tempo' music in their experiment (170 bpm) was so much faster than typical advertisement background music that it became a distraction by being incongruent with what is usually played. Oakes and North also tested the association of musical timbre to musical fit. The consultation of an advertisement agency musician and pretesting determined that the sound of a piano was congruent with the tone of a radio advertisement for cosmetic surgery services, while the sound of a church organ or Caribbean-style steel drums was not. In an experiment, listeners' recall for the intended message was higher when the background music consisted of the piano rather than the other instruments or no background music at all.

The lyrics of a song and perceived mood of the music may also influence the degree of musical fit. In an experiment with Taiwanese college students, Chou and Lien (2010) found that older, familiar Mandarin pop songs in television advertisements not only evoked good moods and favorable nostalgic thoughts, but they also improved attitudes toward an advertisement if the songs had lyrics with high relevance to the advertisement (see also Olsen & Johnson, 2002). Concerning mood, Alpert, Alpert, and Maltz (2005) asked college students to evaluate advertisements of greeting cards for the occasion of either a friend having a birthday (happy occasion) or a friend who was sick in the hospital (sad occasion). Either a happy or sad prelude from Bach's *Well-Tempered Clavier* (determined by pretesting) played in the background during the advertisements. Those who heard the sad music—regardless of the occasion for which they were supposed to be purchasing the card—reported feeling significantly sadder than those who heard the happy music. Participants reported more likelihood of buying the card if the musical mood was congruent with the purchase occasion.

The examples described here are not the only types of musical fit or effects that can occur. Factors such as culture and congruity between visual and audio formal structures could also have an impact (cf. Iwamiya & Hanako, 2004; Shen & Chen, 2006). (This topic is addressed in more detail in Chapter 7 on semantic and formal congruence by Iwamiya, in this volume.)

Constructing meaning

Like pictures and words, music can be associated with concepts of people, values, cultures, and social processes (cf. Barthes, 1985; Shevy & Kristen, 2009). When integrated into advertising, music can help to portray a venue, occasion, activity, or type of person (as exemplified by sex, race, age, appearance, and lifestyle). Some studies have examined how people combine music with images, words, messages, and products to create meanings or make certain product attributes and values salient.

Hung (2000, 2001) conducted a series of experiments showing that changing the type of music in television commercials directed attention to different attributes of the product, location, and people in the commercial. In the first of these studies, participants were shown one of two television coffee advertisements; the music was either culturally congruent or incongruent with the images. Participants who saw a video showing rainforest scenery and what appeared to be Latin American workers with Brazilian music or a video of a European café with European music gave somewhat consistent descriptions of the video images according to the culture represented. However, participants who saw the incongruent stimuli (e.g., European images with Brazilian music) made the music fit with the video in individual ways. For example, the café video with café music was interpreted as a relaxing, social atmosphere, and the coffee was perceived as sophisticated, expensive, and somewhat pretentious. The café video with Brazilian music, however, was interpreted differently by individual participants. Some perceived a mysterious setting with non-conformist coffee drinkers, while others perceived young professional coffee drinkers. The interaction between music and visual images is complex, with each element contributing to the overall meaning constructed (Cohen, 2005; Cook, 1998; Scott, 1990). Zander (2006) found that changing the style of music in a radio advertisement did not influence low-involvement participants' intention to buy a product, but it did change their impression of the brand and the endorser (as measured by a personality inventory).

In relation to the ELM discussed previously, music can increase or decrease one's ability to think about the central argument of a message. It is also possible that motivation and the cognitive demands of the advertisement's argument can influence one's ability to process the music. Drawing from the work of Leonard Meyer (1994), Zhu and Meyers-Levy (2005) studied two types of meaning listeners can construct from music and how cognitive load influences which meaning the music imparts. The first type of meaning, 'embodied,' referred mainly to the 'hedonic value or favorableness' (p. 334) of feelings evoked by the music. The authors stated that embodied meaning should require relatively few cognitive resources because understanding whether a piece of music is pleasant is an easy task. The second type of meaning, 'referential,' involves constructing meaning based on associations between the music and the extra-musical world, which should require more cognitive resources. Zhu and Meyers-Levy (2005) presented travel agency radio advertisements that had either an easy message structure (a lecture) or a demanding structure (a narrative). They found that participant evaluations and open-ended comments about the agency reflected the background music's referential meaning in the easy structure condition and the music's embodied meaning in the difficult structure condition. They concluded that the narrative consumed more cognitive resources, leaving fewer for constructing more taxing meanings from the music. These effects were only present for some participants (i.e., those who were willing to give cognitive effort in the first place).

Priming and conditioning

The associative view depicts memory as a network of associated nodes, with each node representing a concept, word, or similar knowledge construct. When a stimulus activates a node, making it more accessible for use in working memory, other closely associated nodes may also be activated (Anderson, 1983; Dimofte & Yalch, 2011). A group of closely associated concepts is called a *schema*, and the process of activating a concept or schema is called *priming*. Shevy (2008) conducted two experiments showing that the sound of popular music genres is associated with distinct groups of extra-musical concepts, forming 'cognitive genre schemas.' In Shevy's first experiment, participants indicated the meanings they associated with a brief recording of instrumental sections of country or hip-hop music. In comparison to country music, listeners associated hip-hop more strongly with minority ethnicity, youth, and liberal ideology and less with trustworthiness and friendliness. In a second experiment, a different group of participants heard the same music in an audio recording ostensibly of a musician making a persuasive appeal for charity donations at a concert. The genre of music did not directly alter attitude toward the charity, but it did change listeners' perception of the musician. Those who heard the hip-hop music were more likely to think he was of minority ethnicity, urban, younger, and more of an expert (e.g., well-informed, intelligent).

While priming is the activation of existing associations, *conditioning* is a process through which cognitive or affective associations are made between two stimuli, e.g., music and an extra-musical entity such as a brand, behavior, or person (Gorn, 1982). Gorn conducted a seminal experiment in which college students selected pens that had been briefly presented with music they liked (from the movie *Grease*) and avoided selecting pens that had been presented with music they disliked (Indian raga). Gorn's study became a source of controversy when subsequent researchers failed to replicate the results (Kellaris & Cox, 1989). More recent research has provided support for the role of conditioning. Redker and Gibson (2009) presented participants with a Web-based root beer advertisement containing scrolling text and images of the root beer and its logo. For participants who liked country music, the country music accompaniment resulted in a more favorable attitude toward the brand. The researchers concluded that music influenced two types of attitudes: explicit (consciously indicated) and implicit (measured by response time in a task comparing brand names). At the end of the study, participants were allowed to select a bottle of root beer to take home. The combined measures of the explicit and implicit attitudes predicted the chosen root beer brand 75% of the time.

Ziv, Hoftman, and Geyer (2012) tested the influence of background music conditioning on moral judgments through a series of three experiments that presented fictional radio advertisements promoting the unethical activities of cheating on a pension plan or buying a pre-written college seminar paper. The advertisements contained either no music or music that had been shown to convey a positive mood (Mozart's *Eine Kleine Nachtmusik* or James Brown's *I Got You/I Feel Good*) or a negative mood (Albinoni's *Adagio in G minor*) in prior studies and pretesting. The addition of any background music reduced recall of information, but the positive music caused participants to list more advantages and fewer disadvantages of the unethical behavior and made them more likely to recommend the websites to a friend. When participants were motivated to think harder before hearing the advertisement (high involvement), the positive music still led to a more positive evaluation of the cheating behavior. Negative music increased negative evaluations of the cheating behavior. The authors concluded that the music had an affective conditioning effect in which the mood conveyed by the music became associated with the behavior and influenced moral decisions, particularly when participants were not thinking as hard about the advertisement. They suggested that the effect of the music when participants were thinking harder was not necessarily due to conditioning, but other means of biasing thoughts (recall our previous discussion of the ELM central route).

Concerning the role of conditioning in advertisement, North et al. (2004) stated, 'The most prudent conclusion to draw at the moment is simply that the debate over classical conditioning continues' (p. 1677). Our understanding of musical conditioning may be enriched as researchers address moderating variables such as cognitive effort, musical fit, types of association (e.g., semantic imagery or affect), and the number of exposures to the advertisement-music pairing.

Engaging the consumer

The previous sections have centered on psychological processes involved in responses to persuasive multimedia presentations and have mainly focused on television advertisements. This section is organized around three common practices used in advertising to actively engage the consumer: Audio branding conveys a company's identity and image to the public, jingles make slogans appealing by making them 'sing-able,' and the creation of virtual environments such as online shopping sites engage consumers in interactive multimedia. The psychological explanations for how and why these practices work (or do not work) are briefly discussed. Many involve the same psychological processes discussed earlier, though their application to these practices may provide novel insights into the role of music in advertising.

Audio branding

Audio branding, also known as sonic branding or sonic identity (Audiobrain, 2009), is a field of study closely related to conditioning. Audio branding is the formation of cognitive associations between music or other sounds and a logo or other symbol. A well-recognized example of audio branding in the United States is the musical chimes accompanying the NBC television network peacock logo. People who have seen that logo enough times will likely think of NBC when they hear the musical sequence in other places. The principles of forming this kind of association between sound and image are similar to those used in film music such as the dramatic violin motif accompanying the shower scene in *Psycho* or the minor second *leitmotif* used to reference the shark in *Jaws* (Jackson, 2003). In audio branding, musical fit and conditioning serve as strategic principles. Audio brand designers often try to develop an original sound that evokes meanings and feelings that communicate the unique identity and market positioning of an organization or brand.

The cognitive associations in branding include perceptual cues such as music and the visual logo, specific meanings or attributes made salient by the combination of these cues, and generating a positive attitude (Bronner, Hirt, & Ringe, 2010; Wang, 2005; Williams, 1999). Shevy and Kristen (2011) emphasized the importance of music genre meanings when using music in an audio brand. In their study, participants from Germany and the United States indicated the concepts they associated with 'German folksy' (a contemporary representation of German folk), country, punk, and hip-hop music. The results showed significant differences between the genres in concepts that could be important in portraying a brand or organization. For example, punk and hip-hop were associated more with valuing personal independence, whereas country and German folksy were associated more with valuing family. German folksy was associated more with optimism for the future, while punk was associated more with pessimism. These patterns were consistent between the US and German participants, indicating that meaning associated with musical genres has some stability internationally, at least when comparing Western cultures.

Jingles

Jingles are a type of audio branding that have been defined as:

> an identifiable musical or otherwise audio fragment which is associated with a brand name across different ads of the same brand... A jingle is similar to a theme song except that a jingle is short, may or may not contain words or advertising message, is attention-catching and memorable. (Hung & Rice, 1992, p. 225)

Studies consistently show the effectiveness of well-constructed jingles on memory. Yalch (1991) found that people recalled more slogans presented as jingles than slogans that were merely spoken. A set of experiments by Wallace (1994) showed that 'a repeating, simple melody can provide a recall aid above and beyond what is provided in the text alone or in the poetic properties of the text such as rhyme' (p. 1481).

Most jingle research examines the effects of structuring a textual message such as a slogan as part of the music. Jingles may operate primarily at the level of perception and implicit memory, requiring little to no conscious effort (Alexomanolaki et al., 2007). When people hear jingles such as Coca Cola's 'Have a Coke and a smile,' McDonald's 'I'm lovin' it,' or State Farm Insurance's 'Like a good neighbor, State Farm is there,' learning to associate the surface, phonetic features of words with melody may happen without much effort. However, this kind of learning does not assure that listeners understand the meaning of the words. (See similar findings for children and educational media, reviewed by Calvert, Chapter 12, in this volume.)

Yalch (1991) proposed that musical structure (e.g., melody, phrasing, rhythm) can serve as a mnemonic device that improves lyrical memory if two conditions are present: (1) 'constructability' and (2) 'associability.' In order to meet the constructability condition, the musical structure must be accessible during learning and recall of the message (e.g., simple and familiar melodies tend to work better); to meet the associability requirement, the words must be easy to associate with the musical structure. As a mnemonic device, the musical structure can help break the incoming verbal message into chunks that are easier to encode and emphasize certain words to enhance memory for salient information. During recall, memory of the musical melody can help people remember the number and order of words and whether any are missing (Wallace, 1994). Lyric rhyming structure (if used), emotion associated with the melody, and the possibility of the melody leading to increased rehearsal of the words (e.g., singing the words to oneself) also has the potential to improve memory.

An experiment by Alexomanolaki et al. (2007) revealed that the presence of music, particularly a jingle, in a television commercial improved implicit learning and recall of words and images. The authors defined implicit learning and recall as processes of encoding and retrieving information 'without deliberate or conscious reference to what is being learned' or recalled (p. 53). Explicit learning and recall, on the other hand, require conscious effort. Drawing from studies in advertising and film music, Alexomanolaki and colleagues proposed that visual information would be more closely linked to explicit memory and that music would be more closely linked to implicit memory. They also presented literature suggesting that implicit memory processes tend to occur during a state of low attention and that implicit recall may be more accurate than explicit recall for indicating consumer thought and behavior.

In Alexomanolaki et al.'s (2007) experiment, participants watched an episode of a television situation comedy. Embedded within the show were four commercials; three were distractors to facilitate implicit learning by reducing attention to the target advertisement, a commercial for Nescafé coffee. To further facilitate implicit learning of the coffee commercial, the instructions given to the participants purposely avoided mentioning the commercials. Rather, participants were simply told that they would watch a television show and answer questions about what they had seen. To encourage a state of low attention toward the television, participants were minimally supervised and were allowed to eat, drink, and chat during the show.

The coffee commercial was accompanied by one of four soundtracks: (1) the musical jingle that originally accompanied the commercial, (2) instrumental music only, (3) the instrumental music with the words of the jingle spoken as a voiceover, and (4) sound effects (no music) with the spoken jingle voiceover. Implicit memory was assessed by asking participants to quickly select words and images relevant to the commercial visuals and product from larger lists of words and images. Participants were also asked to complete a word fragment that formed the brand name and a phrase fragment that formed the slogan. The participants were given little time to complete these tasks in order to minimize their ability to think. Several questions also explicitly asked about the commercial with no time constraints. Explicit recall did not vary significantly between the conditions, but implicit recall did. Implicit recall was higher for the commercials that contained music in comparison to the no-music version, and the jingle version had the highest implicit recall of all. The authors concluded that the 'jingle seems to be the most effective form of music reinforcement in advertising' (p. 65).

Virtual atmospheres

Marketing researchers study the ways in which sensory stimuli (color, odor, music, etc.), called 'atmospherics,' influence consumer inferences, attitude, and behavior in physical spaces (Lunardo & Mbengue, 2011). Hence, the influence of background music on consumer behavior in places such as restaurants and retail stores has a substantial research history. These studies have advanced our understanding about the use of music as part of this 'atmosphere.' Music with a slow tempo can decrease the traffic speed and increase sales volume in a store (Milliman, 1982). Playing a style of music that fits individual departments within a store can increase the number of shoppers who make a purchase and the amount they spend (Yalch & Spangenberg, 1993). Classical music might persuade consumers to buy more expensive products (Areni & Kim, 1993). Music with prosocial lyrics can cause restaurant patrons to tip more

(Jacob, Guéguen, & Boulbry, 2010), and happy music and music that is liked by participants can increase attitudes toward a store shown in a video (Broekemier, Marquardt, & Gentry, 2008).

As consumers have begun to make purchases using the Internet, researchers have tracked their behaviors. In an experiment involving an online gift shop, Wu, Cheng, and Yen (2008) found that, compared to no music or slow music (72 bpm or less) conditions, faster music (92 bpm or greater) increased shoppers' arousal and pleasure, which correlated with favorable attitudes toward the store and purchase intention. Richard, Chebat, Yang, and Putrevu (2010) created a conceptual model of online consumer behavior in which Web atmospherics contribute affective and cognitive influences to online behavior (website involvement and exploratory behavior) and outcomes (website attitudes and pre-purchase evaluation). In the model proposed by Richard et al., the affective influence of Web atmospherics is via entertainment, which consists of sensory and hedonic elements such as color, music, and interactivity. The cognitive influence is attributable to the structure of the site (e.g., layout), the amount of information on the site, and the currency of information. The extent to which the site presents a challenge that is matched by the user's skill can also influence online behavior.

Lai, Wu, Hsieh, Kung, and Lin (2011) reported that fast-tempo background music on a shopping website caused visitors to shift between Web pages more frequently, and visitors also perceived their browsing time to be shorter. They also reported that playing different music on different Web pages caused more page shifting and longer perceived time compared to conditions in which music continued constantly through the whole site or where the same music replayed on each new page. The researchers also determined that playing the same music continuously through the whole website led to greater recall accuracy. Future research could investigate how music impacts other meaningful aspects of virtual worlds such as colorfulness, simplicity, and relaxedness, as has been done in some video game immersion research (Lipscomb & Zehnder, 2004).

Moderating variables

Although this chapter has focused on the impact of music and message content, these are certainly not the sole determinants of persuasion through media (see Shevy, Chapter 4, in this volume). A number of moderating variables may strengthen, weaken, or otherwise alter the persuasive influence of music. One example, presented earlier, is the way in which a person's level of involvement can increase or reduce the impact of music on attitude. Other examples of moderating variables include music familiarity and preference, the cultural origins of symbol systems and listeners, and other listener traits.

Familiarity with and preference for music may increase interest or arousal, though not always (Carpentier & Potter, 2007). Familiar music may draw fewer cognitive resources away from message processing than unfamiliar music. As discussed previously, Hahn and Hwang (1999) indicated that participants who heard familiar background music during a soap commercial recalled more information than those who heard unfamiliar music, though these results were not replicated in a second experiment. MacInnis and Park (1991) observed that listeners' level of familiarity and preference for a musical selection were correlated with positive emotion, which led to a more positive evaluation of an advertisement. However, they also found that familiar music can also serve as a distraction, decreasing attention to the central message.

Cultural factors can also alter the effects of music. Tavassoli and Lee (2003) found that playing music (instrumental rock/funk and jazz) interfered with bilingual (Chinese and English) Singapore students' ability to learn advertisement text written in English but not in Chinese. The presentation of visual images rather than music had the opposite effect, interfering with Chinese advertisement text, but not English. The researchers argued that this is due to the fact that English uses a primarily sound-based mental code and Chinese is more visual. Concerning persuasion, the authors stated, 'Distraction can enhance or reduce the persuasive impact of a message. Distraction reduces learning of an advertisement's persuasive content and limits message scrutiny' (p. 470). Tavassoli and Lee also observed a parallel cultural effect in which music served as a better recall cue for English text, and visuals improved recall of Chinese text.

Music may also have different connotations for different cultural groups. As discussed earlier, Kristen and Shevy (2009) found that American listeners strongly associate hip-hop with minority ethnicity whereas German listeners do not. A difference in such a salient construct associated with strong attitudes (e.g., cultural identity or prejudice) is an important factor to recognize when creating messages for an international audience.

Individual characteristics and traits can also moderate the effects of music, including gender and cognitive styles. For instance, Kellaris and Rice (1993) found that females responded more positively toward music at lower volumes than males, which could have implications for music presentation in advertising. Richard et al.'s (2010) research investigating online shopping behavior indicated that entertainment atmospherics, including music, increased exploration of a site by women but not men. Meyers-Levy and Zhu (2010) showed that gender and willingness to expend cognitive effort (i.e., 'need for cognition' or NFC, as described earlier) interacted to moderate the musical meaning perceived in a radio advertisement. Meyers-Levy and Zhu measured two types of musical meaning, as introduced earlier: (1) 'embodied meaning,' which listeners construct from attributes of the structural properties of the music itself (e.g., a piece of music may sound solemn and grandiose because of its steady tempo and expansive chords) and (2) 'referential meaning,' which listeners construct from an association between the music and extra-musical ideas (e.g., the piece may bring to mind a coronation or other grand event and therefore seem to have stately and majestic qualities). Prior research had indicated that referential meaning requires more cognitive effort than embodied meaning. In Meyers-Levy and Zhu's (2010) study, men with high NFC were influenced by the referential meaning of background music when forming perceptions of advertised services (a florist and a test preparation service). The perceptions by men with low NFC, on the other hand, were influenced by embodied meanings. Women were sensitive to both referential and embodied meaning regardless of NFC level. Other personality traits (e.g., introversion/extraversion) have also been shown to play a role in the ability to cognitively process background music (e.g., Furnham & Bradley, 1999).

Conclusion

For centuries music has been used for persuasion, yet the central argument in persuasive messages rests predominantly in textual or visual form. Thus, the persuasive power of music often resides in the way that music facilitates or hinders the processing of messages in a multimedia context. Researchers have made substantial strides in understanding persuasive message processing with the Elaboration Likelihood Model as the overarching framework. The ELM has been applied to examine music's effects, both in establishing the amount of elaboration and as an influence within the central and peripheral routes. Particular attention has been given to delineating the way music may attract or detract attention, the motivation and ability for processing the central argument, and the comprehension and attitudinal outcomes of the persuasive message.

Music tempo, lyrics, and familiarity with music, if applied appropriately, could increase the allocation of cognitive resources to the persuasive message. Meanwhile, exposure to music may prime cognitive constructs with which it is previously associated, thereby allowing carefully constructed media presentations to form new associations through conditioning and branding processes. Mood valence and arousal evoked by music may influence people who rely on their gut feelings to make a decision. Indeed, this line of work on music may contribute to persuasion research by sensitizing the research community to the variety of persuasion and decision approaches adopted by different individuals. Additionally, variables such as musical familiarity, gender, and culture may moderate the processing and effects of an advertisement, public service announcement, or online store. A good fit between music and other message elements may reduce cognitive load, create favorable attitudes, and aid consistent meaning construction.

In spite of the gaps and inconsistencies in past research findings, there is great need for more work in this area. This is especially the case as new Internet and mobile formats emerge; gaming, viral marketing, and online shopping are already shaping the next generation of persuasive media. The types of persuasive messages found on social media sites and mobile platforms tend to be more interactive than the media advertising upon which the bulk of our knowledge of musical multimedia persuasion is based. Thus, there is a need to investigate and understand the roles and processes of music in these emergent platforms, especially from the perspectives of interactive persuasion. Such research will surely benefit message producers and consumers navigating the sea of media available to them.

References

Alexomanolaki, M., Loveday, C., & Kennett, C. (2007). Music and memory in advertising: Music as a device of implicit learning and recall. *Music, Sound, and the Moving Image*, *1*(1), 51–71.

Allan, D. (2006). Effects of popular music in advertising on attention and memory. *Journal of Advertising Research*, *46*(4), 434–443.

Allan, D. (2007). Sound advertising: A review of the experimental evidence on the effects of music in commercials on attention, memory, attitudes, and purchase. *Journal of Media Psychology, 12*(3). Retrieved from <http://www.calstatela.edu/faculty/sfischo/>.

Allan, D. (2008). A content analysis of music placement in prime-time television advertising. *Journal of Advertising Research, 48*(3), 404–417.

Alpert, M. I., Alpert, J. I., & Maltz, E. N. (2005). Purchase occasion influence on the role of music in advertising. *Journal of Business Research, 58*(3), 369–376.

Anand, P., & Sternthal, B. (1990). Ease of message processing as a moderator of repetition effects in advertising. *Journal of Marketing Research, 27*(3), 345–353.

Anderson, J. R. (1983). A spreading activation theory of memory. *Journal of Verbal Learning and Verbal Behavior, 22*(3), 261–295.

Areni, C. S., & Kim, D. (1993). The influence of background music on shopping behavior: Classical versus top-forty music in a wine store. *Advances in Consumer Research, 20,* 336–340.

Audiobrain. (2009). *Welcome to Audiobrain: Emmy award-winning sonic branding boutique.* Retrieved from <http://www.audiobrain.com>.

Avramova, Y. R., Stapel, D. A., & Lerouge, D. (2010). Mood and context-dependence: positive mood increases and negative mood decreases the effects of context on perception. *Journal of Personality and Social Psychology, 99*(2), 203–214.

Barthes, R. (1985). *Image-music-text* (S. Heath, Trans.). New York, NY: Hill & Wang.

Bless, H., Bohner, G., Schwarz, N., & Strack, F. (1990). Mood and persuasion. *Personality and Social Psychology Bulletin, 16*(2), 331–345.

Broekemier, G., Marquardt, R., & Gentry, J. W. (2008). An exploration of happy/sad and liked/disliked music effects on shopping intentions in a women's clothing store service setting. *Journal of Services Marketing, 22*(1), 59–67.

Bronner, K., Hirt, R., & Ringe, C. (Eds.). (2010). *Audio Branding Academy Yearbook 2009 / 2010.* Sinzheim, Germany: Nomos.

Bruner, G. C. (1990). Music, mood, and marketing. *Journal of Marketing, 54*(4), 94–104.

Cacioppo, J. T., & Petty, R. E. (1982). The need for cognition. *Journal of Personality and Social Psychology, 42*(1), 116–131.

Calvert, S. L., Huston, A. C., Watkins, B. A., & Wright, J. C. (1982). The relation between selective attention to television forms and children's comprehension of content. *Child Development, 53*(3), 601–610.

Campbell, M. C. (1995). When attention-getting advertising tactics elicit consumer inferences of manipulative intent: The importance of balancing benefits and investments. *Journal of Consumer Psychology, 4*(3), 225–254.

Carpentier, F. D., & Potter, R. F. (2007). Effects of music on physiological arousal: Explorations into tempo and genre. *Media Psychology, 10*(2), 339–363.

Chou, H.-Y., & Lien, N.-H. (2010). Advertising effects of songs' nostalgia and lyrics' relevance. *Asia Pacific Journal of Marketing and Logistics, 22*(3), 314–329.

Cohen, A. J. (2005). How music influences the interpretation of film and video: Approaches from experimental psychology. In R. Kendall & R. Savage (Eds.), *Selected reports in ethnomusicology: Perspectives in systematic musicology* (Vol. 12, pp. 15–36.). Los Angeles, CA: Ethnomusicology Publications, UCLA.

Cohen, A. R., Stotland, E., & Wolfe, D. M. (1955). An experimental investigation of need for cognition. *Journal of Abnormal and Social Psychology, 51*(2), 291–294.

Cook, N. (1998). *Analysing musical multimedia.* Oxford, UK: Oxford University Press.

Cotte, J., Coulter, R. A., & Moore, M. (2005). Enhancing or disrupting guilt: The role of ad credibility and perceived manipulative intent. *Journal of Business Research, 58*(3), 361–368.

Day, R.-F., Lin, C.-H., & Huang, W.-H. (2009). Effects of music tempo and task difficulty on multi-attribute decision-making: An eye-tracking approach. *Computers in Human Behavior, 25*(1), 130–143.

Dimofte, C. V., & Yalch, R. F. (2011). The mere association effect and brand evaluations. *Journal of Consumer Psychology, 21*(1), 24–37.

Eagly, A. H., & Chaiken, S. (1993). *The psychology of attitudes*. Orlando, FL: Harcourt Brace Jovanovich, Inc.

Furnham, A., Abramsky, S., & Gunter, B. (1997). A cross-cultural content analysis of children's television advertisements. *Sex Roles, 37*(1–2), 91–99.

Furnham, A., & Bradley, A. (1999). Music while you work: The differential distraction of background music on the cognitive test performance of introverts and extraverts. *Applied Cognitive Psychology, 11*(5), 445–455.

Gawronski, B., & Bodenhausen, G. V. (2006). Associative and propositional processes in evaluation: An integrative review of implicit and explicit attitude change. *Psychological Bulletin, 132*(5), 692–731.

Gorn G. J. (1982). The effects of music in advertising on choice behavior: A classical conditioning approach. *Journal of Marketing, 46*(1), 94–101.

Gorn G. J., Pham, M. T., & Sin, L. Y. (2001). When arousal influences ad evaluation and valence does not (and vice versa). *Journal of Consumer Psychology, 11*(1), 43–55.

Hahn, M., & Hwang, I. (1999). Effects of tempo and familiarity of background music on message processing in TV advertising: A resource-matching perspective. *Psychology & Marketing, 16*(8), 659–675.

Haugtvedt, C., Petty, R. E., Cacioppo, J. T., & Steidley, T. (1988). Personality and ad effectiveness: Exploring the utility of need for cognition. *Advances in Consumer Research, 15*, 209–212.

Holt, D., Ippolito, P. M., Desrochers, D. M., & Kelley, C. R. (2007). *Children's exposure to TV advertising in 1977 and 2004: Information for the obesity debate.* Washington, DC: Federal Trade Commission, Bureau of Economics Staff Report.

Hung, K. (2000). Narrative music in congruent and incongruent TV advertising. *Journal of Advertising, 29*(1), 25–34.

Hung, K. (2001). Framing meaning perceptions with music: The case of teaser ads. *Journal of Advertising, 30*(3), 39–50.

Hung, K., & Rice, M. (1992, April). *The development and testing of a typology of musical elements in television commercials.* Paper presented at the 1992 Conference of the American Academy of Advertising. Athens, GA.

Iwamiya, S., & Hanako, O. (2004, August). *Formal congruency between image patterns and pitch patterns.* Paper presented at the Eight International Conference on Music Perception & Cognition, Evanston, IL.

Jackson, D. M. (2003). *Sonic branding: An introduction.* New York, NY: Palgrave Macmillan.

Jacob, C., Guéguen, N., & Boulbry, G. (2010). Effects of songs with prosocial lyrics on tipping behavior in a restaurant. *International Journal of Hospitality Management, 29*(4), 761–763.

Kahle, L. R., & Homer, P. M. (1985). Physical attractiveness of the celebrity endorser: A social adaptation perspective. *Journal of Consumer Research, 11*(4), 954–961.

Kellaris, J. J., & Cox, A. D. (1989). The effects of background music in advertising: A reassessment. *The Journal of Consumer Research, 16*(1), 113–118.

Kellaris, J. J., Cox, A. D., & Cox, D. (1993). The effect of background music on ad processing: A contingency explanation. *Journal of Marketing, 57*(4), 114–125.

Kellaris, J. J., & Rice, R. C. (1993). The influence of tempo, loudness, and gender of listener on responses to music. *Psychology and Marketing, 10*(1), 15–29.

Kensinger, E. A. (2009). Remembering the details: Effects of emotion. *Emotion Review, 1*(2), 99–113.

Kristen, S., & Shevy, M. (2009, September). *International meanings of the semantics of popular music: A comparison of the extra-musical associations with country, German folksy music, hip-hop and punk in American versus German listeners.* Paper presented at the Sixth Media Psychology Division Conference of the German Psychological Association. Duisburg, Germany.

Lai, C.-J., Wu, Y.-L., Hsieh, M.-Y., Kung, C.-Y., & Lin, Y.-H. (2011). Effect of background music tempo and playing method on shopping website browsing. In J. Watada, G. Phillips-Wren, L. C. Jain & R. J. Howlett (Eds.), *Intelligent Decision Technologies* (Vol. 10, pp. 439–447). Berlin, Germany: Springer.

Lang, A. (2009). The limited capacity model of motivated media message processing. In R. L. Nabi & M. B. Oliver (Eds.), *The SAGE handbook of media processes and effects* (pp. 193–204). Thousand Oaks, CA: Sage Publications.

Lipscomb, S. D., & Zehnder, S. M. (2004). Immersion in the virtual environment: The effect of a musical score on the video gaming experience. *Journal of Physiological Anthropology and Applied Human Science, 23*(6), 337–343.

Lunardo, R., & Mbengue, A. (2011). When atmospherics lead to inferences of manipulative intent: Its effects on trust and attitude. *Journal of Business Research.* (First published online June 25, 2011.) Retrieved from <http://www.sciencedirect.com/>.

Macinnis, D. J., & Park, C. W. (1991). The differential role of characteristics of music on high- and low- involvement consumers' processing of ads. *Journal of Consumer Research, 18*(2), 161–173.

McGuire, W. J. (1985). Attitudes and attitude change. In G. Lindzey & E. Aronson (Eds.), *Handbook of social psychology* (Vol. 2, pp. 233–346). New York, NY: Random House.

Meyer, L. B. (1994). Emotion and meaning in music. In R. Aiello & J. A. Sloboda (Eds.), *Musical Perceptions* (pp. 3–39). New York, NY: Oxford University Press.

Meyers-Levy, J., & Zhu, R. (2010). Gender differences in the meanings consumers infer from music and other aesthetic stimuli. *Journal of Consumer Psychology, 20*, 495–507.

Milliman, R. E. (1982). Using background music to affect the behavior of supermarket shoppers. *Journal of Marketing, 46*(3), 86–91.

Murray, N. M., & Murray, S. B. (1996). Music and lyrics in commercials: A cross-cultural comparison between commercials run in the Dominican Republic and in the United States. *Journal of Advertising, 25*(2), 51–63.

North, A., & Hargreaves, D. J. (2008). *The social and applied psychology of music.* New York, NY: Oxford University Press.

North, A. C., Mackenzie, L. C., Law, R. M., & Hargreaves, D. J. (2004). The effects of musical and voice 'fit' on responses to advertisements. *Journal of Applied Social Psychology, 34*(8), 1675–1708.

Oakes, S., & North, A. C. (2006). The impact of background musical tempo and timbre congruity upon ad content recall and affective response. *Applied Cognitive Psychology, 20*(4), 505–520.

Olsen, G. D. (1997). The impact of interstimulus interval and background silence on recall. *The Journal of Consumer Research, 23*(4), 295–303.

Olsen, G. D. (2002). Salient stimuli in advertising: The effect of contrast interval length and type on recall. *Journal of Experimental Psychology: Applied*, *8*(3), 168–179.

Olsen, G. D., & Johnson, R. D. (2002). The impact of background lyrics on recall of concurrently presented verbal information in an advertising context. *Advances in Consumer Research*, *29*(1), 147–148.

Park, C. W., & Young, S. M. (1986). Consumer response to television commercials: The impact of involvement and background music on brand attitude formation. *Journal of Marketing Research*, *23*(1), 11–24.

Petty, R. E., Briñol, P., & Priester, J. R. (2009). Mass media attitude change: Implications of the elaboration likelihood model of persuasion. In J. Bryant & M. B. Oliver (Eds.), *Media effects: Advances in theory and research* (3rd ed., pp. 125–164). New York, NY: Routledge.

Petty, R. E., & Cacioppo, J. T. (1979). Issue involvement can increase or decrease persuasion by enhancing message relevant cognitive responses. *Journal of Personality and Social Psychology*, *37*(10), 1915–1926.

Petty, R. E., & Cacioppo, J. T. (1986). The elaboration likelihood model of persuasion. *Advances in Experimental Social Psychology*, *19*, 123–205.

Redker, C. M., & Gibson, B. (2009). Music as an unconditioned stimulus: Positive and negative effects of country music on implicit attitudes, explicit attitudes, and brand choice. *Journal of Applied Social Psychology*, *39*(11), 2689–2705.

Richard, M. O., Chebat, J. C., Yang, Z., & Putrevu, S. (2010). A proposed model of online consumer behavior: Assessing the role of gender. *Journal of Business Research*, *63*(9–10), 926–934.

Scott, L. M. (1990). Understanding jingles and needledrop: A rhetorical approach to music in advertising. *Journal of Consumer Research*, *17*(2), 223–236.

Shen, Y.-C., & Chen, T.-C. (2006). When east meets west: The effect of cultural tone congruity in ad music and message on consumer ad memory and attitude. *International Journal of Advertising*, *25*(1), 51–70.

Shevy, M. (2008). Music genre as cognitive schema: Extramusical associations with country and hip-hop music. *Psychology of Music*, *36*(4), 477–498.

Shevy, M., & Hawkins, R. P. (2008). Attending to mass media. In W. Donsbach (Ed.), *International Encyclopedia of Communication* (Vol. 1, pp. 216–221). Malden, MA: Blackwell Publishing.

Shevy, M., & Kristen, S. (2009, June). *German listeners' music-genre schemas for international and domestic popular music: Differences in cognitive meanings associated with exposure to country, hip-hop, punk, and German folksy music.* Paper presented at the International Communication Association Annual Conference. Chicago, IL.

Shevy, M., & Kristen, S. (2011). Semantic meanings associated with popular music: An international consideration of music genre in branding. In K. Bronner, R. Hirt, & C. Ringe (Eds.), *Audio Branding Academy Yearbook 2010–2011* (pp. 219–229). Sinzheim, Germany: Nomos.

Stewart, D. W., & Furse, D. H. (1986). *Effective television advertising.* Lexington, MA: Lexington Books.

Storbeck, J., & Clore, G. L. (2008). Affective arousal as information: How affective arousal influences judgments, learning, and memory. *Social and Personality Psychology Compass*, *2*, 1824–1843.

Tavassoli, N. T., & Lee, Y. H. (2003). The differential interaction of auditory and visual advertising elements with Chinese and English. *Journal of Marketing Research*, *40*(4), 468–480.

Tormala, Z. L., Briñol, P., & Petty, R. E. (2007). Multiple roles for source credibility under high elaboration: It's all in the timing. *Social Cognition, 25*(4), 536–552.

Trampe, D., Stapel, D. A., Siero, F. W., & Mulder, H. (2010). Beauty as a tool: The effects of model attractiveness, product relevance, and elaboration likelihood on advertising effectiveness. *Psychology & Marketing, 27*(12), 1101–1121.

Wakshlag, J. J., Reitz, R. J., & Zillmann, D. (1982). Selective exposure to and acquisition of information from educational television programs as a function of appeal and tempo of background music. *Journal of Educational Psychology, 74*(5), 666–677.

Wallace, W. T. (1994). Memory for music: Effect of melody on recall of text. *Journal of Experimental Psychology – Learning Memory and Cognition, 20*(6), 1471–1485.

Wang, J. (2005). Youth culture, music, and cell phone branding in China. *Global Media and Communication, 1*(2), 185–201.

Williams, R. (1999). *Secret formulas of the wizard of ads: Turning paupers into princes and lead into gold.* Austin, TX: Bard Press.

Wu, C.-S., Cheng, F.-F., & Yen, D. C. (2008). The atmospheric factors of online storefront environment design: An empirical experiment in Taiwan. *Information & Management, 45*(7), 493–498.

Yalch, R. F. (1991). Memory in a jingle jungle: Music as a mnemonic device in communicating advertising slogans. *Journal of Applied Psychology, 76*(2), 268–275.

Yalch, R. F., & Spangenberg, E. R. (1993). Using store music for retail zoning: A field experiment. In L. McAlister & M. L. Rothschild (Eds.), *Advances in Consumer Research* (Vol. 20, pp. 632–636). Provo, UT: Association for Consumer Research.

Zander, M. F. (2006). Musical influences in advertising: How music modifies first impressions of product endorsers and brands. *Psychology of Music, 34*(4), 465–480.

Zhu, R., & Meyers-Levy, J. (2005). Distinguishing between the meanings of music: When background music affects product perceptions. *Journal of Marketing Research, 42*(3), 333–345.

Ziv, N., Hoftman, M., & Geyer, M. (2012). Music and moral judgment: The effect of background music on the evaluation of ads promoting unethical behavior. *Psychology of Music, 40*(12), 738–760.

Chapter 15

Auditory icons, earcons, and displays: Information and expression through sound

Agnieszka Roginska

New York University, USA

As we enter a time in which the abundance of data can be overwhelming, we face new challenges of data display. Very often, the question is not whether we *have* the information, but rather whether we can *perceive* the information. We are living in a world of numerous gadgets, communications devices, appliances, where information technology can be found in every home and vehicle. We use this data for guidance, information, warning, and entertainment. Stock brokers use multiple screens to monitor stock trading. Intelligent home appliances can tell us when our food is ready, our refrigerator needs restocking, and our laundry needs washing. So the question remains, how do we display this information meaningfully?

Displays are a physical means of communicating information to a person. Several forms of displays can be used to transmit information, including visual, auditory, cutaneous (touch, temperature, pressure), kinesthetic (motion, force), olfactory (smell), and gustatory (taste). Traditionally, the majority of displays have been designed for the human visual system. Visual displays can convey meaning to the recipient, either by using means such as text, graphs, icons, and symbols. However, when visual displays are used, the attention of the user must be on the display in order to perceive information—the eyes must be on the screen. The effectiveness of visual displays can, in some cases, be limited due to the visual system's limited field of view, restricted scope of the number of perceivable channels, and the lower sensitivity of subtle temporal changes as compared to the auditory system. Furthermore, depending on the user, application, and environment, there are occasions when non-visual displays may be more appropriate.

Auditory displays are the most widely used displays after their visual counterpart. An auditory display refers to the use of sound to convey and communicate information to a user (Kramer, 1994). Such displays can have the function of augmenting an already existing graphical display (e.g., Brewster, 1997; Brown, Newsome, & Glinert, 1989), or they can be the principal form of information representation (e.g., Begault, 1993; Loomis, Golledge, & Klatzky, 1998; Mynatt, 1997).

In this chapter, I present an overview of auditory displays and their history, types, and uses in traditional and emerging multimedia technologies. The chapter opens with a description of the different types of auditory displays, including earcons, auditory icons, and speech-based auditory displays, along with their uses and effectiveness as standalone representations of data, and in larger schemes, like sonification. A discussion of the mapping between data and sound displays is presented next. Finally, research investigating applications of auditory displays is presented for uses in navigation/guidance, interaction, alerting, monitoring, and enhancing.

History of auditory displays

Long before the concept of auditory displays was formalized, their use was adopted to represent situational, temporal, or physical information. One of the earliest forms of primitive auditory display are alarms. Auditory alarms date back to ancient times, when instrumental sounds were used to signal warnings of enemy attack, including patterned drumming, animal horns, and trumpets. Alarms were also used in ancient clocks. Dating back to ancient Greece, philosopher Plato (427–347 BCE) had an alarm clock, which was a water-based clock with an alarm that sounded like a water organ. In the 3rd century BCE, inventor Ctesibuius (285–222 BCE) added an elaborate alarm system to his clepsydra, which consisted of a mechanism that would release pebbles at a specified time, which would fall on a gong and generate an attention-grabbing, alarm-type sound (Landels, 1979). Since then, alarms have gone through significant development and the type of sound used, its length, tonal quality, and melodic contour have been customized to fit the situation and meaning it is meant to convey.

Another early example of auditory displays is a representation of Morse code. This early form of communication predates any form of speech transmission across long distances. Morse code, developed by Samuel Morse in 1836, uses a series of dots and dashes that encode alphabetical information. Although the code was originally transmitted as electrical pulses on a telegraph, it is also transmitted through visual signals (on/off lights) and audio tones (long and short). For example,… _ _ _… is 'SOS,' since three consecutive dots (short stimuli) represent an 'S' and three consecutive dashes (long stimuli) represent an 'O.' This auditory display, an encoding of textual information into sound, is used to this day for communication by ham radio operators, radio beacons, and repeaters, the latter of which uses Morse code for identification.

Since the advent of computers and digital sound, auditory displays have seen a rise in use. Starting in the second half of the 20th century, we have seen the emergence of auditory displays in technologies we use every day. In addition to computers and computing devices, communication technologies rely heavily on auditory displays, including home phones, mobile phones, pagers, fax machines, and PDAs. Consumer electronics, such as cameras, printers, media players, controllers, and power strips, incorporate auditory displays to convey information. Many home appliances, including microwaves, washer/dryers, coffee makers, ovens, refrigerators, and smoke detectors, have augmented their technologies and displays with audio. Even motor vehicles (e.g., turn signal, seatbelt, and key in ignition) are taking full advantage of sound to effectively communicate to the user. These days, most electronics incorporate auditory displays.

Information on computers and other machines is usually presented using a visual display. Visual interfaces are often limited by the amount of space allocated for the display. As consumers are looking for smaller and lighter devices, the size of the display is significantly limited. Designers and developers are looking for new ways to reduce the size of the product, often by reducing the size of the display, while maintaining information transmission quality. The attention is now turning to auditory displays to assume some of the tasks previously performed by visual displays while maintaining the same level of information transmission and interaction with the user.

Types of auditory displays

There are many types of auditory displays. From short beeps to lengthy data-driven displays, from speech to non-speech sounds, whether they are natural (sampled) or synthesized, auditory displays are designed to convey information to a listener. The two categories of non-speech auditory displays include 'earcons' and 'auditory icons.' Earcons and auditory icons use music, sound effects, sound gestures, sound symbols, and natural sounds to represent actions or objects—such as the sound of ruffling paper to represent emptying the recycle bin on a computer, or a 'click' when taking a picture on a digital camera which mimics the sound of the opening and closing of the shutter on an analog camera. In contrast, 'spearcons,' 'spindexes,' and other forms of speech-based auditory displays use language to convey information to a listener and can be effectively used on, for example, smartphones and tablets. This section will describe these examples of different types of auditory displays in more detail.

Earcons

Earcons are non-verbal audio messages used in the user-computer interface to provide information to the user about a computer object, operation, or interaction (Blattner, Sumikawa, & Greenberg, 1989). They are the audio counterpart to graphical icons in that they aim to present concise information using sound. Examples of earcons include a 'ping' to indicate the arrival of a new text message, a short sound (e.g., a chord) to indicate computer startup or shutdown, or a 'ding' to inform a driver their seatbelt is not fastened. Earcons are sound symbols and, as is the case with most symbols, these must be learned since there is no intuitive relationship between the symbol and the meaning.

In their initial proposal of earcons, Blattner et al. (1989) used knowledge acquired from their investigations of visual icons to design earcons. Icons can represent much information in a small amount of space. They rely on the human ability to quickly identify and perceive natural form or shape. When icons are used as part of a computer interface, users may be able to make faster decisions and/or selections than when using text-based menus.

Throughout the years, much thought has been given to the design of graphical icons. The concept of 'figural goodness' in Gestalt psychology (Attneave, 1954) helps to judge the characteristics of a 'good icon.' Continuity, closure, simplicity, unity, and symmetry define these characteristics (Easterby, 1970). Similarly, they also define the principles that we use to group stimuli into configurations. Thus, icons that are easy to remember, easily recognizable, and segregate well from other sources will be considered to be 'good' icons. Similarly, earcons must be easy to remember and to be comprehended by all, including those who are not experts in sound or music theory.

Most graphical icons fall into one of three categories: representational, abstract, or semi-abstract. Representational icons graphically represent the object or operation they are associated with. For example, in a text editor, the printer icon invokes the printing action, or the icon of the recycling bin represents a place where one puts unwanted documents. Representational icons are very effective for objects that can be graphically depicted. However, there are certain actions that do not have an obvious pictorial representation. For these, designers must resort to abstract figures. For example, the window actions located at the upper corner of most windows use abstract shapes to signify the 'minimize,' 'restore,' and 'close' actions. Semi-abstract icons are a combination of the representational and abstract icon types, or they used an extremely simplified representation of the object, for example, a folder with an arrow that represents the action of putting items in it.

Like graphical icons, earcons can either be representational or abstract. The former are referred to as 'auditory icons' and use representative sounds to convey meaning. For example, an auditory icon of an email being sent could be the sound of an object 'flying away.' The (abstract) earcon design approach is to use single pitches or groups of pitches as building blocks. The pitches are used in isolation or are combined to create motifs. For example, many cars equipped with alarm systems emit a single-note earcon to signify that the alarm has been turned on, while announcements at airports and train stations are often preceded by a longer, multi-note earcon. Earcons can be composed using any number of notes—single-note earcons are short and convey a message quickly. However, motifs are also often used, since they provide a more memorable signature to the event or object that the earcon represents.

Blattner and colleagues' research (Blattner et al., 1989) showed that there are many advantages of using the approach of motifs in designing audio messages. Their work showed that the modular and systematic approach is straightforward to understand and use, as well as easy to modify and tailor. As such, the modularity allows for the use and re-use of basic building blocks, which may be used to construct larger sets of earcons, leading to groups, or families, of related earcons. Related earcons, which contain motifs that are in one way or another connected by transformation, inheritance, or combinations of smaller earcons, have a similar sound.

Earcon design

Because earcons are designed based on elements of sound, the dimensions inherent to sound, and the way they are manipulated, play an important role in how well an earcon represents its significate. The fundamental dimensions of sound include pitch, loudness, spatial location, duration, and timbre. These dimensions have been studied and used by many in determining how earcons should be designed and which parameters are more and less important.

Pitch is the primary perceptual parameter related to the physical attribute of frequency of a tone, and is an indication of how high or low a tone is. Pitch can be a powerful means of conveying information. Absolute pitches are often of little use unless most of the population had perfect pitch. However, people are quite sensitive to intervals, or relative pitches—since a large portion of the population can carry a tune. Therefore, if two pitches are sequentially organized, most people will be able to judge a simple relationship between the notes (e.g., the first tone is higher than the second tone). The pitches in a motive are usually chosen from a tonal scale and occupy a narrow frequency range, within one octave (Blattner et al., 1989).

Related to pitch, the register of an earcon can be a meaningful parameter in conveying information. Register refers to the position of the motif along the frequency range. The meaning of an earcon can change depending on the register in which it is presented (Brewster, Wright, & Edwards, 1993, 1995). For example, when representing temperature, high pitches can be used for high temperatures, while low pitches would be used for cooler temperatures.

In earcon design, loudness is considered to be a less useful parameter because listeners are not very good at making absolute judgments on loudness (Buxton, Gaver, & Bly, 1991). The overall volume of a device may affect the way in which the loudness of individual notes is perceived. Depending on the pitch of the tone, discrete changes in loudness can also be difficult to perceive. However, a sharp change of loudness (over a short amount of time) may be effective in signaling an event.

The spatial location of an earcon can be a very informative parameter. Not only does spatial separation allow multiple sounds to be presented simultaneously while being well segregated from one another (Bregman, 1990), the location itself can be an information-carrying parameter. For example, when representing files on a computer desktop using earcons, the spatial location of the sound can be correlated to where the file is located on the desktop—e.g., left/right.

Timbre is the most complex characteristic of sound, involving the spectral content, amplitude envelope, and transient attack of a sound. It is the characteristic of sound that allows us to distinguish a flute from a piano when they are playing the same note at the same loudness level. Different timbres are easily recognizable and can be a significant component of earcons when conveying information.

Rhythm is the most prominent characteristic of a motive in an earcon. It is a very powerful tool. Blattner et al. (1989) describe rhythm, or the 'timing and weighting of notes,' as the most crucial feature of music that takes precedence over melody when it comes to creating motifs. In fact, even when spectral and pitch differences are large, earcons can be confused when a similar rhythm is used Patterson (1982). Patterson's research also indicates that sounds that are too short (less than 0.0825 seconds) may go unnoticed unless the earcon contains only one or two notes. As far as the length is concerned, earcons are short. They are sufficiently long to convey information, but no longer—typically two to four notes. Their short length makes them easy to learn, recognize, and remember.

Earcon design issues

Earcons have been constructed using a single element or by placing two or more audio elements in sequence. *One-element earcons* are usually made up of a single note, or a very short motif and are typically reserved for events that are simple, basic, or that occur frequently (e.g., mouse clicks, key actions, or simple error messages). This is not to say that a single-note earcon can only represent a total of one event or object. Changing attributes such as timbre, pitch, or adding dynamics can significantly augment the bank of earcons available. Figure 15.1 is an example of one-element earcons representing the actions *create* and *destroy* and the objects *file* and *string*.

Figure 15.1 Examples of one-element earcons representing the actions *create* and *destroy*, and the objects *file* and *folder*.

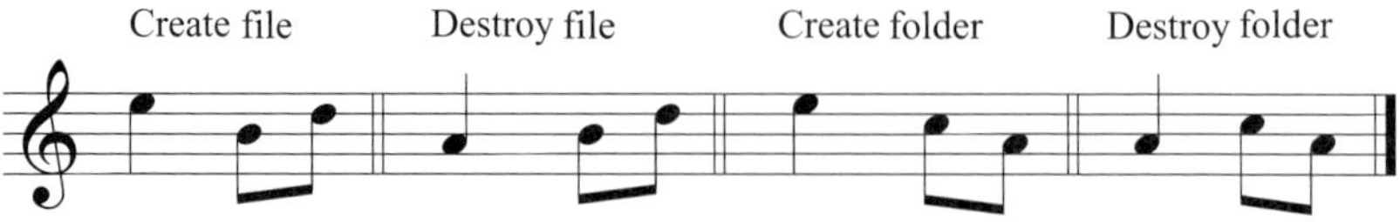

Figure 15.2 Compound earcons created from single-element earcons.

Compound earcons can be created by combining, transforming, or inheriting from other earcons. As shown in Figure 15.2, using single-element earcons defined in Figure 15.2, compound earcons can be constructed by linking two earcons in a sequence. By concatenating short sounds, longer, more complex and meaningful messages can be created.

A number of studies have tested the effectiveness of compound earcons, focusing on applications where visual displays are not possible. Brewster, Raty, and Kortekangas (1996) used hierarchical earcons to provide navigational cues through a menu hierarchy, similarly to a hierarchy in a book menu, for example. Hierarchical earcons use sound parameters such as timbre, pitch, register, and intensity. Each level from the hierarchy inherits the structure from the higher level and then changes it. For example, earcons from level one to level two inherited their continuous sound, but the instrument, pitch and location along the left/right stereo axis was changed. A four-level hierarchy with a total of 27 nodes was used. During a short training session, the compound earcons representing the hierarchy were played. The hypothesis of the authors was that listeners would learn the earcon rules during the training, and apply these to elements in the hierarchy, even if they hadn't heard them before. The goal of this experiment was to test the knowledge of earcons by asking listeners to select where the element representing the earcon fit into the hierarchy. Results showed that 81.5 percent of earcons were identified correctly. Errors indicated that the nodes from the lowest level in the hierarchy had the worst recall, suggesting that hierarchical earcons may have trouble representing hierarchies with a large number of levels.

A follow-up experiment by Brewster, Capriotti, and Hall (1998) challenged hierarchical earcons by evaluating compound earcons that were created by concatenating shorter ones. The same experimental setup was used, as described above, with four levels and 27 nodes. Earcons were constructed of sounds to represent numbers 0 to 4. Each number was a 1-second sound played by a different instrument (sitar for 0, piano for 1, orchestral hit for 2, bell for 3, and flute for 4). In addition, a marimba sound was used to represent a dot. Numbers higher than 4 used the same instrumental mappings as 0 to 4, two octaves higher. Results showed that participants were able to recognize the position of an element in the hierarchy with an accuracy of 97 percent. Furthermore, even earcons that were new to the listener were correctly recognized with a 97 percent accuracy rate, resulting in a significantly more informative representation of hierarchical information for an application with no visual display.

Auditory icons

Gaver (1989) named *representational* earcons as 'auditory icons.' He argued that '*auditory icons* exploit people's tendencies to listen to sources by mapping attributes of everyday sound-producing events to attributes of the model world of computers' (p. 75, emphasis added). For example, in the Mac OS, putting an object in the trash is accompanied by a thumping sound representing throwing something into a bin, or the action of emptying the trash is represented by the sound of crinkling paper.

In contrast to earcons, which are synthetic, abstract, and whose meaning is learned, auditory icons are expected to be intuitive. They are the auditory equivalent of visual icons. If the design of auditory icons follows the analogies of Gaver (1989), their meaning should be easily understood: 'objects in the computer world should be represented by the objects involved in sound-producing events; actions by the interactions that cause sound; and attributes of the system environment (e.g., processing load or available memory) by attributes of the sonic environment (e.g., reverberation time)' (p. 76).

The organization of everyday objects and events can be leveraged in order to create families of auditory icons. Families of auditory icons are created when the same type of sound is used for the same type of object. For example, let us assume that sound files are always represented by a metallic timbre. Creating a family of auditory icons for sound files would imply that, whether a sound file is moved, copied, deleted, opened, or played, the sound associated with the action would have a metallic timbre.

There are several advantages to using auditory icons in interfaces. First, the interface is appealing because it is based on the way people listen to sounds in everyday life. Second, because their meaning can be intuitively extracted, auditory icons are easy to learn and remember (Bonebright & Nees, 2007). Third, auditory icons can be quickly associated with their graphical counterpart, as they both aim at creating a similar analogy to the same action or object.

One of the most serious drawbacks of auditory icons is that it can be difficult to find suitable iconic sounds for all events in an interface—not all events and objects correspond to a sound-producing event in the real world. Forcing auditory icons onto every event would result in inconsistencies and leave room for interpretation of sounds used in the interface.

Understanding, learning, and remembering earcons and auditory icons

As mentioned earlier, earcons use symbolic or metaphorical sounds that must be learned. In contrast, auditory icons use natural auditory associations between a sound source and the sound it produces. An earcon or auditory icon is therefore of little use if a listener does not understand its meaning. First, the significance of the sound must be learned in order to associate the sound with the meaning. Then, the meaning must be remembered. When learning an earcon or auditory icon, the listener must internally code and store the musical/sound units representing the audio message. Let us start with an example taken from the natural world. Many of the objects around us make sounds depending on the actions we perform. As we grow, we learn the type of sound object A makes when action B is performed. For example, the car engine makes a specific sound when it is being started. Because we have heard various car engines start numerous times, we learned to associate that sound with the action 'car engine starts.' We have created a mental bank of templates to which we compare the sounds we hear. If the sequence or sound is similar enough to an existing template, then the listener recognizes the sound as a learned one. Otherwise, the sound is classified as 'new,' and the learning process starts.

Fundamentally, the learning process consists of memorizing information. Pieces of information, or perceptual patterns, are formed internally until they are small enough that they can be easily memorized. Organized groups and related patterns are easier to memorize than unrelated ones (Davies, 1978). When designing an earcon, it is desirable to minimize the level of complexity for each audio message in a computer user interface while maintaining a high level of information transmission. The user should be required to remember as little as possible. Compound earcons are an example of how to reduce the amount of information the user is asked to remember because they are made up by combining one-element earcons.

The difficulty of learning auditory icons versus abstract earcons depends on many factors including the nature of the message, the total number of messages used, and the types of sound representations used (Blattner et al., 1989). If a system requires few sound icons, it is customarily more efficient to use auditory icons, since they can be quickly associated with a representation. Earcons often require more time to be assimilated but can convey more information in a shorter amount of time.

Spatial auditory displays

A unique, and powerful, dimension inherent in sound is its spatial location. Unlike the visual system, the auditory system doesn't have a 'field of view.' Sounds can be heard and perceived anywhere around a listener. A listener does not have to be facing a sound in order to perceive it. Regardless of whether a sound is located in front, behind, above, or below, it can be detected by the listener (Wakefield, Roginska, & Santoro, 2012). When used to process auditory displays (and sonifications, as discussed later in the chapter), spatial sound can be very effective at enhancing a person's listening experience and conveying additional information to the listener.

Spatial auditory displays have used location to represent the absolute location of objects or events. For example, an auditory icon representing an object on a graphic monitor can be played to be perceived at the same location as it appears on the screen—if a graphical icon is located in the lower right corner of the screen, the auditory icon may be presented so that it appears to be emanating from the lower right corner. Similarly, spatial auditory displays can be used as audio beacons to guide people to a target location. These are particularly effective in environments where visual cues may be obstructed or unavailable. For example, vision may be obscured during an evacuation in a smoke-filled room, not allowing evacuees to see the location of the emergency exit. An auditory display alarm positioned at the same spatial location as the exit could guide people to safety by indicating the direction they should be walking (Wijngaarden, Bronkhorst, & Boer, 2004).

In addition to providing location-specific information, when multiple auditory displays are presented concurrently in spatially disparate locations, they can be better segregated into individual streams (e.g., Barreto, Jacko, & Hugh, 2007; Marston, Loomis, Klatzky, Golledge, & Smith, 2006; Shilling, Letowski, & Storms, 2000). Without spatial separation, the multiple sound sources will have a greater tendency to fuse together, making them more difficult to understand. The result is the possibility of presenting multiple auditory displays concurrently, without sacrificing their intelligibility.

Spearcons, spindexes and other speech-based auditory displays

Speech is the most natural and predominant form of modern-day human communication. We use it to convey emotions, actions, intentions, and thoughts. It is an excellent way to convey very specific meaning, messages, and information or more abstract thoughts and ideas. Not only is speech intuitive, requiring little or no formal training to be understood, but it also has a higher level of specificity than music, and non-speech auditory displays.

Some of the issues involved with using earcons or auditory icons relates to the ease with which additional auditory displays can be added, managed, and updated. Applications for which there is a relatively large degree of fluctuation in content, such as phone contact information or filenames on a computer, need to have auditory displays regularly updated to keep up with these changes, and applications that have a need for hierarchical information display could significantly benefit from auditory displays that are primarily speech-based and require little learning.

Walker, Nance, and Lindsay (2006) proposed a form of auditory displays for navigating through menus. *Spearcons* (speech earcons) are short audio clips that are automatically generated by using text-to-speech synthesis. The audio clip is sped up, often to the point where it is no longer identifiable as speech. However, menu items that are similar, invoking similar actions, will sound alike. Menu items such as 'Open… ,' 'Open Recent… ,' 'Open Location… ,' all begin with the same word. As such, their beginning sound will be alike, and they will tend to be categorized as part of the same family of actions. Because spearcons are based on spoken words, only a very short learning stage is necessary to get familiar with their sounds (Palladino & Walker, 2007).

Studies by Palladino and Walker (2007, 2008a, 2008b) and Walker and Kogan (2009) found that navigating through menus on desktop computers as well as mobile phones using spearcons results in a more efficient navigation experience than without them. One of these studies (Palladino & Walker, 2008b) compared the performance of basic text-to-speech (TTS) to spearcon-enhanced TTS in a navigation task through two-dimensional menus (two levels of accessibility). A total of 28 individuals participated in the study. There were two types of stimuli presented: (1) TTS or (2) TTS preceded by a spearcon. TTS sounds were generated using a TTS application. The spearcons were generated using a sped-up version of the TTS. Because the speeding up was logarithmic, longer phrases were more heavily compressed. An auditory menu structure such as the one found in the Nokia N91 mobile phone was used, with six categories: messaging, music, connectivity, tools, camera, and gallery, with five to nine items in each category. Participants used a computer running Windows XP during the experiment and navigated using the keyboard's arrow keys. The task of the participant was to find a target item as quickly and accurately as possible. The speed of navigation to the target for each trial was measured. A total of 220 trials were presented to each subject, divided into ten blocks of 22 trials. Results showed that performance in the conditions with spearcons was significantly faster (mean response time (M) = 3821 milliseconds (ms), standard deviation (SD) = 3917 ms) than in the conditions with TTS only (M = 5344 ms, SD = 3918 ms). This significantly faster performance in two-dimensional menu navigation is in contrast to Palladino and Walker (2008a), involving one-dimensional menu navigation, which resulted in similar performance between the TTS-only and TTS with spearcon conditions. The authors concluded that the benefits of using spearcons come when multidimensional menus are used.

Navigating through menus with a large number of elements (e.g., contacts list, albums list, etc.) could become time consuming if every item is represented by an auditory cue. In such cases, it is beneficial to have a higher-level representation that may be similar to a table of contents or an index. In the visual domain, Beck and Elkerton (1989) have shown that the use of an index can improve the search time when looking through lists of text. Based on this concept, Jeon and Walker (2009, 2011) introduced the 'spindex' as a form of navigating through long lists.

A *spindex* is a short speech audio signal that typically represents the first letter of the word on the menu. For example, the sound of the letter 'J' would be used to represent all the names found in the contacts list that begin with the letter 'J.' When searching through a large quantity of elements, there is no benefit derived from getting complete information about each record during the search. It is most useful to receive enough information to determine whether an element is 'in the zone' or not. This makes the process of reaching the target much faster and more efficient. Then, once a user has arrived in the zone of the target, they require a finer-grained way of going through each menu item separately. Spindexes can be used, for example, on cell phones, to guide a user through a contacts list.

However, there are many disadvantages to using speech as an auditory display. The first is that it is slow. It may take an entire sentence or more to convey the same informational content that a beep might present in a fraction of a second. Particularly for fast-changing information, the speech-based display may become invalid before the completed message is presented. For ongoing processes, speech may be inappropriate. For example, when copying a file onto the system, users would not want a speech-based display to say 'reading, reading, reading—writing, writing, writing.'

There are cases in which speech-based displays may be disturbing, regardless of the meaning or content. When a user is involved in a task that is based on speech or oral communication, additional verbal information may distract the user from the main task. Having concurrent information presented that is speech-based can be problematic from a basic auditory streaming perspective, including the greater difficulty of attending to a source that has a similar spectral content or contour as another source (Bregman, 1990).

Most of the spectral energy of speech is concentrated in the lower frequencies, i.e., below 8 kHz, although there is higher harmonic content information affecting sound quality in the range of 12 kHz and above. This spectral structure has several acoustic and psychoacoustic implications. Miller (1947) investigated the masking of speech by a number of different sources. His studies have shown that speech can easily be masked by noise, especially in the presence of continuous noise with spectral content over the speech frequency range. Unfortunately, because much of the noise we experience in the natural environment is concentrated in low frequencies (where much of the energy of speech is present), the masking of speech by natural sounds can result in missing information.

The concentration of energy in the lower frequencies for speech signals is also an issue for localization. Human localization makes primary use of high frequencies for elevation and front/back discrimination. Without high-frequency content, our ability to determine the absolute location of a source is degraded (Gilkey & Anderson, 1995). For applications that use position as a source of information, lack of location discrimination could lead to missing important data. For all these reasons, speech is often not the best choice of stimulus type to use for applications in auditory displays.

There are some applications in which speech-based auditory displays can prove to be too slow or may not be appropriate to effectively represent the information. In these cases, when a more *analogous* and *continuous* representation of data is beneficial, we look toward 'sonification.'

Sonification

Beyond using short audio clips to represent actions, single elements, and events, auditory displays can be used to create transformations of larger data sets into sound. Kramer et al. (1999) define *sonification* as 'the transformation of data relations into perceived relations in an acoustic signal for the purposes of facilitating communication or interpretation' (p. 3). In general, sonification involves the translation and integration of quantitative data through mapping to a sound model and enables recognition of patterns in data by their auditory signatures, which are perceived by a listener. The goal is to use sound to help listeners gain knowledge about data or events that might otherwise be viewed using graphs, charts, or other representations. For example, stock market data, traditionally shown using bar, pie, XY charts, and other forms of graphical representations, can be mapped on to sound to create an auditory impression of the same data. In this case, a straightforward mapping may be the use of rising and falling pitch to represent the price of a stock, while loudness can be mapped to the stock volume.

There are three general approaches to the transformation of data into sound. In the first, recorded and manipulated environmental sounds (e.g., running water, rain forest ambience, and crickets, to name a few) are used (e.g., Barra et al., 2001; Gilfix & Couch, 2000; Hansen & Rubin, 2001; Mauney & Walker, 2004). In the second, sounds are synthesized which bear a direct relationship to the data being sonified. An example of this work is the uses of synthesized breathing and heartbeats to sonify patient vital statistics (e.g., Fitch & Kramer, 1994). In the third, a musical framework is chosen for these sound relations (e.g., Correia, Deweppe, Demey, & Leman, 2010; Roginska, Childs, & Johnson, 2006). Music is one of the more commonly used systems for the organization of sound. It has many dimensions, such as pitch, timbre, texture, loudness, and duration, as well as short- and long-scale temporal relationships: melody, harmony, rhythm, and motifs.

Over the past 20 years, there have been many explorations and examples of sonifications. Medical applications of sonification have included heart rate monitoring (Ballora, Pennycook, Ivanov, Glass, & Goldberg, 2004), knee-joint signals (Krishnan, Rangayyan, Bell, & Frank, 2001), EEG data (Baier, Hermann, & Stephani, 2007), and others. Geospatial data representing ocean buoys (Sturm, 2005), severe weather data (Childs & Pulkki, 2003), as well as remotely sensed data (Roginska, Childs, & Johnson, 2006), have been the source of sonifications. Monitoring and analysis of financial and stock market data has been explored by Kramer (1994), Neuhoff, Kramer, and Wayand (2002), Nesbitt and Barrass (2002), and Janata and Childs (2004).

Sonifications have been used in data analysis and exploration tasks. For example, a report on sonification commissioned by the National Science Foundation describes a problem during the Voyager 2 space mission while the spacecraft was traversing through the rings of Saturn. Visual displays were not helpful at identifying the problem. When the data were played using sound, a rapid-fire pattern was detected whenever the spacecraft was passing through an area with a higher concentration of dust. The 'machine gun' sound heard after the data were played was linked to high-speed collisions with micrometeoroids (Kramer et al., 1999). In this case, visual display techniques have failed to provide insightful information, whereas the sonification helped with identifying the origin of the problem.

Effectiveness of sonifications

Roginska, Childs, and Johnson (2006) used simulated remote-sensing data in a study that compared the effectiveness of sonification between synthetic and instrumental sounds. The goal of the research was to assess whether instrumental or synthetic sounds were more effective at representing the remote-sensing data and whether presenting the sounds using monophonic, stereophonic, or three-dimensional (3D) audio reproduction methods has a significant effect on the effectiveness of the sonification. Fourteen streams of data were embedded in the remote-sensing dataset, each with a unique characteristic of onset/offset, repetition rate, periodicity, and length. A sonification design was created to represent the 14 channels of real-time data to be monitored. The design sought to maximize: (1) the ease of listening over long periods of time; (2) the ability to distinguish all 14 channels; (3) the ability to perceive rhythmic, harmonic, and contrapuntal interactions and relationships between the streams; and (4) the perception of unusual or out of place events in the texture. Two versions of the sonification were created. The first used synthetic sounds, including band-passed noise, complex tones with different fundamental frequencies and harmonic content. The second version was an orchestration of the data using various musical instruments with distinct articulations. Ten unique instruments were used for the orchestration (flute, oboe, clarinet, bassoon, French horn, trombone, violins (four), viola, cello, and double bass). The four violin parts each used a different articulation and range for easier segregation of melodic lines.

The two sonifications (synthetic and orchestral) were presented to listeners over headphones with three reproduction methods: monophonic, stereo, and 3D. In the mono presentation, the same stream was presented to the left and right ears. The stereo method had the streams panned between the left and right ears, with an even spatial distribution between sound sources. The 3D presentation used head-related transfer functions (HRTF) to process the sounds and spatialize them around the listener on the horizontal plane. Participants were asked to identify the number of distinct sounds they heard during the presentation, as well as indicate the times at which they detected unusual data activity from the perspective of data density and/or irregular events. (To hear excerpts of the music used in this experiment, please visit <http://www.oup.co.uk/companion/tan>.)

A total of 24 untrained listeners participated in the study. Results showed no significant difference between the sonification method used and the significant events identified by the participants (see Figure 15.3), but showed a significant difference in number of streams detected (see Figure 15.4). The instrumental sonification resulted in a significantly greater number of streams identified in the monophonic (M = 7.25, SD = 0.5), stereo (M = 10.75, SD = 0.96), and 3D (M = 11.5, SD = 0. 58), than in the synthetic sonification in monophonic (M = 5.75, SD = 0.96), stereo (M = 8.5, SD = 1.29), and 3D (M = 10.5, SD = 1.29), $p = 0.01$.

The results of this study show that the effectiveness of the sonification method (synthetic versus orchestral) in the number of streams listeners perceive is dependent on the types of sounds used and the richness of the spectral content. However, both sonification methods were equally effective for the identification of significant events, which occurred at unique moments in the timeline and could rely more on the onset characteristic of the sound. The results of this study underline the importance of the spatial panning presentation method in the effectiveness of an auditory display. In a multiple

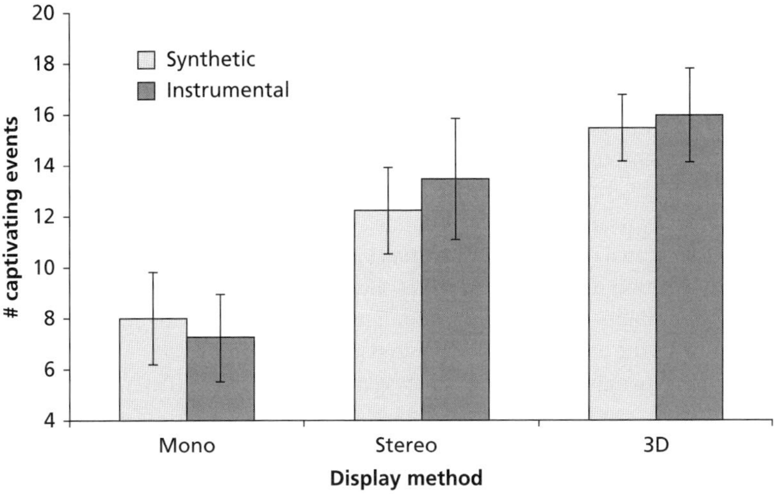

Figure 15.3 Mean number of captivating events detected. Results are displayed as a function of display method and signal type.

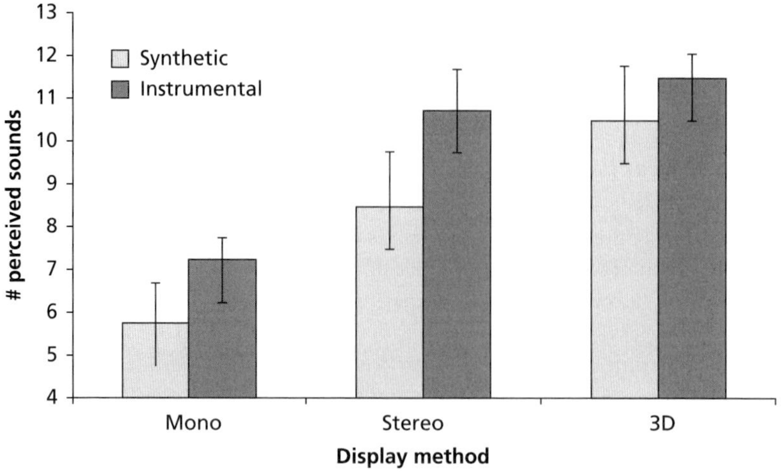

Figure 15.4 Mean number of perceived sound sources as a function of display method and signal type.

sound source environment, much information can go undetected when sounds are positioned at the same location. (See also Kerins, Chapter 16, in this volume for a discussion about multi-channel sound presentation.)

Data mapping

Auditory display design currently has no existing standard of mapping between objects, actions, events, and their corresponding sounds. However, the common goal of all displays is an intuitive audio representation of data. The question is: What makes an auditory display intuitive?

There are two fundamental types of mapping to be considered: 'conceptual' and 'perceptual.' A *conceptual mapping* is one that links aspects of some reality to a model. Let us take the example of a computer. In reality, a computer is a collection of hardware components. From a user's point of view, we rarely conceive of silicon and chips when referring to a computer. Rather, we imagine a screen with a desktop. The 'desktop' is designed to represent a desktop with items placed on it—something to which most people can easily relate. The idea of a desktop representing the organization of a computer is a conceptual mapping. A *conceptual mapping* is a translation from a reality into a conceptualization of a model. However, a conceptual mapping alone will not allow users the accessibility to the model world. A further mapping must be performed, one that transforms the conceptual model into perceptual forms.

A perceptual mapping is one made between the model world (described by the conceptual mapping) and its perceptible display. The nature of a perceptual mapping varies greatly. There are three basic types of perceptual mappings: symbolic, metaphorical, and iconic (Gaver, 1989—derived from Bates, 1979; Peirce, 1932; Heil, 1983). A symbolic mapping is an arbitrary one and strongly relies on some pre-definition of its meaning. For example, to symbolize the deletion of a file, in a visual representation, we might see an icon of a file with an 'x' through it and, in the auditory domain, hear a 'beep.' A metaphorical mapping is one that uses similarities between the actual event and its representation to portray action. For example, a deleted file may be represented by a faded icon or a much softer sound, relying on the relationship between deleting and vanishing. An iconic mapping is one that uses a visual or audio object to represent, as closely as possible, the object at hand. In the case of deleting a file, an iconic representation could involve dragging the file into the recycle bin.

An important consideration in auditory displays is what auditory display dimensions to use for data dimensions that have no intuitive audio representations. For example, how does temperature map onto pitch? Another important issue involves the particular mapping choice on the effect of performance of a task that relies on auditory displays.

In the early days of auditory displays, Walker and Kramer (1996) examined this issue in an experiment investigating how different types of mapping affect performance. Their experimental research on different types of mappings and metaphors incorporated reaction time and accuracy as dependent measures. These experiments looked at the auditory features that can best represent data dimensions, and how the direction of the mapping (direct or inverse) would affect performance. For example, if temperature data get mapped onto pitch, it seems natural to use a rising pitch for a rising temperature.

To investigate this question, participants were presented with an experimental environment of a 'crystal factory.' Four data variables were mapped individually to an audio output. Each participant was trained to associate a data dimension with a dimension of the auditory display (e.g., associate 'pressure' with the 'brightness' of a tone). In addition, participants were trained on the meaning of the direction, or polarity, of the mapping (e.g., if the temperature drops, the pitch will rise). At the beginning of the experiment, the values of the variables used in the auditory display remained fixed for a few seconds—the 'normal' state. Then, one of the values was changed and the auditory representation changed accordingly. When the participant heard this change, he or she was asked to respond as quickly as possible by making a control action. Based on the training they received, the reaction would be different—a participant trained to interpret a rising pitch as a rising temperature might react by turning the heater 'on' if the pitch started falling; if a participant was instructed that a rising pitch signifies a rising pressure, he or she might turn up the pressure knob if a falling pitch was played. Four types of mappings were prefabricated, each one was judged by the authors to be 'intuitive' (most natural), 'okay' (good, but probably not optimal), 'bad' (counterintuitive), or 'random.' For example, an 'intuitive' mapping could be between rising temperature and rising pitch or size and loudness; a 'bad' mapping was defined as relating temperature with onset time and size with pitch.

In general, Walker and Kramer (1996) showed that loudness effectively represented temperature, pitch was good for rate, and tempo was generally not an effective structure. Originally, the authors predicted that mappings based on stronger or more natural metaphors would result in faster and more accurate control reactions. However, the analysis of the results showed that the mapping that resulted in the best performance was not the 'intuitive' one, but rather the 'bad' one. In fact, even the 'random' mapping resulted in better performance than the supposedly 'intuitive' mapping. Although these results were surprising, they underlined two important sensitivities related to sonification. First, what may seem like an intuitive mapping between type of data and sound dimension to one or a group of individuals, may not be perceived as intuitive by other listeners. More research, including cross-cultural research, is necessary to examine data-sound relationships. Second, the polarity of the mapping is an important factor in creating an acceptable mapping—as some listeners may perceive a rising pitch to be an intuitive mapping for increasing size of an object, while others may view it as a decrease in size (since smaller objects tend to make higher pitched sounds). (See also Kendall & Lipscomb, Iwamiya, and Eitan in this volume for other empirical data and approaches connected to patterns, icons, and metaphors.)

Applications of auditory displays in multimedia

Auditory displays are used widely and are becoming increasingly prominent in a greater variety of applications. The use of earcons, auditory icons, sonifications, and other forms of auditory displays can been seen and heard in applications such as home appliances, computers, smartphones, and automotive, aviation, medical, financial, military, and mission-critical applications. Their functionality in multimedia can be divided into five (somewhat interrelated) main areas: interaction and feedback, alerting, monitoring, navigation and guidance, and augmenting reality.

Adding auditory to visual displays poses the question of the effect of multi-modal displays on *cognitive load*, as briefly explained here. At the heart of Paivio's (1986) dual-coding theory and Baddeley's (1998) theory of working memory lies the assumption that we have two separate channels for processing information: auditory and visual. The auditory channel uses auditory working memory to process all auditory/verbal input. The visual channel uses visual working memory to process visual (or pictorial) input (Mayer & Moreno, 1998). A series of studies by Mayer and Moreno (1998), Moreno and Mayer (1999), and Moreno, Mayer, Spires, and Lester (2001) investigated problem-solving performance when students were presented with animation-and-narration in contrast to animation-and-text. Similar experiments were carried out by Mousavi, Low, and Sweller (1995). Results of most of these experiments show strong evidence that cognitive load can be reduced when both the auditory and visual channels of processing information are engaged (referred to as the *modality effect*). It is important, however, when designing multi-modal displays to carefully consider the advantages and limitations of each information-processing channel in order to maximize information transmission and minimize cognitive load.

Auditory displays for interaction and feedback

As the size of screens of many multimedia devices is rapidly shrinking and their use is becoming more extensive and powerful, we turn to auditory displays to offload the visual sense and use sound to interact with devices. We have traditionally not only relied on the visual display, but also on tactile feedback. Typing, for example, has been an experience that included tactile (touch) and auditory feedback (clicking sound of a keyboard). As the devices are shrinking in size, and their keyboards are being replaced by touch-screen alternatives, we are losing the tactile interaction and feedback we used to get from physical keyboards. This can lead to more misspellings or slower writing. However, the lack of tactile feedback can be compensated for by auditory feedback to help with the user-machine interaction, which can improve the experience of interacting with the device.

Auditory displays can become an alternative to visual displays when it comes to interacting with a mobile device. As the research of Walker et al. (2006) and the studies on spearcons suggest, as described earlier, *spearcons* are a viable alternative in navigating through menus (especially multidimensional menus) on a mobile phone.

Auditory displays for alerting

Unlike visual stimuli, sound does not need to be paid attention to or be in the field of view to be perceived. Even when we are in a state of sleep, we are subconsciously processing sounds and, when these are loud or important enough, we awake from our sleep. For these reasons, audio has been the principal choice for alarms, notifications, and alerting, especially in situations in which an operator moves to different locations and can miss information provided on the visual display.

One of the most effective ways of alerting is through auditory alarms. Alarms have been used in numerous applications, and are significantly used on flight decks of military and commercial airplanes, on ship decks, and in submarines. Alarms need to be cautiously designed as they normally occur in emergency situations and should not disrupt speech communication. Patterson (1982, 1990) has carried out significant research related to alarm design, providing guidelines on how to design alarms in cockpit and work environments. Patterson (1982) describes a number of acoustic parameters that can affect the urgency of the warning. He illustrates how the level of auditory alerts in an environment with a constant background noise level can be predicted using a model of auditory threshold. Patterson uses the concept of the auditory filter (Fletcher, 1940), which describes the behavior of the auditory system as a collection of bandpass filters, where the frequency content of the signal will significantly affect its detectability in the presence of a masker. For example, a tone of the same loudness and with a similar frequency as another tone will mask the first tone easier than if the two tones are farther apart in frequency. Using these guidelines, an auditory display alarm can be more effectively designed by selectively choosing the frequency, harmonic content, and level of the alert in order to maximize its detectability without presenting the signal at an excessively high intensity.

Studies investigating the design and implementation of auditory alarms have been performed by many researchers. Among the most significant contributors to the field is Judy Edworthy's work on auditory warnings design. According to Edworthy (1994), the key considerations when designing auditory warning include type, sound levels, psychological appropriateness, learning factor, and urgency mapping. Edworthy suggests that 'there are two central requirements of an ergonomic non-verbal auditory warning: first, it needs to be heard, but it should not be too loud; second, it needs to be psychologically appropriate in some way' (p. 203). A compelling design will create a warning that is not unpleasant, but attention-grabbing so that it communicates the need for action.

Early work on the design of auditory warnings and alarms provided guidelines for creating warnings that map to the urgency of the situation to the auditory display

(Edworthy, 1997; Edworthy, Loxley, & Dennis, 1991; Hellier, Edworthy, & Dennis, 1993). These studies investigated the sound parameters in an auditory alarm that lead to a faster response. Results show that loudness is the most important factor in the perception of urgency in an alarm, and that harmonic content, frequency, rhythm, repetition, speed, duration, and melodic contour also play a significant role. For instance, increasing the pitch, speed, or length of an alarm increases the perception of urgency (Edworthy et al., 1991).

In multimedia, alerts are commonly used for notifying a user about an event or a status change. They are designed in such a way as not to disrupt ongoing tasks but to transmit information to a user about the intended message by using a sound. Beyond just letting the user know that something has happened, auditory alerts can carry information about what the event is through the short earcon or auditory display. For example, many email clients notify their users that a new email has arrived by the use of a characteristically short earcon. When a user hears this sound, which they have learned to associate with the arrival of a new email, they are immediately informed that such an event has happened, even without turning their attention away from the task in which they are involved at the time. They can then choose to take immediate action or wait for a more appropriate time. This is an example of a single alert. Recurring alerts are used to let a user know that they need to interact with a device. For example, the ring of a telephone indicates there is someone trying to establish contact, providing a continuous alert until an action is taken (i.e., a person or a service answers or the person on the other end of the line hangs up). The phone is an example of a persistent alert.

Auditory displays for monitoring

Applications used for monitoring processes, workloads, data, or events, are making an increased use of auditory displays. Auditory displays are effective in these applications because, often, a single individual is tasked with monitoring a significant number of concurrent streams of data. Visual displays are often impractical because the person monitoring has a limited field of view and may not notice a significant event requiring immediate reaction unless their attention is focused on the specifically relevant data stream. Auditory displays, however, can make use of sounds' multiple dimensions and our virtually unlimited auditory field of view to present many streams of data concurrently.

Sonification is a particularly interesting approach taken by many to monitor large quantities of data. Barra et al. (2001) describe a system for monitoring workload and error conditions on Internet web servers. The system combines music chosen by the end user as background music (from CD, MP3, etc.) with server information. Server data are mapped to volume and MIDI-generated sounds. The MIDI sounds are superimposed over the background music while its volume is adjusted based on the server data. The work of Janata and Childs (2004) describes a sonification mechanism to monitor financial information by sonifying real-time stock market data. Using this mechanism, a user can monitor multiple streams of data concurrently while performing other tasks and only turn their attention when the sonification lets them know there is a relevant event happening.

Research of the uses of sonification and auditory displays for monitoring can been seen in many military applications, including spatial auditory displays on US Navy multimodal watch stations (Brock, Stroup, & Ballas, 2001), monitoring of unmanned aerial vehicles (Donmez, Cummings, & Graham, 2009), improving collision avoidance systems (Begault, 1993), and locating targets (Bronkhorst, Veltman, & van Breda, 1996; Glumm, Kehring, & White, 2006). Auditory displays have long been used in Air Force applications, along with haptic displays, to assist pilots in targeting, and improving situational awareness of the presence of enemies (e.g., Nelson et al., 1998; Oving, Veltman, & Bronkhorst, 2004; Tannen, 1999).

Process monitoring in environments where there are numerous media display devices following real-time data can particularly benefit from using auditory displays to track multiple streams of data. For example, a supervisor of a medical care unit station at a hospital can monitor multiple patients' data and seek out relevant changes in the audio signal that would indicate a patient needs attention. Auditory alarms are used in hospital operating rooms to indicate a sudden change in a patient's condition.

Auditory displays for navigation and guidance

The hearing system plays an important role in guiding and alerting us of dangers because it is not bound by the line of sight. Our ancestors have relied on their hearing to warn them of approaching predators. We rely on hearing to warn us of approaching vehicles, especially from behind us, where our visual field is obstructed.

For visually impaired individuals, hearing becomes the primary source of information about the surrounding environment and its contents. Since the adoption of the long cane, there have been many efforts to develop electronic-assisted way-finding technologies, and to make computers and multimedia devices accessible to visually impaired users by developing audio-assisted guidance systems.

Researchers have developed several auditory display mechanisms to give visually impaired users access to graphical interfaces and use them for guidance. One of the earliest examples of adding auditory displays to a user interface was the SonicFinder by Gaver (1989), for which auditory icons were mapped to system events. In this case, sound was added to augment the visual display, not to replace it, demonstrating the beginning efforts of audio-based displays.

Although screen readers are common and widely used, they are limited in their functionality and do not offer an intuitive way to navigate through an interface. One of the first examples of auditory display-based user interfaces specifically designed for visually impaired users was Soundtrack, developed by Edwards (1989). This text editor used non-speech sounds to navigate through the user interface, as well as speech synthesis for navigating through the menu items.

More recent developments have included research in the area of the applications of auditory displays and sonification methods for audio-assisted navigation. Sonifications can augment screen readers and other basic methods in order to accelerate and improve the interaction with an environment, either real or virtual. For example, the System for Wearable Audio Navigation (SWAN) project aims to provide individuals who cannot see due to a visual impairment, or are unable to look, with auditory navigation cues that act as beacons in order to guide them through a real-world environment (Walker

& Lindsay, 2006). The SWAN uses a Global Positioning System (GPS) and head tracker to monitor the location and orientation of the user. This information is transmitted to a computer in which maps of pre-existing areas and objects are stored. This information is used to guide the individual through the environment by playing spatialized, non-speech, auditory icons and earcons (e.g., ping, beeps, tones, noise, jingle, etc.). The auditory displays are transmitted over bone-conduction earphones (rather than headphones) to avoid occluding the user's natural hearing. Sounds are used as beacons (to guide and indicate the path the listener should follow), to represent objects in the environment, and to indicate surface transitions and boundaries. Field tests described in Walker and Lindsay (2006) have shown this to be an effective wayfinding system, where participants in studies were able to stay on course of a path while being guided by beacons. However, the system's effectiveness is dependent on the beacon sounds used as well as the capture radius of the environment.

Auditory displays for augmenting reality

Gone are the days in which we set limits to what our multimedia devices can do or what we can process, based on restricted computing power. We now have access to not only the information we *need*, but also the information we *want*. We have the capability to *augment* our world with information that we receive electronically. Through the use of auditory displays, we can enhance our reality by superimposing sound information that is not heard by the naked ear from our surroundings onto the world we perceive. Based on data obtained from electronic devices, we can increase the type and amount of information the user perceives about the world around them.

GPS information is an example of data that can be used to augment a user's awareness about their environment. This information is readily available on many devices. For example, a car uses GPS to track its location and presents this information to the driver. Because the driver is able to give little visual attention to the device, in this application auditory displays are heavily relied upon to transmit information to the user.

Taking GPS information further, *augmented audio reality* (Cohen, Aoki, & Koizumi, 1993) is a concept that describes the addition of synthesized, virtual sounds, onto real-world audio in an interactive environment. By using virtual content, the human sensory perception of the real world is augmented. Many of these systems are based on mobile platforms, which allow the user to move around and explore an environment. Often, these systems use spatial auditory displays, in which HRTF-based (or similar) processing is used and delivered to the listener over headphones. The user is equipped with a system that plays or synthesizes a spatial audio image while simultaneously navigating a real environment, for example, by presenting historic landmark information within a city as a user points a mobile device in the direction of a given landmark (e.g., Shadel, 2010).

There have been many examples of Augmented Audio Reality (AAR) systems over the past decade. At the Institut de Recherche et Coordination Acoustique/Musique (IRCAM) in Paris, France, Eckel (2001a, 2001b) developed the LISTEN project for studying audio-augmented environments. Using headphones equipped with a head tracking system, Warusfel and Eckel (2004) introduced a platform for navigating through a virtual environment that is superimposed on top of the real environment.

Further work on LISTEN resulted in a personalized, augmented environment for a museum guide (Zimmermann & Lorenz, 2008), in which virtual soundscapes are presented over headphones. These soundscapes are generated based on the user's position and visit history at the exhibition. A more recent example of AAR is provided by virtual audio tours of cities, in which spatially accurate landmarks are represented by 3D auditory displays, providing information about their history, use, and other interesting factoids (Shadel, 2010).

Conclusion

The use of auditory displays in multimedia is rapidly developing and resulting in an advanced use of music, musical phrases, natural sounds, speech, and synthesized sounds for displaying information and improving interaction with multimedia devices. The design of auditory displays and mapping between data and sound is a challenging task and relies heavily on the understanding of the application for which the sounds are designed. Because the goal is to inform the user about an event or object, auditory displays focus on presenting data in an intuitive fashion.

Many principles related to the way we hear and understand music are used in the design and development of auditory displays, such as harmonic relationships, rhythm, pitch, and timbre. Whether we use earcons, auditory icons, or sonification, many studies have shown that a large amount of information can be presented to a listener successfully in a short period of time. As we move in the direction of more powerful electronic devices with shrinking visual displays, we can take advantage of auditory displays to improve the way and the amount of information we perceive, as we navigate through, interact with, receive alerts from, monitor, or enhance the world around us.

References

Attneave, F. (1954). Some informational aspects of visual perception. *Psychological Review, 61*, 183–193.

Baddeley, A. (1998). *Human memory*. Boston, MA: Allyn & Bacon.

Baier, G., Hermann, T., & Stephani, U. (2007). Multi-channel sonification of human EEG. In W. L. Martens (Ed.), *Proceedings of the 2007 International Conference on Auditory Display* (pp. 491–496). Montreal, Canada: Schulich School of Music, McGill University.

Ballora, M., Pennycook, B., Ivanov, P., Glass, L., & Goldberg, A. (2004). Heart rate sonification: a new approach to medical diagnosis. *Leonardo, 37*(1), 41–46.

Barra, M., Cillo, T., De Santis, A., Petrillo, U. F., Negro, A., Scarano, V., *et al.* (2001). Personal Webmelody: Customized sonification of web servers. In J. Hiipakka, N. Zacharov, & T. Takala (Eds.), *Proceedings of the 2001 International Conference on Auditory Display* (pp. 1–9). Espoo, Finland: Helsinki University of Technology.

Barreto, A., Jacko, J. A., & Hugh, P. (2007). Impact of spatial auditory feedback on the efficiency of iconic human-computer interfaces under conditions of visual impairment. *Computers in Human Behavior, 23*(3), 1211–1231.

Bates, E. (1979). *The emergence of symbols: Cognition and communication in infancy*. New York, NY: Academic Press.

Beck, D., & Elkerton, J. (1989). Development and evaluation of direct manipulation list. *Special Interest Group for Computer-Human Interaction (SIGCHI) Bulletin, 20*(3), 72–78.

Begault, D. R. (1993). A head-up auditory display for TCAS advisories. *Human Factors, 35*, 707–717.

Blattner, M. M., Sumikawa, D. A., & Greenberg, R. M. (1989). Earcons and icons: Their structure and common design principles. *Human-Computer Interaction, 4*(1), 11–44.

Bonebright, T. L., & Nees, M. A. (2007). Memory for auditory icons and earcons with localization cues. In W. L. Martens (Ed.), *Proceedings of the 2007 International Conference on Auditory Display* (pp. 419–422). Montreal, Canada: Schulich School of Music, McGill University.

Bregman, A. S. (1990). *Auditory scene analysis: The perceptual organization of sound.* Cambridge, MA: MIT Press.

Brewster, S. A. (1997). Using non-speech sound to overcome information overload. *Displays, 17*, 179–189.

Brewster, S. A., Capriotti, A., & Hall, C. V. (1998). Using compound earcons to represent hierarchies. *Human-Computer Interaction (HCI) Letters, 1*(1), 6–8.

Brewster, S. A., Raty, V. P., & Kortekangas, A. (1996). Earcons as a method of providing navigational cues in a menu hierarchy. In M. A. Sasse, R. J. Cunningham, & R. L. Winder (Eds.), *Proceedings of Human-Computer Interaction 96* (pp. 167–183). London, UK: Springer.

Brewster, S. A., Wright, P. C., & Edwards, A. D. N. (1993). An evaluation of earcons for use in auditory human-computer interfaces. In S. Ashlund, K. Mullet, A. Henderson, E. Hollnagel, & T. White (Eds.), *Proceedings of the Conference on Human Factors in Computing Systems* (pp. 222–227). Amsterdam, the Netherlands: ACM Press, Addison-Wesley.

Brewster, S. A., Wright, P. C., & Edwards, A. D. N. (1995). Parallel earcons: Reducing the length of audio messages. *International Journal of Human-Computer Studies, 43*(22), 153–175.

Brock, D., Stroup, J. L., & Ballas, J. A. (2002). Using an auditory display to manage attention in a dual task, multiscreen environment. In *Proceedings of the 2002 International Conference on Auditory Display*. Kyoto, Japan: Advanced Telecommunications Institute. Retrieved from <http://www.icad.org/websiteV2.0/Conferences/ICAD2002/proceedings/13_DerekBrock.pdf>.

Bronkhorst, A. W., Veltman, J. A., & van Breda, L. (1996). Application of a three-dimensional auditory display in a flight task. *Human Factors, 38*(1), 23–33.

Brown, M. L., Newsome, S. L., & Glinert, E. P. (1989). An experiment into the use of auditory cues to reduce visual workload. In K. Rice & C. Lewis (Eds.), *Proceedings of the SIGCHI Conference on Human Factors in Computing Systems* (pp. 339–346). Austin, TX.

Buxton, W., Gaver, W., & Bly, S. (1991). Tutorial number 8: The use of non-speech audio at the interface. In *Proceedings of InterCHI'91.* New Orleans, LA: ACM Press, Addison-Wesley.

Childs, E., & Pulkki, V. (2003). Using multi-channel spatialization in sonification: A case study with meteorological data. In E. Brazil & B. Shinn-Cunningham (Eds.), *Proceedings of the 2003 International Conference on Auditory Display*. Boston, MA.

Cohen, M., Aoki, S., & Koizumi, N. (1993). Augmented audio reality: Telepresence/VR hybrid acoustic environments. In *Proceedings of the Institute of Electrical and Electronics Engineers (IEEE) International Workshop in Robot and Human Communication* (pp. 361–364). Tokyo, Japan: Institute of Electrical and Electronics Engineers.

Correia Da Silva Diniz, N., Deweppe, A., Demey, M., & Leman, M. (2010, June). A framework for music-based interactive sonification. In E. Brazil (Ed.), *Proceedings of the 2010 International Conference on Auditory Display* (pp. 345–351). Washington, DC.

Davies, J. B. (1978). *The psychology of music.* Stanford, CA: Stanford University Press.

Donmez, B., Cummings, M. L., & Graham, H. D. (2009). Auditory decision aiding in supervisory control of multiple unmanned aerial vehicles. *Human Factors, 51*(5), 718–729.

Eckel, G. (2001a). Immersive audio-augmented environments: the LISTEN project. In E. Elanissi, F. Khosrowshahi, M. Sarfraz, & A. Ursyn (Eds.), *Proceedings of the Fifth International Conference on Information Visualisation* (pp. 571–573). Los Alamitos, CA: The Institute of Electrical and Electronics Engineers.

Eckel, G. (2001b). The vision of the LISTEN project. In H. Thwaites & L. Addison (Eds.), *Proceedings of the Seventh International Conference on Virtual Systems and Multimedia* (pp. 393–396). Los Alamitos, CA: The Institute of Electrical and Electronics Engineers.

Edwards, A. D. N. (1989). Soundtrack: an auditory interface for blind users, *Human-Computer Interaction, 4*(1), 45–66.

Edworthy, J. (1994). The design and implementation of non-verbal auditory warnings. *Applied Ergonomics, 25*, 202–210.

Edworthy, J. (1997). Cognitive compatibility and warning design. *International Journal of Cognitive Ergonomics, 1*(3), 193–209.

Edworthy, J., Loxley, S. , & Dennis, I. (1991). Improving auditory warning design: Relationship between warning sound parameters and perceived urgency. *Human Factors, 33* (2), 205–231.

Easterby, R. S. (1970). The perception of symbols for machine displays. *Ergonomics, 13*(1), 149–158.

Fitch, W. T., & Kramer, G., (1994). Sonifying the body electric: Superiority of an auditory display over a visual display in a complex, multivariate system. In G. Kramer (Ed.), *Auditory display. Sonification, audification, and auditory interfaces* (pp. 307–325). Reading, MA: Addison-Wesley.

Fletcher, H. (1940). Auditory patterns. *Reviews of Modern Physics, 12*, 47–65.

Gaver, W. (1989). The SonicFinder: An interface that uses auditory icons. *Human-Computer Interaction, 4*(1), 67–94.

Gilfix, M., & Couch, A. (2000). Peep (The Network Auralizer): Monitoring your network with sound. In *2000 LISA XIV* (pp. 109–117). New Orleans, LA.

Gilkey, R. H., & Anderson, T. R. (1995). The accuracy of absolute localization judgments for speech stimuli. *Journal of Vestibular Research, 5*, 487–497.

Glumm, M., Kehring, K., & White, T. (2006). *Effects of tactile, visual, and auditory cues about threat location on target acquisition and attention to visual and auditory communications.* Aberdeen Proving Ground, MD: ARL-TR-3863, U.S. Army Research Laboratory.

Hansen, M.H., & Rubin, B. (2001). Babble online: Applying statistics and design to sonify the internet. In J. Hiipakka, N. Zacharov, & T. Takala (Eds.), *Proceedings of the 2001 International Conference on Auditory Display* (pp. 10–15). Espoo, Finland: Helsinki University of Technology.

Heil, J. (1983). *Perception and cognition.* Berkeley, CA: University of California Press.

Hellier, E., Edworthy, J., & Dennis, I. (1993). Improving auditory warning design: quantifying and predicting the effects of different warning parameters on perceived urgency. *Human Factors, 35*(4), 693–706.

Janata, P., & Childs, E. (2004). Marketbuzz: Sonification of real-time financial data, In P. Vickers & K. Stevens (Eds.), *Proceedings of the 2004 International Conference on Auditory Display.* Sydney, Australia.

Jeon, M., & Walker, B. N. (2009). 'Spindex': Accelerated initial speech sounds improve navigation performance in auditory menus. In *Proceedings of the Annual Meeting of the Human Factors and Ergonomics Society (HFES2009)* (pp. 1081–1085). San Antonio, TX.

Jeon, M., & Walker, B. N. (2011). Spindex (speech index) improves auditory menu acceptance and navigation performance. *ACM Transactions on Accessible Computing (TACCESS)*, *3*(3), 10:1–26.

Kramer, G. (1994). Some organizing principles for representing data with sound. In G. Kramer (Ed.), *Auditory display. Sonification, audification, and auditory interfaces* (pp. 185–221). Reading, MA: Addison-Wesley.

Kramer, G., Walker, B., Bonebright, T., Cook, P., Flowers, J., Miner, N., *et al.* (1999). *The Sonification Report: Status of the Field and Research Agenda.* Report prepared for the National Science Foundation by members of the International Community for Auditory Display. Santa Fe, NM: International Community for Auditory Display.

Krishnan, S., Rangayyan, R. M., Bell, G. D., & Frank, C. B. (2001). Auditory display of knee-joint vibration signals. *Journal of the Acoustical Society of America*, *110*(6), 3292–3304.

Landels, J. G. (1979). Water-clocks and time measurement in classical antiquity. *Endeavour*, *3*(1), 32–37.

Loomis, J. M., Golledge, R. G., & Klatzky, R. L. (1998). Navigation system for the blind: Auditory display modes and guidance. *Presence: Teleoperators and Virtual Environments*, *7*, 193–203.

Marston, J. R., Loomis, J. M., Klatzky, R. L., Golledge, R. G., & Smith, E. L. (2006). Evaluation of spatial displays for navigation without sight. *Association for Computing Machinery (ACM) Transactions on Applied Perception*, *3*(2), 110–124.

Mayer, R. E., & Moreno, R. (1998). A split-attention effect in multimedia learning: Evidence for dual processing systems in working memory. *Journal of Educational Psychology*, *90*, 312–320.

Mauney, B. S., & Walker, B. N. (2004). Creating functional and livable soundscapes for peripheral monitoring of dynamic data. In P. Vickers & K. Stevens (Eds.), *Proceedings of the 2004 International Conference on Auditory Display*. Sydney, Australia.

Miller, G. A. (1947). The masking of speech. *Psychological Bulletin*, *44*, 105–129.

Moreno, R., & Mayer, R. E. (1999). Cognitive principles of multimedia learning: The role of modality and contiguity. *Journal of Educational Psychology*, *91*, 358–368.

Moreno, R., Mayer, R. E., Spires, H. A., & Lester, J. C. (2001). The case for social agency in computer-based multimedia learning: Do students learn more deeply when they interact with animated pedagogical agents? *Cognition and Instruction*, *19*, 177–214.

Mousavi, S., Low, R., & Sweller, J. (1995). Reducing cognitive load by mixing auditory and visual presentation modes. *Journal of Educational Psychology*, *87*, 319–334.

Mynatt, E. D. (1997). Transforming graphical interfaces into auditory interfaces for blind users. *Human-Computer Interaction*, *12*, 7–45.

Nelson, W. T., Hettinger, L. J., Cunningham, J. A., Brickman, B. J., Haas, M. W., & McKinley, R. L. (1998). Effects of localized auditory information on visual target detection performance using a helmet-mounted display. *Human Factors*, *40*, 452–460.

Nesbitt, K. V., & Barrass, S. (2002). Evaluation of a multimodal sonification and visualization of depth of stock market data. In K. Nishimoto (Ed.), *Proceedings of the 2002 International Conference on Auditory Display.* Kyoto, Japan.

Neuhoff, J.G., Kramer, G., & Wayand, J. (2002). Pitch and loudness interact in auditory displays: Can the data get lost in the map? *Journal of Experimental Psychology: Applied*, *8*(1), 17–25.

Oving, A. B., Veltman, J. A., & Bronkhorst, A. W. (2004). Effectiveness of 3-D audio for warnings in the cockpit. *International Journal of Aviation Psychology*, *14*(3), 257–276.

Paivio, A. (1986). *Mental representations: A dual coding approach.* Oxford, UK: Oxford University Press.

Palladino, D., & Walker, B. N. (2007). Learning rates for auditory menus enhanced with spearcons versus earcons. In W. L. Martens (Ed.), *Proceedings of the International Conference on Auditory Display* (pp. 274–279). Montreal, Canada.

Palladino, D., & Walker, B. N. (2008a). Efficiency of spearcon-enhanced navigation of onedimensional electronic menus. In P. Susini & O. Warusfel (Eds.), *Proceedings of the 2008 International Conference on Auditory Display*. Paris, France.

Palladino, D., & Walker, B. N. (2008b). Navigation efficiency of two dimensional auditory menus using spearcon enhancements. In *Annual Meeting of the Human Factors and Ergonomics Society (HFES 2008)* (pp. 1262–1266). New York, NY.

Patterson, R. D. (1982). *Guidelines for auditory warning systems on civil aircraft.* London, UK: Civil Aviation Authority.

Patterson, R. D. (1990). Auditory warning sounds in the work environment. *Philosophical Transactions of the Royal Society of London. Series B, Biological Sciences, 327*(1241), 485–492.

Peirce, C. S. (1932). *Collected Papers of Charles Sanders Peirce* (C. Jartshorne & P. Weiss, Eds.). Cambridge, MA: Harvard University Press.

Roginska, A., Childs, E., & Johnson, M. (2006). Monitoring real-time data: a sonification approach. In T. Stockman, L. V. Nickerson, C. Frauenberger, A. Edwards, & D. Brock (Eds.), *Proceedings of the 2006 International Conference on Auditory Display* (pp. 176–181). London, UK.

Shadel, R. B. (2010). *AudioMaps: Augmented reality audio navigation for mobile device.* (Unpublished Master's Thesis.) New York University, NY.

Shilling, R. D., Letowski, T., & Storms R. (2000). Spatial auditory displays for use within attack rotary wing aircraft. In P. R. Cook, J. Ballas, R. Storms, J. Pair, & J. Oliverio (Eds.), *Proceedings of the 2000 International Conference on Auditory Display*. Atlanta, GA.

Sturm, B. (2005). Pulse of an ocean: Sonification of ocean buoy data. *Leonardo, 38*(2), 143–149.

Tannen, R. S. (1999). *Multimodal displays for target localization in a flight test.* (AFRL-HE-WP-TR-2001–0102, 1–51). Wright-Patterson AFB, OH: USAF AMRL.

Wakefield, G. H., Roginska, A., & Santoro, T. S. (2012). Auditory detection of infrapitch signals for several spatial configurations of pink noise maskers. In C. Burroughs & S. Conlon (Eds.), *Proceedings of the 41st International Congress on Noise Control Engineering, Inter-Noise 2012.* New York, NY.

Walker, B. N., & Kogan, A. (2009). Spearcon performance and preference for auditory menus on a mobile phone. Invited paper in C. Stephanidis (Ed.), *Proceedings of the 5th International Conference on Universal Access in Human-Computer Interaction (UAHCI) at Human-Computer Interaction (HCI) International 2009* (pp. 445–454). San Diego, CA.

Walker, B. N., & Kramer, G. (1996). Mappings and metaphors in auditory displays: An experimental assessment. In S. P. Frysinger & G. Kramer (Eds.), *Proceedings of the Third International Conference on Auditory Display*. Palo Alto, CA.

Walker, B. N., & Lindsay, J. (2006). Navigation performance with a virtual auditory display: Effects of beacon sound, capture radius, and practice. *Human Factors, 48*(2), 265–78.

Walker, B. N., Nance, A. G., & Lindsay, J. (2006). Spearcons: Speech-based earcons improve navigation performance in auditory menus. In T. Stockman, L. V. Nickerson, C. Frauenberger, A. Edwards, & D. Brock (Eds.), *Proceedings of the 2006 International Conference on Auditory Display* (pp. 63–68). London, UK.

Warusfel, O., & Eckel, G. (2004). LISTEN—augmenting everyday environments through interactive soundscapes. In *IEEE Workshop on VR for public consumption*. Chicago, IL.

Wijngaarden, S. J., Bronkhorst, A. W., & Boer, L. C. (2004). Auditory evacuation beacons. *Journal of the Audio Engineering Society*, *53*(1–2), 44–53.

Zimmermann, A., & Lorenz, A. (2008). LISTEN: a user adaptive audio-augmented museum guide. *User Modeling and User-Adapted Interaction*, *18*(5), 389–416.

Chapter 16

Understanding the impact of surround sound in multimedia

Mark Kerins

Southern Methodist University, USA

Prerecorded audio is such an integral and accepted part of modern life that its existence is taken for granted—yet its very ubiquity masks the complex ontological nature of recorded sound. Every recording is colored by the recording technology used to capture it, the placement of the microphones relative to the sound sources, the number of tracks recorded and how they were mixed together, the ultimate playback location of the recording, and so on.

One crucial, yet often overlooked, way in which audio recordings differ from live sound is that recording translates a continuous three-dimensional soundscape into a finite number of discrete channels. To be sure, recorded audio using a small number of unique audio channels *can* create the illusion of a complete three-dimensional soundscape (at least for listeners located in the 'sweet spot' between the speakers playing back those channels)—it is simply that doing so requires careful mixing and processing of sounds to multiple channels. Music recordings, for instance, have for decades employed a two-channel stereo configuration (distinct left and right channels of sound) to create a sense of breadth and depth far greater than can be done with a single track of recorded sound. In recent years, even more precisely spatialized recordings have been created through complex 'multichannel sound' systems that expand beyond traditional two-channel stereo to configurations of 5.1 (the .1 referring to a low frequencies-only channel) or more channels.

Today, multichannel soundtracks are commonplace, with 5.1-channel sound the standard format for movies, television, and console games and available on some musical recordings and other media. Historically, most empirical research on prerecorded sound has dealt with monophonic or two-channel stereo reproduction; as multichannel sound has become increasingly common, though, the importance of understanding the unique issues associated with this type of audio has grown as well. Recent years, therefore, have seen a growth in scholarly interest in multichannel sound, specifically in whether it creates a different listening experience than stereo or mono formats—and, if so, *how* the experience is different. This chapter offers an overview of existing empirical research on multichannel sound, outlining what has (and more often has *not*) been accomplished thus far, focusing especially on work relating to the question of how *music* functions in multichannel multimedia. This particular emphasis on the role of music in multimedia, it should be noted, highlights a peculiar limitation of extant empirical work on multichannel sound: *none* of it directly addresses the issue of music's role in audiovisual media. While the experiments discussed in this chapter utilize a variety of stimuli in investigating the impact of multichannel sound, *none* of them utilize as stimuli any *audiovisual* materials with *purely musical* sonic components—in all the stimuli with visual components, the soundtracks include non-musical elements such as dialogue, ambiences, and/or sound effects. The approach taken here, therefore, is to examine the results of studies on multichannel music and studies on multichannel audiovisual media together in order to draw useful hypotheses and conclusions about how music's role in multimedia is affected by multichannel sound.

A brief history of surround sound

The channel configuration used for commercially available prerecorded music has remained remarkably consistent since the late 1950s: two-channel stereo, with discrete left and right channels, first appeared on long-play (LP) records in 1957 (Belton, 1992) and would remain the standard configuration for later formats such as FM radio, cassette tapes, compact discs, and even the vast majority of downloadable digital files. Yet, despite its success and longevity, two-channel stereo is actually a fairly limited format in terms of its ability to create a sense of three-dimensional sonic space; indeed, as far back as 1933, audio engineers recognized that proper spatial reproduction of music required at least three channels (Beck, 2003). Two-channel stereo is particularly bad at creating sounds outside the plane of the two speakers; the format provides decent spatial characteristics in front of the listening position but has limited ability to convincingly portray sounds as originating from beside or behind listeners.

A variety of more complex configurations have attempted to address the shortcomings of two-channel stereo by adding sound sources to the left/right configuration, often including speakers placed next to or behind the listening position to create 'surround sound.' Indeed, it is hardly surprising that the first motion picture released with a surround soundtrack—*Fantasia* (1940)—was musically-driven; the decision to create a new sound system specifically for use with this single film highlights how much the development of new sound systems has historically been driven by the goal of improving reproduction of *musical* sound. Post-Fantasound (Disney's moniker for the *Fantasia* sound system), the film industry experimented with a variety of multichannel systems in the 1950s, but none of these spread beyond theaters or even took root as a standard within cinemas.

The first widely available expanded systems for music playback were the four-channel 'quadraphonic' systems of the 1970s. These 'quad' systems encoded four channels of audio—designed to be played back through four speakers arranged around the listening position—into the two tracks available on LP records. Quad represented a major advance in the spatialization capabilities of recorded music, but consumer confusion about competing (and incompatible) quadraphonic systems, the reluctance of home listeners to crowd their living rooms with more speakers and amplifiers, the higher expense of creating quad recordings, and the technical limitations of the quad encoding processes proved more than the format could overcome. As a result, quad never seriously challenged two-channel stereo for dominance in the marketplace (Beck, 2003). The technology underlying quad sound, however, was quickly adopted by the film industry as the basis for new multichannel formats. As with *Fantasia* three decades earlier, cinema first tested the possibilities of multichannel sound on musical material; *Tommy* (1975)—adapted from the quad-recorded album by The Who—was the first feature film released in a quad-based surround sound format. Music lost its place as the star of multichannel sound, however, when the soundtracks of a succession of high-profile multichannel films (*Star Wars*, 1977; *Superman*, 1978; and *Apocalypse Now*, 1979) were hailed not for their multichannel music mixes but for their use of multichannel to spatialize sound *effects*. Thanks to these and other Dolby Stereo films, many filmmakers and audio engineers came to associate multichannel sound with effects-driven sound design rather than with music (Beck, 2003; Holman, 2000; Kerins, 2010). Tellingly, the multichannel capabilities of Dolby Stereo, the sound system that by the early 1980s had been adopted by the film industry as the theatrical exhibition standard, were designed more to properly match sounds horizontally with their onscreen sources than to create a true three-dimensional space. In fact, its channel configuration originally employed only three channels across the width of the screen before later adding a surround channel behind the audience.

Where music had once been a driving factor behind advancements in multichannel sound, from the introduction of Dolby Stereo onward it would be the film industry that led the way. For instance, after the death of quad, multichannel sound had essentially disappeared as a consumer format. In the 1980s, though, the popularity of Dolby Stereo and the growth of the home video industry gave multichannel a reentry point into homes. Dolby introduced home sound formats (first Dolby Surround, later Dolby Pro Logic) that allowed those with four or five speakers in their homes to hear multichannel film soundtracks essentially as they had played in theaters. These formats, though commonly employed in broadcast television and on home video releases, were never widely used for commercial music releases. In the early 1990s, the film industry again pushed multichannel sound forward with the introduction of the first digitally-encoded film soundtracks, expanding the four-channel Dolby Stereo system into a 5.1-channel configuration of three front channels (left, center, and right), two surround channels (left surround and right surround), and a low-frequency effects channel (the 'point-one' of '5.1') for creating loud bass sounds. Popularized by such implementations as Dolby Digital and DTS, the 5.1-channel configuration quickly became the norm for theatrical film exhibition; when DVD video launched in 1997, 5.1-channel surround was similarly specified as its soundtrack format. In the ensuing DVD boom, the desire of home viewers to experience their DVDs in their full 5.1-channel glory (Sherber, 2001) led increasing numbers of consumers to install some form of home theater system during the first decade of the 2000s. Using its definition of a 'home theater' as an audio system capable of playing back four or more distinct channels of audio over at least four separate speakers, in 2006 the Consumer Electronics Association reported that the percentage of households with home theater systems had more than doubled—to over 36 percent—since the introduction of DVD, and concluded that home multichannel systems 'went main-stream long ago' (Consumer Electronics Association, 'Digital America 2006,' p. 1).

Determining the impact of surround sound

The continued success of 5.1-channel sound in film and in other audiovisual media suggests that multichannel sound must offer some sort of major improvement over simpler soundtrack formats such as mono and two-channel stereo; neither theater owners nor consumers would likely be willing to pay for the surround decoders and multiple speakers necessary to properly reproduce a 5.1-channel soundtrack if they did not expect to receive some benefit from doing so. Yet, as this chapter will detail, empirical studies into *the* fundamental question about multichannel sound—how does multichannel sound alter the listening experience?—have yielded surprisingly little consensus about what, if any, impact the sound system used has on listeners. One reason for this diversity of results is that different researchers have sought quite different types of evidence that the listening experience may have been 'altered' by multichannel sound. Some have explored whether listeners can *identify* differences between different sound systems, while others have instead asked whether listeners *prefer* one sound system over others, and yet another group has sought 'independent' differences in listener ratings that appear even without directly comparing multiple sound systems. These three large-scale approaches to empirical research on multichannel sound occasionally overlap in individual studies, but are distinct enough to serve as a useful organizing device for an overview of extant work on the impact of multichannel audio on the listening experience.

Effect of surround sound on relative ratings

Studies in the first of these three categories tackle the question 'Does multichannel sound alter the listening experience?' with perhaps the most direct method possible: presenting listeners with multiple sound mixes of the same stimuli, having those listeners rate each mix on one or more scales and then analyzing whether the mixes were rated differently. Put another way, these studies explore whether listeners comparing two different versions of a stimulus (e.g., a 5.1-channel mix and a two-channel stereo mix) respond differently to the two versions.

An example of this type of experiment is provided by Lessiter and Freeman (2001) who designed a study to quantify the impact of 5.1-channel sound on the audiovisual experience. This experiment presented participants with a single never-clearly-described video clip three times: once in its original 5.1-channel surround mix, once in a two-channel stereo mixdown, and once in a mono (one-channel) mixdown. Participants then rated each version on over 60 different measures. Analysis revealed a significant main effect of the audio presentation mode in several rating categories, including 'spaciousness/surrounding,' 'engagement,' 'enjoyment,' and 'overall audio rating.' In all areas where presentation mode had a significant main effect, the 5.1 mix was always rated significantly higher than both the stereo and mono mixes.

These results would seem to suggest that 5.1 sound significantly enhanced the experience of seeing and hearing the stimulus clip relative to stereo or mono sound. The authors of this study noted, however, that the results may have been affected by the presence of the LFE channel in the 5.1-channel presentation, a factor for which the authors had not controlled—to be specific, the LFE channel had been turned off during their loudness calibrations, making the 5.1 presentation mode noticeably louder than the other two in the actual experiment. This raised the question of whether the higher ratings for the 5.1 mode were simply an effect of that mode seeming louder or more bass-heavy.

A follow-up study (Lessiter & Freeman, 2001) attempting to examine this question by comparing loudness-matched surround and stereo mixes with and without the LFE channel found that the addition of the LFE channel had a significant positive impact on some 'presence' measures, while the change from two-channel to five-channel had no significant impact on any presence-related characteristics. This implies at least some of the significant main effects of presentation mode found in the initial study represented the impact of the 5.1-channel mode's LFE channel, rather than its increased number of channels. Any results from this study are suspect, though, as its 'loudness'-matching procedures relied upon dB sound pressure levels (SPLs), which do not directly correspond to listeners' *perceptions* of loudness—especially when comparing presentations differing only in the presence or absence of a low-frequency channel. Indeed, the authors themselves acknowledged that 'Sounds of different frequencies, but equivalent dB SPLs are experienced as perceptually different in terms of loudness' (p. 8).

Zacharov and Huopaniemi (1999), another comparison-based study from early in the 5.1-channel era, investigated the impact of the 5.1-channel configuration from a slightly different perspective. First, Zacharov and Huopaniemi focused on the impact of 5.1 sound for *audio-only* stimuli, rather than for audiovisual stimuli. Second, rather than directly considering the difference between 5.1-channel reproduction and two-channel stereo or mono playback, like Lessiter and Freeman (2001), Zacharov and Huopaniemi explicitly *assumed* that the 5.1-channel configuration had increased spatialization capabilities and sought to determine whether those presumed benefits could be replicated using a two-channel stereo setup. As a result, this study compared a discrete 5.1-channel configuration with six 'virtual home theater' (or 'VHT') algorithms that each aimed 'to faithfully reproduce the spatial sound qualities of 5.1 channel audio systems using only two loudspeakers or headphones' (p. 1). Four audio-only stimulus materials were utilized (two soundscapes and two musical selections), with each starting as a 5.1-channel mix then being converted into six different two-channel mixes using the VHT algorithms. Each listener gave responses in an individual session, using a computer interface that allowed the listener to switch among the seven sound mixes at will (and repeat each stimulus and each mix as many times as desired). For each of the four stimuli, all participants ranked the seven sound mixes (ties were allowed) in two separate categories: 'spatial sound quality' and 'timbral quality.'

The results of this study should be viewed with some caution, as its design implies methodological complications that space limitations for the present chapter preclude discussing. That said, Zacharov and Huopaniemi's (1999) analysis of their data revealed a general consensus among the listeners in their rankings of the seven competing systems. Additionally, when examining the mean rankings (and confidence intervals thereof) for spatial quality and timbral quality, both individually for each stimulus and averaged across all stimuli, the authors found that, 'In all cases *the 5 channel system is consistently and significantly superior than* [sic] *any of the VHT systems*' (1999, pp. 5–6, emphasis in original). The authors also discovered a significant effect of the interaction between system and program material, but asserted that this was due to the rankings of the various virtual home theater systems differing across the four program materials, as the five-channel system was always ranked highest regardless of the program material.

Zacharov and Huopaniemi (1999) would appear to provide evidence that the five discrete channel configuration of the 5.1-channel system provides higher perceived quality, at least in some ways, than two-channel presentation. VHT algorithms, though, are designed specifically to create a surround environment without surround speakers, and hence are potentially at a disadvantage relative not only to an actual multichannel system, but also to a two-channel stereo system being used simply to create a frontal (left/right) sound image rather than to simulate a five-channel system. Thus even setting aside any methodological concerns about this study, the results of Zacharov and Huopaniemi—who were specifically investigating the ability of two-channel systems to *replicate* five-channel mixes—may not hold true in the case of two-channel stereo mixes not attempting to emulate a surround environment.

In comparing 5.1-channel sound to two-channel stereo, Zielinski, Rumsey, and Bech (2003) may therefore be more useful. In this study, designed to identify the best downmix approach for applications in which bandwidth limitations prohibit using a full 5.1-channel mix, participants evaluated nine different audio channel configurations without the complicating factor of VHT algorithms. These configurations included single-channel mono, two-channel stereo, a variety of three- and four-channel configurations, and full five-channel surround; the LFE signal was played back with each mix. For each of six short stimuli—three music-only and three audiovisual—a 5.1-channel original soundtrack was downmixed in eight different ways to create the other eight test configurations.

As with the previously described studies, one person at a time took part, and a computer interface allowed the participant to switch freely among the various mixes of each stimulus. In this study, the computer interface also gave participants a button labeled 'reference,' which played the original 5.1-channel mix. Participants were told to rate the 'basic audio quality' of each mix on a scale from 0 to 100, with explicit instructions to consider the 'reference' as a perfect score of 100. 'Basic audio quality' was defined for the participants as a rating 'describing any and all detected differences between the reference and the evaluated excerpts' (Zielinski et al., 2003, p. 786); participants were provided with a long list of attributes that should be considered part of this measurement. Participants rated all nine mixes for each stimulus.

Analysis revealed several significant effects, the most notable (and strongest) being those of the mix used and the interaction between stimulus item and the mix. These results were consistent with the results of Zacharov and Huopaniemi (1999) in that participants *did* perceive significant differences in audio quality among the various mixing configurations, but Zielinski et al. (2003) noted that the precise nature of these differences were not the same across all stimuli. The full 5.1-channel mix received the highest rating for all six stimuli, as would be expected given that participants had been explicitly instructed that the 5.1-channel 'reference' represented a perfect score. On the other end of the spectrum, the mono mix consistently scored the lowest. In between these two extremes, however, the results varied dramatically. For several stimuli the highest-rated of the three different four-channel downmix algorithms was a

'3/1' configuration (three front channels, one surround) preserving the original front soundscape of the 5.1-channel mix while downmixing its stereo surround channels into mono. For other stimuli, this same configuration was rated significantly lower than the other two four-channel mixdowns, both of which preserved the 5.1 mix's stereo surround channels while downmixing the 5.1 mix's three front channels into two. The same held true in the case of the three-channel algorithms, with different downmixes rated higher depending on the stimulus material.

Zielinski et al. (2003) noted a pattern in these results: participant ratings of the various downmixes 'are strongly dependent on the spatial characteristic of the program material' (p. 790). In other words, the style of a stimulus's original 5.1-channel mix largely determined which downmix would receive the highest ratings. In some 5.1-channel mixes, 'foreground' material is present in both the front and rear (i.e., surround) channels, while in others, foreground material is limited to the front channels with the surrounds containing only 'background' sounds such as room response, reverberations, etc. The authors labeled these two broad categories of mixes F-F and F-B, respectively, for foreground-foreground and foreground-background.

Combining data from those stimuli deemed F-F into one group and those deemed F-B into another revealed that the eight downmixing schemes evaluated fell into three distinct categories. Those algorithms that altered the front channels but not the rear channels of the original 5.1-channel mix were consistently rated higher with F-F material than with F-B material. For those that affected the rear channels but not the front channels, the opposite was true: participants gave higher ratings when evaluating F-B material than they did with F-F stimuli. Finally, for the original 5.1-channel mix and for those algorithms that altered both the front and rear channels, participant ratings were not significantly different between F-B material and F-F material. In short, the specific channel configuration of a sound mix *was* important to listener ratings, but no *single type* of downmix was rated the best for all varieties of material. F-B material was robust to downmixing and even elimination of the rear channels, but not to downmixing the front channels; F-F material, meanwhile, was not at all robust to loss of spatial information in the rear channels but was significantly more robust than F-B material to downmixing the front channels alone, perhaps because the additional spatial information in the rear channels of F-F material retained the sense of a complete soundscape even when information from the front channels had been lost.

A follow-up study (Zielinski, Rumsey, Kassier, & Bech, 2005) further demonstrated that the influence of the channel configuration on listeners' ratings of 'basic audio quality' depends heavily on the nature of the original recording. In this study, Zielinski et al. used an experimental method similar to that of Zielinski et al. (2003), which was likewise designed to evaluate different ways of reducing a full 5.1-channel soundtrack into a smaller data stream. In this case, the authors compared several of the highest-rated downmixing algorithms from their previous study with an alternate means of achieving the same data reduction: using a low-pass filter on each of the five channels, thus eliminating higher frequencies and reducing the bandwidth needed for each channel. The study included two conditions: one in which overall bandwidth of the 5.1-channel original was reduced by 40 percent, and a second in which it was reduced by 60 percent. Both conditions included some algorithms that achieved this reduction via downmixing to fewer channels and some that achieved the same data reduction via low-pass filtering (with several different approaches to which frequencies were filtered out of each channel). Curiously, for some reason these researchers chose not to include for comparison common extant data reduction schemes, such as DTS or Dolby Digital, that significantly reduce the amount of data required for a 5.1-channel soundtrack with relatively little loss of perceived audio quality. As in the earlier study, participants were asked to rate the 'basic audio quality' of each data-compressed version of a particular stimulus relative to the original 5.1-channel mix. Twelve stimuli were used, evenly split between music-only (four F-B items and two F-F items) and audiovisual (two F-B items and four F-F items) materials; the study authors provided no explanation as to why differing numbers of F-B and F-F items were used within each of these two categories, rather than using three items of each type.

Analysis of the data from this study confirmed the importance of the F-F/F-B distinction. For all the F-B program materials, downmixing to any configuration with front channels only was invariably preferred to any low-pass filtering algorithm utilized. As the authors explain: 'If one has to limit the overall bandwidth of an uncompressed multichannel recording exhibiting the F-B characteristic [...] it is better, in terms of basic audio quality, to 'sacrifice' the rear channels by downmixing them to the full-bandwidth front channels rather than preserving five channels and limiting their bandwidth' (Zielinski et al., 2005, p. 181). The results were less clear, though, for F-F material. In the condition in which bandwidth was reduced by 60 percent, the two-channel stereo downmix was rated as having significantly higher 'basic audio quality' than any of the low-pass-filtered mixes. When reducing bandwidth by only 40 percent instead of 60 percent, the low-pass algorithms produced similar ratings of 'basic audio quality' to two downmixes: a '3/0' downmix to three front channels only, and a '1/2' downmix (preserving the stereo surrounds while mixing all three front channels down to mono). For the F-F stimuli, in other words, downmixing the original five channels to three was perceived by participants as degrading the overall audio quality in roughly the same degree as applying the 40 percent low-pass filters.

Comparing these divergent results highlights an important fact: multichannel—and specifically surround sound—is far more important to some 5.1-channel mixes than to others. Listener ratings of 'basic audio quality' across different data reduction algorithms were consistently impacted more by removing frequencies than by downmixing *if* the original 5.1 mix was of the F-B type. In the case of F-F material, though, eliminating channels sometimes had as much of an impact on quality ratings as using a low-pass filter.

The results just presented are at least somewhat suspect, given that the design of Zielinski et al. (2005) presented the original 5.1-channel mixes as a defined 'reference' for all stimuli; had the participants in this study not heard the original F-F 5.1 mixes, they might not have given the front-only downmixes of those stimuli such low 'basic audio quality' ratings, just as participants asked to judge the overall picture quality of a black-and-white image might respond quite differently if they knew the image had originally contained a full color palette than if they believed it to have always been black-and-white. Indeed, while this problem is particularly egregious when one mix is defined as a 'reference,' *any* study of sound presentation modes in which participants rate the overall quality (however that might be defined) of multiple versions of the same stimuli suffers from this same potential problem. Zacharov and Huopaniemi (1999), for example, did not include an explicitly labeled 'reference.' Asking listeners to rate the 'spatial sound quality' of sound mixes—specifically pointing out that this includes localization—then letting them switch between a five-channel mix and a variety of two-channel mixes, however, encouraged participants to treat the multichannel mix as the 'best.' In terms of gauging the impact of multichannel presentation, these types of studies are thus likely to induce 'false positives' (in which multichannel presentation is found to alter the audience experience more than it actually does) because participants are specifically listening for *differences* between the original 5.1-channel mix and a variety of downmixed configurations.

Effect of surround sound on media preference

The researchers involved in a second category of studies have attempted to mitigate this risk of false positives through a slightly different experimental design. Rather than ask listeners to *rate* different sound mixes of the same stimuli, they ask listeners to simply indicate their *preference* for one mix over another. In essence, these experiments ask 'Do people prefer one presentation mode over another?' rather than 'Can people identify differences between two or more presentation modes?' This approach not only eliminates such complicating factors as the question of what rating scales will uncover potential differences between sound presentation modes and the possibility of different participants interpreting the same rating scale differently, it subsumes all the varying aspects of sound that may affect the listening experience into a single data point: which do participants *like* better?

The first portion of Lessiter and Freeman (2001, described earlier) actually included one preference-based component, though the study as a whole centered on comparative ratings. After the audiovisual clip had been presented in all three presentation modes (5.1-channel surround, two-channel stereo, and mono), participants had to indicate which one of the three modes was their favorite. Analysis showed that the 5.1-channel mix was chosen as the favorite significantly more frequently than either of the other two mixes. As with other results obtained from this first experiment, though, it is unclear whether this difference reflected actual preference for the surround mix or other factors tied to the study's loudness-matching problems, and the follow-up experiment attempting to correct this oversight did not include a preference component.

Unlike Lessiter and Freeman (2001), Choisel and Wickelmaier (2007) used listener preference data as the fundamental avenue of inquiry. This study compared eight sound system configurations ranging from mono to a full 5.0-channel surround setup (the LFE material was omitted from all mixes). It used as stimuli four audio-only musical excerpts (two classical recordings and two popular music recordings). Instead of directly rating all eight configurations in comparison to each other, this experiment utilized a paired comparisons, forced-choice design, within which participants were presented with two different mixes of the same stimulus at a time and asked to indicate which they preferred. No mix was explicitly designated as the 'original' or 'reference' material. Over the course of the study, each listener was presented with every possible pairing of sound mixes, in every order, for all four of the stimuli.

The authors conducted a two-part analysis of the resulting data. First, they set out to determine whether the preference judgments were transitive—in other words, whether the fact that participants preferred A to B and B to C implied they preferred A to C. They considered three different degrees of transitivity, labeled 'weak,' 'moderate,' and 'strong' to reflect how transitive preferences were. For instance, if P(A,B) is the probability of choosing mix A over mix B, and if P(A,B) ≥0.5 and P(B,C) ≥0.5, then 'weak' transitivity implied that P(A,C) ≥0.5 as well, while 'moderate' and 'strong' transitivity meant that P(A,C) was at least the lesser or greater, respectively, of P(A,B) and P(B,C). The data in this study included almost no violations of weak and moderate transitivity and relatively few violations of strong transitivity. Given this outcome, the authors determined that 'at least an ordinal preference scale may be derived from the choice frequencies' (p. 393).

Second, Choisel and Wickelmaier (2007) tested their data using the Bradley–Terry–Luce (BTL) model (Bradley & Terry, 1952; Luce, 1959), which predicts P(A,B) given the parameters of stimuli A and B. A goodness-of-fit test of the actual data to this model showed the results for all four stimuli were consistent with the BTL model, implying that the few transitivity violations found were random, not systematic. With confirmation that the data fit the BTL model, a preference *ratio* scale could be constructed for each of the four stimuli. These analyses revealed that sound presentation mode *did* have a significant impact on preference judgments. As the authors noted, 'In all conditions... listeners were far from indifferent, but had rather strong preferences for certain reproduction modes' (p. 393). Those preferences, however, were highly dependent on the specific program material used; in particular, the *most* preferred mode varied depending on the specific musical excerpt used. Perhaps most intriguing is that the five-channel presentation mode was not always the most preferred presentation mode; indeed, for one excerpt, this mode was among the *least* preferred, beating only the consistently low-ranked mono and phantom mono modes. Traditional two-channel stereo, on the other hand, was among the most preferred presentation modes for all four of the stimuli, finishing no worse than third most preferred (of eight presentation modes) for any of the four stimuli and, when taking into account the margin of error (with 95 percent confidence intervals), potentially ranked the *most preferred* for all four.

Choisel and Wickelmaier (2007) is the lone extant study of the impact of multichannel sound to eschew *any* sort of individual stimuli ratings in favor of a strictly comparative preference-based method. This one study, though, provides clear evidence that listeners can and do demonstrate consistent preferences for some sound presentation modes over others when given the chance to compare presentation modes directly. And the thorough (if limited in scope) transitivity analysis through which the authors processed their data would seem to minimize the risk that this result is a 'false positive' of the type that comparative rating-based studies can engender. Preference-based experiments, however, do have their own potential pitfalls, notably that preference ratings are potentially more dependent on the individual proclivities of the participants than ratings of spatial quality, timbral quality, or overall audio quality. To be sure, all these measures are subjective, but in different ways. Ratings of specific attributes can at least be defined by the experimenters for all participants in ways tied to the sound itself (e.g., are all frequencies present, do sounds seem placed in different locations around the room, is there any noticeable distortion, etc.); while participant judgments on these remain subjective, researchers at least know the participants are trying to rate the same criteria. Determinations of 'preference,' on the other hand, are made differently by different listeners based on their own personal taste. The film industry provides an excellent specific example of this distinction: some directors are adamant that sounds should envelop the audience from all around the theater, while others think all sounds should come from the front of the theater behind the screen (Kerins, 2010). Both groups would probably provide similar responses to a question of whether all frequencies were present in a particular mix, but when asked for a 'preference' judgment between a five-channel mix and a monophonic one, their answers would almost certainly differ.

Audience expectations and past experience, for example, can significantly affect preference ratings. This is a concern of particular importance in the case of choosing between different sound systems, since most listeners will be more familiar with one type of sound system—usually the one they have at home—than with others (Kirk, 1956). Previous studies (e.g., Geringer & Dunnigan, 2000; Kirk, 1956) revealed that music listeners show preference bias toward the sound presentation mode to which they are most accustomed, even when that mode is compared to technically superior alternatives. Additionally, the more time listeners spend with a particular system, the more they prefer that system (Kirk, 1956, p. 1116). In the case of music, virtually all contemporary pre-recorded music listening experiences involve two-channel stereo mixes, whether heard on a home stereo, through headphones, or in a vehicle. Studies such as Kirk's suggest audiences may, therefore, prefer two-channel stereo over other sound modes simply due to their own past experiences listening to music.

The finding that two-channel stereo was consistently among the most preferred sound systems for the music-only stimuli in Choisel and Wickelmaier (2007), while five-channel surround was not, would be consistent with such an interpretation. Participants in that study—all university students—may simply have been most accustomed to hearing music in two-channel stereo, and hence preferred it to other presentation modes. To their credit, Choisel and Wickelmaier actually attempted to examine the effect of experience and training by repeating the same experiment with the same participants 6 months after their initial study. They found no significant differences between the way participants responded in the initial and later sessions, suggesting that the initial experiment, which could have made participants accustomed to previously unfamiliar presentation modes, did not significantly alter their subsequent impressions of the various sound systems. This study in itself, however, does not negate the possibility that experience played a part in the preference ratings. After all, participation in one listening experiment that included surround sound music would be unlikely to outweigh the participants' extensive prior experience with two-channel stereo.

Effect of surround sound on independent media ratings

As already detailed, both comparative rating-based and preference-based approaches to investigating the impact of multichannel sound can lead to provocative and interesting results, but both also have their potential pitfalls. A third and final approach to studying this topic fundamentally differs from the previous two in that it uses independent group design so that no one listener experiences the same stimulus in multiple presentation modes. This allows participants to judge mixes on their own merits rather than in comparison to others.

An excellent example of this type of study is Skalski and Whitbred (2010), discussed in Chapter 13. In this study, the researchers assessed the impact of different sound and image presentation modes on the experience of playing video games. Participants were divided into four groups, each of which played the same video game with a unique image (high-definition or standard-definition) and sound (5.1-channel surround or two-channel stereo) presentation mode combination. Each participant was given a brief tutorial on gameplay then left alone to play the game for 10 minutes. After the play session was completed, each completed a questionnaire including questions from the Temple Presence Inventory (Lombard, Ditton, & Weinstein, 2009), which assesses several measures of 'presence.' The questionnaire also included eight items intended to measure enjoyment, for which participants rated statements such as 'I would like to play this game again' on a seven-point scale anchored by the terms 'strongly disagree' and 'strongly agree.'

The data were analyzed with image and sound presentation modes as independent variables. Sound presentation mode had a significant effect on ratings of several presence categories, including engagement, spatial presence, and perceived realism; in each of these cases the 5.1-channel condition yielded higher ratings (i.e., more engaging, more spatially present, and more realistic) than the two-channel stereo condition. The 5.1-channel surround presentation also resulted in significantly higher ratings of enjoyment. Intriguingly, Skalski and Whitbred (2010) found no significant interaction between image and sound, nor any significant difference in presence or enjoyment ratings between standard-definition and high-definition video, leading the authors to assert that 'Sound quality may indeed be more important to video game play than image quality' (p. 80).

Another set of three related studies sought to examine the effect of sound presentation mode on non-gaming media using a similar between-subjects method. Lipscomb, Kendall, Moorefield, and Tolchinsky (2003) presented one group of participants with two-channel stereo mixes of ten musical excerpts and another group with 5.1-channel mixes of the same excerpts. All participants rated the excerpts on 12 semantic differential scales. Eleven of these scales were selected to represent the Evaluative, Potency, and Activity dimensions proposed by Osgood, Suci, and Tannenbaum (1957); the other scale was 'abstract' versus 'concrete.' Analyses of these ratings showed that presentation mode did not significantly affect listener ratings on *any* of the twelve rating scales for *any* of the musical excerpts.

A companion study (Kerins & Lipscomb, 2003) employed a similar experimental method using audiovisual stimuli—excerpts from feature films—rather than musical stimuli. In this study participants were split into three independent groups, each hearing sound presentation in only one condition: monophonic, Dolby Stereo (front left, front center, front right, and a single surround channel), or 5.1-channel presentations; these three presentation modes were used rather than the two-channel stereo and 5.1-channel surround modes of Lipscomb et al. (2003) to better match actual theatrical sound system types. Like Lipscomb et al. (2003), this study found no significant effect of presentation mode on any of the rating scales.

Kerins and Lipscomb (2007) conducted a follow-up study, including both musical and cinematic excerpts, that modified the experimental method used in Lipscomb et al. (2003) and in Kerins and Lipscomb (2003) in ways intended to enhance the possibility of illuminating distinctions between presentation modes. The first change was designed to counteract the possibility that listeners in the earlier studies, who heard all excerpts in the same presentation mode, had adjusted their expectations to that particular system. Each listener in Kerins and Lipscomb (2007) heard half of the excerpts played in stereo and the other half played in 5.1, with a randomized excerpt order alternating between stereo and 5.1 presentation; participants were thus exposed to multiple sound presentation modes without ever experiencing the *same* stimulus material in two different presentation modes (a crucial difference from the comparative rating-based studies discussed earlier).

Additionally, participants were given a different set of attributes on which to rate each excerpt than in the earlier studies. The researchers kept one rating scale from each of the Evaluative, Potency, and Activity dimensions (good, heavy, and active, respectively) identified in Osgood et al. (1957), but replaced the others from Lipscomb et al. (2003) with eight new scales based on words chosen for their presumed potential to elicit responses related to changes in the sonic environment, such as 'expansive,' 'immersive,' and 'full.' Additionally, the researchers used the verbal attribute magnitude estimation (VAME) method (Kendall & Carterette, 1993) rather than semantic differential scales; in this method, the rating scales have *exact* opposites at their ends (e.g., 'not good' versus 'good') as opposed to *presumed* opposites (e.g., 'bad' and 'good').

In the case of the musical excerpts, despite the experimental method changes in comparison to Lipscomb et al. (2003) and Kerins and Lipscomb (2003), Kerins and Lipscomb (2007) found presentation mode to have no significant effect on any listener ratings for any of the musical excerpts. Analysis of the data from the cinematic excerpts yielded more intriguing results. First, it showed a significant interaction between presentation mode and excerpt, suggesting (in agreement with the studies cited earlier) that the impact of presentation mode depends on the stimulus material presented. Analyzing the data for each film individually, presentation mode was found to have a significant effect on *overall* VAME ratings for only two of the six film excerpts used, though it did significantly affect listener ratings on *some* of the VAME scales for other excerpts. More specifically, ratings on the VAME scales 'heavy' and 'full' were significantly affected by presentation mode for multiple excerpts, with the 5.1 presentation rated higher (i.e., 'heavier' and 'fuller') in every case.

Experiments such as Kerins and Lipscomb (2007) or Skalski and Whitbred (2010) that employ between-subjects designs, like those in the other two categories discussed earlier, have potential pitfalls. The most significant is probably the danger of 'false negatives'; this is the corollary to the 'false positive' potential of studies in which participants hear and can directly compare multiple mixes of the same original program content (i.e., Choisel & Wickelmaier, 2007; Zacharov & Huopaniemi, 1999; Zielinski et al., 2003, 2005). In other words, the independent group design makes it more likely that a subtle difference between two sound presentation modes would not emerge—one potential reason Kerins and Lipscomb (2007) found a significant effect of presentation mode for cinematic excerpts where Kerins and Lipscomb (2003) did not. The Lessiter and

Freeman (2001) study described earlier provides clear evidence of this type of problem. The authors of that study explain that an earlier, unpublished investigation using independent groups (e.g., each listener heard only one of the three presentation modes) revealed *no* significant differences between the modes, and that it was only when all participants experienced all three presentation modes that presentation mode had a significant impact on ratings.

This demonstrates the potential for studies using between-subjects designs to fail to reveal significant effects of presentation mode that might be found using within-subjects comparative designs. The question, of course, is whether the former result is a false negative, the latter result a false positive, or if, in fact, this difference is an effect of the slightly different research questions being asked by the two types of study. In either case, it highlights the importance of the experiential frame—the subjective limitations participants may place on their responses as a result of the design of the study. If *all* the stimuli a participant experiences utilize the same presentation mode, that mode may be treated as the 'frame' for their responses, in effect eliminating any effect of presentation mode. For example, if participants were asked to rate 'picture quality' of various movie excerpts that were all shown in black and white, they might consider black and white presentation as the frame of reference for that study and not 'downgrade' all the clips for their lack of color. In the same way, studies of multichannel sound utilizing independent groups may not reveal any differences between presentation modes simply because participants do not consider the impact of presentation mode on the material; audiences may not perceive anything as missing from or wrong with a two-channel stereo presentation unless they hear it alongside—and can directly compare it to—a multichannel presentation. While this issue is potentially problematic for *any* audio-based study, experiments dealing with multichannel sound seem likely to be particularly prone to experiential frame issues. As the authors of one study suggest, 'there is an inherent assumption, even among experienced listeners, that audio quality is primarily a nonspatial phenomenon .... Informal comments from some listeners during tests have suggested there is a resistance to considering changes in spatial complexity, envelopment, image quality, and the like as changes in quality' (Zielinski et al., 2005, p. 189).

This experiential frame issue could, therefore, have been one factor influencing the results of Lipscomb et al. (2003) and Kerins and Lipscomb (2003), both of which used independent groups relative to presentation mode and found no significant presentation mode-related differences in participant ratings either of music excerpts (Kerins & Lipscomb, 2007; Lipscomb et al., 2003) or of film clips (Kerins & Lipscomb, 2003). Yet it would not explain why Kerins and Lipscomb (2007) similarly found no significant differences for musical excerpts in ratings between two-channel and 5.1-channel presentation—recall that in this study all participants experienced both presentation modes. Comparing these results with the comparative studies cited above (Choisel & Wickelmaier, 2007; Zacharov & Huopaneimi, 1999; Zielinski et al., 2003, 2005), which all found presentation mode to have a significant impact on participant response to musical stimuli, suggests that it is not enough merely for listeners to experience different presentation *modes*, they must experience them *for the same program material.*

Understanding the impact of multichannel sound

The extant research discussed in the previous section provides ample evidence that sound presentation mode *can* impact audience perceptions of media. The specifics of when and how surround presentation differs from stereo presentation, however, are less clear. Depending on the particular study cited, for instance, it could be argued that for music listening, 5.1 sound is *always significantly better* than stereo sound (Zacharov & Huopaniemi, 1999; Zielinski et al., 2003, 2005), provides *marginal benefit* over stereo sound (Lessiter & Freeman, 2001), is better than stereo sound in some contexts but *worse* than stereo in others (Choisel & Wickelmaier, 2007), or makes *no difference* whatsoever (Kerins & Lipscomb, 2007, 2010; Lipscomb et al., 2003). These seemingly divergent results are not necessarily contradictory; rather, they reveal that a variety of factors come into play in determining the importance of sound presentation mode to the audience experience. As already noted, for example, the precise formulation of a given experiment's research question and its method play a crucial role; studies in which participants hear and can directly compare multiple mixes of the same original stimulus, for instance, are far more likely to reveal presentation mode to have a significant impact on participant ratings and/or preferences. But issues other than experimental design also help determine how sound presentation mode does or does not affect the audience experience.

Context

One key factor influencing audience responses to different sound presentation modes is the context in which they are presented. The potential influence of participants' experiential frame mentioned earlier is a good example of how context can affect study results. Another important contextual factor is the type of *media* in question. Lessiter and Freeman (2001) found that independent groups responded significantly differently to the same video game depending on sound presentation mode. In contrast, no existing studies using independent groups have found similar results for musical stimuli. And Kerins and Lipscomb (2007), using independent groups of participants to respond to both musical and cinematic stimuli, found sound presentation mode to have a significant impact on ratings for certain cinematic excerpts but not for *any* of the musical excerpts.

Studies based on comparative ratings or preference selections *have* found presentation mode to significantly affect participant responses to music-only stimuli—but all these studies have involved participants directly comparing multiple versions of the same stimulus materials. These results suggest that, while sound presentation mode *can* impact the audience experience in a variety of media types, it has a stronger impact on audiovisual stimuli than on music-only stimuli. This is perhaps not surprising. In audiovisual media, the image track can suggest a specific three-dimensional environment, and the spatial accuracy of the soundtrack (one major sonic characteristic affected by channel configuration) is judged at least partially on the basis of its relationship to the onscreen image. In music-only media, on the other hand, no cues outside the soundtrack suggest a 'correct' spatialization.

Zielinski et al. (2003) confirm this hypothesis, finding that the presence or absence of picture content significantly affected participant ratings of different channel configurations. In particular, configurations without a front center channel received significantly lower ratings for audiovisual content than for audio-only content, particularly from off-center listening positions: 'the phenomenon observed supports a view of the high importance of the center channel, especially in the context of audio-visual systems' (p. 794). Indeed, one of the more interesting findings of Zielinski et al. (2005) was a breakdown of all the F-B mixed material by media type. In the case of film excerpts, the stereo downmix was deemed to have *lower* quality than a low-pass-filtered multichannel mix; for musical excerpts, the opposite was true. This suggests that even for similarly front-centric (e.g., F-B) mixes, the presence or absence of an image is of major importance in determining the perceived difference between multichannel and stereo presentation. As the researchers state, 'this observation highlights the special case of center channel dialogue reproduction for movies' (p. 188).

The failure of 5.1-channel surround as a consumer music format, despite its success in television, home video, and gaming also suggests audiences find multichannel sound to be of greater value in audiovisual contexts than in audio-only situations. When the music industry launched two surround sound audio formats in the late 1990s—super audio compact disc (SACD) and DVD-Audio (DVD-A)—it was responding to the success of 5.1-channel surround on DVD and the subsequent growth of home theater. These formats could utilize the setups already in place at many homes and, the industry assumed, would be received enthusiastically by a public that had clearly shown its appreciation for surround sound. As one member of the Recording Academy stated, 'The public has voted. Play them surround, and they like it' (Neuberger, 2006, p. 18). Yet surround sound music never found mainstream success; even at the peak of popularity in 2002 and 2003, SACD and DVD-A sales combined totaled less than two million discs. Five years later, the Recording Industry Association of America determined that SACD and DVD-A sales had fallen too low to continue tracking (RIAA, 2008). Many elements undoubtedly contributed to the low consumer adoption rates of surround sound music technology, including the incompatibility of the two competing formats, the reluctance of consumers to purchase yet another component to add to their increasingly complex home theater systems, and the relative satisfaction of most listeners with the CD format. Even so, it seems likely that if audiences had perceived the same benefit to hearing music in surround as they had to experiencing audiovisual media in surround, SACD and/or DVD-A would have been much more successful. The commercial failure of surround sound music, then, provides market-based support for the conclusion that surround sound simply does not impact audio-only experiences as much as it does audiovisual ones.

Why multichannel sound makes a difference

Context is certainly not the sole factor influencing the importance of presentation mode. In some cases, audiences respond to changes in sound presentation mode quite differently even for stimuli of the same media type (audiovisual or audio-only) presented in the same experiential context; the causes of these differences remain a topic of much interest to those studying the impact of multichannel sound. In fact, most of the experiments already discussed include components designed to go beyond the simple issue of *whether* sound presentation mode significantly alters the audience experience to *how* it does so.

One major impediment to exploring this latter question is that it is difficult to isolate the impact of any *one* element of a soundtrack. As Choisel and Wickelmaier (2007) note, 'The quantification of attributes that play a role in the context of multichannel reproduced sound is a nontrivial problem because of the complex nature of the stimuli that typically gives rise to several timbral and spatial sensations simultaneously' (p. 397). In other words, ratings of overall sound quality or preference inherently combine a wide array of perceptual elements into a single judgment. Furthermore, even when a single factor *can* be identified and isolated, determining its precise role is difficult due to context and other factors complicating the question. When Guastavino and Katz (2004) examined the role of the LFE channel, for instance, they found its effects to vary depending on the stimulus material. For one soundscape, listeners found that the addition of the LFE channel made the soundtrack more realistic; for others, it made the soundtrack *too* rich in low frequencies.

Despite these difficulties, several studies of multichannel sound's impact on listeners have attempted to isolate the effects of presentation mode by having participants provide ratings not only of general quality or preference but also of specific components of these 'overall' ratings. Zielinski et al. (2005), for example, had participants rate all mixes for their timbral fidelity (the term used by the study authors), frontal spatial fidelity, and surround spatial fidelity, in addition to the 'basic audio quality' ratings discussed earlier. For all materials, the researchers found that both downmixing and low-pass-filtering negatively impacted ratings of both timbral and spatial fidelity; not surprisingly, low-pass-filtering (which removes the high frequency overtones that help determine timbre) had a stronger impact on timbral fidelity, while downmixing had a stronger impact on spatial fidelity. While both timbral and spatial fidelity impacted ratings of 'basic audio quality,' timbral fidelity had the stronger effect, which is why 'in general listeners prefer full-bandwidth down-mixed items to fivechannel [sic] low-pass-filtered ones' (p. 183). In other words, while listeners could *perceive* that five-channel mixes had better spatial capabilities than two- or three-channel configurations, this difference was not as important an influence on their ratings of basic audio quality as timbral quality. Additionally, the data showed that *frontal* spatial fidelity was more closely correlated to ratings of basic audio quality than *surround* spatial fidelity. This statistical correspondence helps explain some of the study's more surprising findings, such as the full-bandwidth 2/0 and 3/0 sound mixes receiving high ratings for 'basic audio quality' for all stimuli despite the consistently low ratings of these configurations for 'surround spatial fidelity.' What Zielinski et al. (2005) seem to demonstrate is that the most apparent advantage of 5.1-channel sound—its enhanced *surround* capabilities—simply does not have as much of an impact on overall sound quality as other aural facets of a sound mix.

One potential difficulty with attempting to uncover specific perceptual effects of multichannel sound using any sort of scale-based rating method is that different listeners may interpret or respond to scales in different ways. As noted earlier, even a simple construct such as 'basic audio quality' is open to interpretation. Zielinski et al. (2003), for instance, intentionally specified all the components of 'basic audio quality,' since the researchers were concerned that participants would not automatically consider spatial characteristics as part of this judgment. A multi-part study by Choisel and Wickelmaier (2006) sidestepped the difficulties of rating-based approaches by employing an entirely different experimental method in which descriptors were solicited from participants themselves to discover what criteria they were using to distinguish different presentation modes.

This series of three experiments utilized the same four stimuli as Choisel and Wickelmaier (2007)—two classical music excerpts and two popular music excerpts—to elicit descriptors. In the first experiment, participants listened to sound *triples* (three different downmixes of the same 5.1-channel original stimulus), selected which of the three differed the most from the other two, then gave verbal descriptors explaining '*in what way* the selected sound differed from the other two, and *in what way* the other two were alike' (p. 818, emphasis in original). In the second experiment, a different group of participants heard sound *doubles* of the stimuli and were asked to give words describing perceived differences between the two. Finally, the third experiment (which used yet another independent group of participants) employed a notably different method to elicit descriptors. Participants were presented with triples of sounds, this time ordered as *a*, *b*, and *c*, and had to answer whether or not *a* and *b* shared a feature that *c* did not have. A computer program written by the authors analyzed the responses to identify sets of mixes that had been labeled as sharing common traits; for each of these sets, participants were asked to give a name to the feature that all the mixes in that group shared that the other mixes did not.

These three elicitation methods yielded a wide range of sonic descriptors. Comparing across the different approaches, Choisel and Wickelmaier (2006) found *eight* sonic attributes that appeared the most frequently across all stimuli and in all three experiments: width, envelopment, elevation, spaciousness, brightness, distance, clarity, and naturalness. Choisel and Wickelmaier (2007), as discussed earlier, then included these attributes in a paired comparisons, forced-choice experiment. Participants were presented with two mixes of one program item at a time and were asked which best exhibited each of the eight attributes; for instance, for the 'brightness' attribute, participants responded to the question 'which sound is brighter?' Principal components analysis was used to reduce the eight attributes to two orthogonal components for each of the two loosely-defined musical genres (popular and classical); the resulting components were similar—though not identical—between the popular music and classical stimuli. For both genres, multiple regression on the two components resulted in equations that predicted preference quite well, explaining 95 percent of the variance for the classical excerpts and 84 percent of the variance for the popular music excerpts. For all four stimuli, these equations accurately predicted whether 5.1 or stereo presentation would be preferred overall.

Content

That Choisel and Wickelmaier (2007) were able to identify components that accurately predicted sound mode preference for specific musical excerpts suggests that certain auditory features of sonic stimuli may play a crucial role in determining the degree to which multichannel presentation would make a major difference to audiences hearing that piece. Indeed, the fact that the eight attributes examined in Choisel and Wickelmaier's experiment loaded differently onto orthogonal components for the two musical genres considered demonstrates the importance of *content* when considering the impact of multichannel sound in media. Whether these varied results reflect differences in audience expectations for different musical genres or more fundamental divergences between the genres themselves, it is clear that any discussion of multichannel sound versus traditional two-channel stereo sound must take into account the specific content of the stimuli.

The importance of content is confirmed by results from the studies mentioned earlier. Zielinski et al. (2003) made the broad distinction between F-B and F-F surround mixes, and found that those channel configurations which produced the best results when downmixing F-B material were not the same ones that worked best for downmixing F-F material. Choisel and Wickelmaier (2007) reinforced this distinction, finding that the surround mix was significantly preferred over the stereo mix for only one of the four program materials rated in their study. This particular piece was the lone stimulus to include 'clearly distinct sound sources (e.g., a guitar playing a staccato single-note line) in the surround channels' (p. 395); in other words, the only piece for which surround sound was preferred to stereo was also the only one with an F-F mix. And Guastavino and Katz (2004), in an investigation of how well different multichannel configurations could reproduce real-life soundscapes, similarly noted that different sound systems work better for different types of content, writing that 'the results highlight the fact that there is no single system that is optimal for all conditions' (p. 1105).

Given that the impact of multichannel sound on the audience experience appears to be heavily content-dependent, it is important to carefully consider the specific stimuli used in any study focused on multichannel sound. For instance, most of the studies discussed here compared 5.1-channel surround mixes to two-channel stereo mixes of the same media. Yet, in most of these cases, one of the two mixes was created from the other for the study; in only a few cases were both the stereo and surround stimulus materials professionally created by the artists responsible for the original music or film excerpts. This would seem to inherently bias the results in the same way—to reuse an earlier analogy—as comparing color photos to black-and-white photos, when the 'color' version of the photo had been created from the black-and-white one by the researcher; the black-and-white photo, in that case, may be preferred to the color one due to poor colorization of the latter rather than to any inherent viewer preference for black-and-white over color. In fact, comparing the findings of studies that employed professionally crafted stereo *and* surround mixes to those of studies that did not suggests that just such a bias may exist, at least in the case of musical stimuli. Those experiments that compared 5.1-channel original mixes to algorithm-created downmixes found five-channel music mixes to be consistently rated more favorably than their stereo counterparts (Zacharov & Huopaniemi, 1999; Zielinski et al. 2003, 2005). Two of the three studies employing professional mixes for both the 5.1-channel and stereo conditions, on the other hand, found *no* significant difference in ratings between the two for musical stimuli (Kerins & Lipscomb, 2007; Lipscomb et al., 2003); the third (Choisel & Wickelmaier, 2007) found that stereo presentation was preferred for some musical excerpts while surround was preferred for others. While by no means conclusive, this distinction suggests that the effects of channel configuration found in some past studies may stem not from presentation mode but from comparing carefully crafted professional sound mixes to researcher-created reconfigurations of those mixes.

The role of content in determining multichannel sound's impact is even more complex in audiovisual media due to the presence of an image track. Two investigations of the impact of presentation mode on the cinematic experience (Kerins & Lipscomb, 2007; Kerins, Lipscomb, & Rendahl, 2010) found that 5.1 surround presentation was perceived as significantly different from stereo presentation for two of the six film excerpts presented. What these two excerpts had in common was not the nature of their mixes per se, but the specific ways in which their soundtracks and image tracks *related*. Specifically, these two excerpts exhibited the aesthetic style described by Kerins (2010) as the 'digital surround style,' a set of audiovisual traits that capitalize on the capabilities of 5.1-channel soundtracks to alter the traditional cinematic image-sound relationship. In other words, it may have been the nature of the program material *as a whole* (including sound *and* image) that made 5.1-channel presentation differ significantly from stereo presentation for these excerpts. This result is somewhat surprising, as it suggests that whether experiencing a given film in stereo is significantly different from experiencing it in surround depends as much on that film's visuals as on its soundtrack. Nevertheless, this result is in keeping with a long history of work showing that visual cues affect audience perceptions of sound (e.g., Bertelson & Radeau, 1981; Lipscomb & Kendall, 1994/1996; McGurk & MacDonald, 1976; Stein & Meredith, 1993; Thurlow & Rosenthal, 1976; Valente & Braasch, 2010).

Extant research on the role of multichannel sound in audiovisual media is largely limited to the cinematic context. Based on the results enumerated earlier, it seems likely that the specific way image and sound relate in a particular audiovisual combination is similarly important to determining the impact of multichannel sound in other media forms. Skalski and Whitbred (2010), for instance, found surround sound to significantly impact ratings of presence and enjoyment, but this result was based on participant responses to a single video game. That game, moreover, was a first-person shooter—a gaming genre in which 5.1 surround is often so heavily integrated into game design that players using a surround system have a significant advantage over those using a traditional stereo system (Kerins, 2013). Had Skalski and Whitbred (2010) instead used as its stimulus a game from a genre in which surround sound cues do not have a material impact on the gameplay—a rhythm game, for instance—they may have found no significant difference in ratings between the 5.1-channel and stereo conditions. The same could be said for Lessiter and Freeman (2001), who found no significant difference in ratings of presence or enjoyment between 5.0 and 2.0 mixes in the single-stimulus study described earlier. In fact, the authors themselves obliquely acknowledged this shortcoming, noting that the clip they used 'may not represent the most appropriate stimulus to capitalize on discrete audio channels surrounding the listeners' (p. 8). Certainly provocative results such as those of Lessiter and Freeman or Skalski and Whitbred should not be ignored and are useful in suggesting areas that deserve future investigation, but given the highly content-driven nature of 5.1-channel surround's impact, any results based on a single stimulus can hardly offer generalizable conclusions.

Conclusion: The impact of multichannel on multimedia

This survey of extant empirical work on multichannel sound has made at least one thing clear: the area is ripe for further exploration. Given the varying results of past studies, however, few other general conclusions can be drawn. Several studies have shown that 5.1 surround presentation *can* alter the audience experience relative to stereo presentation; whether and how it does so in any particular situation, though, is difficult to predict from the limited existing work exploring this question. To conclude this chapter, therefore, it seems productive to suggest considerations that would help future research better illuminate the role multichannel sound plays in the audience experience.

First, given that numerous studies have found program content a major influence on the impact of multichannel sound, it is odd that many of the studies conducted thus far seem to have chosen their stimulus materials more or less at random. Future research should include a range of carefully selected content, and those studies must acknowledge that results cannot necessarily be generalized across media forms or genres—indeed, even within the *same* media form and/or genre, results may not be generalizable across different content items. Key content-choosing criteria already mentioned include the F-F versus F-B distinction and the difference between professionally- and algorithmically-created mixes, but other considerations could prove equally valuable in explicating the details of how multichannel sound functions in particular contexts. As one example, an experiment comparing film excerpts with similar sound mixes but different visual styles could provide evidence for or against the post-experiment proposal of Kerins and Lipscomb (2007) that the impact of multichannel sound in a film is determined by a film's use of the 'digital surround style.'

Second, as the organization of this chapter makes clear, researchers must be careful about how they frame the question of primary interest: 'does multichannel sound alter the listening experience?' Asking whether listeners can tell the difference between two mixes of the same program material when comparing them side by side is quite different than asking whether two sound presentation modes provide a significantly *different experience* for the audience or whether one is 'better' than the other. To be sure, investigating any of these issues may reveal something useful, but clarifying the precise focus of any given study will help situate that study within the existing body of research on the effects of multichannel sound.

Finally, and to this author most importantly, research designed to study the effects of multichannel sound in everyday use would be a welcome addition to the field. Even putting aside any other concerns (of which there are plenty) about the methodological approaches used in extant studies, virtually all of those discussed here share a crucial shortcoming: lack of ecological validity. As a result of factors such as the use of expert listeners as participants, the ability of participants to directly compare multiple sound mixes of the same stimuli, the short duration of stimulus materials (only a few seconds in some cases), and the use of perfectly set up and calibrated sound systems, few of these studies give a realistic sense of what everyday listeners might gain from the addition of multichannel sound to their own music listening, gaming, or cinema-going experiences. If anyone is interested in going beyond the question of whether multichannel sound *could* have an impact on audiences to whether it actually *does* have an impact, attempts to study its role in more realistic environments will be a crucial component of further research.

Multichannel sound is becoming more prevalent and complex (Kerins, 2010). Two decades ago, four-channel multichannel soundtracks were common in cinemas and occasionally found in homes; today, six-channel (5.1) sound is the standard for not just movies but also video games, home video, and television broadcasts. Given this ubiquity, better understanding the effects of multichannel sound presentation on audiences would benefit both scholars studying contemporary media and media-makers determining where and how multichannel sound can be used most effectively. Whatever their flaws, the studies discussed in this chapter have provided a meaningful starting point for such future investigations and, as a group, present some provocative results and intriguing questions worthy of additional exploration. Still, the limited general conclusions available from extant work on the impact of multichannel sound signals just how much remains to be done. Research on the role of sound presentation mode in multimedia thus far has merely scratched the surface of the topic; as more researchers begin to tackle the many residual questions in this area, our understanding of nearly all current media forms should be greatly enhanced.

References

Beck, J. (2003). *A quiet revolution: Changes in American film sound practices, 1967–1979.* (Unpublished doctoral dissertation.) University of Iowa, IA.

Belton, J. (1992). 1950's magnetic sound: the frozen revolution. In R. Altman (Ed.), *Sound theory/sound practice* (pp. 154–167). New York, NY: Routledge.

Bertelson, P., & Radeau, M. (1981). Cross-modal bias and perceptual fusion with auditory-visual spatial discordance. *Perception & Psychophysics, 29*(6), 578–584.

Bradley, R. A., & Terry, M. E. (1952). Rank analysis of incomplete block designs: I. The method of paired comparisons. *Biometrika, 39*, 324–345.

Choisel, S., & Wickelmaier, F. (2006). Extraction of auditory features and elicitation of attributes for the assessment of multichannel reproduced sound. *Journal of the Audio Engineering Society, 54*(9), 815–826.

Choisel, S., & Wickelmaier, F. (2007). Evaluation of multichannel reproduced sound: Scaling auditory attributes underlying listener preference. *Journal of the Acoustical Society of America, 121*(1), 388–400.

Consumer Electronics Association. (2006). *Digital America 2006—gone mainstream.* Retrieved from <http://www.ce.org/Press/CEA_Pubs/2080.asp> (accessed September 21, 2011).

Geringer, J. M., & Dunnigan, P. (2000). Listener preferences and perception of digital versus analog live concert recordings. *Bulletin of the Council for Research in Music Education, 145*, 1–13.

Guastavino, C., & Katz, B. F. G. (2004). Perceptual evaluation of multi-dimensional spatial audio reproduction. *Journal of the Acoustical Society of America, 116*(2), 1105–1115.

Holman, T. (2000). *5.1 Surround Sound: Up and running.* Boston, MA: Focal Press.

Kendall, R. A., and Carterette, E. C. (1993). Verbal attributes of simultaneous wind instrument timbres: I. von Bismarck adjectives. *Music Perception, 10*(4), 445–467.

Kerins, M. (2010). *Beyond Dolby (Stereo): Cinema in the Digital Sound Age*. Bloomington, IN: Indiana University Press.

Kerins, M. (2013). Multichannel gaming and the aesthetics of interactive surround. In C. Gorbman, J. Richardson, & C. Vernallis (Eds.), *Oxford handbook of new audiovisual aesthetics*. New York, NY: Oxford University Press.

Kerins, M., & Lipscomb, S. D. (2003, June). *Audience perception of sound modes in cinema.* Paper presented at the conference of the Society for Music Perception & Cognition. Evanston, IL.

Kerins, M., & Lipscomb, S. D. (2007, August). *Presentation mode in the cinematic and music listening experiences: An experimental investigation.* Paper presented at the conference of the Society for Music Perception & Cognition. Montreal, Canada.

Kerins, M., Lipscomb, S. D., & Rendahl, A. (2010). *The influence of 5.1 surround presentation on the cinematic and music listening experiences.* Manuscript submitted for publication.

Kirk, R. E. (1956). Learning: a major factor influencing preferences for high-fidelity reproducing systems. *Journal of the Acoustical Society of America, 28*, 1113–1116.

Lessiter, J., & Freeman, J. (2001, May). *Really hear? The effects of audio quality on presence.* Paper presented at the 4th International Workshop on Presence. Las Vegas, NV.

Lipscomb, S. D., & Kendall, R. A. (1994/1996). Perceptual judgment of the relationship between musical and visual components in film. *Psychomusicology, 13(1)*, 60–98.

Lipscomb, S. D., Kendall, G., Moorefield, V., & Tolchinsky, D. E. (2003, June). *Immersive sound: Does 5.1 surround sound really make a difference in the affective experience of music listening?* Paper presented at the conference of the Society for Music Perception & Cognition. Las Vegas, NV.

Lombard, M., Ditton, T. B., & Weinstein, L. (2009, November). *Measuring (tele)presence: The Temple Presence Inventory.* Paper presented at the 12th Annual International Workshop on Presence. Los Angeles, CA.

Luce, R. D. (1959). *Individual choice behavior: A theoretical analysis.* New York, NY: Wiley.

McGurk, H., & MacDonald, J. (1976). Hearing lips and seeing voices. *Nature, 264*, 746–748.

Neuberger, H. (2006). The end of stereo. *Mix, 30*(6), 18.

Osgood, C. D., Suci, G. J., & Tannenbaum, P. H. (1957). *The measurement of meaning.* Urbana, IL: University of Illinois Press.

Recording Industry Association of America (RIAA) (2008). *2008 U.S. Manufacturers' Unit Shipments and Value Chart.* Retrieved from <http://76.74.24.142/1D212C0E-408B-F730-65A0-C0F5871C369D.pdf> (accessed 18 May 2009).

Sherber, A. (2001). DVD leads a hardware revolution. *Video Store, 23*(42), 1, 11.

Skalski, P., & Whitbred, R. (2010). Image versus sound: A comparison of formal feature effects on presence and video game enjoyment. *PsychNology Journal, 8*(1), 67–84.

Stein, B. E., & Meredith, M. A. (1993). *The merging of the senses.* Cambridge, MA: MIT Press.

Thurlow, W. R. G., & Rosenthal, T. M. (1976). Further study of existence regions of the 'ventriloquist effect.' *Journal of the American Audiology Society, 1*(6), 280–286.

Valente, D., & Braasch, J. (2010). Subjective scaling of spatial room acoustic parameters influenced by visual environmental cues. *Journal of the Acoustical Society of America, 128*(4), 1952–1964.

Zacharov, N., & Huopaniemi, J. (1999, September). *Results of a round robin subjective evaluation of virtual home theatre sound systems.* Paper presented at the 107th convention of the Audio Engineering Society. New York, NY.

Zielinski, S.K., Rumsey, F., & Bech, S. (2003). Effects of down-mix algorithms on quality of surround sound. *Journal of the Audio Engineering Society*, *51*(9), 780–798.

Zielinski, S.K., Rumsey, F., Kassier, R., & Bech, S. (2005). Comparison of basic audio quality and timbral and spatial fidelity changes caused by limitation of bandwidth and by down-mix algorithms in 5.1 surround audio systems. *Journal of the Audio Engineering Society*, *53*(3), 174–192.

Part V

Future Research Directions

Chapter 17

Future research directions for music and sound in multimedia

Siu-Lan Tan, Annabel J. Cohen, Scott D. Lipscomb, and Roger A. Kendall

This book presents the first effort to consolidate a wide range of the empirical research on the psychological processes involved in the integration of sound and image in our engagement with film, television, video, interactive games, and computer interfaces. Prior to this volume, isolated pockets of productivity in various fields were insufficient on their own to form the basis for a book on multimedia experience. Collectively, as represented here, the separate initiatives are sufficiently expansive to warrant the comprehensive treatment that an edited volume offers, both for disseminating the current knowledge base and for inspiring scholarship. The final chapter looks ahead and explores future research directions in our world where multimedia is increasingly pervasive, technology is rapidly advancing, and team scholarship is becoming the order of the day.

In light of the theoretical perspectives presented early in the book, we first consider the possibility of a complete theoretical explanation of the role of music in multimedia. This leads to a discussion of the issues related to defining cross-modal similarity with respect to both structure or syntax and meaning or semantics that are then addressed in the context of studies that carefully control the physical and semantic properties of the multimedia materials presented. The issue of sensory dominance is then revisited, acknowledging the value of studies that involve more than two senses and the value of studying real-world as well as laboratory phenomena. We then discuss the role of music and sound in real-world applications (e.g., computer gaming, television, and online advertising) and teaching and learning, considering also how music might be used most effectively in the multimedia context. We conclude that progress will arise most quickly with the help of interdisciplinary teams representing expertise from many fields that are implicated in comprehensive studies of music in multimedia.

Theories, models, and multidisciplinary perspectives

Part I of the book focused attention on distinct theoretical and disciplinary perspectives: from cognitive psychology, Cohen's Congruence-Association Model (CAM), and the working narrative; from semiotics, Kendall and Lipscomb's experimental approach; from communications studies, Shevy's focus on of mass media and mass audience;

Bashwiner's music theoretic and analytic perspective; and Kuchinke, Kappelhoff, and Koelsch's neuroscientific approach that is also mindful of cognitive film theory. It is noteworthy that although the chapters all discuss the psychology of musical multimedia, there is little overlap among them. This serves to reflect both the scope and infancy of the entire endeavor. The future for research in music and multimedia may well build on these theories, filling in, revising, integrating, and extending them to new applications.

We might then ask whether a single broader perspective could even encompass all of the different viewpoints presented. Could a single theory or framework represent the breadth of media communication described by Shevy (Chapter 4), while at the same time preserving the parsimony of CAM and Kendall and Lipscomb's semiotic approach (Chapters 2 and 3), the detail of musical analysis of Bashwiner (Chapter 5), and Kuchinke et al.'s (Chapter 6) neuroscientific explication of the role of music in emotion? While *the* Grand Theory or even *a* Grand Theory of the psychology of musical multimedia may not be a reasonable goal, arguments can be made to broaden current theories and to suggest that approaches taken now are narrower than necessary, and narrower than what will be in just a decade.

The late eminent cognitive scientist, Allan Newell (2002), argued for unified theories of cognition, for theories of cognition that explained it all. One reason he gave is that a single system, the brain, accomplishes it all, and so therefore should a theory of brain function. There can be competing unified theories, but a theory that is limited to a single mental task is less likely to be as correct as a theory that accomplishes many different kinds of tasks. From this perspective, theorists do well to appreciate general capabilities of the brain, such as its ability to process all audio, visual, and embodied modalities associated with film. A theory of film, of perception, or of cognition that cannot handle music is incomplete. The present book informs the reader that the music of multimedia has many dimensions, be they rhythmic or pitch patterns, semantic meanings, or drivers of emotion. A theory of music processing that addresses only one of these is lacking. To this end, Koelsch's (2012) neural model of music perception is exemplary. The model is based on brain imaging and behavioral data, tracing processes from the sensory periphery to the frontal cortex; however, the model represents only a single part of the complex multimedia cognition process. The model for other aspects of perception such as visual scenes, speech, and embodiment may be even more complex alone or certainly in integration with other systems including that of music.

There remains also the mystery of consciousness. While sometimes thought of as the final frontier, accounting for the contents of consciousness is a critical challenge for a full understanding of the role of music in multimedia. Related to this is the question of how different theories address the ability of music to seamlessly traverse the diegetic/non-diegetic world of film. Indeed very few empirical studies have yet attempted to explore audience response to the same piece of music in a diegetic and non-diegetic function (e.g., Tan, Spackman, & Wakefield, 2008; see also Fujiyama, Ema, & Iwamiya, 2012) and many further studies are needed to follow these pioneering efforts.

Music is but one of three audio channels—the others being speech and sound effects. Much remains to be understood regarding the extraordinary ability of audiences to decode these. There is value in continuing research along two directions: consideration of three separate audio dimensions as CAM implies and consideration of music as part of an integrated single soundtrack combined with speech and sound effects (Lipscomb & Tolchinsky, 2005). Sound designers further distinguish between realistic sound effects and ambient sounds. For example, a particular sound may be appropriate for the scene, but its presentation (e.g., rhythm or intensity pattern) may be non-diegetic (e.g., the use of the sound of the typewriter key in the movie, *Atonement*). Blurring the boundary between music and sound effects appears to be no challenge for an audience and deserves future attention of researchers. Fortunately, a number of specialized tools and analytic procedures are available, such as acoustical, music-theoretic, and linguistic analyses procedures. Similarly, visuo-grammatical analysis and spectral analysis of visual information in a film would be illuminating, especially along with the various kinds of analyses of the audio materials.

While Bashwiner (Chapter 5) focuses on the importance of the music-theoretic analysis, the same specificity of analysis is deserving of the other sources of information in the film. Can tools that work for one domain—for example, music theory—be applied to another domain with success? As an example of this methodological interdisciplinarity, Cohen (2002) proposed the applicability of the musical concept of rondo to the repetitive structure of the *The Red Violin* (1998), and the concept of tonality to the violin itself, the reference 'tone' of the work. But we should not be content with any one approach that might serve more than one domain. A music-theoretic analysis of the score is only one way of considering music. The acoustic analysis of music reveals many important aspects of the music soundtrack that are overlooked by music theory, and conversely.

Although the focus of the book is on the integration of sound and image in our engagement with film, television, video, interactive games, and computer interfaces in the 21st century, multimedia will extend beyond audio and video to the haptic and kinesthetic dimension. Even without these extensions, theoretically music in multimedia extends beyond the representation of sound and image to representation of kinesthetic motion as in musical-related gestures of conductors, dancers, performers (instrumentalists and vocalists), and listeners (Godøy & Leman, 2010).

Following Part I of the book on theoretical and interdisciplinary perspectives are Parts II and III directed separately to structural inter-relations of multimedia and to the influence of music on the interpretation of other media and vice versa. While these concepts are useful from an organizational standpoint, and are also found at the heart of the CAM model (Chapter 2), it is also necessary to consider whether in fact structure and meaning can always be separated this way, as the paper by Kendall and Lipscomb (Chapter 3) reminds us. Psycholinguistics (and linguistics) provides a useful comparison in which structure (e.g., identification of parts of speech) contributes to meaning, and meaning helps to identify structure. For example, the identification of a grammatical component such as a verb requires some understanding of the meaning of the word that distinguishes it from a noun. The topic of meaning has dimensions in philosophy, semiotics, linguistics, film theory, and literary theory. It was possible to only briefly touch on them in the present book, and there is much scope here for further exploration. The field of psychology and literature (Oatley, 2011), cognitive literary studies (Jaén & Simon, 2012), and psychology of narrative represent new branches within cognitive psychology that may inform future studies of music and multimedia.

Cross-modal relations in multimedia

The experience of multimedia requires cross-modal perceptual processing; therefore, the inclusion of the chapters in Part II of the present volume is crucial to understanding how this processing takes place. Multimedia is, in fact, inherently cross-modal. The Introduction (in this volume) described an instrument known as the 'light organ,' created for Scriabin's *Prometheus* (composed in 1910), connecting musical pitch to color perception (empirical studies of chromesthesia include Kelly, 1934, and Haack & Radocy, 1981). This interesting idea formed part of the narrative for the finale to Spielberg's *Close Encounters of the Third Kind*, in which a large light organ communicated to an arriving alien spaceship using a tonal and color language.

Focusing on auditory and visual perception, Handel (2006) discusses cross-modal perception as a process of object identification in which 'the processing of sensory information occurs both simultaneously, in parallel at different neural locations, and successively, serially, as firing patterns converge from these locations' (p. 7). The goal of three related chapters in the present volume by Iwamiya (Chapter 7), Eitan (Chapter 8), and Lipscomb (Chapter 9) was to identify, on the basis of empirical outcomes, the perceptual-cognitive experience of the listener-viewer, which can be considered in terms of two broad categories of congruence: *syntactic* (Iwamiya's 'formal congruency' and Lipscomb's 'accent structure alignment') and *semantic* (Iwamiya's 'semantic congruency' and Lipscomb's 'association judgment'). Eitan focuses primarily on the latter, using a method of 'cross-modal matching' (Stein & Meredith, 1993, p. 15), as he discusses a variety of cross-modal mappings and how they relate to the time-variant pitch height of the auditory component in multimedia. Pioneering studies of sine tones of different frequencies and amplitudes noted that the isomorphism in the sensation of frequency with pitch and amplitude with loudness could be modified to include spatial size (volume) and density (Rich, 1916; Stevens, 1934).

An extensive review of the cross-modal perceptual and cognitive literature by Spence (2011) identifies three categories of cross-modal correspondence: *structural correspondences* related to neural firing (such as loudness and brightness); *statistical correspondences* where couplings are based on experience with regularities in the environment; and *semantic correspondences* emerging from language development and word associations (p. 987). Interactions of these categories suggest that best-fit relations in correspondence will necessarily vary by experimental context, and that a given fit that is 'best' may not be the only fit that is perceived by listener-viewers as valid. Experiments in this volume with temporally organized musical sound and visual variables confirm this fact. For example, when considering cross-modal interactions between monophonic pitch patterns and visual motion patterns, Kendall and Lipscomb (Chapter 3) found that, although the expected fit was often good, many alternative correspondences were nearly equal in best-fit ratings. Eitan (Chapter 8) also found such variability, as did Lipscomb and Kendall 1994, using actual excerpts from a mainstream motion picture.

One area open to future investigation is the systematic variation of the physical properties of temporal, visual, and auditory elements in multimedia to determine the thresholds of stimuli (i.e., the degree to which a given element can be moved temporally without affecting the perceived level of congruence) that closely approximate real film, music, and animation (i.e., ecologically valid stimuli). Very few studies of film, for example, specify the size of the projected image, the brightness level at the participants' reception, the color resolution and dynamic range, and other such variables that might have an impact on ratings of fitness, semantic congruence, or preference.

As stated previously, the vast majority of cross-modal research investigating multimedia perception has been limited to audio and visual stimuli. In order to fully understand the multimedia experience, it will be important to expand beyond vision and hearing, designing research studies that include, at minimum, tactile stimulation and perhaps the involvement of other modalities as suited to the specific type of multimedia. In addition to the various categories of correspondences presented by Spence (2011; see earlier), there are also different types of congruence: *within-modality congruence* (e.g., between loudness and pitch of a tone), *within-modality spatial congruence* (e.g., between the position of visual shapes and their spatial direction), *across-modality perceptual congruence* (e.g., between pitch height and vertical location of an object), and *across-modality spatial congruence* (e.g., between auditory and visual location). While empirical researchers may hope to find a single explanation for all types of congruence, Marks (2004) concluded 'it seems improbable that all of these interactions result from a common mechanism' (p. 103).

Most research that has been completed to the present has been designed to determine *the* way processing occurs for all listener-viewers, rather than operating on the assumption that there may be significant differences between subpopulations of participants or when using stimuli that represent different types of congruence. It will be important for future researchers to design empirical studies that assess the congruency of cross-modal stimuli using conditions that represent the different types of congruency effects described earlier and to utilize ecologically valid stimuli. In addition, addressing areas of multimedia that have little empirical study is called for at this time. Examples of such media include Disney attractions like *Soarin' Over California* involving large-scale video projections, motion seats, air current manipulations, and fragrances (ideas that historically evolve from Sensurround and Smell-O-Vision films).

Interpretation and sensory dominance

The most common line of research in multimedia investigates how sound influences interpretation of visual images—for instance, how changing the musical soundtrack colors perception and memory of events shown in film images (e.g., Hoeckner & Nusbaum) or amplifies the emotional impact of a film scene (Kuchinke, Kappelhoff, & Koelsch), intensifies the excitement of a video game and heighten the player's physiological responses (Grimshaw, Tan, & Lipscomb), or changes consumers' impressions of a product or brand (Shevy & Hung). Less attention has been directed to how visual information influences our perception of music. In the present volume, Boltz (Chapter 10) sheds light on how visual information may actually shape perception and appraisal of music or sound, thus challenging a typically held notion of visual dominance.

Vision is by and large the dominant sense in many circumstances. On the one hand, visual dominance over hearing and other sense modalities has been frequently demonstrated (e.g., Posner, Nissen, & Klein, 1976; Spence, 2009), and a neural basis has been posited for visual dominance in processing audiovisual objects (e.g., Schmid, Büchel, & Rose, 2011; see also Kuchinke et al., Chapter 6). The idea of 'visual dominance' over the sense of hearing has a long history, exemplified by the ventriloquism effect (e.g., Radeau & Bertelson, 1974) and the Colavita effect (Colavita, 1974), referred to in many of the chapters in this book.

On the other hand, auditory dominance has been demonstrated in some situations. Infants and very young children tend to show auditory dominance consistent with the overshadowing of auditory over visual input in the early years (Robinson & Sloutsky, 2004). For instance, Calvert (Chapter 12) describes how audio cues in children's television programming play a key role in directing young children's attention to the screen at key plot points in a story, as the moving visual images alone do not sustain their attention for very long. Auditory dominance has also been found in adults, particularly with respect to time-based abilities such as precise temporal processing (Repp & Penel, 2002), temporal localization (Burr, Banks, & Morrone, 2009), and estimation of time durations (Ortega, Guzman-Martinez, Grabowecky, & Suzuki, 2009). In some cases, auditory information overrides visual information when perceptual cues are discrepant. For instance, a single flash of light is often perceived as multiple flashes when accompanied by a rapid series of auditory beeps (Shams, Kamitani, & Shimojo, 2000). Lipscomb and Kendall (1994) provide another example of auditory dominance in a multimedia context (film). These researchers found that variation in participant semantic differential ratings was influenced more by the musical component than by the visual element.

Particularly interesting in its implications for processing of rich multimedia experiences is Hecht and Reiner's study (2009) pointing to the disappearance of visual dominance when a visual signal is presented simultaneously with an auditory and haptic signal (i.e., as a tri-sensory combination). The authors concluded that 'while vision can dominate both the auditory and the haptic sensory modalities, it is limited to bi-sensory combinations in which the visual signal is combined with another single stimulus' (p. 193). The authors explain this with reference to the brain operating according to principles of Bayesian inference, weighting and combining evidence on the basis of experience, and following Körding et al. (2007) who developed a causal inference model 'probabilistically inferring the causes of cues' (p. e943). Hecht and Reiner (2009, p. 312) state: 'This Bayesian inference approach that does not restrict itself to a rigid linkage of particular sensory systems with special tasks (as the original 'modality appropriateness' proposition) has a better explanatory power for sensory dominance phenomena.' While the CAM model also emphasizes inference, the cue integration model of Körding and colleagues (Trommershauser, Körding, & Landy, 2011) provides a computational model of sensory cue integration. Their model specifically handles auditory-visual localization tasks and could possibly be adapted for more complex stimuli (e.g., musical and visual motion patterns) if a temporal dimension were added.

Multiple sensory modes are engaged in many multimedia experiences, such as scrolling through a long menu while responding to auditory cues such as 'earcons' to guide fine motor responses (Roginska, Chapter 15); playing a video game on the Wii game console with intense visual, auditory and often tactile input (Grimshaw, Tan, & Lipscomb, Chapter 13); or in the scenario of a child who sings or gestures along with an interactive children's program (Calvert, Chapter 12). These real-world contexts incorporate far richer sensory experiences than the artificial laboratory stimuli used in most sensory dominance studies and engage a wider range of sensory modalities. Further, multisensory processing may become more efficient with frequent multimedia use. For instance, college students with extensive video game experience demonstrated significantly better multisensory perception and integration than non-gamers, as indicated by their ability to distinguish audio and visual events that were slightly offset in time (Donohue, Woldorff, & Mitroff, 2010).

The present volume does not directly challenge the idea of 'visual dominance' but encourages readers to be aware of the growing number of studies that show that many factors mediate visual dominance (e.g., Sinnett, Spence, & Soto-Faraco, 2007) and that auditory dominance has been clearly demonstrated in certain conditions. Recent neuroscientific findings also point to cases of multisensory processing in which no single sense 'trumps' the others (see Kuchinke, Kappelhoff, & Koelsch, Chapter 6). The 'visual dominance' bias may restrict creativity when formulating original research questions, designing studies, and interpreting findings of multimedia research. It is only by examining the complex and often mutual interactions of various sensory modalities that we come to a fuller understanding of the integration of rich multimedia in human experience.

Real-world applications: Music and sound in multimedia

Research on music and sound in multimedia has implications for a variety of practical applications. Chapters in Part IV explore the use of multimedia in the context of learning and engaging young minds (Calvert), play and entertainment (Grimshaw, Tan, & Lipscomb), persuasive messages (Shevy & Hung), computer interfaces (Roginska), and the impact of multi-channel sound (Kerins). These all converge on the theme of *cognitive load*, and the burden on working memory. Capacity for cognitive processing is limited and thus there is competition for attentional and cognitive resources. If one is engaged in a challenging task, adding extra information (even if potentially useful) can add 'cognitive load' to an already strained system and therefore may diminish performance (Sweller, 1999). On the other hand, shifting some information to another channel could reduce cognitive load by distributing resources across modalities. When it comes to applications in multimedia, a primary question is whether adding information via more than one sensory mode reduces or adds cognitive load. The researcher's task is to determine what conditions lead to positive versus negative outcomes and how to maximize attentional and cognitive resources in multimedia presentations.

Children's media

Infants and young children are keenly responsive to auditory stimuli—as noted in the discussion on 'auditory dominance' in the early years. The auditory system is more mature than the visual system at birth (and even prenatally) (Pujol & Lavigne-Rebillard, 1985). Infants' orienting behavior is often driven by auditory stimuli, and infants are especially attuned to musical qualities of speech (prosody) in infant-directed speech and singing (Cooper & Aslin, 1990; Nakata & Trehub, 2004). As mentioned earlier, young children's engagement with television is at first guided by auditory cues. They usually play with toys in the vicinity of the television, and only look up at the screen intermittently, often when their attention is captured by salient auditory cues (see Calvert, Chapter 12).

The role of music, speech, and sound effects is particularly sparse in research on educational media and multimedia, though some guidelines based on the existing empirical research have been set forth (e.g., Barron, 2004). In the relatively few studies in which music has been a focus, it is often concluded that the presence of music adds cognitive load and may negatively impact learning (e.g., see Moreno & Mayer, 2000). Visual learning is especially hindered when presented with a combination of relevant spoken narration with unrelated background music (Brünken, Plass, & Leutner, 2004). However, we do not know the extent to which the findings of studies showing detrimental effects of background music on learning are due to the lack of rigorous research on the most effective application of music and sound in multimedia presentations. We also do not know to what extent these findings are generalizable to younger learners, especially the cohort of 'digital natives' (Prensky, 2001) who were born into a world in which electronic multimedia is ubiquitous. They may respond differently from those who grew up a generation earlier, as their developing minds may be shaped by multimedia use (see also Cohen, Chapter 2, and Calvert, Chapter 12).

Video and computer games

In the context of interactive games, it is difficult to determine whether music and sound helps or hinders player performance. Grimshaw, Tan, and Lipscomb (Chapter 13) note that the effects of game audio on game performance are complex and affected by numerous factors—including genre of game and music, player's familiarity with the game, liking for the music, skill level, and other personal traits. Game designers are increasingly tailoring music to individual players, and giving players more choice and control over soundtracks. Familiar music may not add significantly to cognitive load, and allowing players to select their own music track can enhance game performance and enjoyment (e.g., Cassidy & MacDonald, 2009).

Auditory cues are becoming a main focus of research in game design for players with physical or perceptual challenges, such as visual impairment. Especially striking is the development of audio-based software interfaces to assist visually impaired users to transfer learning from virtual to real-world environments. For instance, the *Audio-Based Environment Simulator* (Sánchez, Pascual-Leone, & Merabet, 2009) can create virtual environments modeled after real indoor spaces, such as a school or office. Users follow a guided tour or play games to collect hidden gems with the goal of facilitating navigation of the real environment simulated by the program. Navigation is guided by audio cues such as knocking sounds to one's left or right to indicate the location of a door and a 'where am I?' key using text-to-speech capability to describe current location, orientation, and obstacles in one's way. More recently, footwear-based interaction in virtual environments has been explored, using shoes designed to control a multichannel surround sound system (Nordhal, Serafin, Turchet, & Nilsson, 2011; see also Kerins, Chapter 16). This research has strong practical applications for advancing work related to physical therapy and the rehabilitation of lower limbs, and for enhancing navigational ease, sense of presence and realism in virtual environments in entertainment contexts.

A growing body of research points to cognitive and physical benefits of video games for older adults (Maillot, Perrot, & Hartley, 2011) as well as socioemotional gains (Kahlbaugh, Sperandio, Carlson, & Hauselt, 2011). Some industry manuals on game design provide guidelines to accommodate age-related loss of auditory acuity—such as choosing background music that minimizes the masking of spoken instructions or other auditory cues, doubling audio cues with visual and haptic cues, and avoiding high frequency audio cues associated with age-related hearing loss (e.g., Boot, Nichols, Rogers, & Fisk, 2012; Fozard & Gordon-Salant, 2001). In particular, sound and music should not distract from the current task as cognitive load is of special concern due to reduced working memory capacity potentially associated with aging (Zacks, Hasher, & Li, 2000). Research on the role of sound in video and computer games played by older adults would advance our understanding of sensory and perceptual processing, multisensory integration, auditory working memory, and neuroplasticity in the aging population, while concurrently providing solid psychological and perceptual principles for effective sound design for the current trend of multi-age and inclusive games.

Advertising

Learning and memory also play an important role in persuasive multimedia, such as advertising on television and on the Internet. In the context of persuasive multimedia, freeing up cognitive resources is not always the main goal. For instance, consumers respond more positively to an affective advertisement (as opposed to a highly informative one) and can be less critical of source credibility when they have fewer cognitive resources available due to heavy cognitive load (Shiv & Fedorikhin, 1999). A deep level of processing (Craik, 2011; Craik & Lockhart, 1972) may also not always be the goal as persuasion can take different routes (Petty & Cacioppo, 1986) and even peripheral features of an advertisement (such as whether someone likes the background music in a commercial) may play a role in changing attitude or behavior. For instance, research reviewed by Calvert (Chapter 12) pointed out that when children or adolescents are learning verbal information, singing (versus speaking) the information can be an effective but superficial tool for memorization. However in the case of commercial jingles, the appealing messages to which people are repeatedly exposed do not require deep thought or analysis in order to achieve the goal of 'sticking' in one's mind (Shevy & Hung, Chapter 14). For instance, the whimsical 'sometimes you feel like a nut' jingle for Mounds/Almond Joy television commercials was revived in the United States in 1990 because people remembered the 1970s jingle over a decade after it stopped running (Dagnoli, 1989).

Advertising on the television and Internet often involves *implicit learning* and *implicit memory*. Though attention is focused on the television program, key information about the commercials may be learned and retained at an implicit level, sufficient to be triggered at the sight of brands or products during the next trip to the supermarket. Another advertising strategy involves repeated presentations of a message as familiarity often leads to preference, a principle referred to as the *mere exposure effect* (Zajonc, 1968). For instance, frequent incidental exposure to web-based banners can lead to positive feelings about an advertisement, even when banners are displayed outside the focal area (at the very top of the screen) as participants are reading articles on the computer screen (Xiang, Singh, & Ahluwalia, 2007). While there is a significant research on implicit memory and mere exposure effect in the advertising literature, few studies have focused on the possible role that music may play in implicit memory or the mere exposure effect in multimedia advertising (e.g., Alexomanolaki, Loveday, & Kennett, 2007).

Computer interfaces and auditory displays

Allotting some information to the auditory channel can be an effective way to reduce cognitive load by distributing attentional resources across modalities (Roginska, Chapter 15). For instance, auditory spatial location information has been effectively used for threat assessment in fighter cockpits, using three-dimensional spatial location and a variety of auditory cues to indicate location and type of threat, and diminishing loudness of the sound as the threat diminishes (Sanderson, Anderson, & Watson, 2000). Current developments in the area of auditory displays include investigations into how to effectively use multiple auditory cues concurrently while avoiding masking or interfering with intelligibility of the individual sounds. Solutions include spatializing sound in a multiple sound source environment (see Roginska, Chapter 15, and Kerins, Chapter 16), and applying basic rules of musical counterpoint (Brewster, Wright, & Edwards, 1995) and principles of auditory scene analysis (Bregman, 1990; McGookin & Brewster, 2004) to separate auditory streams.

Although single tones or very short motifs are often employed to convey information, richer structured musical stimuli (or 'earcons') can communicate more complex information. For instance, Alty and Rigas (2005) used pitch, timbre, and rhythm concurrently to convey diagrams comprised of arrangements of several simple shapes to visually impaired adults. Horizontal and vertical coordinates were indicated by pitches of a chromatic scale (with piano or organ timbre differentiating axes), and rhythm indicated features of the outline such as proportion (i.e., in a square, four similar rhythmic units would be played). Adults with post-literate visual impairment were able to correctly interpret locations, shapes, sizes, and configurations of shapes and draw accurate diagrams of the shapes on a grid. None of the participants had prior musical training, supporting previous research that found no differences between musicians' and non-musicians' ability to recognize earcons, even when two earcons are presented simultaneously (e.g., Brewster, Wright, & Edwards, 1995). The full range of possibilities for metaphorical mapping of musical properties of sound to data is just beginning to be explored (McGookin & Brewster, 2011; see also Eitan, Chapter 8). In McGookin and Brewster's words: 'As with much earcon research, the influence of music and musicianship is lacking. A full investigation into how it can be best exploited is a ripe area for future research' (p. 357).

Multimedia applications and ethics

In line with applications of multimedia are issues of ethics that will need to be addressed. Understanding the power of music in multimedia increases the power inherent in those who produce media, for example, advertisers and directors in the entertainment industry, as hinted at by Shevy (Chapter 4). A recent edited book entitled *The Dark Side of Creativity* (Cropley, Cropley, Kaufman, & Runco, 2010) challenges the usual positive notions about creativity. Commercial advertisers, who are prime exploiters of multimedia and music in multimedia, aim to control minds to encourage viewer-listeners to purchase products. The same principles of advertising, however, can be applied for societal good rather than the corporate bottom line—for instance, promoting healthy behaviors (choosing nutritious snacks, using mosquito netting, avoiding contaminated water in third world societies) or encouraging cultural understanding through specially developed DVDs demonstrating songs and cultures so as to foster engagement by others in those cultures. Harnessing empirically confirmed knowledge about the role of music in media for the betterment of society can be a future positive thrust for 21st-century researchers, opening up collaborations with disparate disciplines, including education, medicine, international relations, and social justice, among many others.

Final remarks: A call to interdisciplinarity

While results of past research are essential to assessing the current state of our knowledge, it is the readily apparent need for significantly more research in this arena that becomes the clarion call from authors for the present volume. Three issues are at the forefront as future researchers tackle related issues: the interpretation of apparently contradictory results from extant research investigations, the impact of the context within which multimedia is presented, and the impact of the content of the multimedia stimuli used in empirical studies. Toward this end, it will be important to expand the research stimuli used beyond audiovisual presentations of cinematic excerpts (by far, the primary stimulus type used in past research) into other realms of multimedia experience, including music videos, television, interactive videogames, advertisements, and others. It will also be crucial that interested researchers with expertise in a variety of related disciplines collaborate on pursuing answers to relevant research questions.

Interdisciplinary work is called for, but interdisciplinary work is difficult and complex. To gain power from addressing important issues from perspectives of different disciplines (or from sub-branches within the same discipline) calls for skills in which scholars are seldom trained. The rewards of interdisciplinary research are often much longer in coming than are the rewards of working within one's own familiar framework and paradigm with like-minded researchers. A separate science of interdisciplinary research is evolving so as to understand the nature of interdisciplinary challenges and to capitalize most effectively on interdisciplinary opportunities.

Researchers in the field of music and multimedia would do well to consult such volumes as the *Oxford Handbook of Interdisciplinarity* (Frodeman, Klein, & Mitcham, 2012) or *Interdisciplinary Collaboration* (Derry, Schunn, & Gernsbacher, 2005) to place in perspective the challenges of interdisciplinary endeavor in multimedia research and to appreciate issues arising, such as the different meanings ascribed to the same terms by different disciplines. Interdisciplinarity is challenging in its attempt to integrate different approaches and methods, in contrast to multidisciplinarity, which simply juxtaposes disciplines. The concept of transdisciplinarity extends beyond academia to the community, to government, or to practitioners and is also a key future direction for research in music and multimedia, as this concluding chapter indicates.

Future promise for the study of the psychology of music in multimedia lies in forming collaborative research teams from all relevant areas of knowledge. Most importantly, we must think of the next generation of scholars, the students, who—as a result of the availability of laptop computers and mobile devices—have the capabilities of a multimedia laboratory with them most of the time, allowing for almost instant selection and creation of materials for research and exploratory studies. Professors in introductory courses in behavioral research, film theory, and music are urged to open opportunities for students, encouraging them to carry out projects employing these media and collaborating with peers in other disciplines. It is critical, of course, that faculty *model* the desired behaviors and facilitate the development of skills required to conceive interdisciplinary study, be proactive in finding potential collaborators across campus or in other labs, form and maintain professional relationships with these peers, and communicate effectively across disciplinary boundaries, learning the unique 'language' associated with relevant fields. After all, music is a form of non-verbal communication and, in order to fully understand this universally present phenomenon, we must be able to communicate about it with others who bring a different perspective but are equally passionate about gaining a complete understanding, which is best accomplished through interdisciplinary collaboration.

Further, the use of music in multimedia is not confined to a single dominant culture. Every culture that makes use of multimedia does so in ways that are common to all cultures, but also in ways that are unique to the individual culture. Insight into the mental processes underlying the role of music and audio in multimedia may come from availing ourselves of the media produced in other cultures and, where possible, coming together with experts from cultures different than our own. Such experiences can challenge our assumptions. The chapters of this book, written by contributors who reside in seven different countries and who represent a dozen or so disciplines, provide a start on this multicultural, multidisciplinary mission of using empirical research to enhance our understanding of music in the multimedia context.

References

Alexomanolaki, M., Loveday, C., & Kennett, C. (2007). Music and memory in advertising: Music as a device of implicit learning and recall. *Music, Sound, and the Moving Image, 1*(1), 51–71.

Alty, J. L., & Rigas, D. (2005). Exploring the use of structured musical stimuli to communicate simple diagrams: the role of context. *International Journal of Human-Computer Studies, 62*, 21–40.

Barron, A. E. (2004). Auditory instruction. In D. H. Jonassen (Ed.), *Handbook of research on educational communications and technology* (2nd ed., pp. 949–978). Mahwah, NJ: Lawrence Erlbaum.

Boot, W. R., Nichols, T. A., Rogers, W. A. and Fisk, A. D. (2012). Design for aging. In G. Salvendy (Ed.), *Handbook of human factors and ergonomics* (pp. 1442–1471). Hoboken, NJ: John Wiley.

Bregman, A. S. (1990). *Auditory scene analysis: The perceptual organization of sound.* Cambridge, MA: MIT Press.

Brewster, S. A., Wright, P. C., & Edwards, A. D. N. (1995). Parallel earcons: Reducing the length of audio messages. *International Journal of Human-Computer Studies, 43,* 153–175.

Brünken, R., Plass, J. L., & Leutner, D. (2004). Assessment of cognitive load in multimedia learning with dual-task methodology: Auditory load and modality effects. *Instructional Science, 32,* 115–132.

Burr, D., Banks, M. S., Morrone, M. C. (2009). Auditory dominance over vision in the perception of interval duration. *Experimental Brain Research, 198,* 49–57.

Cassidy, G. G., & MacDonald, R. A. R. (2009). The effects of music choice on task performance: A study of the impact of self-selected and experimenter-selected music on driving game performance and experience. *Musicae Scientiae, 13,* 357–386.

Cohen, A. J. (2002). Music cognition and the cognitive psychology of film structure. *Canadian Psychology, 43,* 215–232.

Colavita, F. B. (1974). Human sensory dominance. *Perception & Psychophysics, 16,* 409–412.

Cooper, R. P., & Aslin, R. N. (1990). Preference for infant-directed speech in the first month after birth. *Child Development, 61,* 1584–1594.

Craik, F. I. M. (2011). Levels of processing in human memory. In M. A. Gernsbacher, R. W. Pew, L. M. Hough, & J. R. Pomerantz (Eds.). *Psychology and the real world: Essays illustrating fundamental contributions to society* (pp. 76–82). New York, NY: Worth.

Craik, F. I. M. & Lockhart, R. S. (1972). Levels of processing: A framework for memory research. *Journal of Verbal Learning and Verbal Behavior, 11,* 671–684.

Cropley, D. H., Cropley, A. J., Kaufman, J. C., & Runco, M. A. (2010). *The dark side of creativity.* Cambridge, UK: Cambridge University Press.

Dagnoli, J. (1989, September). Best-loved themes get sweet reprise. *Advertising Age,* p. 32.

Derry, S. J., Schunn, C. D., & Gernsbacher, M. A. (Eds.) (2005). *Interdisciplinary collaboration.* Mahwah, NJ: Erlbaum.

Donohue, S. E., Woldorff, M. G., & Mitroff, S. R. (2010). Video game players show more precise multisensory temporal processing abilities. *Attention, Perception, & Psychophysics, 72,* 1120–1129.

Fozard, J. L., and Gordon-Salant, S. (2001). *Changes in vision and hearing with aging.* In J. E. Birren & K. W. Schaie (Eds.), *Handbook of the psychology of aging* (pp. 241–266). San Diego, CA: Academic Press.

Frodeman, R., Klein, J. T., & Mitcham, C. (Eds.) (2012). *Oxford handbook of interdisciplinarity.* Oxford, UK: Oxford University Press.

Fujiyama, S., Ema, K., & Iwamiya, S. (2012). Effect of the technique of conflict between music and moving picture using Akira Kurosawa's movies. In *Proceedings of the Spring Meeting of Japanese Society of Music Perception and Cognition,* pp. 85–70. Tokyo, Japan: Acoustical Society of Japan. (In Japanese.)

Godøy, R., & Leman, M. (Eds.) (2010). *Musical gestures: sound, movement, and meaning,* New York, NY: Routledge.

Haack, P., & Radocy, R. (1981). A case study of a chromesthetic. *Journal of Research in Music Education, 29*(2), 85–90.

Handel, S. (2006). *Perceptual coherence.* New York, NY: Oxford University Press.

Hecht, D., & Reiner, M. (2009). Sensory dominance in combinations of audio, visual and haptic stimuli. *Experimental Brain Research, 193,* 307–314.

Jaén, I., & Simon, J. J. (2012). An overview of recent developments in cognitive literary studies. In I. Jaén and J. J. Simon (Eds.), *Cognitive literary studies: Current themes and new directions* (pp. 13–32). Austin, TX: University of Texas Press.

Kahlbaugh, P. E., Sperandio, A. J., Carlson, A. L., & Hauselt, J. (2011). Effects of playing wii on well-being in the elderly: physical activity, loneliness, and mood. *Activities, Adaptation & Aging, 35,* 331–344.

Kelly, E. (1934). An experimental attempt to produce artificial chromaesthesia of the technique of the conditioned response. *Journal of Experimental Psychology, 17* (3), 315–341.

Koelsch, S. (2012). *Brain and music.* Malden, MA: Wiley-Blackwell.

Körding, K. P., Beierholm, U., Ma, W. J., Quartz, S. Tenenbaum, J. B., & Shams, L. (2007). Causal inference in multisensory perception. *PLoS ONE, 2*(9), e943.

Lipscomb, S. D., & Kendall R. A. (1994). Perceptual judgment of the relationship between musical and visual components in film. *Psychomusicology, 13*(1), 60–98.

Lipscomb, S. D., & Tolchinsky, D. E. (2005). The role of music communication in cinema. In D. Miell, R. MacDonald, & D. Hargreaves (Eds.), *Musical communication* (pp. 383–404). Oxford, UK: Oxford University Press.

Maillot, P., Perrot, A., & Hartley, A. (2011). The effects of video games on cognitive aging. *Gériatrie et psychologie neuropsychiatrie du vieillissement, 10,* 83–94. [In French.]

Marks, L. E. (2004). Cross-modal interactions in speeded classification. In G. A. Calvert, C. Spence, & B. E. Stein (Eds.), *The handbook of multisensory processes* (pp. 85–105). Cambridge, MA: MIT Press.

McGookin, D. K., & Brewster, S. A. (2004). Understanding concurrent earcons: applying auditory scene analysis principles to concurrent earcon recognition. *ACM Transactions on Applied Perception, 1,* 130–155.

McGookin, D., & Brewster, S. (2011). Earcons. In T. Hermann, A. Hunt, & J. G. Neuhoff (Eds.), *The sonification handbook* (pp. 339–361). Berlin, Germany: Logos.

Moreno, R., & Mayer, R. E. (2000). A coherence effect in multimedia learning: The case for minimizing irrelevant sounds in the design of multimedia instructional messages. *Journal of Educational Psychology, 92,* 117–320.

Nakata, T., & Trehub, S. E. (2004). Infants' responsiveness to maternal speech and singing. *Infant Behavior & Development, 27,* 455–464.

Newell, A. (2002). Précis of *Unified theories of cognition.* In T. A. Polk & C. M. Seifert (Eds.), *Cognitive Modeling* (pp. 1231–1259). Cambridge, MA: MIT Press.

Nordahl, R., Serafin, S., Turchet, L., & Nilsson, N.C. (2011). A multimodal architecture for simulating natural interactive walking in virtual environments. *PsychNology, 9,* 245–268.

Oatley, K. (2011). *Such stuff as dreams: The psychology of fiction.* Malden, MA: Wiley-Blackwell.

Ortega, L., Guzman-Martinez, E., Grabowecky, M., & Suzuki, S. (2009). Auditory dominance in time perception. *Journal of Vision, 9* (8), 1086.

Petty, R. E., & Cacioppo, J. T. (1986). *Communication and persuasion: Central and peripheral routes to attitude change.* New York, NY: Springer-Verlag.

Posner, M. I., Nissen, M. J., & Klein, R. M. (1976). Visual dominance: an information-processing account of its origins and significance. *Psychological Review, 83,* 157–171.

Prensky, M. (2001). Digital natives, digital immigrants. *On the Horizon, 9,* 1–6.

Pujol, R., & Lavigne-Rebillard, M. (1985). Early stages of innervation and sensory cell differentiation in the human fetal organ of Corti. *Acta Oto-Laryngologica, 424*, 43–50.

Radeau, M., & Bertelson, P. (1974). The after-effects of ventriloquism. *Quarterly Journal of Experimental Psychology, 26*, 63–71.

Repp, B. H., & Penel, A. (2002). Auditory dominance in temporal processing: New evidence from synchronization with simultaneous visual and auditory sequences. *Journal of Experimental Psychology: Human Perception & Performance, 28*, 1085–1099.

Rich, J. (1916). A preliminary study of tonal volume. *Journal of Experimental Psychology, I*, 13–22.

Robinson, C. W., & Sloutsky, V. M. (2004). Auditory dominance and its change in the course of development. *Child Development, 75*, 1387–1401.

Sánchez, J., Pascual-Leone, A., & Merabet, L. (2009). Blind children: Navigation through gaming and associated brain plasticity. In *Proceedings of the International Conference on Virtual Rehabilitation* (pp. 29–36), June 2009 in Haifa, Israel. Piscataway, NJ: IEEE Press.

Sanderson, P. M., Anderson, J.R., & Watson, M. (2000). Extending ecological interface design to auditory displays. In *Proceedings of the 2000 Annual Conference of the Computer-Human Interaction Special Interest Group of the Ergonomics Society of Australia* (pp. 259–266). Sydney, Australia: CSIRO.

Schmid, C., BüNewchel, C., & Rose, M. (2011). The neural basis of visual dominance in the context of audio-visual object processing. *Neuroimage, 55*, 304–311.

Shams, L., Kamitani, Y., & Shimojo, S. (2000). What you see is what you hear. *Nature, 408*, 788.

Shiv, B., & Fedorikhin, A. (1999). Heart and mind in conflict: Interplay of affect and cognition in consumer decision-making. *Journal of Consumer Research, 26*, 278–282.

Sinnett, S., Spence, C., & Soto-Faraco, S. (2007). Visual dominance and attention: the Colavita effect revisited. *Perception & Psychophysics, 69*, 673–686.

Spence, C. (2009). Explaining the Colavita visual dominance effect. *Progress in Brain Research, 176*, 245–258.

Spence, C. (2011). Cross-modal correspondences: A tutorial review. *Attention, Perception & Psychophysics, 73*, 971–995.

Stein, B. E., & Meredith, M. A. (1993). *The merging of the senses.* Cambridge, MA: MIT Press:

Stevens, S. S. (1934). The attributes of tones. *Proceedings of the National Academy of Sciences of the United States of America, 20* (7), 457–459.

Sweller, J. (1999). *Instructional design in technical areas.* Camberwell, Australia: ACER Press.

Tan, S. -L., Spackman, M. P., & Wakefield, E. M. (2008). Effects of diegetic and non-diegetic presentation of film music on viewers' interpretation of film narrative. In K. Miyazaki, Y. Hiraga, M. Adachi, Y. Nakajima, & M. Tsuzaki (Eds.), *Proceedings of the 10th International Conference on Music Perception and Cognition (ICMPC10) Sapporo, Japan* (pp. 588–593) [DVD]. Adelaide, Australia: Causal Productions.

Trommershauser, J., Körding, K., & Landy, M. S. (2011). *Sensory cue integration.* New York, NY: Oxford University Press.

Xiang, F., Singh, S., & Ahluwalia, R. (2007). An examination of different explanations for the mere exposure effect. *Journal of Consumer Research, 34*, 97–103.

Zacks, R. T., Hasher, L., & Li, K. Z. H. (2000). Human memory. In T. A. Salthouse & F. I. M. Craik (Eds.), *Handbook of aging and cognition* (2nd ed., pp. 293–357). Mahwah, NJ: Lawrence Erlbaum.

Zajonc, R. B. (1968). Attitudinal effects of mere exposure. *Journal of Personality and Social Psychology, 9*(2, pt. 2), 1–27.

Author Index

C

D

H

I

J

K

L

M

N

T

X

Y

Z

Subject Index

Note: Page numbers in *italics* indicate references to figures; 'n' following a page number indicates a footnote; a number after 'n' indicates the footnote number if more than one footnote is on a page.

D

E

F

G

H

N